SOCIALLY RESPONSIBLE FINANCE AND INVESTING

The *Robert W. Kolb Series in Finance* provides a comprehensive view of the field of finance in all of its variety and complexity. It covers all major topics and specializations in finance, ranging from investments, to corporate finance, to financial institutions. Each volume is written or edited by a specialist (or specialists) in a particular area of finance and is intended for practicing finance professionals, graduate students, and advanced undergraduate students. The goal of each volume is to encapsulate the current state of knowledge in a particular area of finance so that the reader can quickly achieve a mastery of that discipline.

Please visit www.wiley.com/go/kolbseries to learn about recent and forthcoming titles in the Kolb Series.

SOCIALLY RESPONSIBLE FINANCE AND INVESTING

Financial Institutions, Corporations, Investors, and Activists

Editors

H. Kent Baker
John R. Nofsinger

The Robert W. Kolb Series in Finance

WILEY

John Wiley & Sons, Inc.

Library of Congress Cataloging-in-Publication Data:

Baker, H. Kent (Harold Kent), 1944–
    Socially responsible finance and investing : financial institutions, corporations,
investors, and activists / H. Kent Baker, John R. Nofsinger. – 1st ed.
        p. cm. – (Robert W. Kolb series ; 612)
    Includes index.
    ISBN 978-1-118-10009-7 (hardcover); ISBN 978-1-118-23701-4 (ebk);
    ISBN 978-1-118-26205-4 (ebk); ISBN 978-1-118-22375-8 (ebk)
    1. Investments–Moral and ethical aspects.   I. Nofsinger, John R.   II. Title.
    HG4515.13.B35 2012
    174'.4–dc23

                                                                2012015380

10 9 8 7 6 5 4 3 2 1

Contents

Acknowledgments

Socially Responsible Finance and Investment represents a team effort in which many players made important contributors. A distinguished group of academics and practitioners offered their extensive knowledge and skills in writing and revising their respective chapters. The professional team at John Wiley & Sons helped transform the manuscript into a polished book. Special thanks go to Claire New, our production editor, and others who assisted in this project. We also thank Bob Kolb for including this book in the Robert W. Kolb Series in Finance and Kevin Commins, executive editor at Wiley, for his efforts in gaining approval for this project. H. Kent Baker appreciates the financial support provided by the Kogod School of Business at American University. Finally, we are grateful to our families, especially Linda Baker and Anna Nofsinger, for their patience and support. We dedicate this book to them.

CHAPTER 1

Socially Responsible Finance and Investing: An Overview

H. KENT BAKER
University Professor of Finance and Kogod Research Professor, American University

JOHN R. NOFSINGER
Professor of Finance and Nihoul Faculty Fellow, Washington State University

INTRODUCTION

What is the main goal of a business firm? Many have debated this question over the years. The response largely depends on one's view of to whom the firm is responsible. Some contend that corporations are only responsible to their shareholders and do not have other obligations to society besides complying with applicable laws, ethical standards, and international norms. Hence, corporations should operate to meet the best interests of shareholders within these constraints. Others take the broader view that corporations have responsibilities to stakeholders other than shareholders. *Stakeholders* refer to those who have an interest or concern in the firm because of how its activities affect them. Stakeholders consist of owners, management, employees, suppliers, customers, the local community, and others.

Donaldson and Preston (1995) discuss three versions of stakeholder theory: normative, instrumental, and descriptive. Normative stakeholder theory views a firm's behavior through an idealistic social or moral lens. That is, this version focuses on how firms "should" act. Instrumental stakeholder theory views stakeholder relationships as the means to some end, such as maximizing firm value. By contrast, descriptive stakeholder theory uses the stakeholder model as a tool for describing the activities and interests of the firm. In general, instrumental stakeholder theory seems to fit the needs of performance-oriented investors better than other approaches. Others provide an extensive treatment of stakeholder theory (Friedman and Miles 2006; Freeman, Harrison, Wicks, Parmar, and de Colle 2010; Phillips 2011).

Jensen (2001, p. 8) offers the following observation about a firm's goal:

> How do we want the firms in our economy to measure their own performance? How do we want them to determine what is better versus worse? Most economists would answer simply that managers have a criterion for evaluating performance and deciding between alternative courses of action, and that the criterion should be maximization of the long-term market value of the firm. . . . This Value Maximization proposition has its roots in 200 years of research in economics and finance.

Most financial economists would agree that the fundamental purpose of a business firm, especially a corporation, is to maximize returns to its shareholders. This view is consistent with instrumental stakeholder theory, which considers the stakeholder network as the means to the end of wealth creation. For example, Friedman (1962, 1970) treats shareholders as ends to firm performance and explicitly measures performance as profit. As Friedman (1970, p. 32) notes, the responsibility of business firms "will generally be to make as much money as possible." Proponents of this view contend that the notion of corporate social responsibility (CSR), which is also called corporate conscience, corporate citizenship, social performance, and responsible business, distracts from the economic role of business.

Others, such as Freeman (1984, 1998), have different views. Freeman (1998, p. 126) states that "we must reconceptualize the firm around the following question: For whose benefit and at whose expense should the firm be managed?" He proposes replacing the narrow focus on shareholders with a broader set of obligations. Porter and Kramer (2011) echo this sentiment by proposing that the purpose of the corporation be viewed as creating shared value and not just profit. They maintain that corporations can make more long-term profits by embracing CSR. According to Baker and Powell (2005), achieving shareholder wealth maximization assumes that managers operate in the best interests of shareholders, avoid actions designed to deceive financial markets in order to boost the firm's stock price, and act in a legally and socially responsible manner. Given these assumptions, Baker and Powell (p. 12) state that "shareholder wealth maximization is consistent with the best interest of stakeholders and society in the long run."

Although shareholder wealth maximization has gained considerable traction in the academic and business communities, the concept of social responsibility has also gained momentum. Socially responsible finance includes responsibility from the corporate side (corporate social responsibility) as well as the investor side (socially responsible investing) in the capital markets.

CORPORATE SOCIAL RESPONSIBILITY

In the late twentieth century, an increasing number of corporations started to think about their effect on society at large, mainly because of growing consumer awareness of corporate activities around the world. Some corporations decided to embark on corporate social responsibility programs designed to offset some of their effects on the world while also generally improving corporate practices (Campbell 2007). *Corporate social responsibility* (CSR) is a form of corporate self-regulation integrated into a business model. That is, CSR is the decision-making and implementation process that guides all company activities in protecting and promoting international human rights, labor and environmental standards, and compliance with legal requirements within its operations and in its relations to the societies and communities where it operates (Carroll 1999). CSR involves a commitment to contribute to the economic, environmental, and social sustainability of communities through the ongoing engagement of stakeholders, the active participation of communities affected by company activities, and the public reporting of company policies and performance in the economic, environmental, and social arenas.

In theory, CSR policy functions as a built-in, self-regulating mechanism whereby business should monitor and ensure its support to law, ethical standards, and international norms. Thus, business should embrace responsibility for the impact of its activities on the environment, consumers, employees, communities, stockholders, and all other members of the public sphere. Also, CSR-focused businesses should proactively promote the public interest by encouraging community growth and development, and voluntarily eliminating practices that harm the public sphere, regardless of legality. Norman and MacDonald (2004) show how CSR deliberately attempts to include public interest into corporate decision-making and focuses on a triple bottom line: people, planet, and profit.

The practice of CSR is much debated and criticized. Not surprisingly, CSR has both fans and detractors. Proponents contend that a strong business case exists for CSR. They argue that corporations can benefit in multiple ways by operating with a perspective broader and longer than their own immediate, short-term profits. Critics maintain, however, that CSR distracts from the fundamental economic role of businesses. Others argue that CSR is nothing more than superficial window-dressing while still others contend that it is an attempt to pre-empt the role of governments as a supervisory body over powerful multinational corporations (Archel, Husillos, and Spence 2011; Harrison, Bosse, and Phillips 2010).

SOCIALLY RESPONSIBLE INVESTING

Socially responsible investing (SRI), also called ethical investing and green investing, is an investment that is considered socially responsible because of the nature of the business the company conducts. SRI uses environmental, social, and corporate governance (ESG) criteria to generate long-term, competitive financial returns and positive societal impact (SIF 2010). That is, investors limit their investment alternatives to securities of firms whose products or actions are considered socially acceptable (Bollen 2007). For example, socially responsible investors might avoid investment in companies that produce or sell addictive substances such as tobacco, liquor products, or gambling and might seek out companies engaged in environmental sustainability and alternative energy/clean technology efforts (Statman 2004). Unlike traditional investing that focuses only on financial returns, SRI combines both financial goals and social responsibility (Derwall, Koedijk, and Ter Horst 2011).

Socially conscious investing is growing into a widely-followed practice. For example, retail investors can make socially responsible investments in individual companies, follow SRI indexes, or through a socially conscious mutual fund or exchange-traded fund (ETF). Mutual funds and ETFs provide an added advantage in that investors can gain exposure to multiple companies across many sectors with a single investment. Yet some question whether investors sacrifice performance for the sake of ideology (Hong and Kacperczyk 2009). That is, just because an investment touts itself as socially responsible does not mean that it will provide investors with a good return.

PURPOSE OF THE BOOK

The purpose of this book is to provide a comprehensive view of the growing field of socially responsible finance and investing. It discusses the socially responsible foundations and their applications to finance as determined by the current state of this research. The book is written by noted scholars—both academics and practitioners—who provide a synthesis of what is known about each topic no matter whether the evidence is flattering or not. Of the books currently available in this area, many tend to focus on one narrow topic, such as how to measure socially responsible activities in a firm, and to be written from a proponent's point of view. This is not the case with *Socially Responsible Finance and Investing*, which takes a wide-ranging view and offers multiple perspectives.

The socially responsible framework for viewing business activities is likely to increase in popularity. This movement is already becoming popular with the European business community and scholars there. The ideas are now gaining a foothold in the United States. With a focus on the recent financial collapse, other bailouts, and the environment, the U.S. interest in socially responsible finance is likely to continue increasing.

FEATURES OF THE BOOK

Socially Responsible Finance and Investing has several distinguishing features.

- Perhaps the book's most distinctive feature is that it provides a comprehensive discussion of the theory, empirical work, and practice within the various topics covered in socially responsible finance and investing. The book not only attempts to blend the conceptual world of scholars with the pragmatic view of practitioners, but also to synthesize important and relevant research studies including recent developments. The book takes an objective view and avoids an advocacy position.
- The book contains contributions from numerous authors. The breadth of contributors assures a variety of perspectives and a rich interplay of ideas.
- This volume discusses the results of empirical studies that link theory and practice. The objective is to distill them to their essential content so that they are understandable to the reader.
- Each chapter contains discussion questions that help to reinforce key concepts. This feature should be especially important to faculty and students using the book in classes.

INTENDED AUDIENCE

This book should appeal not only to an academic audience—researchers, professors, and students—but also to industry professionals, lawmakers, and regulators. For example, both academics and practitioners who are interested in socially responsible finance should find this book to be useful given the scope of the work. It should also be appropriate as a stand-alone book for undergraduate or graduate-level business courses related to the topics contained in this book. Further, libraries should find this work to be a suitable reference book.

STRUCTURE OF THE BOOK

The remaining 23 chapters are organized into four sections. A brief synopsis of each chapter by section follows.

Section I. Foundations and Key Concepts

Chapters 2 through 6 provide the foundation for understanding socially responsible finance and investing. Chapter 2 offers an in-depth discussion of stakeholder analysis, while Chapter 3 examines how different business disciplines view CSR. Chapter 4 introduces the concept of business models and social entrepreneurship. Chapter 5 discusses the legal framework in which SRI operates. Chapter 6 concludes this section by examining various international and cultural views toward SRFI.

Chapter 2 Stakeholder Analysis (Lloyd S. Kurtz)
Social investors often incorporate elements of stakeholder theory into their work. Many believe that firms with good stakeholder relationships should be viewed as better managed and therefore likely to offer superior financial performance. Empirical research has strengthened the case for a correlation between good stakeholder management and superior firm-level financial outcomes. These findings strongly suggest that a stakeholder worldview has validity and that analyzing stakeholder relationships can aid in investment analysis. Although many theoretical approaches are available, a modified form of instrumental stakeholder theory seems to fit best with the needs of investors. In this framework, good management may be defined as the efficient allocation of resources to stakeholder management, such that a large surplus remains for owners and managers. Stakeholder analysis of this type aids in assessing management quality and clarifies the relationships among stakeholders, owners, and managers. The resulting insights are often relevant for the valuation of the firm. Stakeholder analysis therefore has the potential to improve fundamental analysis, and stakeholder relationships deserve the attention not just of social investors, but of managers and investors in general.

Chapter 3 Corporate Social Responsibility (Heather Elms and Michelle Westermann-Behaylo)
This chapter identifies varying approaches to CSR in the business ethics, finance, accounting, and marketing literatures. In particular, it identifies a series of current themes in the business ethics literature that are not yet reflected in the finance, accounting, and marketing literatures as evidenced by a review of the articles published in the high-quality journals of these functional disciplines. The analysis suggests that greater consideration of these themes by the functional literatures and greater appreciation of the focus of the functional literatures by the business ethics literature may lead to a better understanding of the CSR phenomenon.

Chapter 4 Business Models and Social Entrepreneurship (Michael A. Pirson)
The 2007–2009 financial crisis caused many to question the basic premises of the current business system and the financial services industry. Some suggest that corporations should aim to regain legitimacy by pursuing shared value rather than mere financial value. Managers may be able to look at the field of social entrepreneurship to learn how to create such shared value. This chapter presents the concept of social entrepreneurship and introduces two areas in which social entrepreneurs have created novel business models: microfinance and social impact investing. The lessons that can be learned for shared value creation are discussed for the financial industry as a whole and those interested in socially responsible finance. The chapter concludes by presenting several caveats.

Chapter 5 Fiduciary and Other Legal Duties (Benjamin J. Richardson)
In common law legal systems, such as in the United Kingdom and the United States, fiduciary duties exert an important influence on institutional investors' latitude to practice SRI. Obligations on fund managers, trustees, and others who have custody of investors' money generally require that they invest prudently in their best financial interests. In limited circumstances, this legal framework may allow SRI such as when these investments offer comparable returns, the fund's constitution mandates SRI, or if beneficiaries consent to SRI. Recent statutory reforms in some jurisdictions have created a more enabling legal environment for SRI than in the past.

Chapter 6 International and Cultural Views (Astrid Juliane Salzmann)
Even though public and corporate interest in investment with social and environmental considerations is growing, the current literature remains vague about the underlying motives of investors. This chapter investigates the effect of the institutional environment on the social and ecological behavior of firms and investors around the world. It reviews four structural theories—legal origin, endowments, religion, and cultural values—and examines their usefulness to explain cross-country differences in social responsibility. Despite some isolated findings, where research has given explanations for developments in the field of sustainable finance, a deeper understanding of their general determinants remains incomplete. Existing research has primarily focused on religion and culture as explanatory factors for ethical issues in finance. Exploring the impact of the legal origin and endowments might also seem fruitful, but elaboration on the relevance of these theories remains a field for future research.

Section II. Society and Finance

The impact of social concerns on financial activities has evolved over time. Some of the nine chapters of this section describe this evolution in different segments of society, while others detail recent financially irresponsible events. Chapter 7 describes the history of the role of social, environmental, trust, and ethical issues in business. The religious aspects of social responsibility for finance are detailed in Chapter 8. Chapter 9 focuses on the development of microfinance and social banking. Managerial compensation has long been a controversial issue in society and is discussed in Chapter 10. Chapter 11 shows how externalities in the financial services industry have led to negative outcomes. A large energy efficiency and sustainability trend occurs in real estate. The aspects of real estate sustainability in society are the focus of Chapter 12. Chapters 13 and 14 describe the roles of federal housing policies and predatory lending to the financial crisis. Lastly, Chapter 15 details the history and recent developments in the financial secrecy industry and its role in society.

Chapter 7 Social, Environmental, and Trust Issues in Business and Finance (Christoph F. Biehl, Andreas G. F. Hoepner, and Jianghong Liu)

This chapter discusses social, environmental, and trust (SET) issues relating to business and finance in a historical context. Social issues relating to the concerned societal groups emerged beginning in the mid-twentieth century and have had an increasing impact on business ever since. Recently, societal groups have voiced anxieties about the trustworthiness of certain businesses, especially large financial institutions. These societal trends can be business relevant in both a positive and negative way. Managing these stakeholder concerns can, for instance, build trust and consumer loyalty, but it also costs corporate resources. Due to a consistently increasing complexity of business and finance and a similarly consistently increasing speed of information exchange among concerned stakeholders (e.g., via social media), trust-based businesses such as financial institutions are likely to increasingly face the challenges and opportunities resulting from societal concerns about SET issues.

Chapter 8 Religion and Finance (Luc Renneboog and Christophe Spaenjers)

Individuals' economic attitudes are frequently observed to vary in a systematic manner with religious affiliation or religiosity. As a consequence, religion is also correlated with a range of financial-economic outcomes. Research has established the importance of religion at the macro-economic level, and has shown that the religious environment may affect the behavior of managers and institutional investors. Much less evidence exists on the role of religion in the financial decision-making process at the household level. Therefore, this chapter uses data from a well-recognized household survey to investigate the relationship among religious affiliation, economic attitudes, and saving and investment decisions in the Netherlands. The evidence shows that differences in economic beliefs and preferences can partially explain the higher propensity to save by all religious households and the lower investments in stocks by Catholic households.

Chapter 9 Social Finance and Banking (Olaf Weber and Yayun Duan)

This chapter describes social banking, impact investment, and microfinance as areas of social finance. Each tries to achieve a positive social impact on society, the environment, or sustainable development through social finance and banking. The data show that social finance is successful in creating both a financial and a social return and has been growing in recent years. Impact measurement indicators have yet to be developed to adequately measure the financial and social impact of social finance. Furthermore, transaction costs have to be reduced to maintain attractive financial returns, and broader client groups have to be addressed to increase the impact of social finance.

Chapter 10 Managerial Compensation (Kose John and Samir Saadi)
This chapter surveys the recent literature on managerial compensation, focusing on the main issues that spurred intense debate in the popular press, academia, and from regulatory agencies. In particular, the literature review discusses whether the high levels of executive compensation are justifiable, and whether executive compensation schemes induce unethical behavior by executives. While most of the empirical evidence supports the view that the high levels of executive compensation are excessive and unethical, an emerging stream of literature provides rational explanations for the observed levels of executive pay. Ample evidence also shows that some compensation packages induce executives to manipulate their pay. This chapter also summarizes a limited, but growing, literature linking managerial compensation to corporate social responsibility. This literature suggests that the structure of managerial compensation matters to corporate social performance.

Chapter 11 Externalities in Financial Decision Making (Janis Sarra)
This chapter examines externalities in financial decision making. It explores how the structure of financial products and services has led to considerable harm to individuals and firms, suggesting that the incentives created by the current structure of financial services need serious re-examination. Socially responsible investment could play an important role in retooling the system to ensure that financial decision making and investment contribute to, rather than detract from, the long-term social, economic, and environmental sustainability of firms.

Chapter 12 Real Estate and Society (Piet Eichholtz and Nils Kok)
Real estate can play a key role in averting further climate change because of its high contribution to pollution and substantial energy consumption. Interest in green and sustainable buildings has grown dramatically in recent years with increasing awareness of these factors. This chapter explores the economic significance of the energy efficiency and sustainability trend in real estate, addressing the financial performance of green buildings, in both the United States and international markets. The behavior of corporations with respect to housing decisions is discussed, analyzing how real estate can be used as a proxy for corporate social responsibility. The chapter then investigates how institutional investors integrate sustainability in their allocations to real estate, measuring the environmental performance of dedicated property fund managers.

Chapter 13 Federal Housing Policies and the Recent Financial Crisis (Ronnie J. Phillips and Kenneth Spong)
The recent financial crisis and housing debacle destroyed wealth for homeowners and resulted in a substantial taxpayer bailout. Some contend that federal housing policies were a major reason for the crisis. In particular, public policies adopted under the goal of promoting greater home ownership, especially among low-income individuals, may have led to much weaker mortgage lending standards and put many homeowners at greater financial risk. This social goal of increasing home ownership, and thereby promoting wealth accumulation by low-income families, has a long history and has been supported by both political parties and a wide range of policy makers. This chapter reviews the key laws and policies adopted to promote homeownership and the manner in which they may have

contributed to weaker lending standards, excessive debt burdens, and, in turn, the housing and financial crisis. Several alternative approaches are suggested to promote the goal of greater homeownership and wealth building among lower-income families without threatening the financial health of such families or putting the financial system and taxpayer at risk.

Chapter 14 Predatory Lending and Socially Responsible Investors (Christopher L. Peterson)

This chapter attempts to provide a simple introduction to the complex finance, law, and policy of consumer credit markets with an eye toward helping responsible investors begin to develop the ability to shun predatory lending. While no consensus exists on what lending practices are socially corrosive, responsible investors looking for opportunities in consumer financial markets have an obligation to make their best effort to identify and avoid predatory loans. This chapter first provides a brief introduction to some of the more controversial current lending practices. Next, it summarizes evidence of self-defeating consumer borrower behavior. Then, it provides a cursory characterization of the rapidly evolving law of consumer finance. Finally, this chapter suggests several warning signs of predatory lending that can serve as a starting point for further investigation.

Chapter 15 Use and Misuse of Financial Secrecy in Global Banking (Ingo Walter)

This chapter explores financial secrecy as a product that is traded in organized and unorganized markets. It examines demand functions based on the disutility of financial disclosure, and supply functions based on the ability to impede financial disclosure. The "price" is defined as the displacement of the risk/return frontier incorporating financial secrecy, as opposed to a benchmark frontier lacking protection against financial disclosure. Agency and enforcement problems are examined in the presence of financial secrecy, with an emphasis on tax evasion and money laundering. The framework developed in the chapter is useful in explaining the behavior of principals active in the market for financial secrecy, namely, strategies of individuals, firms, and countries active in the supply of financial secrecy, civil and criminal enforcement actions, and financial flows across regulatory jurisdictions motivated by financial secrecy considerations.

Section III. Corporate Engagement

This section consists of five chapters dealing with the topic of corporate engagement. Chapter 16 focuses on the role of governance in CSR. Chapter 17 investigates the various ways of measuring CSR from the perspective of different stakeholders. Chapter 18 discusses corporate philanthropy from the perspectives of value enhancement and agency cost. Chapters 19 and 20 examine institutional investor and social activism.

Chapter 16 Corporate Social Responsibility and Governance (Lorenzo Sacconi)

Corporate social responsibility (CSR) is a model of corporate governance (CG) extending fiduciary duties from fulfillment of responsibilities towards the firm's owners to fulfillment of analogous fiduciary duties toward all the firm's stakeholders. After considering the place of CSR in the debate about alternative CG modes, a full-fledged social contract foundation of the multistakeholder and multi-fiduciary model is presented. The chapter shows that CSR is a social norm that would endogenously emerge from the stakeholders' social contract seen as the first move in an equilibrium selection process that reaches the equilibrium state of a CG institution. The social contract provides a model of the impartial mediating reasoning performed by a board of directors striving to balance different claims of stakeholders. It also allows deducing the multistakeholder objective function that socially responsible firms maximize, and then provides a specification of the particular fiduciary duties owed to each stakeholder according to its position.

Chapter 17 Measuring Responsibility to the Different Stakeholders (Amir Rubin and Eran Rubin)

This chapter provides a discussion of the complexity of having an all-encompassing measure that quantifies corporate social responsibility (CSR) performance of a firm. It suggests an approach for measuring the different aspects of CSR, aimed to better align social and corporate goals. The chapter analyzes the different stakeholders associated with CSR and their interrelationships. The chapter contains a survey of the literature on stakeholder specific measures, whose purpose is to provide transparency on how a corporation affects a specific group of stakeholders. The chapter also presents a brief history of stakeholder specific responsibility measures and discusses how these measures are used in both academic work and practice.

Chapter 18 Corporate Philanthropy (Janet Kiholm Smith)

This chapter explores a myriad of issues related to corporate philanthropy. The historical accounts of firm involvement in social causes provide perspective for understanding the empirical evidence regarding the determinants of corporate giving and its impact on firm performance. The two primary hypotheses for giving programs, value enhancement and agency cost, generate testable implications that have been widely studied. Overall, the results suggest that enhanced financial performance is not the overriding concern of managers when authorizing corporate contributions. Instead, most evidence points to the prevalence of agency costs. However, the evidence cannot refute the notion that some firms align their philanthropy with underlying strategy and may be successful at leveraging their giving to differentiate their product or work environment. This chapter identifies various methodological and data-related challenges for research on corporate philanthropy.

Chapter 19 Institutional Investor Activism (Diane Del Guercio and Hai Tran)

For the past quarter century, institutional investors have been frequent activist shareholders on corporate governance issues. A large literature of academic research examines whether this activity is effective in influencing target firms and enhancing the performance of both target firms and activists' portfolios. The importance of this question stems from the role of institutional investors as large and influential investors in the capital markets and as financial fiduciaries who are entrusted with the assets of millions of clients and beneficiaries. This chapter examines the many parallels between the issues that institutions face today in incorporating environmental, social, and governance criteria into their investment and activism programs, and the issues arising 25 years ago in the context of corporate governance. In short, socially responsible activism appears to be in the early stages of gaining momentum and legitimacy among mainstream institutional investors, with a steady stream of academic research likely to follow.

Chapter 20 Social Activism and Nongovernmental Organizations (Jonathan P. Doh and Deborah Zachar)

This chapter provides an overview of the role of social activism in the realm of socially responsible finance and investing. The chapter begins with a brief review of various perspectives on corporate social responsibility, focusing especially on the role of stakeholder theory and stakeholder management. It then documents the emergence of civil society actors such as nongovernmental organizations (NGOs) as critical players in the process by which stakeholders influence financial decisions through their activism. Next, the chapter describes the various mechanisms through which activists influence finance and investments. The chapter concludes with suggestions for further research.

Section IV. Socially Responsible Investing

The four chapters in this section examine the investment aspects of social responsibility. Chapter 21 focuses on the corporate long-term value associated with the firm making socially responsible investments. The last three chapters discuss various aspects of social responsibility in the investment industry. Chapter 22 discusses the risk-adjusted performance of SRI institutional investors and financial companies. This is followed by Chapter 23, which details the historical development of SRI and its investment performance, and concludes with predictions about its future. Lastly, Chapter 24 demonstrates the money flows into and out of SRI funds globally.

Chapter 21 Corporate Socially Responsible Investments (John R. Becker-Blease)

Corporations making socially responsible investments have attracted considerable interest in the popular press over the past several decades. The impact of these decisions on corporate value and the intended beneficiaries is the subject of a substantial academic literature in management and economics, and a small but growing literature in finance. Researchers suggest five potential sources of long-term value from corporate social responsibility (CSR) focused investments. This chapter reviews the literature associated with each potential source of value, and concludes that the preponderance of evidence is consistent with the hypothesis that CSR-focused investments are associated with long-term value creation.

Chapter 22 SRI Mutual Fund and Index Performance (Halil Kiymaz)

This chapter provides a review of the literature on socially responsible investing (SRI) with particular emphasis on empirical evidence of mutual fund and index performance. SRI is no longer a negligible segment of international capital markets. During the last two decades, SRI has increased sharply, reflecting the changes in investor sensitivities in social, environmental, and ethical issues. The main issue for firms is whether providing a risk-adjusted return to investors is possible while being socially or ethically responsible. Although the issue is far from being resolved, the existing literature tends to report that a cost is associated with investors willing to invest in SRI. Further, investors appear to accept lower performance to seek their moral choice of investment.

Chapter 23 Performance Implications of SR Investing: Past versus Future (Nadja Guenster)

This chapter discusses the impact of socially responsible investment (SRI) strategies on portfolio performance. It focuses on two common investment strategies: investing in firms with leading environmental, social, and governance (ESG) policies and shunning firms that are involved in "sinful" business activities. Examples of so-called sinful business activities are tobacco, alcohol, gambling, and weapons. Two opposite effects have influenced the performance of SRI methods over the last decades. First, a strategy of overweighting firms with high ESG standards and underweighting firms with poor standards earned positive abnormal returns. Second, SRI investors lost out on high returns on sin stocks. Although socially responsible investors, in aggregate, often experience similar performance to conventional investors, this is likely to change. In an efficient market, firms with high ESG standards should not earn higher returns than firms with low standards. The empirical evidence suggests that this equilibrium is approaching. Then, socially responsible investors missing out on the high sin stock returns are likely to underperform conventional investors.

Chapter 24 Money Flows of Socially Responsible Investment Funds around the World (Luc Renneboog, Jenke Ter Horst, and Chendi Zhang)

This chapter studies the money flows into and out of socially responsible investment (SRI) funds around the world. In their investment decisions, investors in SRI funds may be more concerned with ethical or social issues than with fund performance. Therefore, SRI money flows are less related to past fund returns. Ethical money is less sensitive to past negative returns than are conventional fund flows, especially when SRI funds primarily use negative or sin/ethical screens. Social attributes of SRI funds weaken the relationship between money inflows and past positive returns. However, money flows into funds with environmental screens are more sensitive to past positive returns than are conventional fund flows. Stock picking based on in-house SRI research increases the money flows. These results give evidence on the role of nonfinancial attributes, which induce heterogeneity of investor clienteles within SRI funds. No evidence of a smart money effect is found, as the funds that receive more inflows neither outperform nor underperform their benchmarks or conventional funds.

SUMMARY AND CONCLUSIONS

Since the late 1960s and early 1970s, CSR and SRI have gained considerable momentum. Since that time much discussion and research has focused on these two areas. According to Sparkes (2002, p. 65), "CSR and SRI are two sides of the same coin. Yet, the two terms differ in that SRI takes a bottom-up approach that focuses mainly on the power of investors, while CSR is a top-down approach that requires more action from corporations than investors."

Both the theory and practice of CSR and SRI have been moving ahead at a rapid pace, and this momentum is likely to continue in the future. Thus, gaining an understanding of the key principles and concepts of CSR and SRI as well as the empirical evidence involving these topics is more important than ever. Although this is a daunting task, this book can help provide the basis for achieving this understanding. Enjoy the trip as you explore the many facets of socially responsible finance and investing.

REFERENCES

Archel, Pablo, Javier Husillos, and Crawford Spence. 2011. "The Institutionalization of Unaccountability: Loading the Dice of Corporate Social Responsibility Discourse." *Accounting, Organizations and Society* 36:6, 327–343.

Baker, H. Kent, and Gary E. Powell. 2005. *Understanding Financial Management: A Practical Guide.* Malden, MA: Blackwell Publishing.

Bollen, Nicolas P. B. 2007. "Mutual Fund Attributes and Investor Behavior." *Journal of Financial and Quantitative Analysis* 42:3, 683–708.

Campbell, John L. 2007. "Why Would Corporations Behave in Socially Responsible Ways? An Institutional Theory of Corporate Social Responsibility." *Academy of Management Review* 32:3, 946–967.

Carroll, Archie B. 1999. "Corporate Social Responsibility: Evolution of a Definitional Construct." *Business & Society* 38:3, 268–295.

Derwall, Jeroen, Kees Koedijk, and Jenke Ter Horst. 2011. A Tale of Values-Driven and Profit-Seeking Social Investors. *Journal of Banking and Finance* 35:8, 2137–2147

Donaldson, Tom, and Lee E. Preston. 1995. "The Stakeholder Theory of the Corporation: Concepts, Evidence and Implications." *Academy of Management, Review* 20:1, 65–91.

Freeman, R. Edward. 1984. *Strategic Management: A Stakeholder Approach.* Marshfield: MA: Pitman Publishing Inc.

Freeman, R. Edward. 1998. "Stakeholder Theory of the Modern Corporation." In Max B. E. Clarkson, ed. *The Corporation and Its Stakeholders,* 123–138. Toronto: University of Toronto Press.

Freeman, R. Edward, Jeffrey S. Harrison, Andrew C. Wicks, Bidhan L. Parmar, and Simone de Colle. 2010. *Stakeholder Theory: The State of the Art.* Cambridge, UK: Cambridge University Press.

Friedman, Milton. 1962. *Capitalism and Freedom.* Chicago: University of Chicago Press.

Friedman, Milton. 1970. "The Social Responsibility of Business Is to Increase Its Profits." *New York Times Magazine,* September 13, 32–33, 122, 126.

Friedman, Andrew L., and Samantha Miles. 2006. *Stakeholders: Theory and Practice.* Oxford, UK: Oxford University Press.

Harrison, Jeffrey S., Douglas A. Bosse, and Robert A. Phillips. 2010. "Managing for Stakeholders, Stakeholder Utility Functions, and Competitive Advantage. *Strategic Management Journal* 30:1, 58–74.

Hong, Harrison, and Marcin Kacperczyk. 2009. "The Price of Sin: The Effects of Social Norms on Markets." *Journal of Financial Economics* 93:1, 15–36.

Jensen, Michael C. 2001. "Value Maximization, Stakeholder Theory, and the Corporate Objective Function." *Journal of Applied Corporate Finance* 14:3, 8–21.

Norman, Wayne, and Chris MacDonald. 2004. "Getting to the Bottom of 'Triple Bottom Line.'" *Business Ethics Quarterly* 14:2, 243–262.

Phillips, Robert A., ed. 2011. *Stakeholder Theory: Impact and Prospects.* Northhampton, MA: Edward Elgar Publishing.

Porter, Michael E., and Mark R. Kramer. 2011. "The Big Idea: Creating Shared Value." *Harvard Business Review* 89:1/2, 62–77.

SIF. 2010. "2010 Report on Socially Responsible Investing Trends in the United States." Social Investment Forum (SIF). Available at http://ussif.org/resources/research/documents/2010 TrendsES.pdf.

Sparkes, Russell. 2002. *Socially Responsible Investment: A Global Revolution*. Chichester, UK: John Wiley & Sons.

Statman, Meir. 2004. "What Do Investors Want?" *Journal of Portfolio Management* 30:5, 153–161.

ABOUT THE EDITORS

H. Kent Baker is a University Professor of Finance and Kogod Research Professor in the Kogod School of Business at American University. Professor Baker has written or edited 19 books including *Survey of International Finance, Survey Research in Corporate Finance, The Art of Capital Restructuring, Capital Budgeting Valuation, Behavioral Finance: Investors, Corporations, and Markets*, and *Corporate Governance: A Synthesis of Theory, Research, and Practice*. As one of the most prolific finance academics, he has published more than 150 refereed articles in such journals as the *Journal of Finance, Journal of Financial and Quantitative Analysis, Financial Management, Financial Analysts Journal, Journal of Portfolio Management*, and *Harvard Business Review*. He has consulting and training experience with more than 100 organizations. Professor Baker holds a BSBA from Georgetown University; M.Ed., MBA, and DBA degrees from the University of Maryland; and an MA, MS, and two Ph.D.s from American University. He also holds CFA and CMA designations.

John R. Nofsinger is a Professor of Finance and Nihoul Faculty Fellow at Washington State University. He is one of the world's leading experts in behavioral finance and is a frequent speaker on this topic and socially responsible finance at investment management conferences, universities, and academic conferences. He has authored (or coauthored) nine scholarly, trade, and text books. His book, *The Psychology of Investing* (4th edition, 2010), is popular in the investment industry. His books have been translated into Arabic, Chinese, Japanese, Korean, Polish, Portuguese, Spanish, and Thai. Professor Nofsinger is also a highly successful scholar, having published more than 50 articles in scholarly and practitioner journals. His research has appeared in the *Journal of Finance, Journal of Business, Journal of Financial and Quantitative Analysis, Journal of Corporate Finance, Journal of Banking and Finance, Financial Management, Financial Analysts Journal, Journal of Behavioral Decision Making*, and many others. Professor Nofsinger earned a Ph.D. (finance) from Washington State University.

PART I

Foundations and Key Concepts

CHAPTER 2

Stakeholder Analysis

LLOYD S. KURTZ
Chief Investment Officer, Nelson Capital Management, Lecturer, University of
California, Berkeley and Santa Clara University

INTRODUCTION

The stakeholder worldview—the idea that the firm is best described as a network
of relationships with a diverse group of constituencies—has great intuitive appeal.
Social investors often incorporate elements of stakeholder theory in their work, and
many believe that stakeholder principles can be used to improve on conventional
investment analysis.

A logical premise is that a company that treats employees well and works hard
to maintain good community relationships would have numerous advantages over
companies that do not make similar efforts. These efforts would likely help the
company's brand image, aid employee retention and new employee recruitment,
and provide an advantageous starting point for negotiations with regulators. Taken
together, these advantages should allow the company to be more productive and
profitable, and therefore be worth more than other firms. The U.S. social investment
firm Pax World Investments (2011), one of the first investment firms to formally
implement a stakeholder framework, puts it this way: "[W]e believe that well-
managed companies that maintain good relations with employees, consumers,
communities, and the natural environment, and that strive to improve in those
areas, will in the long run better serve investors as well."

Implementation of this intuitively appealing idea is challenging, however.
Stakeholder theory has been discussed intensively by management theorists, ethicists, and legal scholars for almost 20 years. But it has so far had little influence on
fundamental analysis, which remains grounded primarily in traditional economics
and finance, as well as in customary practices of the investment industry. Of the
thousands of analysts employed by mainstream investment banks, only a small
fraction specializes in areas requiring stakeholder analysis.

In the past 10 years, however, some social investment firms have sought to
directly incorporate stakeholder information into their investment decision making, particularly with respect to environmental, social, and governance (ESG)
metrics. This is known as ESG integration. Unlike the older practice of values-
based investment, which typically reflects the salient features of a particular religious or ethical paradigm, ESG integration seeks to exploit intangible information
gleaned from stakeholder analysis to obtain an investment advantage. Some social

investors choose only one approach or the other, while others seek to employ elements of both.

Like the field of corporate social responsibility (CSR), which it resembles in many ways, stakeholder analysis seeks to employ a more robust set of metrics than are offered by the traditional toolkit. The differences are primarily of perspective. As Crane and Matten (2010, p. 61) note, "[u]nlike the CSR approach, which strongly focuses on the corporation and its responsibilities, the stakeholder approach starts by looking at various groups to which the corporation has a responsibility." In practice, social investment analysis usually involves using data elements traditionally associated with CSR, such as corporate charitable giving, product safety, and executive pay, but uses frameworks derived from stakeholder analysis to place them in the proper context. CSR provides the data, and stakeholder analysis provides the structure.

Modern stakeholder analysis is therefore concerned with all aspects of a firm's business. Good financial results are appealing, but the stakeholder analyst asks: How have they been achieved? Does the company's superior return on capital result from outstanding labor productivity, or is it due to imposing externalities through environmental pollution or the sale of harmful products? Does the company engage in activities that might harm its reputation? If so, what steps have its managers taken to mitigate these impacts? Social investors employ stakeholder analysis to address these questions and develop a view about management quality and the long-term sustainability of the firm's business model.

The purpose of this chapter is to critically evaluate how stakeholder frameworks may be applied in investment analysis. The rest of this chapter is organized as follows. The remainder of this introduction discusses historical precursors to stakeholder analysis, notably the input/output model. The chapter then reviews the empirical support for a stakeholder worldview and proceeds to a discussion of stakeholder theory. This is followed by a detailed discussion of instrumental stakeholder theory as adapted to investment analysis, with particular attention paid to the relationship between noncontrolling owners and controlling managers and shareholders. The chapter concludes with a brief discussion of the impact of stakeholder information on financial markets.

STAKEHOLDERS VERSUS SHAREHOLDERS

Despite its intuitive appeal, a stakeholder worldview also elicits plausible objections. If the owner of a shop increases worker pay above the market rate for labor, why wouldn't that be a direct subtraction from his or her wealth? Or, if a publicly traded company decides to donate $1 per share to charity, shouldn't the share price rationally be expected to fall by $1? Such expenditures appear to be a poor allocation of resources, particularly to those who view the primary mission of the firm as the maximization of its share price. Micklethwait and Woolridge (2002, p. 187) describe the dispute in the following manner:

> Since the mid-nineteenth century, there has been a battle between two different conceptions of the company: the stakeholder ideal that holds that companies are responsible to a wide range of social groups and the shareholder ideal that holds that they are primarily responsible to their shareholders.

In the shareholder-first narrative, proponents of stakeholder theory hope to reduce shareholder wealth in order to increase the wealth of others. Ironically, some stakeholder theorists seem to agree. For instance, Freeman (1998, p. 126) states that "we must reconceptualize the firm around the following question: For whose benefit and at whose expense should the firm be managed?" Freeman (p. 126) indicates that the narrow focus on shareholders should be replaced with a broader set of obligations:

> [We] can revitalize the concept of managerial capitalism by replacing the notion that managers have a duty to stockholders with the concept managers bear a fiduciary relationship to stakeholders. Stakeholders are those groups who have a stake in or claim on the firm...[including] suppliers, customers, employees, stockholders, and the local community, as well as management in its role as agent for these groups.

In framing the central problem as the division of wealth generated by the firm, both narratives draw attention away from the value-creation process. But surely what the firm does is of greater importance to society and the environment than how it allocates the resulting cash flows. A major polluter might redirect profits away from shareholders and toward community stakeholders, but trying to minimize the pollution in the first place would probably be more sensible.

THE INPUT/OUTPUT MODEL

How does a firm create value? The classical input/output model, in which managers marshal a variety of resources to serve customers, embeds many elements of a stakeholder worldview. Exhibit 2.1 illustrates the model, in which suppliers, shareholders, and employees cooperate to produce goods or services for customers.

Inputs are priced according to the logic of supply and demand, and in equilibrium each supplier earns normal economic profits. Each of the inputs competes continuously with the others for its share of the firm's wealth. If higher costs for

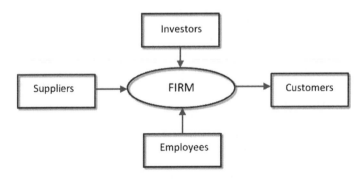

Exhibit 2.1   Input/Output Model
This exhibits shows an input/output model of the interaction between the firm and various parties, specifically investors, suppliers, and employees who provide inputs so that the firm can provide its products and services to its customers.
Source: Modified from Donaldson and Preston (1995).

one input cannot be passed on to customers through a price increase or offset by cost reductions elsewhere, owners will bear the ultimate costs.

This model has considerable practical appeal. Evidence suggests that firms can work this way in the real world. Studies of the auto industry, such as Abowd (1989) and Gorton and Schmid (2000), find that economic benefits for labor such as favorable wage settlements can negatively affect firm value. The Costco Corporation's (2011) Codes of Ethics uses language that closely parallels the input/output model: (1) obey the law; (2) take care of our members; (3) take care of our employees, (4) respect our suppliers; if we do these four things throughout our organization, then we will achieve our ultimate goal, which is to (5) Reward our shareholders.

The input/output model also offers a useful expression of the duties of the firm's managers. Multiple relationships must be negotiated, and wealth creation depends on coordinated effort. Some inputs to the model such as labor have quasi-social characteristics. These elements make the input/output model a useful starting point for discussing stakeholder analysis.

STAKEHOLDERS AND CORPORATE STRATEGY

What would be needed to modify the input/output model to make it more complete? The stakeholder worldview expands the number of relationships associated with value creation. Government, for example, could be added to the diagram, given that companies must pay taxes and maintain good relationships with regulators.

Allowing for the possibility of win/win opportunities would be useful. Increasing worker pay and benefits might be a good idea, for example, if doing so could improve the firm's productivity and profitability. Superficially charitable expenditures might confer important benefits through advertising effects, community goodwill, or strengthening of existing firm competencies.

Some prominent business strategists endorse this idea. Porter and Kramer (2006, p. 56) introduce the idea of strategic corporate responsibility, which "does not treat corporate success and social welfare as a zero-sum game." They note that private firms often have unique capabilities and resources, and therefore have an opportunity to deploy them in ways that can benefit both their strategic position and society at large. In some situations, social challenges may occur where a particular company is the only societal resource with the appropriate combination of assets and expertise to address them.

McElhaney (2008) develops the concept further, classifying the development of firms' CSR activities into five levels of development, from "defensive" to "strategic." At the defensive level, a firm makes CSR investments to repair its reputation after bad behavior or as a reaction to unexpected negative events. At the strategic level, by contrast, a firm makes CSR investments proactively and with a strategic mind-set. As McElhaney (p. 11) notes, "A company at the highest stage of corporate social responsibility embeds CSR into its daily business operations, collaborates with other companies, and attempts to change the rules of the game or attack a problem or social issue at its cause." But firms must carefully choose areas of involvement. McElhaney (p. 42) remarks: "To be an effective business strategy, CSR must be tied to the business objectives of the firm."

EMPIRICAL SUPPORT FOR A STAKEHOLDER WORLDVIEW

If the stakeholder worldview has validity, the advantages for firms with strong stakeholder relations should be observable. That is, market participants should be able to observe both financial and reputational benefits for companies that are particularly attentive to stakeholder management.

A growing body of empirical research suggests that this is indeed the case. Over the past 10 years, researchers report a positive correlation between stakeholder management and financial outcomes. Firms with superior stakeholder performance have had superior financial results on average. They have had greater earning power, better reputations, and in some cases superior stock performance.

Orlitzky, Schmidt, and Rynes (2003), who conduct a meta-analysis of CSR studies, find a positive correlation with financial outcomes, including both reported earnings and stock market performance. One major problem with such studies is that sorting out causality is difficult. Is Wells Fargo the largest corporate giver in California because it is already a large, successful company, or is the company's success due in some way to its generous charitable giving programs? Orlitzky et al. (p. 427) directly address the issue of causality, finding that richer companies are more likely to engage in CSR, but that they appear to earn superior returns from doing so:

> [P]ortraying managers' choices with respect to corporate social performance and corporate financial performance as an either/or trade-off is not justified in light of 30 years of empirical data. [We find]...(1) across studies, Corporate Social Performance is positively correlated with Corporate Financial Performance, (2) the relationship tends to be bidirectional and simultaneous, [and] (3) reputation appears to be an important mediator of the relationship....

Numerous studies show that firms with superior CSR performance have above-average capital efficiency ratios. For example, using similar procedures over different time periods, Waddock and Graves (1997b) and Tsoutsoura (2004) find that a broadly defined CSR measure is correlated with higher returns on assets. Guenster, Derwall, Bauer, and Koedijk (2010) focus on corporate sustainability practices and also find that higher-ranked firms have higher returns on assets.

Some evidence also suggests that good CSR performance is correlated with firm growth, and that positive stakeholder performance in one area may positively affect other areas as well. Lev, Petrovits, and Radhakrishnan (2010) find that generous corporate givers tend to have faster revenue growth. Gong and Grundy's (2011) analysis of corporate matching charitable grants finds that labor productivity is higher at firms with matching schemes and employees are happier working for those firms. Edmans (2011) demonstrates that firms with superior employee relations have a greater propensity to deliver earnings that exceed Wall Street estimates.

Researchers also find that strong CSR performers tend to have better reputations. Waddock and Graves (1997b) report that the *Fortune* magazine "most admired" companies have superior CSR ratings. Graves and Waddock (2000) show that companies featured in the book *Built to Last* by Collins and Porras (1997) also had superior CSR ratings. Apparently, companies that invest aggressively in stakeholder relationships—even those outside the narrow value creation process described by the input/output model—can gain meaningful benefits from doing so.

TYPES OF STAKEHOLDER THEORY

While studies support elements of a stakeholder worldview, theorists differ on the appropriate interpretation of these findings. However, two general points of strong agreement exist. First, virtually all stakeholder theorists believe that the firm is accountable to a broader set of interests than those described in the input/output model. Although details may differ, most theoretical presentations are consistent in their broad outlines with the diagram presented in Exhibit 2.2.

In this visualization the corporation is accountable not only to suppliers, employees, and shareholders, but to other constituencies. Both the nature of the accountability and the identities of various stakeholders and the underlying definition of stakeholder, vary markedly among theorists. Yet, virtually all stakeholder theorists agree that the firm's obligations go beyond the narrow specifications of the input/output model.

Second, most agree that the relationships between firm managers and stakeholders go beyond the basic logic of supply and demand. In his classic work *Exit, Voice, and Loyalty*, Hirschman (1970) persuasively argues that many economic relationships have a substantive social or political dimension. In economic relationships, when one party is confronted with deteriorating or unacceptable quality, he will seek to end the relationship in favor of a more appealing alternative (exit). But relationships may also depend, according to circumstances, on socio-political logic. When that is the case, the party complains and seeks change, possibly using the threat of exit to obtain bargaining leverage (voice). Such decisions are mediated in Hirschman's framework by loyalty, which he defines as a function of a realistic estimate of the probability of change, the cost of switching, and the quality of the alternatives.

Hirschman's (1970) approach appears well suited to stakeholder analysis. Customers who have a bad experience will often complain before switching to another

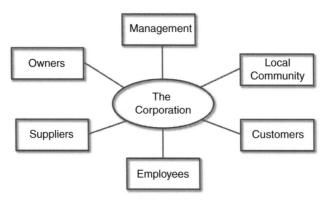

Exhibit 2.2   A Stakeholder Model of the Corporation
Source: Modified from Freeman (1984).

product. Employees who are dissatisfied with their pay may try to negotiate before moving to another employer. Shareholders who dislike some aspect of the firm's behavior may choose to engage firm management rather than sell the stock. In each case, an astute management response may mean the difference between continued success and a negative outcome for the firm. This is why many social investors believe stakeholder analysis can shed fresh light on questions of management quality.

The literature contains many different versions of stakeholder theory. Donaldson and Preston (1995) usefully separate them into three nested categories: normative, instrumental, and descriptive. These are more than academic distinctions because each category focuses on a different purpose, and the definition of a stakeholder varies as well.

Normative Stakeholder Theory

Early iterations of stakeholder theory were normative. In the classic formulation, Freeman (1998, p. 129) describes stakeholders as "groups and individuals who benefit, or are harmed by, and whose rights are violated or respected by, corporate actions. Just as stockholders have a right to demand certain actions by management, so do other stakeholders have a right to make claims." Unlike the input/output model, relationships between the firm and stakeholders are not strictly economic or even quasi-economic as described by Hirschman (1970), but may also be mediated by laws, duties, or expected ethical conduct.

The normative formulation does not attempt to explain how firms work. It is intended instead as a model or idealization of how they should work, according to a particular philosophical viewpoint. As such, normative stakeholder theory does not lend itself to empirical analysis or offer explicit tools for choosing among a set of investment opportunities. This limits its applicability to ESG integration and the search for superior investment performance.

Still, normative stakeholder theory is of great utility to values-based investors who want to systematically describe their social and environmental priorities. It offers a framework whereby they can make their expectations around CSR behavior explicit, and communicate to companies and clients about how they view such issues.

Instrumental Stakeholder Theory

Discussion of normative stakeholder theory has been extensive among management theorists, ethicists, organizational scientists, legal scholars, and others. But investors and economists have made only modest contributions. In their book-length treatment of stakeholder theory, Friedman and Miles (2006) cite more than 500 distinct sources, but fewer than a dozen from contemporary financial or economic journals. Freeman, Harrison, Wicks, Parmar, and de Colle (2010) devote major sections of their book to traditional disciplines of business, ethics, and corporate social responsibility, but not to economics or finance.

Instrumental stakeholder theory retains the stakeholder concept and, like the normative approach, represents the firm as a network of relationships. But instrumental stakeholder theory views the stakeholder network as the means to the end of wealth creation. Jones (1995, p. 235) presents instrumental stakeholder theory as a synthesis of stakeholder conceptions and economic thought:

> [Instrumental stakeholder theory] implies that behavior that is trusting, trustworthy, and cooperative, not opportunistic, will give the firm a competitive advantage. In the process, it may help explain why certain "irrational" or altruistic behaviors turn out to be productive and why firms that engage in those behaviors survive and often thrive.

Therefore, instrumental stakeholder theory fits the needs of performance-oriented investors better than other approaches. In instrumental stakeholder theory, investors are not seen as adversaries, but as the beneficiaries of effective management.

Unlike normative stakeholder theory, instrumental stakeholder theory does not presuppose a particular philosophical viewpoint or legal environment, which is also true of descriptive stakeholder theory, discussed below. This is a major advantage for investors engaged in the analysis of global businesses. A global corporation may interact with dozens of governments, hundreds or thousands of communities, and many different cultural environments. In such a situation, definitions of the firm in terms of a single ethical framework or legal system are unlikely to be of much value.

This is a critical point because many stakeholder theorists view the firm as first and foremost a legal entity. But trading networks recognizable as firms have existed for a thousand years or more, predating modern legal systems, and their underlying dynamics are best explained by economic and reputational dynamics, not legal ones. Gordon (2008, pp. 827–829) describes the experience of a group of traders in 1138:

> Although the partners recognized that Abraham bin Yiju had himself been defrauded, they had no means, legal or otherwise, to recover a bad debt in Mangalore. All they could do to help was to threaten the reputation of the dealer who defaulted. Madmun's cousin suggested this sort of censure in a letter to Abraham. "Perhaps you should threaten him that here in Aden we censure anyone that owes us something and does not fulfill his commitments. Maybe he will be afraid of the censure. If he does not pay, we shall issue an official letter of censure and send it to him, so that he will become aware of his crime."

Reputation was not incidental to the conduct of business for these traders; it was integral and remains so for most businesses today. In a global business environment where firms cannot master the elements of each legal system to which they are exposed, trust and reputation remain paramount. When he assumed the role of chief executive officer (CEO) at Salomon Brothers, Warren Buffett (1991) told employees: "lose money for the firm and I will be understanding; lose a shred of reputation for the firm, and I will be ruthless."

Descriptive Stakeholder Theory

Both normative and instrumental stakeholder theory operate from a relatively narrow perspective. The normative version idealizes firm behavior through a social or moral view. The instrumental version views stakeholder relationships as the means to some objective, such as maximizing firm value. Descriptive stakeholder theory, by contrast, seeks to adopt the broadest possible perspective and use the stakeholder model as a tool for describing the activities and interests of the firm.

- A normative stakeholder theorist might say: Coca-Cola has a duty to protect the environment, so it should pay more attention to its water policies.
- An instrumental stakeholder theorist might say: Coca-Cola should manage its water policies so as to minimize the negative impact of reputational effects on firm value.
- A descriptive stakeholder theorist might say: Coca-Cola's water policies are an important defining characteristic of the firm.

Social investors may, depending on their needs, incorporate normative, instrumental, or descriptive stakeholder approaches into their activities. Values-based investors will use models that are largely normative in character, whereas performance-oriented investors will more likely employ some type of instrumental stakeholder analysis. Policy makers and academics may well prefer the broader perspective of descriptive stakeholder theory. The sections that follow describe an instrumental framework intended to enhance traditional fundamental analysis.

STAKEHOLDER ANALYSIS FOR INVESTORS

Some stakeholder theorists conceive of "the firm" or "the corporation" as the center of the stakeholder network. Exhibit 2.2 is a representative example. Hill and Jones (1992) contribute a crucial refinement to this view. In their account, the firm is a "nexus of contracts" between the controlling managers and other stakeholders. The firm cannot make decisions or enter into contracts on its own. Managers are the only ones with direct control over the decision-making apparatus.

In practice, a control group is at the center of each firm. A *control group* is the group of managers and controlling owners whose consent is required for major investments. Although the control group cannot necessarily be defined in terms of traditional job titles, such as a chief financial officer (CFO), it can be identified by the group's leadership role in capital allocation. The control group, through its allocation of money and management attention, makes the decisions that determine whether the firm's stakeholder relations will be good, bad, or indifferent. Thus, an investment-oriented approach to stakeholder analysis must focus on the activities of this group.

This is consistent with both agency theory and investment practice. There is a market for corporate control. In corporate takeovers, the seller typically demands and receives a control premium. This is in addition to the intrinsic economic value of the target enterprise as defined by the market, and in practice is often large enough to negatively impact the long-term economics of the transaction for the buyer (Sirower 1997).

As a first approximation, the control group might think of itself first in all decisions, while still recognizing the many constraints under which it operates. Each stakeholder relationship requires continuous negotiation, usually some economic investment, and an ongoing assessment of its competitive benefits.

Given the control group's ability to contract for whatever materials and services are needed, one might ask why formal corporate structures are necessary at all. Why cannot the control group simply contract for everything needed on the open market? Williamson (1985, 2009) extensively analyzes this question and concludes that, due to differing transaction costs, in some cases the hierarchical organization and other attributes of the firm allow it to be more efficient than open market contracting. The internal organization and the market are complementary—neither can fully supplant the other. In his Nobel Prize lecture, Williamson (2009, p. 468) concludes that "markets and hierarchies differ in discrete structural ways and we need to come to terms with the strengths and weaknesses of each."

The direct implication is that the control group must assess, for all of the firm's activities, which should be internal and which should be contracted externally. A decision to close a plant and subcontract production work to facilities elsewhere could have major impacts on multiple stakeholders. This is a primary area of interest for stakeholder analysts, who focus on situations where outsourcing or subcontracting could entail operational or reputational risks.

The control group negotiates continuously, through both economic and sociopolitical mechanisms, with three distinct stakeholder types: customers, suppliers, and contextual stakeholders. These will be reviewed briefly in the sections that follow, using the U.S. retailer Wal-Mart as a primary example.

TYPES OF STAKEHOLDERS: CUSTOMERS

Customers are the essential stakeholders of the firm. According to Wyly (2000, p. 279), Sam Walton, the founder of Wal-Mart, said "there is only one boss— the customer. And she can fire everybody in the company from the chairman on down, simply by spending her money somewhere else." In his biography of Walton, Trimble (1990, p. 268) reports "[he] harps constantly that customers must feel 'it is their store' and know they will be 'treated fairly, honestly, and with respect.' Against competitors who employed intermittent promotional strategies ('high/low pricing'), Walton offered customers a compelling alternative: "Always Low Prices."

Customer relationships vary widely, but in most cases reputation is a critical component in the firm's value proposition. A customer is unlikely to buy a product—be it food, tires, or industrial services—without some reference to the reputation of the offering firm. According to Rosenbloom and Barbaro (2009):

> A 2004 report prepared by the consulting firm McKinsey found that 2 percent to 8 percent of Wal-Mart consumers surveyed had ceased shopping at the chain because of "negative press they have heard." Wal-Mart executives and Wall Street analysts began referring to the problem as "headline risk."

The same report also stated that 82 percent of customers expected Wal-Mart to act as a role model for other companies.

When firms are faced with a customer complaint, they have at least three response strategies. The simplest and most straightforward is to modify the product. If a restaurant's food is not very good, investment in a new chef may be the best response. Product modification may be expensive, however, or in some cases even impossible. Many efforts have been made, for example, to make airline travel pleasant and convenient, but the task has defeated even the greatest minds.

Some firms invest in customer service initiatives, offering customers a higher degree of voice through telephone support, feedback surveys, or special training for staff. This must be done judiciously, however, as the most vocal customers may also be the least profitable.

A third option is for the firm to employ its own voice to influence customers. Advertising is powerful and arguably underemphasized by Hirschman (1970) in his original analysis. Rather than modify its products, the company may seek to instead modify customers' opinions of them. This may be as straightforward as employing a celebrity endorser or as complex as rebranding following a major crisis.

TYPES OF STAKEHOLDERS: SUPPLIERS

Even in a simple business, the control group must coordinate the efforts of many suppliers. The input/output model views the firm primarily as a network of supplier relationships, managed for the benefit of the customer and the owner. Fundamental analysis is well-suited to many aspects of these relationships, but some supplier relationships have unique characteristics that are not widely followed by the investment industry. For example, supplier relationships may have important social and environmental impacts. According to Humes (2011, pp. 1320–1321), when Wal-Mart evaluated its environmental footprint in the mid-2000s, management concluded that 90 percent of the firm's environmental impact was transmitted through its supply chain.

Labor is a critical input in many businesses and in some cases, such as software development, may be the dominant supplier relationship. Successful firms often have highly skilled workforces, and therefore must make substantial investments to retain scarce skills. McWilliams and Siegel (2000) demonstrate that some CSR metrics correlate strongly with research and development (R&D) expenditures. They inspect Waddock and Graves's (1997a) finding that high CSR companies are more capital efficient, and show that it disappears when the CSR rating is replaced with a research and development (R&D) variable. This strongly suggests that one reason for the correlation between high CSR and firm profitability is that highly profitable firms are more likely to engage in R&D, and more likely to offer programs and benefits to retain the skilled labor required to conduct it.

Innovative labor practices may make an important difference even in lower-margin businesses, however. Tedlow (2003, pp. 340–341) reports that in the competitive U.S. retail industry of the 1950s and 1960s, Sam Walton placed heavy emphasis on attracting the best possible workforce.

> Walton knew he had to hire the best store managers he could. As he put it, from early in his career Walton would do what he would always "do for the rest of my run in the retail business without any shame or embarrassment: nose around other people's stores searching for good talent." Walton kept the talent loyal to the company by "giving them a piece of the action" in both monetary and psychic terms . . . store managers and later the 'associates' who staffed the stores benefited from a generous profit-sharing program.

The profit-sharing program, in which Wal-Mart stock was allocated to employee retirement accounts, allowed even rank-and-file employees to retire with substantial wealth in the early days of the company. This resulted in an exceptionally loyal and motivated workforce.

Investors may also be viewed as suppliers. The most problematic aspect of the shareholder-first narrative of the firm is that noncontrolling shareholders are essentially just suppliers of a widely available input to production, in this case capital. From a theoretical perspective, why they should expect, or be offered, more than normal economic profits from this exchange is unclear. Because many investors subscribe to the shareholder-first narrative, this makes the relationship between the control group and noncontrolling owners a point of particular interest for stakeholder analysts, and this relationship will be discussed in detail in the section called Owners as Stakeholders.

TYPES OF STAKEHOLDERS: CONTEXTUAL

Contextual stakeholders include local communities, governments, the environment, and the international community. These stakeholders stand outside the normal trading dynamics of the firm, but may nonetheless have large impacts on firm value. While some commentators stress nonfinancial aspects of these relationships, the firm has a direct economic relationship with contextual stakeholders in virtually all cases. The relationship with government, for example, includes tax payments. Community relationships may include fees, incentive payments or tax breaks from the community, or contractual arrangements at the local level. In the case of the environment, the economic components of the relationship include costs of prevention and cleanup, and revenue impacts due to loss of reputation in the case of accidents or excessive pollution.

The most directly powerful contextual stakeholders are governments, which in the event of a poorly managed relationship can pursue remedies up to and including a shutdown of the firm's operations within its jurisdiction. Companies have many resources available to manage these relationships. In some cases, however, firms may actually co-opt those charged with regulating them, a phenomenon known as *regulatory capture*. This in itself may represent a threat to owners' interests, as in the absence of normal safeguards the control group may engage in excessive risk-taking (Taylor 2011).

Governmental relationships are receiving fresh scrutiny in the United States following a Supreme Court decision affirming the right of corporations to actively participate in politics (Liptak 2010). In August 2011, a group of law professors formally petitioned the U.S. Securities and Exchange Commission (SEC) to require companies to disclose their political contributions (Bebchuk and Black 2011). At that time, about 60 percent of the firms in the S&P 100 index voluntarily disclosed their political contributions.

Community relationships likewise embed both opportunity and risk. Hirschman (1970, p. 63) observes that "in addition to maximizing profits, the firm will tend to minimize discontent of its customers, for the highly rational purpose of earning goodwill or reducing hostility in the community of which it is a part." Failure to do so may be costly. Hoge (2006) reports on a unanimous decision by the city council of Hercules, California, to seize a Wal-Mart building site by eminent domain: "the vote caused most of the 300 people who had packed Hercules City Hall for the meeting to break out in cheers and applause." Although Wal-Mart successfully challenged the decision in court, it ultimately relinquished the building site in a negotiated sale.

In the mid-2000s, Wal-Mart's senior management decided to carefully review its sustainability practices. According to Humes (2011, p. 1221), the decision to focus on sustainability first, rather than social relationships, was deliberate:

> [Consultant Jib Ellison said:] "If you really want to take on sustainability with a capital 'S,' it's not just the environment. It's health care, it's wages, it's ethical sourcing, it's globalization. Everything. A sustainable economy, a sustainable society." "Yes," Scott said warily, "but let's start with the environment." Scott knew it was too late to limit Wal-Mart's "exposure" on the sorts of social issues Ellison suggested.

The program began to deliver economic results almost immediately. Humes (pp. 1203–1207) describes the savings achieved by reducing the packaging for a single item sold in the company's stores:

> The minor size reduction would allow a much greater number of toys to be boxed and loaded inside a single shipping container. The same number of toys could be shipped using 497 fewer shipping containers—the trailer-sized metal boxes used to haul goods around the globe. These changes led to $2.4 million in annual savings.... Then [management] started asking...: Where else can we do this?

Although social investors place considerable emphasis on contextual stakeholder relationships, firms may also become very successful before having to put much conscious effort into them. For a small or medium-sized firm, outstanding execution on the relationships described in the input/output model may be all that is needed for the company to achieve good business results. Humes (2011, p. 1298) quotes former Wal-Mart CEO Lee Scott as saying that he enjoyed the early days of the company when it was not so well-known: "[Competitors] ignored us, and we could focus on the core of our business." However, Humes argues (p. 1299) that "the flip side of this inward focus was a kind of tunnel vision that left many in the home office incapable of accepting any criticism of Wal-Mart as constructive, and suspicious of outsiders bearing new ideas." As the firm grows, management of contextual stakeholder relationships becomes unavoidable.

OWNERS AS STAKEHOLDERS

Given the centrality of the control group in stakeholder analysis, the most important and problematic relationship is likely to be between noncontrolling owners and the control group, which is usually centered on the CEO. These relationships are challenging because noncontrolling owners are entrusting their wealth to others, and even in highly developed legal systems may have little recourse if the firm misallocates their money.

In evaluating management quality, research suggests noncontrolling owners should take a close interest at least three distinct areas. Expressed as risks these areas are expropriation, overreach, and overinvestment.

Expropriation

Expropriation is the tendency of the control group to use firm resources for its own benefit. If the relationship is not monitored, the control group has every incentive to arrange the firm's affairs to its own advantage. Abundant evidence indicates that this often happens, negatively affecting shareholder wealth. Analysis by Heron, Lie, and Perry (2007, p. 24) suggest that "slightly less than 30 percent of public companies that used stock options for executive compensation manipulated at least one grant between 1996 and 2005." Bebchuk, Grinstein, and Peyer (2011) find that executives and directors receive an abnormally high percentage of grants at the lowest price of the grant month. As Bebchuk et al. note (p. 1), these "lucky" grants are more "associated with higher CEO compensation from other sources, and are correlated with a lack of majority of independent directors on the board, no independent compensation committee with an outside blockholder, or a long-serving CEO."

Stakeholder-oriented investors must therefore be exceptionally attentive to the integrity of the control group. Gawer (2010) finds that deterioration in corporate governance ratings was a leading indicator of underperformance in the European equity market from 1999 to 2009, although there was not a comparable effect for improving scores. But monitoring may be expensive. In his study of the CalPERS corporate governance program, Barber (2006, p. 4) describes the dilemma this way:

> Absent any monitoring by investors, agency costs take a (relatively) large percentage of [firm] valuation. Investors can reduce the agency cost bite taken out of the valuation pie by monitoring corporations, but monitoring is costly, varies in effectiveness, and, no doubt, has diminishing marginal returns.

Although Barber concludes that the CalPERS program had positive valuation effects on targeted firms, it has not been widely imitated. In 2010, CalPERS substantially modified its program.

In his updated edition of Graham (2004, p. 6491), journalist Jason Zweig speculates on why the noted investor said less about investors' relationship to management in each succeeding edition of the book: "Why did Graham cut away more than three-quarters of his original argument? After decades of exhortation, he evidently had given up hope that investors would ever take any interest in monitoring the behavior of corporate managers." Investors still have the opportunity to take Graham's advice, and the data suggest they would be wise to do so.

Overreach

All leadership positions require self-confidence, but self-confidence is a double-edged sword. *Overreach* refers to the degree to which the control group engages in activities as a result of overconfidence, such as exceeding the contractual authority granted by owners or engaging in self-promotional behavior to the detriment of the business.

Harding (2011) cites New York Stock Exchange (NYSE) data showing that the average holding period for stocks fell from eight years in 1960 to three years in 1990, to about one year in 2000. With the advent of high-frequency trading strategies, this figure has continued to decline, and by 2010 it was approximately six months. Given the ease and low cost of exit, investors typically prefer exit over voice when they are disappointed in management performance.

As owner time horizons continue to shorten, managers have become restive, and some have sought to change the rules of the relationship. Christensen and Anthony (2007) go so far as to argue that managers would be better off ignoring some stockholders:

> Perhaps it is time for companies to adjust the paradigm of management responsibility: "You are investors and speculators, not shareholders, and you temporarily find yourselves holding the securities of our company. You are responsible for maximizing the returns on your investments. Our responsibility is to maximize the long-term value of this company. We will therefore act in the interest of those whose interests coincide with our long-term prospects, namely employees, customers, the communities in which our employees live, and the minority of investors who plan to hold our securities for several years."

But is this responsibility or arrogance? Page (2005, p. 10) argues, along with many others, that final control of the firm must reside with owners, for both legal and moral reasons:

> because they shoulder most of the risk, shareholders have every right—within the law—to exclusively enjoy, benefit from, and dispose of the entity they created. To deny this right would be tantamount to annihilating ownership privileges and would deal a severe blow to individual liberties, something no democratic regime would tolerate.

No matter how fickle or short-term the behavior of owners, managers cannot simply ignore them.

Khurana (2002) contends that shorter time horizons have distorted the CEO selection process in the United States, causing it to overvalue "charismatic" external candidates. In many cases, Khurana (p. 20) says that "less emphasis is placed on the company's strategic situation and how appropriate the background of the candidate is in light of this," at the expense of qualified but less famous or inspiring internal candidates. Malmendier and Tate (2007) find evidence that companies managed by these "superstar CEOs" underperform on average. Bebchuk, Cremers, and Peyer (2011) indirectly arrive at a similar finding, demonstrating that the CEO's pay fraction—the percentage of senior management compensation taken by the CEO—is negatively correlated with risk-adjusted returns for shareholders.

The converse also appears to be true: One striking finding of the Collins (2001) study of companies that had dramatically improved their performance was that in every instance the CEO was not well-known and typically sought to deflect credit to other members of his senior team.

Overinvestment

Given the tensions described above, managers face major temptations to overinvest in stakeholder relationships to advance their own personal interests. Consider CEOs who are planning a political career in a few years' time. Such individuals may want to be seen as generous and civic-minded while in their management role, and might approve excessive expenditures for charitable giving, employee compensation, or other measures likely to benefit their reputations.

Cai, Jo, and Pan (2011, p. 6) test this by comparing CEO pay at high CSR companies to compensation at low CSR companies:

> as their reputations improve, CEOs will enjoy better outside career opportunities and greater bargaining power, which will eventually increase their ability to negotiate a higher level of compensation. If CEOs tend to overinvest in CSR to build their reputations, we would expect a positive association between CSR and CEO compensation.

Their analysis suggests an alternative explanation. High CSR CEOs tend to have lower pay than their low CSR counterparts, which suggests that agency-motivated overinvestment in CSR is not widespread. Cai et al. propose that CSR instead functions as a conflict resolution mechanism among stakeholders, a view consistent with that held by many social investment practitioners.

Few studies appear to support the overinvestment hypothesis. Orlitzky et al.'s (2003) meta-analysis of the CSR literature suggests that firms do not systematically overinvest in stakeholder relationships. Kim and Statman (2011) review the environmental expenditures of large U.S. firms and do not find evidence of overinvestment. Identifying individual cases of overinvestment, however, is a necessary competency of the stakeholder analyst.

Stakeholder Information in Financial Markets

Many types of stakeholder information can be value-relevant, and therefore of interest to financial markets. The first presumption of a financial theorist, however, would be that this information is already correctly incorporated into valuations. Some evidence suggests that this is the case. Kurtz and diBartolomeo (2011) find that, after adjusting for conventional investment factors, a longstanding U.S. social investment index had alpha that was statistically indistinguishable from zero over an 18-year time period. Petrillo (2010) reports positive results for a backtest of an optimized portfolio intended to maximize exposure to CSR, but out-of-sample performance (now known as the iShares MSCI Select ESG Fund) has closely tracked the overall stock market.

In their important study of intangible information in markets, Daniel and Titman (2006, p. 1640) conclude that the search for relevant insights is likely to be a difficult one:

> An interesting avenue for future research would be to explicitly identify sources of intangible information that lead to overreaction. We conjecture that this is information that is related to firms' growth opportunities. In particular, it may be the case that investors overestimate the precision of relatively nebulous information

about future growth opportunities, and as a result, tend to overreact to the information. Unfortunately, testing this possibility is likely to be difficult since, almost by definition, it is difficult to identify and characterize this nebulous information.

A few studies demonstrate how this can work in practice. Derwall, Guenster, Bauer, and Koedijk (2005) find significant unexplained outperformance in portfolios constructed using a widely used assessment of sustainability practices. Edmans (2011) finds that a portfolio consisting of a list of superior employers outperformed the market on a risk-adjusted basis for long time periods. According to Edmans (p. 1), "the stock market does not fully value intangibles, even when independently verified by a highly public survey on large firms."

Stakeholder analysis may also be relevant to portfolio risk management. Kumar (2009) finds that investor mistakes are larger and more frequent when firms are difficult to value, for example, when intangible value represents a large percentage of firm value.

Therefore, stakeholder analysis provides a set of tools that is likely to be useful to investors. The correlation of strong CSR performance and high R&D expenditures is provocative, for example, because high R&D expenditures are also associated with high levels of intangible value. Governance metrics and sustainability initiatives such as the one pursued by Wal-Mart may signal changes in the economics and future prospects of the firms. Stakeholder frameworks can help investors identify, assess, and prioritize situations in which markets have not fully assimilated this intangible information.

SUMMARY AND CONCLUSIONS

Putting stakeholder analysis into practice requires acknowledging that some versions of stakeholder theory are more consistent than others with the economic realities of the firm. The input/output model is a good starting point for investor-oriented stakeholder analysis. Although it depicts the struggle for resources within the firm somewhat simplistically, this model also embeds elements that are consistent with a stakeholder worldview.

Research has strengthened the case for a correlation between good stakeholder management and superior financial outcomes at the firm level. Studies show that firms with superior ESG (environmental, social, and governance) and CSR (corporate social responsibility) performance have, on average, experienced superior financial results. They have had greater earning power, better reputations, and, in the cases of environmental practices and employee relations, superior stock performance as well. These findings strongly suggest that a stakeholder worldview has validity, and that analysis of stakeholder relationships can aid in the analysis of firm-level financial performance.

A modified form of instrumental stakeholder theory lends itself to empirical analysis and fits well with the needs of investors. Under this approach, the firm is viewed as a network of complex economic relationships in which both sociopolitical and financial logic govern most participants' behavior. These relationships are dynamic and continuously negotiated. At the center of the network is the control group, which allocates resources and attention to stakeholder relationships in order to maximize its own wealth. Good management may be defined as the efficient allocation of resources to stakeholder management such that a substantial surplus remains for owners and managers. Modern stakeholder analysis of this type aids in the assessment of management quality. It also clarifies the economic relationships among stakeholders, owners, and managers, and underscores the importance of corporate governance initiatives to protect owners' interests.

The resulting insights are value relevant. While efficient market theory predicts that all available information about the firm is already incorporated in market valuations, a few studies show significant performance effects that appear to be directly attributable to stakeholder relationships. Thus, stakeholder relationships deserve the attention not just of social investors, but of managers and investors generally.

DISCUSSION QUESTIONS

1. Despite being intuitively appealing to many, what are some objections to a stakeholder worldview?
2. What are examples of specific evidence supporting a stakeholder worldview?
3. What are some major points of agreement among stakeholder theorists?
4. Which type of stakeholder theory is most likely to be useful for performance-oriented investors? Why?
5. How might stakeholder analysis be useful in assessing management quality?

REFERENCES

Abowd, John M. 1989. "The Effect of Wage Bargains on the Stock Market Value of the Firm." *American Economic Review* 79:4, 774–800.

Barber, Brad M. 2006. "Monitoring the Monitor: Evaluating CalPERS' Activism." Working Paper, University of California, Davis.

Bebchuk, Lucian, and Bernard Black. 2011. "Petition for Rulemaking." Committee on Disclosure of Corporate Political Spending. Available at www.sec.gov/rules/petitions/2011/petn4–637.pdf.

Bebchuk, Lucian A., K. J. Martijn Cremers, and Urs C. Peyer. 2011. "The CEO Pay Slice." *Journal of Financial Economics* 102:1, 199–221.

Bebchuk, Lucian A., Yaniv Grinstein, and Urs Peyer. 2010. "Lucky CEOs and Lucky Directors." *Journal of Finance* 65:6, 2363–2401.

Buffett, Warren. 1991. "Opening Statement before the Subcommittee on Telecommunications and Finance of the Energy and Commerce Committee of the U.S. House of Representatives," May 1. Available at http://blogs.wsj.com/marketbeat/2010/05/01/buffetts-1991-salomon-testimony/.

Cai, Ye, Hoje Jo, and Carrie Pan. 2011. "Vice or Virtue? The Impact of Corporate Social Responsibility on Executive Compensation." Working Paper, Santa Clara University.

Christensen, Clayton, and Scott D. Anthony. 2007. "Put Owners in Their Place: Why Pander to People Who Now Hold Shares, on Average, Less than 10 Months?" *BusinessWeek*, May 27. Available at www.businessweek.com/magazine/content/07_22/b4036100.htm.

Collins, James C. 2001. *Good to Great: Why Some Companies Make the Leap . . . and Others Don't.* New York: Harper Business.

Collins, James C., and Jerry I. Porras. 1997. *Built to Last: Successful Habits of Visionary Companies.* New York: Harper Business.

Costco Corporation. 2011. "Costco Code of Ethics." Available at https://secure.ethicspoint .com/domain/media/en/gui/28417/index.html.

Crane, Andrew, and Dirk Matten. 2010. *Business Ethics*, 3rd ed. New York: Oxford University Press.

Daniel, Kent, and Sheridan Titman. 2006. "Market Reaction to Tangible and Intangible Information." *Journal of Finance* 61:4, 1605–1643.

Derwall, Jeroen, Nadja Guenster, Rob Bauer, and Kees Koedijk. 2005. "The Eco-Efficiency Premium Puzzle." *Financial Analysts Journal* 61:2, 51–63.

Donaldson, Tom, and Lee E. Preston. 1995. "The Stakeholder Theory of the Corporation: Concepts, Evidence and Implications." *Academy of Management Review* 20:1, 65–91.

Edmans, Alex. 2011. "Does the Stock Market Fully Value Intangibles? Employee Satisfaction and Equity Prices." *Journal of Financial Economics* 101:3, 621–640.

Freeman, R. Edward. 1984. *Strategic Management: A Stakeholder Approach*. Marshfield, MA: Pitman Publishing Inc.

Freeman, R. Edward. 1998. "Stakeholder Theory of the Modern Corporation." In Max B. E. Clarkson, ed. *The Corporation and Its Stakeholders*, 123–138. Toronto: University of Toronto Press.

Freeman, R. Edward, Jeffrey S. Harrison, Andrew C. Wicks, Bidhan L. Parmar, and Simone de Colle. 2010. *Stakeholder Theory: The State of the Art*. Cambridge: Cambridge University Press.

Friedman, Andrew L., and Samantha Miles. 2006. *Stakeholders: Theory and Practice*. Oxford: Oxford University Press.

Gawer, Joseph. 2010. "Corporate Governance Changes, Biases and Stock Returns." Working Paper, Université Paris Dauphine and NATIXIS Asset Management.

Gong, Ning, and Bruce D. Grundy. 2011. "Can Socially Responsible Firms Survive Competition? An Analysis of Corporate Employee Matching Grants." Working Paper, Australian School of Business, University of New South Wales.

Gordon, Stewart. 2008. *When Asia Was the World*. Philadelphia: Da Capo Press.

Gorton, Gary, and Frank Schmid. 2000. "Class Struggle inside the Firm: A Study of German Codetermination." Working Paper, Wharton School Center for Financial Institutions, University of Pennsylvania.

Graham, Benjamin. 2004. *The Intelligent Investor*. Revised Edition. *HarperCollins e-books. Kindle Edition*.

Graves, Samuel B., and Sandra Waddock. 2000. "Beyond 'Built to Last': An Evaluation of Stakeholder Relationships in 'Built-to-Last' Companies." *Business and Society Review* 105:4, 393–418.

Guenster, Nadja, Jeroen Derwall, Rob Bauer, and Kees Koedijk. 2010. "The Economic Value of Corporate Eco-Efficiency." *European Financial* 17:4, 679–704.

Harding, Sy. 2011. "Stock Market Becomes Short Attention Span Theater of Trading." *Forbes*, January. Available at www.forbes.com/greatspectulations/2011/01/21/stock-market-becomes-short-attention-span-theater-of-trading/.

Heron, Randall A., Erik Lie, and Todd Perry. 2007. "On the Use (and Abuse) of Stock Option Grants." *Financial Analysts Journal* 63:3, 17–27.

Hill, Charles W. L., and Thomas M. Jones. 1992. "Stakeholder-Agency Theory." In Max B. E. Clarkson, ed. *The Corporation and Its Stakeholders*, 205–242. Toronto: University of Toronto Press.

Hirschman, Albert. 1970. *Exit, Voice, and Loyalty*. Cambridge, MA: Harvard University Press.

Hoge, Patrick. 2006. "Vote Goes against Wal-Mart: Council Oks Using Eminent Domain to Block Retailer." *San Francisco Chronicle*, May 24. Available at http://articles .sfgate.com/2006–05–24/bay-area/17293735_1_mart-discount-store-eminent-domain.

Humes, Edward. 2011. *Force of Nature: The Unlikely Story of Wal-Mart's Green Revolution*. New York: HarperCollins. Kindle edition.

Jones, Thomas M. 1995. "Instrumental Stakeholder Theory: A Synthesis of Ethics and Economics." *Academy of Management Review* 20:2, 404–437.

Khurana, Rakesh. 2002. *Searching for a Corporate Savior: The Irrational Quest for Charismatic CEOs.* Princeton: Princeton University Press.

Kim, Yongtae, and Meir Statman. 2011. "Do Corporations Invest Enough in Environmental Responsibility?" *Journal of Business Ethics* 103:3, 351–383.

Kumar, Alok. 2009. "Hard-to-Value Stocks, Behavioral Biases, and Informed Trading." *Journal of Financial and Quantitative Analysis* 44:6, 1375–1401.

Kurtz, Lloyd, and Dan diBartolomeo. 2011. "The Long-Term Performance of a Social Investment Universe." *Journal of Investing* 20:3, 95–102.

Lev, Baruch, Christine Petrovits, and Suresh Radhakrishnan. 2010. "Is Doing Good Good for You? How Corporate Charitable Contributions Enhance Revenue Growth." *Strategic Management Journal* 31:2, 182–200.

Liptak, Adam. 2010. "Justices, 5–4, Reject Corporate Spending Limit." *New York Times*, January 21. Available at: www.nytimes.com/2010/01/22/us/politics/22scotus.html.

Malmendier, Ulrike, and Geoffrey A. Tate. 2007. "Superstar CEOs." Working Paper, University of California, Berkeley.

McElhaney, Kellie. 2008. *Just Good Business: The Strategic Guide to Aligning Corporate Responsibility and Brand.* San Francisco: Berrett-Koehler Publishers.

McWilliams, Abagail, and Donald Siegel. 2000. "Corporate Social Responsibility and Financial Performance: Correlation or Misspecification?" *Strategic Management Journal* 21:5, 603–609.

Micklethwait: John, and Adrian Woolridge. 2002. *The Company.* New York: The Modern Library.

Orlitzky, Marc, Frank L. Schmidt, and Sara L. Rynes. 2003. "Corporate Social and Financial Performance: A Meta-analysis." *Organization Studies* 24:3, 403–441.

Page, Jean-Paul. 2005. *Corporate Governance and Value Creation* Charlottesville, VA: Research Foundation of the CFA Institute.

Pax World Investments. 2011. "Key Issues Briefs." Available at www.paxworld.com/investment-approach/sustainability-research/key-issues-briefs.

Petrillo, Alan. 2010. "Q&A with a 'Quant': A Pro's Perspective on ESG Integration into Mathematical Modeling." MSCI *Insights.* Available at www.msci.com/insights/responsible_investing/questions_quant_esg.html.

Porter, Michael E., and Mark R. Kramer. 2006. "Strategy and Society: The Link between Competitive Advantage and Corporate Social Responsibility." *Harvard Business Review* 84:12, 78–92, 163.

Rosenbloom, Stephanie, and Michael Barbaro. 2009. "Green-Light Specials, Now at Wal-Mart." *New York Times*, January 24. Available at www.nytimes.com/2009/01/25/business/25walmart.html?pagewanted=all.

Sirower, Mark L. 1997. *The Synergy Trap.* New York: The Free Press.

Taylor, John B. 2011. "'Reckless Endangerment' by Gretchen Morgenson and Joshua Rosner." Book Review, *Washington Post*, May 27. Available at www.washingtonpost.com/entertainment/books/reckless-endangerment-by-gretchen-morgenson-and-joshua-rosner/2011/05/11/AGs4cqCH_story.html.

Tedlow, Richard S. 2003. *Giants of Enterprise: Seven Business Innovators and the Empires They Built.* New York: HarperBusiness.

Trimble, Vance. 1990. *Sam Walton: The Inside Story of America's Richest Man.* New York: Dutton.

Tsoutsoura, Margarita. 2004. "Corporate Social Responsibility and Financial Performance." Working Paper, University of California, Berkeley.

Waddock, Sandra A., and Samuel B. Graves. 1997a. "The Corporate Social Performance-Financial Performance Link." *Strategic Management Journal* 18:4, 303–319

Waddock, Sandra A., and Samuel B. Graves. 1997b. "Finding the Link between Stakeholder Relations and Quality of Management." *Journal of Investing* 6:4, 20–24.

Williamson, Oliver E. 1985. *The Economic Institutions of Capitalism.* New York: The Free Press.

Williamson, Oliver E. 2009. "Transaction Cost Economics: The Natural Progression." Nobel Prize Lecture. Available at www.nobelprize.org/nobel_prizes/economics/laureates/2009/williamson_lecture.pdf.

Wyly, Sam. 2000. *1000 Dollars and an Idea: Entrepreneur to Billionaire.* New York: New Market Press.

ABOUT THE AUTHOR

Lloyd S. Kurtz is Chief Investment Officer at Nelson Capital Management, an investment firm in Palo Alto, California. He is a lecturer in investments at Santa Clara University, and is also affiliated with the Center for Responsible Business at the Haas School of Business, University of California, Berkeley. At the Center for Responsible Business he oversees the Moskowitz Prize, an annual prize recognizing outstanding studies in the field of social investment, and acts as faculty advisor for the Haas Socially Responsible Investment Fund. He is a Chartered Financial Analyst.

CHAPTER 3

Corporate Social Responsibility

HEATHER ELMS
Associate Professor, Kogod School of Business, American University

MICHELLE WESTERMANN-BEHAYLO
Assistant Professor, Kogod School of Business, American University

INTRODUCTION

Corporate social responsibility (CSR) attracts considerable attention among academics, practitioners, and the popular press. Yet understandings of CSR and the foci of analyses vary across these discussions. This chapter focuses on various academic discussions of CSR among several business disciplines (business ethics, finance, accounting, and marketing). The intention is to further acquaint each of these fields with the others' research, and thus provide each with material for future investigations including interdisciplinary studies. In particular, because other disciplines' literatures do not reflect several key themes in the business ethics literature, the chapter discusses the evolution of CSR thinking in business ethics and identifies several key issues currently at the forefront of the business ethics discussion.

The remainder of the chapter has the following organization. The first section provides an overview of the business ethics literature on CSR. The next two sections discuss how the finance, accounting, and marketing literatures currently reflect the evolution of thinking on CSR in business ethics, including key issues. These sections discuss how greater use of the business ethics literature on CSR might contribute to CSR discussions in each of these functional literatures. The fourth section examines emerging directions of scholarship. Suggestions are provided on how a greater use of these functional literatures may help develop the business ethics literature. In doing so, the hope is also to move discussions in the practitioner and popular arenas forward. This latter aim is particularly appropriate given that many business ethics discussions of CSR begin with Friedman's (1970) article in *The New York Times Magazine*, entitled, "The Social Responsibility of Business Is to Increase Its Profits." The final section provides a summary and conclusions.

THE BUSINESS ETHICS LITERATURE

In reviewing the business ethics literature, this section identifies six key themes in the evolution of, and current thinking in, the business ethics discussion of CSR.

These themes are then pursued in a discussion of the current finance, accounting, and marketing literatures.

Friedman versus Freeman: Stockholders versus Stakeholders

Friedman's (1962, 1970) claims are often juxtaposed in the business ethics literature with various forms and interpretations of Freeman's stakeholder theory (Beauchamp and Bowie 1989; Donaldson, Werhane, and Cording 2002; Donaldson and Werhane 2008; Beauchamp, Bowie, and Arnold 2009). The comprehensive seminal version of Freeman's (1984) theory is, however, explicitly critical of at least certain forms of CSR (Elms, Johnson-Cramer, and Berman 2011). Freeman (1984, p. 40) notes:

> While there have been many criticisms of the research in corporate social responsibility, perhaps the most troubling issue is the very nature of "corporate social responsibility" as if the concept were needed to augment the study of business policy. Corporate social responsibility is often looked at as an "add on" to "business as usual" and the phrase often heard from executives is "corporate social responsibility is fine, if you can afford it." . . .

> We need to understand the complex interconnections between economic and social forces. Isolating "social issues" as separate from the economic impact that they have, and conversely isolating economic issues as if they had no social effect, misses the mark both managerially and intellectually. Actions aimed at one side will not address the concerns of the other. Processes, techniques and theories that do not consider all of these forces will fail to describe and predict the business world as it really is.

While often referenced as a foundational source for CSR, Freeman (1984) avoids making a responsibility-based argument about stakeholders, and instead only suggests that a lack of understanding of stakeholder expectations by managers puts firm performance at risk (Elms et al. 2011). Some later contributions (Evan and Freeman 1989; Freeman 2002) propose a fiduciary duty to stakeholders, but even later contributions (Freeman 2008a, p. 40) suggest only that a stakeholder-theory-based understanding of CSR means that "the primary responsibility of the executive is to create as much value for stakeholders as possible." Freeman, Velamuri, and Moriarty (2006); Freeman, Harrison, and Wicks (2007); and Freeman, Harrison, Wicks, Parmar, and De Colle (2010, p. 236) substitute "company" for "corporate" and "stakeholder" for "social" in CSR—thus rendering it "company stakeholder responsibility." Freeman et al. (2010, p. 236) emphasize that "talking of responsibilities that are contingent on size and success is highly problematic," so all companies need to be included—not just corporations—and that focusing on stakeholders provides greater direction than focusing on society. More recently, Freeman and Elms (2011, p. 1) explicitly suggest that "the social responsibility of business is to create value for stakeholders." Freeman (2008b, p. 162) explicitly attempts "to end the so called 'Friedman-Freeman' debate" by suggesting that a careful reading reveals that the two views are not at odds.

Instrumental versus Intrinsic Approaches

The juxtaposition of Friedman and Freeman as well as the evolution of Freeman's claims highlights one of the key distinctions also present in other CSR discussions. Friedman's (1962, 1970) and Freeman's (1984) claims are essentially instrumental—treating stakeholders as ends to firm performance, although Friedman's measure of performance is explicitly profit, and Freeman's includes both survival and competitive advantage. Freeman (2002) adds intrinsic concerns suggesting the need to treat stakeholders as ends in themselves, given their status both as humans and stakeholders. Phillips (2003, p. 95) emphasizes the additional obligations owed stakeholders given the firm's acceptance of stakeholders' voluntary contributions to the firm, vs. duties "owed by all to all simply by virtue of being human." Other recent contributions revert to an instrumental approach to stakeholders (Porter and Kramer 2011). Like Freeman before them, Porter and Kramer (p. 76) are critical of understandings of CSR that "have only a limited connection to the business." Instead, Porter and Kramer (p. 64, their italics) propose the concept of "creating shared value, which involves creating economic value in a way that *also* creates value for society by addressing its needs and challenges." However, while Porter and Kramer (p. 64) do suggest that "the purpose of the corporation must be redefined as creating shared value and not just profit per se," by at least implicitly prioritizing economic over social value and by proposing, shared value as "a new way to achieve economic success," they remain instrumental in their approach.

The Separation Thesis

Although Porter and Kramer (2011) are concerned about the potential separation of CSR from business, they remain willing to maintain a distinction between economic and social value. Freeman's (1984, p. 40) concern is that the implied separation of social and economic issues was only the "most troubling" of "many criticisms of the research in CSR." This concern foreshadows more recent discussions of what Freeman (1994) for the first time called "the separation thesis" or even later called "the separation fallacy" (Freeman 2008b). Freeman (1994, p. 412) describes the separation thesis as the idea that "The discourse of business and the discourse of ethics can be separated so that sentences like, 'x is a business decision' have no moral content, and 'x is a moral decision' have no business content." Freeman (2008b, p. 163) suggests: "The separation thesis is fairly straightforward, as Sen (1991) and others have suggested. . . . The basic idea is that it's not useful anymore to separate questions of business and questions of ethics." Wicks (1996), Sandberg (2008), and others contribute to the discussion.

Carroll's articles (1979, 1991), both also oft-cited foundations of current CSR research, instead attempt to separate business's social obligations into economic, legal, ethical, and discretionary (philanthropic). Carroll (1979, p. 499) recognizes: "These four categories are not mutually exclusive, nor are they intended to portray a continuum of economic concerns on one end and social concerns on the other. That is, they are neither cumulative nor additive." In distinguishing between ethical and discretionary responsibilities, Carroll also recognizes, however, that ethical responsibilities, like economic and legal responsibilities, are not voluntary. Schwartz and Carroll (2003) emphasize that even philanthropic behaviors may not be discretionary, eliminate this category, and present the other categories as a Venn diagram, rather than as a column (Carroll 1979) or a pyramid (Carroll 1991), both of which suggest a hierarchy of responsibilities, as well as the relative magnitude of each responsibility. The Venn diagram emphasizes the overlap among responsibilities, but also suggests pure economic, legal, and ethical responsibilities, with which Freeman and others might disagree.

Stakeholders versus Society

The contributions of Carroll (1979, 1991) and others also highlight another key distinction in the business ethics literature on CSR: responsibility to stakeholders vs. society. While Freeman and his co-authors' (Freeman et al. 2006, 2007, 2010) substitution of "stakeholders" for "society" in CSR emphasize their concern for responsibility to stakeholders—a subset of society with a specific relationship to the firm—Carroll and other CSR scholars remain concerned with society more broadly (Elms et al. 2011). Much CSR research similarly concerns societal rather than firm/stakeholder outcomes, including the reduction of poverty (Porter and Kramer 2006), conflict (Fort and Schipani 2004; Fort 2007, 2008), and human misery more generally (Margolis and Walsh 2003). Some CSR research remains unclear in its focus. For example, Porter and Kramer (2011) move back and forth between stakeholders and society. Others, including Waddock (2008, p. 30), identify a variety of foci, reduce the term to "corporate responsibility," and look to the "the company's business model and the impacts of the business model, strategies, and practices on stakeholders, nature, and societies." Freeman et al. (2010, p. 260, their italics) identify their position and reasoning, suggesting a need for clarity in CSR research:

> Stakeholder theory enters in the CSR debate by suggesting that the managers of the corporations have a responsibility not simply (and vaguely) to serve the *general interests* of society (which society? In today's global economy, where even small firms have dealings involving partners in several countries, with different social, legal, and ethical contexts, the definition of "society" as if it was a unique entity becomes very problematic), but rather to serve the interests of *the corporation's stakeholders....*

Corporate Social Performance (CSP) versus Corporate Financial Performance (CFP)

Notwithstanding critiques from some corners that corporate social and corporate financial behaviors and performance cannot be separated as both are necessary, not voluntary, components of overall firm performance, the so-called CSP vs. CFP debate continues. Although as noted above, many approaches to CSR are instrumental, Wood (2010, p. 50) notes, "To a large extent, CSP [an operationalization of responsibility] has been equated with 'doing good,' and the search has been on for a statistical relationship between CSP and financial performance (FP) so as to justify or delegitimize the normative calls for managers to pay attention to CSP." Despite the search, Orlitzky (2011, p. 411) states, "Many academic researchers regard the business case for CSP as unresolved ... despite the more optimistic conclusions reached in several meta-analyses ... as well as practitioner publications...."

Margolis and Walsh (2003, p. 277) also note: "A simple compilation of the findings suggests there is a positive association, and certainly very little evidence of a negative association between a company's social performance and its financial performance." A recent meta-analysis of 52 CSP/CFP studies reaches this same substantive conclusion (Orlitzky, Schmidt, and Rynes 2003). Orlitzky (2011, p. 411) further suggests that,

> The typical inference, based on narrative reviews of the literature, is that the empirical evidence is too varied to allow for definitive conclusions. . . . In these reviews, poor measures and weak theory construction are often mentioned as causes of this apparent variability in published findings. . . . More broadly, CSP-CFP research has also been called into question because it has been interpreted to support a thesis (the Separation Thesis) that, from the perspective of pragmatist ethics, is at least questionable—or even obsolete (Freeman 1994).

Margolis and Walsh (2003, p. 278) similarly further note:

> The reviewers see problems of all kinds in this research. They identify sampling problems, concerns about the reliability and validity of the CSP and CFP measures, omission of controls, opportunities to test mediating mechanisms and moderating conditions, and a need for a causal theory to link CSP and CFP. The imperfect nature of these studies makes research on the link between CSP and CFP self-perpetuating: each successive study promises a definitive conclusion, while also revealing the inevitable inadequacies of empirically tackling the question.

But while Orlitzky (2011) proceeds by examining the association between differences in institutional logics across subdisciplines and CSP/CFP cross-study variability, Margolis and Walsh (2003, p. 278) and others suggest that researchers must attempt to get beyond the CSP/CFP debate and instead move on to explore a new set of research questions including addressing "questions about what it is firms are actually doing in response to social misery and what effects corporate actions have, not only on the bottom line but also on society." Margolis and Walsh (2003, p. 285) also comment:

> To make sense of corporate responses to misery and discern the function of those responses, we need to understand which firms respond to which social problems, with what consequences, for both the firms and society. . . . Five areas of inquiry invite descriptive research: how companies extract and appraise the stimuli for action; how companies generate response options; how companies evaluate these options and select a course of action; how the selected course is implemented; and, finally, what consequences follow from corporate efforts to ameliorate social ills.

To Whom versus What, and the Relationship between Corporate and Stakeholder Responsibility

While Wood (2010, p. 51) suggests: "Ever since discussions of CSR began, the primary question has been: "to whom are corporations responsible, and for what, exactly?", much of the work in business ethics stops at identifying to whom corporations are responsible (e.g., which stakeholders), rather than detailing the content of those responsibilities (Phillips 2003; Walsh 2005). Much more work remains to be done in identifying the content of responsibilities to stakeholders other than shareholders (for whom the content has generally been identified as profit maximization—though even here, additional responsibilities might be identified.)

Elms and Phillips (2009, p. 406) and others (Phillips 2003; Palazzo and Scherer 2006; Scherer and Palazzo 2007) emphasize that this content "should be established through discourse between and among companies and stakeholders." Phillips (2003); Bosse, Phillips, and Harrison (2009); and Harrison, Bosse, and Phillips (2010) stress the existence of reciprocal moral obligations between companies and stakeholders. Work on both the extent and content of corporate responsibility note the relationship between corporate and stakeholder responsibility and thus the extent and content of stakeholder responsibility. Goodstein and Wicks (2007) provide examples across several companies and industries, noting that responsibilities will differ across organizational contexts. Elms and Phillips (2009) detail a set of corporate responsibilities specific to a particular industry (private security). This work emphasizes that corporate responsibility requires stakeholders to value that responsibility and to act upon that valuation. As institutions designed to meet demand, corporations are unlikely to behave responsibly without stakeholder responsibility (i.e., demands for responsible behavior from corporations through various decisions). In markets in which stakeholders value responsibility, corporate responsibility becomes endogenous. Friedman (1970, p. 32) notes that the responsibility "which will generally be to make as much money as possible" is "while conforming to the basic rules of the society, both those embodied in law and those embodied in ethical custom." Those laws and ethical customs reflect stakeholder responsibility. Given the relationship between corporate and stakeholder responsibility and the arguable neglect of stakeholder responsibility relative to corporate responsibility, more research on stakeholder responsibility, including what stakeholders do and should value, remains necessary to truly understand corporate responsibility (Elms, Brammer, Harris, and Phillips 2010).

THE FINANCE LITERATURE

Identifying how scholarly finance journals address CSR required searching the top academic finance journals, as shown in Exhibit 3.1, using ABI/Inform and EBSCO to identify articles published between January 2006 and August 2011. These searches involved using such broad terms as *corporate social responsibility*, *corporate responsibility*, *social responsibility*, *socially responsible*, and *responsibility*. Although the initial search yielded 69 articles, careful review reveals that only eight articles are relevant for the final sample.

The limited number of articles discussing CSR published in recent years in the top academic finance journals suggests that this topic does not appear to be a main concern in the finance literature. Where responsibility is mentioned, the concern seems limited to fulfilling fiduciary responsibilities to shareholders as opposed to addressing broader concerns. In the few articles that mention corporate responsibilities to other stakeholders, the discussion tends to be instrumental, developing the shareholder case for how attention to CSR may relate to firm financial performance and increased profits for shareholders in accordance with

Exhibit 3.1 Journals Reviewed for CSR Research during 2006 to 2011

This exhibit shows a list of the finance, accounting, and marketing journals searched using the ABI/Inform and EBSCO databases to identify relevant CSR articles published between January 2006 and August 2011.

Panel A. Finance Journals
Journal of Banking & Finance, Journal of Finance, Journal of Financial and Quantitative Analysis, Journal of Financial Economics, Journal of Financial Intermediation, Journal of International Money and Finance, Journal of Money, Credit, and Banking, and *Review of Financial Studies*

Panel B. Accounting Journals
Accounting Organizations and Society, Behavioral Research in Accounting, Contemporary Accounting Research, International Journal of Accounting, Journal of Accounting & Economics, Journal of Accounting & Public Policy, Journal of Accounting, Auditing & Finance, Journal of Accounting Research, Review of Accounting Studies, and *The Accounting Review*

Panel C. Marketing Journals
International Journal of Research in Marketing, Journal of the Academy of Marketing Science, Journal of Consumer Affairs, Journal of Consumer Psychology, Journal of Consumer Research, Journal of Marketing, Journal of Marketing Research, Journal of Public Policy & Marketing, and *Marketing Science*

Friedman (1962, 1970) and other instrumental perspectives. The exclusive focus on the shareholder case, without reference to the relationship between business and ethics, suggests that finance scholars have not yet rejected the separation thesis discussed above.

On the limited occasions when the finance literature discusses social activities or corporate responsibilities, agency theory concerns are often at issue, and the outcomes assessed frequently relate to the impact on financial performance or shareholder value. In other words, the CSP vs. CFP arguments requiring a shareholder case for CSR appear to underlie any interest in this topic in this field. As Goss and Roberts (2011, p. 1794) note, "The debate over the merits of CSR revolves around whether such investments are value enhancing or whether they are the value-destroying manifestation of agency conflicts." Often referencing Friedman's (1962, 1970) statements about CSR, much of the discussion of CSR in the finance literature revolves around the argument that where CSR does not directly increase shareholder value, it is an inappropriate misallocation or misappropriation of funds.

An "investment" in CSR may be seen as a misallocation of assets in the form of philanthropy. Porter and Kramer (2006) contend that certain types of philanthropy may provide a competitive advantage, and indeed, some finance research finds that giving does enhance shareholder value (Brown, Helland, and Smith 2006). Nevertheless, this outcome is seen as unlikely given that philanthropy is often given without regard to strategic goals or core competencies. Porter and Kramer (2002, p. 58) assert: "the way most corporate philanthropy is practiced today, Friedman is right." Thus, consistent with Friedman's (1962, 1970) arguments, philanthropy in the form of CSR that does not enhance firm value is considered a misallocation because the shareholders themselves should be determining whether and how to donate their funds.

Additionally, an "investment" in CSR may represent an agency conflict where managers benefit by misappropriating funds in the form of overspending on CSR initiatives (Barnea and Rubin 2010). Management is seen to receive personal credit for any investment in CSR beyond the optimal amount that would enhance firm value, while shareholders bear the costs (McWilliams and Siegel 2001). In such cases, overspending on CSR is compared to excessive managerial perquisites such as unnecessary corporate jets (Goss and Roberts 2011).

Given this perspective, CSR is only considered appropriate in the finance literature when seen as enhancing firm value by, for example, mitigating risk, reducing costs, or delivering a price premium. Thus, researchers find that firms that are strong in CSR have lower idiosyncratic risk (Lee and Faff 2009). Moreover, research evidence shows that firms strong in CSR have lower costs of capital (El Ghoul, Guedhami, Kwok, and Mishra 2011) and higher market-to-book ratios (Galema, Plantiga, and Scholtens 2008).

Conversely, the finance literature also features CSR when it decreases firm value by increasing costs. Goss and Roberts (2011) find that major concerns about a company's social responsibility practices (in other words, a record of corporate social irresponsibility) increase the cost of bank loans. Moreover, they find that low-quality borrowers with a record of strong CSR are seen to be engaging in discretionary spending that also increases the costs of borrowing. Moreover, research suggests that the agency problem of entrenched management combined with CSR activities has a particularly negative effect on financial performance (Surroca and Tribó 2008).

As discussed above, the business ethics literature largely rejects the separation thesis, which suggests that business decisions can be completely distinct from ethical or social responsibility. Yet, the recent finance literature still tends to treat CSR as being separate from, and often detrimental to the main purpose of business, which is financial performance. Seeing corporate responsibility and stakeholders other than shareholders as an intrinsic part of business would represent a major shift in financial thinking. This shift involves considering the following: the relationship among shareholders, other stakeholders, and society; the potential merits of CSR; and those to whom additional responsibilities might be directed as well as the content of those responsibilities. How this shift would impact the finance literature is examined after discussing how the literature in other core business disciplines addresses CSR in a similar "Friedmanesque" manner.

THE ACCOUNTING AND MARKETING LITERATURES

Finance is not the only core business discipline that adheres to a mostly shareholder-focused, instrumental approach to CSR. Scholarly publications in fields such as accounting and marketing also tend to discuss CSR as an acceptable activity only when a shareholder case can be made. Using the same procedure as outlined above for the finance literature resulted in initially identifying 217 articles about CSR in top accounting and marketing journals. Further analysis resulted in eliminating all but nine articles (three in accounting publications and six in marketing journals) for this discussion.

In general, the manner in which CSR is addressed in the accounting and marketing literatures is similar to the approach described above in the finance literature. The focus of analysis of CSR activities tends to revolve around the impact on shareholder value rather than the creation of stakeholder value. When considering the effects on nonshareholder stakeholder groups, such as the utility of CSR reporting to multistakeholder groups or the effect of marketing messages on consumers, the authors use an instrumental rather than intrinsic approach with shareholder profit maximization as the ultimate aim. Hence, they see a shareholder case or corporate financial performance as necessary to justify CSR activities, rather than CSP. Apparently, much of the accounting and marketing literature does not appear to reject the separation thesis.

The Accounting Literature

A recent stream of literature in accounting publications explores the expanding phenomenon of CSR reporting. Dhaliwal, Li, Tsang, and Yang (2011) ask, "What is the rationale for the increase in reporting nonfinancial information?" Their findings suggest that CSR reporting decreases the cost of capital by increasing the number of institutional investors and dedicated equity analysts focusing on the firm. Thus, the authors find an instrumental (shareholder case) rationale for CSR reporting in that firms can take advantage of a lower cost of capital.

Cohen, Holder-Webb, Nath and Wood (2011) ask, "How useful are corporate reports of non-financial information to retail (nonprofessional) investors?" Using data from an online survey of 750 nonprofessional investors reveals that a strong majority of retail investors do not value CSR reports, with only 30 percent of respondents using this type of information in their investment decision making. The authors also find that less than 5 percent of respondents value the quality of CSR information when issued by corporations themselves (such as on a corporate web site). By contrast, 24 percent of respondents value CSR information from financial professionals, and 39 percent value CSR information that third-party sources issue, such as nongovernmental organizations and rating agencies. Cohen et al. note that their evidence reveals a disconnect between the supply and demand of CSR information. Regarding this point, Holder-Webb, Cohen, Nath, and Wood (2009) show that corporations primarily disclose their CSR information through their websites and it is primarily self-serving information.

Cohen et al. (2011) suggest that if CSR information were normally audited, investors might have a greater demand for this information in the future, given their findings that younger investors are more interested than older ones in relying on credible CSR information in making future investment decisions. While their interest in the value of CSR reporting recalls business ethicists' interest in what stakeholders do and should value (above), the authors focus only on shareholders. Thus, Cohen et al view the value of CSR reporting to shareholders in an instrumental manner, as opposed to considering the intrinsic value that CSR reporting might have to a broader range of stakeholders.

Other scholars question whether the institutionalization of CSR reporting will actually be beneficial for nonprofessional investors or any other stakeholder groups. Archel, Husillos, and Spence (2011) report that as the government in Spain sought to institutionalize and regulate CSR reporting requirements, the discourse and power dynamics of the multistakeholder process became dominated by business interests and a profit-maximization narrative. Thus, the narrow shareholder profit case for CSR or CSR reporting outweighed concerns over the potential for creating value among a wider group of stakeholders. The authors' interest in exploring the considerable impact that corporate responsibility in accounting has on stakeholders suggests that discussions of CSR in the accounting literature are beginning to grapple with the issues currently debated in the business ethics literature about corporate responsibility beyond shareholder wealth maximization. Nevertheless, the profit case for CSR and the bottom line of shareholder value maximization continue to be prominently featured in the accounting literature.

The Marketing Literature

Similarly, recent marketing scholarship overwhelmingly presents CSR as appropriate only when an instrumental shareholder case can be made for it given outcomes such as increased customer satisfaction and loyalty, favorable firm image, and firm identification (Luo and Bhattacharya 2006). Specifically, the marketing literature often explores how the shareholder case for CSR can be made or destroyed by the manner in which marketing tactics are deployed and CSR activities are communicated. For example, Luo and Bhattacharya (2009) examine how corporate social performance can function as insurance for shareholder wealth by reducing firm idiosyncratic risk and stock price volatility when CSR is combined with higher advertising intensity. However, they find that when high research and development (R&D) spending is combined with advertising intensity and CSR, the increased risk can have a negative effect on the stability of shareholder wealth. Similarly, Simmons and Becker-Olsen (2006) examine the brand impact of social sponsorships as a marketing tactic. They find that where the sponsorships have a good fit with the firm's image, a positive effect is transferred to the market value of the firm's brand, but a poor sponsorship fit can dilute brand equity.

The marketing literature also identifies occasions where CSR messages are less effective or can even harm market value. For example, the lack of fit or lack of innovativeness of CSR marketing messages can actually reduce positive marketing outcomes such as customer satisfaction and market value outcomes in terms of Tobin's q or stock returns (Luo and Bhattacharya 2006). Similarly, CSR messages might not be as influential as other types of messages, such as firm ability or quality messages, in shaping consumer satisfaction and affecting measures of market value. In the types of companies where the responsible corporate action may be to develop advertising campaigns urging moderation in the use of their products including alcohol, tobacco, and snack foods, marketing research shows that such CSR activities can lead to negative company evaluations and decreased product sales (White and Willness 2009). Finally, marketing strategy research suggests ways to overcome perceptions of corporate hypocrisy arising when statements about CSR do not match or overstate CSR actions, including using abstract communication or inoculation strategies (Wagner, Lutz, and Weitz 2009).

This brief review of how CSR is discussed in the accounting and marketing literature shows that the finance discipline is not the only field that requires an instrumental shareholder case to justify engaging in CSR. These business disciplines are still debating the merits of CSR depending upon whether the shareholder case for it can be made, and do not reflect the discussion in the business ethics literature that has moved beyond this debate. When addressing the impacts on stakeholders and CSP in the accounting and marketing literature, it is for the instrumental purpose of maximizing firm value, rather than because relationships with stakeholders are intrinsically valued. Similar to finance, seeing corporate responsibility and stakeholders other than shareholders as an intrinsic part of business would represent a major shift in the accounting and marketing literature. This shift involves considering the relationship among shareholders, stakeholders, and society, the potential merits of CSR, and those to whom additional responsibilities might be directed, as well as the content of those responsibilities. A marketing study by Dobson and Gerstner (2010) begins to do just this by focusing on the intrinsic value of consumer health, the social (negative) impact of marketing strategies beyond shareholder value maximization and for society more generally, and the stakeholder responsibility of governments to regulate.

EMERGING DIRECTIONS IN FINANCE SCHOLARSHIP

The search of the finance literature also reveals some exceptions to the predominantly instrumental, shareholder-focused discussion of responsibility described above. All three of these articles rely in part on Zingales (2000). Zingales reviews how the organizations of today, described as knowledge-based, human capital dependent, and flat, differ fundamentally from the hierarchical asset-based firms of the traditional theory of the firm that underlies most economic finance theory. He discusses the characteristics of a new theory of the firm and the changes it would require in corporate finance practice and research. Among other things, Zingales suggests that firm valuations would have to account for the total surplus value created and captured by stakeholders other than shareholders, and would also have to develop new theories about how the surplus is divided between all financial and nonfinancial stakeholders. In this way, Zingales recognizes how value creation goes beyond a firm's share-based market capitalization to include value allocated to a wide pool of organizational stakeholders. The continued success of the firm is ensured only when the distribution of surplus value sufficiently encourages continued firm-specific investments by all stakeholders. Zingales raises issues worthy of further exploration within the finance literature and beyond.

Following Zingales's (2000) line of inquiry and a long-term perspective (i.e., long-run stock returns), Edmans (2011) finds that CSR investments in human capital contributing to employee satisfaction lead to higher long-run stock returns. This implies that short-term stock market valuations fail to take intangible assets into account, and thereby do not recognize the changing nature of the firm, as discussed by Zingales. Another implication is that socially responsible investment based on employee well-being may bring higher investment performance over the long run.

Jiao (2010), who expands this finding, reports that investments in stakeholder welfare, and particularly with respect to employee and environmental issues, increase the intangible value of the firm. These findings undermine the misappropriation theory, suggesting that managers pursue investments in CSR for their own personal social gain.

In another example of finance research dealing with Zingales's (2000) questions, Hennessy and Livdan (2009) explore the positive externalities that are created through the fulfillment of relational contracts between a firm and its suppliers. The authors suggest that a firm's organizational capital is increased by the amount of this type of intangible asset. They demonstrate how financial theory can be adjusted to accommodate the new realities of today's networked organizations and the implications for the theory of the firm.

SUMMARY AND CONCLUSIONS

The discussion above leads to various suggestions for expanding upon and developing the discussion of CSR that have occurred to date across the business ethics, finance, accounting, and marketing disciplines. These suggestions are made with the hope of not only integrating the concerns evidenced in the business ethics literature about CSR into the functional scholarship on CSR, but also encouraging the business ethics literature to benefit from this functional scholarship. Both would enable greater depth to the debate about the role of business in society across different business disciplines.

Being able to identify the value created for all stakeholders, rather than just shareholders, would eliminate concerns about any focus on shareholders, as well as concerns about the instrumental use of stakeholders in the service of shareholders. Considering how responsibility has intrinsic value to stakeholders takes additional account of the distinction between instrumental and intrinsic value, rejects the separation thesis, moves beyond the simple CSP/CFP debate, and enables a discussion of the relationship between corporate and stakeholder responsibility. Finance, accounting, and marketing's focus on quantifying shareholder returns to CSR might be useful to business ethicists, and collaboration across these fields might facilitate the development of methodologies for measuring total value created.

Besides creating value for stakeholders, firms distribute value. Understanding how value is best shared and distributed to stakeholders to ensure future value creation would further eliminate concerns about any focus on shareholders and the instrumental use of stakeholders in the service of shareholders. Examining the relationship between value distribution and future value creation would better describe the outcomes that the CSP/CFP debate has sought to identify. Again, collaboration across fields with, for example, finance, accounting, and marketing providing measurement expertise and business ethics providing normative expertise, might facilitate growth in our understanding.

Tsai and Ghoshal (1998) suggest that integrity, or consistently adhering to an acceptable set of principles, is clearly important in markets and other institutions reliant on ongoing relationships. The importance of integrity in markets justifies taking a broader view of CSR across the business disciplines. Ghoshal (2005) contends that business schools should heed the real-world effects that result from the theories faculty develop and teach. Rather than furthering seemingly amoral theories that suggest business decisions can be separated from, and determined without consideration of, social impacts, some emerging work across the functional disciplines rejects the separation thesis, admits the value of corporate responsibility, and identifies the relationship between value created and distributed across stakeholders. The development of theories that recognize this relationship among stakeholders could promote a new ethos of professional responsibility among managers, thus promoting the integrity of markets. This ethos would include asking not simply "what's in it for me?" but rather "what impact does this transaction have on stakeholder value creation?" and ultimately "does this transaction strengthen the market or weaken it?" More integrated theories that help quantify stakeholder value creation and distribution could develop the discussion across multiple business disciplines. The long-term security of markets, and of society, is at stake.

DISCUSSION QUESTIONS

1. What distinguishes instrumental from intrinsic approaches to CSR?
2. Define the separation thesis and identify how the business ethics and finance literatures have addressed this thesis.
3. Why might investigating the CSP/CFP relationship be problematic?
4. Why is recognizing the relationship between CSR and stakeholder responsibility important?
5. How has the finance literature tended to approach CSR?
6. How might CSR research be further developed by better integration of the CSR literatures in business ethics, finance, accounting, and marketing?

REFERENCES

Archel, Pablo, Javier Husillos, and Crawford Spence. 2011. "The Institutionalization of Unaccountability: Loading the Dice of Corporate Social Responsibility Discourse." *Accounting, Organizations and Society* 36:6, 327–343.

Barnea, Amir, and Amir Rubin. 2010. "Corporate Social Responsibility as a Conflict between Shareholders." *Journal of Business Ethics* 97:1, 71–86.

Beauchamp, Thomas L., and Norman E. Bowie. 1989. *Ethical Theory and Business*, 3rd ed. Upper Saddle River, NJ: Pearson Prentice Hall.

Beauchamp, Thomas L., Norman E. Bowie, and Denis G. Arnold. 2009. *Ethical Theory and Business*, 8th ed. Upper Saddle River, NJ: Pearson Prentice Hall.

Bosse, Douglas A., Robert A. Phillips, and Jeffrey S. Harrison. 2009. "Stakeholders, Reciprocity, and Firm Performance." *Strategic Management Journal* 30:4, 447–456.

Brown, William O., Eric Helland, and Janet Kiholm Smith. 2006. "Corporate Philanthropic Practices." *Journal of Corporate Finance* 12:5, 855–877.

Carroll, Archie B. 1979. "A Three Dimensional Model of Corporate Performance." *Academy of Management Review* 4:4, 497–505.

Carroll, Archie B. 1991. "The Pyramid of Corporate Social Responsibility: Toward the Moral Management of Organizational Stakeholders." *Business Horizons* 34:4, 39–48.

Cohen, Jeffrey, Lori Holder-Webb, Leda Nath, and David Wood. 2011. "Retail Investors' Perceptions of the Decision-Usefulness of Economic Performance, Governance, and Corporate Social Responsibility Disclosures." *Behavioral Research in Accounting* 23:1, 109–129.

Dhaliwal, Dan S., Oliver Zhen Li, Albert Tsang, and Yong George Yang. 2011. "Voluntary Nonfinancial Disclosure and the Cost of Equity Capital: The Initiation of Corporate Social Responsibility Reporting." *Accounting Review* 86:1, 59–100.

Dobson, Paul W., and Eitan Gerstner. 2010. "For a Few Cents More: Why Supersize Unhealthy Food?" *Marketing Science* 29:4, 770–780.

Donaldson, Thomas, and Patricia H. Werhane. 2008. *Ethical Issues in Business: A Philosophical Approach*, 8th ed. Upper Saddle River, NJ: Pearson Education Inc.

Donaldson, Thomas, Patricia H. Werhane, and Margaret Cording. 2002. *Ethical Issues in Business: A Philosophical Approach*, 7th ed. Upper Saddle River, NJ: Pearson Education Inc.

Edmans, Alex. 2011. "Does the Stock Market Fully Value Intangibles? Employee Satisfaction and Equity Prices." *Journal of Financial Economics* 101:3, 621–640.

El Ghoul, Sadok, Omrane Guedhami, Chuck C. Y. Kwok, and Dev R. Mishra. 2011. "Does Corporate Social Responsibility Affect the Cost of Capital?" *Journal of Banking & Finance* 35:9, 2388–2406.

Elms, Heather, Stephen Brammer, Jared Harris, and Robert A. Phillips. 2010. "New Directions in Strategic Management & Business Ethics." *Business Ethics Quarterly* 20:3 (20th Anniversary Edition), 401–426.

Elms, Heather, Michael Johnson-Cramer, and Shawn Berman. 2011. "Bounding the World's Miseries: Corporate Responsibility and Freeman's Stakeholder Theory." In Robert A. Phillips, ed. *Stakeholder Theory: Impact and Prospects*, 1–38. Northhampton, MA: Edward Elgar Publishing.

Elms, Heather, and Robert A. Phillips. 2009. "Private Security Companies and Institutional Legitimacy: Corporate and Stakeholder Responsibility." *Business Ethics Quarterly* 19:3, 403–432.

Evan, William M., and R. Edward Freeman. 1989. "A Stakeholder Theory of the Modern Corporation: Kantian Capitalism." In Thomas L. Beauchamp and Norman E. Bowie, eds. *Ethical Theory and Business*, 3rd ed., 97–106. Englewood Cliffs, NJ: Prentice-Hall.

Fort, Timothy L. 2007. *Business, Integrity and Peace: Beyond Geopolitical and Disciplinary Boundaries*. New Haven: Yale University Press.

Fort, Timothy L. 2008. *Prophets, Profits, and Peace: The Positive Role of Business in Promoting Religious Tolerance*. Cambridge, UK: Cambridge University Press.

Fort, Timothy L., and Cindy A. Schipani. 2004. *The Role of Business in Fostering Peaceful Societies*. New York: Cambridge University Press.

Freeman, R. Edward. 1984. *Strategic Management: A Stakeholder Approach*. Marshfield, MA: Pitman Publishing Inc.

Freeman, R. Edward. 1994. "The Politics of Stakeholder Theory: Some Future Directions." *Business Ethics Quarterly* 4:4, 409–421.

Freeman, R. Edward. 2002. "Stakeholder Theory of the Modern Corporation." In Thomas Donaldson, Patricia H. Werhane, and Margaret Cording, eds. *Ethical Issues in Business: A Philosophical Approach*, 7th ed., 38–48. Upper Saddle River, NJ: Pearson Education Inc.

Freeman, R. Edward. 2008a. "Managing for Stakeholders." In Thomas Donaldson and Patricia H. Werhane, eds. *Ethical Issues in Business: A Philosophical Approach*, 8th ed., 39–53. Upper Saddle River, NJ: Pearson Education Inc.

Freeman, R. Edward. 2008b. "Ending the So-Called 'Friedman–Freeman' Debate." *Business Ethics Quarterly* 18:2, 153–190.

Freeman, R. Edward, and Heather Elms. 2011. "The Social Responsibility of Business Is to Create Value for Stakeholders." Working Paper, Darden School of Business, University of Virginia, and Kogod School of Business, American University.

Freeman, R. Edward, Jeffrey S. Harrison, and Andrew C. Wicks. 2007. *Managing for Stakeholders: Survival, Reputation and Success*. New Haven: Yale University Press.

Freeman, R. Edward, Jeffrey S. Harrison, Andrew C. Wicks, Bidhan L. Parmar, and Simone De Colle. 2010. *Stakeholder Theory: The State of the Art*. New York: Cambridge University Press.

Freeman, R. Edward, S. Ramakrishna Velamuri, and Brian Moriarty. 2006. "Company Stakeholder Responsibility: A New Approach to CSR." Charlottesville, VA: Business Roundtable Institute for Corporate Ethics.

Friedman, Milton. 1962. *Capitalism and Freedom.* Chicago: University of Chicago Press.

Friedman, Milton. 1970. "The Social Responsibility of Business Is to Increase Its Profits." *New York Times Magazine*, September 13, 32–33, 122, 126.

Galema, Rients, Auke Plantinga, and Bert Scholtens. 2008. "The Stocks at Stake: Return and Risk in Socially Responsible Investment." *Journal of Banking & Finance* 32:12, 2646–2654.

Ghoshal, Sumantra. 2005. "Bad Management Theories Are Destroying Good Management Practices." *Academy of Management Learning & Education* 4:1, 75–91.

Goodstein, Jerry D., and Andrew C. Wicks. 2007. "Corporate and Stakeholder Responsibility: Making Business Ethics a Two-Way Conversation. *Business Ethics Quarterly* 17:3, 375–398.

Goss, Allen, and Gordon S. Roberts. 2011. "The Impact of Corporate Social Responsibility on the Cost of Bank Loans." *Journal of Banking & Finance* 35:7, 1794–1810.

Harrison, Jeffrey S., Douglas A. Bosse, and Robert A. Phillips. 2010. "Managing for Stakeholders, Stakeholder Utility Functions, and Competitive Advantage. *Strategic Management Journal* 30:1, 58–74.

Hennessy, Christopher A., and Dmitryi Livdan. 2009. "Debt, Bargaining, and Credibility in Firm-Supplier Relationships." *Journal of Financial Economics* 93:3, 382–399.

Holder-Webb, Lori, Jeffrey R. Cohen, Leda Nath, and David Wood. 2009. "The Supply of Corporate Social Responsibility Disclosure among U. S. Firms." *Journal of Business Ethics* 84:4, 497–527.

Jiao, Yawen. 2010. "Stakeholder Welfare and Firm Value." *Journal of Banking & Finance* 34:10, 2549–2561.

Lee, Darren, and Robert Faff. 2009. "Corporate Sustainability Performance and Idiosyncratic Risk: A Global Perspective." *Financial Review* 44:2, 213–237.

Luo, Xueming, and C. B. Bhattacharya. 2006. "Corporate Social Responsibility, Customer Satisfaction, and Market Value." *Journal of Marketing* 70:4, 1–18.

Luo, Xueming, and C. B. Bhattacharya. 2009. "The Debate over Doing Good: Corporate Social Performance, Strategic Marketing Levers, and Firm-Idiosyncratic Risk." *Journal of Marketing* 73:6, 198–213.

Margolis, Joshua D., and James P. Walsh. 2003. "Misery Loves Companies: Rethinking Social Initiatives by Business." *Administrative Science Quarterly* 48:2, 268–305.

McWilliams, Abagail, and Donald Siegel. 2001. "Corporate Social Responsibility: A Theory of the Firm Perspective. *Academy of Management Review* 26:1, 117–127.

Orlitzky, Marc. 2011. "Institutional Logics in the Study of Organizations: The Social Construction of the Relationship between Corporate Social and Financial Performance." *Business Ethics Quarterly* 21:3, 409–444.

Orlitzky, Marc, Frank L. Schmidt, and Sara L. Rynes. 2003. "Corporate Social and Financial Performance: A Meta-Analysis." *Organization Studies* 24:40, 3–41.

Palazzo, Guido, and Andreas G. Scherer. 2006. "Corporate Legitimacy as Deliberation: A Communicative Framework." *Journal of Business Ethics* 66:1, 71–88.

Phillips, Robert A. 2003. *Stakeholder Theory and Organizational Ethics.* San Francisco: Berrett Koehler Publishers, Inc.

Porter, Michael E., and Mark R. Kramer. 2002. "The Competitive Advantage of Corporate Philanthropy." *Harvard Business Review* 80:12, 56–68.

Porter, Michael E., and Mark R. Kramer. 2006. "Strategy and Society: The Link between Competitive Advantage and Corporate Social Responsibility." *Harvard Business Review* 84:12, 78–92.

Porter, Michael E., and Mark R. Kramer. 2011. "The Big Idea: Creating Shared Value." *Harvard Business Review* 89:1/2, 62–77.

Sandberg, Joakim. 2008. "Understanding the Separation Thesis." *Business Ethics Quarterly* 18:2, 213–232.

Scherer, Andreas G., and Guido Palazzo. 2007. "Toward a Political Conception of Corporate Responsibility: Business and Society Seen from a Habermasian Perspective." *Academy of Management Review* 32:4, 1096–1120.

Schwartz, Mark S., and Archie B. Carroll. 2003. "Corporate Social Responsibility: A Three Domain Approach." *Business Ethics Quarterly* 13:4, 503–530.

Sen, Amartya. 1991. *On Ethics and Economics.* Malden, MA: Blackwell Publishing.

Simmons, Carolyn J., and Karen L. Becker-Olsen. 2006. "Achieving Marketing Objectives through Social Sponsorships." *Journal of Marketing* 70:4, 154–169.

Surroca, Jordi, and Josep A. Tribó. 2008. "Managerial Entrenchment and Corporate Social Performance." *Journal of Business Finance & Accounting* 35:5, 748–789.

Tsai, Wen Pin, and Sumantra Ghoshal. 1998. "Social Capital and Value Creation: The Role of Intrafirm Networks." *Academy of Management Journal* 41:4, 464–476.

Waddock, Sandra. 2008. "The Development of Corporate Responsibility/Corporate Citizenship." *Organization Management Journal* 5:1, 29–39.

Wagner, Tillmann, Richard J. Lutz, and Barton A. Weitz. 2009. "Corporate Hypocrisy: Overcoming the Threat of Inconsistent Corporate Social Responsibility Perceptions." *Journal of Marketing* 73:6, 77–91.

Walsh, James P. 2005. "Taking Stock of Stakeholder Management." *Academy of Management Review* 30:2, 426–452.

White, Katherine, and Chelsea Willness. 2009. "Consumer Reactions to the Decreased Usage Message: The Role of Elaborative Processing." *Journal of Consumer Psychology* 19:1, 73–87.

Wicks, Andrew C. 1996. "Overcoming the Separation Thesis: The Need for Reconsideration of SIM Research." *Business and Society* 35:1, 89–118.

Wood, Donna J. 2010. "Measuring Corporate Social Performance: A Review." *International Journal of Management Reviews* 12:1, 50–84.

Zingales, Luigi. 2000. "In Search of New Foundations." *Journal of Finance* 55:4, 1621–1653.

ABOUT THE AUTHORS

Heather Elms is Associate Professor of International Business, Kogod Research Professor, and Chair of the International Business Department at the Kogod School of Business, American University, Washington, DC. Her research interests focus on the relationship between corporate and stakeholder responsibility and the content of those responsibilities. She has published in such outlets as the *Academy of Management Review*, *Business Ethics Quarterly*, *Organizational Research Methods*, *Strategic Management Journal*, and *Strategic Organization*. She is an associate editor of *Business Ethics Quarterly* and on the editorial boards of *Business & Society* and *International Journal of Emerging Markets*. Professor Elms received her Ph.D. in Management from the University of California, Los Angeles.

Michelle Westermann-Behaylo is Assistant Professor of Corporate Citizenship at the Kogod School of Business, American University, Washington, D.C. Her specific areas of inquiry include corporate ethical culture, stakeholder management, corporate responsibility, and the role of business in peacebuilding. She has published in *Business & Society*, *Journal of Business Ethics*, and *American Business Law Journal*. Before her academic career, she practiced international business and trade law in both the public and private sectors. She earned her Ph.D. from George Washington University School of Business and her JD from Vanderbilt Law School.

CHAPTER 4

Business Models and Social Entrepreneurship

MICHAEL A. PIRSON
Assistant Professor for Global Sustainability and Social Entrepreneurship, Fordham
University Research Fellow, Harvard University; and Partner, Humanistic
Management Network

INTRODUCTION

The 2007–2008 financial crisis caused many to question the basic premises of the
current business system (Kaletsky 2010). Books and articles on how to rethink the
current business system abound. From notions of Capitalism 3.0 (Barnes 2006) to
moral capitalism (Young 2003) or humanistic management (Pirson and Lawrence
2009), many authors suggest that business needs to reinvent itself to meet the challenges of the twenty-first century. For example, Porter and Kramer (2011) suggest
that the purpose of the corporation needs to be redefined. They posit that the corporation should pursue shared value creation rather than merely pursuing financial
value creation. The authors also suggest that managers should view the corporation as socially embedded and actively uncover potential for value creation for
all stakeholders to remain competitive and secure organizational longevity. Porter
and Kramer basically refurbish the older stakeholder management argument by
stating that economic value can only be created in a sustainable fashion when all
stakeholders, including society, can appreciate the value created. In a certain new
twist to the argument, the authors highlight the example of social entrepreneurs
from which corporations can learn.

Social entrepreneurs are often ahead of established corporations in discovering
shared value opportunities because they are not locked into the narrow traditional
business thinking (Elkington and Hartigan 2008). In a manner unsettling to the
traditional theory of finance, strategy, and economics, these social entrepreneurs
often try to create shared value by pursuing dual objectives (Alter 2006; Rangan,
Quelch, Herrero, and Barton 2007; Pirson 2008). This chapter presents the concept
of social entrepreneurship and discusses several case studies of social enterprises
in the financial sector. The chapter also identifies their business models and highlights how their approaches to shared value creation illuminate socially responsible
financial practices.

The remainder of the chapter is organized as follows. First, the concept of
social entrepreneurship is outlined, followed by a description of various models

of social entrepreneurship. Second, several business models of social enterprises in the financial sector are highlighted with a specific focus on the areas of microfinance and impact investing. Finally, lessons learned and further conclusions are presented for those interested in applying insights of social enterprises in the area of responsible finance.

SOCIAL ENTREPRENEURSHIP AS A BLUEPRINT FOR SHARED VALUE CREATION STRATEGIES

Traditionally, the business model of an organization is understood as a conceptual model rather than a financial model (Teece 2010). Nevertheless, an organization is fundamentally concerned with how value created for customers can be converted into financial profit. This notion is now being challenged in that business models should aim at creating social benefits as well as financial benefits. This section presents the concept of social entrepreneurship as a blueprint for novel business models in the financial sector.

Social entrepreneurship has moved from being a niche concept three decades ago to becoming heralded as a blueprint for corporate development today (Pirson 2008; Porter and Kramer 2011). As social entrepreneurship crosses academic disciplines, it challenges traditional assumptions of economic and business development (Dart 2004; Dacin, Dacin, and Matear 2010). Much of the existing academic literature of social entrepreneurship centers on the definition of social entrepreneurship. Despite the increased interest, Dacin et al. contend that no agreement exists on the domain, boundaries, forms, and meanings of social entrepreneurship.

Much of the debate on social entrepreneurship is a recycled version of the discussion about the purpose of business famously represented by Friedman (1970) and Davis (1973). Mirroring the old debate about the social goals of business, Dees and Elias (1998) suggest that social ventures can oscillate between purely charitable (social mission) and purely commercial (financial mission), depending on the entrepreneurial mission. Tan, Williams, and Tan (2005) similarly indicate that social enterprises can take form on a continuum of descending degrees of altruism that profits society. According to Alter (2006), the hallmark of social entrepreneurship lies in its ability to combine social interests with business practices to effect social change. Hence, the crux of the individual social enterprise lies in the specifics of its dual objectives—the depth and breadth of social impact to be realized, and the amount of money to be earned (the business model).

Simms and Robinson (2009) propose that social entrepreneurs may be involved in both activities for profit and not-for-profit and specifically mention that social enterprises are those that pursue dual or triple bottom line objectives. A similar perspective is taken by Hockerts (2006) and Lasprogata and Cotten (2003) who classify social enterprises as those employing hybrid business models pursuing dual objectives. Mair and Marti (2006) focus on the process of innovative use of resources to catalyze social change. As such, a business creating employment in areas of high unemployment could be considered a social enterprise if it uses resources in innovative ways. Elkington and Hartigan (2008) further expand the notion of social entrepreneurship suggesting that Google is a social enterprise because it has a social mission of making the world's information accessible.

The inclusivity of the above-mentioned definitions of social entrepreneurship highlights the question of the boundaries of social and traditional entrepreneurship. While some definitions include the notion of shared value creation specifically, most scholars maintain that a maximization of social value creation represents the definitional difference of social and traditional entrepreneurship (Dacin et al. 2010). Implicit in many definitions of social entrepreneurship rests the notion of the primacy of social value creation over any kind of financial value creation. Despite the more inclusive perspectives presented above, some scholars, such as Thompson and Doherty (2006), even argue that social entrepreneurship is to be understood as a social value creation concept only and posit that organizational forms should remain in the nonprofit domain. They further suggest that any shared value creation ambition would endanger the legitimacy of the social cause promoted. Foster and Bradach (2005) consider profit seeking entirely inappropriate as it distracts managers from their social mission. Boschee and McClurg (2003) maintain that the difference between the social and traditional entrepreneur lies precisely within the primacy of social performance measures. No matter what role social value generation plays in social enterprises, Porter and Kramer (2011) suggest that companies can learn how to think about social value creation from them.

MODELS OF SOCIAL ENTREPRENEURSHIP

As Dacin et al. (2010, p. 45) state, "the dual mission of social entrepreneurial ventures provides both interesting opportunities and constraints." Even though a wide range of social enterprises has emerged, Alter (2006) suggests that three main categories are defined by the emphasis and priority given to financial and social objectives: external, integrated, and embedded social enterprises.

External Social Enterprise

In external social enterprises, social value creating programs are distinct from profit-oriented business activities. The business enterprise activities are external from the organization's social operations and programs. Businesses can partner with not-for-profit organizations to create external enterprises that fund respective social programs and/or operating costs. This stage represents an incremental adoption of social value creation objectives. Examples for external social enterprises are partnership programs such as ProductRed, which companies can join and sell their products for a markup, which in turn funds the United Nation's Global Fund or similar licensing partnerships with the World Wildlife Foundation (WWF). The relationship between the business activities and social programs is supportive, oftentimes providing financial and nonfinancial resources to the external program.

Integrated Social Enterprise

In integrated social enterprises, social programs overlap with business activities, but are not synonymous. Social and financial programs often share costs, assets, and program attributes. The social enterprise activities are thus integrated even as they are separate from the organization's profit-oriented operations. This type of social enterprise often leverages organizational assets such as expertise, content, relationships, brand, or infrastructure as the foundation for its business (Alter 2006). The Aravind Eye Hospital in Madurai, India, is an example of an integrated social enterprise. It serves cataract patients in a main hospital, where wealthy patients pay a market fee for their surgery. The profit surplus created by these fees is then used to pay for the surgery of poor patients in the free hospital (Rangan, 1993). The relationship between the business activities and the social programs is hence synergistic, adding financial and social value to one another. In the integrated approach, two separate arms of a venture still exist that pursue different but mutually supportive objectives.

Embedded Social Enterprise

In the embedded social enterprise, business activities and social programs are synonymous. Social programs are self-financed through enterprise revenues and thus the embedded social enterprise can also be a stand-alone sustainable program. Because the relationship between business activities and social programs is comprehensive, financial and social benefits are achieved simultaneously. Businesses that serve the base of the pyramid (Prahalad 2005) could be regarded as such embedded social enterprises, and the group of enterprises structured by the Grameen and BRAC (known formerly as the Bangladesh Rehabilitation Assistance Committee) groups present other approaches. BRAC is a development organization dedicated to alleviating poverty by empowering the poor to bring about change in their own lives.

For example, the Grameen Bank model of microloans is based on the disbursement of model microloans to the poorest of the poor without collateral. Because these loans are often the only chance for this clientele, the payback rate with interest is beyond any traditional rates (greater than 90 percent), and profit can be earned. As such, profitability can serve a social goal of eliminating poverty. In recent years, however, more traditional players such as Citibank and Banco Compartamos in Mexico have adopted microfinance models that adapt the original business model to satisfy profit maximization strategies (Rennison 2008).

BUSINESS MODELS OF MICROFINANCE

Examining microfinance, the most mature area of social entrepreneurship, provides a way of highlighting the various business models adopted in the area of social entrepreneurship. This section focuses on two examples: Grameen Bank and Accion International.

Grameen Bank

Pioneered by Muhammad Yunus and Grameen Bank, microfinance has gained increased visibility in the marketplace. Yanus founded the Grameen Bank (the word *grameen* means rural) in Bangladesh in 1983 (www.grameen-info.org). Its business model centers on lending small amounts of money (called microloans) primarily to poor women to enable them to earn a living through self-employment. No material collateral is necessary to take out a loan, but borrowers provide a social form of collateral. That is, borrowers organize in groups of five, and each group member needs to repay his or her loan on time, while ensuring that other group members do the same. Failure for even one borrower to meet a payment jeopardizes the future borrowing possibilities of all. This model establishes a delicate dynamic between peer-pressure and peer-support among Grameen borrowers and is credited with the high loan repayment rate of 95 percent. Despite the delicacy of the business model, the bank had inducted 8.35 million members (96 percent women) in 81,379 Bangladeshi villages by 2011. A stabilizing feature of the business model is the ownership structure of Grameen Bank. Similar to cooperative banks, the poor borrowers largely own the bank (93 to 95 percent), while a small minority (5 to 7 percent) remains in government hands. The fact that the formerly unbankable people now own their own bank strengthens the commitment to the bank and helps explain its success. In that sense, the organization model strengthens the business model.

Looking at the business model more closely, the Grameen Bank provides four types of loans: (1) income-generating loans with an interest rate of 20 percent; (2) housing loans with an interest rate of 8 percent; (3) higher education loans with an interest rate of 5 percent; and (4) a 0 percent interest loan for struggling members of society, namely, beggars. Traditional banks know how to work with the first three types of loans. This section highlights the rationale for a 0 percent loan program for those most deeply afflicted by poverty.

Different from traditional banks, which consider the poor unbankable, Grameen Bank views the poor as future customers who need and deserve banking services like anyone else. Begging is not considered a choice but a last resort. Grameen aims to restore the dignity of its struggling members and to help them find a dignified livelihood, send their children to school, and graduate into becoming regular Grameen Bank members. The bank's ultimate goal is to see that no one in the villages that it serves has to beg for survival. For that reason, the program provides basic support through publicly declaring beggars as members of Grameen Bank. All members receive an identity badge with the Grameen Bank logo to let everybody know that this national institution stands behind them. Further, the members are covered under life insurance and loan insurance programs free of charge, and existing Grameen groups are encouraged to become their mentors. This form of social support is combined with favorable loan conditions, which require only the repayment of the principal in installments according to repayment ability. By 2011, more than 111,297 beggars have joined the program. Grameen states that of the more than USD 20 million disbursed, 80 percent has already been repaid. Additionally, roughly 20,000 have left begging and are making a living in a sales profession. Among them, roughly 10,000 beggars have joined Grameen Bank groups as main-stream borrowers. Here, social value creation reinforces financial value creation through the shared value business model.

Using innovative business models, Grameen Bank has shown that poor people can work themselves out of poverty and can become bankable. In that sense, Grameen is developing its own, highly loyal customers. Grameen Bank is not only serving the needs of the poor, but it is also doing well financially. Grameen Bank declared a 30 percent cash dividend for the year 2010. This is the highest cash dividend declared by any bank in Bangladesh in 2010. Whereas donations and grants largely funded the bank during its early years, the bank has been entirely self-funding and profitable since 1998.

Accion International

As one of the early players in the global microfinance industry, Accion International further developed and refined the microfinance model. In 1961, Accion International started as a "private peace corps" focusing on community development with programs in Brazil, Colombia, Peru, and Venezuela (Quelch and Laidler 2003). During the 1970s, the firm started its first experiments with microcredits in Brazil and then replicated them in Ecuador and Colombia. In the 1980s, Accion International tested Grameen's Solidarity Group model and deployed it widely. Witnessing the power of microcredits for local entrepreneurs, the firm developed a business model based on the belief that microcredit institutions need to be self-sustaining and that the poor can pay commercial rates of interest (Quelch and Laidler 2003; Chu 2005).

The leadership of Accion International considered scaling up operations as a requirement to eradicate poverty. Accordingly, funding from private philanthropy and development agencies was insufficient to reach the millions of poor in Latin America. To reach sufficient scale, the firm emphasized establishing a formal network across Latin America as well as involving commercial banks. Using the vehicle of a U.S. bank–backed credit guarantee, local banks provided loans directly to the local Accion International chapters, which then disbursed the loans to micro-entrepreneurs. In the 1990s, Accion International committed to lending USD 1 billion in five years and accomplished this goal, proving a serious market need (Quelch and Laidler 2003; Chu 2005). Consequently, the firm supported the push towards a commercialization of microfinance.

As microfinance became regulated, Accion International helped to establish commercial microfinance banks. These banks were able to rapidly increase their loan portfolio because the capital markets provided funds through financial instruments, such as bonds and certificates of deposit (CDs), and other commercial banks invested in them using their deposits. Because the return on equity of these microfinance banks often exceeded that of conventional commercial banks, Accion International pushed the commercialization even further. In the 2000s, the firm helped to transform their nongovernmental organization (NGO) based network members to become commercial banks. In some cases, these banks even started publicly listing their stock such as Banco Compartamos in Mexico. These commercial microfinance institutions raised concerns from many traditional players in the banking industry because their returns consistently exceeded the returns of conventional banks by 250 to 500 percent (Chu 2005). As Accion International is aspiring to increase the scale of microfinance even further, it is now advising traditional commercial banks such as ABN Amro, Citibank, and others on how to establish microcredit programs (Quelch and Laidler 2003; Chu 2005).

Lessons Learned for Socially Responsible Finance and Investing

Grameen Bank and Accion International both started with the goal to eradicate poverty. Taking that perspective allowed them to find opportunities where traditional banks did not. In fact, it allowed both organizations to look beyond the existing customer base and create attractive and novel business models. However, while sharing some elements, their business models have led them in very different directions. Grameen Bank mainly pursues an integrated strategy of serving the market in Bangladesh directly. Accion International provides microcredits, acting as a conduit and embraces a very commercial strategy aimed at scale.

The business models in the field of microfinance vary widely. They oscillate from social value creation and poverty reduction to simple for-profit making. For example, many criticized Banco Compartamos because it achieved very high profits by increasing interest rates on its microloans to more than 80 percent per year. In July 2010, India's biggest microfinance institution, SKS Microfinance went public. Soon after, the government shut the firm down because it charged usurious interest rates. In both instances, Muhammad Yunus publicly stated his disagreement with the business model, saying that the poor should be the only beneficiaries of microfinance. By contrast, Michael Chu, former CEO of Accion International, contends that commercial microfinance is the only way to sustainably eradicate poverty. He further states that any cap on interest rates would be counterproductive because profit margins attract more providers and ultimately drive down interest rates (Chu 2005).

Increasingly, companies and organizations in the developed world see developing countries as unexplored high-volume, low-margin markets for their products and services (Hart 2010). According to Sundelin (2009), an unmet demand of roughly $300 billion for microfinance services remains, which presents an opportunity for responsible financial industry players. To pursue this opportunity, traditional players need to study the success factors of existing microfinance institutions and possibly rethink their traditional approaches. As Sundelin suggests, revenue models can be based on interest only or a combination with joining fees and commission fees for both borrowers and lenders. Additional revenues can come from donations, sponsoring partners, or advertisers. To ensure repayment, banks need to learn how to use social collateral instead of financial collateral by developing a system of peer support and peer pressure.

While some organizations, such as Grameen Bank, operate as direct local lenders, others operate by aggregating several lenders to spread the risk. Still others engage by providing interest-bearing financial securities to microfinance institutions. Whereas the former may be harder to implement, such a direct presence may help to increase growth outside the financial service sector. Microfinance organizations that have established brands and high-quality relationships with local entrepreneurs in remote markets can leverage these trust-based relationships as a platform for developing and distributing various products and services (Sundelin 2009). An interesting example is Grameen Shakti in Bangladesh that leverages the brand and infrastructure of Grameen Bank's nationwide microfinance program. It was created in 1996 to reach rural people with clean and affordable energy in a country where 80 percent of the people still do not have access to electricity. The revenue model is often based on several shopkeepers sharing one system, with the electricity enabling new business opportunities. By 2002, Grameen Shakti reached break-even, and by 2008 it had installed more than 180,000 solar home systems, installing more than 8,000 new ones each month. As such, these novel business models become a source of competitive advantage that goes beyond the financial sector and provides opportunities for responsible corporate engagement in general.

THE CASE OF SOCIAL IMPACT INVESTING

Microfinance has paved the way for other types of financial services for the base of the pyramid. Social impact investing has emerged as one of many lessons from microfinance and is elevating several basic insights. Two of the leading organizations in the field of social impact investing are Acumen Fund and Calvert Social Investors. This section provides a discussion of their respective business models and presents lessons for traditional financial players who want to engage in socially responsible finance.

Acumen Fund

Jacquline Novogratz founded Acumen Fund in 2001 with the goal of demonstrating that business acumen together with philanthropic capital can build thriving enterprises that serve vast numbers of the poor (Ebrahim and Rangan 2011). Based on the insight that the markets alone cannot solve the problems of poverty and that charity and aid are not enough, the Acumen Fund developed an approach that seeks to bridge the gap between the efficiency and scale of market-based approaches and the social impact of pure philanthropy.

Acumen Fund labels patient capital as its approach of raising charitable funds from individuals, foundations, and corporations, which it then invests as equity or debt in enterprises serving the base of the pyramid markets. These enterprises could be both for-profit and nonprofit organizations that focus on delivering services to the poor in the areas of water, health care, housing, energy, and agriculture. Besides financing these ventures, Acumen Fund actively engages in capacity building with its investees, much as venture capitalists would. A typical investment ranges from $300,000 to $2.5 million in equity or debt and engenders a five-to-seven-year commitment from Acumen, placing high-potential young professionals with investees to provide onsite capacity building assistance. In contrast to the traditionally much shorter investment spans of grant makers or banks, Acumen refers to its approach as patient capital for impatient people (Novogratz 2007; Friedman 2007). The fund's stated aim in investing patient capital is not to seek high returns, but rather to jump-start the creation of enterprises that improve the ability of the poor to live with dignity. As Novogratz notes, patient capital differentiates itself by the long time horizons, the increased risk tolerance, and the goal of maximizing social rather than financial returns. Further, patient capital provides management support and the flexibility to seek partnerships with governments and corporations through subsidy and co-investment when doing so may benefit low-income customers.

Acumen Fund invests in organizations that have business models capable of bringing affordable, life-changing products and services to parts of the world where markets have previously failed. Many of these businesses create jobs and lead directly to economic growth. Over the past 10 years, the Acumen Fund has affected the lives of more than 40 million people by investing upwards of USD 60 million in 57 enterprises, thereby creating more than 35,000 jobs.

Calvert Social Investment Foundation

The Calvert Group, one of the first socially responsible mutual fund managers, offers individual investors a variety of screened socially responsible portfolios of public equities, bonds, and other money market products (Emerson and Spitzer 2006). In the late 1980s, the Calvert Group began to explore investment strategies that not only screened out social value destruction but also sought to create social value with its investments. This discussion eventually led the fund to commit to investing 1 percent of its assets in community development finance intermediaries. To facilitate this style of investing, the Calvert Group eventually founded the Calvert Social Investment Foundation (Calvert Foundation) in 1995 with the support of national foundations including Ford, MacArthur, and Mott.

The Calvert Foundation aims to affect community investment by refining practice and investments so that individual investors can actively participate in community investing. The Calvert Foundation makes loans to organizations that are effective in developing or rehabilitating affordable homes, financing small businesses, providing essential community services, and creating jobs. These loans represent what the Calvert Foundations labels as community impact investing. Community investing differs from pure philanthropy as it provides loans with interest and differs from traditional microfinance in that the denomination is higher. In the community investing process, interested investors provide capital, and Calvert ensures the due diligence process and provides loans to socially beneficial organizations. Investors receive the principal back and earn interest but possibly at a lower than market rate. Although community impact investment functions like a traditional loan, it creates both a social and financial return on investment.

The business model of such community impact investment can be highlighted through the Calvert Community Investment Note, Calvert Foundation's flagship investment product. Structured as a general recourse obligation of the foundation, the notes are designed to provide average investors with a safe and convenient way to invest directly in community development and other blended value-generating projects and enterprises. The notes are highly customizable and investors can purchase them in increments of $1,000 with a minimum $1,000 investment. Investors can choose the profile of the investments underlying their notes, targeting specific geographic regions and programmatic areas. They can also select the maturity of their notes (ranging from 1 to 10 years) and the interest rate (ranging 0 to 3 percent). The Calvert Foundation can build completely customized community investment portfolios for those investing more than $50,000 in capital (Emerson and Spitzer 2006).

As of 2011, the Calvert Foundation has invested nearly $200 million in 250 community organizations in all 50 U.S. states and over 100 countries. The portfolio comprises investments in a diversified mix of high-impact organizations whose missions cover a range of social causes and innovations including the following: affordable housing, microfinance, Fair Trade coffee, small business development, and the establishment of essential community facilities such as charter schools, daycare centers, and rehabilitation clinics. As of 2011, investors and supporters have helped build or rehabilitate more than 17,000 homes, create 430,000 jobs in both the United States and developing countries, and finance more than 25,000 cooperatives, social enterprises, and community facilities.

Based on the success of Calvert's investments and the increasing demand for such shared value investing opportunities, Citibank has reached out to Calvert. Calvert is now advising Citibank and its customer base, who are mostly high net-worth individuals, to help the investment process. Similar to Accion International, Calvert wants to become a service provider to traditional banks that have difficulty establishing their own products and services for socially responsible investments.

Lessons Learned

Both the Acumen Fund and Calvert Foundation demonstrate that finance can be a vehicle for social change and have a socially desirable impact. Both organizations represent blueprints for those financial sector organizations that are interested in becoming more socially responsible. As the example of Citibank's collaboration with Calvert Foundation demonstrates, a real opportunity exists to collaborate with social entrepreneurs. For those organizations that are interested in developing their own profile of social responsibility, Acumen Fund provides many of the lessons learned in working with socially responsible finance. These lessons extend beyond the sheer mechanics of the business, but are instructive for the entire financial industry searching to engage in socially responsible finance. Below are some lessons learned based on information provided on Acumen's web page (www.acumenfund.org).

- *Dignity is of greater importance to the human spirit than wealth.* Poverty involves more than money. Often people do not realize their full potential because of a lack of choice and opportunity, not due to a lack of money. The task of achieving dignity is inherently more difficult than solving a technical problem. Achieving dignity requires changing the focus from solving problems for poor people to listening to them as agents who want to change their own lives.
- *Problems of poverty are not solely solved through grants or markets.* Solving the problems of poverty requires more than just pouring money on them, sitting back and letting markets take their course, and pretending that an invisible hand will transform billions of poor people's lives. The issue is not about "trade versus aid," but about using the markets wisely as a listening device in order to find the best solution to a problem.
- *Poverty describes a person's economic situation, not the individual.* Those with low income face a different set of constraints because of their economic situation. Like others, they make decisions based on factors other than what is good for them in a purely rational sense. Understanding people requires seeing them as full human beings and not as customers with a series of problems to be solved.
- *The keys to long-term success focus on cultivating local leaders, local money, and strong local communities.* Solving the toughest problems of poverty requires robust local solutions whose long-term viability is based on the support from local teams, capital, and, customers. Although this approach can take longer to execute, it tends to endure.
- *Leadership takes precedence over programs and policies.* Development work often assumes that programs and policies matter more than leadership, which is

often not the case. The personal qualities of the entrepreneurs and their teams are more important than having a business plan, an innovative product, or money in the bank.

- *Technology is not the sole answer.* Most often business and philanthropy focus on great technological innovation. No matter how great a new product or invention is for the poor, it rarely sells itself. People buy services that they understand and not simply technologies. Thus, the needs of dealers, distributors, business partners, employees, and customers must be understood as a critical factor for successful distribution and adoption of the product.
- *Without taking risks and the prospects of failure, success is also ruled out.* Creating new blueprints for social change requires taking calculated risks on innovative business models, entrepreneurs, and emerging leaders. People can learn from these failures and use this experience to improve.
- *Governments are rarely the source of solutions, but they can scale what works.* Although the public sector alone cannot solve large-scale problems of poverty, it can serve as a partner to the market, which can provide the innovative solutions, and can scale what works.
- *The cornerstone of business is trust, and no shortcuts are available to earning it.* Low-income communities often express concern about outsiders trying to solve their problems. Achieving real change requires establishing trust, which is earned by showing real commitment. Building trust takes time but can be destroyed in an instant.
- *Values serve as the foundation for capital investing, not on a series of steps to be followed.* A critical element in capital investing is to build it on a foundation of integrity and respect. The steps followed often differ when lending to different clientele (i.e., the rich and the poor).

SUMMARY AND CONCLUSIONS

While much can be learned from the models used by Grameen Bank, Accion International, Acumen Fund, and the Calvert Foundation, many organizations in the financial sectors will need to venture onto their own learning path. Understanding the business models of socially entrepreneurial organizations can provide a solid starting point, but simply copying these models will probably result in failure. A key element in the success of these ventures arguably lies beyond the business model level. Social entrepreneurs use vastly different mental models from those of their administrative counterparts in established organizations. Much of what social entrepreneurship can provide to traditional organizations is therefore an approach to viewing problems as opportunities.

According to Cooperrider (2008, p. 32), Peter Drucker once said, "Every global and social problem of our time is a business opportunity in disguise." In that sense, social entrepreneurship represents more of a mental model shift, expressed in different business models, than a straight line to socially responsible best practices. Traditional financial organizations could try to adopt alternate mental models to develop novel and socially responsible practices. For that matter, however, the traditional mental models of financial sector organizations need to be challenged.

Learning from social entrepreneurs means identifying large global problems, defining socially desirable goals, and employing effective business models to reach them. In the traditional mindset, the order is usually reversed, and short-term profitability concerns dominate. This mind-set has caused several for-profit micro-finance institutions to lose legitimacy and eventually to close. Financial organizations trying to become more socially responsible might find doing so harder than initially expected, as that transition often requires a fundamental paradigm shift rather than simple operational changes.

DISCUSSION QUESTIONS

1. What is social entrepreneurship?
2. Why is social entrepreneurship heralded as a blueprint for corporate development?
3. Identify and describe three models of social entrepreneurship?
4. Identify two areas that traditional finance could learn from social entrepreneurs.

REFERENCES

Alter, Sutia K. 2006. "Social Enterprise Models and Their Mission and Money Relationships." In Alex Nicholls, ed. *Social Entrepreneurship—New Models for Sustainable Social Change*, 205–232. Oxford, UK: Oxford University Press.

Barnes, Peter. 2006. *Capitalism 3.0.* London: Berrett-Koehler.

Boschee, Jerr, and Jim McClurg. 2003. "Toward a Better Understanding of Social Entrepreneurship: Some Important Distinctions." White Paper, SE-Alliance White Paper.

Chu, Michael. 2005. "ACCION International: Maintaining High Performance through Time." *Harvard Business School Case* 304-095. Boston: Harvard Business School Press.

Cooperrider, David. 2008. "Sustainable Innovation." *BIZED*, July/August, 32.

Dacin, Peter A., Tina M. Dacin, and Margaret Matear. 2010. "Social Entrepreneurship: Why We Don't Need a Theory and How We Move Forward from Here." *Academy of Management Perspectives* 24:3, 37–57.

Dart, Raymond. 2004. "The Legitimacy of Social Enterprise." *Nonprofit Management and Leadership* 14:4, 411–424.

Davis, Keith. 1973. "The Case for and against Business Assumption of Social Responsibilities." *Academy of Management Journal* 16:2, 312–322.

Dees, Gregory, and Jaan Elias. 1998. "The Challenge of Combining Social and Commercial Enterprise." *Business Ethics Quarterly* 8:1, 165–178.

Ebrahim, Alnoor, and Kasturi V. Rangan. 2011. "Acumen Fund: Measurement in Impact Investing (A) and (B)." *Harvard Business School Case* 9-310-011 and 9-106-043. Boston: Harvard Business School Press.

Elkington, John, and Pamela Hartigan. 2008. *The Power of Unreasonable People: How Social Entrepreneurs Create Markets That Change the World*. Boston: Harvard Business School Press.

Emerson, Jed, and Josh Spitzer. 2006. "Blended Value Investing-Capital Opportunities for Social and Environmental Impact." www.thegiin.org, March 1. Available at www.thegiin.org/cgi-bin/iowa/resources/research/40.html.

Foster, William, and Jeffrey Bradach. 2005. "Should Nonprofits Seek Profits?" *Harvard Business Review* 83:2, 1–9.

Friedman, Milton. 1970. "The Social Responsibility of Business Is to Increase Its Profits.' *New York Times*, September 13, 32.

Friedman, Thomas. 2007. "Patient Capital for an Africa that Can't Wait.' *New York Times*, April 20, A23.

Hart, Stuart L. 2010. *Capitalism at the Crossroads: Next Generation Business Strategies for a Post-Crisis World*. Wharton Digital Press.

Hockerts, Kai. 2006. "Entrepreneurial Opportunity in Social Business Ventures." In Johanna Mair, Jeffrey Robinson, and Kai Hockerts, eds. *Social Entrepreneurship*, 142–154. Basingstoke, UK: Palgrave Macmillan.

Kaletsky, Anatole. 2010. *Capitalism 4.0: The Birth of a New Economy in the Aftermath of Crisis*. New York: PublicAffairs.

Lasprogata, Gail A., and Marya N. Cotten. 2003. "Contemplating Enterprise: The Business and Legal Challenges of Social Entrepreneurship." *American Business Law Journal* 41:1, 67–113.

Mair, Johanna, and Ignasi Marti. 2006. "Social Entrepreneurship Research: A Source of Explanation, Prediction, and Delight." *Journal of World Business* 41:1, 36–44.

Novogratz, Jacqueline. 2007. "Meeting Urgent Needs with Patient Capital." *Innovations* 2:1/2, 19–30.

Pirson, Michael. 2008. "Social Entrepreneurship—A Blueprint for Humane Organizations?" In Heiko Spitzeck, Michael Pirson, Wolfgang Amann, Shiban Khan, and Ernst von Kimakowitz, eds. *Humanism in Business: Perspectives on the Development of a Responsible Business Society*, 248–259. Cambridge: Cambridge University Press.

Pirson, Michael, and Paul R. Lawrence. 2009. "Humanism in Business: Towards a Paradigm Shift?" *Journal of Business Ethics* 93:4, 553–565.

Porter, Michael E., and Mark R. Kramer. 2011. "The Big Idea: Creating Shared Value." *Harvard Business Review* 89:2, 1–17.

Prahalad, Coimbatore. K. 2005. *The Fortune at the Bottom of the Pyramid: Eradicating Poverty through Profits*. Philadelphia: Wharton School Publishing.

Quelch, John A., and Nathalie Laidler. 2003. "ACCION International." *Harvard Business School Case* 503–106. Boston: Harvard Business School Press.

Rangan, Kasturi V. 1993. "The Aravind Eye Hospital, Madurai, India: In Service for Sight." *Harvard Business Review Case* 593-098. Boston: Harvard Business School Press

Rangan, Kasturi V., John A. Quelch, Gustavo Herrero, and Brooke Barton. 2007. *Business Solutions for the Global Poor: Creating Social and Economic Value*. Hoboken, NJ: John Wiley & Sons.

Rennison, Amy. 2008. "Mohammad Yunus and Michael Chu Debate: Profiting from Poor People." *The Worldwide Microfinance Forum, Microcapital*. Available at www.microcapital.org/microcapital-special-feature-mohammad-yunus-and-michael-chu-debate-profiting-from-poor-people-at-the-worldwide-microfinance-forum/.

Simms, Shalei V. K., and Jeffrey Robinson. 2009. "Activist or Entrepreneur? An Identity-Based Model of Social Entrepreneurship." In Jeffrey Robinson, Johanna Mair, and Kai Hockerts, eds. *International Perspectives on Social Entrepreneurship*, 9–27. Basingstoke, UK: Palgrave Macmillan.

Sundelin, Anders. 2009. "Microfinance: Providing Capital and Services in New Ways." www.*blogspot.com*, May 15. Available at www.tbmdb.blogspot.com.

Tan, Wee-Liang, John Williams, and Tech-Meng Tan. 2005. "Defining the 'Social' in 'Social Entrepreneurship': Altruism and Entrepreneurship." *International Entrepreneurship and Management Journal* 1:3, 353–365.

Teece, David J. 2010. "Business Models, Business Strategy and Innovation." *Long Range Planning* 43:2/3, 172–194.

Thompson, John, and Bob Doherty. 2006. "The Diverse World of Social Enterprise: A Collection of Social Enterprise Stories." *International Journal of Social Economics* 33:5/6, 399–410.

Young, Stephen. 2003. *Moral Capitalism: Reconciling Private Interest with the Public Good*. London: Berrett-Koehler.

ABOUT THE AUTHOR

Michael A. Pirson is an assistant professor for Sustainable Business and Social Entrepreneurship and the director of the Center for Management Studies at Fordham University Schools of Business. He is also a research fellow at Harvard University and a partner of the Humanistic Management Network, an organization bringing together scholars, practitioners, and policy makers working toward the end of a "life-conducive" economic system. He is the coeditor of a book series at Palgrave-McMillan (Humanism in Business). In his pre-academic career, Professor Pirson worked for an international consulting group for several years, before starting his own private consultancy. He worked for and with governmental organizations, nonprofits, and business organizations. Professor Pirson is the SE track chair for the Oikos-Ashoka Global Case Writing competition in Social Entrepreneurship and serves on the board of three social enterprises. He received his undergraduate degree in economics at the University of Erlangen-Nuernberg, Germany; his joint degree in business and political science (MBA/MPA) in France, Germany, and the United States; and his doctorate in organizational behavior from the University of St. Gallen, Switzerland.

CHAPTER 5

Fiduciary and Other Legal Duties

BENJAMIN J. RICHARDSON
Professor and Canada Research Chair in Environmental Law and Sustainability,
University of British Columbia

INTRODUCTION

Can investors lawfully engage in socially responsible investment (SRI)? When individuals invest on their own behalf, they face few legal restrictions. But when someone else manages their money, such as in a pension plan, the fund's trustees and managers have fiduciary obligations to invest prudently in the best interests of the beneficiaries.

The potential ambit of such legal constraints on SRI has generated much debate and some confusion. According to Stratos (2004, p. 12), a Canadian authority, "current interpretations of the fiduciary duties of pension fund managers may unnecessarily constrain their ability to address the full range of relevant corporate responsibility considerations related to prospective investments." Conversely, research commissioned by the United Nations Environment Program's Finance Initiative (UNEP-FI) suggests that SRI is not precluded or overly hampered by fiduciary duties when SRI addresses financially material considerations (Freshfields Bruckhaus Deringer 2005).

The legal scope for SRI depends somewhat on how *socially responsible* is defined. It is a contentious term full of complexity that mirrors the similarly passionate debates about the meaning of *sustainable development* or *sustainability* (Pezzoli 1997). As those debates reveal, while some believe sustainability is achievable without major structural change to capitalism (World Business Council for Sustainable Development 2007), others such as Flannery (2006) and Monbiot (2007) advocate more fundamental reforms to our economic and social systems. If SRI implies that investment trustees and managers should merely "take into account" environmental and social issues that they perceive to be financially material to investment performance, as SRI is increasingly depicted in financial markets, there is little doubt that such practices are lawful. Indeed, if trustees ignore such issues, and consequently incur avoidable financial losses, legal liabilities might arise.

But what if SRI infers radical changes such as ridding an investment portfolio of all fossil fuel producers or extractive industries? Such a strategy would create a legal dilemma, because why should a fund exclude companies plying a lawful business? If lawmakers want to discourage such activities, presumably they should prohibit or regulate them directly, rather than expect social investors to fill the void as surrogate regulators. SRI historically developed for investors wanting to be in the vanguard of social change when governments had failed to act. The divestment campaign against South Africa's apartheid regime is the quintessential example. But without a financial rationale for such practices, there may be fiduciary law obstacles unless such practices reflect a fund's governing constitution or if beneficiaries provide a mandate. In the retail fund sector, for example, mutual funds are marketed specifically to ethical investors. Such funds are free to cater to their wishes so long as they fully disclose and act according to their investment prospectus. In the institutional sector, some charitable foundations are established with an explicit mandate to invest ethically. The legal difficulties for SRI arise mostly when an institutional fund is created to serve another purpose such as to build retirement savings for employees.

Fiduciary law is not the only area of law that affects the prospects for SRI. For investors in mutual funds, important legal rules in tort and contract law, as well as securities law, serve to protect investors from being misled or cheated. Corporate governance can also affect the prospects for SRI, as it influences the opportunities for shareholders to exert influence within corporations, such as by voting proxies, filing shareholder resolutions, and seeking dialogue with corporate management. Securities law is also relevant to corporate activities, especially in governing how businesses must report their financial affairs, including disclosure of environmental and social impacts. Without such disclosures, investors face difficulties differentiating between corporate laggards and leaders for sustainable development. At a more fundamental level, human rights and environmental regulation influence markets. Indeed, if the social and environmental externalities of the economy such as climate change were optimally controlled, there would be much less need for SRI.

Thus, the legal context to SRI is a complex and detailed subject, of which only a selection of issues can be canvassed in this chapter. It focuses on the fiduciary and trust law duties that govern finance in the institutional sector, including consideration of case law and academic commentary. The chapter concludes with a discussion of some recent statutory reforms that affect fiduciary finance and SRI. The chapter does not consider the legal issues that arise in the retail sector that caters directly to individual investors. Other legal issues that may affect SRI, such as corporate governance, contract law and securities law, are also not examined. Throughout the chapter, a multijurisdictional approach to the subject matter is taken, with some emphasis on legal precedents from the major common law jurisdictions (i.e., United States and United Kingdom), which have among the most developed financial markets and legal rules for SRI.

BASIC FIDUCIARY PRINCIPLES AND THEIR IMPACT ON SRI

The term *fiduciary* is an invention of Roman law and, as a noun, means a person holding the character of a trustee, being charged to act primarily for another's benefit with regard to specific property or affairs. The fiduciary is the entity that acts on behalf of another party, the beneficiary. Essentially, a fiduciary relationship is a bond of responsibility and dependency (Shepherd 1981). The core function of fiduciary law is to control opportunism and self-interested behavior in situations in which an actor has custody of the assets or affairs of another for a specific purpose (Conaglen 2005; Flannigan 2009). Other legal duties arise in fiduciary relationships, depending on their context and purpose. Among various relationships the law has characterized as fiduciary in nature are those in investment institutions between investors and fund custodians. In both common law and legislation, therefore, trustees, fund managers, advisors, and certain other types of decision makers may be impressed with fiduciary status and, consequently, owe specific obligations to beneficiaries.

Fiduciary law is a creature of common law systems. In countries with civil law systems, such as Germany and France, somewhat equivalent norms have been legislated (Preu and Richardson 2011). Some legal harmonization is a result of pressures to forge compatible legal standards to facilitate cross-border financial markets. This approach has gone the furthest in the European Community, such as pursuant to its Occupational Pensions Directive (2003), which posits several investment rules that reflect fiduciary standards, including obligations on pension plan trustees to act in the "best interests" of beneficiaries and to ensure the security, diversification, liquidity, and profitability of the investment portfolio.

The specific fiduciary duties for which investment institutions owe their beneficiaries belong primarily to the realm of trust law, as modified, often substantially, by legislation. The trust differs from other fiduciary relationships because of the presence of trust assets. Essentially, a *trust* is an entity in which property or money is held and managed on behalf of another (Hayton 1999). The trust is an ingenious legal device of English law that divides the attributes of ownership between two persons, the rights of management being in the trustee, and the right of enjoyment in the beneficiary (Waters 1967). Trusts are widely used as the legal structure for pension plans and mutual funds (O'Hagan 2000). A trust may also be established to advance specific purposes, as in a charitable trust without an identifiable group of beneficiaries.

Fiduciary responsibilities materialize in somewhat different ways across the financial sector (Richardson 2008). Trust law is particularly applicable to pension plans, which have clearly defined beneficiaries. Likewise, investments by foundations are governed by trust principles. Commercial banks do not owe their depositors a fiduciary duty in regard to how deposited funds are managed or disbursed, although they are often subject to detailed banking regulations and fiduciary duties that may arise when banks provide financial advice to clients. In most jurisdictions, insurance companies, which are major institutional investors, do not owe a fiduciary duty to insured policyholders regarding their investment activities. But fiduciary responsibilities may arise when insurance companies provide pension-type investment services through contracts with individual savers, although contract and consumer protection law largely govern such relationships. Furthermore, insurers' investment decisions tend to be regulated to protect insurers' loss reserves and to maintain liquidity (Randall 1999). Although fiduciary principles also arise in mutual fund governance, contract law and securities regulation primarily serve to align investment decisions with the interests of fund members. Trustees of mutual funds, pension plans, and other types of investment funds often delegate many of their decision-making powers to professional asset managers. Contrary to the common law prohibition on such delegations, legislation typically authorizes deputation of fund management so long as the fiduciary retains ultimate control and carefully supervises fund managers

The core fiduciary and trust law obligations are: (1) obey the trust deed; (2) act in the best interests of the beneficiaries; (3) treat all beneficiaries even-handedly; and (4) invest prudently with care and skill. These obligations are examined in the following sections. Trustees are potentially liable to beneficiaries for investment decisions that breach these duties (Ho 1998). Trustees could be held liable for the consequences of improper disposal of investments, including losses in the value of the portfolio and transaction costs, as presumably offset by the value and earnings of the replacement assets. But measuring damages when fund managers or trustees fail to fulfill the ethical preferences of beneficiaries, such as in a dedicated SRI fund, would be difficult to assess because there may be no measurable financial loss, only an *ethical loss*.

Fiduciary and trust law allow SRI in essentially four situations, as follows:

1. When environmental, social, and corporate governance issues (abbreviated in industry parlance as ESG issues) are perceived to be financially material to investment performance, this would provide a means of fulfilling the duty of care to invest prudently. Both portfolio screening and corporate engagement would be acceptable methods of SRI, although engagement is more suitable as it does not per se reduce the diversity of an investment portfolio (unless as a result of unsuccessful engagement a recalcitrant firm is excluded). Engagement and active shareholding are also increasing viewed as fiduciary responsibilities on the basis that the underlying shareholder rights are valuable assets.
2. When two investments are equally suitable in financial terms, ethical considerations can be the tie breaker, this is known as the *tie-breaker principle*.
3. The trust deed may provide an explicit or reasonably implicit mandate for SRI. This might be the case for an endowment fund, which is structured to meet specific philanthropic goals.
4. In limited circumstances, trustees may practice SRI when beneficiaries consent. However, some financial institutions are subject to legislation that restricts administrators' latitude to act with regard to nonfinancial criteria, even when demanded by investors.

In most common law jurisdictions, these duties have been codified and modified by legislation. For instance, the United States' federal pension law, the Employee Retirement Income Security Act of 1974 (ERISA), espouses principles that are similar to common law trust standards. Section 404 of ERISA obliges fiduciaries to act, inter alia, solely in the interest of plan participants and beneficiaries; and with the care, skill, prudence, and diligence under the circumstances then prevailing that a prudent man acting in a like capacity. Also, the United States' Uniform Trust Code, which codifies as well as modifies some common law trust rules, has been adopted into legislation in approximately half the states (Cooper 2008).

The following sections examine in more detail the core fiduciary and trust law duties and the consequential scope for SRI.

OBEY THE TRUST DEED

The first of these duties, to obey the trust deed created by the settlor, concerns the instrument that details the rights and powers of the trustees, benefits that accrue to beneficiaries, matters to be disclosed, record keeping, and other procedures and standards. If the deed expressly requires the trustees to invest according to specific or social environmental criteria, then they must heed those criteria. The trust deed is not necessarily determinative of all the responsibilities and powers of trustees. In financial institutions, such as employee pension funds, the trust deed is embedded within a wider legislative framework that elaborates rules especially regarding investment decision making. The trust deed is more decisive for a foundation or eleemosynary institution—so-called mission investors.

Although many charitable foundations lack an explicit ethical investment mission, an implication is that they should not invest contrary to their purpose (Parker, Mellows, and Oakley 1998). One example would be a foundation that promotes research into curing lung cancer. Trustees of such a foundation might agree that they should avoid investing in tobacco companies. Britain's Charity Commission (2001), which supervises British charities pursuant to the Charities Act of 1993, has advised that it may choose investments that do not necessarily seek the best financial returns if it advances the organization's philanthropic mission.

An English court in the case of *Bishop of Oxford v. Church Commissioners for England* (1992) took a somewhat more cautious view about SRI. The bishop wanted the Commissioners to invest more faithfully according to Christian doctrine, even at the risk of some financial loss. Although the Commissioners had an ethical investment policy for the Church's assets, it applied only to the extent that such considerations would not be financially harmful. The court underlined the duty of trustees to act in accordance with the purpose of the trust:

> It is axiomatic that charity trustees, in common with all other trustees, are concerned to further the purposes of the trust of which they have accepted the office of trustee. That is their duty. To enable them the better to discharge that duty, trustees have powers vested in them. Those powers must be exercised for the purpose for which they have been given: to further the purposes of the trust. That is the guiding principle applicable to the issues in these proceedings (*Bishop of Oxford*, 1992, p. 1244).

The Church Commissioners' investment policy stated that "[w]hile financial responsibilities must remain of primary importance (given our position as trustees), as responsible investors . . . we do not invest in companies whose main business is armaments, gambling, alcohol, tobacco and newspapers" (*Bishop of Oxford*, 1992, p. 1248). The court took no issue with the goals behind the charity or the Commissioners' policy of negative screening. But it did find the declarations sought by the plaintiff would go beyond the legal obligations of the trustees, as "[i]n most cases the best interests of the charity require that the trustees' choice of investments should be made solely on the basis of well-established investment criteria, having taken expert advice where appropriate and having due regard to such matters as the need to diversify, the need to balance income against capital growth, and the need to balance risk against return" (*Bishop of Oxford*, 1992, p. 1246). The court felt that where the aims of the charity and the objects of investment would directly conflict, the trustees must balance the extent of financial loss from offended supporters of the Church against the financial risks of SRI.

DUTY OF LOYALTY TO BENEFICIARIES

Trustees must act only in the interests of beneficiaries, as opposed to acting for their self-interest or any third-party interests. In the United States, authorities have expressed this duty as one of "undivided loyalty" (*Meinhard v. Salmon*, 1928), requiring a trustee "to administer the trust solely in the interest of beneficiaries" (Serota and Brodie 1995, p. 25). Various constituent elements of this duty have been developed over the years, including the obligation on trustees to avoid conflict of interests, the duty not to delegate responsibility, and the duty to act impartially towards different beneficiaries. In the case of a charitable trust, fidelity is owed to the purposes of the trust rather than to any specific class of beneficiaries.

Fiduciary law does not prescribe what beneficiaries' interests are. Rather, their interests depend on the terms of the governing trust deed and the overall purpose and context of the trust. In investment institutions, the duty of loyalty is commonly interpreted as promoting the financial interests of beneficiaries. Depending on the context, scholars believe trustees may also consider nonfinancial criteria (Scott and Fratcher 1988). If beneficiaries share a moral objection to a particular form of investment, they may benefit if their trust avoids that investment, possibly even at the cost of a lower financial return.

The duty of loyalty may also allow trustees to make investments that provide incidental or collateral benefits to others (e.g., to a local community) so long as beneficiaries are not adversely affected. In the United States, ERISA has been interpreted by the Department of Labor as "not preclud[ing] consideration of collateral benefits, such as those offered by a 'socially-responsible' fund" (Doyle 1998, p. 2). In *Donovan v. Walton* (1995, p. 1245) the court observed: "ERISA . . . simply does not prohibit a party other than a plan's participants and beneficiaries from benefiting in some measure from a prudent transaction with the plan."

Crucially, however, allowing trustees to consider the interests of third parties does not give them any enforceable rights. Their interests are simply discretionary considerations for trustees. This limitation is illustrated by the unsuccessful lawsuit in *Associated Students of the University of Oregon v. Oregon Investment Council* (1987). The student organizations sought a judicial declaration that the Investment Council could not invest higher education endowment funds in corporations doing business in South Africa, Zimbabwe, and Namibia. However, the court never addressed the substantive legal issues. In denying the students standing, the Court of Appeals of Oregon, as noted in this case (1987, p. 150), stated "they do not allege any legally recognized injury, and neither agreement with plaintiffs' opposition to apartheid nor the desirability of encouraging students to become concerned with social and moral wrongs and to seek to right them can turn the alleged 'injuries' into legally recognized ones."

The British case of *Cowan v. Scargill* (1985) considered the duty of loyalty to beneficiaries. In this case, trustees appointed jointly by the National Coal Board and the National Union of Mine Workers disagreed about the investment strategy for the workers' pension plan in question. Union trustees disapproved of the proposed investment plan unless it prohibited any increase in foreign investment and, in particular, any investment in energy industries in competition with coal mining. The Coal Board trustees commenced legal proceedings against the union trustees claiming that they were in breach of fiduciary duties by insisting on the proposed restrictions. The judge, Vice-Chancellor Robert Megarry, agreed with the National Coal Board trustees. Starting from the proposition that trustees must treat the interests of the beneficiaries as paramount, where the trust purpose is to provide financial benefits for the beneficiaries, he reasoned, the best interests of the beneficiaries normally mean their financial interests. If the actual or potential beneficiaries of a trust were only those individuals with strict views on moral or social matters, such as "condemning all forms of alcohol, tobacco and popular entertainment, as well as armaments" (*Cowan v. Scargill* 1985, p. 288), Megarry conceded that investing in certain problematic activities just to maximize financial return may not be for their "benefit."

Some financial institutions have interpreted the *Cowan* case to mean that trustees are under a duty to obtain the highest rate of return attainable and that trustees "and their fund managers and advisers [are precluded] from having regard to any considerations, other than the maximization of financial returns" (Freshfields Bruckhaus Deringer 2005, p. 88). However, the Freshfields Report cites several persuasive reasons the *Cowan* ruling does not provide a good authority for the profit maximization argument. First, the case turns heavily on its facts, where the union trustees were trying to prop up an entire industry, namely the failing British coal industry, which was "clearly not in the interests of all the beneficiaries." Second, the judge had no previous authority upon which to rely on, and the ruling is only that of an English lower court. Third, the mining union trustees' proposal sought a complete ban on certain investments rather than a more nuanced policy, and the proposal "bore little or no resemblance to a modern ESG investment policy" (Freshfields Bruckhaus Deringer 2005, p. 89).

BENEFICIARIES' VIEWS AND THE DUTY OF IMPARTIALITY

Financial fiduciaries must not only act in beneficiaries' best interests but also treat all beneficiaries even-handedly. This duty of impartiality has important implications for SRI because if beneficiaries may consent to trustees practising SRI, presumably they must all consent.

Many important legal and practical issues concern this basis to SRI. That trust law may countenance SRI if it fulfils the will of beneficiaries was acknowledged by the seminal Freshfields Report (Freshfields Bruckhaus Deringer 2005, p. 12), which advised that "a decision-maker may integrate ESG considerations into an investment decision to give effect to the views of the beneficiaries in relation to matters beyond financial return." While this conclusion would seem a logical extension of trustees' duty of loyalty, it is seemingly at odds with the passive role beneficiaries have traditionally assumed in fund governance as a matter of practice and legal precedent. A widespread assumption in financial markets is that investment management is a complex, specialist activity that few lay persons could competently undertake (Richardson 2011). In contrast, the trend towards shifting investment risk to beneficiaries, such as in pension plans offered to employees on a defined-contribution basis, presumptively justifies giving beneficiaries greater voice in fund governance.

Beneficiaries are legally entitled to be informed about the administration of the trust assets, but traditionally they have not enjoyed unqualified rights to be consulted or to instruct trustees. Trustees, unlike an agent who is subject to control of his or her principal, are generally not legally obliged to consult with beneficiaries. They only need to act in their "best interests," without necessarily being obliged to enquire what those best interests are. In Canada, the Ontario Law Reform Commission (1984, p. 74) observed that "[t]o allow beneficiaries to direct the ongoing administration of the trust confuses the role of trustee and beneficiary and is inconsistent with the trust concept. If the creator of a trust wishes the beneficiary to be actively involved in the administration of the trust, such person may always be appointed as trustee."

Trust law in some jurisdictions recognizes that beneficiaries may instruct trustees only in limited circumstances, such as when the trust in question is a small, intimate arrangement, as in a private family trust, and where all the beneficiaries are adults with full legal capacity. In *Cowan v. Scargill* (1985, p. 288), the judge gave one example: "Thus if the only actual or potential beneficiaries of a trust are all adults with very strict views on moral and social matters, condemning all forms of alcohol, tobacco and popular entertainment, as well as armaments, I can well understand that it might not be for the 'benefit' of such beneficiaries to know that they are obtaining rather larger financial returns." But modern investment institutions hardly resemble such a situation, and many are subject to legislation that restricts the ability of trustees to heed any nonfinancial preferences of beneficiaries. For instance, British Columbia's Pension Benefits Standards Act (1996, s. 44(1)) provides that "pension plan investments ... must be made ... in the *best financial* interests of plan members, former members and other plan beneficiaries."

There are various drawbacks and limitations to any legal mandate to respond to the will of beneficiaries. If beneficiaries can instruct trustees and thereby influence investment decisions, trustees might be considered their agents and consequently beneficiaries might be liable as principals to third parties for any compensable losses. Further, the practicality of ascertaining what their will is, especially if they are not unanimous in their views, must be overcome. The trust law duty of impartiality requires a trustee to treat beneficiaries even-handedly. In *Bishop of Oxford v. Church Commissioners for England* (1992, p. 1247), the court ruled: "trustees should not make investment decisions on the basis of preferring one view of whether on moral grounds an investment conflicts with the objects of the charity over another. This is so even when one view is more widely supported than the other." The likelihood of beneficiaries of a particular fund holding similar views on the desirability of SRI is far-fetched.

Disagreements over social values are rife in modern society (Zimmerman 1994). Disputes often arise over the environmental consequences of economic developments, which human rights deserve respect, and a host of other ethical issues. Investors have similarly diverse values. Academic research on the psychological and socio-economic characteristics of individual social investors and their opinions on various ethical matters suggests that ethical deliberation must bridge some major differences of opinion. Some empirical studies suggest that many such investors are unwilling to be altruistic if they would incur a financial loss (McLachlan and Gardner 2004; Nilsson 2008). Research also highlights differences among social investors concerning which SRI issues they care about the most. One study identified military equipment, tobacco, and gambling as common concerns (Anand and Cowton 1993), while another concluded that environmental protection and labor relations were more salient (Rosen, Sandler, and Shani 1991). Presumably, the heterogeneity of values among conventional investors is even greater than that among social investors.

Another way trustees might act on the will of beneficiaries, albeit indirectly, is by responding to the broader societal values to which they belong. The Freshfields Report (Freshfields Bruckhaus Deringer 2005, p. 96) suggests that trustees could rely on well-established social customs as a proxy for the values of the beneficiaries, such as to exclude "investments that are linked to clear breaches of widely recognised norms, such as international conventions on human rights, labor conditions, tackling corruption and environmental protection." One reason such social customs could be considered a proxy is, as Gifford (2004, p. 141) explains, because "[g]iven the ubiquity of pension fund membership, especially in the developed world, it can also be argued that the interests of members of funds are broadly consistent with those of the society in which the members live."

Numerous international treaties govern issues of interest to social investors including environmental protection (at least 500 such treaties and other international instruments), human rights (some 300 instruments), and labor standards (nearly 200 treaties). Some are widely ratified and thus putatively reflect a near-consensus of international opinion. However, reliance on international treaties or national legislation as evidence of social custom is not without shortcomings. First, while certain social norms embodied in such legal instruments may reflect democratically-determined decisions, invariably not everyone agrees with them. Second, many standards embodied in such treaties and laws are drafted too vaguely to provide concrete guidance for financial decision makers in hard cases.

In some countries, procedures that mandate consultation with beneficiaries or even appointment of their representatives to the governing boards of investment institutions may help convey beneficiaries' views. Among examples, in Britain, the Pensions Act (2004, s. 241(1)(a)) prescribes that "at least one-third" of the trustees must be "member-nominated," and the government may enact regulations to raise this number to one-half member-nominated trustees. Australia's Superannuation Industry (Supervision) (SIS) Act (1993) mandates 50 percent beneficiary representation on trustee boards of funds that have at least five members. Being a representative of beneficiaries, however, does legally per se allow a trustee to consider him or herself an agent of the beneficiaries, acting only according to instructions given. Trustees remain obliged to respect the purpose of the fund and overriding statutory requirements such as to invest prudently.

One legislative approach to improve beneficiaries' voice in fund governance is to create segregated portfolios that give members some choice regarding their investments including SRI. This arrangement has been proposed as an amendment to the United States' ERISA, and as of June 2010, at least 17 states already offer their employees the option of investing retirement dollars in such funds (U.S. Social Investment Forum 2010). A similar approach has been adopted in Australia for employee pension funds, which are known as superannuation funds, pursuant to the

Superannuation Legislation Amendment (Choice of Superannuation Funds) Act (2005). Such democratic reforms, however, do not necessarily make SRI more likely. Some anecdotal evidence suggests that more democratically-governed funds are at the forefront of SRI, such as public sector pension plans' investment in urban renewal and community economic development (Clark, Hebb, and Hagerman 2004). But apart from such economically targeted investment, any correlation appears to be modest.

DUTY OF CARE

The duty of care requires fiduciaries to exercise reasonable care, skill, and caution that a person in a like position should do under similar circumstances. The traditional formulation of the *prudent investor standard*, as this duty is often expressed, effectively precluded any investment that posed an unusual risk, as courts expected a trustee to assess and justify each investment individually (Ali and Yano 2004). Under the influence of modern portfolio theory, this understanding of prudent investment has ceded to the view that optimal returns derive from a large, diversified portfolio that generally carries lower financial risks than the risk attaching to each investment taken in isolation (Haskell 1990). Consequently, inclusion of investments selected for their social benefit might be easier to justify within a large portfolio than on a case-by-case basis.

The duty of care also requires obtaining professional advice. In the Scottish case of *Martin v. Edinburgh District Council* (1988), a majority of the Edinburgh District Council trustees decided to divest from South African–based assets owing to their ethical concerns about apartheid. Their policy was successfully challenged. The court concluded that the trustees of the municipality's fund acted unlawfully by implementing a policy of divestment without expressly considering the best interests of the beneficiaries and without obtaining professional advice.

The duty of care may also allow SRI when ethical considerations are a tie-breaker. The concept has been recognized in courts. In the *Bishop of Oxford* case, discussed above, the judge ruled that trustees choosing between two investments of equal suitability according to conventional principles of prudent investment might account for the ethical considerations as the deciding factor (the *tie-breaker principle*). The court viewed the Church Commissioners' ethical investment policy as proper, but it would be improper for them to have adopted a more restrictive policy burdened with greater financial risks.

The American case of *Board of Trustees of Employee Retirement System of the City of Baltimore v. City of Baltimore* (1989) considered a similar issue. The Maryland Court of Appeal examined the City's ordinances requiring its four municipal pension funds to divest from companies doing business in South Africa. The trustees of the funds argued that the ordinances unlawfully altered their common law duty of care by substantially reducing the universe of eligible investments. While the court agreed that the ordinances excluded a "not insignificant segment of the investment universe" (1989, p. 103), it believed the reduced returns expected from the divestiture in South Africa would only amount to about 10 basis points each year, and that the measured way the divestments were to occur meant that they did not undermine the trustees' prudential duties. The court explained: "thus, if . . . social investment yields economically competitive returns at a comparable level of risk, the investment should not be deemed imprudent" (1989, p. 107). It also found the ordinances acceptable so long as the cost of investing according to social responsibility precepts was *de minimis*. The court explained that a trustee's duty is not to maximize return on investments, but to secure a "just" and "reasonable" return, while avoiding undue risk.

The tie-breaker principle, however, is not easily applied because trustees typically manage investments on a portfolio-wide basis rather than assess investments on a case-by-case basis. Moreover, a precise comparative evaluation of the performance of investments can only be accurately made with the benefit of hindsight.

The methods for practicing SRI also have some bearing on its legality. The SRI policy should be implemented without burdensome and costly administrative procedures. Some SRI funds carry higher expenses and charges due to the additional research required (Croome-Carther 2007). The financial performance of SRI-focused funds has also been subject to much scrutiny, and some researchers believe that fund managers and trustees are likely to breach their fiduciary duties if they practice SRI, especially in economic downturns (Copp, Kremmer, and Roca 2010). Other research suggests SRI can outperform the market (Kiernan 2008), and portfolio diversification has become easier because SRI funds are now available across a broad range of asset classes and economic sectors (U.S. Social Investment Forum 2006). SRI is likely to be most compatible with the duty of care when it is implemented through corporate engagement and shareholder activism, rather than strict exclusionary screening. In this way, funds can maintain reasonably diversified portfolios in accordance with the principles of modern portfolio theory. However, engagement and activism can be time consuming and expensive to administer, and therefore might undermine compliance with fiduciary standards if undertaken extensively.

In recent years, the investment community has increasingly recognized the potential financial materiality of corporate social and environmental performance, and thus SRI has shifted somewhat from its ethical roots to an instrumental business consideration. The influential United Nations Environment Programme—Finance Initiative (UNEP-FI) (2006, p. 4) explained in its report, *Show Me the Money*, that "[t]he first—and arguably for investors the most important reason to integrate [SRI] issues is, simply, to make more money." In another UNEPFI (2004, p. 5) report, financial analysts are advised to demonstrate "material links to business value; ... [and] avoid moral arguments." This shift in thinking has implications for fiduciary responsibilities. As Woods (2011, p. 6) explains, "the fulfillment of the primary mandate [of fiduciaries to promote the best interests of the beneficiary] is likely to suffer if trustees ignore the long-term consequences of financing environmental degradation." Yaron (2001, p. 2), a Canadian lawyer, comments that "there is significant legal and empirical support for viewing socially responsible investment practices as a requisite element of prudent and loyal trusteeship." Climate change has been identified as one example. Mercer Investment Consulting (2005, pp. 18−19) has advised: "Climate risk can have a real impact on portfolio holdings. There is a growing case for trustees to attain some level of knowledge around these issues, and to take steps to mitigate any negative consequences of not taking action ... we suggest that it is consistent with fiduciary responsibility to address climate change risk."

STATUTORY REFORM

Fiduciary law's affect on SRI is sometimes modified by legislation. In most cases, it merely codifies common law standards, but occasionally it modifies them in ways that may hinder SRI. For example, the Uniform Trust Code, which has been adopted by many state governments in the United States, may prevent trust settlors from placing restrictions on investment decision making that would override the duty to act as a prudent investor. The assumption is that financial prudence dictates what is in beneficiaries' interests. Consequently, this standard could undermine a trust settlor's ability to safeguard his or her beneficiaries' nonmonetary ethical values through restraints on trust investments (Cooper 2008). A few jurisdictions in the United States have gone further by attempting explicitly to ban SRI in some cases. For example, Nebraska's statutory duties of the Investment Council state that "[n]o assets of the retirement systems... shall be invested or reinvested if the sole or primary investment objective is for economic development or social purposes or objectives" (Nebraska Revised Statutes, 2007, p. s. 72-1239.01).

There is also somewhat of a countervailing legislative trend in some jurisdictions to acknowledge SRI as a legitimate investment practice. So far, such regulation commonly involves informational and incentive-based policy mechanisms to stimulate, but not direct, SRI. Some governments have introduced green investment tax concessions (e.g., the Netherlands' 1996 Green Investment Directive), which aim to improve the cost-benefit equation in favor of sustainable development. Others have focused on getting financiers to report their SRI policies, proxy voting activities, and environmental impacts of financial significance. These requirements may enable the assessment, verification, and communication of performance and, in theory, thereby put pressure on environmental laggards to change or reward leaders through competitive market advantages. In 2000, for example, regulations in Britain came into effect modifying the Pensions Act's statement of investment principles requirement by requiring occupational pension fund trustees to disclose what role, if any, ESG criteria has in their investment decision making (Occupational Pension Schemes (Investment, and Assignment, Forfeiture, Bankruptcy) Amendment Regulations, 1999). This reform inspired similar legislation in several other European Union states and Australia (Richardson 2002). Many pension funds have responded to the disclosure regulation with vigor by adopting an SRI policy, although the quality of implementation of such policies has tended to be less satisfactory (U.K. Sustainable Investment and Finance Association 2009, 2010). Reformers in North America focused on mutual funds, legislating requirements that they disclose their proxy voting policies and voting records when acting as shareholders (Securities Exchange Commission 2003, Canadian Securities Administrators 2005).

Some Canadian provinces have also modified fiduciary rules to give more latitude for SRI. Manitoban legislation stipulates that unless the pension plan or trust instrument dictates otherwise, an investment decision partially motivated by nonfinancial criteria is permissible so long as trustees follow the duty of care (Trustee Act 1995). A more pro-SRI reform was Ontario's South African Trust Investments Act (1990), which essentially allowed divestiture from South African investments, even if such action resulted in lower returns. The Act absolved trustees from their fiduciary and other legal duties in "refusing to acquire a South African investment" or "disposing of a South African investment even if the value of the property for which the trustee is responsible decreases or fails to increase sufficiently as a result" (South African Trust Investments Act, 1990, s. 3(a)-(b)), so long as trustees had consulted with beneficiaries and had at least a majority's support. However, both the Manitoban and Ontarian (now repealed) provisions are couched in negative terms, indicating that a trustee will not breach fiduciary duties by considering nonfinancial factors, rather than creating a positive duty on trustees to invest ethically.

While regulations to permit SRI in the private sector are becoming more prevalent, explicit legal duties for socially conscious investing have only been imposed on public financial institutions (Richardson 2008). The first precedents were adopted in the 1980s by some states and municipalities in the United States, which sought to restrict government pension funds from investing in apartheid South Africa (McCarroll 1980–1981) or in strife-torn Northern Ireland (Conway 2002). Since 2000, sovereign wealth funds of Sweden, Norway, New Zealand, and France have been subject to legislative direction to invest ethically, with obligations that are more comprehensive and ambitious than the American precedents. The Norwegian Government Pension Fund—Global is obliged by its ethical guidelines, on the advice of the independent Council of Ethics, to exclude companies from its investment portfolio "if there is an unacceptable risk that the company contributes to or is responsible for a) serious or systematic human rights violations . . . b) serious violations of the rights of individuals in situations of war or conflict: c) severe environmental damage; d) gross corruption; e) other particularly serious violations of fundamental ethical norms" (Guidelines for Observation and Exclusion from the Government Pension Fund Global's Investment Universe, 2010, s. 2(3)). The New Zealand legislation has a qualified and less prescriptive obligation to invest ethically. The Guardians of the New Zealand Superannuation Fund's primary duty is to invest the Fund on a "prudent, commercial basis . . . in a manner consistent with . . . avoiding prejudice to New Zealand's reputation as a responsible member of the world community" (New Zealand Superannuation and Retirement Income Act, 2001, s. 58(2)(c)). The New Zealand legislation thus gives little guidance as to what constitutes ethical investment compared to Norway's legislation. A limitation of both countries' legislation is the absence of a positive duty on the funds to promote SRI; rather, their focus is limited to avoiding the funds' complicity with unethical activities.

SUMMARY AND CONCLUSIONS

Fiduciary and trust law governs how institutional funds manage their assets on behalf of their beneficial owners. In most common law jurisdictions, these legal rules have been codified or modified by legislation, and their precise manifestation varies somewhat between pension funds, insurance companies, mutual funds, and other types of financial institutions. The duty of prudence or care has been interpreted as requiring trustees to assess investments not in isolation but by reference to their contribution to the whole investment portfolio, to create a diverse portfolio, and to take professional advice. Further, the key fiduciary duty—the duty of loyalty—requires that fiduciaries advance the best interests of the beneficiaries and has been interpreted so as to ensure that fiduciaries act honestly and exclusively for the beneficiaries, thereby preventing fiduciaries from acting for their own or third-party interests.

Fiduciary and trust law allow SRI in essentially four situations: (1) when environmental, social, and corporate governance issues are financially material to investment performance; (2) where two investments are equally suitable in financial terms, then ethical considerations can be the tie breaker; (3) where the settlor's trust deed provides mandate for SRI, as in the case with charitable foundations; and (4) when beneficiaries consent to SRI.

The legal framework for fiduciary finance will likely continue to evolve, especially as pressures grow to address the intertwined financial market and ecological crises that affect the global economy (Joly 2011). Reforms in some jurisdictions such as in Canada and Britain are already revamping the fiduciary standards that apply at the level of ordinary business corporations in an effort to promote greater consideration of environmental and community interests as factors that can shape the prosperity of companies (Bone 2009). Fiduciary standards that encourage long-term, sustainable investing might help reduce the harmful myopic and speculative tendencies of financial markets while channeling capital into environmentally beneficial development.

DISCUSSION QUESTIONS

1. In what ways do the core fiduciary and trust duties of loyalty and care facilitate or hinder SRI?

2. Should trustees be able to practice SRI if that is the will of beneficiaries, even if it might lower financial returns? By what means can trustees ascertain the views of beneficiaries, and what are the consequences if beneficiaries are not unanimous?

3. Can and should trustees only heed the interests of the beneficiaries of an investment fund, or should trustees also consider the wider interests of society in managing an investment portfolio? Explain.

4. How can governments most effectively reform fiduciary law to facilitate socially responsible investment? What are the advantages and disadvantages of available policy tools such as information disclosure, taxation incentives, or statutory obligations to invest ethically?

REFERENCES

Ali, Paul, and Kanako Yano. 2004. *Eco-Finance*. The Hague: Kluwer Law.

Anand, Paul, and Christopher Cowton. 1993. "The Ethical Investor: Exploring Dimensions of Investment Behavior." *Journal of Economic Psychology* 14:2, 377–385.

Associated Students of the University of Oregon v. Oregon Investment Council. 1987. 82 Or. App. 145, 728 P.2d 30.

Bishop of Oxford v. Church Commissioners for England. 1992. 1 WLR 1241.

Board of Trustees of Employee Retirement System of the City of Baltimore v. City of Baltimore. 1989. 317 Md. 72; 562 A.2d 720.

Bone, Jeffrey. 2009. "Corporate Environmental Responsibility in the Wake of the Supreme Court Decision of BCE Inc. and Bell Canada." *Windsor Review of Legal and Social Issues* 27 (May), 5–30.

Canadian Securities Administrators (CSA). 2005. *National Instrument 81-106 Investment Fund Continuous Disclosure and Companion Policy 81-106CP.* Montreal: CSA.

Charity Commission. 2001. *Guidance on Programme-Related Investment*. London: Charity Commission.

Clark, Gordon, Tessa Hebb, and Lisa Hagerman. 2004. *U.S. Public Sector Pension Funds and Urban Revitalization: An Overview of Policy and Programs*. Oxford: University of Oxford, School of Geography and Environment.

Conaglen, Matthew. 2005. "The Nature and Function of Fiduciary Loyalty." *Law Quarterly Review* 121: 452–480.

Conway, Neil J. 2002. "Investment Responsibility in Northern Ireland: The MacBride Principles of Fair Employment." *Loyola of Los Angeles International and Comparative Law Review* 24:1, 1–18.

Cooper, Jeffery A. 2008. "Empty Promises: Settlor's Intent, the Uniform Trust Code, and the Future of Trust Investment Law." *Boston University Law Review* 88:5, 1165–1216.

Copp, Richard, Michael L. Kremmer, and Eduardo Roca. 2010. "Should Funds Invest in Socially Responsible Investments During Downturns?: Financial and Legal Implications of the Fund Manager's Dilemma." *Accounting Research Journal* 23:3, 254–266.

Cowan v. Scargill. 1985. Ch. 270.

Croome-Carther, Shauna. 2007. "Funds with Values." *FORBES.COM*, November 14. Available at www.forbes.com/investoreducation/2007/11/14/sri-funds-domini-pf-education-in_sc_1114investopedia_inl.html.

Donovan v. Walton. 1985. 609 F. Supp. 1221 (D.C. Fla.), 1245.

Doyle, Robert J. 1998. *Advisory Opinion*. Washington, DC: Pension and Welfare Benefits Administration, Office of Regulations and Interpretations.

Flannery, Tim. 2006. *The Weather Makers*. Toronto: HarperCollins.

Flannigan, Robert. 2009. "The Core Nature of Fiduciary Accountability." *New Zealand Law Review* 3: 375–429.

Freshfields Bruckhaus Deringer. 2005. *A Legal Framework for the Integration of Environmental, Social and Governance Issues into Institutional Investment*. Geneva: UNEP-FI.

Gifford, James. 2004. "Measuring the Social, Environmental and Ethical Performance of Pension Funds." *Journal of Australian Political Economy* 53 (June), 139–160.

Guidelines for Observation and Exclusion from the Government Pension Fund Global's Investment Universe. 2010. Norwegian Storting.

Haskell, Paul G. 1990. "The Prudent Person Rule for Trustee Investment and Modern Portfolio Theory." *North Carolina Law Review* 69:1, 87–112.

Hayton, David. 1999. "English Fiduciary Standards and Trust Law." *Vanderbilt Journal of Transnational Law* 32:3, 555–612.

Ho, Lusina. 1998. "Attributing Losses to a Breach of Fiduciary Duty." *Trust Law International* 12:1, 66–76.

Joly, Carlos. 2011. "Reality and Potential of Responsible Investment." *Issues in Business Ethics* 31:193–210.

Kiernan, Matthew. 2008. *Investing in a Sustainable World: Why Green Is the New Color of Money on Wall Street*. New York: AMACOM.

Martin v. Edinburgh District Council. 1988. S.L.T. 329.

McCarroll, Patricia. 1980–1981. "Socially Responsible Investment of Public Pension Funds: The South Africa Issue and State Law." *Review of Law and Social Change* 10:2, 407–434.

McLachlan, Jonathan, and John Gardner. 2004. "A Comparison of Socially Responsible and Conventional Investors." *Journal of Business Ethics* 52:1, 11–25.

Meinhard v. Salmon. 1928. 164 N.E. 545 (N.Y.).

Mercer Investment Consulting (MIC). 2005. *A Climate for Change: A Trustee's Guide to Understanding and Addressing Climate Risk*. Toronto: MIC.

Monbiot, George. 2007. *Heat: How to Stop the Planet from Burning*. New York: South End Press.

Nebraska Revised Statutes. 2007. c. 72.

New Zealand Superannuation and Retirement Income Act. 2001, no. 84.

Nilsson, Jonas. 2008. "Investment with a Conscience." *Journal of Business Ethics* 83:2, 307–325.

Occupational Pensions Directive. 2003. 2003/41/EC.

Occupational Pension Schemes (Investment, and Assignment, Forfeiture, Bankruptcy) Amendment Regulations. 1999. no. 1849.

O'Hagan, Patrick. 2000. "The Use of Trusts in Finance Structures." *Journal of International Tax, Trust and Corporate Planning* 8:2, 85–92.

Ontario Law Reform Commission. 1984. *Report on the Law of Trusts.* Toronto: Ontario Law Reform Commission.

Parker, David B., Anthony R. Mellows, and A. J. Oakley, 1998. *Parker and Mellows: The Modern Law of Trusts.* London: Sweet and Maxwell.

Pensions Act. 2004. c. 35, Laws UK.

Pension Benefits Standards Act. 1996. R.S.B.C., c. 352.

Pezzoli, Keith. 1997. "Sustainable Development: A Transdisciplinary Overview of the Literature." *Journal of Environmental Planning and Management* 40:5, 549–574.

Preu, Johanna, and Benjamin J. Richardson. 2011. "German Socially Responsible Investment: Barriers and Opportunities." *German Law Journal* 12:3, 865–900.

Randall, Susan. 1999. "Insurance Regulation in the United States." *Florida State University Law Review* 26:3, 625–699.

Richardson, Benjamin J. 2002. "Pensions Law Reform and Environmental Policy: A New Role for Institutional Investors?" *Journal of International Financial Markets: Law and Regulation* 3:5, 159–169.

Richardson, Benjamin J. 2008. *Socially Responsible Investment Law: Regulating the Unseen Polluters.* New York: Oxford University Press.

Richardson, Benjamin J. 2011. "Fiduciary Relationships for Socially Responsible Investing: A Multinational Perspective." *American Journal of Business Law* 48:3, 597–640.

Rosen, Barry, Dennis Sandler, and David Shani. 1991. "Social Issues and Socially Responsible Investment Behavior: A Preliminary Empirical Investigation." *Journal of Consumer Affairs,* 25:2:, 221–234.

Scott, Austin W., and William F. Fratcher. 1988. *The Law of Trusts.* 4th ed. Boston: Little Brown and Company.

Securities Exchange Commission (SEC). 2003. "Disclosure of Proxy Voting Policies and Proxy Voting Records by Registered Management Investment Companies." Washington DC: SEC.

Serota, Susan, and Frederick Brodie. 1995. *ERISA Fiduciary Law.* Edison, NJ: BNA Books.

Shepherd, J. C. 1981. "Towards a Unified Concept of Fiduciary Relationships." *Law Quarterly Review* 97 (January): 51–79.

South African Trust Investments Act. 1990. R.S.O. c. S.16.

Stratos. 2004. *Corporate Disclosure and Capital Markets.* Ottawa: National Roundtable on the Environment and Economy.

Superannuation Legislation Amendment (Choice of Superannuation Funds) Act. 2005. (Cth).

Superannuation Industry (Supervision) (SIS) Act. 1993. (Cth).

Trustee Act. 1995. S.M. c.14.

United Nations Environment Programme—Finance Initiative (UNEP-FI). 2004. *The Materiality of Social, Environmental and Corporate Governance Issues in Equity Pricing.* Geneva: UNEP-FI.

United Nations Environment Programme—Finance Initiative (UNEP-FI). 2006. *Show Me the Money: Linking Environmental, Social and Governance Issues to Company Value.* Geneva: UNEP-FI.

U.K. Sustainable Investment and Finance Association (UKSIF). 2009. *How the Pension Funds of the UK's Corporate Responsibility Leaders are Approaching Responsible Investment*. London: UKSIF.

U.K. Sustainable Investment and Finance Association (UKSIF). 2010. *Focused on the Future: 2000–2010 Celebrating Ten Years of Responsible Investment Disclosure by UK Occupational Pension Funds*. London: UKSIF.

U.S. Social Investment Forum (SIF). 2006. *2005 Report on Socially Responsible Investing Trends in The United States*. Washington DC: SIF.

U.S. Social Investment Forum (SIF). 2010. "Social Investment Forum Applauds Introduction of Bill Allowing Federal Employees to Select SRI Retirement Option." Press Release, September 21. Washington, DC: SIF.

Waters, Donovan W. M. 1997. "The Nature of the Trust Beneficiary's Interest." *Canadian Bar Review* 45:2, 219–283.

Woods, Claire. 2011. "Funding Climate Change: How Pension Fund Fiduciary Duty Masks Trustee Inertia and Short-Termism." In James Hawley, Shyam Kamath and Andrew T. Williams, eds. *Corporate Governance Failures: The Role of Institutional Investors in the Global Financial Crisis*, 242–277. Philadelphia: University of Pennsylvania Press.

World Business Council for Sustainable Development (WBCSD). 2007. *Catalyzing Change: A Short History of the WBCSD*. Geneva: WBCSD.

Yaron, Gil. 2001. *The Responsible Pension Trustee: Reinterpreting the Principles of Prudence and Loyalty in the Context of Socially Responsible Institutional Investing*. Vancouver: Canadian Shareholder Association for Research and Education.

Zimmerman, Michael. 1994. *Contesting Earth's Future: Radical Ecology and Postmodernity*. Berkeley: University of California Press.

ABOUT THE AUTHOR

Benjamin J. Richardson holds the Senior Canada Research Chair in Environmental Law & Sustainability, at the Faculty of Law, University of British Columbia. Previously, he was a professor at Osgoode Hall Law School of York University (2003–2010) and before then he taught at the law faculties of the University of Manchester and University of Auckland. Before working in academia, Professor Richardson was a policy advisor to the NSW National Parks and Wildlife Service in Australia, and a legal consultant to the International Union for Conservation of Nature (IUCN) in Nepal and Kenya. Professor Richardson's principal research area is socially responsible investment and its regulation, and he is the author of *Socially Responsible Investment Law* (Oxford University Press 2008).

CHAPTER 6

International and Cultural Views

ASTRID JULIANE SALZMANN
Research Associate, RWTH Aachen University

INTRODUCTION

As a response to social and environmental challenges imposed through globalization and industrialization, private, institutional, and corporate investors adopted a new mind-set and increased interest in investment with social and environmental considerations. A huge literature in the field of business ethics has emerged with growing evidence of systematic attempts to combine moral or ecological factors with conventional criteria in financial decision making (Egri and Ralston 2008). Although evidence exists that social responsibility in financial markets is growing, the literature remains vague about the underlying motives of investors (Agle and Van Buren 1999).

Until recently, the finance literature has largely ignored a country's national characteristics such as the cultural, social, legal, and political environment. Lately, however, an extensive body of work has been advanced and documented that national features are fundamental sources of differences in financial development among nations (Aggarwal and Goodell 2009). But what are the specific factors that drive developments in sustainable finance and investment? The literature fails to provide a comprehensive answer to this question. This chapter investigates the effect of differences in the institutional environment on the social and ecological behavior of firms and investors around the world. It examines four structural theories to explain cross-country differences in social responsibility: legal origin, endowments, religion, and cultural values. The following sections review these theories and assess their relative importance as fundamentals in socially responsible finance across countries.

Besides referring to anecdotal evidence and relying on established empirical studies where possible, this chapter additionally assesses institutional theories in terms of their explanatory power for socially responsible finance and investment. Unfortunately, data about the overall state of a country regarding socially responsible finance and investing (SRFI) are particularly hard to obtain. The following considerations employ an index on the ethical behavior of firms obtained from the World Economics Forum's Global Competitiveness Report 2009–2010. The report lays out data from the Executive Opinion Survey, in which real-world business practitioners provide their expert opinions on general aspects of their countries' economic environment. The survey covers 139 countries, and the sample includes a total of 13,607 questionnaires. This represents an average of 98 respondents per country with a median country sample size of 87 responses. The data have been collected from January to May 2010. Notwithstanding its exceptional sample size both in terms of country coverage and received responses, the survey reports a high level of consistency in data collection across countries. Despite some skepticism among researchers, the use of survey data is gaining popularity in economics, as it offers timely and unique measures that can hardly be obtained otherwise.

The index on the ethical behavior of firms evaluates the answers to the question: "How would you compare the corporate ethics of firms in your country with those of other countries in the world? (1 = among the worst in the world; 7 = among the best in the world)." Though the index is rather vague on what to consider as ethical behavior and probably covers a broad range of aspects in social responsibility in finance and investment, it is certainly a useful indicator for the relevance of sustainable finance. Due to the large number of participating countries and the large sample size, the data provide a rare source of insight into each country's environment and allows for comparisons across nations. Exhibit 6.1 overviews ethical behavior across countries.

The remainder of the chapter is organized as follows. The next section portrays the theory on law and finance and discusses potential consequences on ethical behavior. The third section focuses on endowments and evaluates their usefulness for explaining cross-national diversity in SFRI. Section four reviews the literature on religion as a determinant for issues in ethical finance and investment. The fifth section introduces major cultural models and assesses whether national culture is an important factor for sustainable finance. The final section concludes with a brief summary and suggestions for future research.

LEGAL ORIGIN

At the end of the last century, Rafael La Porta and his associates started to publish a series of articles focusing on the economic consequences of the level of legal investor protection in a country (La Porta, Lopez-de-Silanes, Shleifer, and Vishny 1997, 1998). Their research resulted in a myriad of follow-up papers and established the so-called law and finance theory. The law and finance theory is based on differences between the two prevailing legal traditions—the British common law and the French civil law—and predicts that the historically inherited legal system is an important determinant of international variations in financial development today. This approach is certainly one of the most influential theories to explain cross-country differences in finance today.

The law and finance theory holds that the two basic legal systems differ fundamentally in the degree of investor protection originating from their basic underlying ideas about law and its purpose. The British common law developed to protect owners of private property against the crown, whereas the French civil law evolved to strengthen state power against a corrupt judiciary. The resultant emphasis of private property rights by the common law tradition supports financial

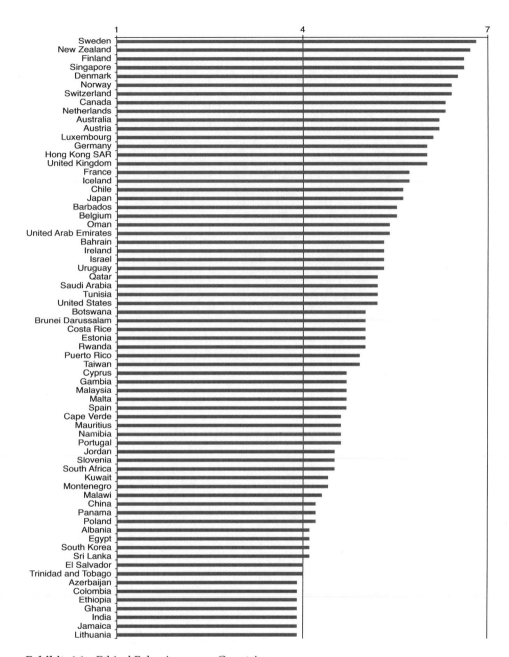

Exhibit 6.1 Ethical Behavior across Countries

The figure illustrates the varying levels of ethical behavior across countries. The index on the ethical behavior of firms evaluates the answers to the question: "How would you compare the corporate ethics of firms in your country with those of other countries in the world? (1 = among the worst in the world; 7 = among the best in the world)."

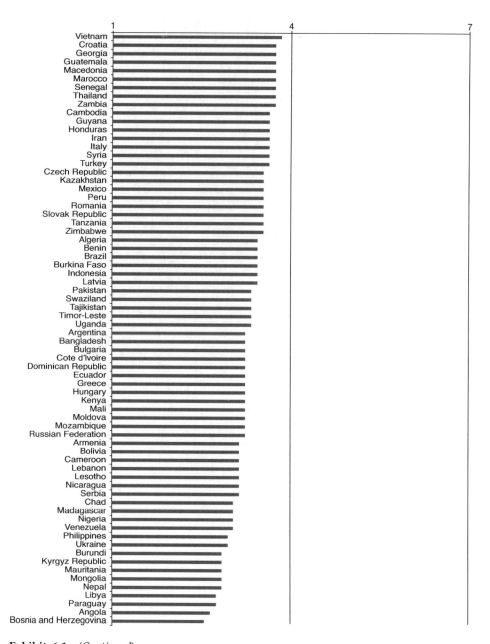

Exhibit 6.1 (*Continued*)

development, and countries that have adopted the common law system generally exhibit better developed financial markets than countries with a civil law tradition (Beck, Demirgüç-Kunt, and Levine 2003a).

The two major legal traditions spread to various countries through conquest and colonization, and despite local legal evolution, the fundamentals of each legal tradition have survived. The British promoted a legal system that fosters financial development, whereas the French shared a legal tradition that is less favorable to financial development. The common law legal system evolved in England and was introduced to the British colonies, including the United States, Canada, Australia, India, South Africa, and many other countries. The civil law legal system emerged from Roman law and was predominantly formed in France during the French Revolution. Napoleon brought the civil law codes to Belgium, the Netherlands, Italy, and parts of Germany. Later, France imposed these legal rules to its colonies in the Near East and Northern Africa, Indochina, Oceania, and the French Caribbean. Napoleon's codes also influenced Portugal and Spain, and these nations instituted the civil law system in their colonies in Latin America. The Russian Empire adopted the French civil law code, too, and influenced many countries in the region. Although socialist law was established in these countries after the Russian Revolution, most countries returned to the civil law system after the fall of the Berlin Wall. The German legal tradition further spread the civil law system to Austria, Greece, Italy, Switzerland, Japan, China, and Korea. Apparently, the civil law tradition is the most widely dispersed around the world (La Porta, Lopez-de-Silanes, and Shleifer 2008).

The Economic Consequences of Legal Origin

The economic consequences of legal institutions are pervasive. La Porta et al. (1998) pioneered this research by observing that the level of investor protection provided through the legal system is a strong predictor for bank and stock market development. Subsequent research relates legal traditions to access to finance (Demirgüç-Kunt and Maksimovic 1998), capital structure (Demirgüç-Kunt and Maksimovic 1999), and corporate valuations (La Porta, Lopez-de-Silanes, Shleifer, and Vishny 2002). A large body of work shows that the influence of the legal system is not restricted to financial markets and extends it to market entry regulations (Djankov, La Porta, Lopez-de-Silanes, and Shleifer 2002), judicial institutions (Djankov, La Porta, Lopez-de-Silanes, and Shleifer 2003), and labor market outcomes (Botero, Djankov, La Porta, Lopez-de-Silanes, and Shleifer 2004). Finally, Levine (1999) documents that legal traditions effect long-run economic growth. Although this list is far from complete, it highlights that the law and finance theory is of utmost importance in the literature.

Legal Origin and Ethical Behavior

So far, scholars have not yet addressed the impact of the legal system on issues in socially responsible finance. However, anticipating at least some coherence, regarding the vast influence of legal origin on economic outcomes across many fields of economic studies, seems only natural.

As financial responsibility may be regarded as a particular and potentially superior form of financial development, one might conclude that common law countries would foster SRFI as well, along with their tendency to support financial development in general. Furthermore, the social and ecological environment can be regarded as some special kind of "private property," and should correspondingly be protected in countries with a common law tradition. Finally, the findings are in line with the literature review from the preceding paragraph, which highlights that, on average, common law countries tend to better developed. One might suspect that developments in social issues might presuppose a certain level of general economic development, so that the legal origin could likewise serve as a mediating variable from advanced overall financial development to specific progress in socially responsible finance. In this vein, Jones (1999) argues that socio-economic development is usually related to greater material prosperity and increased human capital development. Accordingly, more developed societies have higher economic and human capital to contend claims for social responsibility.

The empirical investigation in Exhibit 6.2, based on the variable for ethical behavior introduced above, supports the suggested link. Ethical behavior is measured on a scale of 1 to 7, with lower values indicating poor ethical behavior. Common law countries report an average value of ethical behavior of 4.5, which is considerably higher than the mean value for civil law countries of 4.1. The difference is statistically significant, and becomes equally apparent from the median value of 4.1 for the common law countries but only 3.8 for the civil law countries. The underlying cumulative distribution functions for each group of legal origins support these findings as well, as the distribution function for civil law countries tends to rise faster than that for common law countries. Accordingly, common law countries seem to foster developments in SRFI.

Exhibit 6.2   Legal System and Ethical Behavior

	Common Law Countries	Civil Law Countries
Median	4.5	4.1
Mean	4.1	3.8
Test of means (t-statistics)	1.5904	
p-value	0.0571	
Ethical behavior (cumulative distribution function) (%)		
≤ 1.5	0.00	0.00
≤ 2.0	0.00	0.00
≤ 2.5	0.00	0.00
≤ 3.0	5.41	6.98
≤ 3.5	21.62	36.05
≤ 4.0	45.95	61.63
≤ 4.5	56.76	70.93
≤ 5.0	70.27	79.07
≤ 5.5	81.08	86.05
≤ 6.0	89.19	90.70
≤ 6.5	94.59	97.67
≤ 7.0	100.00	100.00

The table presents some descriptive information on ethical behavior in common and civil law countries. The index on the ethical behavior ranges from 1 to 7, with lower values indicating poor ethical behavior. Common law countries exhibit considerably higher values and therefore tend to foster ethical behavior compared to civil law countries.

ENDOWMENTS

Similar to the law and finance theory introduced above, the endowment theory emanates from the institutions established by colonizers. Yet, it emphasizes a completely distinct causal mechanism focusing on the conditions of the colonies and the disease environment faced by the European settlers. If colonialists encountered favorable endowments where they could settle safely, they created good institutions supportive to long-term financial development. If the environment was not feasible for settlement, they created worse institutions and aimed to extract as much from the colony as possible.

The endowment theory goes back to Acemoglu, Johnson, and Robinson (2001), who observed that European settlers experienced very different environments when they colonized the world. In some regions, the colonizers came across hospitable environments where settling was convenient (e.g., the United States, Australia, Canada, and New Zealand). In other places, they faced awkward conditions with a high disease environment and died in large numbers (e.g., Congo, Ivory Coast, and Latin America). Depending on the feasibility of settlement, the Europeans followed different colonization policies leading to different types of institutions. In hospitable locations, they established sound institutions that secured property rights and constrained the power of the government. In inhospitable environments, they established institutions that facilitated government control and extractive states. The main aim was to transfer as much of the resources of the colony to the colonizer. The colonial institutions endured after independence and continue to influence financial development today (Beck, Demirgüç-Kunt, and Levine 2003b).

The Economic Consequences of Endowments

The endowment theory has attracted less attention than the theory of law and finance, which might be due to lack of appropriate data to measure endowments. Acemoglu et al. (2001) use rare data on the mortality rates of soldiers, clergy, and sailors positioned in the colonies. Later studies proxy endowments through the geographical latitude as absolute value of the latitude of a country. Countries with smaller values lie closer to the equator and generally exhibit a more tropical climate unfavorable to European colonizers.

Acemoglu et al. (2001) estimate large effects on income per capita. Beck et al. (2003b) provide evidence that countries with poor geographical endowments tend to have less developed financial intermediaries, less developed stock markets, and weaker property rights protection. Additionally, they document that endowments are more robustly associated with financial development than legal origin and can explain more of the cross-country variations of financial markets. Ayyagari, Demirgüç-Kunt, and Maksimovic (2008) show that endowments can explain firms' perceptions of property rights protection.

A major shortcoming of the endowment theory arises from the fact that it is actually only applicable to countries that have been formerly colonized. The foundations of the theory lie in the institutions developed by European colonizers, and thus particularly fail to explain developments in the European countries themselves. Whether the extension of the theory through considering climate conditions as a proxy for geographical endowments is appropriate and can overcome this drawback needs to be shown in future research.

Endowments and Ethical Behavior

Although the literature has not yet tackled the relationships between endowments and SRFI, the connection seems rather straightforward. In countries where institutions are primarily extractive, developments in SRFI are likely minimal. Moreover, a society needs to satisfy its member's basic needs first, before it can approach higher-level needs in areas such as sustainability (Jones 1999). When people face unfavorable environments with awkward living conditions, superior developments of any kind appear to be a struggle. Thus, they are unlikely to exert additional efforts to increase performance in sustainability issues.

Exhibit 6.3 plots the variable for ethical behavior against the logarithm of the settler mortality rates per thousand. It shows a negative correlation ($\rho = -0.2194$) with a significance level of $p = 0.1109$. Colonies where the European settlers faced higher mortality rates exhibit less ethical considerations than hospitable regions. Results become much stronger when using latitude as a proxy for endowments, with a positive correlation ($\rho = 0.3416$) and significance level of $p = 0.0000$. Countries that are more distant from the equator have better ethical behavior.

RELIGION

Although the literature now often emphasizes cultural differences, less priority is given to moral values held in common by many cultures. Individuals have certain moral principles that they explicitly or implicitly accept. The source of moral standards can be sought in religion. When considering religion and its fundamentals, a clear implication is that shared values across cultures exist.

In fact, almost all principles associated with religious belief are the same in every religion. Batson, Lishner, Carpenter, Dulin, Harjusola-Webb, Stocks, Gale, Hassan, and Sampat (2003) acknowledge that the golden rule "Do unto to others as you would have them do unto you"—which has been advanced by various religious teachers—is the antecedent of all moral action. The universal ethics have been reported similarly in major religions. Values common to most great world religions are respect for persons, justice, trustworthiness, honesty, compassion, generosity, hospitality, and peace. Jesus, Buddha, Muhammad, and other religious leaders spread these values in earlier days, but have not become less essential for people of today (Moses 2001).

The relevance of the underlying religious values is central when determining the outcomes of religiosity. McDaniel and Burnett (1990) characterize religiosity as a belief in God combined with a commitment to follow principles believed to be set by God. Vitell and Paolillo (2003) claim that faith provides the foundation for a moral life built on religion. Magill (1992) associates religiosity with a personal background against which the ethical nature of behavior is judged. Weaver and Agle (2002) observe influences of religiosity both on attitudes and human behavior.

Guiso, Sapienza, and Zingales (2003) state that hardly any aspect of a society's life is unaffected by religion, including economics. Agle and Van Buren (1999),

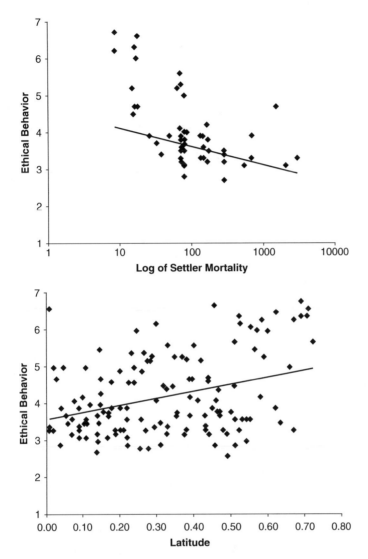

Exhibit 6.3   Relationship between Ethical Behavior and Endowments
The graph plots two alternative measures for endowments against the ethical behavior of firms in a
country. Endowments are proxied through the logarithm of settler mortality and the absolute value of
the latitude of a country. Higher values on the index of ethical behavior denote good ethical behavior.
Countries with better endowments show better ethical behavior.

who find that few people would deny a link between the life of faith as well as
contemporary life or economic decision making, support this viewpoint. Etzioni
(1988) translates this as the claim that economics has a moral dimension, indicating
that economics concerns more than simple optimality. Although this does not
convey that economic decisions are prone to be irrational, it merely expresses that
economic decision making may consider what is right as well as what is most
profitable (Webley, Lewis, and Mackenzie 2001).

The Economic Consequences of Religion

Despite the fact that religion has been identified as an important factor for economic behavior, the debate on the economic effects of religion is far from settled (Iannaccone 1998). Barro and McCleary (2003) document a positive relationship between economic growth and stronger religious beliefs. Stulz and Williamson (2003) observe that Catholic countries tend to protect creditors' rights less, and therefore have less developed external capital markets. Yet, Guiso et al. (2003) find that Catholics foster private ownership considerably more than Protestants. Furthermore, Christian religions are generally more positively connected with attitudes that support economic growth, while Muslim religion is negatively connected. The ranking between Catholicism and Protestantism is, however, not clear. Grullon, Kanatas, and Weston (2010) find that religious norms are an important factor for explaining cross-country differences in managerial compensation, which could not completely be explained by firms' fundamentals alone in earlier studies. According to Renneboog and Spaenjers (2012), religious households are more likely to save, and that Catholic households invest less frequently in the stock market than other religions.

Religion and Ethical Behavior

The idea that religiousness might influence ethical beliefs, judgments, and behavior appears to be intuitive, and scholars have explored various connections between religion and business ethics. Yet, the literature provides no consensus on the impact of religious values for ethical behavior (Vitell, Paolillo, and Singh 2005).

Webley et al. (2001) observe that ethical investment is primarily based on ideology and indeed not on return considerations, and ethical investors stay committed to their investment even if it performs negatively. Kennedy and Lawton (1998) report a negative relationship between religiousness and the willingness to behave unethically, and document a stronger relationship for Protestants than for Catholics. Grullon et al. (2010) find that firms with more religious employees exhibit greater monitoring and control of corporate managers. They examine whether religion mitigates unethical behavior using securities fraud lawsuits filed against the firm, aggressive earnings manipulation, option back-dating, and seemingly excessive executive compensation as corresponding proxies. The authors find considerable support that religiosity reduces the likelihood of such unethical behavior with results strongest for Protestant religious beliefs.

Others investigate religion and ethical behavior. For example, Agle and Van Buren (1999) analyze the impact of religious belief on various attitudes toward corporate social responsibility. However, contrary to the strong findings reported beforehand, the actual effects of religious beliefs are far from clear in their study. Hence, they conclude that religion has only a marginal effect on managerial attitudes and decision making. Terpstra, Rozell, and Robinson (1993) examine the influence of religious beliefs on insider trading among agnostics, atheists, and religiously affiliated individuals. Interestingly, they find that atheists are least likely to engage in insider trading, and agnostics are most likely to do so. Guth, Green, Kellstedt, and Smidt (1995) relate religious perspectives to environmentalism and discover that religious commitment is even negatively associated to environmentalism. Angelidis and Ibrahim (2004) examine the relationship between the degree

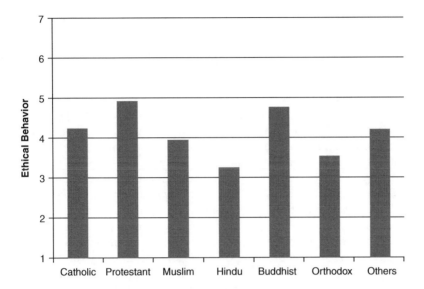

Exhibit 6.4 Ethical Behavior and Religious Denominations
The figure compares ethical behavior across major religious denominations. Protestant and Buddhist countries maintain considerable concerns for ethical issues, whereas Muslim, Hindu, and Orthodox countries exhibit poor ethical behavior.

of religious belief and the corporate social responsiveness orientation of individuals. Their analysis focuses on four different factors of corporate responsibility: economic, legal, ethical, and discretionary. They find a significant relationship between the strength of religiousness and attitudes toward the economic and ethical components of corporate social responsibility.

As a key personal characteristic, religiosity is expected to influence ethical beliefs in a positive way (Vitell and Paolilo 2003). Moreover, a reasonable assumption is that religious beliefs might have stronger predictive power about attitudes toward ethical behavior than other intrinsic values (Agle and Van Buren 1999). However, the above literature review demonstrates that although religiosity has an important impact on attitudes and behavior, whether religion has a mitigating effect on undesirable ethical behavior is unclear. In this vein, Hood, Spilka, Hunsberger, and Gorsuch (1996, p. 371) portray their research on religion and ethical behavior as "something of a roller-coaster" ride. Whereas the link between religiosity and ethical behavior seems straightforward on some issues, the relationships on other issues are more complex (Weaver and Agle 2002).

Exhibit 6.4 supports the finding that different religious thoughts have different effects on ethical behavior. The mean value for the sample of ethical behavior across countries is 4.2 on a scale of 1 to 7. Protestant and Buddhist countries report above-average ethical behavior ($\mu = 5.89$, $p = 0.01$, and $\mu = 4.75$, $p = 0.12$, respectively), whereas Muslim, Hindu, and Orthodox countries exhibit less interest in ethical issues ($\mu = 3.95$, $p = 0.04$, $\mu = 3.23$, $p = 0.05$, and $\mu = 3.53$, $p = 0.00$, respectively).

CULTURAL VALUES

There has been an increasing awareness of the necessity to integrate cultural values into economic theory, and the impact of culture on economic outcomes has been the subject of much recent research. Although in times of globalization, convergence of business activities can hardly be overlooked in some areas, major divergence in national cultures persists (Leung, Bhagat, Buchan, Erez, and Gibson, 2005). According to the cultural view, differences in culture can help explain differences in economic outcomes.

Hofstede (1980, p. 25) defines *culture* as "the collective programming of the mind." Culture is composed of certain basic, inherited values that people adopt as principles to guide their life. An individual designates them as providing "value" for guiding actions and behaviors in all aspects of life. Values are labeled *values* specifically because they are valuable to an individual. Cultural values produce beliefs, norms, and attitudes, which shape behavioral patterns as well as the perception of the world. Cultural values direct individuals when taking decisions or choosing between actions to be undertaken. Therefore, cultural values are determining factors for economic action and have economic consequences. This rationale is the main intuition behind the cultural analysis of economic decision making.

Although some studies use religion as a proxy for national culture, so-called cultural dimensions identify systematic differences in individuals' values and preferences and allow for a more refined measurement of national culture. Hofstede (1983) developed one of the most influential frameworks to characterize cultures, which has subsequently revolutionized research in cultural economics. In his cross-country research on organizational culture, Hofstede conducts a questionnaire survey among employees in national subsidiaries of IBM from 1967 to 1973. He identifies four cultural dimensions along which the values of individuals in various countries differed.

1. *Power distance* is the extent to which different societies handle human inequality differently.
2. *Uncertainty avoidance* measures a society's tolerance for uncertainty and ambiguity and refers to its search for truth.
3. *Individualism and collectivism* describe the relationship between the individual and the collectivity that prevails in a given society.
4. *Masculinity and femininity* refer to the distribution of roles between the genders.

Hofstede (2001) adds one more dimension, *long-term versus short-term orientation*, which captures the society's time horizon and reflects to what extent it has a dynamic and future-oriented ability.

Following the work of Hofstede (1983), several researchers have attempted to advance an improved framework to measure national culture. Focusing on a broad set of underlying basic values, Schwartz (1994) recognizes seven culture-level dimensions.

1. *Conservatism* stresses maintenance of the status quo, propriety, and restraint of actions or inclinations that might disrupt the solidary group or the traditional order and is concerned with the values security, conformity, and tradition.
2. *Intellectual autonomy* articulates the desirability of individuals independently pursuing their own ideas and intellectual direction, and draws on the values of curiosity, broadmindedness, and creativity.

3. *Affective autonomy* underlines the desirability of individuals independently pursuing affectively positive experience and relies on the values of pleasure, exciting life, and varied life.

4. *Hierarchy* indicates the legitimacy of an unequal distribution of power, roles, and resources, and applies to the values of social power, authority, humility, and wealth.

5. *Egalitarianism* relates to the transcendence of selfish interests in favor of voluntary commitment to promoting the welfare of others and bears on the values of equality, social justice, freedom, responsibility, and honesty.

6. *Mastery* supports getting ahead through active self-assertion and refers to the values of ambition, success, daring, and competence.

7. *Harmony* points to fitting harmoniously into the environment and rests on the values of unity with nature, protecting the environment, and world of beauty.

Other frameworks describing cultural paradigms that have been developed recently include the GLOBE study (House, Hanges, Javidan, Dorfman, and Gupta 2004), the survey of cultural values (Smith, Peterson, and Schwartz 2002), and the World Values Survey (Inglehart, Basanez, and Moreno 1998).

The Economic Consequences of Cultural Values

The idea that the development of markets and institutions is related to the surrounding social environment dates back to Granovetter (1985), who supposed that all kinds of economic relationships among individuals or corporations do not exist in an abstract idealized market, but are embedded in the social context. Although national culture has long been neglected in economic research, the cultural view has gained momentum in the last decade through establishing the above-mentioned cultural frameworks. The development of cultural dimensions enables identifying systematic differences in individuals' preferences, so that hypotheses can be formulated and tested empirically (Guiso, Sapienza, and Zingales 2006). Subsequently, interest in how cross-national differences in societal values affect business practices increased. Researchers extended their analyses on the relationship between national culture and economic outcomes to virtually all areas of business studies. Today, a multitude of papers offers culturally based explanations for the understanding of economic phenomena.

Hofstede (1980) pioneered this research field by documenting that management practices depend on the cultural background of a country. Licht, Goldschmidt, and Schwartz (2005) demonstrate that corporate governance laws relate systematically to the prevailing culture. Haxhi and van Ees (2010) contend that particular cultural dimensions affect corporate governance best practices. Doupnik and Tsakumis (2004) find that culture may be relevant in explaining systemic differences in financial reporting attributes across countries. Han, Kang, Salter, and Yoo (2010) document that national culture is an important factor to explain corporate managers' earnings discretion practices. Richardson (2008) uses culture as an explanatory of international tax compliance diversity. Tabellini (2008) observes that culture is a core determinant of economic development.

The idea that culture matters has also been gaining ground in the finance literature. Kwok and Tadesse (2006) maintain that national culture plays an important role for the configuration of financial systems. Chui, Lloyd, and Kwok (2002) suggest that national culture affects corporate capital structures. Ramirez and Tadesse (2009) document an important effect of culture on the levels of cash holding. Shao, Kwok, and Guedhami (2010) find that culture relates to dividend payouts. Zheng, El Ghoul, Guedhami, and Kwok (2012) reveal that national culture helps explain cross-country variations in the maturity structure of debt. Chui and Kwok (2008) show that national culture has a significant effect on life insurance consumption. Chui, Titman, and Wei (2010) examine how cultural differences influence the returns of momentum strategies. Beugelsdijk and Frijns (2010) provide a cultural explanation of the foreign bias in asset allocation.

Cultural Values and Ethical Behavior

The relevance of cultural values for the concept of business ethics has triggered a salient debate. The main argument has been that the concept of social responsibility is inherently context-specific, with cultural values playing an important part in influencing ethical behavior (Ringov and Zollo 2007). Although, as globalization hastens and business practices are turning increasingly uniform, attitudes toward ethical conduct remain stunningly local, suggesting that an individual's understanding of ethics is likely to be rooted in a particular culture. People from different cultural backgrounds seem to have different beliefs about right and wrong, which will necessarily lead to variations in ethical decision making across countries (Jackson 2001).

In fact, many researchers regard cultural values as a principal antecedent of ethical decision making and behavior. Bommer, Gratto, Gravander, and Tuttle (1987) propose that the social environment, particularly cultural and societal values, influences ethicality. They hypothesize that these values affect behavior through the mediating structure of the individual's decision-making process. Cohen and Nelson (1993) contend that the link between culture and the environment lies in the mechanism that culture affects normative ethical beliefs about what is morally correct behavior. This view is consistent with Elgin (1994), who suggests that attitudes regarding environmental sustainability are rooted at the cultural level. Husted (2005) contends that the willingness of a nation to pursue proper environmental policies relies upon the idiosyncratic cultural values of a country. Individuals will act in a socially responsible way if social responsibility is a key part of their cultural value system.

In this vein, research shows that values and ideology primarily influence socially responsible investment (Jansson and Biel 2012). However, investors rarely invest in ethical stocks exclusively, but rather have a mixed portfolio in which they combine a wide range of stocks to balance risk and return in order to do financially well but at the same time being good (Lewis and McKenzie 2000). Correspondingly, socially responsible investment can be regarded as an investment style that combines the traditional investment strategy of profit maximization with a value-based component for nonfinancial benefits.

Research further suggests that national culture can have a substantial effect on ethical beliefs and views of acceptable business practices. Park, Russell, and Lee

(2007) conjecture that sociocultural factors influence the will and ability to protect the environment. They contend that if individuals are more culturally aware of environmental issues, a higher level of environmental sustainability can be maintained. National culture is assumed to shape environmental conditions by influencing people's attitudes about natural resources and environments. Using the Hofstede (1983) cultural dimensions, Husted (2005) presents evidence that countries with low levels of power distance, low levels of masculinity, and high levels of individualism, have a higher social and institutional capacity for sustainability. He bases his results on an empirical investigation across 52 countries.

Likewise, Park et al. (2007) uncover a clear link between national culture and environmental issues. Using a sample of 43 countries, they find that both power distance and masculinity are significantly negatively related to environmental sustainability. The results are consistent with Ringov and Zollo (2007), who test whether the cultural background in its home country influences corporate social responsible behavior. In an empirical study of 23 countries, they find that power distance and masculinity have a significantly negative effect on corporate social and environmental performance. They explain that social and environmental issues are more likely to emerge and be openly discussed if power distance is low. Masculinity has a negative impact, as highly masculine societies place low value on caring for others or cooperation.

Waldman, de Luque, Washburn, and House (2006) employ the GLOBE study to predict corporate social responsibility values of top management. They analyze data from 15 countries and illustrate a positive relationship for institutional collectivism and a negative relationship for power distance. Hence, all studies reveal a moderate but important role of culture in determining ethical behavior.

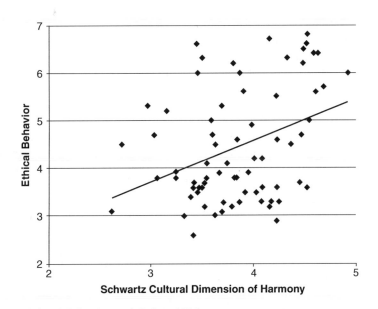

Exhibit 6.5 Ethical Behavior and Cultural Values
The graph plots the relationship between ethical behavior and the Schwartz's (1994) Harmony index. Countries that score higher on the cultural dimension of Harmony tend to have better ethical behavior.

A cultural dimension that could be of supreme importance for ethical issues is Schwartz's (1994) Harmony index. *Harmony* refers to a harmonious relationship with the surrounding environment and is therefore likely to be positively related to business ethics. This link is indeed supported by the data set used in this chapter. Exhibit 6.5 indicates that countries that score higher on the cultural dimension of Harmony tend to have better ethical behavior ($\rho = 0.3638$, p $= 0.0015$).

SUMMARY AND CONCLUSIONS

This review presents four major structural theories—legal origin, endowments, religion, and cultural values—and analyzes their relevance to explain variations in social responsibility around the world. Existing research shows that these theories indicate powerful determinants of economic behavior and have sustained their usefulness to explain differences in business practices and economic outcomes across countries.

The chapter documents several meaningful contributions. First, the literature in the field of international sustainable finance is rather scarce. Relatively little cross-country research analyzes the determinants of the international diffusion of corporate responsibility concepts and practice, as very few studies have a global focus (Aguilera, Rupp, Williams, and Ganapathi 2007). The majority of research in the field of SRFI consists of single-country studies and hence lacks a cross-country comparative perspective (Egri and Ralston 2008). Second, research in sustainability issues has been difficult due to a lack of a clear definition or consideration of dimensionality. The overall approach has been piecemeal, and research in social responsibility is lacking coherence. Much of the literature in this field is scattered, addressing various topics in an unsystematic manner (Rowley and Bergman 2000). Consequentially, scholars have increasingly called for multilevel research, systematically investigating determinants for cross-country differences in sustainable finance (Hitt, Beamish, Jackson, and Mathieu, 2007). Third, existing research primarily focuses on religion and cultural values as explanatory variables for varying levels of social responsibility. The usefulness of these theories seems plausible, as both concepts rest on intrinsic values—internalized either religiously or culturally—which are likely to guide attitudes toward ethical issues (Cullen, Parboteeah, and Hoegl 2004). Although the relevance of the legal system and endowments for ethical behavior has not yet been tackled in the literature, the impact that both theories make in the finance literature suggests that they might exert an influence on sustainable finance as well. More elaboration on the relevance of these theories remains a field for future research.

Despite some specific findings where research provides some explanations for developments in the field of sustainable finance, a deeper understanding of the general determinants remains incomplete. As the field of ethical finance and investing is undoubtedly growing, inherent difficulties associated with measuring sustainability might be overcome by new measures provided through social rating agencies, paving the way for international comparative studies (Ringov and Zollo 2007).

Religion and culture may be most fruitful as explanatory factors for ethical issues in finance. Until now, findings on how religion affects ethical behavior remain mixed, necessitating further research. A large and reliable database on sustainable finance across the world could clarify whether religion is indeed a useful determinant for ethical behavior, and whether some religious denominations behave socially responsibly in particular. Research on the impact of cultural dimensions needs to be extended to the area of socially responsible investing. Further, a need exists to comprehensively identify the dimensions of national culture that are most relevant for ethical behavior, applying other cultural models besides the Hofstede (2001) framework. Furthermore, alternative well-known structural theories as the legal and endowments theory should not be neglected, as the contribution of religious and cultural values for social responsibility may be complementary to other institutions. Insights from any of these theories will be useful in developing a fuller understanding of issues in SRFI.

DISCUSSION QUESTIONS

1. Identify four institutional theories that have been used to explain differences in financial developments around the world.
2. Which theories are most likely to exert an influence on developments in SRFI? Why?
3. What is the major difference between the legal origin and the endowments theory?
4. Discuss some measurements of national culture and their usefulness to explain differences in financial responsibility.

REFERENCES

Acemoglu, Daron, Simon Johnson, and James A. Robinson. 2001. "The Colonial Origins of Comparative Development: An Empirical Investigation." *American Economic Review* 91:5, 1369–1401.

Aggarwal, Raj, and John Goodell. 2009. "Markets and Institutions in Financial Intermediation: National Characteristics as Determinants." *Journal of Banking and Finance* 33:10, 1770–1780.

Agle, Bradley R., and Harry J. Van Buren. 1999. "God and Mammon: The Modern Relationship." *Business Ethics Quarterly* 9:4, 563–582.

Aguilera, Ruth V., Deborah E. Rupp, Cynthia A. Williams, and Jyoti Ganapathi. 2007. "Putting the S Back in Corporate Social Responsibility: A Multi-Level Theory of Social Change in Organizations." *Academy of Management Review* 32:3, 836–863.

Angelidis, John, and Nabil Ibrahim. 2004. "An Exploratory Study of the Impact of Degree of Religiousness upon an Individual's Corporate Social Responsiveness Orientation." *Journal of Business Ethics* 51:2, 119–128.

Ayyagari, Meghana, Asli Demirgüç-Kunt, and Vojislav Maksimovic. 2008. "How Well Do Institutional Theories Explain Firms' Perceptions of Property Rights." *Review of Financial Studies* 21:4, 1833–1871.

Barro, Robert, and Rachel McCleary. 2003. "Religion and Economic Growth." *American Sociological Review* 68:5, 760–778.

Batson, C. Daniel, David A. Lishner, Amy Carpenter, Luis Dulin, Sanna Harjusola-Webb, E. L. Stocks, Shawna Gale, Omar Hassan, and Brenda Sampat. 2003. "As You Would Have Them Do unto You: Does Imaging Yourself in the Other's Place Stimulate Moral Actions?" *Personality and Social Psychology Bulletin* 29:9, 1190–1201.

Beck, Thorsten, Asli Demirgüç-Kunt, and Ross Levine. 2003a. "Law and Finance: Why Does Legal Origin Matter?" *Journal of Comparative Economics* 31:4, 653–675.

Beck, Thorsten, Asli Demirgüç-Kunt, and Ross Levine. 2003b. "Law, Endowments, and Finance." *Journal of Financial Economics* 70:2, 137–181.

Beugelsdijk, Sjoerd, and Bart Frijns. 2010 "A Cultural Explanation of the Foreign Bias in International Asset Allocation." *Journal of Banking and Finance* 34:9, 2121–2131.

Bommer, Michael, Clarence Gratto, Jerry Gravander, and Mark Tuttle. 1987. "A Behavioral Model of Ethical and Unethical Decision Making." *Journal of Business Ethics* 6:4, 265–280.

Botero, Juan C., Simeon Djankov, Rafael La Porta, Florencio Lopez-de-Silanes, and Andrei Shleifer. 2004. "The Regulation of Labor." *Quarterly Journal of Economics* 119:4, 1339–1382.

Chui, Andy C. W., and Chuck C. Y. Kwok. 2008. "National Culture and Life Insurance Consumption." *Journal of International Business Studies* 39:1, 88–101.

Chui, Andy C. W., Alison E. Lloyd, and Chuck C. Y. Kwok. 2002. "The Determination of Capital Structure: Is National Culture a Missing Piece to the Puzzle?" *Journal of International Business Studies* 33:1, 99–127.

Chui, Andy C. W., Sheridan Titman, and K. C. John Wei. 2010. "Individualism and Momentum around the World." *Journal of Finance* 65:1, 361–392.

Cohen, Deborah V., and Katherine Nelson. 1993. "Multinational Ethics Programs: Cases in Corporate Practice." In W. Michael Hoffman, Judith W. Kamm, Robert E. Frederick, and Edward S. Petry, eds. *Emerging Global Business Ethics*, 151–162. Westport, CT: Quorum Books.

Cullen, John B., K. Praveen Parboteeah, and Martin Hoegl. 2004. "Cross-National Differences in Managers' Willingness to Justify Ethically Suspect Behaviors: A Test of Institutional Anomie Theory." *Academy of Management Journal* 47:3, 411–421.

Demirgüç-Kunt, Asli, and Vojislav Maksimovic. 1998. "Law, Finance, and Firm Growth." *Journal of Finance* 53:6, 2107–2137.

Demirgüç-Kunt, Asli, and Vojislav Maksimovic. 1999. "Institutions, Financial Markets, and Firm Debt Maturity." *Journal of Financial Economics* 54:3, 295–336.

Djankov, Simeon, Rafael La Porta, Florencio Lopez-de-Silanes, and Andrei Shleifer. 2002. "The Regulation of Entry." *Quarterly Journal of Economics* 117:1, 1–37.

Djankov, Simeon, Rafael La Porta, Florencio Lopez-de-Silanes, and Andrei Shleifer. 2003. "Courts." *Quarterly Journal of Economics* 118:2, 453–517.

Doupnik, Timothy S., and George Tsakumis. 2004. "A Critical Review of Tests of Gray's Theory of Cultural Relevance and Suggestions for Future Research." *Journal of Accounting Literature* 23:1, 1–48.

Egri, Carolyn P., and David A. Ralston. 2008. "Corporate Responsibility: A Review of International Management Research from 1998 to 2007." *Journal of International Management* 14:4, 319–339.

Elgin, Duane. 1994. "Building a Sustainable Species-Civilization: A Challenge of Culture and Consciousness." *Futures* 26:2, 234–245.

Etzioni, Amitai. 1988. *The Moral Dimension: Toward a New Economics*. New York: Free Press.

Granovetter, Mark. 1985. "Economic Action and Social Structure: The Problem of Embeddedness." *American Journal of Sociology* 91:3, 481–510.

Grullon, Gustavo, George Kanatas, and James Weston. 2010. "Religion and Corporate (Mis)Behavior." Available at http://ssrn.com/abstract=1472118.

Guiso, Luigi, Paola Sapienza, and Luigi Zingales. 2003. "People's Opium? Religion and Economic Attitudes." *Journal of Monetary Economics* 50:1, 225–282.

Guiso, Luigi, Paola Sapienza, and Luigi Zingales. 2006. "Does Culture Affect Economic Outcomes?" *Journal of Economic Perspectives* 20:2, 23–48.

Guth, James L., John C. Green, Lyman A. Kellstedt, and Corwin E. Smidt. 1995. "Faith and the Environment: Religious Beliefs and Attitudes on Environmental Policy." *American Journal of Political Science* 39:2, 364–382.

Han, Sam, Tony Kang, Stephen Salter, and Yong K. Yoo. 2010. "A Cross-Country Study on the Effects of National Culture and Earnings Management." *Journal of International Business Studies* 41:1, 123–141.

Haxhi, Ilir, and Hans van Ees. 2010. "Explaining Diversity in the Worldwide Diffusion of Codes of Good Governance." *Journal of International Business Studies* 41:4, 710–726.

Hitt, Michael A., Paul W. Beamish, Susan E. Jackson, and John E. Mathieu. 2007. "Building Theoretical and Empirical Bridges across Levels: Multilevel Research in Management." *Academy of Management Journal* 50:6, 1385–1399.

Hofstede, Geert. 1980. *Culture's Consequences: International Differences in Work-Related Values.* Newbury Park, CA: Sage Publications.

Hofstede, Geert. 1983. "The Cultural Relativity of Organizational Practices and Theories." *Journal of International Business Studies* 14:2, 75–89.

Hofstede, Geert. 2001. *Culture's Consequences: Comparing Values, Behaviors, Institutions, and Organizations across Nations.* Thousand Oaks, CA: Sage Publications.

Hood, Ralph W., Bernard Spilka, Bruce Hunsberger, and Richard Gorsuch. 1996. *The Psychology of Religion: An Empirical Approach.* New York: Guilford Press.

House, Robert, Paul Hanges, Mansour Javidan, Peter Dorfman, and Vipin Gupta. 2004. *Culture, Leadership, and Organizations: The GLOBE Study of 62 Societies.* Thousand Oaks, CA: Sage Publications.

Husted, Bryan W. 2005. "Culture and Ecology: A Cross-National Study of the Determinants of Environmental Sustainability." *Management International Review* 45:3, 349–371.

Iannaccone, Laurence R. 1998. "Introduction to the Economics of Religion." *Journal of Economic Literature* 36:3, 1465–1496.

Inglehart, Ronald, Miguel Basanez, and Alejandro Moreno. 1998. *Human Beliefs and Values: A Cross-Cultural Sourcebook.* Ann Arbor: University of Michigan Press.

Jackson, Terence. 2001. "Cultural Values and Management Ethics: A 10 Nation Study." *Human Relations* 54:10, 1267–1302.

Jansson, Magnus, and Anders Biel. 2012. "Investment Institutions' Beliefs about and Attitudes toward Socially Responsible Investment (SRI): A Comparison between SRI and Non-SRI Management." *Sustainable Development.*

Jones, Marc T. 1999. "The Institutional Determinants of Social Responsibility." *Journal of Business Ethics* 20:2, 163–179.

Kennedy, Ellen J., and Leigh Lawton. 1998. "Religiousness and Business Ethics." *Journal of Business Ethics* 17:2, 163–175.

Kwok, Chuck C. Y., and Solomon Tadesse. 2006. "National Culture and Financial Systems." *Journal of International Business Studies* 37:2, 227–247.

La Porta, Rafael, Florencio Lopez-de-Silanes, and Andrei Shleifer. 2008. "The Economic Consequences of Legal Origins." *Journal of Economic Literature* 46:2, 285–332.

La Porta, Rafael, Florencio Lopez-de-Silanes, Andrei Shleifer, and Robert W. Vishny. 1997. "Legal Determinants of External Finance." *Journal of Finance* 52:3, 1131–1150.

La Porta, Rafael, Florencio Lopez-de-Silanes, Andrei Shleifer, and Robert W. Vishny. 1998. "Law and Finance." *Journal of Political Economy* 106:6, 1113–1155.

La Porta, Rafael, Florencio Lopez-de-Silanes, Andrei Shleifer, and Robert W. Vishny. 2002. "Investor Protection and Corporate Valuation." *Journal of Finance* 57:3, 1147–1170.

Leung, Kwok, Rabi S. Bhagat, Nancy R. Buchan, Miriam Erez, and Cristina B. Gibson. 2005. "Culture and International Business: Recent Advances and Their Implications for Future Research." *Journal of International Business Studies* 36:4, 357–378.

Levine, Ross. 1999. "Law, Finance, and Economic Growth." *Journal of Financial Intermediation* 8:1/2, 36–67.

Lewis, Alan, and Craig Mackenzie. 2000. "Morals, Money, Ethical Investing and Economic Psychology." *Human Relations* 53:2, 179–191.

Licht, Amir N., Chanan Goldschmidt, and Shalom H. Schwartz. 2005. "Culture, Law, and Corporate Governance." *International Review of Law and Economics* 25:2, 229–255.

Magill, Gerard. 1992. "Theology in Business Ethics: Appealing to the Religious Imagination." *Journal of Business Ethics* 11:2, 129–135.

McDaniel, Stephen W., and John J. Burnett. 1990. "Consumer Religiosity and Retail Store Evaluation Criteria." *Journal of the Academy of Marketing Science* 18:2, 101–112.

Moses, Jeffrey. 2001. *Oneness: Great Principles Shared by All Religions*. New York: Ballantine Books.

Park, Hoon, Clifford Russell, and Junsoo Lee. 2007. "National Culture and Environmental Sustainability: A Cross-National Analysis." *Journal of Economics and Finance* 31:1, 104–121.

Ramirez, Andrés, and Solomon Tadesse. 2009. "Corporate Cash Holdings, Uncertainty Avoidance, and the Multinationality of Firms." *International Business Review*, 18:4, 387–403.

Renneboog, Luc, and Christophe Spaenjers. 2012. "Religion, Economic Attitudes, and Household Finance." *Oxford Economic Papers*, 64:1, 103–127.

Richardson, Grant. 2008. "The Relationship between Culture and Tax Evasion across Countries: Additional Evidence and Extensions." *Journal of International Accounting, Auditing, and Taxation* 17:2, 67–78.

Ringov, Dimo, and Maurizio Zollo. 2007. "The Impact of National Culture on Corporate Social Performance." *Corporate Governance* 7:4, 476–485.

Rowley, Tim, and Shawn Berman. 2000. "A Brand New Brand of Corporate Social Performance." *Business and Society* 39:4, 397–418.

Schwartz, Shalom. 1994. "Beyond Individualism/Collectivism: New Cultural Dimensions of Values." In Uichol Kim, Harry C. Triandis, Cigdem Kagitcibasi, Sang-Chin Choi, and Gene Yoon, eds. *Individualism and Collectivism: Theory, Method, and Applications*, 85–99. Beverly Hills, CA: Sage Publications.

Shao, Liang, Chuck C. Y. Kwok, and Omrane Guedhami. 2010. "National Culture and Dividend Policy." *Journal of International Business Studies*, 41:8, 1391–1414.

Smith, Peter, Mark Peterson, and Shalom Schwartz. 2002. "Cultural Values, Sources of Guidance, and their Relevance to Managerial Behavior: A 47-Nation Study." *Journal of Cross-Cultural Psychology* 33:2, 188–202.

Stulz, René M., and Rohan Williamson. 2003. "Culture, Openness, and Finance." *Journal of Financial Economics* 70:3, 313–349.

Tabellini, Guido. 2008. "Institutions and Culture." *Journal of the European Economic Association* 6:2/3, 255–294.

Terpstra, David E., Elizabeth J. Rozell, and Robert K. Robinson. 1993. "The Influence of Personality and Demographic Variables on Ethical Decisions Related to Insider Trading." *Journal of Psychology* 127:4, 375–389.

Vitell, Scott J., and Joseph G. P. Paolillo. 2003. "Consumer Ethics: The Role of Religiosity." *Journal of Business Ethics* 46:2, 151–162.

Vitell, Scott J., Joseph G. P. Paolillo, and Jatinder J. Singh. 2005. "Religiosity and Consumer Ethics." *Journal of Business Ethics* 57:2, 175–181.

Waldman, David A., Mary S. de Luque, Nathan Washburn, and J. House Robert. 2006. "Cultural and Leadership Predictors of Corporate Social Responsibility Values of Top Management: A Globe Study of 15 Countries." *Journal of International Business Studies* 37:6, 823–837.

Weaver, Gary R., and Bradley R. Agle. 2002. "Religiosity and Ethical Behavior in Organizations: A Symbolic Interactionist Perspective." *Academy of Management Review* 27:1, 77–97.

Webley, Paul, Alan Lewis, and Craig Mackenzie. 2001. "Commitment among Ethical Investors: An Experimental Approach." *Journal of Economic Psychology* 22:1, 27–42.

Zheng, Xiaolan, Sadok El Ghoul, Omrane Guedhami, and Chuck C. Y. Kwok. 2012. "National Culture and Corporate Debt Maturity." *Journal of Banking and Finance*, 36:2, 468–488.

ABOUT THE AUTHOR

Astrid Juliane Salzmann is a research associate at the Department of Finance in the Faculty of Business and Economics at the RWTH Aachen University in Germany. She has been teaching Finance at the RWTH Aachen University since 2006. Her research interests focus on international finance and cross-cultural research. She studied Management Mathematics at the University of Kaiserslautern and the National University of Singapore and received her Ph.D. in 2010 from the RWTH Aachen University.

PART II

Finance and Society

CHAPTER 7

Social, Environmental, and Trust Issues in Business and Finance

CHRISTOPH F. BIEHL
Ph.D. Candidate, Centre for Responsible Banking and Finance, School of Management, University of St Andrews and Academic Network Knowledge Manager, United Nations–backed Principles for Responsible Investment

ANDREAS G. F. HOEPNER
Lecturer in Banking and Finance and Deputy Director, Centre for Responsible Banking and Finance, School of Management, University of St Andrews and Academic Fellow, Principles for Responsible Investment, United Nations

JIANGHONG LIU
Ph.D. Candidate, Centre for Responsible Banking and Finance, School of Management, University of St Andrews

INTRODUCTION

Some commentators might believe as though social, environmental, and trust (SET) issues came from nowhere in the last few years to rapidly surge on the agenda of business and financial institutions. However, SET concerns in business and finance existed long before Enron, the subprime mortgage crisis, or the BP oil spill. This chapter analyzes SET development in three steps.

First, the chapter discusses SET issues and their impact on business and finance throughout history. For this purpose, a manual review of the literature finds 154 SET records, which serve as a basis for the analysis. The SET issues are found to emerge and advance over time. Initially, concerns centered around social issues with direct influence on people in the region and had an increasing impact on business and finance through unions and pension funds. Over time, environmental factors became increasingly important, and even some social factors emerged without direct influence on the concerned people themselves. These new factors, especially some environmental disasters, have influenced business through new legislation. Recently, trust issues emerged as a direct reaction to the financial crisis. They are very important to business and especially the financial services industry.

Second, this chapter discusses the financial performance and risk management challenges and opportunities resulting from SET issues in the current context. Critics point to the cost of managing SET issues without a sufficient reward to justify them. Proponents, however, report various incentives for integrating SET issues into business and investment processes, including business opportunities (e.g., renewable energies or green real estate), more advanced risk management in an increasingly nervous environment, and consumer loyalty gains.

Finally, the chapter offers an outlook on future opportunities resulting from the integration of SET concepts into business and finance. This chapter contends that SET considerations appear to be less a flavor of the moment than performance relevant aspects in business and finance. The basis of this perspective involves two gradual changes in contextual factors. First, corporations, especially financial institutions, have become increasingly complex, which has led to concern for societies and their elected representatives. Second, the instant exchange of opinions on social networking web sites has led societies to become more critical and collaborative. Both developments increase the likelihood of social critiques of perceived misbehavior of businesses, specifically for financial institutions. Such critiques can lead to a loss in client trust, which is particularly relevant, because trust is a key product differentiation factor of many (financial) service providers.

HISTORICAL CONTEXT OF SET ISSUES

This section provides a chronological overview of the development of SET issues over time. The discussion centers on the general atmosphere and highlights how SET issues influence business activities and investment. Exhibit 7.1 provides a detailed list of SET events. The exhibit provides background for the chapter and serves as a complementary resource. The analysis distinguishes between near social and far social issues. In this conceptual framework, near social issues directly influence the group voicing the concerns, while far social issues emanate from those not directly influenced by the issue. Others might conceptualize far social issues as being ethical in nature.

Pre-1940s: The Early Centuries

The idea of fairness and responsibility during a transaction is most likely as old as mankind. Several religions, such as Judaism through the Torah, indirectly provide the first evidence of fair trade guidelines around 1312 BC. Apart from the religious basis, Aristotle wrote down a moral philosophical guideline for responsible trade around 330 BC. He created a framework that guarantees fair and responsible business transactions. The concept *justice in trade* appears in his work *The Nicomachean Ethics* (Aristotle 1911).

The activism of individuals or small groups dominates this era. For example, in 1688 the Quakers decided not to participate in the slave trade because they felt that their beliefs did not permit such behavior (Cadbury 1942). Similarly, in 1760, John Wesley, cofounder of the Methodist church, laid down guidelines for the responsible use of money (Sparkes 2002). In both cases, the guidelines prohibited trade and investment in business activities that harm "god's creation." These guidelines

Exhibit 7.1   Social, Environmental, and Trust Issues: A Chronological Overview

Panel A. Pre-1940s: The Early Centuries

Year	Category Number	Topic Category	Description	References
1688	S1	Religious	Boycott of slavery (Quaker).	Cadbury (1942)
1760	S2	Religious	John Wesley (Methodists) Guidelines for the "Responsible Use of Money."	Sparkes (2002)
1919	S3	Policy	U.S. prohibition.	Tyrrell (1997); Sparkes (2002)
1920	S4	Religious	Methodist Church avoids alcohol and gambling investments.	Guay, Doh, and Sinclair (2004)
1920	S5	Religious	Quakers avoid investments in weapon manufacturers.	Guay, Doh, and Sinclair (2004)

Panel B. 1940s: The Post–World War II Era

Year	Category Number	Topic Category	Description	References
1948	S6	Religious	U.K. church invests ethically.	Luxton (1992); Sparkes (2002)
1948	S7	Human rights	United Nations Declaration of Human Rights.	Sparkes (2002)

Panel C. 1950s: The Discovery of Pension Funds as a Tool

Year	Category Number	Topic Category	Description	References
1952	E1	Pollution	16,000 people die of smog in London from December 1952 until February 1953.	Bell and Davis (2001); Sparkes (2002)
1954	S8	Labor movement, shareholder activism	Teamsters Union buys $1 million of Montgomery stocks and threatens proxy fight; results in union being allowed to organize the company.	Gray (1983)
1956	E2	Policy	Clean Air Act (United Kingdom), world's first piece of environmental legislation (response to 1952s smog catastrophe).	Sparkes (2002)
1958	S9	SRI	United Auto Workers proposal to invest pension fund for the benefit of Ford workers.	Gray (1983)

(continued)

Exhibit 7.1 (*Continued*)

Panel D. 1960s: The Movement Decade

Year	Category Number	Topic Category	Description	References
1960s–1970s	S10	Gender equality	Gender equality movement.	Milkman (1985)
1960	S11	Anti-Apartheid	Sharpeville massacre leads to increasing international pressure.	Kidd (1988)
1960s	S12	Anti-Apartheid	Anti-Apartheid CSR, shareholder activism, and ethical investment initiatives with focus on pension funds.	Gray (1983)
1963	S13	Labor movement	Lane Kirkland states in his handbook that pension funds' investment should benefit the workers, e.g., housing, impact investment.	Gray (1983)
1964; 1965	S14	Civil rights	Civil Rights Act; Voting Rights Act.	Berg (1964); Sparkes (2002); Landsberg (2007)
1965–1974	S15	Vietnam War	Vietnam War movement.	Sparkes (2002); Schueth (2003)
1965	S16	Labor movement, SRI	New York Times Co. Pension Plans: joint union managed trusteeship forced through strike.	Gray (1983)
1965	S17	SRI, religious	ANSVAR SRI Fund created in Sweden; partly funded by religious groups.	Guay, Doh, and Sinclair (2004)
1966	S18	Consumer rights	Publication of Ralph Nader's book *Unsafe at Any Speed*; targeting safety issues at General Motors.	Nader (1965)
1967	S19	Civil rights, shareholder activism	FIGHT initiates protests concerning Eastman Kodak's civil rights policy.	Wadhwani (1997); Sparkes (2002);
1969	S20	Vietnam War, shareholder activism	First submission of responsible shareholder resolution at the AGM of Dow Chemicals.	Sparkes (2002); Guay, Doh, and Sinclair (2004)
1969	S21, E3	General	Council for Economic Priorities (CEP): First company to carry out in-depth social and environmental research	Sparkes (2002); Brown, de Jong, and Lessidrenska (2009)

Exhibit 7.1 (*Continued*)

Panel E. 1970s: The Organization and Implementation Decade

Year	Category Number	Topic Category	Description	References
1970	S22	Vietnam War	Yale debate on SRI.	Sparkes (2002)
1970s	S23	Labor movement	Improvements of working standards.	Gray (1983)
1970	E4	General environment	World Earth Day—informing about and raising awareness for environmental problems.	Gallagher (1997)
1970	E5	General environment, policy	Federal Environmental Protection Agency established in the United States.	Gallagher (1997)
1970	E6	General environment, policy	Natural Environmental Policy Act—first environmental legislation passed in the United States.	Gallagher (1997)
1970	S24	Consumer rights	First social responsibility issue to appear at a proxy ballot (Ralph Nader—General Motors).	Schwartz (1971); Sparkes (2002)
1970	S25	SRI	Ray Schotland provides legal foundation of alternative investments.	Schotland (1980); Gray (1983)
1970s	S26	SRI, ethical Investment	Publication of *The Ethical Investor: Universities and Corporate Responsibility.*	Simon, Powers, and Gunnemann (1972); Gray (1983)
1970s	S27	Shareholder activism	Breach of Wall Street Rule, i.e., institutional investors vote against management in proxies.	Gray (1983)
1971	S28	Vietnam War, SRI	Pax World Fund—first modern SRI fund in the United States.	Sparkes (2002); Guay, Doh, and Sinclair (2004)
1971, 1973	S29, E7	General	Creation of Corporate Responsibility Centers (ICCR and IRRC).	Sparkes (2002)
1972	E8	Global Growth	"The Limits to Growth"; Club of Rome publishes a forecast concerning the (environmental) consequences of global growth.	Club of Rome (1974); Sparkes (2002)

(*continued*)

Exhibit 7.1 (*Continued*)

Panel E. 1970s: The Organization and Implementation Decade

Year	Category Number	Topic Category	Description	References
1973	S30	Gender equality	AFL-CIO (largest union federation in the United States): Equal Rights Amendment.	Milkman (1985)
1973	S31	SRI	First attempt to create a U.K. ethical unit trust.	Sparkes (2002)
1975	E9	Global warming	Article about global warming: "Are We on the Brink of a Pronounced Global Warming?" in *Science*.	Broecker (1975)
1976	E10	Pollution (accident)	Seveso dioxin leak in Italy; Seveso had to cover the costs of evacuating 600 people and treating 2,000 because of dioxin poisoning and the decontamination of the area.	Sparkes (2002); Cavanagh and Linn (2006)
1977	S32	Anti-Apartheid	Sullivan Principles—ethical guidelines for companies conducting business with South Africa.	Sullivan (1983); Sparkes (2002)
1977	S33; E11	Consumer, policy	Ban of chemicals that lead to cell mutations (DDT, PCB).	Sparkes (2002)
1978	E12	Pollution	Love Canal area is declared a national emergency (toxic waste land fill in the 1930s and 1940s); leads to the creation of a superfund for toxic clean-up ($1.6 billion), the government's permission to sue companies for clean-up costs and up to $50 million fine.	Sparkes (2002); Kahn (2007)
1978	S34	Labor movement	Rifkin and Barker state that investment of pension funds harms union workers.	Gray (1983)
1978	S35	SRI	(Impact) investment within Massachusetts.	Coltman and Metzenbaum (1979); Gray (1983)
1978	S36	SRI	(Impact) investment within Wisconsin.	Smart (1979); Gray (1983)

Exhibit 7.1   *(Continued)*

Panel E. 1970s: The Organization and Implementation Decade

Year	Category Number	Topic Category	Description	References
1979	E13	Nuclear power	Three Mile Island and Pittsburgh Incident: End of construction of commercial nuclear power plants in the United States; leads to increase in regulations.	Sparkes (2002); Kahn (2007)
1979	S37	SRI, legal framework	Labor Department (head of all state pension funds) states that alternative investments do not violate the prudence rule per se.	Gray (1983)
1979	S38	SRI, legal framework	"[T]he federal prudence and diversification rules neither absolutely preclude nor specifically authorize the selection of investments that have been affected by nonfinancial considerations" (Gray, 1984, p. 55).	Hutchinson and Cole (1980); Gray (1983)
1979	S39	Labor movement, SRI	Chrysler pension fund: joint union-management advisory board.	Gray (1983)
1979	S40	Labor movement, SRI	P.F. Laboratories pension fund: joint union-management control.	Gray (1983)
1979–1982	S41	Anti-apartheid	Massachusetts stops the public pension funds from investing in companies doing business with repressive regimes.	Gray (1983)
1979	S42	SRI	Corporate Data, Exchange Report: "Pension Investments: A Social Audit," find that exclusion takes place on an ad-hoc basis.	Gray (1983)
1979	S43	Social performance	Control Data report on pension funds' social performance policy.	Gray (1983)

(continued)

Exhibit 7.1 *(Continued)*

Panel F. 1980s: The Decade of Societal and Political Attention

Year	Category Number	Topic Category	Description	References
1980s	S44	Anti-apartheid	Mainstream phase of anti-apartheid movement.	Posnikoff (1997); Sparkes (2002)
1980	S45	Labor Movement	AFL-CIO adopts employee participation	Gray (1983)
1980	S46	SRI, legal framework	ERISA framework; "The concept of 'benefits,' however need not be limited to payments that a participant or beneficiary would receive upon retirement, i.e. pure economic return to an investment. It is arguably broad enough to include numerous types of positive returns, e.g., job security and improved working conditions. Thus, this provision can be construed to promote non-traditional objectives at the expense of adequate return and corpus safety if the investment produces a direct 'other benefit'"(Gray 1983, p. 57).	Ravikoff and Curzan (1980); Gray (1983)
1980	S47	SRI, legal framework	"The Labor Department has taken the position that nonfinancial criteria that affect profitability can legally be used to make investment decisions" (Gray 1983, p. 58).	Gray (1983)
1980	S48	Labor movement, SRI	Heileman Brewery pension fund: joint union-management administration	Gray (1983)
1980	S49, E14	SRI	Connecticut Policy—"However, it has become increasingly apparent that the standard of prudence and responsibility should be considered in light of this additional criterion, social and environmental policies of the corporations in which the state owns or contemplates owning investment" (Gray 1983, p. 93).	Gray (1983)

Exhibit 7.1   (*Continued*)

Panel F. 1980s: The Decade of Societal and Political Attention

Year	Category Number	Topic Category	Description	References
1980	S50	Anti-apartheid	Connecticut prohibit investment in South Africa unless the company signs the Sullivan principles.	Gray (1983)
1980	S51, E15	Shareholder activism	The New York State Retirement System starts voting in favor of ESG at proxies.	Gray (1983)
1981	S52	Labor movement, human rights, SRI	National Conference of Public Employee Retirement Systems: avoidance of any anti-labor company, any country, government, or regime that does not respect human dignity.	Gray (1983)
1981, 1983	S53	SRI, legal framework	Labor Department vs. Operating Engineers Pension Fund (OEPF) concerning alternative investments; OEPF wins indicating a ruling pro alternative investments.	Gray (1983)
1981	S54, E16	SRI	U.S. Trust Co. of Boston—investment program to attract alternative investors.	Gray (1983)
1981	S55	Anti-apartheid. shareholder activism	The Public Employers Retirement System of California and State of New Jersey Division of Investment contact management of companies about their investment in South Africa.	Gray (1983)
1982	S56	Anti-apartheid	Connecticut establishes social performance criteria for state investment indicating that companies investing in South Africa need to follow the Sullivan Principles.	Sparkes (2002)
1982	S57, E17	SRI	Calvert Group introduces mutual funds with social and environmental screening approach.	Gray (1983); Guay, Doh, and Sinclair (2004)
1982	S58, E18	Shareholder activism	The New York Employers Retirement System releases an official ESG proxy voting policy.	Gray (1983)

(continued)

Exhibit 7.1 *(Continued)*

Panel F. 1980s: The Decade of Societal and Political Attention

Year	Category Number	Topic Category	Description	References
1983	E19	NGOs	UN World Commission on Environment and Development—Brundtland Report ("Our Common Future").	Sparkes (2002)
1983	S59	Labor movement, SRI	Eastern Air Lines pension fund: two union representatives on board of trustees.	Gray (1983)
1983	S60	SRI	Shearson/American Express introduces mutual fund with social screening approach.	Gray (1983)
1984	S61	SRI	First ethically screened mutual fund in the United Kingdom: Friends Provident Stewardship Funds.	Sparkes (2002); Guay, Doh, and Sinclair (2004)
1984	E20	Pollution (accident)	Toxic gas leak in Bhopal kills 3,500 and injures 50,000 (subsidiary of U.S. chemical company); leads to increase in regulations; costs about $527 million.	Sparkes (2002); Kahn (2007)
1984	E21	Policy	National database on toxic chemical production as a reaction to Bhopal leak.	Sparkes (2002)
1985	S62	Anti-apartheid	Opposition against apartheid increases because the "case of emergency" law is used by the South African regime.	Sparkes (2002)
1986	E22	Nuclear power	Nuclear power incident in Chernobyl.	Sparkes (2002); Kahn (2007)
1986	E23	Pollution (accident)	Leak in Sandoz chemical plant leads to severe pollution of the Rhine close to Basel; costs about $85 million.	Sparkes (2002); Knight and Pretty (1997)
1986	S63	SRI, shareholder activism	First shareholder resolution sponsored by a mutual found (Calvert).	Guay, Doh, and Sinclair (2004)
1986	S64	SRI	First Canadian SRI Fund (Ethical Growth Fund).	Guay, Doh, and Sinclair (2004)

Exhibit 7.1   (*Continued*)

Panel F. 1980s: The Decade of Societal and Political Attention

Year	Category Number	Topic Category	Description	References
1987	E24	Ozone layer	Montreal Protocol leads to ban of CFC production in developed countries.	Sparkes (2002); Velders, Andersen, Daniel, Fahey, and McFarland (2007)
1988, 1990	E25	Biodiversity	Heinz Food gives into consumer pressure and shareholder resolutions concerning dolphin-friendly fishing nets.	Frooman (1999); Sparkes (2002)
1988	E26	NGOs	CERES (Coalition for Environmentally Responsible Economies)—increasing impact after Exxon Valdez incident in 1989.	Sparkes (2002)
1988	E27	SRI	U.K. environmental funds, e.g., Merlin Jupiter Green Fund.	Sparkes (2002)
1989	S65, E28	SRI	First SRI in the Rockies Conference.	The Ethical Partnership (2011)
1989	E29	Pollution (accident)	*Exxon Valdez* disaster—11 million gallons of crude oil spilled; besides direct costs, payment of $150 million fine and $900 million civil settlement: total cost about $11,500 million; leads to increase in regulation.	Knight and Pretty (1997); Sparkes (2002); Cavanagh and Linn (2006); Kahn (2007);
1989– 1990	E30	General; policy	Green Tide in whole of Europe during European Elections; 15 percent for Green Party in the United Kingdom leads Margaret Thatcher to adopt environmental profile.	Sparkes (2002); Curtice (1989)
1989	E31	SRI	Launch of Green Norway (Gront Norge).	Guay, Doh, and Sinclair (2004)
1989	S66	SRI	First Australian trust to offer SRI: Australia Ethical Investment.	Guay, Doh, and Sinclair (2004)

(*continued*)

Exhibit 7.1 *(Continued)*

Panel G. 1990s: SET Issues Reach Finance

Year	Category Number	Topic Category	Description	References
1990	S67	SRI	Domini Social Index.	Domini Social Investments (2011)
1990s	S68, E32	Consumer	Beginning of Ethical Consumerism, e.g., fair trade and organic food.	Irving, Harrison, and Rayner (2002); Sparkes (2002)
1992	E33	General	Earth Summit in Rio; process started by the meeting leads to increasing number of international environmental laws.	Freestone (1994); Sparkes (2002)
1992	E34	Biodiversity	Convention on Biological Diversity signed by 158 countries; legally binding document in December 1993.	Cropper (1993); Sparkes (2002)
1992	S69, E35	SRI	First SRI fund in South Africa: UNITY.	Guay, Doh, and Sinclair (2004)
1993	E36	SRI	Green Project Fund (Groenprojectenfonds) launched in the Netherlands: ASN Aandelenfonds.	Guay, Doh, and Sinclair (2004)
1994	S70, E37	Consumer	Launch of Fair Trade Foundation (consumer label)	Sparkes (2002)
1996	S71, E38	SRI	Moskowitz Prize (SRI in the Rockies Conference) for excellent academic research in the field of sustainable and responsible investment.	US SIF (2011)
1996	S72, E39	SRI	Global Principle Fund launched in Norway: Storebrand developed with Amnesty International, Human Rights Watch, and University of Oslo.	Guay, Doh, and Sinclair (2004)
1997, 2005	E40	Global Warming	Kyoto Protocol—37 countries commit themselves to a reduction of greenhouse gases.	Sparkes (2002)
1998	E41	Pollution (accident)	Longford liquefied petroleum gas processing plant (Esso) accident: $1.3 billion total estimated cost for the industry due to the disruption in the gas supply.	Cavanagh and Linn (2006)

Exhibit 7.1   (*Continued*)

Panel G. 1990s: SET Issues Reach Finance

Year	Category Number	Topic Category	Description	References
1999	E42	Consumer, genetically modified	Tight genetically modified ingredients labeling in the United Kingdom; major supermarkets ban GM ingredients.	BBC News (1999); Sparkes (2002)
1999	S73, E43	SRI	First Asian SRI fund launched in Singapore (United Global Unifem Fund).	Guay, Doh, and Sinclair (2004)
1999	E44	SRI	First Japanese SRI fund (Eco-Fund).	Guay, Doh, and Sinclair (2004)
1999	S74, E45	SRI	Dow Jones Sustainability Development Indices.	Guay, Doh, and Sinclair (2004)

Panel H. 2000s: The Era of Responsible Investment Starts

Year	Category Number	Topic Category	Description	References
2000s	T1	Globalization	Concerns over globalization and deregulation and resulting increase of power of companies; lack of trust towards companies leads to loss of trust in the system.	Sparkes (2002)
2000	T2	Globalization	The Lisbon EU Head of State Summit stressed the role of CSR to target the problems of globalization and increase trust.	Sparkes (2002)
2000	S75, E46	SRI	Specific SRI section during EU Summit on Corporate Social Responsibility in Brussels.	Sparkes (2002)
2000	E47	Nuclear power	Germany introduces legislation and a schedule to close down all nuclear power plants.	*Independent* (2000); Sparkes (2002)
2000	E48	Religious, genetically modified	Church of England bans GM trial from land owned by the church.	Sparkes (2002)
2000s	E49	Renewable energy	Governmental incentives to invest in solar, wind, geothermal, biofuel, biomass, or hydropower lead to increasing investment.	Sparkes (2002)

(*continued*)

Exhibit 7.1 (*Continued*)

Panel H. 2000s: The Era of Responsible Investment Starts

Year	Category Number	Topic Category	Description	References
2000	E50	SRI	Merrill Lynch launches the First Renewable Energy Fund.	Sparkes (2002)
2000s	S76	Renewable energy	Higher-profit opportunities of biofuel plants in comparison to food' plants lead to substitution of food plants with biofuel plants and higher food prices.	Evans (2009)
2000	S77, E51	SRI, policy	Consideration of social, ethical, and environmental aspects added to the U.K. Pensions Act	Guay, Doh, and Sinclair (2004)
2001	S78, E52	SRI	First SRI fund in an emerging market (ABN AMRO, Brazil).	ABN AMRO (2007)
2001	E53	Pollution, legal	Asbestos liabilities reduce up to 50 percent of companies' market capitalization in 2001 leading to the bankruptcy of several companies.	Sparkes (2002)
2001	S79, E54	SRI, policy	SRI clause included in German pension legislation.	Guay, Doh, and Sinclair (2004)
2002	S80, E55	SRI, policy	Australian investment firms have to report the degree to which they take social and environmental criteria into account: Financial Services Reform Act.	Guay, Doh, and Sinclair (2004)
2005	E56	Global warming	ETS largest emissions trading scheme in the world.	European Union (2010)
2006	S81	Darfur Divestment	Darfur Divestment Task Force.	Bechky (2009, 2010)
2006	S82, E57	SRI	Kofi Annan launches Principles for Responsible Investment (PRI).	Principles for Responsible Investment (2011)
2007	S83	Darfur divestment	U.S. Sudan Accountability and Divestment Act of 2007.	Bechky (2010)
late 2000s	T3	Subprime mortgage crisis	Loss of trust in financial system.	Carey (2009)

Exhibit 7.1 (*Continued*)

Panel H. 2000s: The Era of Responsible Investment Starts

Year	Category Number	Topic Category	Description	References
2008	E58	Pollution (accident)	Dioxin found in Italian cheese.	Traynor (2008)
2009	S84	Human rights	UN Resolution concerning severe human rights violations in Burma.	U.N. General Assembly (2009)

Panel I. 2010s: Trust Issues Enter the Stage and Social and Environmental Issues Enter the Mainstream

Year	Category Number	Topic Category	Description	References
2010	E59	Pollution (accident)	*Deepwater Horizon* oil spill in the Gulf of Mexico; BP sets aside $41 billion, equaling 2.5 times 2009 profit.	Mervin (2011)
2010	E60	Nuclear power	Mass protests in German after the new government's decision to revoke the legislation concerning the shut-down of all nuclear power plants.	Pidd (2011)
2010	E61	Biodiversity	Creation of palm oil plantations (subsidized by the EU and others) for renewable diesel lead to the destruction of rainforest and the killing of rare species.	Sheil, Casson, Meijaard, Van Nordwijk, Gaskell, Sunderland-Groves, Wertz, and Kanninen (2009)
2011	E62	Nuclear power	Nuclear power incident in Fukushima; Tepco loses £9.4 billion mainly due to incident.	Campell and Pancesvski (2011); Layne and Uranaka (2011)
2011	E63	General; policy	First Green Party governor of a German federal state; national Christian Democratic Government is forced to adopt greener profile.	Campell and Pancesvski (2011)
2011	E64	Nuclear power	After the Fukushima incident the German government decides to start the process of shutting-down all nuclear power plants.	Pidd (2011)

(*continued*)

Exhibit 7.1   *(Continued)*

Panel I. 2010s: Trust Issues Enter the Stage and Social and Environmental Issues Enter the Mainstream

Year	Category Number	Topic Category	Description	References
2011	E65	Pollution (accident)	Dioxin is found in German eggs; scandal leads to bankruptcy of responsible company.	Brandt, Fröhlingsdorf, Klawitter, Koch, Loeckx, and Ludwig (2011)
2011	E66	Pollution (accident)	Rising costs for natural disasters; companies held liable for damage such as the BP for *Deepwater Horizon* incident.	Sparkes (2002)
2011	T4	Eurozone crisis	Financial crisis in Eurozone (with Greece as the main actor) results in loss of trust in the financial system.	Sapienza and Zingales (2011)

The table consists of (1) the year when the SET event or issue started to arise, (2) the category (S = social, E = environmental, and T = trust) and a continuous numbering, (3) a short description of the SET issue or event, and (4) references supporting the description that are recommended for further reading. The SET issues and events in the table are chosen because they play an important role in the development of the SET categories. The selection of the SET events is based on, but not limited to, Gray (1983), Sparkes (2002), and Guay, et al. (2004).

created the first social and environmental exclusion rules, which are later called *negative screens*.

The ethical motivation influenced business activities and investment in various ways. For example, due to the introduction of negative screens, parts of society did not participate in certain business activities anymore. This process, which was motivated by the consideration of ethical guidelines, still occupies a niche in the modern SET investment industry, for example, the Ave Maria Mutual Fund (Ave Maria Mutual Funds 2011).

1940s: The Post–World War II Era

The events of World War II dominated the 1940s. The war crimes and the unspeakable horrors of the Holocaust convinced global leaders to change strategy and to create universal rules in order to guarantee peaceful interactions and transactions among nations. Besides the moral consequences of the war, another consequence became apparent, namely, the scarcity of workers (Gray 1983).

Based on the experiences of World War II, the United Nations General Assembly adopted the Declaration of Human Rights in 1948 (Sparkes 2002). For the first time in the history of mankind, an international document existed that guaranteed every human being a set of inherited rights. During this period, *near social issues*, i.e., those directly concerning the group raising them—dominated the SET landscape. In post–World War II Europe, social problems outweighed all other areas of concern.

At this time, two main challenges entered the stage. First, due to the existence of a ratified catalog of human rights, business activities and investments could be compared to a new, nonfinancial benchmark. Second, labor unions benefitted from the scarcity of workers. Consequently, the bargaining power of labor unions increased during negotiations with companies. Unions started to request such benefits as better working conditions and pension plans for their members. This means that near social issues entered mainstream companies through the new bargaining power of labor unions (Gray 1983).

1950s: The Discovery of Pension Funds as a Tool

In the 1950s, the development begun during the 1940s continued. Labor unions discovered their power and started to use new (business) tools in order to support their near social claims. In the 1950s, scarcity of housing was the main near social issue. Labor unions adopted this problem on their agendas and tried to use their power to directly and indirectly involve the employers in solutions (Gray 1983).

The labor unions adopted new tools as the following two examples illustrate. First, as Panel C of Exhibit 7.1 shows, the Teamsters Union bought $1 million worth of Montgomery stocks and threatened to start a proxy fight if the company continued its "nonunion" policy. As a direct consequence of the threat, the company allowed unionization. This was one of the first cases of shareholder engagement to achieve a social goal. Second, Panel C of Exhibit 7.1 also shows that in 1958, the United Auto Workers filed a proposal requesting that the investment of the Ford workers' pension fund should directly benefit Ford workers. Thus, pension funds can serve as a tool to create social and not just financial benefits for their members (Gray 1983).

As Exhibit 7.2 shows, environmental issues also surfaced on the societal and political agenda. The reason lies in the London smog catastrophe during the winter of 1952 and 1953, in which 16,000 people died because of smog caused by coal fire emissions (Bell and Davis 2001; Sparkes 2002). As a result of the London

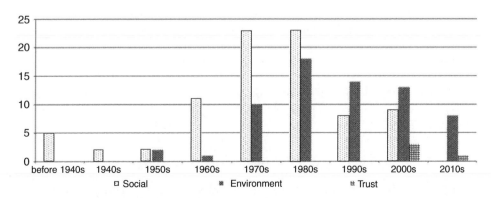

Exhibit 7.2   Distribution of SET Issues over Time
This graph illustrates the distribution of the SET issues listed in Exhibit 7.1 and shows how the focus changes over time from social to environmental and trust issues.

smog catastrophe, the British parliament created the first piece of environmental legislation in 1956 called the Clean Air Act. One consequence of this legislation was that power stations had to be relocated to rural areas. Therefore, this was the first time that an environmental catastrophe led to tighter legislation, which directly affected business activities and investments (Gray 1983; Sparkes 2002).

1960s: The Movement Decade

The 1960s marked a decade of near social movements: the civil rights movement, consumer rights movement, and anti–Vietnam war movement. This movement decade serves as the bridge between the 1950s, when the social issue first surfaced, and the 1970s when some of the issues reached the mainstream of society and policy. The social protest symbolized by the different movements directly influenced business activities and investments in numerous ways.

The civil rights movement demanded equal rights for all citizens. Major achievements for the movement are the Civil Rights Act and the Voting Rights Act (Berg 1964; Sparkes 2002; Landsberg 2007). Followers of the civil rights movement targeted Eastman Kodak because of its civil rights policy. The impact of the protest on Eastman Kodak's business activities forced the management to change its civil rights policy (Wadhwani 1997).

The anti–Vietnam war movement voiced concerns over the Vietnam War and denounced war crimes, such as using napalm against civilians (Sparkes 2002; Schueth 2003; Guay, Doh, and Sinclair 2004). In this movement, activists used various tools such as shareholder engagement. In 1969, the first responsible shareholder resolution was filed at an annual General Meeting of Dow Chemicals, the producer of napalm and agent orange, which are active ingredients of firebombs and defoliants, respectively. This marks the next step in shareholder engagement (Sparkes 2002; Guay et al. 2004).

The consumer rights movement became a voice through Ralph Nader and his campaign against the trade-off of safety for profit (Nader 1965). Nader directly targeted General Motors with his book *Unsafe at Any Speed*, revealing the impact of profit maximization on the safety of the consumer.

The labor rights movement pushed for stronger participation of employees in companies (Gray 1983). Labor unions continued to gain influence over pension funds. For example, a union-led strike action led to establishing a joint union-managed trusteeship at the New York Times Co. pension plan (Gray 1983).

Besides tools such as strikes and boycotts that directly influence companies, an investment tool considering SET issues was launched in Sweden in 1965, namely, the ANSVAR SRI fund. This fund, which religious groups partially funded, allows investors to invest their money while taking social criteria into account (Guay et al. 2004) and serves as a first step towards indirectly influencing companies through investment tools.

1970s: The Organization and Implementation Decade

In the 1970s, the SET ideas previously introduced were beginning to get formally organized and implemented in societal and political systems. During this decade, many social demands concerning near social issues start to get satisfied. As

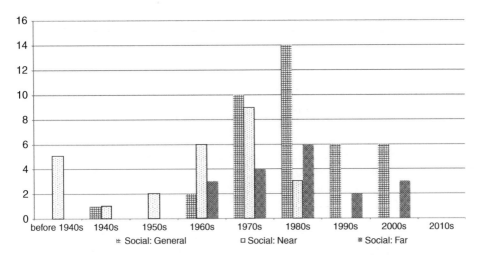

Exhibit 7.3 Visualization of the Shift of Focus within the Social Category
This graph shows the changing focus within the category of social issues and illustrates that the focus changes from social-near issues to social-far issues over time. Social near issues are issues that have a direct impact on the person raising the issues. With social far issues, the person raising the issue does not directly benefit from the outcome. Social-general consists of all issues that cannot be classified as social near or social far.

Exhibit 7.3 shows, this led to a shift in the focus from near to far social issues such as anti-apartheid. Besides this change within the social agenda, environmental issues surfaced and received the attention of both the mainstream and policy makers. The publication of the Club of Rome Report called *The Limit to Growth*, in which a forecast of the world's oil reserve created an urgency of change, drew attention to the environment. People realized that the current economic growth came with a price and was unsustainable (Club of Rome 1974; Sparkes 2002).

Social issues about the Vietnam War influenced business activities and investment. For example, in 1970, a debate on socially responsible investment took place at Yale, which represented an initial step towards establishing nonfinancial investment criteria (Simon, Powers, and Gunnemann 1972; Malkiel 1973; Sparkes 2002). Although investments using SET criteria occupied only a small niche at this time, the introduction of the first SET investment funds provided investors with a choice that was previously unavailable (Guay et al. 2004).

Labor unions continued to gain influence over pension funds, such as the Chrysler pension fund in 1979. This process drove another important change. Until the 1970s, a guideline called The Wall Street Rule was in place. This rule stated that institutional investors either voted with management on shareholder resolutions or sold their stock. In the 1970s, pension funds started to ignore this rule and voted against management on shareholder resolutions concerning SET issues (Gray 1983). This shows a general increase in sensitivity towards SET issues. In this atmosphere of skepticism, the nuclear accident at the Three Mile Island power plant occurred, resulting in approximate costs of more than $2 billion. Due to a change in regulations, this accident marked the end of the construction era of commercial nuclear power plants in the United States (Sparkes 2002; Kahn 2007).

1980s: The Decade of Societal and Political Attention

By the 1980s, the social movements of the 1960s and the rise of environmental concerns during the 1970s had already shaped general public opinion. Problems caused during the 1980s by irresponsible economic growth become apparent through environmental accidents and scandals. The results of the European elections at the end of the decade show that environmental issues had reached the mainstream of society and policy (Curtice 1989). The shift from near-social towards far-social and environmental issues continued.

The dominant social issue was South Africa and its apartheid regime. The process started with the Sullivan Principles, which provided a guideline of how to engage in business with South African companies. Although established in 1977, these principles did not reach the mainstream of society, business, and policy until the 1980s (Sullivan 1983; Posnikoff 1997; Sparkes 2002).

Concerning environmental issues, a series of accidents and scandals occurred. For example, Sparkes (2002) and Kahn (2007) note the following: (1) in 1984, a toxic gas leak in Bhopal killed 3,500 and left 50,000 injured; (2) in 1986, a nuclear meltdown in Chernobyl spread dangerous radiation over large parts of Europe; and (3) in 1989, the *Exxon Valdez* ran aground and spilled 11 million gallons of crude oil (Knight and Pretty 1997; Cavanagh and Linn 2006). The European elections at the end of that decade reflected the public reaction to these accidents. For example, the Green Party in the United Kingdom reached 15 percent in European elections, forcing Margaret Thatcher to add environmental issues to her profile (Curtice 1989; Sparkes 2002).

Social and environmental issues affected not only policy but also business activities and investment. Socially responsible investment reached a milestone when the U.S. Department of Labor legally permitted the use of nonfinancial criteria to make investment decisions (Gray 1983). In the light of these developments, the Public Employees Retirement System of California and the State of New Jersey Division of Investment began contacting the management of companies in their portfolios in order to find out about their investments in South Africa (Gray 1983).

Furthermore, environmental issues gained importance. The accidents during the 1980s dramatically illustrated the costs of environmental ignorance. For example, the *Exxon Valdez* spill cost $11.5 billion and the Bhopal leak cost $527 million (Kahn 2007). The new green trend in politics directly influenced the investment environment because investors feared the costs of tighter environmental regulations. These events resulted in introducing SET criteria in the decision-making process of funds and launching of specialized environmental funds (Sparkes 2002; Guay et al. 2004). At the end of the 1980s, the focus changed from social to environmental issues.

1990s: SET Issues Reach Finance

Environmental concerns dominated the SET agenda of the 1990s. Although investments considering SET issues slowly entered the stage in the 1980s, this growing trend gained traction in the financial markets during the 1990s.

One change regarding consumers was the development of a holistic responsibility. While in the past, most issues were SET related, the movement of ethical consumerism connected all three areas of concern. For example, the FAIR TRADE label certifies and promotes sustainability. In order to reach this aim of sustainably high social and environmental standards, the applicant needs to overcome hurdles to receive the FAIR TRADE label. Due to the fact that an independent association awards this label to companies, a level of trust needs to be created (Irving, Harrison, and Rayner 2002; Sparkes 2002).

The societal discovery of the bargaining power of consumption for environmental issues also reached the interstate level. International attention during the 1990s focused mainly on two treaties: the Kyoto Protocol and the Convention on Biological Diversity. The Kyoto Protocol became a synonym for the fight against climate change. In 1997, 37 countries committed to reduce their greenhouse gas emissions starting in 2005. By 1982, 158 countries had signed the Convention on Biological Diversity, which became a legally binding document of international law in 1993. The target of the convention was to fight the rapidly increasing extinction of animal and plant species in order to preserve a sustainable ecosystem (Cropper 1993; Sparkes 2002).

Concerning the influence of SET issues on business activities and investment during the 1990s, three major developments occurred. First, through the creation of certified labels such as FAIR TRADE, the consumer could directly consider and promote SET concerns through consumption. For example, coffee producers and wholesalers not certified by the fair trade association experienced a direct financial impact (Irving et al. 2002; Sparkes 2002). Second, as the Kyoto Protocol and the Convention on Biological Diversity show, international regulations were rapidly increasing. These regulations directly influenced business activities, such as the Kyoto Protocol's limitation of greenhouse gas emissions (Sparkes 2002). Third, the process to *price the environmental risk* started in the financial markets. The increasing numbers of green investment products, such as the launch of the Green Project Fund Netherlands or the Eco-Fund Japan, reflect results of this process (Guay et al. 2004).

2000s: The Era of Responsible Investment Starts

At the end of the 1990s, environmental concerns were the dominating SET issues, while social concerns played a secondary role. In the 2000s, trust issues entered the stage and changed the SET landscape yet again.

The reasons for the rise of trust issues in society lie in the change of the global business structure. In the 2000s, the consequences of globalization became apparent. The power of companies increased through deregulation and globalization of markets. Companies took over former public services and gained influence in areas of society that the state had previously controlled and protected. This development created skepticism amongst large parts of the population (Sparkes 2002). In this atmosphere of skepticism, the Big Bang of trust occurred—the subprime crisis itself and its direct consequence, namely the economic crisis and global recession. People felt that companies, especially banks and other financial institutions, had abused the new freedom of deregulation (Hall 2008; Fariborz 2011). In the court of public opinion, the consequences of the economic crisis, such as the loss of employment, was directly linked to banks and the financial sector in general.

Besides this new set of concerns, environmental issues kept emerging. In 2005, the European Union (EU) launched the largest multinational trading scheme for greenhouse gas emissions (European Union 2010). Also in the 2000s, the

German government introduced legislation that led to a shutdown of all nuclear power plants over the next decades, depending on their age (*Independent* 2000; Sparkes 2002). The legislation not only entails the closure of all nuclear power plants but also comprises the promotion and subsidization of renewable forms of energy production.

In terms of business activities and investment, the 2000s marked the beginning of a new era. In 2005, Kofi Annan, the United Nation's (UN) secretary general, launched the Principles for Responsible Investment (PRI). This UN initiative works together with its signatories to put the six underlying principles in practice. In 2011, the signatories held $30 billion of assets under management, which represents about 20 percent of the entire global market. Through the PRI, SET issues have reached the mainstream investment industry (Principles for Responsible Investment 2011).

The costs of environmental negligence also became apparent as, for example, evidenced by the settlement of law suits against construction firms producing and using asbestos products. As a consequence of these settlements, many firms had to declare bankruptcy, and environmental negligence became a severe business risk (Sparkes 2002). The changing German legislation concerning nuclear power plants and the introduction of the EU Emissions Trading Scheme revealed other business risks related to the natural environment.

2010s: Trust Issues Enter the Stage, and Social and Environmental Issues Enter the Mainstream

The shift of attention away from social issues towards environmental and trust issues has continued during the current decade. Environmental catastrophes dominate the beginning of the decade. In 2010, the BP oil rig called *Deepwater Horizon* exploded and sunk. Because the emergency systems failed to stop the oil flow, more than 4 million barrels of crude oil leaked into the Gulf of Mexico (Mervin 2011). In 2011, an earthquake and tsunami led to a core meltdown in the Tepco nuclear power plant in Fukushima, Japan (Campbell 2007; Campbell and Pancesvski 2011; Layne and Uranaka 2011). Both events led to a global increase in regulations concerning deep sea drilling and nuclear power, respectively. Shortly after the Fukushima catastrophe, and for the first time in history, a member of a Green party was elected as governor of a developed country state, Baden-Wuerttemberg in Germany (Campell and Pancesvski 2011).

Given the environmental consequences of the catastrophes, understanding the involvement of an important trust issue is essential. These catastrophes occurred after other events at the start of the twenty-first century had already damaged the general trust in businesses and financial institutions. Besides the aforementioned environmental disasters, a severe financial crisis shook the Eurozone in 2011, which is partly blamed on banks, rating agencies, and excessive consumer spending. As a direct reaction to these events, the global Occupy Movement became a symbol of the lack of trust in financial institutions (Sapienza and Zingales 2011).

The impact of the occupy movement and the consequences of the Eurozone crisis can only be determined ex post. The financial consequences of the BP and Tepco disasters, however, can be approximated. In order to cover the clean-up costs, as well as the compensation of those involved in the fishing industry and other directly affected persons, BP set aside $41 billion. This equals 2.5 times its 2009 profit (Mervin 2011). Concerning the Fukushima disaster, Tepco reported a £9.4 billion loss almost exclusively caused by the meltdown (Campell and Pancesvski 2011; Layne and Uranaka 2011). Besides these direct financial consequences, the effects of the events on societal and political opinion are likely to lead to further material consequences.

SET CHALLENGES AND OPPORTUNITIES IN BUSINESS AND FINANCE

An ongoing debate continues about the value relevance of SET issues for financial institutions. In general, scholars have set forth three hypotheses (Hamilton, Jo, and Statman 1993; Kurtz 2005):

1. Certain SET issues are value enhancing, at least in some circumstances.
2. Certain SET issues are value destroying, at least in some circumstances.
3. Certain SET issues are value irrelevant in many or all circumstances as benefits and costs of certain SET issues cancel out, or as certain SET issues simply have no relation to financial value.

The following section discusses the first two hypotheses individually for each SET issue. They are discussed jointly from two perspectives: (1) as applied by financial institutions and (2) as invested in by asset managers. The first banking perspective refers only to financial institutions, while the second investment perspective refers to all types of investable assets, but for the purpose of this chapter, especially equities.

Social Issues

Proponents claim that considering social issues can be value enhancing for financial institutions for at least three reasons. First, communicating an authentic social responsibility can help firms to smooth cash flows through consumer goodwill and consumer loyalty (Mintzberg 1983; Carrol 1999; Carroll and Shabana 2010). Similarly, mutual funds can increase investor loyalty by displaying social responsibility (Bollen 2007). Second, displaying some social responsibility can be seen as a strategy to minimize transaction costs and potential conflicts with stakeholders, reduce risks, and establish corporation reputation (Freeman 1984). Indeed, Godfrey, Merrill, and Hansen (2009) observe an insurance-like protection for firms with a high degree of social responsibility during unexpected legal investigations. Third, social responsibility can be understood as a nonwage benefit for employees (Akerlof 1982; Shapiro and Stiglitz 1984; Yellen 1984). Edmans (2011) confirms this by finding that good employee relations enhance various financial outcomes and especially lead to significantly abnormal positive stock returns.

Simpson and Kohers (2002) and Callado-Muñoz and Utrero-Gonzalez (2011) generally support these arguments. Simpson and Kohers, who analyze Community Reinvestment Act ratings of 385 U.S. banks over the period 1993 to 1994, find a better rating leads to significantly higher return on assets and significantly lower loan losses. Callado-Muñoz and Utrero-Gonzalez investigate the effect of corporate social responsibility (CSR) on financial institutions' competitive outcomes in the deposit and mortgage market. They develop a theoretical model from which they derive two testable hypotheses. First, they hypothesize that if consumers highly value CSR, the more socially responsible Spanish savings banks will have larger market shares than their less socially responsible commercial banking counterparts. Second, the authors assume that under the same condition that consumers value CSR, interest rates will be less relevant to consumer decision making. Based on a Spanish data set from 1999 to 2004, their evidence supports the first hypothesis. Specifically, depositors appear to experience a significant value from CSR activities relating to cultural, environmental, and heritage activities, while mortgage borrowers significantly value culturally related CSR. Their findings also appear to support their second hypothesis as differences in real interest rates do not appear to significantly influence Spanish consumers' deposit and mortgage decisions.

The main argument of the critics of CSR is that many CSR activities simply represent costs without sufficient benefits. They argue that managers have an incentive to display CSR beyond the level justified by shareholder value, as managers receive personal positive spillover effects from social responsibility such as enhanced reputation, which they might not receive from alternative cash outflows of the corporation. Critics believe that evidence displaying a negative relationship between CSR and insider ownership supports their argument (Friedman 1970; Ingram and Frazier 1983; Jaggi and Freedman 1992; Preston and O'Bannon 1997; Waddock and Graves 1997; Jensen 2001; Barnea and Rubin 2006; Becchetti, Ciciretti, and Hasan 2009).

Environmental Issues

Critics of corporate environmental responsibility use similar arguments as those of corporate social responsibility. They consider corporate environmental responsibility costly and a distraction from a firm's core competences. Furthermore, they believe that nonfinancial corporations, financial institutions, and investors are not well advised to internalize costs that business could externalize on society (Friedman 1970; Ingram and Frazier 1983; Jaggi and Freedman 1992; Preston and O'Bannon 1997; Waddock and Graves 1997; Jensen 2001; Barnea and Rubin 2006; Becchetti et al. 2009).

Proponents have addressed this critical view with four arguments. First, they contend that being greener has reputational benefits, especially in many European countries such as Germany. Second, proponents maintain that considering environmental risk is a crucial part of a firm's credit risk assessment, especially regarding real estate collateral. Third, firms engaging in environmental responsibility are probably better prepared for incoming environmental legislation and can minimize their adoption costs. Fourth, financial institutions with real estate operations experience a win-win scenario by developing more energy-efficient office buildings, as they gain on the energy cost reductions and the reputational benefits (United Nations Environment Programme 1992, 1995; Coulson and Dixon 1995; Wanless 1995; Case 1996; Thompson 1998a, 1998b; Weber, Fenchel, and Scholz 2008; Eichholtz, Kok, and Quigley 2010).

Trust Issues

The positive influences of trust in such collaborative activities as business, banking, or finance are simple to argue. Proponents contend that any financial contract is evidence of promises and mutual trust. They emphasize that trust is especially important in inaugural business collaborations (Mayer, Davis, and Schoorman 1995; Sapienza and Zingales 2009). Empirical evidence also clearly shows the high relevance of trust for business operations. Research evidence shows that trust levels are positively related to a multitude of economic activities, including bilateral trade, access to credit, use of checks, lower interest rate margins, stock market capitalization, households investments in stocks and deeper and more efficient financial markets in general (La Porta, Lopez-de-Silanes, Shleifer, and Vishny 1997; Calderon, Chong, and Galindo 2002; Guiso, Sapienza, and Zingales 2004, 2008, 2009; Knell and Stix 2009).

Critics do not offer arguments to challenge the relevance of trust and its positive effects for business. At best, they point out that trust might be an epiphenomenon of good institutions and may in itself not cause positive economic outcomes (Fehr 2009). However, while good strategic planning may be the cause of trust-building activities, the nature of business and contracts suggests that trust would have useful effects for business, banking, and finance.

SUMMARY AND OUTLOOK

Consider the high degree of trust in 2007 bestowed on Lehman Brothers, AIG, Federal National Mortgage Association (Fannie Mae), Federal Home Loan Mortgage Corporation (Freddie Mac), BP (*Deepwater Horizon*), Greece, Portugal, Ireland, Tepco (Fukushima), U.S. government bonds, and Italy. Today, each of them stands for yet another crisis. Many might believe as though the world, and certainly the news, constantly increased its pace. With wireless connections everywhere and many members of the business community consuming news multiple times a day, morning news seems outdated by the evening. Living for the moment appears all too often the vision of many workers. Financial institutions, however, cannot live for the moment, even though many of their employees may. The core competence of financial institutions is to preserve and build value over time.

This competence requires trust in at least three ways. Financial institutions have to trust their own capabilities such as employees, statistical models, or business networks. Clients have to trust a financial institution, even though they often have no means of assessing financial services until years or even decades after their purchasing decision. As financial services are often conceptually very similar, client trust appears to be a primary differentiation factor. Finally, governments also have to trust financial institutions, as their failure to at least preserve value over time can have severe consequences for economies due to the enormous interlinkages among financial institutions, and between these institutions and nonfinancial businesses.

Trust is built on understanding, preferably an understanding of someone's actions but at least an understanding of someone's ambitions and considerations. As financial institutions are becoming increasingly complex, clients often lack a reasonable understanding of their actions. Hence, the ambitions and considerations are becoming very relevant. The ambitions of financial institutions are often revealed by their legal form, which implies that savings banks might be in a better position to build trust than commercial banks (Callado-Muñoz and Utrero-Gonzalez 2011). However, any financial institution could build trust more successfully than its peers based on its publicly voiced considerations, assuming that these considerations are authentic and match its actions and ambitions. To build trust with governments, societies, and potential and existing clients, financial institutions, like many other businesses, are increasingly disclosing their social, environmental, and ethical considerations to the public in official reports or through various implicit or explicit comments or actions. For instance, financial institutions holding assets worth more than US\$ 30 trillion have signed the United Nation's Principles for Responsible Investment. Recently, one of the world's biggest investment management companies, Pacific Investment Management Company (PIMCO), signed the principles, which highlights that some social and environmental considerations have become mainstream investment practices.

In this context, this chapter contends that SET considerations appear to be less a flavor of the moment than performance-relevant aspects in business and finance. The basis of this view is two gradual changes in contextual factors. First, corporations, especially financial institutions, have become increasingly complex, which creates societal concerns. Second, the instant exchange of opinions on social networking websites is leading societies to become increasingly critical and collaborative. Both developments increase the likelihood of making societal critique of perceived misbehavior of businesses in general and financial institutions in particular. Such critique can lead to losses in client trust, which appear highly performance relevant, because trust is a key product differentiation factor of many financial service providers.

DISCUSSION QUESTIONS

1. Which changes have occurred within the SET issues over time?
2. Discuss possible reasons for changes in SET issues over time.
3. What do these changes in SET issues mean for the future?
4. Discuss the opportunities and challenges of SET issues for financial institutions and consumer product businesses.

REFERENCES

ABN AMRO. 2007. *Sustainability Review.* ABN AMRO Group. Available at www.abnamro .com/en/images/010_About_ABN_AMRO/035_Reports_and_reviews/2007_Sustaina ble_Review_pdf.pdf.

Akerlof, George A. 1982. "Labor Contracts as Partial Gift Exchange." *Quarterly Journal of Economics* 97:4, 543–569.

Aristotle. 1911. *The Nichomachean Ethics.* London: Dent & Sons.

Ave Maria Mutual Funds. 2011. *Ave Maria Mutual Funds—Our Funds.* Available at http://avemariafunds.com/funds/.

Barnea, Amir, and Amir Rubin. 2006. "Corporate Social Responsibility as a Conflict between Shareholders." Working Paper, Simon Fraser University and HEC Montreal. Available at http://papers.ssrn.com/sol3/papers.cfm?abstract_id=686606.

BBC News. 1999. "UK Supermarket Goes GM-free." *BBC Online Network*, July 19. Available at http://news.bbc.co.uk/1/hi/uk/397927.stm.

Becchetti, Leonardo, Rocco Ciciretti, and Iftekhar Hasan. 2009. "Corporate Social Responsibility and Shareholder's Value: An Event Study Analysis." Federal Reserve Bank of Atlanta Working Paper No. 2007-6. Available at http://papers.ssrn.com/sol3/papers.cfm?abstract_id=928557.

Bechky, Perry S. 2009. "Darfur, Divestment, and Dialogue." *The University of Pennsylvania Journal of International Law* 30:3, 823–904.

_____. 2010. "The Politics of Divestment." In Tomer Broude, ed. *The Politics of International Economic Law*, 337–362. Cambridge, UK: Cambridge University Press.

Bell, Michelle L., and Devra Lee Davis. 2001. "Reassessment of the Lethal London Fog of 1952: Novel Indicators of Acute and Chronic Consequences of Acute Exposure to Air Pollution." *Environmental Health Perspectives* 109 (Supplement 3), 389–394.

Berg, Richard K. 1964. "Equal Employment Opportunity under the Civil Rights Act of 1964." *Brooklyn Law Review* 31:1, 62–97.

Bollen, Nicolas P. B. 2007. "Mutual Fund Attributes and Investor Behavior." *Journal of Financial and Quantitative Analysis* 42:3, 683–708.

Brandt, Andra, Michael Fröhlingsdorf, Nils Klawitter, Julia Koch, Michael Loeckx, and Udo Ludwig. 2011. "Inside the Dioxin Scandal: The Criminal Machinations of the Feed Industry." *Spiegel Online International*, January 10. Available at www.spiegel.de/international/germany/0,1518,738610,00.html.

Broecker, Wallace S. 1975. "Climatic Change: Are We on the Brink of a Pronounced Global Warming?" *Science* 189:4201, 460–463.

Brown, Halina S., Martin de Jong, and Teodorina Lessidrenska. 2009. "The Rise of the Global Reporting Initiative: A Case of Institutional Entrepreneurship." *Environmental Politics* 18:2, 182–200.

Cadbury, Henry J. 1942. "Another Early Quaker Anti-Slavery Document." *Journal of Negro History* 27:2, 210–215.

Calderon, César, Alberto Chong, and Arturo Galindo. 2002. "Development and Efficiency of the Financial Sector and Links with Trust: Cross-Country Evidence." *Economic Development and Cultural Change* 51:1, 189–204.

Callado-Muñoz, Francisco J., and Natalia Utrero-Gonzalez. 2011. "Does It Pay to Be Socially Responsible? Evidence from Spain's Retail Banking Sector." *European Financial Management* 17:4, 755–787.

Campbell, John L. 2007. "Why Would Corporations Behave in Socially Responsible Ways? An Institutional Theory of Corporate Social Responsibility." *Academy of Management Review* 32:3, 946–967.

Campell, Matthew, and Bojan Pancesvski. 2011. "Fukushima Turns Germans Green." *Sunday Times* (London), April 3.

Carey, Nick. 2009. "Survey Finds Little Trust in U.S. Financial System." *Reuters*, January 27. Available at www.reuters.com/article/2009/01/27/us-financial-markets-trust-idUSTRE50Q6ME20090127.

Carroll, Archie B. 1999. "Corporate Social Responsibility: Evolution of a Definitional Construct." *Business & Society* 38:3, 268–295.

Carroll, Archie B., and Kareem M. Shabana. 2010. "The Business Case for Corporate Social Responsibility: A Review of Concepts, Research and Practice." *International Journal of Management Reviews* 12:1, 85–105.

Case, P. 1996. "Land, Lending and Liability." *Chartered Banker* 2:4, 44–49.

Cavanagh, Nic, and Jeremy Linn. 2006. "Process Business Risk—A Methodology for Assessing and Mitigating the Financial Impact of Process Plant Accidents." Center for Chemical Process Safety International Conference, Orlando, FL, April 26.

Club of Rome. 1974. *The Limits to Growth: A Report for the Club of Rome's Project on the Predicament of Mankind.* New York: Universe Books.

Coltman, Edward, and Shelley Metzenbaum. 1979. *Investing in Ourselves: Strategies for Massachusetts.* Boston: Massachusetts Social and Economic Opportunity Council.

Coulson, Andrea B., and Rob Dixon. 1995. "Environmental Risk and Marketing Strategy: Implications for Financial Institutions." *International Journal of Bank Marketing* 13:2, 22–29.

Cropper, Angela. 1993. "Convention on Biological Diversity." *Environmental Conservation* 20:4, 364–364.

Curtice, John. 1989. "The 1989 European Election: Protest or Green Tide?" *Electoral Studies* 8:3, 217–230.

Domini Social Investments. 2011. "Milestones." Available at www.domini.com/about-domini/Milestones/index.htm.

Edmans, Alex. 2011. "Does the Stock Market Fully Value Intangibles? Employee Satisfaction and Equity Prices." *Journal of Financial Economics* 101:3, 621–640.

Eichholtz, Piet, Nils Kok, and John M. Quigley. 2010. "Doing Well by Doing Good? Green Office Buildings." *American Economic Review* 100:5, 2492–2509.

European Union. 2010. "Emissions Trading System (EU ETS)." European Commission on Climate Action. Available at http://ec.europa.eu/clima/policies/ets/index_en.htm.

Evans, Alex. 2009. *The Feeding of the Nine Billion—Global Food Security for the 21st Century.* New York: New York University, Royal Institute of International Affairs.

Fariborz, Moshirian. 2011. "The Global Financial Crisis and the Evolution of Markets, Institutions and Regulation." *Journal of Banking and Finance* 35:3, 502–511.

Fehr, Ernst. 2009. "On the Economics and Biology of Trust." *Journal of the European Economic Association* 7:2/3, 235–266.

Freeman, R. Edward. 1984. *Strategic Management: A Stakeholder Approach.* Boston: Pitman.

Freestone, David. 1994. "The Road from Rio—International Environmental Law after the Earth Summit." *Journal of Environmental Law* 6:2, 193–218.

Friedman, Milton. 1970. "The Social Responsibility of Business Is to Increase Its Profits." *New York Times Magazine*, September 13, SM17.

Frooman, Jeff. 1999. "Stakeholder Influence Strategies." *Academy of Management Review* 24:2, 191–205.

Gallagher, Carole L. 1997. "The Movement to Create an Environmental Bill of Rights: From Earth Day, 1970 to the Present." *Fordham Environmental Law Journal* 9:1, 107–154.

Godfrey, Paul C., Craig B. Merrill, and Jared M. Hansen. 2009. "The Relationship between Corporate Social Responsibility and Shareholder Value: An Empirical Test of the Risk Management Hypothesis." *Strategic Management Journal* 30:4, 425–445.

Gray, Hillel. 1983. *New Directions in the Investment and Control of Pension Funds.* Washington, DC: IRRC.

Guay, Terance, Jonathan P. Doh, and Graham Sinclair. 2004. "Non-Governmental Organizations, Shareholder Activism, and Socially Responsible Investments: Ethical, Strategic, and Governance Implicatons." *Journal of Business Ethics* 52:1, 125–139.

Guiso, Luigi, Paola Sapienza, and Luigi Zingales. 2004. "The Role of Social Capital in Financial Development." *American Economic Review* 94:3, 526–556.

Guiso, Luigi, Paola Sapienza, and Luigi Zingales. 2008. "Trusting the Stock Market." *Journal of Finance* 64:6, 2557–2599.

Guiso, Luigi, Paola Sapienza, and Luigi Zingales. 2009. "Cultural Biases in Economic Exchange." *Quarterly Journal of Economics* 124:3, 1095–1113.

Hall, Maximilian J. B. 2008. "The Sub-Prime Crisis, the Credit Squeeze and Northern Rock: The Lessons to Be Learned." *Journal of Financial Regulation & Compliance* 16:1, 19–34.

Hamilton, Sally, Hoje Jo, and Meir Statman. 1993. "Doing Well While Doing Good? The Investment Performance of Socially Responsible Mutual Funds." *Financial Analysts Journal* 49:6, 62–66.

Hutchinson, James D., and Charles G. Cole. 1980. "Legal Standards Governing Investment of Pension Assets for Social and Political Goals." *University of Pennsylvania Law Review* 128:6, 1340–1388.

Independent. 2000. "Germany to Go Nuclear Free." *Euronews.* Available at www.euronews .net/2011/05/30/germany-to-go-nuclear-free/.

Ingram, Robert, and Katherine Beal Frazier. 1983. "Environmental Performance and Corporate Disclosure." *Journal of Accounting Research* 18:2, 614–622.

Irving, Sarah, Rob Harrison, and Mary Rayner. 2002. "Ethical Consumerism—Democracy through the Wallet." *Journal of Research for Consumers* 3, 1–20.

Jaggi, Bikki, and Martin Freeman. 1992. "An Examination of the Impact of Pollution Performance on Economic and Market Performance: Pulp and Paper Firms." *Journal of Business Finance and Accounting* 19:5, 697–713.

Jensen, Michael C. 2001. "Value Maximization, Stakeholder Theory, and the Corporate Objective Function." *Journal of Applied Corporate Finance* 14:3, 8–21.

Kahn, Matthew E. 2007. "Environmental Disasters as Risk Regulation Catalysts? The Role of Bhopal, Chernobyl, Exxon Valdez, Love Canal, and Three Mile Island in Shaping U.S. Environmental Law." *Journal of Risk and Uncertainty* 35:1, 17–43.

Kidd, Bruce. 1988. "The Campaign against Sport in South Africa." *International Journal* 43:4, 643–664.

Knell, Markus, and Helmut Stix. 2009. "Trust in Banks? Evidence from Normal Times and from Times of Crises." Working Paper No. 158, Oesterreichische Nationalbank.

Knight, Rory F., and Deborah J. Pretty. 1997. "The Impact of Catastrophes on Shareholder Value." *Oxford Executive Research Briefings.* Oxford: Templeton College.

Kurtz, Lloyd. 2005. "Answers to Four Questions." *Journal of Investing* 14:3, 125–139.

La Porta, Rafael, Florencio Lopez-de-Silanes, Andrei Shleifer, and Robert W. Vishny. 1997. "Trust in Large Organizations." *American Economic Review* 87:2, 333–338.

Landsberg, Brian K. 2007. *Free at Last to Vote: The Alabama Origins of the 1965 Voting Rights Act.* Lawrence, KS: University Press of Kansas.

Layne, Nathan, and Taiga Uranaka. 2011. "Tepco Chief Quits after £9 Billion Loss on Nuclear Crisis." *Reuters,* May 20. Available at http://uk.reuters.com/article/2011/05/20/uk-tepco-idUKTRE74J05Z20110520.

Luxton, Peter. 1992. "Ethical Investment in Hard Times." *Modern Law Review* 55:4, 587–593.

Malkiel, Burton G. 1973. "Book Review: The Ethical Investor: Universities and Corporate Social Responsibility." *Journal of Business* 46:4, 637–639.

Mayer, Roger C., James H. Davis, and F. David Schoorman. 1995. "An Integrative Model of Organizational Trust." *Academy of Management Review* 20:3, 709–734.

Mervin, John. 2011. "Counting the Cost of the BP Disaster One Year On." BBC News, April 19. Available at www.bbc.co.uk/news/business-13120605.

Milkman, Ruth. 1985. "Women Workers, Feminism and the Labor Movement since the 1960s." In Ruth Milkman, ed. *Women, Work and Protest: A Century of US Women's Labor History,* 300–322. London: Routledge and Kegan Paul.

Mintzberg, Henry. 1983. "The Case for Corporate Social Responsibility." *Journal of Business Strategy* 4:2, 3–15.

Nader, Ralph. 1965. *Unsafe at Any Speed: The Designed-In Dangers of the American Automobile.* New York: Grossman.

Pidd, Helen. 2011. "Germany to Shut all Nuclear Reactors." *The Guardian,* May 30. Available at www.guardian.co.uk/world/2011/may/30/germany-to-shut-nuclear-reactors.

Posnikoff, Judith F. 1997. "Disinvestment from South Africa: They Did Well by Doing Good." *Journal of Investing* 15:1, 76–86.

Preston, Lee, and Douglas O'Bannon. 1997. "The Corporate Social-Financial Performance Relationship: A Typology and Analysis." *Business and Society* 36:4, 419–434.

Principles for Responsible Investment. 2011. "UNPRI—About Us." United Nations-Backed Principles for Responsible Investment Initiative. Available at www.unpri.org/about/.

Ravikoff, Ronald B., and Myron P. Curzan. 1980. "Social-Responsibility in Investment Policy and the Prudent Man Rule." *California Law Review* 68:3, 518–546.

Sapienza, Paola, and Luigi Zingales. 2009. "A Trust Crisis." Working Paper, University of Chicago. Available at http://faculty.chicagobooth.edu/brian.barry/igm/atrustcrisis.pdf.

Sapienza, Paola, and Luigi Zingales. 2011. "Financial Trust Index." Chicago Booth/Kellogg School Financial Trust Index. Available at www.financialtrustindex.org/.

Schotland, Roy A. 1980. "Divergent Investing for Pension Funds." *Financial Analysts Journal* 36:5, 29–39.

Schueth, Steven. 2003. "Socially Responsible Investing in the United States." *Journal of Business Ethics* 43:3, 189–194.

Schwartz, Donald E. 1971. "Proxy Power and Social Goals—How Campaign GM Succeeded." *St. John's Law Review* 45:3, 764–771.

Shapiro, Carl, and Joseph E. Stiglitz. 1984. "Equilibrium Unemployment as a Worker Discipline Device." *American Economic Review* 74:3, 433–444.

Sheil, Douglas, Anne Casson, Erik Meijaard, Miene Van Nordwijk, Joanne Gaskell, Jacqui Sunderland-Groves, Karah Wertz, and Markku Kanninen. 2009. *The Impacts and Opportunities of Oil Palm in Southeast Asia: What Do We Know and What Do We Need to Know?* Bogor, Indonesia: Center for International Forestry Research.

Simon, John G., Charles W. Powers, and Jon P. Gunnemann. 1972. *The Ethical Investor: Universities and Corporate Social Responsibility.* New Haven: Yale University Press.

Simpson, W. Gary, and Theodor Kohers. 2002. "The Link between Corporate Social and Financial Performance: Evidence from the Banking Industry." *Journal of Business Ethics* 35:2, 97–109.

Smart, Donald A. 1979. *Investment Targeting: A Wisconsin Case Study.* Madison: Wisconsin Center for Public Policy.

Sparkes, Russell. 2002. *Socially Responsible Investment: A Global Revolution.* Chicester, UK: John Wiley & Sons.

Sullivan, Leon. 1983. "Agents for Change: The Mobilization of Multinational Companies in South Africa." *Law & Policy in International Business* 15:2, 427–444.

The Ethical Partnership. 2011. "The History of Socially Responsible and Ethical Investment." Available at www.the-ethical-partnership.co.uk/HistoryofEthicalInvestment.htm.

Thompson, Paul. 1998a. "Assessing the Environmental Risk Exposure of UK Banks." *International Journal of Bank Marketing* 16:3, 129–139.

Thompson, Paul. 1998b. "Bank Lending and the Environment: Policies and Opportunities." *International Journal of Bank Marketing* 16:6, 243–252.

Traynor, Ian. 2008. "Ultimatum for Italy in Cheese Dioxin Scare." *The Guardian*, March 27. Available at www.guardian.co.uk/environment/2008/mar/28/food.italy.

Tyrrell, Ian. 1997. "The US Prohibition Experiment: Myths, History and Implications." *Addiction* 92:11, 1405–1409.

United Nations General Assembly. 2009. 64th Session. "Resolution 238 (2009) [Situation of human rights in Myanmar]" (A/64/439/Add.3). 24 December 2009.

United Nations Environment Programme. 1992. *Statement by Banks on the Environment and Sustainable Development.* UNEP: Rio de Janeiro.

United Nations Environment Programme. 1995. *Environmental Policies and Practices of the Financial Services Sector.* UNEP: Geneva.

US SIF. 2011. "Moskowitz Prize Competition." Forum for Sustainable and Responsible Investment. Available at http://ussif.org/resources/research/Archive.cfm.

Velders, Guus J. M., Stephen O. Andersen, John S. Daniel, David W. Fahey, and Mack McFarland. 2007. "The Importance of the Montreal Protocol in Protecting Climate."

Proceedings of the National Academy of Sciences of the United States of America 104:12, 4814–4819.

Waddock, Sandra A., and Samuel B. Graves. 1997. "The Corporate Social Performance-Financial Performance Link." *Strategic Management Journal* 18:4, 303–319.

Wadhwani, R. D. G. 1997. "Kodak, Fight and the Definition of Civil Rights in Rochester, New York 1966–1967." *Historian* 60:1, 59–75.

Wanless, Derek. 1995. *The Gilbert Lecture 1995: Banking and the Environment*. London: Chartered Institute of Bankers.

Weber, Olaf, Marcus Fenchel, and Roland W. Scholz. 2008. "Empirical Analysis of the Integration of Environmental Risks into the Credit Risk Management Process of European Banks." *Business Strategy and the Environment* 17:3, 149–159.

Yellen, Janet L. 1984. "Efficiency Wage Models of Unemployment." *American Economic Review* 74:2, 200–205.

ACKNOWLEDGMENTS

The authors thank Qian Li and John Wilson for participating in discussions during early stages of this chapter. Any remaining errors or omissions are the sole responsibility of the authors. The views expressed in this chapter are not necessarily shared by the Principles for Responsible Investment. Authors are listed alphabetically.

ABOUT THE AUTHORS

Christoph F. Biehl is a member of the Centre for Responsible Banking and Finance at the University of St Andrews. His main research focus is the relationship between SET issues and the financial performance of companies. Besides his academic work, he works as the Academic Network Knowledge Manager at the United Nations–backed Principles for Responsible Investment.

Andreas G. F. Hoepner is a lecturer in Banking and Finance at the School of Management of the University of St Andrews, where he is also Deputy Director of the Centre for Responsible Banking and Finance. His research focuses on numeric/performance–related concepts, such as business, environmental science, finance or statistics, and value-driven concepts, such as corporate social responsibility, culture, or social media. He is also currently serving as Academic Fellow to the United Nation's Principles for Responsible Investment.

Jianghong Liu is a Ph.D. candidate of banking and finance at the School of Management at the University of St Andrews. She is also a member of the Centre for Responsible Banking and Finance at the University of St Andrews. Her research interest particularly focuses on SET issues in banking and finance.

CHAPTER 8

Religion and Finance

LUC RENNEBOOG
Professor of Corporate Finance, Tilburg University

CHRISTOPHE SPAENJERS
Assistant Professor of Finance, HEC Paris

INTRODUCTION

Religion is a powerful force in society that influences many types of social behavior including criminal activity and marriage (Iannaccone 1998). In recent years, growing evidence suggests that religion may shape individuals' attitudes towards the importance of saving, risk, financial responsibility, and other economically relevant concepts. In turn, differences in economic beliefs and preferences across religious groups may also affect economic outcomes. An established strand of the literature has investigated the link between the religious composition of a region and its macro-economic growth. Most of this work argues that Protestant areas have known faster economic development. Recent research also documents that the religious environment may affect corporate decision making and institutional investment, mainly because of the correlation between religiosity and risk aversion. Still other studies examine the role of religion in explaining cross-regional variation in aggregate financial behavior. Unfortunately, little research is available on the impact of religion at the micro-level of the individual household.

The remainder of this chapter consists of three main parts. The next section reviews the literature on the relationship between religion and economic attitudes and outcomes. The chapter then turns to an empirical analysis based on Renneboog and Spaenjers (2012) that uses Dutch household survey data to answer three related questions. First, do households belonging to specific religious denominations indeed have different economic attitudes from nonreligious households, as suggested by recent papers? Second, do they make different financial decisions? Third, can the differences in economic attitudes explain the differences in financial decisions? The final section provides a summary and conclusions.

This chapter mainly focuses on Catholics and Protestants, in line with the bulk of the existing literature. An essential difference between the two groups is that the former relies on salvation by works with enforcement by the Church, whereas the latter believes that salvation comes from divine grace with enforcement from social interaction (Arruñada 2010).

LITERATURE REVIEW

This section reviews the literature on how religion affects economic attitudes of individuals, and on how it correlates with economic development. It also discusses the impact of religion on decision making by households, corporate managers, and mutual fund managers.

Religion and Economic Attitudes

In the early twentieth century, Max Weber famously claimed that the Protestant work-and-save ethic led to a *spirit of capitalism* in Protestant regions. Weber's thesis has been the subject of fierce debates in the literature ever since he espoused this notion. Iannaccone (1998, p. 1474) writes that "the most noteworthy feature of the Protestant ethic thesis is its absence of empirical support." Also Arruñada (2010) rejects the work ethic hypothesis, but argues that a Protestant social ethic favors market transactions. Indeed, despite the doubts about the validity of Weber's thesis, various recent studies suggest that religion has an important impact on a range of economically relevant beliefs and preferences. Cross-sectional variation in these attitudes may affect both aggregate economic outcomes and financial decision making at the micro-level.

First, based on data from the World Value Survey, Guiso, Sapienza, and Zingales (2003) find that religiosity is associated with a higher emphasis on the importance of saving. Keister (2003, p. 181) notes that "religious doctrine seldom discourages saving and nearly always encourages correct and conventional living." Guiso et al. also report that Catholics appear to value thrift more than Protestants. This finding contradicts the Weberian claim that Protestant thriftiness mainly stimulated the growth of capitalism.

Second, research shows that religiosity is in general positively related to risk aversion (Miller and Hoffmann 1995). Intriguingly, Hilary and Hui (2009) find that individuals are more likely to avoid risks after reading a text about religious architecture. However, the strength of the relationship between religion and risk aversion may differ between denominations. Based on survey results from the Health and Retirement Study, Barsky, Juster, Kimball, and Shapiro (1997) report that American Catholics are more risk tolerant than Protestants but less so than Jews. Using a methodology similar to that of Hilary and Hui, Benjamin, Choi, and Fisher (2010) find that Catholicism even decreases risk aversion. Furthermore, Kumar (2009) reports that Catholics and Jews are more active participants in lotteries.

Third, religious beliefs may be correlated with different views on the degree to which life's outcomes depend upon one's own behavior (internal locus of control) or external forces (external locus of control). Intuitively, individuals with religious beliefs—and especially Protestants, who believe in predestination—are expected to have a more external locus of control. At the same time, however, evidence suggests that religious people have a "greater sense of individual responsibility" and "are more likely to believe that people are in need because they are lazy and lack willpower" (Guiso et al. 2003, p. 250). This sense of individual responsibility may be particularly relevant in Protestantism, in which "each individual determines on his own what is right" (Stulz and Williamson 2003, p. 318).

Fourth, the relationship between religion and trust has been studied rather frequently, but the evidence is mixed. Using data on individuals, Alesina and La Ferrara (2002) and Bellemare and Kröger (2007) report that religious beliefs do not affect the level of trust. In contrast, Welch, Sikkink, and Loveland (2007) and Arruñada (2010) find that Protestants are more likely to trust people with whom they are not acquainted. Guiso et al. (2003) find that religious upbringing negatively affects trust for Catholics, while more religious participation seems associated with more trust in all religions. Also when based on country-level data, the results are somewhat conflicting. McCleary and Barro (2006) find that beliefs have no effect on trust. Yet, La Porta, Lopez-de-Silanes, Shleifer, and Vishny (1997) find lower trust when a hierarchical religion such as Catholicism dominates in a country. Using a much broader sample of countries than many previous studies, Berggren and Bjørnskov (2011) conclude that trust generally has a negative association with religiosity.

Fifth, and last, religion may induce different views on intergenerational transfers and planning horizons. According to Fink and Redaelli (2005), Catholic households are more likely to leave a bequest. These households may also have longer time horizons (Christelis, Jappelli, and Padula 2010).

These five important categories will return in the empirical analysis in the next section. Clearly, however, more relevant attitudes can be identified—see, for example, Iannaccone (1998) and Guiso et al. (2003).

Religion and Economic Development

Guiso et al. (2003) find that, in general, religious people have economic attitudes that are favorable to economic development. Not surprisingly, Barro and McCleary (2003) conclude that economic growth is positively influenced by *believing* (for example, in heaven and hell), although it responds negatively to the degree of *belonging* (church attendance) across countries.

Much other research has focused on differences in economic development between Catholic and Protestant regions. Building on the Weberian claim of a Protestant work-and-save ethic, Landes (1998) contends that religious differences can partially explain the differences in economic growth between nations. In a similar vein, Grier (1997) finds that ex-colonies from Catholic countries have lower growth rates and income levels than former British (and thus Protestant) colonies. Yet, the author adds that religion is not the only determinant of the differences in development.

Blum and Dudley (2001), who examine the relationship between religious beliefs and economic growth in early-modern Europe, conclude that Protestant cities constructed beneficial economic networks. Their model suggests that these networks may have been made possible by the high cost of contract breach in Protestantism: Any defection could weaken the individual's conviction that he was predestined to be saved. Arruñada (2010) argues that Catholicism relies more on personalized trade, whereas Protestants favor anonymous trade and markets. Stulz and Williamson (2003) find that Catholic countries have significantly weaker creditor rights than Protestant countries.

Becker and Woessmann (2009) provide an alternative theory for the possible stronger growth in Protestant regions. The authors document Martin Luther's stress on the importance of education, and contend that the resulting higher literacy of Protestants enabled faster economic development in Protestant regions, at least in nineteenth-century Prussia.

However, the issue is still not completely settled. For example, using six centuries of data and a homogeneous cultural setting, Cantoni (2010) finds no differences in long-run economic growth between Catholic and Protestant cities and regions in Germany, in contrast to much previous work.

Religion, Firms, and Mutual Funds

Various papers also focus on the role of religion in firms and financial markets, using data at the county level in the United States. Most of this research is driven by the observation that religious affiliation or religiosity is correlated with variation in risk preferences, and the assumption that local cultural norms may affect managers' or institutional investors' behavior.

Hilary and Hui (2009) investigate how the religiosity of a firm's environment affects its investment decisions. Firms located in highly religious areas exhibit lower risk exposures, investment rates, and growth rates, but higher undiscounted profits. The effects are the strongest in counties with large shares of Protestants, but the results are significant for Catholics as well. Shu, Sulaeman, and Yeung (2011) also link local religiosity to organizational risk taking. They find that mutual funds located in regions with low Protestant (or high Catholic) population shares have higher return volatilities, mainly because of less diversification and more aggressive trading. However, this higher (idiosyncratic) volatility is not compensated by higher returns.

Kumar, Page, and Spalt (2011) see religion as an instrument for gambling propensity, which they conjecture to be higher in regions with large shares of Catholics. The authors then relate geographical heterogeneity in religion to differences in various financial outcomes. Consistent with their expectations, Kumar et al. find more ownership of lottery-type stocks by institutional investors and more widespread use of employee stock option plans in regions with a high Catholic-Protestant ratio.

Golombick, Kumar, and Parwada (2011) look at differences in ownership of *Catholic value* stocks—as determined by a religious authority—between mutual fund managers in Catholic and Protestant regions. Although Catholic fund managers tilt their portfolio towards Catholic stocks, they trade in these stocks as in non-Catholic stocks with similar financial characteristics.

Religion and Household Finance

Following the increased accessibility and democratization of financial markets during the 1990s, the analysis of household finance has become a fast-growing academic area (Guiso, Haliassos, and Jappelli 2002). Evidence shows that both demographic variables (such as age, gender, family size, and education) and background risk factors (such as private business risk and health) are important determinants of households' portfolio decisions (Campbell 2006). Over the last few years, an expanding literature has not only explored the roles played by optimism (Puri and Robinson 2007) and cognitive abilities and biases (Stango and Zinman 2009; Christelis et al. 2010), but also considered socio-cultural forces. For example, Hong, Kubik, and Stein (2004) and Brown, Ivković, Smith, and Weisbenner (2008) study the impact of social interaction and peer effects on stock market participation in the United States. Guiso, Sapienza, and Zingales (2008) find that trusting individuals are more likely to own stocks. Georgarakos and Pasini (2010) confirm the positive effects of both sociability and trust. Breuer and Salzmann (2010) examine the impact of national culture on the portfolio structure in a cross-country comparison. They find that a country's cultural values, as measured along dimensions such as *egalitarianism* (versus *hierarchy*) or *autonomy* (versus *embeddedness*) are related to the use of deposits, debt securities, life insurance, and pension funds.

In this literature on household finance, religion and religiosity have mainly been mentioned in passing. Hong et al. (2004) use church attendance as a measure of social interaction, while Guiso et al. (2008) note that a person's trust may be influenced by his ethnic and religious background. Nevertheless, some research also exploits regional variation in religious beliefs. In a European cross-country study, Salaber (2009) relates the religious environment to the ownership and returns of *sin stocks* (i.e., stocks in companies associated with alcohol, tobacco, or gambling). Protestants appear to be more sin averse than Catholics. Hood, Nofsinger, and Varma (2010) confirm the higher ownership of sin stocks by Catholics for the United States. Kumar et al. (2011) show that Catholic regions invest more in lottery-type securities, and also report lower returns on such stocks for firms located in Catholic counties. In another recent contribution, Peifer (2011) examines the market for religiously affiliated mutual funds. He shows that investors in religious socially responsible investing (SRI) funds are less responsive to past return performance than those in secular SRI funds. This illustrates how religious morality can affect investors' behavior in financial markets.

Some studies consider other aspects of household finance such as debt repayment and home ownership. Georgarakos and Fürth (2011) find a positive correlation between the fraction of religious people and timely repayment of loans in Europe. Crowe (2009) documents a negative relationship between the population share of evangelical Protestants and regional house price volatility in the United States. He maintains that the reduced boom-bust cycle in more evangelical regions is partly thanks to the inhabitants' lack of speculative motives.

Despite these efforts, however, there is a lack of research on whether individual differences in religious background are also translated into differences in general savings and investment decisions at the level of the household. Therefore, this chapter now turns to an empirical study of the relationship among religious affiliation, economic attitudes, and household finance.

EMPIRICAL ANALYSIS OF RELIGION AND FINANCIAL DECISION MAKING

The main issue examined is to empirically verify whether religious households indeed have different economic attitudes as suggested by previous research, and take other financial decisions from nonreligious households, which is something that has not been explicitly investigated previously. Moreover, by combining religion, economic attitudes, and household finance into one analysis, this study tries to assess whether the different economic beliefs and preferences may explain the differences in savings and investment decisions.

The data for this research come from a reputable Dutch household survey. The Netherlands is an interesting country to study the effect of religion on individual decision making for two different reasons. First, there is considerable variety in types of religious beliefs. As a consequence of the sixteenth-century religion-based wars between the Catholic Spanish rulers and Protestants rebels, the Dutch population has traditionally been half Protestant and half Catholic. Since the 1950s, however, the Netherlands have quickly turned into one of the most secularized countries in Europe. Nowadays, a small majority of the Dutch population is religious. Second, the distinction between religious and nonreligious individuals is probably easier to make in the Netherlands than in other countries. Generally, those who declare that they belong to a specific religious denomination also practice religion, whereas adults, who have been raised within a religious tradition but do not believe, do not consider themselves as religiously affiliated (Halman, Luijkx, and van Zundert 2005).

The remainder of this section, which is based on Renneboog and Spaenjers (2012), first gives more details about the data. It then presents different sets of results, before outlining some of the study's limitations.

Data

The basis for this study is the DNB Household Survey, which is managed by CentERdata at Tilburg University. This survey collects detailed information on a yearly updated sample of about 2,000 Dutch households, by means of weekly questionnaires. The panel is representative of the Dutch-speaking population of the Netherlands and changes slowly over the years. In the past, the survey has also been used to study the effects of trust (Guiso et al. 2008), loss aversion (Dimmock and Kouwenberg 2010), and financial literacy (Van Rooij, Lusardi, and Alessie 2011) on stock market participation. The data for this chapter cover the period 1995 to 2008. The information for the household head (or main wage earner) is used for the household. The following discussion outlines the variables used in this study.

With respect to religion, a distinction exists between CATHOLIC, PROTESTANT, and OTHER RELIGION. The main focus of this study is on the first two categories; the last category contains Muslims and other smaller religious groups. The religion variable measures affiliation, in contrast to some previous studies (Guiso et al. 2003; Arruñada 2010), which capture upbringing and religious attendance. Unreported analysis shows, however, that the religious affiliation variables used here are good proxies for upbringing and church attendance.

Consider next the number of different economic attitudes. The survey asked all individuals whether they agree with the statement "Being careful with money is an important character trait." The resulting variable THRIFT takes values between 1 (totally disagree) and 7 (totally agree). RISK AVERSION measures the agreement with the statement "I think it is more important to have safe investments and guaranteed returns, than to take a risk to have a chance to get the highest possible returns." The variable INTERNAL LOCUS indicates to which degree the respondent agrees with the statement "My life is determined by my own actions." LOW RESPONSIBILITY focuses on the sense of individual financial responsibility: "It is chiefly a matter of fate whether I become rich or poor." The next variable measures (self-reported) DISTRUST on a scale of 1 (trusting, credulous) to 7 (suspicious). The variable BEQUEST MOTIVE measures how important parents believe it is "to save so I can leave a house and/or other valuable assets to my children" on a scale from 1 (very unimportant) to 7 (very important). The variable TIME HORIZON contains the answer to the question "Which of the time-horizons mentioned below is in your household most important with regard to planning expenditures and savings?" on a scale from 1 (the next couple of months) to 5 (more than 10 years from now). Not all variables are available for the full time period. Most notably, data for DISTRUST are unavailable for a time frame that overlaps with that of the other variables.

Finally, a number of different financial decisions are used as dependent variables in the analysis. The variable SAVED is a dummy variable that equals 1 if the respondent indicates that the household has put some money aside over the last 12 months. The dummy variable STOCKS equals 1 if a household invests in individual stocks. Finally, % STOCKS measures the share of total financial assets invested in stocks.

A wide range of demographic control variables is considered, starting with AGE and the dummy variable MALE. The composition of the household is measured by the dummy variable PARTNER (which equals 1 if the household head has a partner who is also part of the household) and the variable CHILDREN (the number of children in the household). BAD HEALTH is a dummy variable that equals 1 if the respondent indicates his health to be "fair," "not so good" or "poor," as opposed to "excellent" or "good." The employment status of the household head is captured by the dummy variables EMPLOYED (on a contractual basis), SELF-EMPLOYED (in own business, on a freelance basis, etc.), and RETIRED, where the left-out category includes all other unemployed household heads. Three dummy variables capture the level of completed education by the household head: UNIVERSITY, VOCATIONAL (degree from a vocational college), and PRE-UNIVERSITY (scientific secondary or high school degree). The left-out category includes all individuals with another degree or none at all. The natural log of the total net income of the household is indicated by LN(INCOME + 1). The log of each household's net wealth is computed as LN(NET WORTH + 1). Net worth is calculated as the value of all assets (except private business equity) minus debts and mortgages, but is censored below at zero. All income and net worth figures are first transformed to euros for the years before to the introduction of the European currency, and to real terms using the official consumer price index of Statistics Netherlands.

Exhibit 8.1 gives the descriptive statistics (number of observations, mean, standard deviation, minimum, median, and maximum) for the variables outlined above and based on the panel consisting of household-year observations. Exhibit 8.1 shows that in 71 percent of the cases the household has saved in the preceding year, and in 13 percent of the observations the household owns stocks. Slightly more than half of the sample data points concern households with a religious head. The biggest religious group is the Catholic one, followed by the Protestants.

Exhibit 8.1 Descriptive Statistics for the Household Study

Variable	N	Mean	Standard Deviation	Minimum	Median	Maximum
Religion						
CATHOLIC	27,381	0.3059	0.4608	0	0	1
PROTESTANT	27,381	0.2047	0.4035	0	0	1
OTHER RELIGION	27,381	0.0716	0.2579	0	0	1
Economic attitudes						
THRIFT	5,238	5.8624	1.0442	1	6	7
RISK AVERSION	16,408	5.0223	1.6943	1	5	7
INTERNAL LOCUS	3,848	4.9914	1.2618	1	5	7
LOW RESPONSIBILITY	3,847	3.2298	1.5227	1	3	7
DISTRUST	8,655	4.1334	1.2355	1	4	7
BEQUEST MOTIVE	18,394	2.7158	1.7769	1	2	7
TIME HORIZON	18,598	2.2331	1.1818	1	2	5
Financial decisions						
SAVED	18,660	0.7115	0.4531	0	1	1
STOCKS	21,629	0.1315	0.3380	0	0	1
% STOCKS	20,627	0.0352	0.1354	0	0	1
Control variables						
AGE	27,924	48.7544	14.4653	14	47	95
MALE	27,926	0.7947	0.4039	0	1	1
PARTNER	27,927	0.7225	0.4478	0	1	1
CHILDREN	27,927	0.7775	1.1084	0	0	7
BAD HEALTH	20,404	0.2050	0.4037	0	0	1
EMPLOYED	27,854	0.6380	0.4806	0	1	1
SELF-EMPLOYED	27,854	0.0421	0.2008	0	0	1
RETIRED	27,854	0.1692	0.3749	0	0	1
UNIVERSITY	27,925	0.1317	0.3382	0	0	1
VOCATIONAL	27,925	0.2571	0.4370	0	0	1
PRE-UNIVERSITY	27,925	0.1073	0.3095	0	0	1
LN(INCOME + 1)	18,600	10.1156	0.8478	0.4337	10.2435	14.2058
LN(NET WORTH + 1)	19,255	10.4389	3.6670	0.0000	11.7747	18.3029

This exhibit gives the descriptive statistics (number of observations, mean, standard deviation, minimum, median, and maximum) for the variables used in this study. All variables are defined in the chapter.

Results: Religion and Economic Attitudes

The study first investigates to what degree religiosity is associated with differences in economic attitudes. The following multivariate model is estimated:

$$E_{it} = \alpha_1 + X'_{it}\beta + C'_{it}\gamma + T + \varepsilon_{1it} \tag{8.1}$$

where E_{it} is the economic attitude of interest (e.g., THRIFT) for household i in year t and X_{it} are the religion dummy variables (e.g., CATHOLIC). C_{it} denotes controls for the age, income, and net worth variables, as well as squared terms. In all equations, T stands for year fixed effects. Given the nature of the dependent variables, ordered probit models are estimated. In line with Petersen (2009), the standard errors are clustered per household to account for unobserved household effects: residuals may be correlated across time for the same household. Of main interest is the coefficient β, which gives information on the relationship between religiosity and economic attitudes.

Exhibit 8.2 outlines the results of the ordered probit estimation of Equation 8.1, with the number of observations, the pseudo R^2, and the results for a joint significance Wald test and a similar test on the equality of the coefficients for CATHOLIC and PROTESTANT reported at the bottom.

The results in Exhibit 8.2 confirm that different religious denominations are associated with different economic attitudes, even when controlling for a wide range of demographic and background characteristics. Catholic households attach significantly more importance to thrift. Holding all controls constant at the mean, a calculation of the marginal effects (not reported) shows that Catholics have a chance to "totally agree" that "being careful with money is an important character trait" that is 5.3 percentage points above that of non-Catholics. In the overall population, about 30 percent of all respondents "totally agree" with this statement, making the effect also economically significant. In line with this result, there is a highly significant positive coefficient on CATHOLIC in the model on RISK AVERSION. Next, and not surprisingly, the results on the INTERNAL LOCUS model indicate that Protestants are less likely to "totally agree" that their life is determined by their own actions; a Protestant affiliation decreases the probability with 4.6 percentage points. At the same time, the results for LOW RESPONSIBILITY indicate that Protestants still find assuming responsibility over financial decisions important. The results show significantly negative coefficients on the religion dummies in the DISTRUST model: both Catholics and Protestants are more trusting than the overall population. They also have stronger bequest motives; the coefficient on CATHOLIC implies a 10.1 percentage point lower likelihood of leaving money or other assets to their children as "very unimportant." Finally, Catholics and Protestants have significantly longer planning horizons than nonreligious households.

The test statistics at the bottom of Exhibit 8.2 indicate that in all cases, the coefficients on CATHOLIC and PROTESTANT are jointly significant at the 0.10 level. The equality of coefficients is rejected in the models that explain INTERNAL LOCUS, LOW RESPONSIBILITY, and BEQUEST MOTIVE. Protestants have a significantly more external locus of control, higher sense of financial responsibility, and weaker bequest motive than Catholics.

The evidence indicates strong effects on the religion variables. This is striking given the inclusion of control variables. With respect to these controls, the oldest people are thriftier and less trusting, and have a stronger bequest motive and shorter time horizon. The coefficients also suggest that males consider themselves less risk averse and more suspicious, in line with previous research (e.g., Kulich, Trojanowski, Ryan, Haslam, and Renneboog 2011). Another result is that people in bad health have a more external locus of control, are more likely to agree that becoming rich or poor is mainly "a matter of fate," and are less trusting. Self-employed people attach less importance to thrift, strongly believe that life is what you make of it, and are more trusting. People with a higher education seem to have a higher awareness of individual financial responsibility, a lower bequest motive, and a longer time horizon. Income and net worth variables are also strongly significant in many of the models.

Exhibit 8.2 Religion and Economic Attitudes

	Thrift	Risk Aversion	Internal Locus	Low Responsibility	Distrust	Bequest Motive	Time Horizon
CATHOLIC	0.1497**	0.1171***	-0.0525	-0.0010	-0.2003***	0.2724***	0.0923***
	0.0642	0.0382	0.0587	0.0600	0.0459	0.0408	0.0360
PROTESTANT	0.0931	0.0620	-0.3796***	-0.1409**	-0.2470***	0.1266***	0.0717*
	0.0672	0.0431	0.0674	0.0657	0.0500	0.0449	0.0390
OTHER RELIGION	-0.0038	0.0044	-0.2369**	-0.1793*	-0.2877***	0.2631***	0.0005
	0.0948	0.0653	0.1090	0.0949	0.0736	0.0751	0.0604
AGE	-0.0444***	0.0066	0.0001	0.0256**	-0.0243**	-0.0503***	0.0440***
	0.0137	0.0086	0.0128	0.0116	0.0103	0.0088	0.0074
AGE^2	0.0005***	0.0000	0.0000	-0.0001	0.0003***	0.0005***	-0.0005***
	0.0001	0.0001	0.0001	0.0001	0.0001	0.0001	0.0001
MALE	-0.0467	-0.2789***	-0.0244	0.1167*	0.1160**	0.0292	-0.0228
	0.0693	0.0479	0.0693	0.0649	0.0572	0.0512	0.0437
PARTNER	0.0105	0.0598	-0.0856	0.1654***	0.0577	0.0425	0.0488
	0.0643	0.0452	0.0670	0.0622	0.0525	0.0470	0.0392
CHILDREN	0.0053	-0.0192	-0.0372	0.0505*	0.0044	0.2058***	-0.0346**
	0.0297	0.0154	0.0311	0.0273	0.0189	0.0163	0.0153
BAD HEALTH	-0.0928	-0.0165	-0.2354***	0.2394***	0.1269***	0.0009	0.0411
	0.0580	0.0371	0.0633	0.0580	0.0467	0.0385	0.0340
EMPLOYED	-0.0933	0.0132	0.2547***	-0.0559	-0.0624	-0.1447***	0.0307
	0.0846	0.0539	0.0990	0.0866	0.0630	0.0521	0.0498
SELF-EMPLOYED	-0.4108**	-0.0055	0.3847**	-0.0185	-0.2500**	-0.0164	0.1082
	0.1918	0.0818	0.1527	0.1463	0.1127	0.0900	0.0820

	(1)	(2)	(3)	(4)	(5)	(6)	(7)
RETIRED	-0.0078	-0.0321	0.3424 ***	-0.2608 ***	-0.0676	-0.0004	-0.0370
	0.1111	0.0594	0.1160	0.1013	0.0676	0.0557	0.0514
UNIVERSITY	-0.1066	-0.0534	0.0139	-0.3064 ***	0.0006	-0.1507 ***	0.1649 ***
	0.0753	0.0453	0.0740	0.0763	0.0575	0.0498	0.0429
VOCATIONAL	-0.0652	-0.0114	0.0617	-0.2412 ***	0.0373	-0.1625 ***	0.1231 ***
	0.0629	0.0384	0.0607	0.0601	0.0463	0.0406	0.0345
PRE-UNIVERSITY	-0.0900	-0.0992 *	0.0260	-0.1987 ***	0.0667	-0.1020 *	0.0935 *
	0.0883	0.0524	0.0821	0.0775	0.0579	0.0534	0.0507
LN(INCOME + 1)	0.3961 ***	0.3617 ***	-0.0986	0.2092	0.0337	0.0753	-0.1540 *
	0.1054	0.1088	0.1994	0.2110	0.1313	0.1004	0.0864
LN(INCOME + 1)^2	-0.0229 ***	-0.0190 ***	0.0071	-0.0164	-0.0020	-0.0061	0.0107 **
	0.0068	0.0061	0.0110	0.0114	0.0075	0.0058	0.0050
LN(NET WORTH + 1)	-0.0724 ***	-0.0017	-0.0463 *	0.0704 ***	-0.0283	-0.1306 ***	-0.0825 ***
	0.0262	0.0160	0.0255	0.0267	0.0181	0.0156	0.0150
LN(NET WORTH + 1)^2	0.0072 ***	0.0011	0.0026	-0.0078 ***	0.0024 *	0.0114 ***	0.0095 ***
	0.0020	0.0012	0.0019	0.0019	0.0014	0.0012	0.0011
N	3,606	11,435	2,762	2,761	5,535	12,416	12,526
(Pseudo) R^2	0.02	0.01	0.02	0.03	0.01	0.03	0.03
H$_0$: C = P = 0	5.68 *	9.46 ***	33.57 ***	5.32 *	31.73 ***	44.58 ***	7.42 **
H$_0$: C = P	0.62	1.55	21.60 ***	3.95 **	0.75	9.92 ***	0.25

This exhibit shows the results of a multivariate ordered probit regression analysis, with the economic attitudes as dependent variables (Equation 8.1). The model also includes a constant and year dummies. Standard errors (shown below the coefficients) are clustered on the household level. The bottom of the exhibit shows the results for chi-square Wald tests on the joint significance and equality of the coefficients on CATHOLIC (C) and PROTESTANT (P). ***, **, and * denote statistical significance at the 0.01, 0.05, and 0.10 level, respectively.

Results: Religion and Household Finance

The reduced-form relationship between religion and financial decision making is estimated as:

$$Y_{it} = \alpha_2 + X'_{it}\lambda + C'_{it}\mu + T + \varepsilon_{2it} \tag{8.2}$$

where Y_{it} captures the household finance variable (e.g., SAVED), while X_{it}, C_{it}, and T stand for the same religion dummies, control variables, and time fixed effects as before. The coefficients λ measure the correlation between religious background and financial decisions. These estimated models use probit (for the dummy variables SAVED and STOCKS) or tobit (for the variable % STOCKS) model. Again, standard errors are clustered per household. Exhibit 8.3 shows the results.

Exhibit 8.3 shows that Catholic and Protestant household heads are more likely to put aside money (SAVED), even when controlling for age, gender of the respondent, household structure, health status, employment status, educational level, income, net worth, and year effects. The effect is similar in magnitude for Catholic and Protestant households: the probit coefficients imply that both household types have about 3 percentage point higher probabilities to have saved than nonreligious ones, holding all other variables constant at their mean. Catholics are significantly less likely to invest in stocks. Only 13.2 percent of the overall population holds stocks, but being Catholic decreases the likelihood of stock ownership with a substantial 2.3 percentage points. The same pattern emerges when considering the share of financial assets invested in stocks (% STOCKS).

The coefficients on CATHOLIC and PROTESTANT are also jointly significant in the three models presented in Exhibit 8.3. However, while the equality of coefficients in the case of the savings decision cannot be rejected, Catholics and Protestants seem to display an important difference in their attitude regarding stocks.

The financial decisions to save and to invest in stocks are also correlated with most of the demographic and background risk factors included in the analysis. Male household heads are more likely to invest in stocks, but this behavior is attenuated in two-partner households. The presence of children and poor health seem to make saving money more difficult, while retired household heads are more likely to save. More highly educated individuals are more likely to invest in stocks, even when controlling for the employment status and income. As expected, households with a very high net income or net worth are much more likely to own risky assets such as stocks.

Results: Religion, Economic Attitudes, and Household Finance

The next analysis investigates whether the economic attitudes can serve as channels through which religion "affects" household finance. Equation 8.2 is expanded with the economic attitude variables:

$$Y_{it} = \alpha_3 + E'_{it}\kappa + X'_{it}\lambda^* + C'_{it}\mu^* + T + \varepsilon_{3it} \tag{8.3}$$

Exhibit 8.3   Religion and Household Finance

	Saved	Stocks	% Stocks
CATHOLIC	0.0910 *	−0.1278 *	−0.0572 *
	0.0480	0.0668	0.0296
PROTESTANT	0.1054 **	0.0437	0.0318
	0.0538	0.0715	0.0315
OTHER RELIGION	0.0722	0.1674	0.0741
	0.0842	0.1156	0.0506
AGE	−0.0101	−0.0303 **	−0.0184 ***
	0.0099	0.0129	0.0058
AGE^2	0.0000	0.0003 **	0.0002 ***
	0.0001	0.0001	0.0001
MALE	−0.1010 *	0.1997 **	0.0894 **
	0.0575	0.0832	0.0395
PARTNER	0.1487 ***	−0.1691 **	−0.0974 ***
	0.0542	0.0762	0.0358
CHILDREN	−0.1353 ***	0.0053	0.0016
	0.0192	0.0280	0.0127
BAD HEALTH	−0.0995 **	−0.0027	−0.0161
	0.0435	0.0617	0.0274
EMPLOYED	0.4331 ***	−0.1394	−0.0543
	0.0589	0.0939	0.0423
SELF-EMPLOYED	−0.0837	−0.1600	−0.0475
	0.1002	0.1303	0.0585
RETIRED	0.1822 ***	−0.0593	−0.0161
	0.0663	0.0886	0.0383
UNIVERSITY	0.0324	0.2318 ***	0.1027 ***
	0.0584	0.0792	0.0346
VOCATIONAL	0.0614	0.1810 ***	0.0691 **
	0.0483	0.0657	0.0289
PRE-UNIVERSITY	−0.1035 *	0.3006 ***	0.1358 ***
	0.0625	0.0864	0.0392
LN(INCOME + 1)	−0.5012 ***	−0.3353 ***	−0.1869 ***
	0.1729	0.1224	0.0598
LN(INCOME + 1)^2	0.0350 ***	0.0265 ***	0.0132 ***
	0.0096	0.0072	0.0034
LN(NET WORTH + 1)	0.0643 ***	−0.2783 ***	−0.1313 ***
	0.0183	0.0289	0.0135
LN(NET WORTH + 1)^2	0.0003	0.0283 ***	0.0131 ***
	0.0014	0.0023	0.0011
N	12,543	14,010	13,726
(Pseudo) R^2	0.09	0.15	0.16
H$_0$: C = P = 0	5.47 *	6.02 **	3.74 **
H$_0$: C = P	0.06	5.22 **	7.02 ***

This exhibit shows the results of a multivariate regression analysis, with the financial decisions as dependent variables (Equation 8.2). The first two models are estimated using the probit technique, while the third model is estimated using a tobit regression. The models also include a constant and year dummies. Standard errors (shown below the coefficients) are clustered on the household level. The bottom of the exhibit shows the results for chi-square Wald tests on the joint significance and equality of the coefficients on CATHOLIC (C) and PROTESTANT (P). ***, **, and * denote statistical significance at the 0.01, 0.05, and 0.10 level, respectively.

Exhibit 8.4 Religion, Economic Attitudes, and Household Finance

	Saved	Stocks	% Stocks
THRIFT	0.0377	0.0551	0.0133
	0.0317	0.0431	0.0157
RISK AVERSION	0.0061	−0.1493 ***	−0.0600 ***
	0.0193	0.0245	0.0101
INTERNAL LOCUS	0.0176	0.0539	0.0173
	0.0251	0.0367	0.0148
LOW RESPONSIBILITY	−0.0568 ***	−0.0587 **	−0.0260 **
	0.0219	0.0288	0.0117
BEQUEST	−0.0388 **	−0.0232	−0.0063
	0.0197	0.0266	0.0106
HORIZON	0.1220 ***	0.0490	0.0030
	0.0293	0.0347	0.0137
CATHOLIC	0.0492	−0.0626	0.0056
	0.0842	0.1222	0.0457
PROTESTANT	0.1013	0.0908	0.0630
	0.1020	0.1342	0.0539
Control variables	Yes	Yes	Yes
N	2,485	2,485	2,471
(Pseudo) R^2	0.10	0.16	0.17
$H_0: C = P = 0$	1.05	1.18	0.72
$H_0: C = P$	0.24	1.18	0.97

This exhibit shows the results of a multivariate regression analysis, with the financial decisions as dependent variables (Equation 8.3). The first two models are estimated using the probit technique, while the third model is estimated using a tobit regression. The models also include a constant, year dummies, and all previously used control variables. Standard errors (shown below the coefficients) are clustered on the household level. The bottom of the figures shows the results for chi-square Wald tests on the joint significance and equality of the coefficients on CATHOLIC (C) and PROTESTANT (P). ***, **, and * denote statistical significance at the 0.01, 0.05, and 0.10 level, respectively.

The main point of interest is how the coefficients on the religious affiliation dummies change (from λ to λ^*) after controlling for the economic attitudes. Exhibit 8.4 shows the results. All economic attitudes are included jointly, except DISTRUST. All control variables are included in the estimation, but the coefficients on these variables are not reported for reasons of conciseness.

Exhibit 8.4 shows that a higher sense of financial responsibility and a longer horizon are significantly correlated with the decision to save. Surprisingly, there is a small negative coefficient on BEQUEST. The coefficient on CATHOLIC is no longer statistically significant. The magnitude of the coefficient is about half that of the coefficient reported in Exhibit 8.3, which does not control for differences in attitudes. Economic attitudes thus help in explaining the higher propensity to save by Catholic households. For Protestants, the results are somewhat less convincing. Although the coefficient is not significantly different from zero, it is very similar to that in the original model.

The second column presents the results for the models with STOCKS as a dependent variable. The risk aversion and the awareness of financial responsibility are particularly important in explaining the decision to invest in stocks. Comparing the results to those in Exhibit 8.3, the coefficient on CATHOLIC is no longer significantly different from zero. The different economic beliefs and preferences of Catholics thus also partially rationalize their lower stock market participation. Again, the results show a coefficient that is about half the previously reported one. Also the coefficient on PROTESTANT is not significantly different from zero.

The results in the third column generally confirm the previous findings. Risk aversion and the sense of financial responsibility significantly affect the decision whether and how much to invest in stocks. The coefficient on CATHOLIC is now very close to zero.

In summary, many of the economic attitudes that have been considered seem relevant in the context of religion and household finance, in the sense that they are useful in explaining the higher (lower) propensity to save (invest in stocks) of Catholic households. Weaker evidence is found that they also explain Protestants' savings behavior.

Limitations

This empirical study has two limitations that need to be mentioned. The first limitation involves the issue of causality. Because the data used are self-reported and many variables are correlated, causal relationships are hard to pin down. This is a problem of much of the research in the field (Guiso et al. 2003). One exception is the recent study by Benjamin et al. (2010), which creates exogenous variation in religiosity in a controlled laboratory setting. Most of the results shown here should thus be interpreted as precisely estimated correlations rather than causal relationships.

The second limitation involves whether the results can be generalized worldwide. Indeed, the finding that especially Catholics are more risk averse goes against recent evidence for the United States that Catholics (or firms in Catholic regions) exhibit less risk aversion than Protestants (Kumar et al. 2011; Shu et al. 2011). More generally, the results shown here cast doubt on the external validity of all country-specific studies on the economic effects of religious beliefs. Future research should thus consider more explicitly the possibility that the impact of religiosity may differ not only across denominations but also across regions.

SUMMARY AND CONCLUSIONS

This chapter has two main objectives. First, it reviews the existing literature on the relationship between religion and finance. Motivated by the observation that economically relevant attitudes can vary across religious groups, several papers have examined the role of religion in cross-regional variation in economic development. More recently, various studies have also demonstrated that the locally dominant religion can have a significant effect on the behavior of managers and institutional investors. Unfortunately, however, less research exists on the effect of religion on savings or investment decisions at the micro-level of the household.

Second, this chapter presents the results of new research on the variation in economic attitudes and financial decisions across individuals of different religious affiliations in the Netherlands. With respect to economic attitudes, the evidence shows that Catholics and Protestants consider themselves more trusting, care more about leaving money to their children, and have longer planning horizons than nonreligious households. Additionally, Catholics attach more importance to thrift and are relatively averse to taking risks, while Protestants have a relatively greater sense of individual responsibility. Religious household heads are more likely to put aside money than nonreligious individuals, and especially Catholic households are less likely to invest in stocks. Finally, differences in economic beliefs and preferences can largely explain the higher propensity to save and lower stock market participation of Catholics.

DISCUSSION QUESTIONS

1. Explain Weber's thesis and discuss whether it is supported by empirical evidence.
2. Give two examples of how local religious norms affect the behavior of institutional investors or managers.
3. Discuss what research exists on the role of religion in household finance. What is the main gap in the literature?
4. What are the main differences in savings and investment behavior between Catholics, Protestants, and nonreligious household heads in the Netherlands? Discuss whether these findings can be easily generalized worldwide.

REFERENCES

Alesina, Alberto, and Eliana La Ferrara. 2002. "Who Trusts Others?" *Journal of Public Economics* 85:2, 207–234.

Arruñada, Benito. 2010. "Protestants and Catholics: Similar Work Ethic, Different Social Ethic." *Economic Journal* 120:547, 890–918.

Barro, Robert J., and Rachel M. McCleary. 2003. "Religion and Economic Growth across Countries." *American Sociological Review* 68:5, 760–781.

Barsky, Robert B., F. Thomas Juster, Miles S. Kimball, and Matthew D. Shapiro. 1997. "Preference Parameters and Behavioral Heterogeneity: An Experimental Approach in the Health and Retirement Study." *Quarterly Journal of Economics* 112:2, 537–579.

Becker, Sascha O., and Ludger Woessmann. 2009. "Was Weber Wrong? A Human Capital Theory of Protestant Economic History." *Quarterly Journal of Economics* 124:2, 531–596.

Bellemare, Charles, and Sabine Kröger. 2007. "On Representative Social Capital." *European Economic Review* 51:1, 183–202.

Benjamin, Daniel J., James J. Choi, and Geoffrey Fisher. 2010. "Religious Identity and Economic Behavior." NBER Working Paper No. 15925, November.

Berggren, Niclas, and Christian Bjørnskov. 2011. "Is the Importance of Religion in Daily Life Related to Social Trust? Cross-Country and Cross-State Comparisons." *Journal of Economic Behavior & Organization* 80:3, 459–480.

Blum, Ulrich, and Leonard Dudley. 2001. "Religion and Economic Growth: Was Weber Right?" *Journal of Evolutionary Economics* 11:2, 207–230.

Breuer, Wolfgang, and Astrid J. Salzmann. 2010. "National Culture and Household Finance." Working Paper, RWTH Aachen University.

Brown, Jeffrey R., Zoran Ivković, Paul A. Smith, and Scott Weisbenner. 2008. "Neighbors Matter: Causal Community Effects and Stock Market Participation." *Journal of Finance* 63:3, 1509–1531.

Campbell, John Y. 2006. "Household Finance." *Journal of Finance* 61:4, 1553–1604.

Cantoni, Davide. 2010. "The Economic Effects of the Protestant Reformation: Testing the Weber Hypothesis in the German Lands." Working Paper, Universitat Pompeu Fabra.

Christelis, Dimitris, Tullio Jappelli, and Mario Padula. 2010. "Cognitive Abilities and Portfolio Choice." *European Economic Review* 54:1, 18–39.

Crowe, Christopher. 2009. "Irrational Exuberance in the U.S. Housing Market: Were Evangelicals Left Behind?" Working Paper, International Monetary Fund.

Dimmock, Stephen G., and Roy Kouwenberg. 2010. "Loss-Aversion and Household Portfolio Choice." *Journal of Empirical Finance* 17:3, 441–459.

Fink, Günther, and Silvia Redaelli. 2005. "Understanding Bequest Motives: An Empirical Analysis of Intergenerational Transfers." Working Paper, De Nederlandsche Bank.

Georgarakos, Dimitris, and Sven Fürth. 2011. "Household Repayment Behavior: The Role of Social Capital, Institutional, Political, and Religious Beliefs." Working Paper, Goethe University Frankfurt.

Georgarakos, Dimitris, and Giacomo Pasini. 2010. "Trust, Sociability and Stock Market Participation." Working Paper, Goethe University Frankfurt.

Golombick, Joshua, Alok Kumar, and Jerry T. Parwada. 2011. "Does Religion Affect Stock Markets and Institutional Investor Behavior?" Working Paper, University of New South Wales.

Grier, Robin. 1997. "The Effect of Religion on Economic Development: A Cross National Study of 63 Former Colonies." *Kyklos* 50:1, 47–62.

Guiso, Luigi, Michael Haliassos, and Tullio Jappelli, eds. 2002. *Household Portfolios*. Cambridge, MA: MIT Press.

Guiso, Luigi, Paola Sapienza, and Luigi Zingales. 2003. "People's Opium? Religion and Economic Attitudes." *Journal of Monetary Economics* 50:1, 225–282.

Guiso, Luigi, Paola Sapienza, and Luigi Zingales. 2008. "Trusting the Stock Market." *Journal of Finance* 63:6, 2557–2600.

Halman, Loek, Ruud Luijkx, and Marga van Zundert. 2005. *Atlas of European Values*. Leiden, The Netherlands: Brill Academic Publishers.

Hilary, Gilles, and Kai W. Hui. 2009. "Does Religion Matter in Corporate Decision Making in America?" *Journal of Financial Economics* 93:3, 455–473.

Hong, Harrison, Jeffrey D. Kubik, and Jeremy C. Stein. 2004. "Social Interaction and Stock Market Participation." *Journal of Finance* 59:1, 137–163.

Hood, Matthew, John R. Nofsinger, and Abhishek Varma. 2010. "Conservation, Discrimination, and Salvation: Investors' Social Concerns in the Stock Market." Working Paper, Washington State University.

Iannaccone, Laurence R. 1998. "Introduction to the Economics of Religion." *Journal of Economic Literature* 36:3, 1465–1495.

Keister, Lisa A. 2003. "Religion and Wealth: The Role of Religious Affiliation and Participation in Early Adult Asset Accumulation." *Social Forces* 82:1, 175–207.

Kulich, Clara, Grzegorz Trojanowski, Michelle K. Ryan, S. Alexander Haslam, and Luc D. R. Renneboog. 2011. "Who Gets the Carrot and Who Gets the Stick? Evidence of Gender Disparities in Executive Remuneration." *Strategic Management Journal* 32:3, 301–321.

Kumar, Alok. 2009. "Who Gambles in the Stock Market?" *Journal of Finance* 64:4, 1889–1933.

Kumar, Alok, Jeremy K. Page, and Oliver G. Spalt. 2011. "Religious Beliefs, Gambling Attitudes, and Financial Market Outcomes." *Journal of Financial Economics* 102:3, 671–708.

La Porta, Rafael, Florencio Lopez-de-Silanes, Andrei Shleifer, and Robert W. Vishny. 1997. "Trust in Large Organizations." *American Economic Review* 87:2, 333–338.

Landes, David S. 1998. *The Wealth and Poverty of Nations: Why Some Are So Rich and Some So Poor*. New York: W. W. Norton & Company.

McCleary, Rachel M., and Robert J. Barro. 2006. "Religion and Economy." *Journal of Economic Perspectives* 20:2, 49–72.

Miller, Alan S., and John P. Hoffmann. 1995. "Risk and Religion: An Explanation of Gender Differences in Religiosity." *Journal for the Scientific Study of Religion* 34:1, 63–75.

Peifer, Jared L. 2011. "Morality in the Financial Market? A Look at Religiously Affiliated Mutual Funds in the USA." *Socio-Economic Review* 9:2, 235–259.

Petersen, Mitchell A. 2009. "Estimating Standard Errors in Finance Panel Data Sets: Comparing Approaches." *Review of Financial Studies* 22:1, 435–480.

Puri, Manju, and David T. Robinson. 2007. "Optimism and Economic Choice." *Journal of Financial Economics* 86:1, 71–99.

Renneboog, Luc, and Christophe Spaenjers. 2012. "Religion, Economic Attitudes, and Household Finance." *Oxford Economic Papers* 64:1, 103–127.

Salaber, Julie. 2009. "The Determinants of Sin Stock Returns: Evidence on the European Market." Working Paper, Université Paris-Dauphine.

Shu, Tao, Johan Sulaeman, and Eric Yeung. 2011. "Local Religious Beliefs and Mutual Fund Risk-Taking Behaviors." Working Paper, University of Georgia.

Stango, Victor, and Jonathan Zinman. 2009. "Exponential Growth Bias and Household Finance." *Journal of Finance* 64:6, 2807–2849.

Stulz, René M., and Rohan Williamson. 2003. "Culture, Openness, and Finance." *Journal of Financial Economics* 70:3, 313–349.

Van Rooij, Maarten, Annamaria Lusardi, and Rob Alessie. 2011. "Financial Literacy and Stock Market Participation." *Journal of Financial Economics* 101:2, 449–472.

Welch, Michael R., David Sikkink, and Matthew T. Loveland. 2007. "The Radius of Trust: Religion, Social Embeddedness and Trust in Strangers." *Social Forces* 86:1, 23–46.

ABOUT THE AUTHORS

Luc Renneboog is a professor of Corporate Finance at Tilburg University. His research areas include corporate finance, corporate governance, initial public offerings, mergers and acquisitions, rights issues, law and economics, the economics of sports, ethical investing, financial distress, and the economics of art. He has published in journals such as the *Journal of Finance, Journal of Financial Intermediation, Journal of Law and Economics, Journal of Corporate Finance, Strategic Management Journal, Management Science, American Economic Review, Oxford Economic Papers*, and *Journal of Banking and Finance*. He holds an MSc in Management Engineering and a BA in Philosophy from the Catholic University of Leuven, an MBA from the University of Chicago, and a Ph.D. from the London Business School.

Christophe Spaenjers is an assistant professor of Finance at HEC Paris. His research interests include investments, investor behavior, international finance, household finance, corporate finance, financial history, culture, and networks. He has published in journals such as the *Journal of Financial Economics, Management Science, American Economic Review*, and *Oxford Economic Papers*. He holds an MSc from Ghent University and a Ph.D. from Tilburg University.

CHAPTER 9

Social Finance and Banking

OLAF WEBER
Associate Professor, Export Development Canada Chair in Environmental Finance,
University of Waterloo

YAYUN DUAN
Co-op Student, University of Waterloo

INTRODUCTION

What are social finance and social banking? Generally, social finance and banking try to achieve a positive social impact through finance and banking. A positive social impact includes an impact on society, the environment, or sustainable development. Social finance and banking attempt to achieve this impact by offering products and services such as loans, investments, venture capital, and microfinance.

In contrast to social finance, socially responsible investment (SRI) integrates social or environmental criteria into the set of investment indicators (Koellner, Suh, Weber, Moser, and Scholz 2007). SRI attempts to create a financial return outperformance compared to conventional investments that do not integrate social, environmental, or sustainability performance criteria into the investment process (Weber 2006; Buttle 2007; Sandberg, Juravle, Hedesström, and Hamilton 2009; Weber, Mansfeld, and Schirrmann 2011). SRI includes "social" screening, community investment, and shareholder advocacy (O'Rourke 2003).

How are social finance and its subgroups such as impact investing or social banking defined? The Monitor Institute (2009, p. 3) defines *impact investment* as "making investments that generate social and environmental value as well as financial return." Jones (2010, p. 418) defines impact investment more generally as "the use of for-profit investment to address social and environmental problems."

Some authors prefer to use the term *social finance* instead of impact finance. The Canadian forum socialfinance.ca (SocialFinance.ca 2010) defines social finance as:

> [. . .] an approach to managing money that delivers social and/or environmental benefits, and in most cases, a financial return. Social finance encourages positive social or environmental solutions at a scale that neither purely philanthropic supports nor traditional investment can reach.

Another report defines social finance "as the application of tools, instruments and strategies where capital deliberately and intentionally seeks a blended value (economic, social and/or environmental) return" (Harji and Hebb 2009, p. 2). Kaeufer (2010, p. 2) looks at social banks and summarizes its goals as "addressing some of the most pressing issues of our time."

To summarize the definitions and the spectrum of social finance, Chertok, Hamaoui, and Jamison (2008) distinguish between the emphasis on financial and social returns. For them, conventional finance is located on one end of a spectrum and conventional nonprofit investment (Meehan, Kilmer, and O'Flanagan 2004) is located on the other end with social finance in the middle. Thus, the main distinction of social finance is to use financial products and services as a way to achieve a positive impact on society, the environment, or sustainable development.

TYPES OF SOCIAL FINANCE

Social finance can be categorized in three categories: (1) social banking, (2) impact investment, and (3) microfinance. Social banking is conducted by social, ethical, or alternative banks, and partly by cooperative banks and credit unions. Usually, these types of banks exclusively offer products and services related to social banking, such as loans for social enterprises, renewable energy projects, or social housing. In contrast to conventional banks, social banks provide loans in order to create a social or environmental benefit (Edery 2006; da Silva 2007).

Representatives of this group are the Dutch Triodos. In the United States, the most well-known banks using the concept of social finance are One Pacific Coast Bank and the New Resource Bank. A credit union dedicated to social banking is VanCity Savings based in Vancouver, Canada (VanCity 2010).

Impact investing is conducted by both commercial and philanthropic investors. Impact investors typically invest in the equity of social enterprises or charitable organizations. A recent report (J. P. Morgan 2010) lists the Commonwealth Development Corporation in the United Kingdom and the Prudential Insurance Company as impact finance institutions.

Probably the best-known type of social finance is microfinance. Since microfinance pioneer Muhammad Yunus was awarded the Nobel Prize for Peace in 2006, microfinance, and especially microcredit, has become known as a social finance product for fighting poverty. The United Nations even declared the year 2005 as the International Year of Microcredit. Rhyne (2009) classifies microfinance as a "blue ocean" opportunity (Kim and Mauborgne 2004) because many people in developing countries still do not have access to capital to create businesses for their own income. Probably the most well-known example of a microfinance institution is the Grameen Bank in Bangladesh. Recently, some microfinance institutions such as SKS Microfinance and Compartamos even listed on stock exchanges. Typical microfinance products are microcredits, microsavings, and microinsurance.

Social Banking

Social banks are institutions that offer products and services that should create a social impact. A review of the members of the Global Alliance for Banking on Values

Exhibit 9.1   Member Institutions of the Global Alliance for Banking on Values

Bank	Country of Origin	Total Assets $ billion	Loans $ billion	Loans / Assets (%)	BIS Ratio (%)	Net Profit in $ million	ROE (%)
VanCity	Canada	13.70	11.60	84.52		51.0	7.30
Triodos Bank	The Netherlands	4.30	2.40	55.60	16.30	18.0	4.20
GLS Bank	Germany	1.90	1.00	52.54	10.90	7.0	7.40
Mibanco	Peru	1.60	1.30	82.04		34.6	27.40
BRAC Bank	Bangladesh	1.40	0.90	67.79	12.70	19.0	19.20
Banca Etica	Italy	1.00	0.51	52.11	12.40	0.0	0.10
Alternative Bank	Switzerland	0.90	0.66	73.83	6.30	0.0	0.10
Banco Sol	Bolivia	0.50	0.35	71.11	13.00	12.0	38.30
Merkur	Denmark	0.30	0.20	66.90	16.10	1.0	0.20
Xac Bank	Mongolia	0.20	0.14	61.43	16.90	2.0	11.60
New Resource Bank	United States	0.15	0.09	57.86	17.70	−5.0	
One Pacific Coast Bank	United States	0.10	0.05	46.46	13.10	−2.0	−15.40
Cultura Bank	Norway	0.06	0.05	71.21	16.00	0.2	2.70
Sum		26.2	19.30			137.8	
Average		3.70	2.80	64.88	13.76	19.7	8.59

The exhibit presents the member institutions of the Global Alliance for Banking on Values, their country of origin, total assets, loans, loans/assets, BIS ratio, net profit, and ROE.

(GABV) helps to provide some insight into the mission, products and services, and size of social banks. Exhibit 9.1 presents the member banks, including their country of origin, balance sheet, total loans, loans/balance sheet, Bank for International Settlements (BIS) ratio (the ratio of risk-bearing capital to risk-weighted assets), net profit, and return on equity (ROE).

Although the members of the GABV come from all continents except Australia, they comprise social banks operating in industrialized countries and microfinance institutions. With total assets of $26.2 billion and an average of $3.7 billion, the sum of all the banks in the group is very small. The median bank has only $898 million in total assets. As a comparison, the average total assets of all members of the World Council of Credit Unions in North America are $130.2 million. Most of the social banks are savings and loan banks, but their loans-to-assets rates vary from 46 percent to 85 percent. This indicates that only a part of the clients' savings are invested in loans. The BIS ratio, which describes the healthiness of a bank, varies from 6.3 percent to 17.7 percent. According to the Bank for International Settlements (2005), the minimum should not be lower than 4 percent.

Some very profitable banks provide ROEs higher than 25 percent. However, this is valid for two of the microfinance institutions. The international player Deutsche Bank strives for an ROE of 25 percent, and Citigroup achieved an ROE of 8.5 percent in 2009. The latter is similar to the average of the social banks. The credit unions of the German Savings Banks Association achieved a ROE of 4.8 percent in the same year (www.dsgv.de).

The results of Exhibit 9.1 suggest that social banks are profitable and can channel their assets to loans that have a societal or environmental impact. In contrast, they are still very small and serve a minuscule fraction of potential banking clients.

What are the mission, products, and services of these banks? The mission of the Alternative Bank Switzerland (www.abs.ch) states that ethical principles take precedence over maximizing profits. The bank is a savings and loans bank that claims to be transparent, publishes all approved loans, and grants loans to support environmental and social projects. It enables loans to be granted at reduced rates of interest by offering special bonds whose funds are channelled into different areas such as renewable energy, organic farming, or social housing. The Italian Banca Popolare Etica, a similar bank, wants to be a place where savers may meet socio-economic initiatives based on the values of sustainable social and human development.

Other European social banks with similar missions and strategies are the German GLS Bank and the Scandinavian Cultura and Merkur Bank. Triodos Bank is the biggest social bank in Europe. Its mission is to help create a society that promotes quality of life and has human dignity at its core. Triodos Bank also wants to enable individuals, institutions, and businesses to use money more consciously and to offer customers sustainable financial products and high-quality services. The bank offers dedicated savings products and specific investment funds, payment services, debit and credit cards, Internet banking, investment and private banking services, as well as mortgages. Furthermore, it creates and offers investment funds that invest based on social, environmental, and sustainability criteria.

As a designated community development financial institution, OnePacific-Coast Bank (www.onepacificcoastbank.com) aims to improve economic opportunity for low-to-moderate income communities throughout California. The bank partners with community institutions to provide banking services to small to medium-size businesses, nonprofit organizations, community facilities, affordable-housing developers, individuals, and families. It supports nonprofit organizations and integrates financial literacy, technical assistance, and business education into its banking services. The bank uses a triple-bottom-line focus, meaning it bases its prosperity on a balance of economic, social, and environmental success. OnePacificCoast Bank offers a wide range of loan and deposit products to serve the needs of its customers with a focus on supporting affordable housing and green industries. For example, it provides deposit products specifically tailored to previously unbanked and underbanked customers. The bank also offers mission-based deposit products that allow individuals, businesses, and nonprofits to support the bank by accepting below-market interest rates.

New Resource Bank, another U.S.-based social bank, develops new programs to more efficiently finance green projects and green businesses and also to introduce green incentives to everyday community banking clients. The bank is active in market development for green businesses and green projects through engaging in sustainability-related policies and movements. Additionally, it offers banking services and other strategic services for nonprofit organizations. One of its product lines is a community rewards program from which nonprofit organizations can generate income from New Resource Bank donations that are funded by its clients' exchange fees collected from debit card activities.

Consider the microfinance institutions of the GABV. BRAC bank is a socially responsible financial institution focused on markets and businesses with growth potential. It strives to assist building a "just, enlightened, healthy, democratic and poverty free Bangladesh" (www.gabv.org). As a microfinance institution, BRAC offers collateral-free financing, especially for women, in both rural and urban areas as well as savings accounts. BRAC provides security for old age and serves as a contingency fund during natural disasters.

Mibanco provides support to microbusiness entrepreneurs through specialized financial services. It offers working capital, investment, and housing loans to small businesses, as well as current accounts, savings, and deposit accounts to private individuals. Another microfinance, savings and loan bank named XAC provides equitable access to transparent, reliable and responsive banking products and services to its clients, including microenterprises, as well as small and medium-sized enterprises (SMEs). Its mission is to contribute to sustainable development in Mongolia. Furthermore, the bank provides financial services for the low-income segment of the population in urban and remote rural areas.

BancoSol is a microfinance bank that offers opportunities to the lowest-income sectors and provides high-quality, integrated financial services. Its core clients are entrepreneurs, especially women, with a small capital base, but with dynamic adjustment capabilities. BancoSol focuses on young clients with low levels of formal education who operate in the informal economy.

VanCity is a credit union based in Vancouver, BC, Canada. It strives to be a democratic, ethical, and innovative provider of financial services to its members (www.vancity.ca). The credit union maintains its commitment to the triple bottom line. Through strong financial performance, VanCity wants to serve as a catalyst for the self-reliance and economic well-being of its membership and community through strong financial performance. For community investment members, VanCity supports impact financing.

Generally, these cases show that all of these banks are driven by a mission based on a positive societal impact, an effect on the environment, or sustainable development. Some banks emphasize the need to serve unbanked or underbanked customers and to support them in starting or maintaining their businesses. Technically, these banks are savings and loans institutions connecting relatively conventional products with their social missions and goals.

Impact Investment

Impact investment can mainly be found in the United States. However, impact investment institutions are also in Canada, Europe, and Asia-Pacific. *Impact investment* is defined as "making investments that generate social and environmental value as well as financial return" (Monitor Institute 2009, p. 3). Jones (2010, p. 418) defines impact investment in a more general way as "the use of for-profit investment to address social and environmental problems." Thus, these definitions have in common the achievement of a positive societal, environmental, or sustainability impact by capital investments.

Impact investing can be placed on a scale of blended returns between pure financial return and pure social return. Prudent impact investing tries to maximize both social and financial return. This is based on the concepts of blended return

(Emerson 2003) or the shared value proposition (Porter and Kramer 2011). Both state that social and financial returns are not a trade-off but may be concurrently maximized.

But what are the advantages of impact investing compared to donations, charity, or philanthropy? Obviously, impact investing provides financial returns in addition to social returns. Thus, it provides the opportunity to invest capital to create societal impacts for those needing or wanting to gain financial returns. Additionally, impact investment is able to use capital more efficiently because it will be paid back or even creates an additional financial return. Thus, impact investing uses the leveraging effect of loans, investments, and other financial services. Furthermore, it supports the financial feasibility of social or environmental projects or enterprises. Finally, impact investing acknowledges both the ability and willingness of a borrower or a project to take responsibility for the achievement of the project's or social enterprise's goals. It integrates social enterprises and projects into the economic system and thus can create sustainable social and environmental innovations.

Consider the following examples of impact investors. The Global Impact Investing Network (GIIN) lists 40 members (see www.thegiin.org). They come from different fields including charitable organizations (e.g., Bill and Melinda Gates Foundation), financial organizations (e.g., J. P. Morgan), microfinance (ACCION) or commercial impact investors (e.g., Sarona).

Exhibit 9.2 presents the members of the GIIN, the type of organization, the mission, and the products' scope. The GIIN is a network of impact investors dedicated to increasing the effectiveness of impact investing. Impact investments aim "to solve social or environmental challenges while generating financial profit" (Global Impact Investing Network 2011).

As Exhibit 9.2 shows, impact investing is conducted from different perspectives and follows different goals. Out of 37 organizations that provided data, 20 conduct impact investing for profit, and thus create both social and financial return. Another 14 impact investment organizations focus on poverty reduction, development, or microfinance in developing countries. Another goal for four institutions is to provide access to financial services for nonserved or underserved people at the bottom of the socio-economic pyramid.

Impact investors also have other missions. Some of the U.S.-based organizations focus on improving the life situation or education for children in the United States, such as Annie E. Casey Foundation, W. K. Kellogg Foundation, and Packard Foundation. Others focus on community development, such as Deutsche Bank and Gray Ghost Ventures. A few of the impact investors try to change the way financial services are offered. For example, Armonia uses the triple-bottom-line concept (Schaltegger and Burritt 2010) as an investment criterion, and the Capricorn Investment Group conducts ethical, fair, and long-termed investments. Shorebank International strives for an inclusive global financial system. Another investment topic is the environment. Wolfensohn & Company focuses on low-carbon energy solutions and The Rockefeller Foundation aims to contribute to strengthening resilience to environmental challenges.

Impact investors have products and services to meet their missions and targets. As expected, most of them offer investments, either in the form of funds, such as Capricorn Investment and Triodos Investments Management, or direct

Exhibit 9.2 Impact Investment Organizations

Impact Investment Organization	Type	Mission	Commercial vs. Nonprofit	Product Scope
Accion	private	give people financial tools	nonprofit	microfinance
Acumen Fund	global venture	end poverty	nonprofit	investments in developing countries
Annie E. Casey Foundation	philanthropic foundation	build better futures for disabled children in the United States	nonprofit	grants and investments
Armonia (Lunt Family Office)	family office	offer investments based on the triple-bottom-line concept	for profit	investments
Calvert Foundation	foundation	lift people out of poverty	for profit	loans
Capricorn Investment Group	private investment firm	provide ethical, fair, and long-termed investments	for profit	investment funds and direct investment
Citi Foundation	foundation of financial service organization	support individual and family economic empowerment	nonprofit	financing MFIs
Deutsche Bank	foundation of financial service organization	support community development and microfinance	for profit	loans and investments
DOEN Foundation	foundation	support innovative, social, cultural, and sustainable initiatives	nonprofit	grants, guarantees, investments
Equilibrium Capital	investment management firm	finance sustainable real estate, land-based resource management, agriculture, energy efficiency, and water	for profit	investing
Ford Foundation	foundation	strengthen democratic values, reduce poverty and injustice, promote international cooperation, and advance human achievement	nonprofit	grants
Generation Investment Management	private investment firm	sustainable investing	for profit	investments
Gray Ghost Ventures	impact investment firm	address the needs of low-income communities in emerging markets	for profit	investments

(continued)

Exhibit 9.2 (*Continued*)

Impact Investment Organization	Type	Mission	Commercial vs. Nonprofit	Product Scope
IGNIA	venture capital firm	support start-up and expansion of high-growth social enterprises serving the base of the socio-economic pyramid in Latin America	for profit	investments
J. P. Morgan	financial services organization	provide investment and capital market services to social enterprises and funds, foundations, nongovernment organizations, development financial institutions, and other investors serving the base of the economic pyramid	for profit	investments and capital market services
Leapfrog Investments	microinsurance fund	provide affordable insurance to low-income and vulnerable people	for profit	investments
Lundin For Africa	philanthropic foundation	enable sustainable agricultural livelihoods and support SME development across sub-Saharan Africa	nonprofit	investments
Morgan Stanley	financial services organization	enhance environmental sustainability, advance economic opportunity, and support community development	for profit	investments and capital market services
National Community Investment Fund	private equity trust	increase the flow of resources into the most distressed markets around the country	nonprofit	investments
Omidyar Network	philanthropic investment firm	harness the power of markets to create opportunity for people to improve their lives	nonprofit	investments, facilitating deposits, building capacity
Overseas Private Investment Corporation	governmental development finance institution	help solve critical world challenges	nonprofit	investments

Packard Foundation	private foundation	conserve and restore the earth's natural systems, improve the lives of children, advance reproductive health, and invest in its local community	nonprofit	investments, loans, and guarantees
Prudential	financial services organization	support domestic economic development and education sectors	for profit	investments
Root Capital	social investment fund	pioneer finance for grassroots businesses in rural areas of developing countries	nonprofit	investments
RSF Social Finance	financial services organization	change the way the world works with money	nonprofit	loans, investments
Sarona Asset Management	private equity manager	generate solid financial returns with positive economic and social impact by investing in small and medium business in poor communities in developing countries	for profit	investments
ShoreBank International	financial services organization	expand access to capital, information, and financial services for unserved and underserved small businesses, entrepreneurs, and households to build a more inclusive global financial system	for profit	financial services
SNS Impact Investing	financial services organization	create value for clients, investees, and society by developing, promoting, and/or distributing impact investment solutions	for profit	funds
The Bill and Melinda Gates Foundation	foundation	help people to lead healthy and productive lives	nonprofit	grants and investments
The Gatsby Charitable Foundation	endowment trust	support research on plant science and neuroscience, science and engineering education, government effectiveness, and mental health, the arts and African economic development	nonprofit	grants
The Rockefeller Foundation	philanthropic organization	expand opportunity and strengthen resilience to social, economic, health, and environmental challenges	nonprofit	grants, loans, equity, guarantees

(continued)

Exhibit 9.2 (*Continued*)

Impact Investment Organization	Type	Mission	Commercial vs. Nonprofit	Product Scope
TIAA–CREF	financial services organization	target investments that offer a combination of competitive returns and positive social impact	for profit	investments
Trans-Century	investment company	invest in underserved sectors in order to achieve both strong investor returns and tangible economic development by raising gross domestic product (GDP), jobs, and exports	for profit	investments
Triodos Investment Management	financial services organization	allow individuals and institutions to invest directly in sustainable sectors, including microfinance, sustainable trade, sustainable real estate, renewable energy, organic agriculture, conservation, and cultural projects	for profit	investment funds
UBS	financial services organization	support ultra-high net worth clients in aligning their environmental and social values with their portfolios	for profit	portfolio screening, socially responsible investing, thematic investments, and impact investing
W. K. Kellogg Foundation	private foundation	focus on the welfare of vulnerable children, support families and communities as they strengthen and create conditions that help children at risk achieve success as individuals and as contributors to the larger community and society	nonprofit	investing, cash, fixed income, private equity
Wolfensohn & Company	private equity manager	focus on low carbon energy solutions	for profit	investments

This exhibit shows members of the Global Network for Impact Investing, their investment type, mission, commercial strategy, and product scope.

investments, such as Gray Ghost Ventures and IGNIA. Some of these investments focus on developing countries (e.g., Acumen Fund), microfinance (e.g., ACCION), or conduct domestic investments (e.g., W. K. Kellogg Foundation). Other commercial products of impact investors are loans. The loans are granted for both domestic and international projects and enterprises, such as the DOEN Foundation and the Packard Foundation. Various impact investors provide grants or guarantees as well, mostly in addition to other products and services, but as a stand-alone service.

Though the total investment amounts cannot be extracted from the data of the members of GIIN, the Monitor Institute (2009) estimates that the total amount of impact investing in the United States alone in 2007 was $26 billion. The report estimates that the potential for the next 5 to 10 years as about 1 percent of total investments. This equals $500 billion globally and is higher than the total philanthropic giving in the United States. Therefore, impact investors have many opportunities available to them as the first column of Exhibit 9.3 shows.

Impact investors can achieve financial returns because of the success of the financed projects and the economic growth in developing countries. Furthermore, impact investing can provide track records to demonstrate the financial returns and to prove that it is an effective solution for societal and environmental challenges. As the second column of Exhibit 9.3 indicates, impact investing also presents challenges. First, impact investing, and especially the social and environmental rating procedures, is still relatively inefficient and costly. Second, the infrastructure that is needed to invest efficiently is often missing. Third, there is a lack of projects for investment because many of these are exposed to high risks. Fourth, some societal and environmental challenges may only be solved by activities that do not offer any kind of financial return and thus will never be targeted by impact investors. Fifth, as the market grows, the task of clearly defining impact investment and distinguishing between impact investment and conventional investment becomes more difficult. Thus, indicators that measure the social return of impact investing are still needed. This also bears the risk of *feel good* rather than *do good* investing (Monitor Institute 2009), similar to the phenomenon of green washing (TerraChoice Environmental Marketing Inc. 2007).

Exhibit 9.3 Opportunities and Challenges of Impact Investing

Opportunities	Challenges
Create financial returns	Efficiency
Offer effective solutions for environmental and societal challenges	Infrastructure
Provide a track record that demonstrates success	Number of investable projects
	Challenges that cannot be solved by impact investing
	Measure the effect of impact investing

This exhibit indicates the opportunities and challenges that impact investors will face in the future.

Microfinance

Muhammad Yunus describes microfinance as a poverty-reduction tool, which grants loans to different segments of the poor (da Silva 2007). In his opinion, microfinance should be used to alleviate social problems and provide the poor with financial assistance to help them improve their quality of life (Yunus and Weber 2007). As the most fundamental mission of microfinance is poverty alleviation, different microfinance institutions (MFIs) have distinct objectives in achieving this mission, such as expanding financing channels, social justice, self-development, and boosting the rural economy.

Before the creation of MFIs, bank loans were unavailable for poor people, and money lenders exploited many of these people (da Silva 2007). Today, microfinance facilitates financial inclusion and linkage (Karmakar 2008) and expands financing channels for vulnerable groups (Lu 2010). For example, ASA, a world-famous microfinance institution based in Dhaka, Bangladesh, follows this principle and wants to "support and strengthen the economy at the bottom of the socio-economic pyramid by improving access to financial services for the poor" (ASA, Mission, Vision and Objectives 2010).

Furthermore, microfinance spreads the idea of democracy and human rights, and aims to improve women's social status. According to da Silva (2007, p. 71), "One of the most important features of microfinance in India is that it enables women, who do not have access to lending institutions, to borrow at bank rates to start a small business." Many MFIs, such as ACA and Khushhali, reach out to women and increase their decision-making and financial planning abilities (Montgomery 2011) by offering them affordable microloans.

In terms of quality of life, MFIs care about the health and education of the family. Thus, Montgomery (2011) finds a relationship between being a microfinance borrower and better medical treatment, nutrition, and education for the borrower's family.

Women's empowerment leads to the discussion about social equity. Even though the Millennium Development Goals organization believes men and women should have the same rights and status (Montgomery 2011), conventional banks frequently give substantially more loans to men, assuming they have greater abilities to develop businesses. One outcome for the microfinance lenders is that the default rates of the loans granted to women are very low (Weber 2010).

Traditional financial institutions and many economists focus purely on profit maximization. In contrast, microfinance enables economists to think about human capabilities, their creativity, and potential to serve society (Yunus and Weber 2007). Cultivating the poor to be professional, productive and profitable, and providing microcredit loans to help people establish self-sustaining businesses seems to have become the focus of many MFIs. As an increasing number of the members at the bottom of the economic pyramid gain employment or start their own business, the empowerment, self-esteem, and leadership characteristics of the poor develop as well.

Still, Song, Xue, and Zhong (2010, p. 1756) claim that "the poor would be much better served through their integration into the market systems as producers rather than consumers." This concept could support the goal to achieve an independence of many poor people from donations and the grants of others.

Through microfinance, rural productivity could also be improved (Moules 2010). MFIs mobilize rural savings and invest these savings in productive activities, which encourage the growth of farms and enterprises. They undercut exploitative moneylenders and catalyze the economic transformation to saving, planning, and budgeting.

Agriculture is the core business in rural areas. To overcome the financial risks of agriculture, microfinance institutions offer farmers loans to ensure the stability of their business. For instance, Swarnajayanti Gram Swarojaar Yojana, a microfinance program in India, assists farmers in bringing them above the poverty line (da Silva 2007). Microfinance in China improves the income and consumption level of the farmers and helps them avoid risks (Song et al., 2010). Microfinance programs can support farmers in selecting those crops that create a higher income and are demanded by the market. A change to different crops often requires new investment. MFIs are able to provide the necessary investment capital.

Some researchers claim that capital is not the predominant problem for some agricultural households and that knowledge, leadership, product price, and risk are the major hurdles. Therefore, MFIs should have an objective target to collaborate with economic development projects to educate farmers and facilitate the development in the countryside (Song et al., 2010). This must not be a contradiction to the concept explained above. A combination between investment capital and education will be the most successful way to help farmers out of poverty.

Originally, microfinance set a double-bottom-line objective to achieve poverty reduction in combination with financial sustainability. Financial risks are the key to obtaining financial sustainability. Thus, many MFIs commit to effectively control the loan default rate and are relatively successful as the low default rates show. Still, without collateral, microcredit loan repayment is highly associated with trust and control. Therefore, Bubna and Chowdhry (2010) promote a coalition strategy to control loan defaults. They suggest that the local financial organizations form a coalition and keep the financial records of all their clients. Defaulting on a loan, or having unpaid debts, will exclude the person from getting any financial services. Furthermore, a mixed portfolio could be a strategy to distribute and mitigate financial risks (Aubert, Janvery, and Sadoulet 2009).

To avoid donor reliance and to scale up the lending business, some MFIs cooperate with traditional banks and become commercialized or even go public to increase their capital basis. Because of this link to traditional capitalism, economists worry that microfinance will depart from its social mission and only focus on financial returns. This change is called mission drift (Roy 2010) and often happens because of the challenge to scale up the business and to control the costs of lending (Hishigsuren 2007).

Mersland and Strøm (2010) contend that the consequences of higher profits lead to lower outreach. In order to gain higher financial returns, microfinance prefers doing business with wealthier customers (Song et al., 2010). In contrast, Roy claims that commercialized microfinance gives more chances to explore new markets, and that high operation costs prevent microfinance from launching higher numbers of loans. Because a gap exists in the academic analysis of this question, determining whether profitability and social impact in microfinance are a trade-off is unclear (Hahn, Figge, Pinkse, and Preuss 2010) or correlate as the representatives of the blended (Emerson 2003) or shared (Porter and Kramer 2011) value proposition claim.

Many studies show that most MFIs do not have a large mission drift and can achieve high cost efficiency (Roy 2010). Yet, in the future a need will exist to distinguish between MFIs working on the concept of impact investment (J. P. Morgan 2010) and pure commercial lenders who are addressing clients from the economic bottom of the pyramid due to commercial reasons (Rhyne 2009).

To date, few appropriate social indicators are available to measure the performance of microfinance institutions. Also, an imbalance between financial indicators and social indicators is possibly diluting the social responsibilities of microfinance (Copestake 2007). The tension between the social mission of overcoming poverty and the financial pressure of increasing profits to attract capital and to make the institution self-sustaining is obvious (Barnett 2011). Questions about the achievement of the double bottom line goals are not yet answered.

After introducing the theoretical and conceptual background of microfinance, some empirical data about the respective institutions are presented. On mixmarket.org, 1,806 microfinance institutions can be found. Of these institutions, 23.6 percent are based in Latin America and the Caribbean; 21.8 percent are from Eastern Europe and Central Asia; 21.7 percent are located in Africa; 17 percent are from South Asia; 12 percent are based in East Asia and the Pacific; and 3.9 percent are located in the Middle East and North Africa. Regarding their mission, 62.9 percent of the MFIs are nonprofit institutions and 37.1 percent are for profit. Thus, the majority of the MFIs are nonprofit. Of the institutions, 48.6 percent have a low end target market (average loan size < US $150); 40.5 percent address a broad market (depth between 20 percent and 149 percent); 5.6 percent focus on a high end market (depth between 150 percent and 250 percent); and 5.6 percent define small business (depth over 250 percent) as their target market. *Depth* is defined as average loan balance per borrower divided by GNI per capita. These data suggest that MFIs target the bottom of the economic pyramid as clients.

What about the organizational and financial structure of the MFIs? Exhibit 9.4 presents data on the gross loan portfolio, the average loan balance per borrower, total assets and number of active borrowers, deposits and depositors. The data were gathered from mixmarket.org and are based on the most recent data of the respective MFIs (Microfinance data 2011).

Exhibit 9.4 Data for Microfinance Institutions Based on www.mixmarket.org

Region	Assets in U.S. $ billion	Active Borrowers	Number of Depositors
Africa	9.3	9,226,403	22,500,000
East Asia and the Pacific	6.9	14,500,000	6,192,063
Eastern Europe and Central Asia	15.1	3,053,299	2,148,428
Latin America and the Caribbean	55.8	14,100,000	10,300,000
Middle East and North Africa	0.9	2,735,335	89,456
South Asia	10.4	52,300,000	37,200,000
Total	4.0	96,000,000	78,500,000

This exhibit shows the region, assets, active borrowers, and number of depositors of microfinance institutions worldwide.

Exhibit 9.4 shows that in total, the MFIs have US $98.5 billion of assets, serve 96 million active borrowers, and have 78.5 million depositors. By far the highest activity seems to take place in Latin America and the Caribbean with assets of US $55.8 billion. Although Eastern Europe and Central Asia are not the regions where microfinance is usually active, these regions are already a big market with assets of US $15.1 billion. Surprisingly, the African microfinance market is relatively small, given the number of poor people in this region. Furthermore, MFIs serve more active borrowers than depositors.

Additionally, Microfinance data (2011) from mixmarket.org shows that the deposits-to-loan relation is around 47 percent and gross loan portfolio to total assets is 74.4 percent. As often described in the literature (Rhyne 2009), the loan loss rate is relatively low with an average of 0.76 percent.

A more detailed look into the different regions and countries reveals that East Asia and the Pacific have an outstanding portfolio of more than U.S. $24.4 billion, and the most important contributor is the People's Republic of China. This is due to government participation in the MFIs in China. MFIs work together with the state-owned banks, which have abundant capital to support the microcredit loans (Zhou, Xing, and Tong 2009).

MFIs in Eastern Europe and Central Asia (ECA) have the shortest history in the global industry, but their financial performance is the strongest (Berryman 2004). They provide fewer loans with a low number of active borrowers, but they serve higher-income clients. According to Berryman (p. 3), "MFIs in this region offer a loan that is on average five times the size of loans offered by their peers in Asia and almost two times the size of the average loan offered by all MFIs." The majority of MFIs in ECA provide loans to micro- and small enterprises, such as the MFIs in Azerbaijan and Mongolia, and thus do not target the bottom of the economic pyramid.

In contrast to Eastern Europe and Central Asia, Latin America and the Caribbean have a mature microfinance market. Since the late 1980s, microfinance services have expanded rapidly and reached 14.2 million low-income households in this region in 2009 (Navajas and Tejerina 2006). MFIs in this region earned the highest assets, totalling US $24.8 billion in 2009, and they remain above the average loan balance per borrower.

India and Bangladesh contribute most to microfinance in South Asia. India exceeds the other regions by the number of active borrowers, and the modern microfinance movement originated in Bangladesh in the 1970s. Compared to the MFIs in Latin America, they have different features. Most MFIs in Latin America serve microenterprises rather than the truly poor, while in South Asia, the MFIs target poorer people (World Bank Staff 2006). Both of these regions started the microfinance movement in the 1970s, but the scale of MFIs in Latin America is much larger than the one in South Asia.

Africa and the Middle East lag behind the other regions in terms of the gross loan portfolio. In Africa, most microfinance institutions are concentrated in the south-western part, and some of them remain unstructured and informal (Micro-finance in Africa 2008). About 76 MFIs serve 2.5 million people across the region, and the active loans are concentrated in Egypt and Morocco (Gonzalez 2008).

Microfinance is committed to poverty eradication, and different regions have specific objectives to reach this target. Mission drift and the balance between social missions and financial sustainability are the major challenges. Because poverty alleviation is a complex mission, solely depending on microfinance to solve this problem is unrealistic. Africa still seems to be underserved by MFIs, and the question remains whether this continent will be able to use the rich sources of commodities to increase the income of the people.

SUMMARY AND CONCLUSIONS

This chapter discusses social banking, impact finance, and microfinance. All three concepts belong to the topic of social finance, which tries to achieve a positive social impact by means of finance and banking. A positive social impact refers to an effect on society, the environment, or sustainable development. Social banking is conducted by social, ethical, or alternative banks, and partly by cooperative banks and credit unions. Usually, these types of banks offer products and services related to social banking, such as loans for social enterprises, renewable energy, projects, or social housing. They provide loans in order to create a social or environmental benefit. Both commercial and philanthropic investors conduct impact investing. They typically invest in equity or grant loans to social enterprises or charitable organizations. Microfinance and especially microcredit became well known as a social finance product that can fight poverty by providing small loans to support people to set up their own business to be able to generate an income to improve their quality of life.

Social finance can generate both a financial return and a social return. Governments are also participating to find investors to invest in social projects. Important examples are social impact bonds in which foundations, donors, or other impact investors invest upfront in a project or institution that provides a certain social service, such as support to those leaving prison in order to reduce re-offending. Good projects will be able to reduce the costs for the government and achieve a higher financial return. As such, the government couples the repayment of the investment and the amount of the financial return with the social success of the program (Mulgan, Reeder, Aylott, and Bo'sher 2011). Social impact bonds make sense for projects that lead to cost savings for governments and public services.

Measuring the success of such projects (and generally the success of social finance) requires conducting a social return on investment (SROI) analysis (Nicholls, Lawlor, Neitzert, and Goodspeed 2009). SROI is a set of practices and indicators that are used to measure the social impact of a business or an activity. It can be used to measure both positive and negative impacts on society. According to Lingane and Olsen (2004), the development of SROI indicators consists of collecting social performance data, prioritizing the data with respect to their importance, incorporating these data in decision-making processes and reporting, and valuing the amount of social values that are created or destroyed. Based on SROI decisions on channelling, activities or capital can be made. Furthermore, SROI can show the efficiency of social finance and can help investors make the right investment decision.

The size of social finance is still very small compared to conventional investment. Social finance will only have a substantial impact if more investments based on this concept are made in the future. In order to achieve this goal, products and services that address the needs of both institutional and private investors must be developed. This should lead to an increase in the perception of social finance as an investment that creates both social and financial return.

Regarding strategies to attract future clients, North American impact investors are probably in a better situation than European social banks. European social banks often originated from different movements, including environmentalist, unionist, or anthroposophist groups, and have to broaden their original customer base. New groups of clients, such as pension funds, young clients, or retail clients, have to be addressed with new types of products and services.

Social finance, impact investing, and microfinance still come with high transactions costs. In the microfinance business, the administrative costs are about 30 percent of the loan sum (see www.themix.org). The administrative costs for impact investing and social finance are also relatively high because of the integration of additional social or environmental criteria into the investment processes (Meehan et al., 2004). Despite these costs, social finance will guarantee the capital flow between those who want to support social or environmental projects and the projects.

Furthermore, the communication of a potential positive correlation between social impact and financial return will be important for the success of social finance. On the one hand, more background studies are needed to analyze the relationship, and, on the other hand, indicators such as SROI have to be developed to communicate the impact and financial success of social finance. Studies demonstrate that the ROE of microfinance institutions is 8.9 percent (Gonzales 2009), and the balance sheet growth of the three biggest European Social Banks between 2006 and 2008 was between 15 percent and 55 percent (Remer 2011). Other impact investors, such as Sarona, show large positive financial returns over a long period (see www.saronafunds.com). But these facts have to be communicated to a wider public.

Furthermore, social finance should remain distinct and keep a distance from conventional banks or investors and the SRI products that they offer. Social finance and impact investors have always been the innovators in socially responsible finance and banking (Weber 2006) and should keep this role in the future. The appearance of negative news about microfinance could be an indicator that more conventional institutions are entering social finance without maintaining the original ethical principles. In order to maintain the unique market position of social finance, impact investment, and microfinance, the sector should expand the range of products with a specific social impact based on positive criteria and then expand the products and services to a bigger group of clients (Weber and Remer 2011).

DISCUSSION QUESTIONS

1. What is the difference between SRI and social finance?
2. What are the products and services that social banks usually offer? Explain.
3. What are the different goals of impact finance?
4. Describe mission drift as a phenomenon in microfinance and its implications.
5. Is measuring the impact of social finance possible? Explain.

REFERENCES

ASA. "Mission, Vision and Objectives." 2011. Available at www.asa.org.bd/about_mission .html.

Aubert, Cécile, Alain de Janvry, and Elisabeth Sadoulet. 2009. "Designing Credit Agent Incentives to Prevent Mission Drift in Pro-Poor Microfinance Institutions." *Journal of Development Economics* 90:4, 153–162.

Bank for International Settlements. 2005. *International Convergence of Capital Measurement and Capital Standards ("Basel II")*. Basel: Basel Committee on Banking Supervision.

Barnett, Bryan. 2011. "The Economics of Microfinance." *Cato Journal* 31:1, 166–170.

Berryman, Mark. 2004. "Benchmarking Microfinance in Eastern Europe and Central Asia. Microfinance Information Exchange." Available at www.mfc.org.pl/doc/Publication/ ECA_Benchmarking.pdf.

Bubna, Amit, and Bhagwan Chowdhry. 2010. "Franchising Microfinance." *Review of Finance* 14:3, 451–476.

Buttle, Martin. 2007. "'I'm Not in It for the Money': Constructing and Mediating Ethical Reconnections in UK Social Banking." *Geoforum* 38:6, 1076–1088.

Chertok, Michael, Jeff Hamaoui, and Eliott Jamison. 2008. "The Funding Gap." *Stanford Social Innovation Review* 6:2, 44–51.

Copestake, James. 2007. "Mainstreaming Microfinance: Social Performance Management or Mission Drift?" *World Development* 35:10, 1721–1738.

da Silva, Amandio F. C. 2007. "Social Banking: The Need of the Hour." In Amandio F. C. da Silva, ed. *Social Banking—Perspectives and Experiences*, 3–9. Hyderabad, India: The Icfai University Press.

Edery, Yared. 2006. "Ethical Developments in Finance: Implications for Charities and Social Enterprise." *Social Enterprise Journal* 2:1, 82–100.

Emerson, Jed. 2003. "The Blended Value Proposition: Integrating Social and Financial Returns." *California Management Review* 45:4, 35–51.

Global Impact Investing Network. 2011. "Global Impact Investing Network." Available at www.thegiin.org.

Gonzalez, Adrian. 2008. *How Many Borrowers and Microfinance Institutions Exist?* Washington, DC: Microfinance Information Exchange.

Gonzales, Adrian. 2009. *Microfinance at a Glance*. Washington, DC: Microfinance Information Exchange.

Hahn, Tobias, Frank Figge, Jonatan Pinkse, and Lutz Preuss. 2010. "Trade-Offs in Corporate Sustainability: You Can't Have Your Cake and Eat It." *Business Strategy and the Environment* 19:2, 217–229.

Harji, Karim, and Tessa Hebb. 2009. *The Quest for Blended Value Returns: Investor Perspectives on Social Finance in Canada*. Ottawa: Carleton Centre for Community Innovation.

Hishigsuren, Gaamaa. 2007. "Evaluating Mission Drift in Microfinance Lessons for Programs with Social Mission." *Evaluation Review* 31:3, 203–206.

J. P. Morgan. 2010. *Impact Investments: An Emerging Asset Class*. New York: J. P. Morgan Global Research and Rockefeller Foundations.

Jones, John F. 2010. "Social Finance: Commerce and Community in Developing Countries." *International Journal of Social Economics* 37:6, 415–428.

Kaeufer, Katrin. 2010. *Banking as a Vehicle for Socio-Economic Development and Change: Case Studies of Socially Responsible and Green Banks*. Cambridge, MA: Presencing Institute.

Karmakar, K. G. 2008. *Microfinance in India*. Los Angeles and London: Sage Publications.

Kim, W. Chan, and Renee Mauborgne. 2004. "Blue Ocean Strategy." *Harvard Business Review* 82:10, 76–84.

Koellner, Thomas, Sangwon Suh, Olaf Weber, Corinne Moser, and Roland W. Scholz. 2007. "Environmental Impacts of Conventional and Sustainable Investment Funds

Compared Using Input-Output Life-Cycle Assessment." *Journal of Industrial Ecology* 11:3, 41–60.

Lingane, Alison, and Sara Olsen. 2004. "Guidelines for Social Return on Investment." *California Management Review* 46:3, 116–135.

Lu, Yuguang. 2010. "How to Break Predicament of NGOs for Microcredit in China." Available at www.hi.chinanews.com/zt/2010/0901/7960.html.

Meehan, William F. III, Derek Kilmer, and Maisie O'Flanagan. 2004. "Investing in Society." *Stanford Social Innovation Review* 2004:1, 34–43.

Mersland, Roy, and Strøm, R. Øystein. 2010. "Microfinance Mission Drift?" *World Development* 38:1, 28–36.

Microfinance data. 2011. "Mix Market." Available at http://mixmarket.org.

Microfinance in Africa. 2008. "Combining the Best Practices of Traditional and Modern Microfinance Approaches towards Poverty Eradication." Available at www.un.org/esa/africa/microfinanceinafrica.pdf.

Monitor Institute. 2009. *Investing for Social and Environmental Impact*. Cambridge, MA: Monitor Institute.

Montgomery, Heather. 2011. "Can Commercially-Oriented Microfinance Help Meet the Millennium Development Goals? Evidence from Pakistan." *World Development* 39:1, 87–109.

Moules, Jonathan. 2010. "Microfinance Sees Demand Leap." *Financial Times*, September 12, www.ft.com/intl/cms/s/0/804be24c-be97-11df-a755-00144feab49a.html#axzz1XI89dpQE.

Mulgan, Geoff, Neil Reeder, Mhairi Aylott, and Luke Bo'sher. 2011. *Social Impact Investment: The Challenge and Opportunity of Social Impact Bonds*. London: The Young Foundation.

Navajas, Sergio, and Luis Tejerina. 2006. "Microfinance in Latin America and the Caribbean: How Large Is the Market?" Washington, DC: Inter-American Development Bank.

Nicholls, Jeremy, Eilis Lawlor, Eva Neitzert, and Tim Goodspeed. 2009. *A Guide to Social Return on Investment—An Introduction*. Edinburgh: The Cabinet Office.

O'Rourke, Andrea. 2003. "The Message and Methods of Ethical Investment." *Journal of Cleaner Production* 11: 6, 683–693.

Porter, Michael E., and Mark R. Kramer. 2011. "Creating Shared Value." *Harvard Business Review* 89:1/2, 62–77.

Remer, Sven. 2011. "Social Banking at the Crossroads." In Olaf Weber and Sven Remer, eds., *Social Banks and the Future of Sustainable Finance*, 136–195. London: Routledge.

Rhyne, Elisabeth. 2009. *Microfinance for Bankers and Investors*. New York: McGraw Hill.

Sandberg, Joakim, Carmen Juravle, Ted Hedesström, and Ian Hamilton. 2009. "The Heterogeneity of Socially Responsible Investment." *Journal of Business Ethics* 87:4, 519–533.

Schaltegger, Stefan, and Roger L. Burritt. 2010. "Sustainability Accounting for Companies: Catchphrase or Decision Support for Business Leaders?" *Journal of World Business* 45:4, 375–384.

SocialFinance.ca. 2010. "What Is Social Finance?" Available at http://socialfinance.ca/what-is-social-finance.

Song, Wei, Xuna Xue, and Luya Zhong. 2010. "Microfinance Performance in China's Rural Areas: A Perspective of Regional Differences." *2010 International Conference on Financial Theory and Engineering*, 1–7.

TerraChoice Environmental Marketing Inc. 2007. *The Six Sins of Greenwashing*. Ottawa, ON: TerraChoice Environmental Marketing Inc.

The World Bank Staff. 2006. *Microfinance in South Asia: Toward Financial Inclusion for the Poor*. Washington, DC: The World Bank.

VanCity. 2010. "About Us." Available at www.vancity.com/AboutUs/.

Weber, Olaf. 2005. "Sustainability Benchmarking of European Banks and Financial Service Organizations." *Corporate Social Responsibility and Environmental Management* 12:2, 73–87.

Weber, Olaf. 2006. "Investment and Environmental Management: The Interaction between Environmentally Responsible Investment and Environmental Management Practices." *International Journal of Sustainable Development* 9:4, 336–354.

Weber, Olaf. 2010. "Microfinance." *Management Ethics*, Summer, 4–6.

Weber, Olaf, and Sven Remer. 2011. "Social Banks and the Future of Sustainable Finance." *The World Financial Review*, May–June, 4–7.

Weber, Olaf, Marco Mansfeld, and Eric Schirrmann. 2011. "The Financial Performance of RI Funds after 2000." In Wim Vandekerckhove, Jos Leys, Kristian Alm, Bert Scholtens, Silvana Signori, and Henry Schaefer, eds. *Responsible Investment in Times of Turmoil*, 75–91. Berlin: Springer.

Yunus, Muhammad, and Karl Weber. 2007. *Creating a World without Poverty*. New York: Public Affairs.

Zhou, Jianghua, Xiaoqiang Xing, and Yunhuan Tong. 2009. *Serving the Low-Income Group with Microfinance in China*. PICMET 2009 Proceedings. Portland, Oregon.

ABOUT THE AUTHORS

Olaf Weber holds the Export Development Canada Chair in Environmental Finance and is an associate professor at the School for Environment, Enterprise and Development (SEED) at the Faculty for Environment, University of Waterloo, Canada. His research and teaching interests are environment and business, and environmental and sustainable finance with a focus on sustainable credit risk management, social finance, SRI, social banking, and the link between sustainability and financial performance of enterprises. He is a past president of the board of the Institute for Social Banking and was a member of the board of Alternative Bank, a Swiss-based social bank. He has a master's degree in psychology and a Ph.D. in computer science.

Yayun Duan, a third-year international student, studies Environment and Business at the University of Waterloo. As a 2 + 2 student, she studied two years at the Nanjing University of Finance and Economics in China, and came to Canada in 2010 to finish her undergraduate studies. In the summer of 2010, she worked as a microfinance officer at the Postal Saving Bank of China. During this time, she surveyed small-size enterprises, self-employed businessmen and farmers on a weekly basis, and developed strong research interests in microfinance. In 2011, she began assisting Professor Weber with a microfinance project and is responsible for tracking the performance of microfinance institutions and writing reports.

CHAPTER 10

Managerial Compensation

KOSE JOHN
Charles William Gerstenberg Professor of Banking
and Finance, New York University

SAMIR SAADI
Ph.D Candidate, Queen's University

INTRODUCTION

The level and structure of managerial compensation has long been a subject of intense debate. In 2009, and after labeling the sizeable bonus awarded to chief executive officers (CEOs) of companies seeking government bailout as "shameful," President Obama said that such behavior is "exactly the kind of disregard for the costs and consequences of their actions that brought about this crisis—a culture of narrow self-interest and short-term gain at the expense of everything else." (Obama 2009, p. 1) Several commentators and academics have expressed concerns over the rising CEO pay level, which cannot be explained by the flat pattern in the firms' performance and economic conditions over the same period. This leads to higher income inequality and lower shareholders' value. The high level of CEO pay is widely perceived as unethical and as a form of rent extraction by powerful managers. On the other hand, proponents of higher CEO compensation argue that if rising CEO pay is tied to improving corporate performance, workers and shareholders might be better off if CEOs were paid more, and hence, the observed level of CEO pay is the result of optimal contracting.

A limited, though growing, number of studies has also examined the relationship between managerial compensation and corporate social performance. Corporate social responsibility (CSR) is the firm's commitment to sustainable economic development by finding ways to strike a balance among its economic, legal, ethical, environmental, and social responsibilities. Several studies document that increasing societal and stakeholder pressure led to a growing interest by corporate boards in aligning firm objectives not only with its shareholders' interests, but also with the interests of others diverse stakeholders groups. One way for the board to induce executives to behave in a socially responsible manner is to tie executive compensation partly to a CSR metric.

This chapter reviews the main issues related to managerial compensation and, in particular, whether the observed executive compensation is justifiable, and whether executive compensation schemes induce unethical behavior by executives. Because the CEO compensation literature is large, this chapter mainly emphasizes the empirical work of U.S. studies. Furthermore, the primarily focus is on long-term compensation packages, including stock options, as they have represented a major portion of CEO compensation since the late 1990s and have led to sizeable levels of CEO compensation that attracted much attention from academics, media, and regulators (Murphy 1999; Elson 2003; Bebchuk and Grinstein 2005; Frydman and Jenter 2010).

The rest of the chapter is organized as follows. The next section discusses the structure and level of executive compensation. The third section examines the determinants of stock options compensation. The fourth section focuses on the association between CEO pay and firm performance. The fifth section reviews the literature on stock options manipulations. The sixth section discusses the relationship between managerial compensation and CSR. The final section concludes the chapter.

STRUCTURE AND LEVEL OF EXECUTIVE COMPENSATION

Although substantial differences in terms of pay practices exist across firms, executive compensation packages consist typically of five main components:

1. *Salary.* Salary represents a base fixed salary that is set by the compensation committee after examining base salary at a group of preselected peers within the same industry.
2. *Annual bonus.* The bonus is set as a function of the firm's performance as measured in terms of a particular performance metric.
3. *Restricted stock options grants.* Stock options give executives the right to buy the firm's shares at a prespecified price (i.e., the "strike" or "exercise" price), which is typically set as the stock's closing price on the grant date. Executives can exercise their stock options only after the options vest.
4. *Restricted stock grants.* These grants give the executive the right to receive the firm's common stock upon satisfying prespecified vesting requirements.
5. *Long-term incentive plans.* These are incentive plans that reward executives based on long-term (three to five years) key performance factors.

Besides these five major components, the executive compensation package can include other important incentives in the form of pensions, severance payments, and perquisites.

The financial economics literature widely investigates the level and structure of executive compensation. The dramatic change in the level and composition of CEO pay over the last three decades has attracted much attention from academics and the media. With respect to the level of CEO compensation, several studies document that CEO total pay exhibits an exponential increase starting from early 1990s (Murphy 1999; Bebchuk and Grinstein 2005; Frydman and Jenter 2010; Conyon, Fernandes, Ferreira, Matos, and Murphy 2011). For instance, Frydman and Jenter examine total executive compensation in large U.S. firms from 1936 to 2005, as measured by the sum of annual base salary, current bonuses, and payouts from long-term incentives plans. They report a J-shaped pattern in executive compensation with total pay experiencing low annual growth of 0.8 percent from the early 1950s to the mid-1970s, and high annual growth of about 10 percent afterward. Frydman and Jenter report similar J-patterns for the two next highest-paid executives, but the average pay gap between the annual compensation of the non-CEO executives and CEO pay has widened since the mid-1990s.

To put things in perspective, the median (average) CEO pay in the S&P 500 firms was around $2.3 ($3.0) million in 1992 and hit a peak of $7.2 ($12.0) million in 2001, which equates to a 213 percent (300 percent) increase in 10 years. After 2001, however, growth in CEO pay remained relatively flat with a median (average) ranging between $6.0 ($8.0) million and $7.0 ($9.1) million. The median (average) CEO pay in S&P 500 firms over the period 2002 to 2008 was about $6.5 ($8.8) million.

The substantial increase in CEO compensation in the last three decades has been partly attributed to changes in the structure of executive compensation, and in particular the surge in stock options. This pattern has been widely documented by Frydman and Jenter (2010), Conyon et al. (2011), and others. According to Frydman and Jenter, base salaries in 1992 accounted for 42 percent of the $2.3 million median total CEO pay in large U.S. firms, while stock options and restricted stocks accounted for 28 percent and 20 percent, respectively. By 2001, the share of base salary and restricted stock in total CEO compensation fell to 17 percent and 7 percent, respectively. Yet stock options became the dominant pay component, accounting for about 50 percent of the CEO pay compensation package. After the 2000 bubble burst, the use of stock options started to lose its appeal and was gradually replaced by restricted stock. Restricted stock dominated stock options in 2006 and became the most important element in the CEO compensation package in 2008, accounting for 32 percent, while stock options and base salary accounted for 25 percent and 17 percent, respectively.

Although the level of CEO pay has increased over time for all firm sizes, it is the largest firms that experienced the most dramatic rise in CEO pay (Frydman and Jenter 2010). In fact, median CEO pay for MidCap 400 firms was $1.4 million in 1994 and reached $3 million in 2008 (i.e., a growth of 114 percent). The growth is even weaker for SmallCap 600 firms, where median CEO pay was $0.9 million in 1994 and grew to $1.4 million in 2008 (i.e., a growth of 56 percent). Although much of the surge in executive compensation is skewed towards large firms, the level of CEO pay and its steep upward trend (which started in the early 1990s) have attracted much criticism from popular media and some academics.

Most of the criticism of managerial compensation focuses on the following issues. First, current levels of executive compensation are unjustifiable and unfair (i.e., too high). Second, executive compensation does not reflect the firm's performance (weak pay-performance sensitivity). Third, CEOs have too much power and set high compensation for themselves (i.e., weak corporate governance and lack of regulation that curb CEO excess power and compensation). Fourth, executive pay structure is too dependent on stock options and other equity-based incentives, which tends to reward performance that is market driven, and could also induce CEOs to exhibit excessive risk-taking behavior and engage in earnings management and/or stock option manipulations.

According to *Business Week* annual executive surveys, CEO compensation in the United States increased from 42 times that of an average worker in 1980 to 107 times in 1990 and then to 344 times that of an average worker in 2007. At its highest level in 2000, CEO pay amounted to 525 times that of an average worker (Sahadi 2007). In a recent study, Desai, Palmer, George, and Brief (2011) show that increasing pay disparity between executives and employees within a firm leads to top managerial perceptions of possessing greater power, which in turn results in poor treatment of employees.

The executive compensation literature is inconclusive on whether the observed level and trend in CEO pay is justifiable. One important stream of studies holds the view that the high levels of executive compensation results from excessive managerial power that allows CEOs to set their own pay and engage in rent extraction (e.g., Bebchuk and Fried 2004). In contrast, another line of research views the surge in executive compensation as the result of optimal/efficient contracting (e.g. Core, Guay, and Thomas 2005; Murphy and Zábojník 2007).

Because the high levels of CEO pay are originally due to the drastic increase in the popularity of stock option grants starting from early 1990s, the next section discusses the determinants of stock option grants.

DETERMINANTS OF STOCK OPTION COMPENSATION

The managerial compensation literature identifies several determinants of stock option compensation. This section discusses the main determinants, and in particular, growth opportunities, firm size, risk, capital structure, managerial horizon, CEO tenure, ownership structure, and liquidity constraints.

Growth Opportunities

Assuming information asymmetry between management and shareholders, CEO monitoring in high growth firms is a difficult task. Indeed, managers are likely to hold inside information about the value of growth opportunities (Smith and Watts 1992). As a result, firms experiencing high growth opportunities should offer more stock-based compensation to their CEOs. Nonetheless, empirical evidence is mixed. While Lewellen, Loderer, and Martin (1987), Matsunaga (1995), Mehran (1995), and Ittner, Lambert, and Larcker (2003) find a positive relationship between growth opportunities and the level of CEO stock-based compensation, Yermack (1995) finds a negative relationship.

Firm Size

Jensen and Meckling (1976) contend that the difficulty of monitoring management's actions increases with firm size. Consequently, the need for incentive plans is more pronounced in large firms. The empirical studies are inconclusive, however. While Smith and Watts (1992) and Core and Guay (1999) find a positive relationship between stock option awards and firm size, Murphy (1985) reports a negative relationship. Others, including Matsunaga (1995) and Mehran (1995), fail to find any significant relationship between stock option awards and firm size.

Risk

Agency theory predicts the existence of a trade-off between risk and incentives. The sensitivity of compensation to performance should fall when risk rises (Holmstrom and Milgrom 1987). The contingence of compensation on firm performance transfers risk from well-diversified shareholders to executives who are not diversified. Therefore, in high-risk firms, contingent compensation could cause a decrease in shareholder value (Dee, Lulseged, and Nowlin 2005). Hence, a negative relationship between risk and incentives should be expected. Yet the empirical results are inconclusive. Lambert and Larcker (1987), Jin (2002), and Dee et al. (2005) document evidence in accordance with the hypothesis of a trade-off between risk and incentives, while Yermack (1995) fails to find a significant relationship.

Capital Structure

Jensen and Meckling (1976) show that debt helps mitigate agency conflicts between stockholders and managers. Easterbrook (1984) adds that the use of debt enhances managers' monitoring, which in turn reduces management discretion. However, debt could generate a conflict between shareholders and bondholders. When executives are granted some stock-based incentives, they should have the same objectives as the firm's shareholders and thus lean toward investing in riskier projects to the detriment of bondholders. This hypothesis is supported by DeFusco, Johnson, and Zorn (1990), who report an increase in stock return volatility and a negative (positive) stock market (bond market) reaction following stock option plan adoption. John and John (1993) develop a model in which pay-performance sensitivity should decrease as leverage increases in an attempt to reduce agency costs of debt. They argue that, in order to lessen agency conflicts between bondholders and shareholders, highly leveraged firms are less likely to relate incentives to a firm's stock price.

The above discussion suggests that the higher the level of debt in the capital structure, the lower should be the likelihood of using stock-based incentives. At the empirical level, however, the nature of the relationship between financial leverage and managerial compensation is still a controversial issue. For instance, while Lewellen et al. (1987) report a positive association between stock option awards and financial leverage, Matsunaga (1995), Mehran (1995), and Yermack (1995) find no relationship between stock option awards and financial leverage. Yet Bryan, Hwang, and Lilien (2000) and Ittner et al. (2003) report a decrease in stock option-based awards when financial leverage increases.

Managerial Horizon

Smith and Watts (1992) propose the so-called horizon problem, which hypothesizes that as CEOs get closer to retirement, they are likely to reject positive net present value (NPV) projects as well as valuable research and development (R&D) investments. Accordingly, when executive compensation is based on accounting performance measures, current CEOs are penalized and their successors are rewarded.

Since investors capitalize expected returns, the horizon problem can be offset by offering more stock-based awards to older CEOs. Empirical evidence is mixed, however. Yermack (1995) finds no significant association between the level of stock option awards and CEO age. By contrast, Lewellen et al. (1987) find a positive and significant relationship. According to Ryan and Wiggins (2001), the horizon problem is not limited to CEOs nearing retirement because it also applies to young CEOs who strive to build a sound reputation in order to boost their value in the labor market. Because both young and old CEOs attempt to fulfill their goals in the shortest possible time horizon, Ryan and Wiggins maintain that firms should use more stock-based compensation for the oldest, as well as the youngest, executives. Thus, they suggest a convex relationship between CEO age and equity-based pay (stock options and restricted stock). Nevertheless, their empirical results do not support their prediction.

CEO Tenure

The CEO accumulates more stock in the firm as his tenure increases. Thus, his interests become more aligned with those of shareholders, resulting in less need for incentives. In line with this claim, Ryan and Wiggins (2001) find a negative relationship between CEO tenure and stock option awards.

Ownership Structure

The modern finance literature recognizes the link between a firm's ownership structure and its executive compensation package. In a corporate governance system such as those of the United States and the United Kingdom where ownership is highly dispersed, managers tend to pursue their own goals (i.e., managerial entrenchment), which may lead to several distortions including excessive CEO pay and lack of a strong pay-for-performance sensitivity (Murphy 1999). In corporate governance systems such as those in Canada, the high level of ownership concentration serves as a monitoring device leading to a more efficient CEO compensation mechanism and can be viewed as a substitute to giving incentives to managers. Accordingly, firms will compensate their executives less with stock options in the presence of blockholders.

At the empirical level, Mehran (1995) finds a negative relationship between equity-based compensation and blockholder ownership. Ryan and Wiggins (2001) find that outside block ownership is negatively related to stock option compensation. In a subsample of new economy firms, Ittner et al. (2003) conclude that block ownership percentage is negatively associated with equity grants to CEOs and vice presidents. Bebchuk and Fried (2004), however, argue that the managerial power approach to executive compensation predicts that in the presence of a blockholder, firms will design executive compensation to serve the interests of shareholders. Hence, pay will be more sensitive to firm performance.

The classic agency problem is due to the separation of management and ownership. The seminal work by Berle and Means (1932) and Jensen and Meckling

(1976) on the agency problem have led several theorists to suggest that CEO ownership in the company should be taken into account when designing compensation contracts. In particular, the larger the CEO's personal stock ownership, the lower is the need for stock option awards as an incentive device. However, the empirical results are inconclusive. For instance, while Mehran (1995) and Bryan et al. (2000) report a negative association between executive ownership and incentives provided by stock options awards, Matsunaga (1995) and Yermack (1995) find no relationship.

Liquidity Constraints

Contrary to salary and bonuses, stock options do not require the current outlay of cash by the firm, allowing firms to preserve liquidity. Therefore, stock option compensation should be more prevalent in firms facing scarcity of cash. Several empirical studies, such as Yermack (1995) and Bryan et al. (2000), support this view. Matsunaga (1995), however, fails to find any association between liquidity and stock-based compensation. In a more recent study, Ittner et al. (2003) find results contrary to expectations.

IS CEO COMPENSATION JUSTIFIABLE?

CEO compensation is one of the important and often debated components of the corporate governance mechanism that a firm uses to align the conflicting interests of agents and principals (Core, Guay, and Larcker 2003). A firm has to compensate its top executives in various ways to motivate them to work for the benefits of shareholders. The general consensus in the literature is that performance-based compensation for top managers leads to higher market values of a firm (Mehran 1995; Carpenter and Sanders 2002) and CEO pay has a strong relationship with firm performance (Yermack 1996). Disagreement exists about how sensitive CEO compensation is to performance. In an earlier study, Jensen and Murphy (1990) show that overall pay-performance sensitivity is quite low to motivate CEOs effectively. Some of the more recent studies (Boschen and Smith 1995; Hall and Liebman 1998), however, suggest that Jensen and Murphy may have underestimated the average pay-performance sensitivity.

Hall and Liebman (1998) further report that pay-performance sensitivity have increased in U.S. firms over the last 20 years. The driving force underlying this change is the increasing use of equity-based grants, such as stock options and restricted stock awards. Murphy (1999) observes that pay-performance sensitivities differ substantially across firms. Recent studies also document mixed results while reporting the impact of various factors (such as risk, investment opportunities, CEO ownership, board independence, and liquidity constraint) on CEO pay and pay-performance sensitivity. For example, Yermack (1996); Conyon and Peck (1998); and Core, Holthausen, and Larker (1999) examine the effect of board structure. Mehran (1995), Yermack (1995), Bryan et al. (2000), and Ittner et al. (2003) study the effect of ownership while Bizjak, Brickley, and Coles (1993), Smith and Watts (1992), Yermack (1995), and Bryan et al. (2000) investigate the effect of investment opportunities. Yermack (1995), Aggarwal and Samwick (1999), Bryan et al. (2000), Prendergast (2002), and Dee et al. (2005) consider the effect of risk. Others, including industry observers, practitioners, and academicians have questioned the overall CEO compensation level and argue that CEOs receive excessive pay.

One possible explanation for CEO excess pay and inconsistent results with respect to the impact of various factors on CEO pay and pay-performance sensitivity is "flaws in the internal process by which top management compensation is determined by company boards and their compensation committees" (Veliyath 1999, p. 125). In other words, board structure is likely to play a vital role in determining the CEO pay level and can significantly affect the pay-performance sensitivity.

The board of directors is composed of both outside and inside directors. Fama (1980) and Fama and Jensen (1983) suggest that outside directors are in competition and therefore are incited to develop a good reputation in monitoring management. Pfeffer (1981) contends that inside directors are loyal to the CEO because of the power the CEO has over them. Accordingly, most studies consider outside directors as independent (unrelated), while inside directors as co-opted. Nevertheless, despite the belief that outside directors are efficient monitors, the results obtained at the empirical level are mixed. In a sample of 193 firms, Boyd (1994) finds that the ratio of insiders is negatively related to CEO compensation, while Grinstein and Hribar (2004) conclude that the ratio of insiders is not a significant determinant of bonuses perceived by CEOs in mergers and acquisitions (M&As).

In a sample of 153 manufacturing firms over the period 1979 to 1980, Mehran (1995) finds that the use of equity-based compensation is greater in firms with more outside directors on the board. Newman and Mozes (1999, p. 50) state that " . . . the relation between CEO compensation and firm performance is more favorable toward CEOs of insider-influenced firms than it is to CEOs of outsider influenced firms." The mixed results identified in prior work may be explained by the fact that outside board members may not be independent (Main, O'Reilly, and Wade 1995), or that they do not have the time, expertise, or motivation to monitor managers (Gilson and Kraakman 1991). In most cases, the CEO may influence the selection of board members. In fact, Shivdasani and Yermack (1999) show that the CEO has a direct influence in the director nomination process in more than 50 percent of the firms sampled.

In many firms, the CEO is also the chairman of the board. For instance, Shivdasani and Yermack (1999) find dissociation between the two functions in only 16 percent of their sample. The CEO who assumes the position of board chair may use his power to select the board members, control the agenda, filter information available to the board, and manage the directors. Hence, the expectation is that board control will be lower in the case of CEO duality. In accordance with this argument, Jensen (1993) suggests separating the chairman and CEO position. Several papers study the impact of CEO/chair duality on the level of compensation received. The results are mixed. Mallette, Middlemist, and Hopkins (1995), Sridharan (1996), Core et al. (1999), and Conyon and Murphy (2000) find that CEO compensation is higher when the CEO is also the board chairman. However, Angbazo and Naraynan (1997) as well as Cordeiro and Veliyath (2003) fail to find any significant relationship, and Cheung, Stouraitis, and Wong (2005) find a negative relationship between CEO/chair duality and CEO compensation.

Jensen (1993) suggests that when the board of directors is composed of more than seven or eight members, the board will be less efficient and the CEO can more easily control the members. In this case, the CEO may influence his compensation.

The empirical evidence on the effect of board size on management compensation is inconclusive. Holthausen and Larcker (1993) and Core et al. (1999) find a positive relationship between board size and CEO compensation. In particular, Core et al. find that total CEO compensation increases by $30,601 when adding a member to the board. On the other hand, in a sample of commercial banks during the year 1989, Angbazo and Narayanan (1997) fail to find any significant relationship between board size and CEO compensation. Contrary to prediction, Grinstein and Hribar (2004) obtain a negative and significant relationship between board size and bonuses received by CEOs in M&As. The studies investigating the effect of board size on the pay performance sensitivity are scarce. Yermack (1996), examining a sample of 452 U.S. firms over the period 1984 to 1991, concludes that sensitivity decreases as board size increases.

On the other side of the executive compensation debate, there is a growing stream of studies arguing that the observed CEO pay-for-performance sensitivity is actually the outcome of an efficient labor market (e.g. Himmelberg and Hubbard 2000; Murphy and Zábojník 2004, 2007; Core, Guay, and Thomas 2005; Rajgopal et al. 2006; and Gabaix and Landier 2008b). Gabaix and Landier (2008a) provide a comprehensive survey of recent theories on optimal contracting. For instance, Gabaix and Landier (2008b) develop a superstar model of the market for executives that attributes the recent rise in CEO pay to the considerable increase in firm size. Empirically, they show that the six-fold rise in CEO pay between 1980 and 2003 can be fully explained by the six-fold increase in market capitalization of large companies during that period. Frydman and Jenter (2010) argue, however, that Gabaix and Landier's explanation does not hold over the period 1940–1970.

STOCK OPTION GRANT MANIPULATION

Yermack (1997) was the first to point out the issue of stock-option manipulation by opportunistic managers, showing that stock prices exhibit positive abnormal returns immediately after a CEO option grant date. Yermack interprets his findings as CEOs opportunistically timing stock-option grants to benefit from positive corporate news (e.g., strong earnings) that would drive up companies' stock prices, and consequently the value of their stock options. Consistent with Yermack's findings, Aboody, and Kasznik (2000) find positive abnormal returns after a grant date of scheduled CEOs' stock option grants. Chauvin and Shenoy (2001) document negative abnormal returns before CEOs' option grant dates. Both studies interpret these results as evidence that CEOs opportunistically time information disclosure around option grants, as opposed to Yermack's timing of option grants argument. More precisely, CEOs would delay any grant just after the disclosure of bad news and/or accelerate a grant shortly after the release of good news.

Unlike the timing of information disclosure, the timing of option grants relative to future market returns ascribes to opportunistic CEOs an outstanding ability to forecast future market movements. Although some studies, such as Lakonishok and Lee (2001) and Narayanan and Seyhun (2008), provide evidence consistent with the view that some CEOs are capable of forecasting future market movements, the large and increasing number of companies currently under investigation by the Securities and Exchange Commission (SEC) for possible manipulation of their option grants casts some doubt on this view. In fact, Lie (2005) provides a new explanation that requires much lower skills than market forecasting. Lie reports negative abnormal returns before a grant's date and positive abnormal returns afterward. While the author documents the same returns pattern for both unscheduled and scheduled option grants, he finds significantly stronger (negative and positive) returns for the former. Lie interprets these results as evidence that CEOs influence the compensation committee to time option grants retroactively by choosing a date when their share price was low, a practice known as *backdating*. The results of Lie do not, however, rule out the timing of information disclosure and the timing of option grant dates explanations. In other words, Lie's findings do not tell to what extent backdating explains the abnormal returns pattern around stock options grants.

Heron and Lie (2007) investigate this issue and find that backdating explains most of the abnormal returns pattern around stock option grant dates. Heron and Lie (2009) report that 23.0 percent of unscheduled CEOs stock options granted before the two-day filing requirement that took effect on August 29, 2002, were backdated or otherwise manipulated and 10.0 percent afterward.

Another stream of studies looks at the underlying causes of the backdating practice in the United States and shows that weaker corporate governance encourages opportunistic and powerful CEOs to engage in such rent extraction behavior. Bebchuk, Grinstein, and Peyer (2010), for instance, find that the documented practice of CEOs' stock option grant manipulation is also prevalent among outside directors' option grants, particularly within firms with weak corporate governance. Collins, Gong, and Li (2009) show that backdating firms are more likely to have boards dominated by dependent directors and outside directors that have some sort of affiliation with the firms. This may cause a conflict of interest (i.e., gray directors), a higher proportion of outside directors appointed by the incumbent CEO, and higher incidence of the CEO also serving as the chairman of the board.

In a recent study, Bizjak, Lemmon, and Whitby (2009) show that interlocking boards play a major role in the spreading of the backdating practice across U.S. public firms. However, the authors find weak evidence that backdating is systematically related to weak corporate governance. Heron and Lie (2007, 2009) document evidence of backdating even after the endorsement of the Sarbanes-Oxley Act (SOX), which emerged to fix several critical deficiencies in U.S. corporate governance practices, including the stock option grant manipulation.

Lie's (2005) groundbreaking study received very little attention from the media and regulators even after he notified the SEC about the backdating practice (Ritter 2008). A front-page article in the *Wall Street Journal* on March 18, 2006, put option backdating in the spotlight, triggering large-scale public scrutiny of hundreds of public firms (Forelle and Bandler 2006). As of June 14, 2007, the research firm Glass-Lewis & Co. reported that at least 271 publicly-traded companies either had announced an internal investigation or had been the subject of SEC and/or Department of Justice inquiries, and more than 135 companies were the target of shareholders' lawsuits. By end of 2007, at least 90 executives and directors at more than 50 companies had been fired, demoted, or resigned. As of November 2010, a total of 12 corporate executives received criminal sentences, five of them with prison terms, and the remaining executives were sentenced to probation (Lattman 2010).

The option backdating scandal has even created a fugitive, Jacob Alexander, the former CEO of Comverse Technology Inc, who fled to Namibia to avoid prosecution over stock option backdating. On November 23, 2010, still fighting extradition to the United States, Alexander has agreed to pay nearly $48 million to settle a civil action by the U.S. Attorney's office (Kaplan 2010). The funds will be used to settle a $225 million shareholder lawsuit against the company and several former officers and directors. Alexander has also agreed to pay a $6 million civil penalty to the SEC. So far, the largest settlement involves William McGuire, the former chairman and CEO of UnitedHealth Group Inc, who agreed to pay $468 million in civil fines and restitution to the company.

MANAGERIAL COMPENSATION AND CSR

Corporate social responsibility (CSR) is the firm's commitment to contribute to sustainable economic development by finding ways to strike a balance among its economic, legal, ethical, environmental, and social responsibilities (Carroll 1979, 1999; Hill, Ainscough, Shank, and Manullang 2007). Several studies document that the increasing societal and stakeholder pressure led to a growing interest by corporate boards in aligning the firm's objectives, not only with its shareholder interests, but also with the interests of other diverse stakeholder groups (Craighead, Magnan, and Thorne 2004). One way for the board to induce executives to behave in a socially responsible manner is to tie executive compensation partly to a CSR metric. A limited, though growing, number of studies examines the relationship between managerial compensation and corporate social performance (CSP). This is an important issue to address given the ethical concerns and criticisms toward the widening disparity between executive pay and that of an average worker, and also between the CEO's pay and employees' pay within the same firm.

McGuire, Dow, and Argheyd (2003) use a sample of 375 large U.S. firms to examine the relationship between CEO compensation and CSP measured through the ratings of Kinder, Lindenberg, and Domini. The authors find that high levels of salary and long-term incentives are related to poor social performance, but fail to report a statistically significant association between incentives and strong CSP.

Using a sample of 77 Canadian firms, Mahoney and Thorne (2006) investigate the relationship between executive compensation and CSR obtained from the Canadian Social Investment Database. The authors report a positive association between base salary and CSR weaknesses, between annual bonus and CSR strengths, and between stock options and the total CSR rating, as well as CSR strengths. Mahoney and Thorne's findings suggest that the structure of managerial compensation matters to CSP. Thorne, Mahoney, and Bobek (2010) show that the difference in firm size between U.S. and Canadian firms is the main reason behind the different reported relationship between managerial compensation and CSR in the United States (McGuire et al. 2003) and Canada (Mahoney and Thorne 2006). Thorne et al. also find a positive relationship between long-term incentives (stock options) and CSR.

SUMMARY AND CONCLUSIONS

Managerial compensation is an important and often debated component of the corporate governance mechanism. This chapter focuses on the main issues that have spurred intense debate and attracted much attention in the popular press, academia, and from regulatory agencies. In particular, the review discusses whether the high levels of executive compensation are justifiable, and whether executive compensation schemes induce unethical behavior by executives. The literature is inconclusive as to whether the observed level of managerial compensation is justifiable. Ample evidence also shows that executives manipulate their pay such as in the option backdating scandal. A limited, but growing, literature linking managerial compensation to CSR is examined. The evidence suggests that the structure of managerial compensation matters to CSP.

DISCUSSION QUESTIONS

1. What component of the executive compensation package spurred the stiff criticism of CEO pay?
2. Are CEOs in the United States paid higher than their counterparts in other developed countries?
3. Are the levels of CEO compensation justifiable? Explain.
4. What is the source of the documented executive compensation manipulation schemes?

REFERENCES

Aboody, David, and Ron Kasznik. 2000. "CEO Stock Options Awards and the Timing of Corporate Voluntary Disclosures." *Journal of Accounting and Economics* 29:1, 73–100.

Aggarwal, Rajesh K., and Andrew A. Samwick. 1999. "The Other Side of the Trade-off: The Impact of Risk on Executive Compensation." *Journal of Political Economy* 107:1, 65–105.

Angbazo, Lazarus, and Ranga Narayanan. 1997. "Top Management Compensation and the Structure of the Board of Directors in Commercial Banks." *European Finance Review* 1:3, 239–259.

Bebchuk, Lucian A., and Jesse M. Fried. 2004. *Pay without Performance: The Unfulfilled Promise of Executive Compensation.* Cambridge and London: Harvard University Press.

Bebchuk, Lucian A., and Yaniv Grinstein. 2005. "The Growth of Executive Pay." *Oxford Review of Economic Policy* 21:2, 283–303.

Bebchuk, Lucian A., Yaniv Grinstein, and Urs Peyer. 2010. "Lucky CEO and Lucky Directors." *Journal of Finance* 65:6, 2363–2401.

Berle, Adolf, and Gardiner Means. 1932. *The Modern Corporation and Private Property.* New York: Macmillan.

Bizjak, John, James A. Brickley, and Jeffrey L. Coles. 1993. "Stock-Based Incentive Compensation and Investment Behavior." *Journal of Accounting and Economics* 16:1–3, 349–372.

Bizjak, John, Mike Lemmon, and Ryan Whitby. 2009. "Option Backdating and Board Interlocks." *Review of Financial Studies* 22:11, 4821–4847.

Boschen, John F., and Kimberly J. Smith. 1995. "You Can Pay Me Now and You Can Pay Me Later: The Dynamic Response of Executive Compensation to Firm Performance." *Journal of Business* 68:4, 577–608.

Boyd, Brian K. 1994. "Board Control and CEO Compensation." *Strategic Management Journal* 15:5, 335–344.

Bryan, Stephen, LeeSeok Hwang, and Steven Lilien. 2000. "CEO Stock–Based Compensation: An Empirical Analysis of Incentive–Intensity, Relative Mix, and Economic Determinants." *Journal of Business* 73:4, 661–693.

Carpenter, Mason A., and Gerard Sanders. 2002. "Top Management Team Compensation: The Missing Link between CEO Pay and Firm Performance?" *Strategic Management Journal* 23:4, 367–375.

Carroll, Archie B. 1979. "A Three–Dimensional Conceptual Model of Corporate Performance." *Academy of Management Review* 4:4, 497–505.

Carroll, Archie B. 1999. "Corporate Social Responsibility: Evolution of a Definitional Construct." *Business and Society* 38:3, 268–295.

Chauvin, Keith W., and Catherine Shenoy. 2001. "Stock Price Decreases Prior to Executive Stock Option Grants." *Journal of Corporate Finance* 7:1, 53–76.

Cheung, Yan-Leung, Aris Stouraitis, and Anita W. S. Wong. 2005. "Ownership Concentration and Executive Compensation in Closely Held Firms: Evidence from Hong Kong." *Journal of Empirical Finance* 12:4, 511–532.

Collins, Daniel W., Guojin Gong, and Haidan Li. 2009. "Corporate Governance and the Backdating of Executive Stock Options." *Contemporary Accounting Research* 26:2, 403–445.

Conyon, Martin J., Nuno Fernandes, Miguel A. Ferreira, Pedro Matos, and Kevin J. Murphy. 2011. "The Executive Compensation Controversy: A Transatlantic Analysis." Working Paper, University of Southern California.

Conyon, Martin J., and Kevin J. Murphy. 2000. "The Prince and the Pauper? CEO Pay in the US and UK." *Economic Journal* 110:2, 640–671.

Conyon, Martin J., and Simon I. Peck. 1998. "Board Control, Remuneration Committees, and Top Management Compensation." *Academy of Management Journal* 41:2, 640–671.

Cordeiro, James J., and Rajam Veliyath. 2003. "Beyond Pay for Performance: A Panel Study of the Determinants of CEO Compensation." *American Business Review* 21:1, 56–66.

Core, John E., and Wayne R. Guay. 1999. "The Use of Equity Grants to Manage Optimal Equity Incentive Levels." Working Paper, University of Pennsylvania Wharton School.

Core, John E., Wayne R. Guay, and David F. Larcker. 2003. "Executive Equity Compensation and Incentives: A Survey." *Federal Reserve Economic Policy Review* 9:1, 27–50.

Core, John E., Wayne R. Guay, and Randall S. Thomas. 2005. "Is CEO Compensation Inefficient Pay Without Performance?" *University of Michigan Law Review* 103:6, 1141–1185.

Core, John E., Robert W. Holthausen, and David F. Larcker. 1999. "Corporate Governance, Chief Executive Officer Compensation, and Firm Performance." *Journal of Financial Economics* 51:3, 371–406.

Craighead, Jane, Michel Magnan, and Linda Thorne. 2004. "The Impact of Mandated Disclosure on Performance-based CEO Compensation." *Contemporary Accounting Review* 21:2, 369–397.

Dee, Carol Callaway, Ayalew Lulseged, and Tanya S. Nowlin. 2005. "Executive Compensation and Risk: The Case of Internet Firms." *Journal of Corporate Finance* 12:1, 80–96.

DeFusco, Richard A., Robert R. Johnson, and Thomas S. Zorn. 1990. "The Effect of Executive Stock Option Plans on Stockholders and Bondholders." *Journal of Finance* 45:2, 617–627.

Desai, Sreedhari D., Donald Palmer, Jennifer George, and Arthur Brief. 2011. "When Executives Rake in Millions: The Callous Treatment of Lower Level Employees." Working Paper, Harvard University.

Easterbrook, Frank H. 1984. "Two Agency-Cost Explanations of Dividends." *American Economic Review* 74:4, 650–659.

Elson, Charles. 2003. "What's Wrong with Executive Compensation?" *Harvard Business Review* 81:1, 68–77.

Fama, Eugene F. 1980. "Agency Problems and the Theory of the Firm." *Journal of Political Economy* 88:21, 288–307.

Fama, Eugene F., and Michael C. Jensen. 1983. "Separation of Ownership and Control." *Journal of Law and Economics* 26:2, 301–325.

Forelle, Charles, and James Bandler. 2006. "The Perfect Payday." *Wall Street Journal*, March 18, A1.

Frydman, Carola, and Dirk Jenter. 2010. "CEO Compensation." *Annual Review of Financial Economics* 2: 75–102.

Gabaix, Xavier, and Augustin Landier. 2008a. "Is CEO Pay Really Inefficient? A Survey of New Optimal Contracting Theories." European Financial Management, 15:3, 486–496.

Gabaix, Xavier, and Augustin Landier. 2008b. "Why has CEO Pay Increased so Much?" *Quarterly Journal of Economics* 123:1, 49–100.

Gilson, Ronald J., and Reinier Kraakman. 1991. "Reinventing the Outside Director: An Agenda for Institutional Investors." *Stanford Law Review* 43:4, 863–906.

Grinstein, Yaniv, and Paul Hribar. 2004. "CEO Compensation and Incentives: Evidence from M&A Bonuses." *Journal of Financial Economics* 73:1, 119–143.

Hall, Brian, and Jeffrey Liebman. 1998. "Are CEOs Really Paid Like Bureaucrats?" *Quarterly Journal of Economics* 103:3, 653–691.

Heron, Randall A., and Eric Lie. 2007. "Does Backdating Explain the Stock Price Pattern around Executive Stock Option Grants?" *Journal of Financial Economics* 83:2, 271–295.

Heron, Randall A., and Eric Lie. 2009. "What Fraction of Stock Option Grants to Top Executives Have Been Backdated or Manipulated?" *Management Science* 55:4, 513–525.

Hill, Ronald, Thomas Ainscough, Todd Shank, and Daryl Manullang. 2007. "Corporate Social Responsibility and Socially Responsible Investing: A Global Perspective." *Journal of Business Ethics* 70:2, 165–174.

Himmelberg, Charles P., Hubbard R. Glenn, Darius Palia. 1999. "Understanding the Determinants of Managerial Ownership and Performance." *Journal of Financial Economics* 53:3, 333–384.

Holmstrom, Bengt, and Paul R. Milgrom. 1987. "Aggregation and Linearity in the Provision of Intertemporal Incentives." *Econometrica* 55:2, 303–328.

Holthausen, Robert W., and David F. Larcker. 1993. "Board of Directors, Ownership Structure and CEO Compensation." Working Paper, University of Pennsylvania.

Ittner, Christopher D., Richard A. Lambert, and David F. Larcker. 2003. "The Structure and Performance Consequences of Equity Grants to Employees of New Economy Firms." *Journal of Accounting and Economics* 34:1–3, 89–127.

Jensen, Michael C. 1993. "The Modern Industrial Revolution, Exit, and the Failure of Internal Control Systems." *Journal of Finance* 48:3, 831–880.

Jensen, Michael C., and William H. Meckling. 1976. "Theory of the Firm: Managerial Behavior, Agency Costs and Ownership Structure." *Journal of Financial Economics* 3:4, 305–360.

Jensen, Michael C., and Kevin Murphy. 1990. "Performance Pay and Top-Management Incentives." *Journal of Political Economy* 98:2, 225–264.

Jin, Li. 2002. "CEO Compensation, Diversification, and Incentives." *Journal of Financial Economics* 66:1, 29–63.

John, Kose, and Teresa A. John. 1993. "Top–Management Compensation and Capital Structure." *Journal of Finance* 48:3, 949–974.

Kaplan, Thomas. 2010. "Ex-Comverse Chief Settles U.S. Charges." *New York Times*, November 24. Available at http://query.nytimes.com/gst/fullpage.html?res=9C06E2DA113DF 937A15752C1A9669D8B63&ref=jacobalexander.

Lakonishok, Josef, and Inmoo Lee. 2001. "Are Insiders' Trades Informative?" *Review of Financial Studies* 14:1, 79–111.

Lambert, Richard A., and David F. Larcker. 1987. "An Analysis of the Use of Accounting and Market Measures of Performance in Executive Compensation." *Journal of Accounting Research* 25:Supplement, 85–125.

Lattman, Peter. 2010. "Prosecutions in Backdating Scandal Bring Mixed Results." *New York Times*, November 12, 24.

Lewellen Wilbur, Claudio Loderer, and Kenneth Martin. 1987. "Executive Compensation Contracts and Executive Incentive Problems: An Empirical Analysis." *Journal of Accounting and Economics* 10:3, 287–310.

Lie, Eric. 2005. "On the Timing of CEO Stock Option Awards." *Management Science* 51:5, 802–812.

Mahoney, Lois S., and Linda Thorne. 2006. "An Examination of the Structure of Executive Compensation and Corporate Social Responsibility: A Canadian Investigation." *Journal of Business Ethics* 69:2, 149–162.

Main, Brian, Charles A. O'Reilly, and James Wade. 1995. "The CEO, the Board of Directors and Executive Compensation: Economic and Psychological Perspectives." *Industrial and Corporate Change* 4:2, 293–332.

Mallette, Paul, Dennis R. Middlemist, and Willie E. Hopkins. 1995. "Social, Political, and Economic Determinants of Chief Executive Compensation." *Journal of Managerial Issues* 7:3, 253–276.

Matsunaga, Steven R. 1995. "The Effects of Financial Reporting Costs on the Use of Employee Stock Options." *Accounting Review* 70:1, 1–26.

McGuire, Jean, Sandra Dow, and Kamal Argheyd. 2003. "CEO Incentives and Corporate Social Performance." *Journal of Business Ethics* 45:4, 341–359.

Mehran, Hamid. 1995. "Executive Compensation Structure, Ownership, and Firm Performance." *Journal of Financial Economics* 38:2, 163–184.

Murphy, Kevin J. 1985. "Corporate Performance and Managerial Remuneration: An Empirical Analysis." *Journal of Accounting and Economics* 7:1–3, 11–42.

Murphy, Kevin J. 1999. "Executive Compensation." In Otlry Ashenfelter and David Card, eds. *Handbook of Labor Economics*, volume 3b, 2485–2563. New York and Oxford: Elsevier Science North Holland.

Murphy Kevin J., and Jan Zábojník. 2004. "CEO Pay and Appointments: A Market-Based Explanation for Recent Trends." *American Economic Review* 94:2, 192–196.

Murphy Kevin J., and Jan Zábojník. 2007. "Managerial Capital and the Market for CEOs." Working Paper, University of Southern California.

Narayanan, M. P., and Hasan N. Seyhun. 2008. "Do Managers Influence Their Pay? Evidence from Stock Price Reversals around Executive Option Grants." *Review of Financial Studies* 21:5, 1907–1945.

Newman, Harry A., and Haim Mozes. 1999. "Does the Composition of the Compensation Committee Influence CEO Compensation Practices." *Financial Management* 28:3, 41–53.

Obama, Barack. 2009. "Remarks on the Economy and Executive Pay." Speech, Washington D.C., February 4. Available at www.presidentialrhetoric.com/speeches/02.04.09.html.

Pfeffer, Jeffrey. 1981. *Power in Organizations*. Boston: Pitman.

Prendergast, Canice J. 2002. "The Tenuous Trade-off between Risk and Incentives." *Journal of Political Economy* 110:5, 1071–1102.

Rajgopal, Shivaram; Shevlin, Terry, and Valentina Zamora. 2006. "CEOs' Outside Employment Opportunities and the Lack of Relative Performance Evaluation in Compensation Contracts." *Journal of Finance* 61:4, 1813–1844.

Ritter, Jay R. 2008. "Forensic Finance." *Journal of Economic Perspectives* 22:3, 127–147.

Ryan, Harley, and Roy Wiggins. 2001. "The Influence of Firm and Manager-Specific Characteristics on the Structure of Executive Compensation." *Journal of Corporate Finance* 7:2, 101–123.

Sahadi, Jeanne. 2007. "CEO Pay: 364 Times More than Workers." CNNMoney.com, Available at http://money.cnn.com/2007/08/28/news/economy/ceo_pay_workers/index.htm.

Shivdasani, Anil, and David Yermack. 1999. "CEO Involvement in the Selection of New Board Members: An Empirical Analysis." *Journal of Finance* 54:5, 1829–1854.

Smith, Clifford, and Ross Watts. 1992. "The Investment Opportunity Set and Corporate Financing, Dividend and Compensation Policies." *Journal of Financial Economics* 31:3, 263–292.

Sridharan, Uma V. 1996. "CEO Influence and Executive Compensation." *Financial Review* 31:1, 51–66.

Thorne, Linda, Lois S. Mahoney, and Donna Bobek 2010. "A Comparison of the Association between Corporate Social Responsibility and Executive Compensation: United States versus Canada." *Research on Professional Responsibility and Ethics in Accounting* 14, 37–56.

Veliyath, Rajaram. 1999. "Top Management Compensation and Shareholder Returns: Unraveling Different Models of the Relationship." *Journal of Management Studies* 36:1, 123–143.

Yermack, David. 1995. "Do Corporations Award CEO Stock Options Effectively?" *Journal of Financial Economics* 39:2, 237–269.

Yermack, David. 1996. "Higher Market Valuation of Companies with a Small Board of Directors." *Journal of Financial Economics* 40:2, 185–211.

Yermack, David. 1997. "Good Timing: CEO Stock Option Awards and Company News Announcements." *Journal of Finance* 52:2, 449–476.

ABOUT THE AUTHORS

Kose John is the Charles William Gerstenberg Professor of Banking and Finance at the New York University Stern School of Business and teaches courses in corporate finance. His recent areas of research include corporate governance, corporate bankruptcy, executive compensation, and corporate disclosure. He has also done research in the areas of financial markets and financial theory. He has published more than 100 articles in several top journals including *American Economic Review, Journal of Financial Economics, Journal of Finance, Review of Financial Studies*, and *Financial Management*. He was awarded the prestigious Jensen Prize for the best paper published in *Journal of Financial Economics* in 2000. Besides his research, Professor John has been recognized for his excellence in teaching and received the Citibank Excellence in Teaching Award in 1996.

Samir Saadi is a Ph.D. candidate in Finance at Queen's University. He was a Visiting Scholar at the Stern School of Business, New York University and also a Visiting Researcher at INSEAD (Fontainebleau campus). His research interests include corporate finance, corporate governance, executive compensation, M&As, and corporate payout policy. Along with several book chapters, Mr. Saadi has published several papers in journals such as *Financial Management, Contemporary Accounting Research, Journal of Business Ethics, Journal of International Financial Markets, Institutions and Money, Journal of Theoretical and Applied Finance*, and *Journal of Applied Finance*. He is the recipient of several conference best paper awards and numerous prestigious awards and scholarships from, among others, Queen's University, Social Sciences and Humanities Research Council of Canada (SSHRC), Europlace Institute of Finance (EIF), and American Finance Association (AFA). Before joining Queen's University, he served as a consultant for several companies, mainly on aspects of value-based management and export financing.

CHAPTER 11

Externalities in Financial Decision Making

JANIS SARRA
Professor of Law, University of British Columbia

INTRODUCTION

Any shift towards socially responsible investing (SRI) should take into account the externalities created by the choice of investment. Those externalities can be positive, in that sophisticated and well-resourced investors who want to support socially and environmentally sustainable activities can signal to others in the market the soundness of their particular investment choices. Equally, however, the externalities created by supporting particular products and services can be negative, imposing substantial costs on both individuals and society at large. This chapter illustrates how financial markets, as currently structured, cause negative externalities. In particular, it examines three types of financial strategies that produce negative externalities: derivatives, securitization, and syndication. This chapter also explores the social and economic harm generated when investors fail to appreciate that the speculative returns generated through investment in these products can work against broader goals of sustainable businesses.

In most instances relating to the 2008–2009 global financial crisis, the externalities were highly negative, imposing substantial losses on broad numbers of people who did not bargain for these outcomes. Further, the individuals who engaged in activities that caused the negative outcomes did not bear the costs. Within the financial services framework, securitization, syndication, and derivatives activities were all initially designed to manage risk, and thus provide a net social benefit. Yet all of these products have been used in recent years to create new negative externalities. A critical component of advancing a socially responsible finance and investment strategy is an appreciation of how externalities function and what options socially responsible investors have in dampening the negative effects of such financial products and services.

This chapter first offers a working definition of externality and discusses some of the positive externalities associated with the development of the structured financial products market. It then examines the increase and continuing persistence of negative externalities, on the debt and equity side, as well as the role played by risk taking and risk managing. Finally, the chapter discusses the implications for SRI. The last section provides a summary and conclusions.

EXTERNALITIES CAN BE POSITIVE OR NEGATIVE

Externalities occur in financial decision making when the decision to invest supports an activity or product that causes an external benefit or cost to third-party stakeholders that were not directly involved in the transaction. An *externality* is a cost generated by the activities of one or more market players, where the cost is borne by individuals or groups that did not agree to the activities. Externalities are the social effects of economic activity derived from productive or other activity that affect parties other than the originator of such activity, which do not work through the price system (Laffont 2008). A simple example is the environmental harm caused by a production plant located in a community. Individuals in that community, who did not contract in any way with the production company, may suffer negative health effects from toxic substances in the air, soil, or water, and economic consequences from depressed house values or increased health care costs from environmental contaminants. In such instances, the company is profiting from its productive activities, but is externalizing the costs of environmental prevention, protection, and remediation, placing the costs of those activities and the negative environmental outcomes on community members who did not agree to bear the costs of those polluting activities.

Externalities associated with financial decision making were initially not so easily discernible. In the financial markets, externalities caused by a financial institution can impose costs on individuals, other financial institutions, or society at large. A systemic externality is an externality whose impact depends not only on the institution that generates it, but also on the state of the financial system at the time the externality is imposed (Wagner 2010). For example, Wagner suggests that a bank should take into account the fact that if it operates with considerably more risk than other firms, its failure would impose costs on society. Otherwise, a social consequence is that unregulated banks will take too much risk.

POSITIVE EXTERNALITIES IN FINANCIAL MARKETS

Externalities in financial services shifted considerably in the decade before commencement of the 2008–2009 financial crisis. Hence, briefly examining their development and the shift from a positive contribution to negative impact is helpful.

History

Historically, deposit-taking commercial banks were the primary lenders for both business and individuals. They were often located in communities and made economic decisions aimed at profit, but also took into account the bank's stake in the community. There were many positive externalities associated with this type of commercial bank lending. Banks were important in monitoring and correcting governance problems of companies. Their superior access to information, their ability to directly intervene under loan covenants, and their ability to decline credit when the business plan was inadequate, provided a signal about the company's financial health. Commercial banks generated positive externalities in that consumers, trade suppliers, and employees, who could not access that internal firm information or exercise any default control rights, benefited from the resources expended by the bank to engage in the oversight (Sarra 2008). Investors also benefited from the costs borne by the bank in this governance role. Even where companies relied increasingly on the public debt markets, while the indenture trustee often had limited responsibility to monitor compliance, investors frequently required companies to back their commercial paper with lines of credit from banks, with the banks serving a similar governance role (Triantis and Daniels 1995).

Hence, the screening and monitoring activities of a lender produced externalities that benefited numerous stakeholders with an interest in the corporation, through the following: (1) the bank's decision to lend, which signaled to potential and existing stakeholders the quality of the borrower; (2) the imposition of fixed obligations under the loan agreement that prevented managerial slack; (3) security rights that constrained the ability of managers to liquidate noncash assets or unilaterally sell more debt; and (4) loan covenants and monitoring of specified prohibited types of behavior. Triantis and Daniels (1995) called this feature "interdependent screening" to describe externalities that flow not only among creditors, but also from lenders to investors, employees, and other stakeholders.

In the past decade, however, bank practices shifted in response to competitive market pressure from participants such as hedge funds that operated in the nonregulated shadow banking sector, so-named because these funds engaged in investment and lending activities that shadowed the types offered by traditional commercial banks without the prudential obligations or the regulatory framework in which the banks were required to operate. These market players and the new financial products generated by their demand for short-term returns accelerated the shift away from the positive externalities, as discussed below.

Derivatives and Securitization Developed as Risk Management Tools

Credit derivatives were initially developed as a tool for banks to manage their credit risk in businesses for which they had directly invested, diversifying their risk of loan default by cushioning any losses. Protection buyers used credit derivatives to manage portfolio uncertainties, including to hedge over concentrations in loan portfolios, free up economic or regulatory capital, and avoid sales of bond holdings (Sarra 2008). Protection sellers were often in the market to increase exposure to sectors, diversify investment portfolios, exploit yield alternatives, and provide capital arbitrage. Fixed-income asset managers use credit derivatives to adjust credit exposures. Bank portfolio managers use credit default swaps (CDS) to manage concentrations of risk to their largest borrowers. Underwriters use CDS to manage risk, benefiting companies and investors who do not directly use credit derivatives (Parkinson 2008).

Similarly, securitization through collateralized debt obligations (CDO) was developed to manage risk. Securitization allows financial market players to take debt they have acquired, break it into tranches of varying degrees of risk, and sell it to purchasers at prices commensurate with the potential risk and return. The originating lender under this "originate and distribute" model of financing arguably had hedged its own risk and was able to free up that capital to relend into the market. Besides the initial risk management function, banks generated considerable income from the fees generated by originating the initial loan, and then also the revenue from the distribution and sale of the loans in the various bundles in the market.

Initially, securitization appeared as if it would generate positive externalities. Purchasers of the tranches believed that they could rely on the originating lender to conduct the due diligence associated with the loans, believing that the risk was being appropriately assessed and priced by both the originator of the loans and the credit rating agency. Under the current structure where the issuer pays for the credit rating, purchasers were to benefit from those ratings in the selected tranche of debt that was appropriate to their investment priorities and risk profile. However, as discussed in the next section, securitization led instead to negative externalities that harmed individuals far beyond the financial services participants.

On the equity side of finance and investment, equity swaps are a type of derivative purchased to hedge against the potential loss of equity investment. Equity derivatives are generally over-the-counter (OTC) structured financial products, and include equity swaps, options, and futures. An investor can purchase shares and then manage the economic risk by purchasing equity derivatives. The products are complex, ever-changing, and often not easily discernable. What Canada and the United States refer to as equity swaps, are called "contracts for differences" in the United Kingdom. Canadian regulators also use the term "equity monetization" to refer to a variety of sophisticated derivative-based strategies that permit investors to dispose of equity risk without transferring ownership. In some cases, the products are essentially the same, with different terminology used to describe them. In other instances, the products hold different bundles of economic and legal rights. The actual economic interest held in such products is difficult to quantify at any given moment. However, as discussed below, their explosive growth has, in a number of instances, generated new externalities that may detract from socially responsible finance and investing goals.

The further development and use of all these products started to shift around 2002. The original objective of managing risk of direct investment under lending portfolios was overtaken by a speculative market for buying and selling derivatives in multiples of the value of the underlying reference assets or entities, resulting in a large trading market that was fueled by high fees and profits from derivatives trading (Sarra 2008). The vast majority of credit derivatives had been executed bilaterally with derivatives dealers in OTC markets, involving primarily dealers in large, globally active commercial and investment banks (Parkinson 2008).

Trading in CDS was increasingly concentrated in dealers, hedge fund asset managers, and asset managers of investment companies. For example, AIG's CDS-related revenues grew to USD 3.26 billion in 2005 from USD 737 million five years prior (AIG 2009). Overall, bank market share declined as hedge funds increasingly took a greater share of both the buy side and sell side of the derivatives market. In 2000, banks accounted for 81 percent of the buy side and hedge funds only 3 percent. Six years later, bank activity had dropped by 25 percent and hedge funds now had 28 percent of the market. A similar shift occurred on the sell side. Hedge fund market share of the sell side grew from 5 percent to 32 percent in the same period (Murphy, Sarra, and Creber 2006). Those derivatives were then hedged in further derivatives at multiples of the value of the originating reference entities. To enhance returns, hedge funds shifted to more speculative investment grades and unrated exposures. In 2002, 36 percent of all credit derivatives globally were rated at AA or AAA, whereas only 8 percent were rated as below investment grade. Just four years later, only 17 percent of credit derivatives globally were rated at AA or better, whereas 31 percent were rated as below investment grade (Murphy et al. 2006).

Hedge funds and other derivatives traders engaged in market trading that speculated heavily on the reference entity's risk. Many outstanding derivative contracts aggregated 10 times, 20 times or more the amount of creditor claims (Murphy et al. 2006). Most credit derivative transactions were not funded and were subject to margin and collateral arrangements depending on the counterparty. Although counterparties to below-investment-grade derivatives transactions required, in a number of cases, collateral agreements with initial and variation margin requirements, there was still considerable operational risk to effectiveness of the market. When the financial markets began to seriously deteriorate, the CDS exposures of counterparties became evident, with a major crisis in the ability of protection sellers to ensure coverage. Together, these changes substantially altered the credit derivatives market, without any jurisdiction seriously assessing the public policy implications.

Hedge funds and other financial intermediaries in the shadow banking sector also engaged in securitization without any requirement to maintain a level of capital adequacy, given that they were largely unregulated. Originating lenders were securitizing loans so that returns to their principals were immediate or short term, with parties reselling the tranches in the same manner. Investors in search of quick returns created a market for subprime mortgage and asset-backed commercial paper tranches. Executive compensation that rewarded short-term high returns exacerbated the incentives. Gersbach and Roche (2011) observe a moral hazard issue in that lenders could shirk the monitoring that they were supposed to be undertaking of the small- and medium-sized enterprises that borrowed from them.

INCREASED NEGATIVE EXTERNALITIES

These developments led to a substantial increase in negative externalities, both in respect to debt and equity investment, in turn creating new challenges for advancing SRI objectives. This section explores recent trends and the implications for SRI.

On the Debt Side

Credit derivatives and securitization have shifted the externalities in a way that may diminish potential positive effects of socially responsible finance and investing. The negative externalities persist today. First, the disconnection between economic interest and residual control rights can create new incentives in that originating lenders are less willing to expend the time and resources to undertake due diligence in undertaking credit arrangements, as risk is laid off through purchase of CDS or under the originate-and-distribute model. Hence, the signaling to the market that occurred with the decision to lend is no longer reliable as a measure of the firm's value (Sarra 2008). Second, in the purchase and sale of credit derivatives, parties have frequently given up the negotiation of terms and conditions, including monitoring, restrictive covenants, and default control rights, because they know that they will offset their own risk through other structured financial products. Hence, prior positive externality is often lost as senior creditors no longer undertake monitoring and strategic intervention (Sarra 2008). When a company becomes financially distressed, either because of poor governance or a broader market downturn, corporate stakeholders no longer share a common goal of maximizing firm value and constraining managerial slack because the originating lender has hedged its risk and multiple subsequent counterparties have done the same. Stakeholders that could previously rely on the governance role of banks can no longer do so. Given the diverse nature of their interests, information asymmetries, and collective action problems, they are unlikely to be able to fill this governance gap.

Multiplied many times through complex derivative transactions and multiple swaps, previous positive externalities are lost, and new negative externalities are created, generating more systemic risks across the market. The current move to standardize derivatives contracts, while arguably efficient in terms of controlling transaction costs, may exacerbate this risk through the reduction or elimination of debt governance covenants. Moreover, the signaling that occurred through exit or other creditor reactions to the debtor's decisions is diminished because major lenders may be fully hedged. Yet that fact is not transparent to equity investors, employees, trade suppliers, and others who may still look for such signaling. Given the global nature of credit derivatives, the externalities create systemic problems that require more broad-based intervention than merely improving disclosure.

Securitization of debt through CDO and other products creates incentives for the originating lender not to be duly diligent in its lending decisions, as it can offload the risk to the purchasers of various tranches of the debt. The subprime mortgage lending in the United States and consequent foreclosure and housing crisis is an example. Securitization generates few incentives for the originating lender to exact protective covenants, or to undertake monitoring on an ongoing basis, given that risk of default is borne by other parties. Over multiple similar transactions, these disincentives caused a market crisis.

Akerlof and Shiller (2009) suggest that the amount of securitization engaged in by participants in the shadow banking sector imposed serious negative externalities on the financial system and the real economy. Zawadowski (2011) argues for requiring such lenders to buy default insurance on their counterparties from the other banks in the system or from an outside seller, implemented by prefunded CDS. He suggests that even though banks use OTC contracts to hedge risks and thereby expose themselves to counterparty risk, they are unwilling to insure against counterparty default because the externalities inflicted on others through derivative contracts are not internalized. Gauthier, He, and Souissi (2010) observe that system stability takes on the attributes of a public good and one needs a tractable framework that incorporates financing externalities, suggesting that a regulatory framework that properly controls for systemic risk should consider capital, liquid asset holdings, and short-term liability in a holistic way.

The Basel Committee on Banking Supervision (2009) recommends that banks and other financial institutions should retain a sufficiently strong economic interest in their securitized products. In general, this requirement would mean retaining some exposure to securitization cash flows where payoffs are especially sensitive to how well the bank performs its origination, monitoring, and servicing activities. The Dodd-Frank Act (2010) in the United States requires companies that sell products such as mortgage-backed securities to retain at least 5 percent of the credit risk, unless the underlying loans meet standards that reduce riskiness. It requires issuers to disclose more information and analyze the quality of the underlying assets. Regulators in various other jurisdictions are also considering this 5 percent threshold of retained credit risk in respect to securitization (European Commission 2009). Yet, requiring 5 percent "skin in the game" may be limited in its effectiveness in creating appropriate incentives to monitor the products. If the threshold of retaining economic interest is so low, market participants may simply view it as the price of participating in the market, and not create the hoped for incentives to monitor the quality of credit decisions.

On the Equity Side

Equity swaps are particularly troublesome for corporate governance, as the very decision makers of the corporation are increasingly hedging their own risk through the purchase of such swaps (Sarra 2011a). Equity derivatives represent a challenge to SRI because they have the effect of separating shareholder votes from economic interest. The underlying premise of equity investors having control rights and the ability to vote is that such investors have a direct economic stake in the corporation. To the extent that SRI is attempting to expand the number of factors taken into account in the governance of companies and the sustainability of their economic and productive activities, it must account for the growing and nontransparent practice of uncoupling economic interest from voting rights for equity holders.

For equity investors with substantial holdings, there has historically been a greater incentive to explore mechanisms to influence corporate governance, particularly where the investors are interested in longer-term and socially responsible investment in the firm rather than short-term holdings and return on capital. The development of equity derivatives is a major change to the nature of economic interest held by shareholders of a corporation. The widespread use of equity swaps poses questions for governance on both the officer side and the investor side of the socially responsible investment relationship. Directors and officers that are hedging risk of their equity investments through equity swaps have an incentive to shirk their responsibilities, which in turn may prejudice shareholder interests and exacerbate negative externalities arising from corporate conduct.

On the investor side, the traditional corporate law norm is that shareholders have a bundle of rights that reflects their status as residual economic claimants of the corporation, including voting rights, rights to disclosure, rights to any dividends declared, the ability to trade or sell shares, and on wind-up of a financially solvent company, the right to a proportional share of the economic value of the company. This bundle of rights was designed to reflect the economic interests of investors arising from their equity investment. The degree of interest was viewed as commensurate with the number of shares held. The bundle of shareholder rights assumes a direct link between the shareholder's legal interest and economic interest. Yet derivatives challenge that fundamental notion as they uncouple economic interest and legal interest in specific circumstances. For example, for cash-settled equity swaps, the shareholder retains legal title to the shares, and thus the bundle of shareholder rights, but is paid out the cash value of the swap on the occurrence of certain events. Thus, for example, in a takeover situation or other fundamental transaction for which shareholders are given a vote, the shareholder may hold 10 percent of the votes as the registered owner, but may have no economic interest as the shareholder has fully hedged its risk through the purchase of equity swaps. The shareholder can also have a negative economic interest by overhedging, purchasing a swap of greater value than the underlying shares on which the swap is based. In the case of a fully or overcovered equity swap, the investor often does not have to disclose the lack of any economic interest or risk. Directors and officers do not necessarily know who holds the economic interest in the company (Hu and Black 2008; Sarra 2008).

Physically settled equity swaps are slightly less problematic, as on occurrence of one of the specified events, the ownership and voting rights of the shares are traded for cash in the settlement of the equity swap. In such cases, the new shareholder is required to disclose its shareholdings when the concentration reaches a specified amount. The corporation has new shareholders that it must be responsive to, but they are known. However, even in this case, there can be issues where, at settlement of a sizeable number of swaps, the corporation may find it has a very large new shareholder with 10, 20 percent, or more of holdings. Financial services legislation in many jurisdictions requires disclosure of incremental changes in equity ownership through the threshold disclosure requirements. Yet this increasingly common practice negates the transparency sought by such requirements.

Equity swaps are not considered securities in many jurisdictions or are considered part of the exempt market, and thus frequently are not subject to disclosure and investor protection provisions unless they fall within materiality requirements in issuer or management-disclosure obligations. In some instances, where the investor holds the economic benefit of the shares but not the voting rights, the investor can unwind the swap as per a prior agreement with the dealer and acquire voting rights, or it can, in some cases, instruct the dealer how to vote the shares (Hu and Black 2008). Where there are formal rights to unwind a swap or to direct the dealer to vote a particular way, the shareholder will likely come within the disclosure requirements of financial services law. However, where the voting rights are not legally enforceable, and relational-based or implicit, there is often no requirement for disclosure. The arrangement also can bypass prohibitions in some jurisdictions in respect to vote buying in situations where intrinsic fairness is not associated with the purpose of the transaction (Hu and Black 2008).

A variety of other strategies currently uncouple legal and economic interest in equity investment. Hu and Black (2008) observe that such practices have become prevalent on a low-cost and large-scale basis in the United States; for example, the market for share lending includes 20 percent or more of all the outstanding shares of most large U.S. corporations. The authors suggest that this soft parking of shares means that shares are held in friendly hands that have voting rights but no economic ownership, but provide access to shareholder rights when desired under an informal arrangement either to vote as directed or unwind the shares back to the hidden owner. The Hedge Fund Working Group (2008) in the United Kingdom has recommended a ban on using borrowed shares for empty voting purposes. Hu and Black also discuss "record date capture," in which the investor borrows the shares in the stock loan market just before the record date and returns the shares afterward. In such a case, the investor has no economic interest at risk but has acquired the voting rights for the purpose of the particular meeting or transaction for which the record date was set.

One can see why these growing practices are problematic for SRI. Shareholders with substantial shareholdings are in a position to potentially influence the decisions of directors and officers because of their voting power, even though they may have no economic risk in the outcome of those decisions. For fundamental transactions, this disconnection may mean that votes on such transactions do not truly represent the wishes of those whose interest is allied with the corporation's long-term sustainability. Equally important, large shareholders are in a position to informally influence directors and officers through meetings, media statements, and policy positions. Where they have little or no economic interest, this influence may not be in the best interests of investors or the corporation, and is likely to detract from investing that is aimed at socially responsible behavior by the company. In turn, negative externalities exist for the employees, smaller investors, and the community in which the company is located.

For large investors, the purchase of swaps to hedge risk and the resultant disconnection between legal ownership of the share and economic risk creates disincentives for the shareholder to act to monitor the activities of directors and officers. It creates negative externalities, in that small shareholders, who could previously rely on the monitoring and governance role of institutional shareholders, will be unaware that their incentives to monitor have reduced. The previous signaling by institutional shareholders, either from their proxy activities, media statements, or shifting of sizable investment, may no longer be reliable and may remove an important part of the synergistic aspects of investor oversight of the activities of directors and officers.

Hu and Black (2008) argue for shareholder attestation requirements, requiring large shareholders to file ownership disclosure reports attesting that voted shares do not exceed economically owned shares by a specified amount or threshold. The authors suggest that corporate law should be amended to allow firms to adopt provisions in their corporate charters to limit empty voting. These and other suggestions are in need of an extensive public policy discussion. Any new approach will need to grapple with the fundamental notion that shareholders can vote as they choose and corporate law does not intervene to require disclosure either of their reasons for voting a particular way or tempering such behavior, aligning any policy decisions with the historical reasons for such nonintervention.

A principal objective of corporate governance is to maximize the wealth-generating capacity of the corporation, and for SRI, that objective is overlaid with the goal of maximizing wealth in a manner that is socially responsible and aimed at long-term economic, social, and environmental sustainability. The unifying notion is that directors have a fiduciary obligation to act in the best interests of the corporation and hence to maximize enterprise value through oversight of managerial activity in the effective use of corporate assets. These objectives may require new transparency and accountability norms to ensure that directors and officers do act in the company's best interests, with a view to long-term socially responsible and sustainable activities of the corporation.

Syndication as the New Lending Norm

Socially responsible finance and investing also needs to take account of the changing structure of lending globally. Commercial lending is no longer based on a traditional relationship model with a bank or a small group of lenders providing money at par. Now the principal interface between lenders and companies is syndicated creditors. Syndicates with the same agent under one set of credit documents can include multiple borrowers; different participants in separate tranches with differing maturities; first lien and second lien interests; and original issue discount (OID) or debt not issued at par, in multiple currencies. Large syndicates can have in excess of 200 members, and may include investment funds at the syndication stage (Sarra 2011b). There is substantial growth in secondary market trading of syndicated debt. Investment funds are the primary purchasers, and intercreditor agreements have developed. While initial lenders may still have relationships with the company or investments in local communities, syndicated lenders today often have no relationship with the company, no investments in local communities, and are unconcerned about collateral impacts of any financial downturn faced by the company. They are typically looking to avoid or minimize a loss, and to keep the company leveraged. Syndicated lenders are not prepared to convert debt to equity, although they will sometimes amend credit facilities and provide bulge facilities.

Secondary holders and indenture holders typically have no relationship with the company and provide no ancillary services. Thus, they are indifferent to the consequences of the company's financial situation. They have no investments in local communities and are unconcerned about collateral impacts of any default. Often, such lenders hold the debt at a substantial discount to its face value and simply want a return. Indenture debt can be privately placed, public debt, and have zero relationship with the initial and secondary holder. Retail investors typically never participate in negotiations where an accommodation or insolvency restructuring is necessary, other than delivering a proxy vote through a broker, if solicited. Indenture debt holders have many of the characteristics of syndicated debt in terms of a more passive interest in the debtor company. They represent a range of interests in terms of willingness to sell in the secondary market or to agree to a restructuring plan that provides for a debt-to-equity swap. Decisions are made between the indenture trustee and the debtor company. However, the company is at the mercy of whatever decision or voting process is set out in the indenture agreement, without generally having the ability to negotiate directly with these creditors.

Syndication of bank loans is a longstanding practice; however, participants to the syndication have changed markedly in recent years. Traditionally, banks, and in some instances pension funds, were the primary participants. They have been surpassed by the presence of hedge funds, which now comprise one-third of the syndicated loan market (Baird and Rasmussen 2005). Today, large loan syndicates can have hundreds of diverse types of lenders. Coffey, Milam, Torrado, and Piorowski (2007) have observed that secondary trading by hedge funds in the syndicated loan market grew from 10 percent in 2000 to 30 percent of trading volume five years later. The practical result is that hedge funds purchase enough tranches in the secondary market so that they have the power to block any waiver of default, proposed amendment to the credit facility, or restructuring plan that does not meet with their approval. The hedge fund may have a loan-to-own strategy, using its veto to create a default on the part of the debtor company. Such hold-out positions can seriously harm the ability of the debtor company to continue business, as syndicated lenders are less likely to have relationships with the local community that generate an interest in maintaining the business.

Another shift is the nature and extent of second lien loans, which differ from traditional subordinated debt as their security is on the same assets as the senior syndicated loan, but are a claim on the residual value of the assets after that loan is satisfied. The right to payment is usually not subordinated to the senior debt and maturity schedules are set so that the borrower is required to make payments on both loans. Second lien lenders can seek to be repaid at the same time as the debtor company is repaying the senior lending syndicate. The senior lender must agree to the second lien, and it is often willing to do so as it brings more capital into the debtor company, which can be used to enhance the business and meet its claims. Unlike subordinated debt, second lienholders do not have to pay any monies that they collect to the senior debt; rather, they are second only in terms of their claim on the collateral package when it is sold for cash. Second lien loan financings with hedge funds are now widely used, often by debtors in lieu of unsecured high yield debt or traditional unsecured mezzanine financing (Hanrahan and Teh 2007).

The complexity and diversity of interests represented in syndicated transactions means that the relational aspects of the lending relationship are diminished or nonexistent. In terms of SRI, if the investor is part of the syndicated agreement, the ability to influence the other participants is negligible. There are too many players with too little at risk for them to be concerned with the long-term activities and sustainability of the companies for which the syndicated loans have been given. If the socially responsible investor has made an equity investment in the business and issues arise as to the company's capacity to service its debt obligations, syndication means that the likelihood of negotiating a workout and business plan going forward are substantially reduced. One can expect that normative goals of socially responsible activities are unlikely to be placed on the agenda. All businesses require financing, and most businesses require some level of debt. The changes to the debt markets, as discussed above, work against shifting corporate governance towards a vision of the corporation that is socially situated, environmentally responsible, and accountable to larger numbers of stakeholders.

The Role of Risk in These Changes

Whether investment is through debt or equity, all investment, including socially responsible investment, contains a measure of risk. Arrow (1962) observed that the economic system has devices for shifting risk, but they are limited and imperfect; and that while increasing the variety of such devices is worthwhile, the moral factor creates a limit to their potential. His example was fire insurance, which shifts the risk of loss from the person buying the insurance policy to the insurer. For the cost of the premium, the insured is hedging risk of loss. Absent limits on the amount of insurance, if the value of the property destroyed was greater than the current value, it would create an incentive for arson or carelessness. Arguably, Arrow writes, even when a fire insurance policy is limited to the value of the goods covered, it weakens the motivation for fire prevention. As Arrow notes, co-insurance, which extends insurance only to part of the amount at risk, represents a compromise between incentive effects and allocation of risk bearing.

This reasoning becomes important in thinking about derivatives, as the ability of protection buyers to fully or overhedge their risk creates skewed incentives in their behavior where they are also creditors of the reference company. If the value of a CDS purchased is many times the value of the underlying reference entity, it shifts the incentive system to encourage the lender to precipitate a default on the loan in order to create the credit event that triggers a payout in multiples of the value of the loan itself. Devices for managing risk must take account of the moral hazard in such risk-shifting strategies, and hence should create incentives for conduct that does not unnecessarily harm market participants and others.

Failure to fully account for both individual and systemic risks also contributed to recent negative externalities arising from use of structured financial products. Knight (1921) argued that people differ in their capacity to form accurate judgments as to potential risk, future course of events, and forecasting the conduct of others. He argued that there is a cognitive attitude, in that some individuals will hardly "take chances" at all, while others prefer uncertainty. These different capacities influence individual ability to perceive risk, to calculate the likelihood of particular events or losses, and to willingly act to reduce or hedge against such risk. Knight's analysis resonates.

Many investors failed completely to appreciate both individual and systemic risks of their investments in these products. Even where some market participants discerned that a potential crash of the structured financial products market was likely, their actions were driven by short-term profits, high fees, and their ability to externalize their risk. Business attracts entrepreneurs; the essence of innovation in business is drawn from a willingness and ability to take some chances, design new products, and enter new markets. Yet arguably, these very capacities may work to reduce individual ability to perceive risk, to calculate the likelihood of particular events or losses, and willingness to act to prevent or reduce such risks. Moreover, the ability to shed risk through derivatives, securitization, and syndication creates the conditions for even less attention to be paid to the company's risk management and mitigation. Knight (1921) alerts us to the notion that risk shifting is a complex process that engages more than simply willingness to reduce uncertainty, and that individual capacity to understand and control for risk varies considerably.

Korinek (2011) observes that government lump-sum transfers, i.e., bailouts—create the conditions for increased risk taking and externalities, as market participants simply increase their exposure to those risks from which they expect to be bailed out. He suggests that the effect can be to introduce an externality into the economy that leads to an undervaluation of liquidity that in turn leads bankers to take on excessive risk and buy insufficient insurance on their financing decisions.

Risk managing and risk shedding are thus of great interest to advocates for SRI. To date, governments have proven largely ineffective at controlling these developments, and regulatory debates and initiatives in 2011 were relatively timid in their efforts to address the above-noted problems. Beck (1999) discusses the "global risk society," where current economic, social, and political developments have resulted in economic ownership and activity that eludes the protective institutions in society, leaving society largely uninsured against harms. Beck observes that risks that could previously be managed are now too extensive and nontransparent, so that they are difficult or impossible to control, socialize, and compensate for harms. Thus, such risk now undermines established safety systems of the welfare state's existing risk calculations and results in greater social harms.

SUMMARY AND CONCLUSIONS

What are the implications of these developments in structured financial products for socially responsible finance and investing? The contours of SRI are examined extensively elsewhere in this book. From the perspective of the aspirational goals of SRI, a first and basic step is that investors should avoid buying derivatives products that are part of the speculative market and that lead to negative externalities. SRI could also mean that any assessment of potential investment in a company includes requiring disclosure of the degree to which the firm is invested in derivatives and the degree to which it has the capital to back any calls on its liquidity. A policy choice could be to invest where derivatives activities manage risk, but decline to invest where the activities are aimed at maximizing short-term return and externalizing financial risk to innocent third parties or the system as a whole. Such a decision requires an understanding of when such externalities are generated and a choice to forgo short-term returns that cause harms to others.

Socially responsible investors could also ensure that investments in firms engaging in securitization require those firms to retain sufficient economic interest in the distributed loans that incentives are present to conduct the due diligence, monitoring, and oversight of the debtor company's governance and finance.

Socially responsible investors could advocate for corporate compensation structures that reduce incentives to take excessive risk and create negative externalities; instead, rewarding effective oversight of regulatory compliance, independent monitoring of audit and operational functions, and long-term sustainability. Officers should be incentivized to better identify risks of particular structured financial products; understand inappropriate risk concentration; shift risk stress tests from focusing on past events to identifying new risks and potential outcomes; and ensure a continuous understanding the firm's risk position. Socially responsible investors could also advocate remuneration systems that focus on staff whose activities can have a material impact on both the risk exposure of the company and on its externalizing activities.

The rise of the shadow banking sector was in large measure to bypass regulatory oversight in its quest for short-term returns, generating serious negative externalities. Until that sector is brought within the oversight of the state, financial market participants will continue to search for ways to externalize costs of their market activities. Hence, investors can potentially make an important public policy contribution by pressing for a regulatory framework that brings the activities of these market participants into line with oversight of other systemically important entities. Socially responsible investors could go one step further and use the occasion of the recent serious market disruptions and current regulatory debates to advocate for a different normative approach to financial markets. They could advocate for an approach that truly incorporates social and environmental sustainability goals in regulatory outcomes sought, and that seeks to internalize the costs of particular financial decisions.

This short chapter is unable to discuss the intricacies of the relationship between issuers of debt and equity securities and credit rating agencies, a subject much explored elsewhere. However, of particular note is that the first regulatory skirmishes in the United States under the Dodd-Frank Act to make such agencies accountable by imposing some liability risk have resulted in a serious push back from the agencies themselves, leading the U.S. Securities and Exchange Commission to already retreat from its initial accountability measures (Pragyan, Manning, Murphy, Penalver, and Troth 2011). Socially responsible investors could offer a counter-pressure to this resistance, making regulators understand that each aspect of the financial and capital markets needs attention in respect of current negative externalities.

Socially responsible investors could thus influence private market activities, through their decision to link investment choices to socially responsible risk management activities, i.e., investing in firms that use structured financial products to manage risk but do not use them for speculative activities that result in serious negative externalities. They could also press governments to engage in a broader assessment of how the failure to regulate with a view to social and environmental responsibility has resulted in negative externalities to broad numbers of stakeholders and society at large. If the regulatory agenda could be linked to a new, broader set of goals regarding the role of firms and their long-term sustainability, the outcomes sought could reduce the harmful effects of externalities. Achievement of private market or public policy change will require a serious commitment of time and resources, as well as a normative choice that short-term profit will be exchanged for the objective and realization of longer-term, sustainable, and more equitable returns from productive and financial activities in the marketplace.

DISCUSSION QUESTIONS

1. What are externalities?
2. Why does securitization generate negative externalities?
3. What is meant by *share lending*, and why do such practices affect the potential for SRI?
4. What could SRI offer to address some of the issues associated with negative externalities?

REFERENCES

AIG. 2009. *2009 Annual Report*. March 27. Available at www.aigcorporate.com/investors/2010_April/2009AnnualReport.pdf.

Akerlof, George, and Robert Shiller. 2009. *Animal Spirits—How Human Psychology Drives the Economy, and Why It Matters for Global Capitalism*. Princeton: Princeton University Press.

Arrow, Kenneth J. 1962. "Economic Welfare and the Allocation of Resources for Invention." In Richard R. Nelson, ed., *The Rate and Direction of Inventive Activity: Economic and Social Factors*, 43–86. Princeton, NJ: Princeton University Press.

Baird, Douglas, and Robert Rasmussen. 2005. "Anti-Bankruptcy." University of Southern California Law and Economics Research Paper No. C09-8 and University of Chicago Olin Law and Economics Program Research Paper No. 470. Available at http://ssrn.com/abstract=1396827.

Basel Committee on Banking Supervision. 2009. "Findings on the Interaction of Market and Credit Risk." Working Paper 16, May. Basel Committee on Banking Supervision.

Beck, Ulrich. 1999. *World Risk Society*. Cambridge: Polity Press.

Coffey, Meredith, Robert Milam, Laura Torrado, and Michele Piorowski. 2007. "The Secondary Loan Market." In Allison Taylor and Alicia Sansone, eds., *The Handbook of Loan Syndications and Trading*, 186–191. New York: McGraw-Hill.

Dodd-Frank Act. 2010. *The Wall Street Reform and Consumer Protection Act*. Pub. L. 111-203, H.R. 4173. Available at www.opencongress.org/bill/111-h4173/text.

European Commission. 2009. *Directive 2009/111/EC Amending Directives 2006/48/EC, 2006/49/EC and 2007/64/EC*. The European Parliament and the Council of the European Union. Available at http://eur-lex.europa.eu/LexUriServ/LexUriServ .do?uri=OJ:L:2009:302:0097:0119:EN:PDF.

Gauthier, Céline, Zhongfang He, and Moez Souissi. 2010. "Understanding Systemic Risk: The Trade-Offs between Capital, Short-Term Funding and Liquid Asset Holdings." Working Paper, Bank of Canada. Available at www.bankofcanada.ca/wp-content/uploads/2010/11/wp10-29.pdf.

Gersbach, Hans, and Jean-Charles Roche. 2011. "Aggregate Investment Externalities and Macroprudential Regulation." Working Paper, University of Zurich.

Hanrahan, Marc, and David Teh. 2007. "Second Lien Loans." In Allison Taylor and Alicia Sansone, eds., *The Handbook of Loan Syndications and Trading*, 55–70. New York: McGraw-Hill.

Hedge Fund Working Group. 2008. "Guidelines on Best Practice." London: Hedge Fund Working Group. Available at www.pellin.co.uk/HFWG/HFWG-FINAL-REPORT .pdf.

Hu, Henry, and Bernard Black. 2008. "Debt, Equity and Hybrid Decoupling: Governance and Systemic Risk Implications." *European Financial Management* 14:4, 663–709.

Knight, Frank H. 1921. "Structures and Methods for Meeting Uncertainty." In Frank H. Knight, *Risk, Uncertainty, and Profit*. Boston: Houghton Mifflin Co. Available at www.econlib.org/library/Knight/knRUP.html.

Korinek, Anton. 2011. "Systemic Risk-Taking Amplification Effects, Externalities and Regulatory Responses." Working Paper No. 1345, European Central Bank. Available at http://ssrn.com/abstract_id=1838600.

Laffont, Jean-Jacques. 2008. "Externalities." In Steven Durlauf and Lawrence Blume, eds., *The New Palgrave Dictionary of Economics*, 2nd ed., 287–290. Hampshire, UK: Palgrave Macmillan.

Murphy, Elizabeth, Janis Sarra, and Michael Creber. 2006. "Credit Derivatives in Canadian Insolvency Proceedings: The Devil Will Be in the Details." In Janis Sarra, ed., *Annual Review of Insolvency Law*, 187–235. Toronto: Carswell.

Parkinson, Patrick. 2008. "Over-the-counter Derivatives." Testimony Before the Subcommittee on Securities, Insurance, and Investment, Committee on Banking, Housing, and Urban Affairs, United States Senate. July 9. Available at www.federalreserve .gov/newsevents/testimony/parkinson20080709a.htm.

Pragyan, Deb, Mark Manning, Gareth Murphy, Adrian Penalver, and Aron Toth. 2011. "Whither the Credit Ratings Industry?" Bank of England Financial Stability Paper No. 9, March.

Sarra, Janis. 2008. *Credit Derivatives Market Design, Creating Fairness and Sustainability*. London: Network for Sustainable Financial Markets.

Sarra, Janis. 2011a. "New Governance, Old Norms, and the Potential for Corporate Governance Reform." *Law and Policy* 33:4, 576–602.

Sarra, Janis. 2011b. "Manoeuvring through the Insolvency Maze: Shifting Stakeholder Identities and Implications for CCAA Restructurings." *Banking and Finance Law Review (Canada)*, forthcoming.

Triantis, George C., and Ronald Daniels. 1995. "The Role of Debt in Interactive Corporate Governance." *University of California Law Review* 83:2, 1073–1113.

Wagner, Wolf. 2010. "In the Quest of Systemic Externalities: A Review of the Literature." *CESifo Economic Studies* 56:1, 96–111.

Zawadowski, Adam. 2011. "Entangled Financial Systems." Research Paper No. 2011-2, Boston University School of Management. Available at http://ssrn.com/abstract= 1765993.

ABOUT THE AUTHOR

Janis Sarra is Professor of Law at the University of British Columbia Faculty of Law, Vancouver, Canada, and founding director of the National Centre for Business Law. She has been awarded the title of Distinguished University Scholar for her scholarship in the area of securities law and finance and has written extensively in the areas of corporate finance, corporate governance, securities law and commercial insolvency law, including publication of more than 10 books. Before entering the academy, she was a commercial arbitrator and taught part-time at the Ryerson University Faculty of Business in Toronto, Canada. She was recently appointed Director of the Peter Wall Institute for Advanced Studies at the University of British Columbia. Professor Sarra holds an Honours BA and MA in politics and economics from the University of Toronto and a LLB, LLM, and SJD from the Faculty of Law University of Toronto.

CHAPTER 12

Real Estate and Society

PIET EICHHOLTZ
Professor of Finance and Real Estate, Maastricht University

NILS KOK
Associate Professor of Finance and Real Estate, Maastricht University

INTRODUCTION

On average, people spend 80 to 90 percent of their time in homes or offices that have to be heated or cooled, require lighting, and incorporate various energy-consuming appliances. In the United States, for example, buildings account for 71 percent of all electricity consumption (U.S. Energy Information Administration 2011). This translates into buildings generating some 30 to 40 percent of global greenhouse gas emissions. Not surprisingly, in the debate on climate change, carbon emissions, and saving resources, the built environment often emerges as offering great potential for greenhouse gas abatement. This is, for example, demonstrated in a study by the Intergovernmental Panel on Climate Change (2007) and influential work by Stern (2008).

The carbon cost abatement curve developed by McKinsey also shows that energy efficiency investments in buildings save energy in a cost-effective way (Enkvist, Nauclér, and Rosander 2007). Energy-saving can be a value-destroying proposition in some sectors because it requires more money than it saves. In the case of buildings, many of the necessary investments can readily be financed because they actually create value. The market can execute investments in energy efficiency without the need for government interference or regulation because they are already profitable now at current energy prices and with currently available technology.

For both tenants and owners, whether of private homes or commercial buildings, energy is a very substantial cost item, accounting for some 30 percent of operating expenses. As energy prices increase in the long run in the face of scarcer resources, these costs are likely to increase. Buildings that are more efficient will consume less energy, yielding direct cost savings. Recently, insurance companies have started to offer lower rates on buildings that are more energy efficient. Additionally, more sustainable buildings might have a higher value for an investor, as tenants' preferences for such buildings drive higher occupancy rates and higher rents.

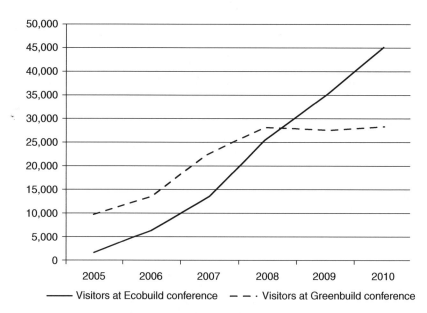

Exhibit 12.1 Attendance at the Ecobuild (United Kingdom) and Greenbuild (United States) Conferences (2005 to 2010)
This graph shows the increase in popular attention to green building with rapidly growing attendance rates at annual conventions related to energy efficiency and sustainability
Source: Ecobuild in the United Kingdom and Greenbuild in North America.

From a risk-mitigation perspective, the construction of a new building at a higher level of efficiency than prescribed by current standards will lead to being well positioned for the future. If the government introduces higher efficiency requirements, this building will already be in compliance, while its competitors still have to catch up. Refurbishing an existing building and making it energy-efficient is much more expensive than constructing a building as more energy-efficient in the first place. In the renovation of existing buildings, if a building's lifecycle renovation is due, the owner will benefit from bringing the building up to a high standard right away because of the high fixed costs involved. That is, overdoing the renovation make sense in order to make the building future-proof and reduce the risk of obsolescence.

Legislation has been an important component of the green movement, especially in Europe, where the Energy Performance of Buildings Directive (EPBD) has resulted in the European Union (EU) system of energy labels. Pan-European regulations on building codes are also becoming more stringent, and by 2020, all new buildings will have to be carbon neutral. In the United Kingdom, an important initiative is the Carbon Reduction Commitment (CRC), a carbon tax on large building owners that is based on their carbon emissions.

Meanwhile, the growing interest in greenness and sustainability in the real estate industry is illustrated by soaring attendance at, for example, the United Kingdom's key Ecobuild conference and the Greenbuild conference in the United States. As Exhibit 12.1 shows, the attendance at Ecobuild has climbed to more than 40,000 since 2005 and it is still growing. This level of attendance is more than double the 16,000 visitors to the biggest annual European real estate trade fair.

Energy-efficient, sustainable buildings, or green buildings, seem to have a bright future. The main purpose of this chapter is to examine the economic performance of such buildings. The remainder of the chapter is organized as follows. The next section addresses energy efficiency, sustainability, and building performance, and concludes that green buildings have better occupancy and command higher rents and prices. Some tenants seem to have a preference for sustainable buildings. Thus, the third section on corporate behavior explores which tenants value sustainable buildings and are willing to pay the price. The fourth section investigates whether real estate investors are moving toward more greenness and sustainability, using the newly developed Global Real Estate Sustainability Benchmark (GRESB) as a measure of environmental performance. The final section provides a summary and conclusions.

THE ECONOMIC PERFORMANCE OF GREEN BUILDINGS

The Energy Star and the Leadership in Energy and Environmental Design (LEED) labels form the basis for measures on the sustainability of buildings in the United States. The U.S. Environmental Protection Agency (EPA) introduced Energy Star initially for appliances and later for homes and commercial buildings. If a building is in the top 25 percent of the most efficient buildings in the United States, it can apply for an Energy Star. A professional engineer then verifies the building's energy consumption data and the EPS awards the label.

The U.S. Green Building Council (USGBC), a nonprofit organization, introduced a broader green building label, LEED. This is a scoring system for existing and new buildings that is based on six components of sustainability. Energy efficiency is just one of the components; the system also includes materials, sustainability of the location, indoor air quality, water, and waste. For new buildings, the system is based on design-stage models of how the building is expected to perform, verified after construction. For existing buildings, the system addresses current operational efficiency. Where Energy Star is a dedicated energy label, LEED, is more holistic and includes some more qualitative components.

Use of these labels in the U.S. market has grown rapidly over the past decade. Exhibit 12.2 shows that by 2010, Energy Star labeled 30 percent of total office space and 10 percent of all office buildings, whereas LEED labeled 10 percent of office space and 5 percent of all office buildings (Kok, McGraw, and Quigley 2011). This trend, a movement initiated by the property industry itself, is accelerating, explosively in the case of LEED, as indicated by another 27,000 buildings in the process of acquiring a LEED label, which amounts to 6 billion square feet of space.

A limited, but fast-growing, body of literature exists on the economic significance of sustainability in commercial and residential buildings. Initial evidence comes, for example, from Eichholtz, Kok, and Quigley (2010) and Fuerst and McAllister (2011). This section presents the evidence for both the United States and the international market, providing market-based results on the value

Panel A. Energy Star

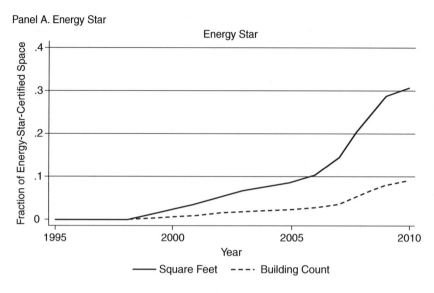

Panel B. LEED

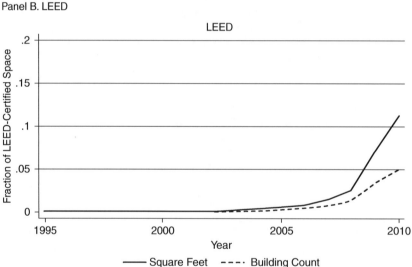

Exhibit 12.2   LEED and Energy Star Dynamics (1995 to 2010)
This graph shows the fraction of commercial office space in the United States that is certified by the
Environmental Protection Agency (Panel A) or the U.S. Green Building Council (Panel B), from 1995
to 2010. The bold line depicts the fraction of total square footage, whereas the dotted line depicts the
fraction of the total number of buildings.

implications of more efficient buildings, using large samples of data to ensure
statistically meaningful conclusions.

The methodology presented below focuses on establishing whether a difference occurs in financial performance for buildings based on green features. Because
directly observing which buildings are efficient is impossible, certification is used
as a proxy for greenness. Rigorous controls for the type of building further ensure

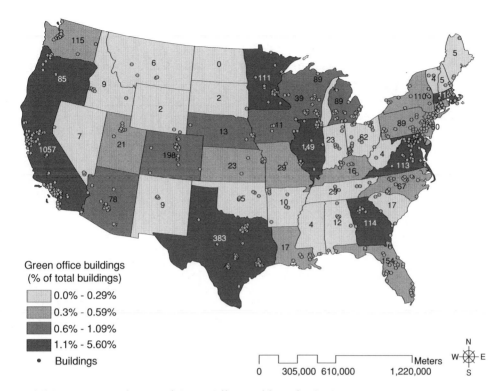

Exhibit 12.3   Distribution of Green Office Buildings by State

The map presents for each U.S. state the fraction of the commercial office stock that has been labeled with an Energy Star and/or LEED label. The darker the state, the higher is the fraction.

similar building comparisons. An important characteristic is age, as new buildings generally have higher rents and higher valuations. Buildings are also compared in the same location to account for the proverbially crucial real estate factor of location, location, location. If all other characteristics, such as building quality, height, maintenance, and renovation are filtered out, what is left is the greenness of a building. Thus, a reasonably safe conclusion is that any value, rent, or occupancy effect can be attributed to this factor. A hedonic pricing model is used to filter out all statistical differences between sustainable and nonsustainable properties in order to arrive at the average difference in occupancy rates and prices. A *hedonic pricing model* is a statistical model (i.e., a multiple regression model) of the sales prices of properties, showing how the prices are related to key characteristics that influence the value of the property.

Green Office Buildings in the United States

The research on green buildings in the United States is based on a sample of 28,000 office buildings (a 2009 cross-section), including 3,000 certified by EPA's Energy Star label or the USGBC's LEED and 25,000 nonlabeled buildings, all at similar locations. The geographical spread of green office stock in Exhibit 12.3

Exhibit 12.4   Green Ratings, Rents, and Sales Prices

Dependent Variable	Rent (per square foot)		Effective Rent (per square foot)		Sales Price (per square foot)	
	(1)	(2)	(3)	(4)	(5)	(6)
Green Rating (1 = yes)	0.026***		0.076***		0.133***	
	[0.007]		[0.010]		[0.017]	
Energy Star (1 = yes)		0.021***		0.065***		0.129***
		[0.005]		[0.007]		[0.0191]
Label Vintage (years)		−0.004**		−0.010***		−0.017*
		[0.002]		[0.002]		[0.011]
LEED (1 = yes)		0.058***		0.060***		0.111***
		[0.010]		[0.015]		[0.0419]
Quality Controls	Yes	Yes	Yes	Yes	Yes	Yes
Location Clusters	Yes	Yes	Yes	Yes	Yes	Yes
Time-Fixed Effects	No	No	No	No	Yes	Yes
N	20,801	20,801	20,801	20,801	5,993	5,993
R^2	0.833	0.834	0.736	0.736	0.662	0.662
Adjusted R^2	0.816	0.817	0.709	0.710	0.616	0.616

*, **, and *** indicate significance at the 0.10, 0.05, and 0.01 levels, respectively.
The table presents regression results relating rents (Columns 1 and 2), effective rents (Columns 3 and 4), and transaction prices (Columns 5 and 6) to physical characteristics of commercial office buildings, their location, and measures of greenness. Effective rent equals the contract rent multiplied by the occupancy rate. Each regression also includes a set of dummy variables, one for each cluster observed in 2009 containing a rated building and nearby nonrated buildings. There are 1,943 dummy variables for clusters containing rated rental buildings and 744 dummy variables for clusters containing rated buildings sold between 2004 and 2009. The observations are propensity-score weighted, and the results are based on a 2009 sample. The control sample consists of all commercial office buildings within a 0.25 mile radius of each rated building for which comparable data are available. All observations are current as of October 2009. Standard errors are in brackets.

shows that some states have a relatively high proportion of certified properties, up to 28 percent. This comes as no surprise in California, for example, with its strong environmental focus and relatively strict regulation. Similarly, the strong green credentials of Massachusetts could be related to the greenness of the state. However, Texas is not generally known for its hard-core environmental culture, but it emerges among the greenest states, which may be driven by a relatively high amount of recent real estate developments.

The market implications of greenness are demonstrated by the regression results in Exhibit 12.4. These show that buildings labeled as energy-efficient or sustainable achieved a 2.3 to 3 percent higher contract rent at the end of 2009, indicating that green labels are valuable for occupiers. In the second column, the data allow for further distinguishing between Energy Star, representing solely energy efficiency, and the more holistic LEED. The Energy Star rental premium is 2 percent, while for LEED the rental premium is higher at 6 percent. Tenants appear to be willing to pay more for sustainability than for energy efficiency alone.

Rent and occupancy multiplied together provide the cash flow, or effective rent that a building generates. The results in Exhibit 12.4 show that cash flows in buildings certified as sustainable are about 7.5 percent higher. Thus, certified buildings not only command a higher rent, but also higher occupancy rates. The occupancy effect is stronger for Energy Star than for LEED, as many LEED-certified buildings were developed at the height of the real estate boom, and came on the market during the subsequent bust. The limited effect of LEED on occupancy rates may be temporary, as occupancy could rise over time.

This chapter also addresses whether the market recognized greenness when a building is transacted. The last column in Exhibit 12.4 shows that transaction prices are some 13 percent higher for labeled versus nonlabeled buildings, demonstrating that investing in a building to make it green and to obtain an Energy Star or LEED label is indeed recognized when the property is transacted. These results have hitherto not been demonstrated in the real estate market with such rigor. Although real estate appraisers may currently not consciously take the sustainability of a property into account, and may not be aware of the effect of sustainability on the value of real estate, a property valuation should reflect a building's cash flow. If cash flows are, on average, 6 percent higher in sustainable buildings, this should translate into a higher valuation, whether the appraiser is aware of a building's green credentials or not.

In conclusion, eco-investment in the U.S. real estate sector is not simply doing good. It is also doing well, as the rent and price premiums can be translated into dollars. The average nongreen building in the rental sample would be worth $5.6 million more if it were converted to green, and the average nongreen building sold in 2004 to 2009 would have been worth $11.1 million more if it had been converted to green. Finally, sustainable buildings also seem to be less risky. The implied capitalization rate (i.e., discount rate) of 3 percent suggests that property investors also value the lower risk premium inherent in certified office buildings. This finding is in line with the hypothesis that if a building is more efficient now, it may protect value going forward.

Whether tenants and investors are willing to pay more just for the green label is addressed next. That is, whether a greater degree of greenness matters. Exhibit 12.5 shows the LEED score of certified buildings (x-axis) and the rent or transaction premium commanded in the marketplace (y-axis). The higher the LEED score, the higher is the effective rent, but this relation holds only up to a certain maximum. Apparently, tenants and investors have an upper limit, beyond which the extra greenness is perhaps seen as a waste of money. The grey area for LEED transaction increments in Exhibit 12.5 shows lower transaction prices for LEED Platinum than for the less stratospheric LEED labels, but estimates in this area are statistically less robust and should be interpreted with caution. The conclusion is that both tenants and investors seem to believe that the level of sustainability can be overdone, but investors seem to think this at a somewhat lower level than tenants.

What is the relationship between energy bills and rent? Are tenants willing to pay a dollar more in rent if they pay a dollar less for energy? The premium paid for each of the 1,819 Energy Star-rated buildings shows that saving one dollar in energy costs per year is associated with an increase in the effective rent of 95 cents, which is very close to a one-for-one exchange. For investors, a one dollar saving in energy costs is associated with a 4.9 percent premium in market capitalization, equivalent to $13 per square foot. Thus, both tenants and investors factor in energy efficiency when leasing or purchasing buildings. If energy costs are lower, both are willing to pay more, or vice versa. The market appears to be efficient, and energy

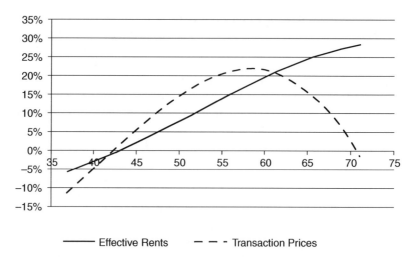

Exhibit 12.5   The Greenness of Buildings and Market Premiums

The figure relates the greenness score of LEED-certified office buildings (x-axis) to the premiums in rents and transaction prices (y-axis) that these buildings command in the marketplace. Buildings with more green features have higher rents and prices, but the relation is nonlinear, reaching a maximum at the LEED Gold level.

savings are quite efficiently incorporated into both rents and transaction prices. The direct capitalization of energy efficiency is also important for investments in building retrofits. The fact that the outcomes of such retrofits, in terms of energy efficiency, are priced implies that building owners can calculate returns rather than payback periods, enabling many more investments than are currently feasible.

One prediction about sustainability in buildings has been that when the market is saturated with green buildings, the premium will disappear. Also, because the initial wave of green building investment was made in a rising market, some could argue that when a crisis arrives—as it indeed has—tenants and investors could no longer afford to do good. Fortunately, data from 2007 to 2009 provide an ideal basis to check for differences between precrisis and postcrisis effects of green certification on commercial building performance.

During this crisis period, unemployment rose to above 10 percent, leading office vacancy rates to climb. For example, Manhattan vacancy rates rose by some 40 percent, while rents plunged by 30 percent. Meanwhile, a wave of buildings certified as green came onto the market. Results documented by Eichholtz, Kok, and Quigley (2011b) show that rents in green buildings went down by about 3 percent more, compared to nongreen buildings. However, as green buildings are generally up-market, centrally-located and newer, they could be expected to be more vulnerable to price declines. After filtering out differences due to quality and location, the difference in rent disappears between 2007 and 2010 in green and non-green buildings. The authors conclude that neither a deteriorating market situation nor an increase in the number of green buildings affected financial premiums paid for green buildings in the U.S. commercial property market. Tenants and investors seem to act regardless of market sentiment or supply of green buildings. Pricing also remains similar, nullifying the idea of greenness in the property sector as fad or fashion.

International Comparisons: Commercial Properties in the United Kingdom

The environmental building label of choice in the United Kingdom is the Building Research Establishment Environmental Assessment Method (BREEAM) labeling system, which dates back to 1999 and is the precursor of and comparable to the LEED system. Scoring is based on 10 components of energy efficiency and sustainability, and the system has five rating levels—outstanding, excellent, very good, good, and pass—and unclassified.

Chegut, Eichholtz, and Kok (2012) collected a sample of 1,150 BREEAM-certified rental transactions for sustainable office properties in London (a 2005 to 2009 cross-section), and compared it with transactions in noncertified buildings. In line with the U.S. research, the aim was to investigate whether tenants and investors recognize sustainability when they make their respective decisions on occupancy and investments, and whether an increase in the number of green buildings affects this willingness to pay.

The authors develop five models of hedonic and propensity-weighted results for rents and transaction prices, all producing the same results. Rents are some 21 to 25 percent higher for green-labeled than conventional buildings and transaction prices show a 26 to 35 percent premium. However, unlike in the United States, where very elaborate checks can be executed to control for quality and other building characteristics (filtering out everything except the green effect), less data are available on building quality in the United Kingdom. This lack of data implies that the results are likely to be somewhat overstated due to building quality effects embedded in the BREEAM certification. The green premium should thus be taken as an upper limit rather than a baseline, precise estimate.

Translating the results into pounds sterling shows the annual rent increment on an average-size (1,268 square meter) certified office building is about £1.4 million, and the transaction increment is about £8.9 million, ceteris paribus (other things being equal). The average rent per square meter for the London rental sample is £400 a year, and the premium for a certified building is approximately £9.4 million. Again, caution is necessary here because proper controls for building quality are lacking.

International Comparisons: Office Buildings in the Netherlands

According to the Energy Performance of Buildings Directive (EPBD), the EU energy label is mandatory throughout the EU. The energy label indicates the energy efficiency of appliances, cars, housing, or commercial buildings, showing how much energy they, in theory, consume. Exhibit 12.6 provides an example. Thus, for tenants, an A label implies that the utility bill should be relatively low. From the economist's point of view, the question is to what extent this label is valuable to the marketplace, and to what extent it provides a reliable signal to tenants in commercial buildings and to homeowners in residential buildings.

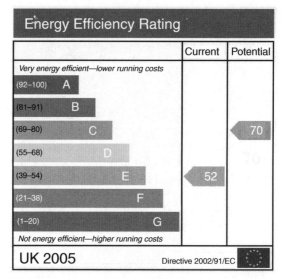

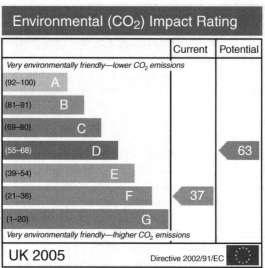

Exhibit 12.6 Energy Labels in the European Union
The energy performance certificate (EPC) is used throughout Europe and displays the level of energy efficiency for residential and commercial buildings. This particular example is from the United Kingdom.

Kok and Jennen (2012) investigate the effect of energy efficiency on commercial buildings in Holland in the same vein as the U.S. and U.K. studies discussed above. The authors collect information on rent transactions in office buildings in the Netherlands, making a distinction between buildings labeled A, B, or C, and buildings labeled as E, F, and G.

The authors compare rental developments over the past five years, controlling for location and building quality. Exhibit 12.7 illustrates that in 2006, still a buoyant

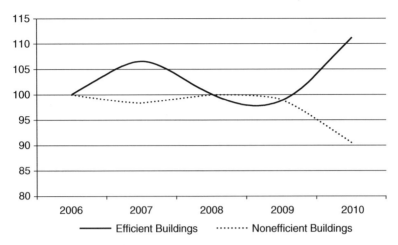

Exhibit 12.7   Rent Index Efficient Office Buildings (Labels A, B, and C) and Nonefficient Office Buildings (Labels D and Lower)

The graph shows the developments in achieved rents for a sample of office buildings certified as efficient (bold line) and a sample of office buildings that are certified as less efficient (dotted line). The graph is based on transactions in the Netherlands during the 2005 to 2010 period. Results are based on a regression that controls for building quality and building location.

period for the office market, tenant preference for buildings certified as efficient was somewhat higher and rents went up faster than in nongreen buildings. But rents also went down a bit more rapidly when the crisis started. In 2009, however, a clear shift in the market started, with rents about 10 percent higher in buildings labeled energy-efficient but dropping 10 percent in buildings labeled as inefficient. This results in a total rent difference of 20 percent, providing some evidence that the market currently awards discounts for nongreen, inefficient buildings as well as premiums for more efficient, green buildings. This evidence also reinforces the results presented for the United States and United Kingdom. An important finding for building owners is that insufficient environmental credentials constitute a risk factor.

International Comparisons: Dutch Housing

All the studies discussed so far have focused on office properties. However, the housing market dominates in the built environment and can therefore have the greatest impact on global energy demand and carbon emissions. An important question is, therefore, whether private home owners care about and make decisions based on energy bills, and whether an energy label helps them to make informed decisions. Brouwen and Kok (2011) employ a methodology similar to the previously discussed commercial studies, based on a large sample of homes sold in the Netherlands with an energy label. The data distinguish between the type of home (apartment, detached, corner, or terrace) and for quality characteristics of homes, allowing for analysis of transaction prices of homes based on their energy label. The results show that efficient homes sell at a premium of about 3.5 percent, on average. The average Dutch home sells for about 240,000 euros, and a premium of about 9,000 euros is obtained simply from having a label A, B, or C. Further analysis uses the D label as the midpoint and shows that A-label homes sell at a premium of 10 percent and B and C labels at slightly lower premiums, while E, F, and G label homes sell at a discount. Here too, the picture that emerges is about discounts as well as premiums. The study documents an almost linear, continuous relationship with price increments for each label step.

An important conclusion of this study is that introducing energy-saving systems in a private home creates a double benefit. That is, homeowners profit from direct energy-cost savings and seeing the selling price go up. The research suggests that private homeowners behave rationally and use the energy label as information in their decision-making process.

International Comparisons: Housing in Asia

Research on non-Western markets is slowly starting to appear. In Japan, Yoshida and Sugiura's (2011) study is the sole study to claim that the market does not value green buildings above comparable conventional buildings. The paper focuses on the housing market, and finds that given proper quality controls, buyers of condos in Japan do not value a green label. In fact, they actually value such a building less.

In an attempt to tease out the reason for this, the study finds that the green attributes are not attributes that save money, but actually cost extra money because the systems for greening the condominiums require substantial maintenance. Japanese homes are already relatively efficient, and the green attributes in this case actually imply an extra financial burden. This is in line with the LEED curve in Exhibit 12.5 showing that when extra greenness adds elements that no longer improve the bottom line, values decline. So, consumers seem to behave rationally in the light of green property investments, even if the effect of that behavior on pricing differs from that in Europe and the United States.

In China, a study by Zheng, Wu, Kahn, and Deng (2011) investigates the relevance of sustainability for a sample of Chinese apartment developments. China has not formally adopted green rating standards. In the absence of such standards, developers are competing with each other based on their own self-reported indicators of their buildings' greenness. The authors create an index using Google search key words to rank housing complexes with respect to their marketing greenness and document that these green units sell for a price premium at the presale stage, but they subsequently resell or rent for a price discount. This corroborates the findings of studies conducted by Chinese engineers who contend that the technologies, including central air conditioning, that are embedded in green buildings actually consume more electricity.

In 2005, Singapore became the first Asian country to adopt a system of green labeling for newly constructed and rehabilitated buildings. The system, called Green Mark, has been widely publicized in the city-state. Deng, Li, and Quigley (2011) study condominiums with the Singapore labeling standard. Based on nearest one-to-one neighbor matching between control and treatment samples, the authors find a significant premium in selling prices for dwellings with Green Mark Certification even after controlling for community amenities. The estimated premium is larger for dwellings certified at higher levels in the Green Mark process, namely Platinum, Gold Plus, and Gold-rated dwellings.

WHY DO CORPORATIONS PAY A PREMIUM FOR GREEN?

This section addresses the behavior of corporate tenants as it relates to housing choices. For corporations, reasons to pay a premium for green offices include the possible noneconomic motivation of flagging their corporate social responsibility (CSR) commitment.

Understanding preferences for green space and the motivation behind it is clearly useful in relation to undertaking green development and for improved prediction of potential demand. It should also demonstrate the scope for voluntary measures to promote green investments and help in formulating policies needed to nudge corporations to go green. Management may, however, also use green real estate as a proxy for real ecological responsiveness; corporations naturally want to present themselves as responsible and engage in headline-grabbing activities such as giving money to good causes. But looking under the hood at the buildings corporations actually use, particularly outside of their headquarters, may tell the true story about their ecological deeds.

The research presented here builds on the theoretical framework provided by a seminal paper of Bansal and Roth (2000) and their classification of motivation posited for renting green buildings. The first motivational factor is improved profitability. Green space may be cheaper to occupy, as it may have lower energy bills, and net rents paid can be slightly higher. Evidence from the medical literature also suggests that people in more healthy green buildings are less prone to such complaints as headaches, nausea, and general fatigue, and may therefore be more productive, improving the output of corporations (Oldham and Rotchford 1983; Bitner 1992).

Secondly, green buildings offer indirect economic benefits. Companies are active in the capital market where they meet investors, the labor market for employees, and the market for their goods where they meet customers. All these groups may value environmental responsibility or be put off by irresponsibility. Employees, for example, may prefer to work for a company that displays shades of green, and customers may prefer to buy or pay premium prices for products from a greener company. These factors also receive factual support in the literature.

These are not trivial factors. Institutional investors, such as pension funds and insurance companies, increasingly scrutinize the environmental credentials of the companies in which they invest. This means that the company's environmental reputation can negatively (e.g., a risk of oil spills) or positively affect its ability to attract capital via an initial public offering, secondary offering, or private placement. For employers in the western European market, at least where unemployment rates have remained relatively low during the recent economic downturn, competition for talent is increasingly important. Talent is known to be attracted by a pleasant space in which to work, with good indoor environmental quality, and other positive attributes that are associated with green buildings.

The third motivational factor is risk avoidance. Environmental issues can give rise to insurance claims, for instance, in the past for asbestos. But damages claims can also arise in relation to the sick building syndrome if employees have respiratory problems such as asthma. Housing employees in a better building also means that a corporate owner is less likely to suffer from government intrusion or increased regulation and legislation.

The final underlying factor suggested as a motivation for renting green space is ethical behavior. For some individuals, corporations, and institutions, green behavior is simply the right thing to do. Research shows that foundations, government, and environmental bodies occupy many green buildings, often with the express intention of leading by example. The Dutch government, for example, targets only space with a C label or higher, while in the United States, federal and local government want to be in buildings certified by the USGBC. These are large organizations, creating substantial demand and absorbing a large proportion of green buildings.

Building on the four major motives for renting sustainable office space, the study of Eichholtz, Kok, and Quigley (2011a) aims to define different groups that are more, or less, likely to go green. Besides nonprofit institutions and governments, green candidates could, for example, be industries where human capital and productivity are key factors, such as financial services, or alternatively dirty industries striving to offset their otherwise nongreen image by green-washing. The research seeks to verify these hypotheses.

The study is based on 286 LEED-rated green office buildings and 1,045 Energy Star rated offices in the United States. Using information on the five biggest tenants in each building, this yields a total sample of 3,179 unique tenants. These are compared with 4,400 conventional, nonlabeled buildings, yielding approximately 8,000 unique tenants. For each of those tenants, data are available on their industry and how much space they occupy.

The results in Exhibit 12.8 show the U.S. government (over 2 million square feet), as well as the State of California, the U.S. Department of Health and Human Science, and the California Environmental Protection Agency (Cal/EPA), high up in the Top 20. In terms of the proportion of all the space occupied that is green, the U.S. government comes out at about 17 percent, California at 28 percent, Health and Human Science at an impressive 87 percent, while Cal/EPA hits appropriately 100 percent in its single, very large green building. Hence, Cal/EPA practices what it preaches. As expected, government is indeed a substantial green tenant.

The findings also confirm that large financial institutions, including Wells Fargo, Bank of America, ABN AMRO (now RBS), American Express, the Vanguard Group, and JP Morgan Chase are substantial occupiers of green space. Telephone interviews reveal that Wells Fargo, for example, known for its ethical behavior, has a corporate policy of occupying green space, and also of renovating existing offices to green standards. Real estate is an essential part of its overall corporate stance. The same is true of Bank of America, which recently occupied an elite LEED Platinum office tower in New York, 1 Bryant Park, one of the greenest buildings in New York. Other big financial institutions, such as insurers Blue Cross & Blue Shield, are also large green tenants. Overall, 7 of the top 20 are financial institutions, in line with the hypothesis that green is attractive for human capital—an important basis of these companies. Satisfying their staff is important for productivity as well as for reputation effects.

Exhibit 12.8 Fraction of Firm Office Space Housed in Green Buildings

Tenant Name	Industry Description	(1) Green Office Space (x 1000 square feet)	(2) Fraction of Total Green Space (%)	(3) Cumulative Fraction of Total Green Space (%)	(4) Total Space CoStar (x 1000 square feet)	(5) Green Space as Fraction of Total Space Rentals (%)
				Space Occupied		
Wells Fargo Bank	National commercial banks	2,741	1.61	1.61	7,343	37.33
U.S. Government	General government	2,415	1.42	3.03	14,631	16.50
Bank of America	National commercial banks	2,124	1.25	4.28	18,695	11.36
ABN AMRO	State commercial banks	1,724	1.01	5.29	2,993	57.60
State of California	General government	1,568	0.92	6.21	5,706	27.49
Deloitte and Touche	Accounting, auditing, and bookkeeping	1,554	0.91	7.13	5,131	30.28
Best Buy	Radio, television, and consumer electronics	1,500	0.88	8.01	2,104	71.31
U.S. Department of Health and Human Services.	General government	1,442	0.85	8.86	1,662	86.72
Shell	Petroleum and gas	1,362	0.80	9.66	3,989	34.14
Chevron	Petroleum and gas	1,229	0.72	10.38	6,181	19.88
Blue Cross and Blue Shield	Hospital and medical service plans	1,211	0.71	11.09	12,251	9.89
Adobe Systems	Prepackaged software	1,158	0.68	11.77	1,388	83.43
Compuware Corporation	Prepackaged software	1,094	0.64	12.41	1,300	84.18
American Express	Personal credit institutions	1,018	0.60	13.01	6,754	15.07
The Vanguard Group	Investment advice	990	0.58	13.59	1,569	63.07
Cal/EPA	Land, mineral, wildlife, and forest conservation	950	0.56	14.15	950	100.00
Mitre Corporation	Commercial physical and biological research	944	0.55	14.71	1,293	73.02
JP Morgan Chase	Investment advice	907	0.53	15.24	10,670	8.50
Skadden Arps	Legal services	889	0.52	15.76	1,751	50.77
Ernst and Young	Accounting, auditing, and bookkeeping	864	0.51	16.27	4,149	20.83

The largest tenants of office space rated as green by the U.S. Green Building Council and the Environmental Protection Agency. The office space is measured in absolute square footage (Column 1) and as a fraction of total office space leased by tenant (Column 5).

Another prominent group in the Top 20 is oil and gas, with Shell and Chevron as prominent tenants in LEED-certified space. Chevron, with a LEED-certified campus in Louisiana built to its standards, prides itself in being a responsible corporate citizen. This evidence shows that these companies aim to come across as efficient and green in their operations. This may be in line with the green-washing hypothesis, but it may also be a reflection of true corporate citizenship. The green real estate preferences of the oil industry may also be an explanation for the high percentage of green buildings in Texas.

In some industries, companies are, on average, small, but the industry as a whole could still be an important green space user. Thus, Exhibit 12.9 looks at the top 20 industries. Here, legal services, mostly a nonconcentrated industry with just one firm in the Top 20, comes to the top with 25 million square feet, again in line with the human capital effect. Law firms in the United States are typically located in the best buildings in town, nowadays typically a LEED-certified building.

The other industries in the top three are banks and executive, legislative, and general office, with the crude petroleum and gas industry again featuring in fourth place. Its remarkably high proportion of green buildings (62.6 percent), however, reflects its relatively low proportion of office buildings to manufacturing facilities. Also featuring high up on the list is fabricated rubber products, another polluting industry, suggesting a similar green-washing motivation.

In summary, green building occupancy is higher in large financial companies and the legal profession, the public sector, mining and construction, and generally in occupations with more productive and more expensive employees. Organizations and industries seem to use green buildings as a flag of ecological responsiveness. Further research shows that green building occupancy is also higher in areas where such employees are based. Variables on sales and payroll per employee show that green building occupancy is higher in areas with higher sales per employee and payroll per employee. Companies and industries based on high-value employees clearly do want to house their workforce in better buildings.

IMPLICATIONS FOR INSTITUTIONAL INVESTORS: THE GRESB BENCHMARK

The evidence presented in this chapter thus far shows that more efficient, sustainable buildings command higher rents, and that distinct groups of corporate tenants are willing to pay these higher rents. This situation may create an interesting investment opportunity. The fiduciary responsibility of institutional investors does not seem to conflict, but is in line with investors' aims to implement sustainability factors into their real estate investment policy. The final section of this chapter considers how institutional investors take account of greenness and sustainability and incorporate them in their day-to-day investment practices by explaining the creation of a new sustainability benchmark for measuring the greenness of property investment companies and funds (Bauer, Eichholtz, Kok, and Quigley 2011).

To better understand real estate investment decisions requires knowing that the capital flowing into the real estate investment industry ultimately comes largely from institutional investors. In the past, these institutions used to own real estate directly, but they have increasingly come to regard real estate as an asset that

Exhibit 12.9 Fraction of Office Space Housed in Green Buildings by Four-Digit SIC

		(1)	(2)	(3)	(4)	(5)
				Space Occupied		
SIC Code	Industry Description	Green Office Space (x 1000 square feet)	Fraction of Total Green Space (%)	Cumulative Fraction of Total Green Space (%)	Total Office Space CoStar (x 1000 square feet)	Green Space as Fraction of Total Space Rentals (%)
8111	Legal services	25,593	15.04	15.04	217,097	11.79
6021	National commercial banks	9,436	5.55	20.59	86,782	10.87
9199	Executive, legislative, and general office	9,035	5.31	25.90	67,081	13.47
1311	Crude petroleum and gas	7,076	4.16	30.06	11,304	62.60
6282	Investment advice	6,532	3.84	33.90	100,939	6.47
8721	Accounting, auditing, and bookkeeping services	5,158	3.03	36.93	136,766	3.77
5731	Radio, television, and consumer electronics stores	1,531	0.90	37.83	3,888	39.37
9311	Public finance, taxation, and monetary policy	822	0.48	38.31	14,491	5.67
7373	Computer integrated systems design	816	0.48	38.79	19,487	4.19
3812	Search, detection, navigation, and guidance	291	0.17	38.96	4,869	5.97
2759	Commercial printing, NEC	287	0.17	39.13	3,996	7.17
3069	Fabricated rubber products, NEC	285	0.17	39.30	769	37.08
4731	Arrangement transportation of freight and cargo	282	0.17	39.46	8,348	3.38
9621	Regulations and administration of transportation programs	280	0.16	39.63	9,115	3.07
7997	Membership sports and recreation clubs	274	0.16	39.79	1,696	16.15
8641	Civic, social, and fraternal associations	274	0.16	39.95	14,362	1.91
2086	Bottled and canned soft drinks and carbonated waters	261	0.15	40.10	5,037	5.19
5411	Grocery stores	253	0.15	40.25	8,363	3.03
4724	Travel agencies	252	0.15	40.40	7,539	3.34
6552	Land subdividers and developers	250	0.15	40.55	9,676	2.58

Industries with the largest fraction of office space rated as green by the U.S. Green Building Council and the Environmental Protection Agency. Office space is measured in absolute square footage (Column 1) and as a fraction of total office space leased by industry (Column 5).

demands entrepreneurship and prefer to hold real estate via listed property companies and/or private real estate funds run by industry experts who presumably know how to maximize income and value.

This means that if a pension fund has sustainability policies that it wants to incorporate in its property investments, the investors cannot directly execute the implementation of those sustainability plans, but have to engage with the funds and companies in which the funds invests. Ultimately, institutional investors want to minimize risk while maximizing returns. They observe the increased demand from corporate tenants for efficient buildings and observe more and stricter environmental regulation in the building industry. Investors may thus conclude that greenness can boost net income, and crucially, that more efficient buildings mitigate risk.

However, since institutional investors do not invest directly in buildings, they need to be able to measure the sustainability performance of the companies and funds in which they invest. In other words, a green label is needed not just for buildings, but also for companies and funds. Thus, a clear need exists for a sustainability rating for real estate funds and companies that can be used by the institutional investors.

This background leads to the authors' creating the Global Real Estate Sustainability Benchmark (GRESB). Backed by 24 pension funds and industry associations, representing $1.7 trillion of combined assets, GRESB measures sustainability at the portfolio level. The approach used is applicable globally, via a survey especially designed to be relevant for real estate. The sponsoring pension funds use GRESB as a tool for engaging with real estate companies and funds. These pension funds can use this measure to enter into an informed dialogue and if necessary, point out deficiencies in some issues and give the companies and funds an appropriate timeframe to make changes. GRESB can also be used as part of the due diligence process for making initial investments.

GRESB is executed via an online survey with 55 questions. The science-based sustainability benchmark is based on industry best practices from the GRI Construction and Real Estate Sector Supplement (CRESS) and the European Public Real Estate Association's Best Practices Reporting (EPRA BPR). Among other aspects, the questions cover management issues such as whether the board looks at sustainability on a regular basis. Implementation is also covered, such as whether water and energy use and greenhouse gas emissions are measured with the aim of reducing them and whether they are so reduced.

The philosophical underpinning of GRESB is that investments into better environmental performance may improve the financial performance of the property funds and companies at the same time. Allocating points and scoring on performance is, therefore, from the standpoint of whether improving the environmental performance is also likely to boost financial performance or to minimize risk. Ultimately, pension funds that sponsor GRESB have both a fiduciary responsibility and a responsibility to society, but legally their fiduciary responsibility comes first.

The GRESB score uses eight dimensions of sustainability that are grouped into two broader categories: management and policy, making up 30 percent of the overall score, and implementation and measurement, constituting the remaining 70 percent. So green walk receives more weight than green talk.

Exhibit 12.10 GRESB Response Overview

	Number of Respondents	Market Coverage (value-weighted) (%)	Gross Asset Value ($ billion)
Listed (Total)	**69**	**35**	**483**
North America	15	37	133
Europe	32	75	170
Asia	12	12	40
Australia	10	80	141
Private (Total)	**271**		**445**
North America	45		129
South America	4		5
Europe	162		205
Asia	37		52
Australia	23		54
Grand Total	**340**		**928**

This exhibit shows responses to the 2011 GRESB survey. The data are presented by investment type (listed property companies and private property funds) and split out by region. The market coverage presents the fraction of the FTSE EPRA/NAREIT Index that is covered by the respondents.

Exhibit 12.10 depicts the response rate to the GRESB 2011 survey, which climbed by 70 percent from the first survey in 2009 (Kok, Bauer, and Eichholtz 2011). The property companies and funds surveyed represent almost 1 trillion dollars of gross asset value. The sample includes 69 listed companies and 271 private property funds. The listed companies in the sample are large, and 75 percent of all listed companies are covered in terms of market capitalization in Europe and 80 percent in Australia. In North America, the figure is 37 percent, with Asia as the lowest at 12 percent. The survey achieved substantial coverage in most markets, covering 35 percent of all listed real estate companies by market capitalization worldwide.

Among the 271 private companies surveyed, the majority of the companies are in Europe, but a fair number of them are in Asia and North America. Ascertaining the market coverage on the basis of valuation is impossible because the total market valuation of private property funds is an unknown factor.

Exhibit 12.11 shows the key results. The GRESB four-quadrant model, with the scores from the management and policy set of questions on the x-axis, represents the talking-the-talk dimension of companies' green credentials. On the y-axis are the scores from the implementation and measurement set of questions, representing concrete action, or walking the walk. Respondents are grouped into quadrants of the graph, with the northeast quadrant including the funds that score higher than 50 percent on both dimensions. These so-called Green Stars are still a small minority of the total sample. Comparing the results of the 2009 survey to those of the 2011 survey shows that firms are moving to this quadrant. The number of Green Stars is up, not only absolutely, which could be driven by the much higher response rate, but also relatively.

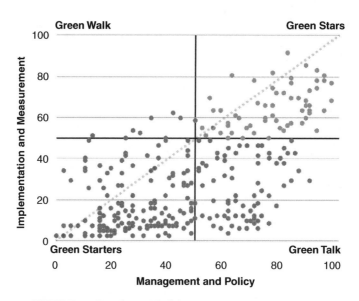

Exhibit 12.11 GRESB Four Quadrant Model

Figure 12.11 shows the position of each respondent to the 2011 GRESB survey in the GRESB Four Quadrant Model of sustainability performance. This performance is measured on two dimensions: Management & Policy (x-axis) and Implementation & Measurement (y-axis).

The Green Stars, with high implementation and measurement scores, are the gallery that every company should aspire to join. The Green Star is the hallmark of sustainability performance of companies with policies and management in place to optimize sustainability via measurement and improvement.

The bulk of companies are still in the two bottom quadrants, the southwest quadrant with management and policy scores between 0 and 50, dubbed Green Starters, and the southeast quadrant companies in the Green Talk category. But importantly, Green Starters can also be viewed as having substantial upside potential, with much low-hanging fruit in energy efficiency improvements to be picked. Some two-thirds of the respondents are in these two quadrants and have considerable room for environmental and financial improvement.

A regional breakdown of the data shows that Green Stars are most likely to be found among Australia's listed companies, but Australian private funds are also performing well. Both groups are, on average, Green Stars. For sustainability in real estate at least, Australia is the world champion. For Europe, the survey shows a wide gap between listed and private companies, with listed scoring above 50 on management and policy, and also quite high on implementation at nearly 40. But the private funds score only just above 20 on implementation, and below 50 on management and policy. Also lagging in the southwest quadrant are listed and unlisted Asian companies, signaling much potential to be harnessed there. North America is currently positioned between listed and private respondents from Europe.

In terms of property types, shopping malls do best, performing as Green Talkers but close to Green Stars. One reason shopping malls and also offices outperform

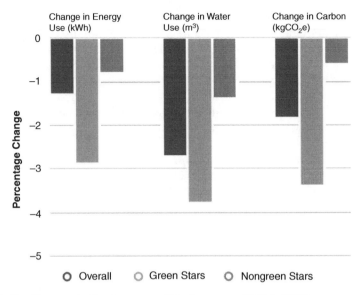

Exhibit 12.12 Changes in Environmental Performance (2009 to 2010)
The graph shows the aggregate 2009 to 2010 change in resource consumption of the respondents to the 2011 GRESB survey. Results are presented separately for the full sample, for "Green Stars" (i.e., those respondents in the top-right quadrant of 12.11), and for respondents that are not considered Green Stars.

other property types may be because owners have more scope to intervene directly in improving the sustainability of buildings, without the help of tenants. Shopping malls and offices have large common areas, such as arcades, entrance areas, and elevators, where the landlord has control. In main-street retail, residential or logistics real estate, the landlord has less control and will need to work in partnership with tenants to undertake action. Another factor is that existing labeling schemes such as LEED and BREEAM are tailored more for offices and shopping malls and less so for other types of real estate.

GRESB has been created to represent a benchmark of greenness and to provide a new sustainability rating at the property fund level. So the final key question is whether GRESB scores are relevant, and whether respondents are actually improving their sustainability performance. Does the fact that some funds have the infrastructure in place as Green Stars mean anything in terms of their actual energy, waste, or water consumption, and is the industry improving in these areas?

Exhibit 12.12 rates companies on changes in energy and water use and carbon emissions in two subgroups of companies, Green Stars and non–Green Stars, plus the overall group. Each respondent is requested to submit information on energy use, water consumption, and carbon emissions in 2009 and 2010 so that the percentage change can be calculated based on like-for-like portfolios. The exhibit shows that the overall property sector surveyed, worth about $1 trillion, reduced its energy consumption by 1.2 percent, a substantial figure in view of the size of the industry and also impressive in view of the fact that new buildings are a tiny proportion of the total, since 99 percent are existing real estate.

The Green Star subgroup shows outperformance in the area of energy consumption by achieving an impressive 3 percent reduction in 2010. For water use and carbon emissions, the pattern is the same. Where the overall sample reduced water use by about 2.5 percent, this was almost 4 percent for the Green Stars. The overall sample reduced carbon emissions by almost 2 percent, whereas the Green Stars reductions were over 3 percent.

This means that a Green Star GRESB rating does indeed show that a company is a leader in terms of environmental performance. Also important is the fact that these Green Stars are mostly mainstream real estate companies (i.e., companies that do not occupy any special niche of greenness, but just aim for superior financial performance using a method that seems to work). This finding implies that all the other respondents, the Green Starters as well as the Green Talkers, can emulate them; they represent the best practices among peers, rather than some elite group catering to an elite audience.

The GRESB scores define measurable environmental performance in terms of energy consumption, water use, and carbon emissions. The surveys show that the commercial property sector has started to improve its environmental performance, though many respondents still have a long way to go. For investors, this implies that screening property funds and companies on their sustainability offers an opportunity to reap the benefits of improving environmental performance of their investments.

SUMMARY AND CONCLUSIONS

One lesson that can be learned from this chapter is that the environmental characteristics of a building are an increasingly important risk factor. Greenness and sustainability are becoming mainstream in the property industry, the percentage of green buildings in the industry is growing fast, and these buildings are associated with the better-quality part of the industry. Investors who do not incorporate this trend into business operations may risk their buildings becoming obsolete and facing structural vacancy.

Evidence on the implications of energy efficiency and sustainability can be observed in the United States, but also in the Netherlands and in the United Kingdom. In countries where the labor population is shrinking, less office space will be needed in the future. The market will be split in two, with a viable part where tenants are willing to pay high rents and a nonviable part with structural vacancy, where buildings will be harder to rent, depreciate rapidly, and will eventually be torn down. Thus, quality will increasingly be the driving force for financial performance, and as sustainability is now a key quality factor, it will be essential to incorporate elements of sustainability or risk having a building that is impossible to rent.

The market seems to be relatively efficient in the pricing aspects of sustainability, and this holds for residential as well as commercial real estate. The word *green* has sometimes been associated with environmental ideology in the past, rather than with maximizing returns. But in real estate, the term is directly associated with tangible aspects such as energy efficiency and indoor environmental quality, and has a direct relationship with tenant comfort and the bottom line.

This irreversible trend also has some policy implications. Considering the increase in private as well as public-sector-initiated labels, these appear to be effective in conveying a message on the quality of buildings. Energy labels in Europe and the United States are all picked up by the market and valued both by the commercial sector and also by homeowners, who are perhaps less widely perceived as rational decision makers. This helps reduce energy consumption and emissions, and the trend is given a further boost by investor preferences for more sustainable buildings.

Such labels could be an interesting, relatively cheap way forward for policy makers. They do not represent a tax burden, such as a carbon tax, which is politically impossible to impose in most countries. These labels do not represent subsidies, which are equally difficult to enact. Importantly, the United States is now considering an energy label similar to the label in the EU. Labels provide information to the market and then allow the market to act, nudging it in the desired direction without policy intervention.

A further conclusion is that from the point of view of vendors or building managers, solely considering the direct payback period of investments in energy efficiency is too narrow a metric. If better windows, insulation, or more efficient heating/cooling systems are installed, this will be directly reflected in lower costs, but also in higher rents and occupancy rates and the competitiveness of the building. On top of this, when the building is transacted, the research presented in this chapter suggests that the investment in environmental improvements will be reflected in the price of the commercial building or home. If solar panels are installed on the roof of a dwelling, recouping the investment may theoretically take 25 years, but if the owner later sells the house, after enjoying the savings year by year, the value of the solar panels will also be reflected in the transaction price (Dastrup, Graff Zivin, Costa, and Kahn 2011). This indirect return on green property investments not only changes the investment decision but also further boosts the energy efficiency of existing homes and buildings.

DISCUSSION QUESTIONS

1. Explain whether a conflict exists between the fiduciary responsibility of institutional investors and a sustainable real estate investment policy.

2. Why are green buildings likely to be less risky than conventional but otherwise comparable buildings?

3. Why is controlling for building quality and age important when estimating the economic and financial effects of sustainable building characteristics?

4. To what extent is government interference necessary to steer the real estate sector towards greener practices? Think about informational nudges, incentives, and regulation.

5. Do commercial property investors and private homeowners make rational choices involving sustainability investments in their buildings?

REFERENCES

Bansal, Pratima, and Kendall Roth. 2000. "Why Companies Go Green: A Model of Ecological Responsiveness." *Academy of Management Journal* 43:4, 717–37.

Bauer, Rob, Piet M. Eichholtz, Nils Kok, and John M. Quigley. 2011. "How Green Is Your Property Portfolio? The Global Real Estate Sustainability Benchmark." *Rotman International Journal for Pension Management* 4:1, 34–43.

Bitner, Mary J. 1992. "Serviscapes: The Impact of Physical Surroundings on Customers and Employees." *Journal of Marketing* 56:2, 57–1.

Brounen, Dirk, and Nils Kok. 2011. "On the Economics of Energy Labels in the Housing Market." *Journal of Environmental Economics and Management* 62:2, 166–179.

Chegut, Andrea, Piet M. Eichholtz, and Nils Kok. 2012. "Supply, Demand, and the Value of Green Buildings." Working Paper, Maastricht University.

Dastrup, Samuel, Joshua S. Graff Zivin, Dora L. Costa, and Matthew E. Kahn. 2011. "Understanding the Solar Home Premium: Electricity Generation and 'Green' Social Status." *European Economic Review*, forthcoming.

Deng, Yongheng, Zhiliang Li, and John M. Quigley. 2011. "Economic Returns to Energy-Efficient Investments in the Housing Market: Evidence from Singapore." *Regional Science and Urban Economics*, forthcoming.

Eichholtz, Piet M. A., Nils Kok, and John M. Quigley. 2010. "Doing Well by Doing Good: Green Office Buildings." *American Economic Review* 100:5, 2494–2511.

Eichholtz, Piet M. A., Nils Kok, and John M. Quigley. 2011a. "Who Rents Green? Ecological Responsiveness and Corporate Real Estate." Working Paper, University of California, Berkeley.

Eichholtz, Piet M. A., Nils Kok, and John M. Quigley. 2011b. "The Economics of Green Building." *Review of Economics and Statistics*, forthcoming.

Enkvist, Per-Anders, Thomas Nauclér, and Jerker Rosander. 2007. "A Cost Curve for Greenhouse Gas Reduction." *McKinsey Quarterly* 1, 35–45.

Fuerst, Franz, and Patrick McAllister. 2011. "Green Noise or Green Value? Measuring the Effects of Environmental Certification on Office Values." *Real Estate Economics* 39:1, 45–69.

Intergovernmental Panel on Climate Change. 2007. *Climate Change 2007: The Physical Science Basis*. Cambridge: Cambridge University Press.

Kok, Nils, Rob Bauer, and Piet M. Eichholtz. 2011. "GRESB Research Report." Maastricht: GRESB Foundation.

Kok, Nils, and Maarten G. J. Jennen. 2012. "The Impact of Energy Labels and Accessibility on Office Rents." Energy Policy 46: 489–497.

Kok, Nils, Marquise McGraw, and John M. Quigley. 2011. "The Diffusion of Energy Efficiency in Building." *American Economic Review* 101:3, 77–82.

Oldham, Greg R., and Nancy L. Rotchford. 1983. "Relationships between Office Characteristics and Employee Reactions: A Study of the Physical Environment." *Administrative Science Quarterly* 28:4 542–556.

Stern, Nicholas. 2008. "The Economics of Climate Change." *American Economic Review* 98:2, 1–37.

U.S. Energy Information Administration. 2011. State Energy Data. Available at http://205.254.135.24/state/seds/.

Yoshida, Jiro, and Ayako Sugiura. 2011. "Which Greenness Is Valued? Evidence from Green Condominiums in Tokyo." *46th Annual AREUEA Conference Paper*. Denver, CO.

Zheng, Siqi, Jing Wu, Matthew E. Kahn, and Yongheng Deng. 2011. "The Nascent Market for 'Green' Real Estate in Beijing." European Economic Review, forthcoming.

ABOUT THE AUTHORS

Piet M. A. Eichholtz is a professor of Real Estate and Finance and chair of the Finance Department at Maastricht University in the Netherlands. Most of his work regards real estate markets with a focus on international investment, portfolio management, and housing markets. His research has been published in such journals as the *American Economic Review*, *Journal of International Money and Finance*, *Real Estate Economics*, and *Financial Analysts Journal*. Besides his academic career,

Professor Eichholtz is also as an entrepreneur. After having gained practical experience at pension fund ABP and NIB Capital, he started Global Property Research, an international consultancy firm specializing in property companies, which he sold in 2001. In 2004, he was a co-founder of Finance Ideas, a financial consultancy company. In 2011, he was among the founders of the Global Real Estate Sustainability Benchmark. Professor Eichholtz holds a Ph.D. in Finance from Maastricht University.

Nils Kok is an associate professor in Finance and Real Estate at Maastricht University. He is also an affiliated faculty at the Berkeley Program on Housing and Urban Policy. His research has appeared in leading academic journals such as the *American Economic Review, Review of Economics and Statistics, European Economic Review, Real Estate Economics*, and *Journal of Environmental Economics and Management*. Besides his academic work, Professor Kok communicates his ideas and findings in the international arena as a frequent speaker on academic and industry conferences and actively shares his expertise through workshops with investment practitioners and policy makers. He is the co-founder of the Global Real Estate Sustainability Benchmark, an investor-led initiative to assess the environmental performance of the global real estate investment industry. Professor Kok holds a Ph.D. in Finance from Maastricht University.

CHAPTER 13

Federal Housing Policies and the Recent Financial Crisis

RONNIE J. PHILLIPS
Senior Fellow, Networks Financial Institute

KENNETH SPONG
Assistant Vice President and Economist, Federal Reserve Bank of Kansas City

INTRODUCTION

Since the 1930s, the U.S. government has sought to expand home ownership to a wider range of households and income groups. This objective was pursued through the creation of government lending agencies, the passage of supportive legislation by Congress, and through regulation and supervision of financial institutions. However, as a result of the recent financial crisis, the federal government's role in promoting home ownership has come under criticism. Public efforts to expand home ownership and access to housing finance put many households at substantial financial risk, and the housing collapse destroyed nearly $7 trillion in housing equity held by homeowners.

The taxpayer bailout of the Federal National Mortgage Association (Fannie Mae) and the Federal Home Loan Mortgage Association (Freddie Mac) also has many wondering whether these government-sponsored enterprises (GSEs) should continue to exist. Moreover, some have suggested that certain banking laws passed by Congress and implemented by the bank regulatory agencies contributed to the depth of the financial crisis. The boom and bust of housing prices, combined with government's involvement in the provision of mortgage credit, has thus resulted in an enormous taxpayer bailout of the financial system. It also likely changed, on a fundamental level, the role many believe the government should have in the housing industry.

This chapter focuses on federal housing policies and regulations that may have contributed to the crisis. The first part includes a discussion of the role of public policymakers in pursuing social objectives in housing. The second section is an overview of the housing collapse and the financial crisis. An examination follows of federal housing policies and their contribution to the crisis. A final analysis looks at alternative policy recommendations that could help both with expanding home ownership among lower income families and reducing financial risk for homeowners and taxpayers. The last section summarizes and concludes the chapter.

239

PUBLIC POLICYMAKERS AND SOCIAL OBJECTIVES IN HOUSING

Economists since Adam Smith have presumed that the profit-making decisions made by individual firms in a market economy will in general be welfare enhancing for society. Though often cited, but rarely quoted, Smith's (1776, p. 423) words are worth remembering:

> As every individual, therefore, endeavors as much as he can both to employ his capital in the support of domestic industry, and so to direct that industry that its produce may be of the greatest value; every individual necessarily labors to render the annual revenue of the society as great as he can. He generally, indeed, neither intends to promote the public interest, nor knows how much he is promoting it. By preferring the support of domestic to that of foreign industry, he intends only his own security; and by directing that industry in such a manner as its produce may be of the greatest value, he intends only his own gain, and he is in this, as in many other cases, led by an invisible hand to promote an end which was no part of his intention.

However, with regard to housing and home ownership, public policymakers in the United States have made substantial interventions since the 1930s in an effort to promote greater levels of home ownership than might otherwise occur through private market forces. These efforts expanded greatly over the past several decades until the recent financial crisis raised questions about the direction and effectiveness of these public policies. The words of Smith (1776, p. 250) also contain an important warning about such use of laws and regulations to redirect commerce. This warning was about laws emanating from the business sector and private interests, but the same warning could be extended to public policies in housing and the interests of the broader housing industry and its public proponents:

> The proposal of any new law or regulation of commerce which comes from this order, ought always to be listened to with great precaution, and ought never to be adopted till after having been long and carefully examined, not only with the most scrupulous, but with the most suspicious attention. It comes from an order of men, whose interest is never exactly the same with that of the public, who have generally an interest to deceive and even to oppress the public, and who accordingly have, upon many occasions, both deceived and oppressed it.

Smith (1776) thus expresses a concern that those proposing laws may not have the same interest as the general public. How much of a role such influences may have played in the housing collapse is unclear. Certainly, all parts of the housing industry, such as realtors, homebuilders, building suppliers, lenders, and community organizations, had their own private interests at stake and were actively engaged in public efforts to promote the housing sector and extend home ownership to a wider segment of the population. At the same time, certain aspects of the housing and financial crisis may, in retrospect, be traced to well-meaning policies that now appear to have been simply misguided.

In either case, Smith's (1776) admonition to not adopt policies until after a long and careful examination—with the most scrupulous and suspicious attention—clearly applies to federal housing policies. Policymakers, in their rush to expand home ownership, may have ignored many cautionary signs and paid inadequate attention to weakening credit quality and rising financial risk for home-owners. The goals of home ownership and wealth building for low-income individuals remain valid, but Smith suggests the need to look more carefully at how those goals can be achieved to ensure a closer connection between private and public interest.

THE HOUSING COLLAPSE AND THE FINANCIAL CRISIS

The federal government promoted home ownership to achieve both economic and social goals. Clearly, building single-family homes creates employment and stimulates the economy. At the same time, for most Americans, home ownership fulfills the basic need for housing and also represents a substantial portion of their net wealth. Owning a home thus promotes wealth accumulation by more Americans, especially those in the lower-income brackets.

The federal government first became involved in reviving home ownership in the Great Depression for two important reasons. The first was to stimulate the economy by preventing further collapse and loss of wealth in the housing sector and by putting people back to work in building houses. At a time of nearly 25 percent unemployment, this was an important goal of housing policies. The second goal, which was both social and political, was the desire to give more people a stake in the American way of life at a time when political extremism and Communist agitation were quite strong in many countries.

Since the 1930s, federal policy makers have taken many other steps to promote home ownership, including a number of actions in the period leading up to the recent financial crisis. This crisis reached full-blown status in the fall of 2008 due to a period of low interest rates, easy credit, weak regulation, and toxic mortgages. The failure of Lehman Brothers, collapse of American International Group (AIG), and weakened balance sheets and conservatorship of Fannie Mae and Freddie Mac in September reinforced the idea that the crisis was of epic proportions. That prompted dramatic actions by the federal government and the Federal Reserve System.

Everyone can agree on two facts about the recent financial crisis. As Exhibit 13.1 shows, the crisis resulted from the boom then bust in housing prices and the role of the federal government was important in exacerbating the crisis. The Finance Crisis Inquiry Commission (FCIC) (2011), however, disagreed about whether the crisis was a direct result of federal government housing policies or negligence and serious weaknesses in federal oversight and supervision of the financial sector. On the one side, the report to Congress on the causes of the financial crisis pointed to the creation of unregulated financial instruments. The way to prevent a similar crisis in the future, in this view, is to do a better job of regulating financial innovation.

However, only six of the commissioners agreed to the final report, with four strongly dissenting from the majority position. Three of the dissenters claimed that it was too simplistic to say that inadequate regulation caused the crisis or that such factors as derivatives, the Community Reinvestment Act, or the removal of

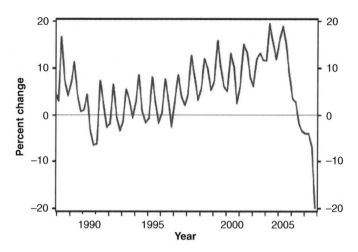

Exhibit 13.1   Case-Shiller Index of Home Prices, 1988 to 2007 (Percent Change at an Annual Rate in Home Prices)

The graph shows the annual percent change in the Case-Shiller Index of home prices from 1988 to 2007. After growing at rates averaging around 10 percent in the years 2000 to 2005, a steep decline began in 2006 with the index falling at a 20 percent rate in 2007. Since 2007, prices have fallen at slower rates, but housing prices are nowhere near their pre-financial crisis highs.

Glass-Steagall firewalls were major contributors (FCIC 2011). The dissenters also suggested that other countries with vastly different regulatory structures suffered some of the same housing and financial problems as did the United States.

Peter Wallison of the American Enterprise Institute also submitted a dissenting statement to the FCIC report. Wallison contended that the primary cause of the crisis was federal housing policy (Wallison 2011a). He asserted that all of the other explanations, such as low interest rates, deregulation, shadow banking, and risk management, were inadequate either by themselves or taken collectively to explain the dramatic changes that occurred in U.S. mortgage markets, including the rapid growth in subprime mortgages. Exhibit 13.2 shows that subprime mortgage originations rose to more than 20 percent of total mortgage originations by 2006 while prime mortgages fell to less than 60 percent. Wallison (2011b) also provides evidence that the recent housing bubble largely stood alone in U.S. history in terms of both its overall size and duration. For Wallison, the appropriate remedy would be to reduce or eliminate the government's role in the residential mortgage markets (FCIC 2011).

FEDERAL HOUSING POLICY

A critical question is how much of a role did public policy play in the recent financial and housing crisis? In the United States, the federal government has long been involved in various aspects of housing finance, beginning, not surprisingly, with the creation of various institutions during the Great Depression to help restore mortgage lending. In fact, several of these institutions have remained in operation and are viewed by some people as playing a key role in the recent crisis.

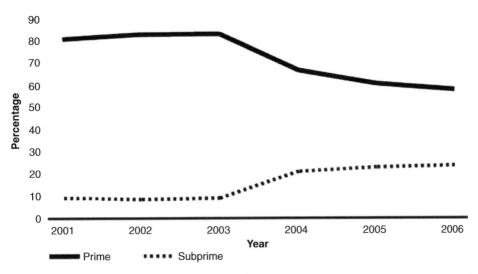

Exhibit 13.2 Percent of Prime and Subprime Mortgage Originations (In Percentage Terms)
The graph shows the percentage of home mortgages that were prime or subprime in the period 2001 to 2006. The percent of prime mortgages peaked at just over 80 percent in 2003 and declined to under 60 percent by 2006. At the same time, the percentage of mortgage loans that were subprime rose from under 10 percent to just over 20 percent by 2006.
Source: GAO analysis of data from Inside Mortgage Credit.

In the 1930s, half of mortgage debt was in default, and the federal government took major public policy steps to help support real estate markets. Congress created the Federal Home Loan Banks in 1932 with the intent of providing liquidity for member institutions holding home mortgages. Next, Congress established the Home Owners' Loan Corporation in 1933 to assist mortgage lenders and to refinance home mortgages that were in default and convert these loans into longer-term mortgages (Harriss 1951; Pollock 2007). This lending continued until the authorized funding ran out in 1935, with more than a million households receiving assistance. In 1934, Congress set up the Federal Housing Administration (FHA) to insure mortgages issued by private lenders and, accordingly, to support the housing market and to bring about more favorable lending terms. A final step in 1938 was to establish the Federal National Mortgage Administration, commonly known as Fannie Mae, an entity intended to create a secondary mortgage market and give lenders a conduit for their home lending. These public policy actions thus served to put the federal government into a much stronger role in supporting the housing sector, which is an objective that has continued to grow in many ways.

Overall Public Policy Focus

Over the past few decades, expanding home ownership to a broader segment of the population has been an acknowledged goal of public policy that has extended across both political parties in the United States. In 1995, for instance, the Clinton administration announced a goal of increasing the number of new homeowners by 8 million by the end of 2000 and, in turn, raising the U.S. home ownership rate to 67.5 percent. A key focus in this goal was increasing the availability of mortgage financing. The U.S. Department of Housing and Urban Development (1995, pp. 4-1, 4-4) described the resulting strategy as follows:

> For many potential homebuyers, the lack of cash available to accumulate the required down payment and closing costs is the major impediment to purchasing a home. Other households do not have sufficient available income to make the monthly payments on mortgages financed at market interest rates for standard loan terms. Financing strategies, fueled by the creativity and resources of the private and public sectors should address both of these financial barriers to home ownership.... Reduce down payment requirements... and reform the basic contract between borrowers and lenders to reduce interest costs.

The George W. Bush Administration also emphasized the goal of expanding home ownership. More specifically, President Bush set a goal of increasing the number of minority homeowners by at least 5.5 million by the end of 2010 and closing the gap in home ownership rates between minority and white Americans (Bush 2002). To reach this goal, the Bush administration recommended legislation to assist low-income families with down payments, increase the supply of affordable homes through tax credits for home construction and development, simplify the home buying and closing process, and increase home buyer education programs. The Bush administration also encouraged leaders in the housing industry to expand access to housing finance and the supply of affordable homes, while also taking steps to eliminate other barriers to home ownership.

Consequently, these goals indicate the general direction of public policies over the past two decades. Various legislative acts, regulatory steps, and tax policies also reflect these specific goals and an even broader support for the overall housing industry. Some of these policy approaches include the housing GSEs, Community Reinvestment Act, federal tax policy allowing deductions for mortgage interest and property tax payments, and other housing-related legislation and policies.

Federal Housing GSEs and Agencies

Fannie Mae, Freddie Mac, and the FHA have been the mainstays in federal efforts to increase home ownership. By converting Fannie Mae to a private shareholder corporation in 1968, Congress, in effect, created a GSE that investors implicitly assumed was backed by the federal government; i.e., the general taxpayer. Congress then added another GSE, Freddie Mac in 1970. Freddie Mac and Fannie Mae eventually came to have very similar powers, thus leading to a framework of two privately owned GSEs, with implicit federal backing, competing with each other and in some cases with private mortgage lenders. The intent behind this structure was to create a stronger and more efficient secondary mortgage market as a means of reaching a wide range of investors and bringing more money into housing finance.

Fannie Mae and Freddie Mac's role in expanding home ownership, particularly with regard to affordable housing, became a legislative mandate with the Federal Housing Enterprises Financial Safety and Soundness Act of 1992. This act stated that Fannie Mae and Freddie Mac "have an affirmative obligation to facilitate

Exhibit 13.3 Affordable Housing Goals for Fannie Mae and Freddie Mac, 1993 to 2008 (In Percentage Terms)

	1993 to 1995	1996	1997 to 2000	2001 to 2004	2005	2006	2007	2008
Low- and moderate-income goal[a]	30	40	42	50	52	53	55	56
Special affordable goal[b]		12	14	20	22	23	25	27
Underserved goal[c]		21	24	31	37	38	38	39

[a]Owner-occupied units financed by Fannie Mae or Freddie Mac would count for this goal if the borrower's income did not exceed the area median income. Rental units would also count if the rent, adjusted for the unit size, was not more than 30 percent of area median income.

[b]Owner-occupied units financed by Fannie Mae or Freddie Mac would count for this goal if the borrower's income did not exceed 60 percent of area median income or 80 percent of area median income if located in a low-income census tract (median tract income no more than 80 percent of area median income) or low-income nonmetropolitan county. Rental units affordable at these income levels could also be included.

[c]Owner-occupied or rental units financed by Fannie Mae or Freddie Mac would count for this goal if they were located in metropolitan census tracts or nonmetropolitan counties with median incomes no more than 90 percent of area median income or no more than 120 percent of area median income with a minority population of at least 30 percent of the total population.

The affordable housing goals for Fannie Mae and Freddie Mac are set so that at least the above-specified percentage of the total units financed by each of these GSEs must satisfy the standards of the particular affordable housing goal. For the 1993 to 1995 transition period, the special affordable goal was measured in billions of dollars rather than as a percentage, and a central city goal was used in place of the underserved goal.

the financing of affordable housing for low- and moderate-income families in a manner consistent with their overall public purposes, while maintaining a strong financial condition and a reasonable economic return (U.S. Public Law 1992). The act also directed the secretary of Housing and Urban Development (HUD) to establish annual goals for purchases by the GSEs of home mortgages for low- and moderate-income families. These goals were to include a low- and moderate-income goal, a special affordable housing goal to address the needs of very low-income households and low-income households in low-income areas, and a goal for central cities, rural areas, and other underserved areas. Exhibit 13.3 describes these affordable housing goals and shows that all of these goals were increased substantially until 2008.

Various people now claim that the escalation in these goals was a primary factor in the declining lending standards and rapid growth in subprime lending that led to the crisis (Pinto 2011; Wallison 2011b). Wallison (p. 544), in remarking on the large volume of subprime loans held by Fannie Mae and Freddie Mac, stated that "This makes it very clear that the bubble of 1997–2007 did not develop naturally as an ordinary bubble; it was driven by a government social policy intended to increase home ownership in the United States." In recognition of the likelihood of substantial losses in their portfolios, the Federal Housing Finance Agency placed both GSEs into conservatorship on September 7, 2008, and replaced their chief executive officers. The current estimated cost to the public in cleaning up the two GSEs is as much as $311 billion, which provides support for the idea that they were a factor in declining lending standards and the financial crisis.

The FHA has also played a role in expanding home ownership by insuring mortgage loans that meet its prescribed standards and are made by banks and other approved lenders. Historically, the FHA's role has been in insuring mortgages with low down payments, commonly made to households with moderate incomes. Through the mid-1990s, the FHA was the prominent player in loans with low down payments, but the rapid expansion of other lenders in this segment of the market—lenders who offered larger loans, more flexible terms, and less income documentation—left the FHA with a very small market share just before the crisis and a relatively small role in it (Pinto 2011). The FHA, though, is one of the few active lenders left in this market and has taken on a major role and substantial risks in the aftermath of the crisis.

Community Reinvestment Act

Congress passed the Community Reinvestment Act (CRA) in 1977 with the intent of encouraging depository institutions to help meet the credit and development needs of their communities, especially the needs of low- and moderate-income neighborhoods or households, small businesses, and small farms. The Act reflects a congressional belief that depository institutions have an obligation to serve the communities where they are located and from which they take deposits.

In 1995, the federal banking agencies substantially revised the regulations implementing the CRA. These revisions reflected legislative provisions enacted in 1994, along with a major effort by the banking agencies to make the regulations less burdensome for depository institutions, more objective, and much more reflective of an institution's actual performance in meeting community financial needs.

CRA performances are evaluated under one of four possible scenarios: (1) streamlined procedures for small institutions, (2) a three-tiered test for larger retail institutions, (3) a limited-scope test for special-purpose institutions, and (4) strategic CRA plans (Spong 2000). Regardless of the evaluation system used, emphasis is placed on the institution's record within its assessment areas (i.e., where it has deposit-taking offices) of making loans to low- or moderate- income persons, in low- or moderate-income areas, and to small businesses and farms. Institutions also receive CRA credit for community development loans, investments, and services. An institution's supervisor gives it one of four possible ratings: outstanding, satisfactory, needs to improve, or substantial noncompliance. These ratings have been disclosed to the public since 1990. From an enforcement standpoint, regulators must consider an institution's CRA performance when the institution or its parent company applies to open a branch or other deposit facility, acquire or merge with another institution, or form a bank holding company.

Whether the CRA played a major role in the crisis is unclear. Under the CRA, community needs are to be met in a manner consistent with the safe and sound operation of the institution, and the resulting loans must meet various bank supervisory standards, including supervisory guidance on appropriate loan-to-value limits for real estate loans. Consequently, depository institutions may have faced more risk constraints than other entities lending to new and low-income homebuyers. Moreover, data on higher-priced loans to lower-income borrowers suggest that depository institutions covered by the CRA may have played only a modest role in this segment of the market (Board of Governors of the Federal Reserve System 2008).

Yet Pinto (2011) and others contend that efforts by depository institutions to expand their low-income lending undoubtedly increased competition in this portion of the market, and thus may have forced other lenders to go further out on the risk curve to obtain business. They also note that the bank merger boom of the past few decades increased the importance of expansion-minded banks maintaining a good CRA record to ease the approval process on acquisitions and limit protests by community groups. For instance, the National Community Reinvestment Coalition (2007) reports that depository institutions, primarily the largest banks, made nearly $4.5 trillion in CRA commitments for community lending between 1995 and 2007 compared to less than $60 billion in commitments between 1977 and 1994. Overall, the CRA may have had an indirect effect on the financial crisis and brought about some increased community lending. But lending from other sources, and in response to other public policies, is likely to have played a much larger role in the crisis.

Home Mortgage Disclosure Act

The Home Mortgage Disclosure Act of 1975 (HMDA) only contains disclosure requirements. However, it plays a key role in providing data on mortgage lending that community groups, researchers, mortgage lenders, regulators, and the U.S. Department of Justice can use as a starting point for assessing the record of mortgage lenders and their compliance with fair housing laws and the CRA.

The HMDA disclosure requirements apply to any mortgage lender with more than a minimal level of activity in an urban area. These lenders must maintain a quarterly register that records data on each home purchase, refinance, or improvement loan application they receive. These registers must include, in part, the loan purpose, loan amount, property location, and final disposition of each loan requested. Most lenders must also record each applicant's gender, race, and income level. The Dodd-Frank Wall Street Reform and Consumer Protection Act of 2010 expands these reporting requirements to include such information as the applicant's credit score, age, the value of the house, origination channel, and other data on loan pricing, prepayments, amortization features, and maturity of the loan.

These disclosures thus provide insights into each mortgage lender's record of serving lower-income borrowers and neighborhoods, and several highly publicized studies based on HMDA data have sent a strong message to lenders that their lending patterns will receive public attention. While the HMDA did not have a direct effect on the financial crisis, it provided an incentive for lenders to serve a wider range of customers.

Federal Tax Policy Regarding Housing

Homeowners receive a number of benefits under federal and most state tax laws. First and foremost, they can take a deduction against their federal taxable income for the mortgage interest and property taxes that they pay as homeowners, provided that their total itemized deductions exceed the standard deduction. Furthermore, homeowners can take these deductions without having to declare an imputed rental income to match the type of rental income a landlord would have to declare for tax purposes on houses that are rented. Many state tax laws allow essentially the same type of mortgage interest and property tax deductions for homeowners. Besides these benefits, homeowners may exclude up to $250,000 ($500,000 for married taxpayers filing jointly) in capital gains from selling a home, assuming they have lived in the home for at least two of the prior five years.

The overall tax benefits that flow to homeowners from these provisions are extremely large. The U.S. Congress Joint Committee on Taxation (JCT) (2010) estimates that tax deductions for mortgage interest and property taxes on owner-occupied homes and the exclusion of capital gains on homes will result in total tax expenditures (or a reduction in tax liabilities) of $133 billion for 2011. According to the JCT estimates, these tax benefits are not only large, but also are heavily concentrated among higher-income taxpayers, with over 69 percent of the tax savings from deducting mortgage interest in 2009 going to taxpayers with incomes of more than $100,000, while a little more than 5 percent of the savings goes to those with incomes under $50,000.

Several factors can explain this disparity in tax benefits between lower-income and higher-income taxpayers. First, higher-income taxpayers are likely to have larger and higher-priced homes, resulting in much higher mortgage interest and property tax payments to be deducted. Second, the value of the tax savings is directly tied to a homeowner's tax bracket. Under current federal tax rates, higher-income households can get back in the form of lower taxes as much as 35 percent of what they pay for mortgage interest and property taxes, while lower-income households get back at most 10 or 15 percent. Third, the tax benefits depend on whether a taxpayer has enough deductions to itemize rather than taking the standard deduction, and in many cases, lower-income homeowners may get nothing back because they do not have sufficient itemized deductions. Thus, over time, these tax subsidies will enable higher-income families to afford larger homes than they otherwise could, while lower-income households are forced to pay proportionately more on an after-tax basis to finance and own a home.

A wide range of studies has looked at homeowner tax deductions and their effects in terms of economic efficiency, equity across different groups of taxpayers, and the role they are thought to play in encouraging home ownership. According to Gyourko and Sinai (2001) and Brady, Cronon, and Houser (2003), those receiving the largest subsidies are concentrated in areas with higher-priced homes and among higher-income households along the west and east coasts. Gyourko and Sinai also find that homeowners in suburban areas generally receive larger benefits than those in inner city neighborhoods. Edmiston and Spong (2008) calculate homeowner tax subsidies by individual census tracts in the Kansas City metropolitan area and then group these tracts according to their median income levels. They find that average tax subsidies, home ownership rates, and housing values in low-income census tracts greatly lag behind those in higher-income tracts.

Thus, these studies indicate that low-income homeowners are unlikely to receive the same level of housing tax incentives as other income groups. As a result, the housing tax incentives may do little to increase home ownership rates because the vast majority of the tax benefits flow to households that should be able to purchase homes without such assistance. A good case could be made for reducing or eliminating homeowner tax deductions and lowering tax rates in a revenue-neutral manner. However, a politically strong real estate lobby and misperceptions about how much the average taxpayer benefits from such deductions have stood in the way of such reform. This result reflects many of the concerns Adam Smith expressed about private interests and public policy.

From the standpoint of the financial crisis, homeowner tax deductions do provide additional motivation for households to take on more debt, although this incentive may be fairly small for lower-income families. These tax deductions have been available for many years, but the lowering of lending standards during the run up to the crisis allowed homeowners to more fully exploit such incentives. Also, the 1986 federal tax reforms, which phased out the deductions for other forms of interest paid by households, encouraged homeowners to take on more mortgage debt through cash out refinancings and home equity loans as a substitute for other borrowings that no longer carried tax advantages. The resulting increase in debt relative to home equity not only made low down payment loans seem less unusual, but also left homeowners and lenders in a much weaker position to withstand the eventual declines in housing prices.

Other Federal Laws and Policies Influencing Home Ownership

Several other federal laws address home ownership and related public policy objectives. These laws deal with such issues as discrimination in lending (Fair Housing Act and Equal Credit Opportunity Act), accurate and timely credit disclosures (Truth in Lending Act and Real Estate Settlement Procedures Act), and various other aspects (Home Ownership and Equity Protection Act and Homeowners Protection Act). For instance, antidiscrimination laws prohibit lenders from considering any factors in their credit decisions that are unrelated to a person's creditworthiness, such as race, color, national origin, religion, sex, handicap, and familial status (Spong 2000). These laws may have helped to expand home ownership to a broader segment of the population, but their objectives have little to do with the factors underlying the financial crisis. One outcome of the financial crisis is a change in how these laws will be written, overseen, and enforced with the creation of the Bureau of Consumer Financial Protection under the Dodd-Frank Wall Street Reform and Consumer Protection Act of 2010.

Some contend that another aspect of public policy, namely, monetary policy, played a notable role in the financial crisis and in encouraging a housing bubble (Taylor 2008). According to this view, policymakers kept short-term interest rates too low before the crisis and thus encouraged too much debt to be built up in the housing sector, along with the development of riskier financial strategies, such as borrowing short and lending long. Others, however, contend that monetary policy was appropriate before the crisis and did not lead to the housing collapse (Bernanke 2010).

ALTERNATIVE APPROACHES FOR EXPANDING HOME OWNERSHIP

Public policy over the last decade or two sought to expand home ownership to a larger group of households primarily by making housing finance more accessible and under more liberal lending terms. The financial crisis demonstrates that the outcome of such policies was to put both mortgage markets and homeowners at greater financial risk. In fact, housing policies intended to promote wealth building among lower-income homeowners became linked with one of the most dramatic reductions in housing wealth in U.S. history. These policies also had the effect of bringing many financially vulnerable households into the market at the peak of the housing boom when homes were least affordable. Consequently, this experience raises the question of whether alternative ways are available to achieve the public policy objective of expanding home ownership without triggering a repeat of recent problems.

Several policy alternatives could potentially help increase low-income home ownership and wealth-building opportunities, while helping households to maintain a sound financial condition. Among such policies are (1) replacing the current set of homeowner tax deductions with a homeowner tax credit; (2) creating first-time homeowner grants or down payment assistance; and (3) using better-designed mortgage instruments. While no magic way exists to greatly reduce the cost of home ownership or to bring home ownership to households without sufficient creditworthiness and financial resources, these alternatives or other similar policies could offer some key benefits compared to recent housing policies. Most important, new approaches are needed to improve the structure and affordability of housing finance, provide a better path toward building up household assets and wealth through home ownership, and to enable first-time homebuyers to step in at an earlier stage and at less financial risk.

Homeowner Tax Credits

Current tax policy allowing households to deduct mortgage interest and property tax payments against taxable income directs most of the benefits toward higher-income taxpayers. Higher-income households will not only be more likely to itemize, but also will receive a much greater benefit when using these deductions to reduce taxable income because of their higher marginal tax rates. Replacing the current set of deductions with a tax credit would extend the tax benefits beyond just those who can itemize under the existing system. Also, if a tax credit were to be set at a fixed percentage of mortgage interest expenses and perhaps with a fixed dollar limit, the benefits would be distributed more evenly across homeowners. As a result, low-income households could receive substantially larger tax benefits from home ownership than they do now.

The 2005 President's Advisory Panel on Federal Tax Reform recommended replacing the existing tax framework with a "home credit" available to all homeowners and equal to 15 percent of the interest paid on a principal residence (President's Advisory Panel on Tax Reform 2005). The Advisory Panel also recommended an upper limit on the amount of the tax credit and suggested this cap be based on a home valued at 125 percent of the median sale price in that region of the country. The Panel's stated objective for this cap was "to encourage home ownership without subsidizing overinvestment in housing" and "to encourage home ownership, not big homes" (President's Advisory Panel on Tax Reform, p. 74). To be fair to homeowners who have already purchased homes, the Panel recommended a five-year, phase-in period for existing mortgages. This home credit was to be part of a larger effort to simplify the tax code in a revenue-neutral manner by eliminating many deductions and special provisions while lowering marginal tax rates.

Several studies examine housing tax credits and generally conclude that these credits would shift more tax benefits to lower-income homeowners and encourage greater home ownership rates among such households (Green and Vandell 1999; Carosso, Steuerle, and Bell 2005). Green and Vandell, for instance, find that home ownership rates could be increased by 8.4 percentage points among minorities and 7.9 percentage points among low-income groups by adopting a revenue-neutral tax credit of $1,100 and assuming the new homeowners could obtain acceptable financing.

Thus, tax credits appear to be an effective way to help increase home ownership rates among low-income households. Additionally, the greater tax savings and higher after-tax income that tax credits could bring to lower-income homeowners could contribute to less financial risk compared to recent policies.

First-Time Homeowner Grants or Down Payment Assistance

Perhaps the most direct means of helping first-time homebuyers is through one-time grants or down payment assistance. Such assistance would offer substantial help to prospective homeowners at a time when their finances are most likely to be constrained. In fact, several studies (Linneman and Wachter 1989; Di and Liu 2005) conclude that down payment and wealth constraints provide an even greater barrier to home ownership than income constraints. Savage (2009) also finds that down payment assistant in the amounts of $7,500 to $10,000 would more than double the share of renters that could afford a modestly priced home, while alternative programs to lower mortgage rates or reduce required down payments would be of only marginal effectiveness. Down payment assistance would be of further benefit as a strong impetus to wealth building among low-income households while also helping to reduce borrowing needs and, accordingly, their financial exposure. Moreover, by providing an immediate source of home equity, such assistance would give first-time homeowners a real incentive to protect their home investment and stay current on mortgage payments.

This approach has been used in several instances. In 2000, the Australian federal government introduced a first-time homeowner grant of A$7,000 (in Australian dollars or around $4,000 in U.S. dollars in 2000). The grant is available to all first-time homebuyers and can be used as a down payment, if the lender permits, or to cover other costs in purchasing a home. During the financial crisis, the Australian federal government raised the grant to A$14,000 on existing homes and A$21,000 on newly-constructed homes. This grant was one of the factors helping to increase home ownership rates to an all-time high in Australia.

In the United States, the American Dream Downpayment Act of 2003 provided targeted assistance on down payments and closing costs for low-income, first-time homebuyers. Also, the Housing and Economic Recovery Act of 2008 introduced a $7,500 tax credit for first-time homebuyers, which took the form of an interest-free loan that a homebuyer had to repay over the next 15 years through additional taxes. The American Recovery and Reinvestment Act of 2009 extended this tax credit through December 2009, with the amount raised to $8,000 and the repayment requirement removed. Various state and local governments have introduced down payment programs.

A key question regarding down payment assistance is what the cost of such a policy might be compared to other approaches. In the years before the financial crisis, the annual number of first-time homebuyers typically ranged between 2 to 2.5 million. Consequently, if $8,000 in down payment assistance had been extended to all first-time homebuyers, the annual cost would have ranged between $16 and $20 billion—a substantial amount, but much less than the estimated $116 billion that will be lost in tax revenues in 2011 due to homeowner mortgage interest and property tax deductions (U.S. Congress Joint Committee on Taxation 2010). The overall cost of any down payment assistance proposal could be held below the above amounts by phasing out such payments above a specified income level or by requiring some of this assistance to be repaid on a gradual basis. This alternative may also raise questions about unequal treatment of renters compared to homeowners, but the existing tax treatment of homeowners and other public policies designed to support homeowners and housing finance would appear to be far more costly and of less benefit to first-time and lower-income homebuyers.

Alternative Mortgage Instruments

The recent subprime lending collapse has pointed out the need for better-designed mortgage instruments for low-income homebuyers, most specifically, home loans without substantial jumps in payments and without large prepayment penalties. Recent revisions to the regulations implementing the Home Ownership and Equity Protection Act of 1994 and provisions in the Dodd-Frank Act of 2010 may help to address some of these concerns and restore a borrower's repayment ability as the critical element in mortgage lending decisions.

Before the recent housing cycle, housing researchers had suggested alternative mortgage products that might provide a better match over time between mortgage payments and incomes for low-income and first-time homebuyers (Scott, Houston, and Do 1993). A typical feature of such products was mortgage payments that start at a lower level, thus making home ownership more affordable for income-constrained households. Payments would then slowly rise in step with expected increases in a borrower's nominal income and/or housing values. Several examples of these alternative mortgage instruments include price-level adjusted mortgages and graduated-payment mortgages.

While there is some financial risk that actual incomes and housing values may not always match the assumed values underlying these mortgage products, the gradual nature of the payment increases over a 30-year mortgage would make such instruments far less risky than many recent subprime loans and the abrupt payment jumps they contained. Moreover, the lower beginning payments would mean that lower-income homebuyers would not have to expose themselves to as much financial risk during the initial years of their loan contracts, and subsequent payment increases would reflect realistic expectations of trends in income and home values.

Recently, some have also advocated using shared-appreciation and shared-equity down payment assistance mortgages (Caplin, Cunningham, Engler, and Pollock 2008; Abromowitz and Ratcliff 2010). With such mortgages, investors, lenders, governmental agencies, or nonprofit entities would put up part of the down payment or would offer a shared appreciation mortgage with a portion of the payments deferred. In return, these parties would share in any appreciation that might occur in the value of the house. The advantages of this sharing arrangement are that payments would be lower, ownership risks would be shared, and the combined down payment or initial investment could be larger, thus making home ownership more affordable and less risky for first-time and lower-income households.

SUMMARY AND CONCLUSIONS

The housing market has had a long history of federal government involvement, but public policy became particularly active over the past two decades in an attempt to increase home ownership rates among lower-income households and give other income groups a chance to move further up the housing ladder. Much of this public policy focus was directed toward making housing finance more accessible through easier and more flexible lending terms and through an expansion in mortgage lending markets.

The financial crisis, however, indicates that an outgrowth of these public policies may have been unsustainable housing trends that put homeowners and lenders at excessive financial risk. Moreover, the huge taxpayer bailouts of Fannie Mae and Freddie Mac, as well as other parts of the housing finance market, are a key example of how public housing policies may have been misguided. High mortgage delinquency and foreclosure rates and a nearly $7 trillion decline in home equity among U.S. homeowners also indicate a need to rethink these policies.

Adam Smith's (1776, p. 250) admonition many years ago seems particularly relevant for public policies regarding home ownership—"ought never to be adopted till after having been long and carefully examined, not only with the most scrupulous, but with the most suspicious attention." In accordance with Smith's warning, public housing policies will succeed only if they closely follow appropriate policy objectives and are not driven in directions that primarily serve selected private interests or provide perverse incentives to market participants.

This chapter contains several alternatives to current policies, including homeowner tax credits, first-time homeowner grants and down payment assistance, and alternative mortgage instruments. These policies could be more carefully focused than recent policies were and involve far less public intervention into mortgage markets. These alternatives would also entail less financial risk on the part of first-time and lower-income homebuyers, thus helping to provide a better path for building household wealth and financial security. Other ways are certainly available to make home ownership more affordable, but the key tests for any new proposals should be whether they are consistent with sustainable housing markets, avoid putting homeowners and lenders at undue risk, and provide a supportive and appropriate blend of public and private interests.

DISCLAIMER

The views expressed are those of the authors and do not necessarily reflect those of Networks Financial Institute, the Federal Reserve Bank of Kansas City, or the Federal Reserve System.

DISCUSSION QUESTIONS

1. Why has the federal government promoted home ownership?
2. Explain whether the Community Reinvestment Act was an important contributor to the financial crisis of 2008.
3. Explain whether current tax policies promote home ownership benefits for everyone equally.
4. What alternative policies could achieve the social goal of promoting home ownership and wealth building among low-income families?

REFERENCES

Abromowitz, David, and Janneke Ratcliffe. 2010. "Homeownership Done Right: What Experience and Research Teaches Us." Center for American Progress. Available at www.americanprogress.org/issues/2010/04/homeownership_right.html.

Bernanke, Ben S. 2010. "Monetary Policy and the Housing Bubble." Remarks at the Annual Meeting of the American Economic Association. Atlanta, Georgia, January 3.

Board of Governors of the Federal Reserve System. 2008. "Staff Analysis of the Relationship between the CRA and the Subprime Crisis." Division of Research and Statistics, November 21. Washington, DC Available at www.federalreserve.gov/news events/speech/20081203_analysis.pdf.

Brady, Peter, Julie-Anne Cronon, and Scott Houser. 2003. "Regional Differences in the Utilization of the Mortgage Interest Deduction." *Public Finance Review* 31:4, 327–366.

Bush, George W. 2002. "A Home of Your Own: Expanding Opportunities for All Americans." Remarks at St. Paul AME Church in Atlanta, Georgia, June 17. Available at http://georgewbush-whitehouse.archives.gov/infocus/homeownership/toc.html.

Caplin, Andrew, Noël Cunningham, Mitchell Engler, and Frederick Pollock. 2008. "Facilitating Shared Appreciation Mortgages to Prevent Housing Crashes and Affordability Crises." Discussion Paper 2008-12, The Brookings Institution.

Carosso, Adam C., Eugene Steuerle, and Elizabeth Bell. 2005. "Making Tax Incentives for Homeownership More Equitable and Efficient." Discussion Paper No. 21, The Urban Institute.

Di, Zhu Xiao, and Xiaodong Liu. 2005. "The Importance of Wealth and Income in the Transition to Homeownership." W05-6 (July), Joint Center for Housing Studies, Harvard University.

Edmiston, Kelly, and Kenneth Spong. 2008. "The Income Geography of Tax Incentives for Homeownership: Evidence from the Kansas City Metropolitan Area." *Proceedings of the 99th Annual Conference on Taxation, National Tax Association*, 263–271.

Financial Crisis Inquiry Commission (FCIC). 2011. *Final Report of the National Commission on the Causes of the Financial and Economic Crisis in the United States Pursuant to Public Law 111-21.* January. Washington, DC: Government Printing Office.

Green, Richard K., and Kerry D. Vandell. 1999. "Giving Households Credit: How Changes in the U.S. Tax Code Could Promote Homeownership." *Regional Science and Urban Economics* 29:4, 419–444.

Gyourko, Joseph, and Todd Sinai. 2001. "The Spatial Distribution of Housing-Related Tax Benefits in the United States." Working Paper 8165, National Bureau of Economic Research.

Harriss, C. Lowell. 1951. *History and Policies of the Home Owners' Loan Corporation.* New York: National Bureau of Economic Research.

Linneman, Peter, and Susan Wachter. 1989. "The Impacts of Borrowing Constraints on Homeownership." *Journal of the American Real Estate & Urban Economics Association* 17:4, 389–402.

National Community Reinvestment Coalition. 2007. *CRA Commitments*. Washington, DC: National Community Reinvestment Coalition.

Pinto, Edward J. 2011. "Government Housing Policies in the Lead-up to the Financial Crisis: A Forensic Study." Papers and Studies, American Enterprise Institute. Available www.aei.org/files/2011/02/05/Pinto-Government-Housing-Policies-in-the-Lead-up-to-the-Financial-Crisis-Word-2003-2.5.11.pdf.

Pollock, Alex J. 2007. *Crisis Intervention in Housing Finance: The Home Owners Loan Corporation*. Washington, DC: American Enterprise Institute. Available at http://wei.org/article/economics/financial-services/crisis-intervention-in-housing-finance/.

President's Advisory Panel on Tax Reform. 2005. "Simple, Fair, and Pro-Growth: Proposals to Fix America's Tax System." *Report of the President's Advisory Panel on Federal Tax Reform*, November. Available at http://govinfo.library.unt.edu/taxreformpanel/final-report/index.html.

Savage, Howard A. 2009. "Who Could Afford to Buy a Home in 2004?" *Current Housing Reports*. Washington, DC: U.S. Census Bureau.

Scott, Jr., William H., Arthur L. Houston, Jr., and A. Quang Do. 1993. "Inflation Risk, Payment Tilt, and the Design of Partially Indexed Affordable Mortgages." *Journal of the American Real Estate and Urban Economics Association* 21:1, 1–25.

Smith, Adam. 1776. *An Inquiry into the Nature and Causes of the Wealth of Nations*. New York: Modern Library.

Spong, Kenneth. 2000. *Banking Regulation: Its Purposes, Implementation, and Effects*, 5th ed. Kansas City, MO: Federal Reserve Bank of Kansas City.

Taylor, John B. 2008. "The Financial Crisis and the Policy Responses: An Empirical Analysis of What Went Wrong." Working Paper, Stanford University. Available at www.stanford.edu/~johntayl/FCPR.pdf.

U.S. Congress Joint Committee on Taxation. 2010. *Estimates of Federal Tax Expenditures for Fiscal Years 2010–2014*. JCS-3-10. Washington, DC: Government Printing Office.

U.S. Department of Housing and Urban Development. 1995. "The National Homeownership Strategy: Partners in the American Dream." Washington, DC: Government Printing Office.

U.S. Public Law. 1992. *Pub. L. 102-550, Title XIII, Sec. 1302, 106 Stat. 3941*. Washington, DC: Government Printing Office. Available at http://uscode.house.gov/download/pls/12C46.txt.

Wallison, Peter J. 2011a. "The True Story of the Financial Crisis." *American Spectator*, May. Available at http://spectator.org/archives/2011/05/13/the-true-story-of-the-financia.

Wallison, Peter J. 2011b. "Three Narratives about the Financial Crisis." *Cato Journal* 31:3, 535–549.

ABOUT THE AUTHORS

Ronnie J. Phillips is a Senior Fellow at Networks Financial Institute and a professor emeritus of Economics at Colorado State University. A past president of the Association for Evolutionary Economics, he has been a Scholar in Residence at the Ewing Marion Kauffman Foundation, Visiting Research Fellow at the American Institute for Economic Research, Visiting Scholar in the Division of Research and Insurance at the Federal Deposit Insurance Corporation, Visiting Scholar at the Office of the Comptroller of the Currency, and a Resident Scholar at the Levy Economics Institute of Bard College. Dr. Phillips also taught at Texas A&M University in College Station, Texas. He has published widely on banking issues, entrepreneurship, and public policy in books, academic journals, newspapers, magazines, and public policy briefs. Dr. Phillips received his BA in Urban Studies from the University of Oklahoma and his Ph.D. in Economics from The University of Texas at Austin.

Kenneth Spong is an assistant vice president and economist at the Federal Reserve Bank of Kansas City. Mr. Spong has been with the Federal Reserve since 1973 and is engaged in research on various topics related to the regulation, supervision, and performance of banks and other financial institutions. This research includes corporate governance and the ownership and management structure of banks, large banks and too-big-to-fail concerns, small business lending, interstate banking, and home financing and home ownership issues among low-income households. His research has been published in various Federal Reserve, academic, and banking trade publications. Mr. Spong has also written a book on bank regulation entitled *Banking Regulation: Its Purposes, Implementation, and Effects,* which is now in its fifth edition. Mr. Spong has a MA in economics from the University of Chicago and a BA in mathematics and economics from the University of Kansas.

CHAPTER 14

Predatory Lending and Socially Responsible Investors

CHRISTOPHER L. PETERSON
Associate Dean for Academic Affairs and Professor of Law, University of Utah

INTRODUCTION

Contemporary financiers and investors naturally place faith in the ability of markets to resolve to efficient outcomes. This self-assurance in the welfare gains from uninhibited consumer financial services has created a skeptical lens through which investors tend to view evidence of unfair, abusive, and fraudulent loans. In the default world view, every individual is expected to make self-interested decisions that collectively create the best possible policy outcomes reasonably expected. Adam Smith (1776) described the phenomenon of self-interested individual decisions creating collective welfare as "an invisible hand" guiding the allocation of resources to an optimal outcome. Firms accused of predatory lending argue that their loans provide an opportunity to smooth consumption over financial crises as well as acquire and retain assets that borrowers could not otherwise possess. Lenders, and many economists, tend to argue that their customers freely choose to borrow and that government intervention in these contracts is paternalistic and ultimately doomed to fail. And, in turn, investors in consumer lending businesses have tended to indulge themselves in the belief that, if the investment is profitable, it will also be socially responsible.

However, the collapse of the American residential mortgage market has shaken the convictions of even the most ardent market conventionalists. Goldman Sachs analysts have predicted 12 million home mortgage foreclosures over the course of the market's readjustment to a new American residential reality (Goldman Sachs Global ECS Research 2009). Assuming only one evicted individual per household, this translates to a larger group of economically displaced individuals than the combined populations of 11 states: Vermont, North Dakota, Alaska, South Dakota, Delaware, Montana, Rhode Island, Hawaii, Maine, New Hampshire, and Idaho (United States Census Bureau 2009). The national foreclosure crisis has resulted in more economic refugees than one would expect from a civil war or cataclysmic natural disaster. With this as a backdrop, surely a fair query is to examine whether *laissez-faire* regulatory advocacy is in service to a free market or market anarchy.

Thus, socially responsible investors looking for opportunities in consumer financial markets face the formidable challenge of attempting to identify and avoid socially corrosive lending products. This task demands at least a passing familiarity with the contentious and inveterate debate over predatory lending. The difficulty therein lies in the complex potential for consumer finance to both empower, but also to constrain, impoverish, and hurt. The purpose of this chapter is to lay a foundation for students and practitioners of socially responsible investing to thoughtfully engage on the predatory lending issue in policy discussion and business planning. As such, this chapter provides an introduction to the predatory lending debate, but will not suffice to resolve it. Instead, this chapter first describes some of the most controversial credit products currently offered in the market. Second, it highlights some of the behavioral research that casts doubt on the ability of markets to naturally inhibit predatory lending. Third, this chapter provides a necessarily brief summary of the evolving legal landscape governing predatory lending. And finally, this chapter suggests some guidelines that socially responsible investors can use to begin a process of identifying predatory financial products.

IN THE EYE OF THE BEHOLDER: CONTROVERSIAL CREDIT PRODUCTS

The definition of the term *predatory lending* has been controversial. Most generally speaking, predatory lending is the practice of extracting unfair or abusive loan contracts from borrowers. What is difficult to define is not predatory lending, but rather, which underwriting strategies, collection practices, and contractual terms warrant the label's approbation. Conclusively establishing which loan products deserve designation as predatory loans is beyond the scope of this brief chapter. But, at the same time, this chapter requires some simple context regarding what products, rightly or wrongly, the predatory lending controversy has followed.

Perhaps most emblematic, consumer advocates frequently argue that "payday loans" are among the most predatory products commonly offered today. A contemporary payday loan usually involves an initial balance of between $100 and $500, with a principle of $325 and a finance charge of about $50 being typical (King, Parrish, and Tanik 2006). Generally, the consumer borrows by writing a personal check or authorizing a future debit by the lender for the loan amount plus an additional fee. Where a check is used, the borrower post-dates the check by writing the due date of the loan one or two weeks in the future, rather than the day on which the consumer actually writes the check. An initial duration of 14 days is the industry norm. Payday lenders generally do not rely upon, nor report to, the three national credit reporting companies. Instead, payday lenders generally verify the borrower's identity and employment. When the duration of the loan has expired, the lender is repaid by depositing the borrower's check or debiting the borrower's account. If the debtor cannot repay, payday lenders generally try to collect the interest on the loan and extend its duration for another two weeks. Because many borrowers have difficulty paying off the entire loan balance while still meeting their other obligations, payday loans often devolve into longer-term repeat borrowing patterns. The vast majority of payday loans refinance a previous payday loan in one form or another. Nationally, average payday lending interest rates are around 400 percent—nearly double the interest rates customarily charged by the New York City mafia (Peterson 2008). Importantly, some banks and credit unions offer overdraft protection policies that have similar pricing and terms to payday loans. Also similar to payday loans, each year consumer advocates bitterly criticize tax refund anticipation loans made or brokered by income tax preparation companies and repaid out of the proceeds of borrowers' federal income tax refunds.

Many consumer advocates have also criticized a variety of loan products secured by automobiles. In the car purchase market, "buy here, pay here" car dealerships specialize in selling and financing used cars. Typical customers in this market have problematic credit histories, as well as limited income and education. As might be expected, these contracts often include high rates and fees, and sharp default penalties (Fox and Guy 2005). Where dealerships merely broker purchase money loans from financial institutions, consumer advocates have criticized the use of overages or yield spread premiums. Here, the car dealership arranges a purchase money loan at an interest rate that is higher than the borrower qualifies for in exchange for a kickback from the lender (Davis and Frank 2011). Car title lenders, also known as *auto-pawn lenders*, typically make triple-digit interest rate, non–purchase money loans to car owners. Critics of these loans argue that they trap borrowers that can neither afford to extinguish the principle and interest, nor stop paying without losing the transportation they need to remain employed (Martin 2010).

While credit cards are a mainstream product, criticism has followed some industry practices. Critics of credit card finance point to various tricks and traps sometimes included in complex credit card contracts (Warren 2008). Complaints have included signing up customers for expensive optional products and charging costly fees without the customer's knowledge or consent; aggressive marketing to college students; circumventing federal consumer protection laws by marketing cards as commercial lines of credit; and retroactively hiking interest rates on previous purchases (National Consumer Law Center, Center for Responsible Lending, Consumer Action, Consumer Federation of America, Consumers Union, Empire Justice Center, New York Legal Assistance Group, and the Sargent Shriver Center on Poverty Law 2011). Moreover, while credit cards tend to have lower interest rates than payday or car title loans, some subprime credit cards have interest rates that now exceed traditional American usury limits.

The problem of predatory mortgage lending has proven resistant to generalization and even more resistant to regulation. For many decades, lenders and brokers have aggressively marketed refinance loans to marginally qualified consumers with significant home equity. Using a combination of high fees, high interest rates, prepayment penalties, and repeated refinancing, lenders could strip out the equity in a family home and be protected from losses by the threat of foreclosure. With the illusion of steady appreciation in home values, this type of predatory mortgage finance was profitable for both portfolio lenders and for those that passed on their loans to investors—typically through private label securitization on Wall Street.

As a result of a gradual change in the late 1990s coupled with tremendously increasing volume in the early twenty-first century, mortgage lenders and brokers watered down their traditional underwriting practices in a new form of predatory structured finance that targeted both borrowers and investors (Peterson 2007). Financiers developed new loan products that required little or no documented income and began to tolerate increasingly higher debt-to-income and loan-to-value ratios. Lenders and mortgage brokers pressured home appraisers to deliver inflated appraisals in order to facilitate the deals upon which their commissions relied. Exotic, interest-only, hybrid adjustable rate, and negatively amortizing pay option mortgage loans set up millions of families for unexpected payment shocks when their short-term teaser interest rates expired. In a frenzy of commission and originate-to-distribute-driven volume, traditional paperwork and documentation practices were ignored throughout the industry. Brokers and loan officers pushed through millions of loans to families that did not have enough income to repay and whose homes were not valuable enough to secure their debt. A controversial and incoherent book entry system of interfacing with county property records, known as the Mortgage Electronic Registration System (MERS), trimmed minor costs off of the securitization process, but left a legacy of confusion and state property law litigation.

At the same time, investment bankers at larger financial institutions bought up millions of problematic loans, reaping fabulous short-term profits and commissions. Hedge funds sold credit-default-swaps insuring residential mortgage securities that had the effect of spreading risk from borrower defaults through financial institutions around the world. Fannie Mae and Freddie Mac naively purchased doomed mortgage-backed securities (MBSs) from Wall Street at the same time that they were lowering their own direct mortgage purchasing underwriting guidelines and paying their executives absurdly lavish salaries. Credit rating agencies pocketed substantial fees for issuing top tier ratings to securities that later proved worthless. Ideologue economists, lawyers, and accountants won undeserved renown by assuring everyone that things were fine.

As loan quality continued to deteriorate, foreclosures increased, and a dissenting national chorus of warning rose. Federal banking regulators and Congress issued milquetoast regulation and actively thwarted those state legislatures and attorneys general that tried to stop the impending catastrophe. Perhaps most ironically of all, some socially responsible investors suffered significant losses because they had purchased securities drawn on subprime mortgage, believing that they were *helping* underserved communities.

Since the other shoe dropped in the summer of 2007, private-label securitization of home mortgage loans has virtually halted. To prevent gridlock in the American economy, the federal government stepped in to purchase around 90 percent of newly originated residential mortgages. Today, the housing finance market and regulatory system remain in flux while markets wait for a backlog of millions of foreclosures to work their way through a system now crippled by paperwork short cuts and MERS-related legal questions. Financial institutions are held captive by the illiquid residential MBSs that they had counted on for their regulatory capital. Hundreds of banks have failed. The crisis wiped out the vast majority of the mortgage brokerage business. Some of those who lost their predatory lending jobs have turned to foreclosure-rescue scams that squeeze the very last resources out of families that are already losing their homes. All this said, a new national cynicism has made making or selling a predatory mortgage more difficult—at least for the time being.

A PALSY IN THE INVISIBLE HAND: DISTORTED CONSUMER FINANCE MARKETS

The national foreclosure crisis, as well as the much longer history of smaller unsecured and automobile-related predatory loans, calls into question the traditional faith in the ability of financial services markets to screen out predatory loans. A growing body of social science suggests that the traditional characterization of financial services markets is highly inaccurate (Peterson 2004; McCoy 2005; Willis 2006; Estelami 2009; Stark and Choplin 2010). While some borrowers make rational, self-interested, informed decisions on the value of each loan in comparison to its opportunity cost, many do not. Moreover, whether welfare-maximizing shoppers have sufficient market power to discipline firms into homogeneously efficient financial product offerings is unclear. At least seven common human psychological patterns create opportunities for predatory lenders to induce contracts that may not be in the best long-term interests of their borrowers.

First, consumers from all walks of life systematically underestimate their exposure to human problems and overestimate their ability to make risk judgments. Because people have difficulty accepting their own vulnerability, most chronically underestimate their chances of heart attacks, asthma, lung cancer, being fired from a job, divorcing within five years after marriage, attempting suicide, and contracting a venereal disease (Weinstein 1980; Weinstein and Lachendro 1982; Weinstein 1987; Weinstein 1989; Taylor 1990). Workers overestimate their legal protections against employers' arbitrary firings (Kim 1997). Even sophisticated managers are prone to treat decisions as unique, generating unreasonably optimistic forecasts by ignoring or minimizing past results (Kahneman and Lovallo 1993; Coelho 2010).

Similarly, consumers chronically underestimate their chances of losing property in floods and earthquakes as compared to objective probabilities. In the flood and earthquake insurance market, instead of relying on objectively verifiable risk, empirical data indicate that consumers rely almost exclusively upon past experience with floods or earthquakes (either personally or through acquaintances). Moreover, even when consumers actually overestimate the probability of a catastrophe, they typically "think that they personally are peculiarly less susceptible to such events" (Sunstein 1997, p. 1184). Consumers tend to be unrealistically optimistic even when negative events have happened to them in the past (Burger and Palmer 1992) and when a real, immediate, and visually vivid risk is present (Harris, Middleton, and Surman 1996). Indeed, the diviner of the invisible hand himself, Adam Smith, recognized the oft-replicated pattern of overconfidence in financial decision making: "The overweening conceit which the greater part of men have of their abilities is an ancient evil remarked by the philosophers and moralists of all ages.... The chance of gain is by every man more or less over-valued and the chance of loss by most men undervalued ..." (Smith 1776, p. 164).

This natural tendency leaves borrowers systematically vulnerable to exploitative lending. The probability of many of the events that people tend to underestimate, such as sickness, divorce, and job loss, are precisely those events that are the leading causes of insolvency (Sullivan, Warren, and Westbrook 2001). Moreover, borrowers chronically underestimate the cost of credit, even in the face of price disclosures (Juster and Shay 1964; National Commission on Consumer Finance 1972; Kinsey and McAlister 1981; Stango and Zinman 2011). Credit card borrowers tend to make foolish choices about contractual terms because they are systematically unrealistically optimistic about their future card use and personal circumstances (Yang, Markoczy, and Qi 2007). According to Durkin (2000, p. 628), Federal Reserve Board researchers looking at data for the past 30 years in all demographic groups find credit cardholders' opinions "about their own experiences are almost the reverse of their views about consumers' experiences in general, suggesting considerable concern over the behavior of others and a belief that 'I can handle credit cards, but other people cannot.'" A study relying on point-of-sale interviews reports that triple- and quadruple-digit interest-rate payday loan borrowers were "hopelessly optimistic in terms of when they expected to be able to repay the loan, particularly at the beginning of the relationship" (Martin 2010, p. 605). Many lenders seek to exacerbate this tendency by shrouding interest rates—leading borrowers to make life-altering decisions with their biased intuitions, rather than careful financial reflection (Stango and Zinman 2011).

Second, many consumers tend to focus on the present benefits of their actions, while underestimating or ignoring longer-term drawbacks. People have an innate difficulty maintaining self-control in the face of immediate gratification. They tend to prefer a benefit that arrives sooner rather than later, in effect discounting the value of the later reward (Thaler 1981). While there are large variations in the rates at which people discount the value of future benefits, decades of empirical research confirm a strong present bias among many consumers (Frederick, Loewenstein, and O'Donoghue 2002). This bias creates difficulty for consumers in attempting to order their financial affairs. The abstract nature of financial pricing makes self-control particularly difficult (Gifford 2002). For example, saving when an asset is highly liquid is hard (Laibson 1997). Employees are much more likely to accumulate retirement savings when automatically enrolled in 401(k) savings plans—illustrating the power of suggestion and inertia and the relatively minor role the cognitive process of opportunity cost comparison plays in actual financial decision-making (Madrian and Shea 2001). Rather than carefully weighing the serious long-term consequences of their borrowing, many debtors are irrationally "payment-myopic," focusing on whether they can make bi-weekly or monthly payments instead of whether the contract as a whole is a wise decision. Because the negative aspects of debt occur in the future, these outcomes appear less problematic than they actually will be (Chapman 1996).

Third, consumer lending markets are likely to be distorted by distressed abbreviated reasoning patterns. Psychologists report consumers who are suffering from emotional distress, embarrassment, desperation, or fear frequently make poor decisions regarding values and risk (Leith and Baumeister 1996; Baumeister 1997). People's impulse control breaks down when they face emotional distress (Tice, Bratslavsky, and Baumeister 2001). Most people have limited attention capacity. When they use this attention to cope with a stressor, many consumers use truncated reasoning to quickly escape the stressful situation by seizing on the first minimally-acceptable option available to them (Keinan 1987; Willis 2006). Because many consumers are in the market to borrow money precisely to deal with some financial threat, they are likely to lack the attention required to resist the temptation of a temporary financial quick-fix. Moreover, the most vulnerable loan applicants tend to have problematic credit histories, which lead them to evaluate loan pricing while fearing the embarrassment and rejection. These conditions are likely to inhibit loan applicants' ability to adjust their perceptions of price as they learn about loan terms (Kassam, Koslov, and Mendes 2009).

Fourth, even those borrowers who are not shopping for credit under distress have great difficulty understanding and comparing credit prices. Research shows that consumers tend to reduce the amount of effort they expend on making sound decisions when those decisions become more complex—a phenomenon known as *information overload* (Payne, Bettman, and Luce 1996; Agnew and Szykman 2005). When faced with complex credit price disclosures and boilerplate contracts, borrowers tend to focus on only a few salient aspects of the decision, or even fail to try to understand the information at all (Davis 1977). Moreover, when borrowers lack experience or understanding of financial and legal terms of loan contracts, the opportunity cost of comparing shopping from multiple creditors can be quite high, suggesting that careful comparison may not even be rational for borrowers who have literacy and numeracy challenges. The U.S. Department of Education's most recent national survey of adult literacy finds that 22 percent of American adults lack even the most basic quantitative literacy skills (United States Department of Education 2003). These citizens have difficulty performing basic quantitative tasks such as using or understanding numbers included in print materials. Thus, they are systematically vulnerable to deceptive and misleading credit pricing tactics. Indeed, at least one analysis of the subprime mortgage crisis reports a strong correlation between numerical ability and foreclosure (Gerardi, Goette, and Meier 2010).

Fifth, the language, terminology, and marketing practices used to present credit contracts can strongly influence how borrowers perceive prices. Compelling evidence suggests that the way pricing and risk information is presented, or framed, can consistently influence human choices (Tversky and Kahneman 1981). For example, people are more averse to medical treatments when identical risk data are framed as a mortality rate than when framed as a survival rate (McNiel, Pauker, Sox, and Tversky 1982; Tversky and Kahneman 1986). Consumers treat identical investment risks differently depending on whether they are presented as a gamble or insurance (Hershey and Schoemaker 1980). These patterns exist and can be manipulated in consumer financial services markets. For example, "[i]ndividuals will perceive a penalty for using credit cards as a loss and a bonus for using cash as a gain; this although the two situations are, from an economic and end-state perspective, identical" (McCaffery, Kahneman, and Spitzer 2000, p. 262). Payday lenders prefer to describe their loan prices as a percentage of the loan principal, rather than with a simple nominal annual interest rate because, for example, borrowers are likely to perceive a two-week loan with a price of 15 percent of the amount financed as less expensive than the same loan with a 391 percent simple nominal annual interest rate—even though these prices are in fact identical (Peterson 2008).

Moreover, people tend to rely too heavily on first impressions when assessing risk and value (Rabin and Schrag, 1999). This is to say, people tend to anchor on early estimates and fail to sufficiently revise their perception of price or risk when further information comes to light (Tversky and Kahneman 1974; Hogarth 1981; Einhorn and Hogarth 1987; Thaler 1994). For example, research suggests anchoring on the early estimate of the value of a lawsuit tends to disrupt later settlement negotiation (Kahneman and Tversky 1995). Even accountants conducting audits anchor on early estimates and insufficiently correct their judgments (Kinney and

Uecker 1982). Marketing professionals have absorbed these lessons and systematically design sales tactics to exploit this pattern in judgment making (Wansink, Kent, and Hoch 1998; Estelami 2009; Stark and Choplin 2010).

Sixth, an impressive body of empirical research indicates that most people are irrationally averse to losses. The classical economic account of rational decision making suggests individuals should value their out-of-pocket costs in the same manner as they value forgone opportunities. This is to say, people should not be more displeased with losses than they are pleased with equivalent gains. But, some data indicate consumers are actually roughly twice as displeased with losses as they are pleased with equivalent gains. A related tendency makes consumers willing to assume an objectively inordinate amount of risk when facing the loss of something they already possess. For example, people who have owned antique furniture or vintage wine for a long period of time commonly refuse to sell their possessions for prices far greater than market value—even though they could buy a replacement and pocket the difference. Some economists explain this is because the owners have endowed their possessions with personal value (Kahneman, Knetsch, and Thaler 1990; Devers, Wiseman, and Holmes 2007). Similarly, many firms sell products with "a thirty-day trial offer" with a "no questions money back guarantee," where the consumer does not have to pay until after the temporary period expires. The seller realizes the buyer will pay a higher price after endowing the product with personal value, or stated differently, buyers will pay more to avoid losing a product they already have. By holding on too tightly to the things they possess, many consumers exhibit a classically irrational bias for preserving the status quo (Kahneman, Knetsch, and Thaler 1991). In the high cost credit market, lenders have learned to exploit loss aversion. For example, car title lenders, also called *auto pawn* companies, often extract more payment out of consumers who do not want to lose their cars than the cars themselves are worth (Peterson 2004). Similarly, homeowners that have fallen behind on mortgage payments will often agree to onerous terms refinancing their homes in order to avoid foreclosure.

Finally seventh, credit contracts generally, and high-interest consumer financial products in particular, have the potential to exacerbate the harm of addictive and compulsive consumer behavior. A reality in modern life is that many Americans suffer from addictions and compulsive behavior. The problems of alcoholism, pathological gambling, and compulsive shopping all have the potential to be negatively interrelated with consumer credit (Faber and O'Guinn 1988; Lesieur 1992; Tokunaga 1993). Addicted and compulsive consumers can use exhaustion of their financial resources as a self-control mechanism—terminating a gambling binge, for example, once the consumer has no more money left. Consumer credit, particularly when offered on predatory terms can create the constant possibility of relapse. Market forces do not protect this large and vulnerable segment of the population from onerous debt problems.

Collectively, these behavioral patterns suggest a very different picture of the free market from the portrait painted by advocates of passive government. Moreover, these behavioral weaknesses may be more pronounced in consumer finance markets than the markets for some other products and services. Unlike the homogeneous pricing of most goods, consumer loans are underwritten to the needs and abilities of individual borrowers, giving lenders the opportunity to heterogeneously price loans based on the inabilities and misunderstanding of loan applicants. In many markets, shoppers discipline pricing and quality. But in consumer finance markets, lenders can segment the market based on consumer vulnerability, rather than on product quality (Engel and McCoy 2011).

THE EVOLVING LAW OF PREDATORY LENDING: A BRIEF OVERVIEW

Consumer financial services regulations are notoriously complex. Rules governing consumer credit are a synthesis of state and federal law and often vary, based on the type of lender. Statutes are often the result of last-minute political compromise, and are subject to repeated amendment over time and conflicting judicial interpretations. Accordingly, this chapter can only hope to generally characterize some of the most basic laws, including credit pricing limits, federal disclosure statutes, deceptive trade practices rules, and some of the more recent (and still evolving) changes in Dodd-Frank Wall Street Reform and Consumer Protection Act.

For hundreds of years, the backbone of American consumer credit protection was usury law capping interest rates on consumer loans in every state. But, in 1978 the U.S. Supreme Court adopted a historically controversial interpretation of a Civil War era banking law holding that a national bank could apply the usury limit of the bank's home state when making a loan to a consumer in another state. This sparked a race-to-the-bottom where South Dakota and Delaware eliminated their usury laws to attract financial services jobs (White 2000). Although a solid majority of the American people still supports traditional usury limits, there are now no effective generally applicable interest rate caps on banks in any American state. Nondepository lenders, however, are still required to comply with state usury limits and criminal loan sharking laws. Trade associations had success in the late 1990s in convincing state legislatures to adopt special usury limits authorizing triple-digit interest rate payday loans in a majority of states. In recent years, this trend has reversed itself, with states such as North Carolina, Georgia, Oregon, New Hampshire, Arizona, and Montana reestablishing more traditional usury limits. Moreover, concerned with evidence that payday lenders were harmfully targeting military personnel, Congress adopted a 36 percent interest rate cap for loans to military service members.

Nevertheless, for civilians, federal consumer credit law has tended to focus on price disclosure supplemented with restrictions on a handful of particularly problematic practices. In 1968, Congress passed the Truth in Lending Act, which attempted to create a uniform terminology for disclosing credit prices. This law created the *annual percentage rate* (APR), which is a yearly expression of the finance charge associated with a loan. Under federal law, a finance charge includes the interest rate, as well as most fees incident to the extension of credit. Thus, Congress hoped that the APR disclosure would create a uniform, easily compared price figure that would assist consumers in shopping for credit. Unfortunately, evidence has since shown that most borrowers have difficulty understanding the term, and many financial products derive much of their revenue from contingent fees or recasting prices that are not meaningfully captured by the term (Stark and Choplin 2010).

With respect to mortgage loans, the Truth in Lending Act was supplemented by the Real Estate Settlement Procedures Act (RESPA) and, later on, the Home

Ownership and Equity Protection Act (HOEPA). RESPA required that home mortgage lenders provide a good faith estimate of closing costs to borrowers before closing as well as a final disclosure form listing all closing charges at the settlement. The law has required these forms in addition to the Truth in Lending Act's forms that disclose some but not all of the same costs. In 1994, HOEPA added some enhanced penalties, a slightly more pointed warning statement, and prohibited a few more particularly egregious practices. However, this statute's rules only applied to loans with prices that exceed either a fee or an interest rate trigger—both of which were set so high that the statute was mostly irrelevant during the mortgage lending boom years (Peterson 2007). While the Federal Reserve Board of Governors (Fed) had broad authority to regulate deceptive and unfair mortgage lending practices under this statute, the Fed effectively ignored these powers in the years leading up to the mortgage bust (Needham 2010). Many states have adopted their own state statutes that are modeled on somewhat expanded HOEPA.

Of course, fraudulent credit sales tactics have always been illegal. But, proving fraud in court, including the lender's intent to deceive, is notoriously difficult and time consuming. The Federal Trade Commission Act lowers the evidentiary hurdles in proving some fraud-like behavior. That federal statute prohibits "unfair and deceptive" sales tactics, and gave the Federal Trade Commission (FTC) permission to adopt regulations specifically articulating examples of deceptive behavior. Almost every state has a "little-FTC" statute that similarly prohibits misleading or deceptive advertising of credit terms. These state statutes, which are usually enforced by state attorneys general, or in some cases private lawsuits, have been one of the most effective deterrents to deceptive consumer credit.

The law of consumer credit, particularly with respect to mortgage loans, is now very much in flux. In 2010, Congress passed the Dodd-Frank Wall Street Reform and Consumer Protection Act. This long and complex statute changed much of the national financial regulatory apparatus, including restructuring the oversight and supervision of financial institutions; creating a new resolution procedure for large financial company insolvencies; imposing more stringent regulatory capital requirements on financial institutions; overhauling the regulation of over-the-counter derivatives; restricting proprietary trading by banks and financial companies; and requiring registration of advisers to some private investment funds. Regarding the problem of predatory lending, the statute's most topical changes included the imposition of a skin-in-the-game requirement for originators of securitized loans and the creation of a new Consumer Financial Protection Bureau (CFPB) responsible for implementing and enforcing compliance with federal consumer credit laws.

The Dodd-Frank Act's new credit retention rules for securitization attempt to better align the incentives of investors and borrowers with those who make and package securitized loans. Under this portion of the Act, securitizers of asset-backed securities must maintain 5 percent of the credit risk in assets transferred, sold, or conveyed through the issuance of asset-backed securities. But regulators can temper this 5 percent skin-in-the-game rule for securitizers who follow heightened underwriting guidelines crafted for different types of asset classes. Asset classes include residential mortgages, commercial mortgages, commercial loans, automobile loans, and any other class of assets deemed appropriate. For home mortgages, the Act also carves out a special exception for "qualified residential mortgages" that will not be subject to the 5 percent risk retention rule. The federal banking regulators are in the process of a hotly contested regulatory rulemaking process to define what underwriting guidelines will be required of securitizers before they can originate loans for distribution to investors while retaining no risk of those loans.

Congress has set up the Consumer Financial Protection Bureau (CFPB) as an "independent bureau" within the Federal Reserve System. Perhaps reflecting congressional disappointment with the Fed's regulatory passivity in the mortgage boom years, the CFPB is funded by the Federal Reserve System, but the Federal Reserve Governors do not have authority to challenge the Bureau's enforcement actions or rulemaking processes. The Act does create a special exemption prohibiting the CFPB from engaging in enforcement actions against smaller financial institutions with assets of less than $10 billion. Among other powers, the CFPB has the authority to thoroughly revise the Truth in Lending and RESPA model home mortgage disclosure forms. Perhaps, most importantly, the CFPB is empowered to identify as unlawful any unfair, deceptive, or abusive acts or practices in connection with any consumer financial product or service transaction in the American economy. In the future, the Bureau is likely to be the primary government watchdog in identifying and prohibiting predatory lending.

PREDATORY WARNING SIGNS FOR THE SOCIALLY RESPONSIBLE INVESTOR

Socially responsible investors face the difficult task of finding consumer financial services that meaningfully help those in need without exposing invested assets to unreasonable risk. At the most basic level, consumer finance generally, but socially progressive consumer finance in particular, demands a healthy dose of level-headed factual skepticism about both the facts and the law. Consumer finance inherently turns on the ability of ordinary people to pay tomorrow what they do not have today. The speculative nature of this endeavor means that those who aspire to be responsible must be highly certain of the value of assets, the source of borrowers' income, and the lender's attention to law and ethical practices. Even though a loan is arguably legal, purchasing it is not necessarily socially responsible. The technology of commerce is constantly evolving, and the law is very often one step behind. Besides illegal lending practices, socially responsible investors should give each lender and loan product a thoughtful review. Despite a lack of consensus on the criteria that define predatory practices, socially responsible investors should consider at least five warning signs of predatory lending. This list of five general warning signs is by no means comprehensive and serves simply as a starting point for discussion.

First, socially responsible investors should not invest in consumer loans with interest rates higher than 36 percent per annum. The rate of 36 percent was the median state interest rate limit on small consumer loans throughout the middle of the twentieth century (Peterson 2008). Moreover, Congress has chosen the rate as the upper limit for military service members. Opinion polls, as well as every recent state public ballot measure on the question, find overwhelming public support for a traditional interest rate limit of this type. Although payday loans, car title loans (as well as some of the more expensive credit cards) may be legal at prices above this rate in many states, socially responsible investors ought not to invest in usurious loans.

Second, socially responsible investors should rigorously screen out loan products that generate substantial revenue from nonsalient pricing features. Junk fees charged at origination, including administration fees, underwriting fees, application fees, review fees, sign-up fees, and commitment fees are all difficult to compare across multiple lenders and frustrate effective shopping. Similarly, contingent charges such as excessive late payment fees, over-the-limit fees, penalty interest rates, and prepayment penalties all meaningfully change the value of loans in a way that is difficult for individual borrowers to quantify and compare (Renuart 2004). Socially responsible lenders should skeptically view ancillary products such as credit insurance and default protection, which rarely provide good value to borrowers. Because borrowers have difficulty comparing prices and predicting how and when they will have the means to repay their debts, socially responsible loans should have simple, easily compared prices.

Third, socially responsible lenders should monitor whether borrowers have a reasonable ability to repay their debts by carefully adhering to traditional debt-to-income (DTI) ratios. While many factors are necessary in underwriting to protect the lenders' profit margin, the absence of a meaningfully enforced DTI limit exposes borrowers to austerity. DTI ratios are important because they answer a simple, forceful, and nearly universally important question: Will the borrower have sufficient income to make monthly payments (Delgadillo and Gallagher 2006)? Historically, the national benchmark DTI limits were a front-end ratio of 28 percent for a homeowner's monthly housing-related payments and a back-end ratio of 36 percent for all of the borrower's debts. Financial planners and consumer financial counselors are extremely skeptical of back-end total DTI ratios of more than 36 percent. They are nearly universal in their agreement that undertaking credit obligations in excess of 36 percent of a household's gross monthly income exposes families to unacceptable risks of insolvency and hardship as well as to a decreased likelihood of meeting long-term financial goals (Little 2007). Socially responsible lenders should be skeptical of DTI ratios above the traditional national benchmarks, but even considering compensating factors they should draw a hard line at a 45 percent back-end DTI.

Fourth, socially responsible lenders should take reasonable precautions to avoid making loans likely to result in negative equity on the borrower's collateral. Identifying a reasonable loan-to-value (LTV) ratio that makes sense for different types of loans is dependent on the nature of the collateral. For example, collateral LTV ratios in pawn-broker loans are likely to be lower than in mortgage lending because of steeper depreciation curves for used durable consumer goods than those that are ordinarily prevalent for residential land. Similarly, socially responsible automobile lenders should take care to adopt underwriting where repayments will amortize the loan more quickly than market conditions depreciate the value of the car. With respect to mortgage loans, traditional mortgage lending practices focused on a cautious and stable 80 percent LTV ratio. While some programs, such as the federal housing administration, have had success at lending at higher LTVs in combination with mortgage insurance, in no event should combined LTVs ever exceed 97 percent. At an absolute minimum, mortgage borrowers should have a small nest-egg of home equity to assist them with closing costs in the event they need to refinance or sell their home.

Fifth, socially responsible lenders should not make negatively amortizing loans, and should treat interest-only loans with great skepticism. *Negatively amortizing loans* are loans that grow larger rather than smaller over time. Such loans create the potential for payment shock once the loan resets to an amortizing payment (McCoy 2007). Once the loan begins to amortize, the borrower starts paying both principal and interest, but these post-reset payments are higher than they would have been under a traditionally amortizing loan because less time remains within the loan's duration to pay down the principal. Negatively amortizing and interest-only loans are dangerous when combined with borrowers' tendency to overestimate their ability to repay debts and their tendency to underestimate prices because they obscure the reality borrowers will eventually face. Socially responsible loans should provide a direct and simple path toward successful repayment.

SUMMARY AND CONCLUSIONS

This chapter provides a simple introduction to the extremely complex law and policy of consumer finance with an eye toward helping responsible investors begin developing the ability to shun predatory lending. Socially responsible investing must recognize that many consumers lack the financial, cognitive, and emotional resources to identify and avoid predatory loans. Neither the market nor the current legal system prevents socially destructive consumer loans. Nevertheless, investors can do their part to ameliorate this situation by refusing to provide capital to lenders that make predatory loans.

DISCUSSION QUESTIONS

1. From 2004 to 2007, home mortgage lenders made millions of loans that borrowers were unable to repay. Why did this happen?

2. What behavioral characteristics of borrowers tend to create inefficiency in consumer finance markets?

3. Congress and state legislatures have attempted to outlaw many forms of predatory lending. Does this mean that socially responsible investors can justify their due diligence with a legal opinion? Explain.

4. Discuss some characteristics that can make a loan socially harmful.

REFERENCES

Agnew, Julie R., and Lisa R. Szykman. 2005. "Asset Allocation and Information Overload: The Influence of Information Display, Asset Choice, and Investor Experience." *Journal of Behavioral Finance* 6:2, 57–70.

Baumeister, Roy F. 1997. "Esteem Threat, Self-Regulatory Breakdown, and Emotional Distress as Factors in Self-Defeating Behavior." *Review of General Psychology* 1:2, 145–174.

Burger, Jerry M., and Michele L. Palmer. 1992. "Changes in and Generalization of Unrealistic Optimism Following Experiences with Stressful Events: Reactions to the 1989 California Earthquake." *Personality and Social Psychology Bulletin* 18:1, 39–43.

Chapman, Gretchen B. 1996. "Temporal Discounting and Utility for Health and Money." *Experimental Psychology: Learning, Memory, and Cognition* 22:3, 771–791.

Coelho, Marta P. 2010. "Unrealistic Optimism: Still a Neglected Trait." *Journal of Business Psychology* 25:3, 397–408.

Davis, Delvin, and Joshua M. Frank. 2011. "Under the Hood: Auto Loan Interest Rate Hikes Inflate Consumer Costs and Loan Losses." Center for Responsible Lending. Available at www.responsiblelending.org/other-consumer-loans/auto-financing/research-analysis/Under-the-Hood-Auto-Dealer-Rate-Markups.pdf.

Davis, Jeffrey. 1977. "Protecting Consumers from Overdisclosure and Gobbledygook: An Empirical Look at the Codification of Consumer Credit Contracts." *Virginia Law Review* 63:6, 841–920.

Delgadillo, Lucy, and Amber Gallagher. 2006. "Borrower- and Mortgage-Related Factors Associated with FHA Foreclosures." *Family and Consumer Sciences Research Journal* 34:3, 204–222.

Devers, Cynthia E., Robert M. Wiseman, and R. Michael Holmes. 2007. "The Effects of Endowment and Loss Aversion in Managerial Stock Option Valuation." *Academy of Management Journal* 50:1, 191–208.

Durkin, Thomas A. 2000. "Credit Cards: Use and Consumer Attitudes, 1970–2000." *Federal Reserve Bulletin* 86:9, 623–634.

Einhorn, Hillel J., and Robin M. Hogarth. 1987. "Decision Making under Ambiguity." In Robin M. Hogarth and Melvin W. Reder, eds. *Rational Choice: The Contrast between Economics and Psychology*, 41–66. Chicago: University of Chicago Press.

Engel, Kathleen C., and Patricia A. McCoy. 2011. *Subprime Virus: Reckless Credit, Regulatory Failure, and Next Steps.* New York: Oxford University Press.

Estelami, Hooman. 2009. "Cognitive Drivers of Suboptimal Financial Decisions: Implications for Financial Literacy Campaigns." *Journal of Financial Services Marketing* 13:4, 273–283.

Faber, Ronald J., and Thomas C. O'Guinn. 1988. "Compulsive Consumption and Credit Abuse." *Journal of Consumer Policy* 11:1, 97–109.

Fox, Jean Ann, and Elizabeth Guy. 2005. "Driven into Debt: CFA Car Title Loan Store and Online Survey." Consumer Federation of America. November. Available at www.consumerfed.org/pdfs/Car_Title_Loan_Report_111705.pdf.

Frederick, Shane, George Loewenstein, and Ted O'Donoghue. 2002. "Time Discounting and Time Preference: A Critical Review." *Journal of Economic Literature* 40:2, 351–401.

Gerardi, Kristopher, Lorenz Goette, and Stephan Meier. 2010. "Financial Literacy and Subprime Mortgage Delinquency: Evidence from a Survey Matched to Administrative Data." Working Paper, Federal Reserve Bank of Atlanta Working Paper Series.

Gifford, Adam, Jr. 2002. "Emotion & Self-Control." *Journal of Economic Behavior and Organization* 49:1, 113–130.

Goldman Sachs Global ECS Research. 2009. "Home Prices and Credit Losses: Projections and Policy Options." January 13. Available at http://books.google.com/books/about/Home_Prices_and_Credit_Losses.html?id=NE6TYgEACAAJ.

Harris, Peter, Wendy Middleton, and Mark Surman. 1996. "Give'em Enough Rope: Perceptions of Health and Safety Risks in Bungee Jumping." *Journal of Social and Clinical Psychology* 15:1, 9–52.

Hershey, John C., and Paul J. H. Schoemaker. 1980. "Risk Taking and Problem Context in the Domain of Losses: An Expected Utility Analysis." *Journal of Risk and Insurance* 47:1, 111–132.

Hogarth, Robin M. 1981. "Beyond Discrete Biases: Functional and Dysfunctional Aspects of Judgmental Heuristics." *Psychological Bulletin* 90:4, 197–217.

Juster, F. Thomas, and Robert Shay. 1964. "Consumer Sensitivity to Finance Rates: An Empirical and Analytical Investigation." *National Bureau of Economic Research Occasional Paper no. 88*, 6–45.

Kahneman, Daniel, Jack L. Knetsch, and Richard H. Thaler. 1990. "Experimental Tests of the Endowment Effect and the Coase Theorem." *Journal of Political Economy* 98:6, 1325–1348.

Kahneman, Daniel, Jack L. Knetsch, and Richard H. Thaler. 1991. "Anomalies: The Endowment Effect, Loss Aversion, and Status Quo Bias." *Journal of Economic Perspectives* 5:1, 193–206.

Kahneman, Daniel, and Dan Lovallo. 1993. "Timid Choices and Bold Forecasts: A Cognitive Perspective on Risk Taking." *Management Science* 39:1, 17–31.

Kahneman, Daniel, and Amos Tversky. 1995. "Conflict Resolution: A Cognitive Perspective." In Kenneth J. Arrow et al., eds. *Barriers to Conflict Resolution*, 44–62. New York: W.W. Norton & Company, Inc.

Keinan, Giora. 1987. "Decision Making under Stress: Scanning of Alternatives under Controllable and Uncontrollable Threats." *Journal of Personality and Social Psychology* 52:3, 639–644.

Kassam, Karim S., Katrina Koslov, and Wendy Berry Mendes. 2009. "Decisions under Distress: Stress Profiles Influence Anchoring and Adjustment." *Psychological Science* 20:11, 1394–1399.

Kim, Pauline T. 1997. "Bargaining with Imperfect Information: A Study of Worker Perception of Legal Protection in an At-Will World." *Cornell Law Review* 83:1, 105–160.

King, Uriah, Leslie Parrish, and Ozlem Tanik. 2006. "Financial Quicksand: Payday Lending Sinks Borrowers in Debt with $4.2 Billion in Predatory Fees Every Year." Center for Responsible Lending. Available at www.responsiblelending.org/payday-lending/research-analysis/rr012-Financial_Quicksand-1106.pdf.

Kinney, William R., Jr., and Wilfred C. Uecker. 1982. "Mitigating the Consequences of Anchoring in Auditor Judgments." *Accounting Review* 57:1, 55–69.

Kinsey, Jean, and Ray McAlister. 1981. "Consumer Knowledge of the Cost of Open-End Credit." *Journal of Consumer Research* 15:2, 248–270.

Laibson, David. 1997. "Golden Eggs and Hyperbolic Discounting." *Quarterly Journal of Economics* 112:2, 443–477.

Leith, Karen Pezza, and Roy F. Baumeister. 1996. "Why Do Bad Moods Increase Self-Defeating Behavior? Emotion, Risk Taking, and Self-Regulation." *Journal of Personality and Social Psychology* 71:6, 1250–1267.

Lesieur, Henry R. 1992. "Compulsive Gambling." *Society* 29:4, 43–50.

Little, Kenneth E. 2007. *The Personal Finance Desk Reference.* New York: Penguin.

Madrian, Bridgette C., and Dennis F. Shea. 2001. "The Power of Suggestion: Inertia in 401(k) Participation and Savings Behavior." *Quarterly Journal of Economics* 116:4, 1149–1187.

Martin, Nathalie. 2010. "1,000% Interest—Good While Supplies Last: A Study of Payday Loan Practices and Solutions." *Arizona Law Review* 52:3, 563–622.

McCaffery, Edward J., Daniel J. Kahneman, and Mathew L. Spitzer. 2000. "Framing the Jury: Cognitive Perspectives on Pain and Suffering Awards." In Cass R. Sunstein, ed., *Behavioral Law and Economics*, 259–287. Cambridge, United Kingdom: Cambridge University Press.

McCoy, Patricia A. 2005. "A Behavioral Analysis of Predatory Lending." *Akron Law Review* 38:4 725–739.

McCoy, Patricia A. 2007. "Rethinking Disclosure in a World of Risk-Based Pricing." *Harvard Journal on Legislation* 44:1, 123–166.

McNiel, Barbara J., Stephen G. Pauker, Harold C. Sox, and Amos Tversky. 1982. "On the Elicitation of Preferences for Alternative Therapies." *New England Journal of Medicine* 306:21, 1259–1262.

National Commission on Consumer Finance. 1972. "Consumer Credit in the United States." Washington, DC: U.S. Government Printing Office.

National Consumer Law Center, Center for Responsible Lending, Consumer Action, Consumer Federation of America, Consumers Union, Empire Justice Center, New York Legal Assistance Group, and the Sargent Shriver Center on Poverty Law. 2011. "Comments Regarding Notice of Proposed Rulemaking Amendments to Regulation Z Provisions

Implementing the Credit Card Accountability, Responsibility and Disclosure Act of 2009." Federal Reserve System 12 CFR Part 226, Docket No. R-1393, RIN No. 7100-AD55.

Needham, Carol A. 2010. "Listening to Cassandra: The Difficulty of Recognizing Risks and Taking Action." *Fordham Law Review* 78:5, 2329–2355.

Payne, John W., James R. Bettman, and Mary Frances Luce. 1996. "When Time Is Money: Decision Behavior under Opportunity-Cost Time Pressure." *Organizational Behavior and Human Decision Processes* 66:2, 131–152.

Peterson, Christopher L. 2004. *Taming the Sharks: Towards a Cure for the High Cost Credit Market*. Akron, OH: University of Akron Press.

Peterson, Christopher L. 2007. "Predatory Structured Finance." *Cardozo Law Review* 28:5, 2185–2282.

Peterson, Christopher L. 2008. "Usury Law, Payday Loans, and Statutory Sleight of Hand: Salience Distortion in American Credit Pricing Limits." *Minnesota Law Review* 92:4, 1110–1164.

Rabin, Matthew, and Joel L. Schrag. 1999. "First Impressions Matter: A Model of Confirmatory Bias." *Quarterly Journal of Economics* 114:1, 37–82.

Renuart, Elizabeth. 2004. "An Overview of the Predatory Mortgage Lending Process." *Housing Policy Debate* 15:3, 467–502.

Smith, Adam. 1776. *The Wealth of Nations*. London: W. Strahan and T. Cadell.

Stango, Victor, and Jonathan Zinman. 2011. "Fuzzy Math, Disclosure Regulation and Credit Market Outcomes: Evidence from Truth in Lending Reform." *Review of Financial Studies* 24:2, 506–534.

Stark, Debra Pogrund, and Jessica M. Choplin. 2010. "A Cognitive and Social Psychological Analysis of Disclosure Laws and Call for Mortgage Counseling to Prevent Predatory Lending." *Psychology, Public Policy and Law* 16:1, 85–131.

Sullivan, Teresa A., Elizabeth Warren, and Jay Lawrence Westbrook. 2001. *The Fragile Middle Class: Americans in Debt*. New Haven: Yale University Press.

Sunstein, Cass R. 1997. "Behavioral Analysis of Law." *University of Chicago Law Review* 64:4, 1175–1195.

Taylor, Shelley E. 1990. *Positive Illusions: Creative Self-Deception and the Healthy Mind*. New York: Basic Books.

Thaler, Richard. H. 1981. "Some Empirical Evidence on Dynamic Inconsistency." *Economic Letters* 8:3, 201–207.

Thaler, Richard H. 1994. "The Psychology of Choice and the Assumption of Economics." In Richard Thaler, ed., *Quasi Rational Economics*, 137–167. New York: Russell Sage Foundation.

Tice, Dianne, M. Ellen Bratslavsky, and Roy F. Baumeister. 2001. "Emotional Distress Regulation Takes Precedence Over Impulse Control: If You Feel Bad, Do It!" *Journal of Personality and Social Psychology* 80:1, 53–67.

Tokunaga, Howard. 1993. "The Use and Abuse of Consumer Credit: Applications of Psychological Theory and Research." *Journal of Economic Psychology* 14:2, 285–316.

Tversky, Amos, and Daniel Kahneman. 1974. "Judgment under Uncertainty: Heuristics and Biases." *Science* 185:4157, 1124–1131.

Tversky, Amos, and Daniel Kahneman. 1981. "The Framing of Decisions and the Psychology of Choice." *Science* 211:4481, 453–458.

Tversky, Amos, and Daniel Kahneman. 1986. "Rational Choice and the Framing of Decisions." *Journal of Business* 59:4, S251–S278.

United States Census Bureau. 2009. *Annual Estimates of the Resident Population for the United States, Regions, States, and Puerto Rico: April 1, 2000 to July 1, 2009* (NST-EST2009–01). Available at www.census.gov/popest/states/NST-ann-est.html.

United States Department of Education. 2003. *National Assessment of Adult Literacy*. Available at http://nces.ed.gov/naal/kf_demographics.asp.

Wansink, Brian, Robert J. Kent, and Stephen J. Hoch. 1998. "An Anchoring and Adjustment Model of Purchase Quantity Decisions." *Journal of Marketing Research* 35:1, 71–81.

Warren, Elizabeth. 2008. "Product Safety Regulation as a Model for Financial Services Regulation." *Journal of Consumer Affairs* 42:3, 452–460.

Weinstein, Neil D. 1980. "Unrealistic Optimism about Future Life Events." *Journal of Personality and Social Psychology* 39:5, 806–820.

Weinstein, Neil D. 1987. "Unrealistic Optimism about Susceptibility to Health Problems: Conclusions from a Community-Wide Sample." *Journal of Behavioral Medicine* 10:5, 481–500.

Weinstein, Neil D. 1989. "Optimistic Biases about Personal Risks." *Science* 246:4935, 1232–1233.

Weinstein, Neil D., and Elizabeth Lachendro, 1982. "Egocentrism as a Source of Unrealistic Optimism." *Personality and Social Psychology Bulletin* 8:2, 195–200.

White, James J. 2000. "The Usury Trompe l'Oeil." *South Carolina Law Review* 51:3, 445–466.

Willis, Lauren E. 2006. "Decisionmaking and the Limits of Disclosure: The Problem of Predatory Lending: Price." *Maryland Law Review* 65:3 707–840.

Yang, Sha, Livia Markoczy, and Min Qi. 2007. "Unrealistic Optimism in Consumer Credit Card Adoption." *Journal of Economic Psychology* 28:2, 170–185.

ABOUT THE AUTHOR

Christopher L. Peterson is the Associate Dean for Academic Affairs and a Professor of Law in the S. J. Quinney College of Law at the University of Utah. His research focuses on the law and policy of consumer financial services regulation. He is a fellow of the American Bar Association's Consumer Financial Services Committee, has been named the National Consumer Advocate of the Year by the National Association of Consumer Agency Administrators, and has received multiple national awards for his research. Professor Peterson has frequently testified in Congressional Committees, and has presented his research at the Federal Deposit Insurance Corporation, the Federal Reserve, and at the White House. He holds a JD from the University of Utah.

CHAPTER 15

Use and Misuse of Financial Secrecy in Global Banking

INGO WALTER
Seymour Milstein Professor of Finance, Corporate Governance and Ethics,
New York University

MICROECONOMICS OF FINANCIAL SECRECY

Financial confidentiality involving nondisclosure of financial information concerning individuals, firms, financial institutions, and governments, represents an integral part of the market for all banking and financial services, fiduciary relationships, and regulatory structures. It also constitutes a "product" that has intrinsic value, and that can be bought and sold separately or in conjunction with other financial services. At the same time, financial nondisclosure can also be used in a multitude of ways that damage society as a whole. For example, confidentiality is required for tax evasion, money laundering, evading national currency policies, political corruption, and a host of other activities that generate negative externalities and cause damage to society.

This chapter examines financial secrecy as a business policy engaged in by international financial institutions, as well as countries seeking to benefit from their role as secrecy havens. It begins with a discussion of the microeconomics of secrecy—demand, supply, equilibrium, and consumer and producer surplus—which are some of the most familiar concepts of economics in a rather unfamiliar guise. The chapter proceeds to discuss the two important applications of financial secrecy: money laundering and tax evasion. The chapter concludes with a discussion of efforts to rein in financial secrecy and mitigate its social costs.

Like any commercial service in the economy, financial confidentiality operates in a market context. Some think that they need confidentiality. The more they need it, the more they are willing to pay. Some people and institutions are in a position to provide protection from disclosure for financial flows or accumulated assets and want to use this position to extract payments. They turn out to be agents—fiduciaries in the shadowy world of financial secrecy. In effect, they are "secret agents."

The Demand for Financial Confidentiality

Many motivations drive the desire for financial confidentiality. Different groups of people are willing to pay for the assured nondisclosure of financial information:

- Personal financial confidentiality usually remains in substantial compliance with applicable laws and regulations. Long-standing traditions of banking confidentiality have served many countries well. Indeed, some people regard personal financial confidentiality as a cornerstone of individual liberty.
- Business financial confidentiality involves withholding financial information from competitors, suppliers, employees, creditors, and customers. Release of such information is undertaken only in a tightly controlled manner and, where possible, in a way that benefits the enterprise. Financial information is proprietary. It is capitalized in the value of a business to its shareholders.
- Tax evasion is a classic source of demand for financial confidentiality. Some people are exposed to high levels of income taxation. Others are hit by confiscatory wealth taxes or death taxes. Still others feel forced by high indirect taxes or quasi-taxes such as price controls to escape into the underground economy. For some people, the only "fair" tax is zero. Tax evasion requires varying degrees of financial confidentiality to work.
- Criminals, such as drug traffickers, not only accumulate large amounts of cash, but also regularly deal in a variety of financial instruments and foreign currencies. The same can be said for gun runners, terrorists, and organized and unorganized crime (robbery, burglary, theft, illegal gambling, prostitution, loan sharking, protection, extortion, and other forms of racketeering). These crimes require ways to launder funds and eliminate paper trails that might be taken as evidence of criminal activity. Political and business bribery and corruption also require financial confidentiality.
- Capital flight normally refers to an unfavorable change in the risk/return profile associated with a portfolio of assets held in a particular country deemed to be sufficient to warrant active redeployment. It usually involves major conflict between the objectives of asset holders and their governments, though it may or may not violate the law. Authorities always consider capital flight to be dysfunctional.

No matter what the motivation, the value of confidentiality depends on what may happen if the confidentiality cover is blown, the "damage function," and the probability of disclosure. Damage can range from execution, exile, prison, and political ostracism to confiscation of assets, fines, incremental taxes, social opprobrium, and familial tension. Avoidance of damage is what the confidentiality-seeker is after. Since damage usually is a matter of probabilities, the attitude toward the risk of exposure is a critical factor in how people value this benefit (Walter 1990).

The Supply of Financial Confidentiality

As with the demand for confidentiality, the supply of confidentiality-oriented financial services encompasses a complex patchwork of intermediaries, conduits, and assets that provide varying degrees of safety from unwanted disclosure. Supply dimensions can be classified into onshore financial assets, offshore financial assets, and physical assets held either onshore or offshore.

Onshore financial assets include bank deposits and certificates, cashier's checks, equity shares, bonds, and notes of public or private issuers. All of these financial assets normally yield "market" rates of return, yet provide the asset holder with some degree of protection from unwanted disclosure. Traditional banking practice in most countries provides for confidentiality with respect to unauthorized inquiries, which gives adequate shielding for "personal" and "business" needs for protection from disclosure. Once the law gets involved, however, either in civil, tax, or criminal matters, much of this protection is lost.

Under proper legal procedures, the state can force disclosure in the event of divorce proceedings, creditor suits, inheritance matters, tax cases, and criminal actions. Although a certain amount of added protection can be obtained through "bearer" certificates of various types, this runs the risk of theft, loss, or accidental destruction (Skousen 1983; Blum 1984). Onshore beneficial ownership can be hidden by placing financial assets in the names of friends, associates, or family members, which can also provide greater protection, assuming the third parties can be trusted and will not themselves face legal or other costs as a result. Additionally, shell companies and legitimate business fronts can be used.

Foreign financial assets may offer considerably more confidentiality because national sovereignty halts at the border. Extraterritorial investigation normally requires that terms be carefully and often reciprocally negotiated between governments. Bank deposits may be held abroad in, ideally, tax haven jurisdictions (Kwitney 1987). Foreign equities and debt instruments may provide similar security, yet may be subject to host country tax withholding and the risk of negotiated disclosure at the request of the home country. Bearer certificates, beneficial ownership, and foreign shell companies may provide added protection and increase the complexity of any future paper chase. In all cases, the confidentiality attributes of the host country are of critical importance, as evidenced by its history, traditions, and proneness to corruption.

True offshore assets provide an alternative to financial confidentiality sought in the domestic financial environments of other countries (Legarda 1984). These may be held in the form of bank deposits or certificates in euro-banking or booking centers ranging from New York to London, from Singapore to Panama, and from the Cayman Islands to Luxembourg. All provide substantial exemption from taxation as well. However, confidentiality may be eroded if deposits in offshore branches of home-country banks are involved (or foreign banks that do business domestically), and authorities can force disclosure through the domestic entity. Deposits in offshore branches of foreign banks that do not do business domestically may avoid this problem, but could in some cases be more risky. Eurobonds, available in bearer form, which can be purchased by individuals, provide another form of offshore assets. Individuals and other entities can use offshore shell companies and beneficial ownership structures to further draw the veil of financial confidentiality (O'Neill 1983; Richpuran 1984).

All sellers of financial confidentiality, whether individuals or financial institutions, have an important stake in doing their best to limit disclosure as much as possible to avoid damaging the value of what they have to sell (Chambost 1983). Governmental jurisdictions responsible for the confidentiality vendors tend to be on much the same wavelength, depending on the importance of the confidentiality business in generating real economic gains in the form of employment, income, and taxes.

Lastly, there are physical assets kept in the form of collectibles, precious metals and stones, other forms of tangible property, or banknotes (domestic and foreign). These assets can be secreted away in walls, mattresses, safe deposit boxes, and holes in the ground. Physical assets may be held offshore, consigned to an individual or an institution. All such assets provide effective confidentiality as long as they remain undiscovered, yet may put the owner at risk of theft, fraud, extortion, or other injury.

Market Distortions and the Supply of Confidentiality

Market frictions such as taxes, exchange controls, interest-rate controls, price controls, and trade barriers all give rise to economic incentives for the formation of parallel markets intended to avoid or evade them. These parallel markets are often very narrow, inefficient, and highly profitable. The same is true of public procurement not characterized by open competitive bidding, the awarding of permits to do business, and the administration of health and safety standards. Parallel markets can even develop for police protection, other public services, and the market for controlled substances such as alcoholic beverages and drugs. The symptoms are familiar enough: smuggling, thriving domestic and cross-border black markets, tax evasion, bribery, and corruption of public officials. All are ultimately traceable to regulation-induced market inefficiencies that can throw off enormous amounts of cash.

Tapping into such market inefficiencies means, logically, finding the most heavily distorted national economies and then ferreting out viable ways to do business in them. The obvious choices have been lodged in developing countries pursuing misguided macroeconomic policies using direct controls, often with heavily overvalued currencies, where many public and private transactions are undertaken far removed from transparent markets. Bribery and corruption have always thrived in such environments because market inefficiencies generate more than enough profits to support even extortionate payoffs.

Of course, such market distortions are not confined only to heavily controlled economies; they exist also in economies organized along free-market lines. Taxation is universally applied in order to finance public expenditures. Specific products such as cigarettes and alcoholic beverages are often exceedingly heavily taxed for revenue reasons and to discourage their use. Regulation of various aspects of economic life, ranging from pollution control, to the number of taxis permitted, to bank safety and soundness, exist even in the most liberal economies to cope with perceived market failures, moral hazard, adverse selection, and social costs. Regulation exists, perhaps, to achieve greater equity among different groups in society, even at the cost of economic efficiency. A whole range of criminal activities also exist including the sale and use of controlled substances.

Yet banned or restricted activities continue to be carried out in organized and unorganized fashion where there is demand, even against the risk of arrest and punishment, through what are often highly sophisticated underground channels renowned for their market imperfection and extreme profitability (Cornwell 1983). The kind of financial confidentiality required to make rent-seeking work in highly distorted economies is equally likely to be associated with distorted sectors of market-oriented economies.

Product Differentiation

While secret physical and domestic financial assets are generally available to anyone, this is not true of many of the types of offshore assets that may be less susceptible to disclosure. Lack of information and financial sophistication, exchange controls, inertia, fear of getting caught, and size of the necessary transactions are some of the factors that inhibit people's access to confidentiality alternatives available around the world. This leads to considerable market segmentation, which in turn gives rise to both constraints and profit opportunities in the international confidentiality business.

List prices such as bank interest rates, bond yields, and equity returns are established by broad market forces that extend well beyond seekers of confidentiality. The returns involved may well represent an opportunity cost on the confidentiality-seeker, yet still be higher than what individuals would have been willing to sacrifice in order to achieve the degree of financial confidentiality actually obtained. They thus enjoy the unearned benefit confidentiality seeker's surplus (SSS).

Financial products specifically tailored to the confidentiality market involve substantially higher opportunity costs and hence smaller SSS. Numbered bank accounts abroad, for example, tend to have correspondingly high opportunity costs. Yet even these are in large part list-priced so that, despite the expense, much of the SSS may remain intact.

The SSS may not remain intact in the case of custom-tailored confidentiality services whose prices are set largely through bargaining. The confidentiality vendor tries to ascertain how much an offered product is worth, given the apparent motivations of the individual confidentiality-seeker. The seller adjusts the asking price accordingly, and an interval of negotiation may elapse before reaching final agreement. The seller will never, of course, threaten to breach the confidential relationship because this would seriously and perhaps fatally impair the value of the secrecy product. In the final negotiated price, much of the SSS to the buyer may evaporate—it is drawn off by the vendor.

Thus, widely divergent confidentiality products and vendors are available, many of whom compete with one another. A few vendors have products with no good substitutes, so the demand for them may well be quite inelastic. Some traditional confidentiality products, including gold, dummy companies in the Caribbean, and holes in the ground are easily available in some places but less so elsewhere. Others have been built up over the generations as secure repositories and can command high premiums. But high premiums also attract competitors, whose entry may alter the structure of the market. A safe assumption is that higher levels of confidentiality involve successively greater degrees of monopoly power in the competitive structure and organization of the market for financial confidentiality.

Market Interactions in Financial Confidentiality

As with any other financial service, confidentiality is bought and sold in an active market, defined by supply and demand characteristics similar to those of "ordinary" markets. Holders of financial assets, broadly defined, are generally thought to be driven by considerations related primarily to the nature of risks and returns. The behavioral characteristics of asset holders are thoroughly addressed in modern portfolio theory. Investor behavior also may be conditioned by confidentiality regarding the nature, location, and composition of financial or other assets that comprise a portfolio.

If confidentiality is not a free good, it must be "purchased" by putting together a portfolio of assets (or a single asset) that yields the desired level of nondisclosure. One "cost" of confidentiality to the asset holder requiring confidentiality is thus the difference between the expected yield on the confidentiality-oriented portfolio and the yield on a "benchmark portfolio," which is a similar portfolio wherein confidentiality is not a consideration.

Besides the cost of confidentiality that may be imbedded in the differential expected real returns on assets, there is also the matter of differential risk. Portfolios of assets containing greater degrees of financial confidentiality may also be more risky. For example, assets may have to be held directly or indirectly in certain countries, resulting in increased foreign exchange risk and/or country risk. Or the portfolio may be forced into a configuration that is susceptible to increased interest-rate risk. Various ways of hedging risk, including the ability to diversify or shift risk by means of futures and options markets, may be unavailable to portfolios subject to a high degree of confidentiality. One could argue that the degree of risk, defined as the covariance of expected future returns on the assets contained in the portfolio, will tend to increase with the confidentiality content of the portfolio.

Conventional views on the creation of "efficient" portfolios can easily be adapted to take confidentiality considerations into account. An *efficient portfolio* is one that maximizes investor returns, subject to a risk constraint, or minimizes risk given a particular return target. Both the individual's attitude toward risk, or risk preference, together with the risks and returns available in asset markets, are the basic elements in the design of efficient portfolios. What happens when one incorporates confidentiality considerations? The asset holder should be willing to accept a reduced rate of return and/or be willing to be exposed to a higher level of risk. From a risk/return perspective, the investor will be worse off. But the welfare gains from the enhanced degree of confidentiality may well outweigh the welfare losses incurred in the risk/return dimension. An optimum combination can be defined once the individual's preferences in each of the three dimensions, as well as the availability and cost of alternatives in the market, are known.

Beyond portfolio effects, charges levied by suppliers of confidentiality can add to the cost of confidentiality. Banking fees may be raised for asset holders known to be driven by the confidentiality motive. Transactions may have to be routed in clandestine ways, through narrow markets with wide spreads and high transaction costs, via inefficient conduits. Foreign exchange transactions, perhaps repeated several times or involving black markets, may add further costs. People may have to be bribed. Third parties, beneficial owners, and shell companies may have to be used to enhance confidentiality, all of which involve costs. Since many of the counterparties understand the value of their services, they may not be shy about pricing their services. Such charges must be added to any yield differential in ascertaining the cost of confidentiality (Smith and Walter 1997).

The acquisition of external assets in the presence of confidentiality can thus be thought of as a rational process. This process balances various costs against benefits in which the confidentiality factor is likely to alter behavior in rather predictable ways. If confidentiality-seeking asset holders are normally risk averse, they will tend to prefer portfolios incorporating greater confidentiality together with lower covariances in expected future total returns. That is, they will prefer a rather conservative portfolio, both because of the reduced probability of disclosure and heavy exposure to risk in other ways (Diamond and Diamond 1984).

The Agency Problem in Financial Confidentiality

Finally, agency problems represent a cost to the confidentiality-seeking asset holder. An agency relationship exists whenever an asset holder delegates decision-making authority to the manager of a discretionary account. If such a relationship exists, positive monitoring and bonding costs will be present. These can be monetary or nonmonetary in nature. Further, some divergence between the agent's actual decisions and decisions that would maximize the welfare of the principal will often occur. The principal will thus incur a "residual loss." Usually, contracts between principals and agents provide appropriate incentives for the agent to make decisions that will maximize the principal's welfare, given existing market uncertainties. Financial confidentiality raises some unique agency issues.

Ordinarily, the agent will have to interpret the investor's wishes and carry them out as best he can. But interpreting these wishes may be difficult and can lead to serious future disputes. Additionally, the investor's objectives may change, either explicitly or implicitly, with the agent being uninformed or poorly advised. The investor may also psychologically reposition his objectives after the fact, especially if the value of his assets has underperformed an alternative portfolio, thereby assigning undeserved blame to the agent. Alternatively, the agent may abuse his or her mandate by churning the portfolio to bolster commission income, for example, or by stuffing it with substandard securities that management wants to discard. Lastly, the agent simply may not be very competent.

Clearly, if confidentiality is added to the agent's mandate, the job becomes much more complex. The agent must do all in her power to safeguard confidentiality within the limits of (and sometimes outside of) the law. Violation of this fiduciary role, at least in the eyes of the principal, includes violating the confidentiality mandate and potentially triggering serious disputes between the two parties. Disputes may cause damage to the agent through erosion in the value of her confidentiality-oriented financial services (Smith, Walter, and De Long 2012).

However, the agent has some leverage too. Ordinarily, agency-related disputes can be taken into court in civil suits, which then supersede other forms of dispute settlement that have proven unsuccessful. But how can the confidentiality seeker take the agent to court when a foreign legal jurisdiction is involved, when that jurisdiction is unclear, or when such an action would compromise the very confidentiality being sought? Consequently, the agent acquires certain immunity from the sort of redress usually available to asset holders confronted by agent misconduct. This could tempt the agent to abuse the agency function for self-enrichment at the expense of the confidentiality-seeking asset holder.

The real question is whether the quasi-immunity attributable to confidentiality influences the behavior of the agent. On the one hand, a strong incentive exists for agents to maximize their own welfare because they are at least partially protected from retribution. Further, confidentiality-seekers are fully prepared to pay any normal agency costs that come with confidentiality, as long as they do not sustain large unaccountable losses. On the other hand, the competition confidentiality vendors face from other sellers, as well as traditions of prudence and competence, tend to impose constraints on abusive behavior. Still, this problem puts a real premium on selection of an agent, who must be depended upon to carry out fiduciary responsibilities with great care and sensitivity to client desires when they are subject to change, yet without succumbing to the temptations that derive from his potential leverage as a "secret agent."

Market Equilibrium

Supply and demand interact in the market for financial confidentiality, just as they do in any other market. A hierarchy of differentiated products exists, each with its own market characteristics: the greater the demand, the higher the price. The more intense the competition among vendors and the easier the substitutability of other confidentiality products, the lower the price. Rational confidentiality seekers will presumably shop around, insofar as their position is not jeopardized as a result, to acquire an optimum mix of products at a cost (including agency costs) that makes the whole exercise worthwhile. How much confidentiality should one buy? Buy just enough so that the marginal cost of financial confidentiality equals its marginal benefit, where both are risk adjusted.

Money Laundering

A key application of financial secrecy in banking and finance is *money laundering*, which can be defined as the process of converting the proceeds of illegal activities into real or financial assets whose origins are effectively hidden from law enforcement officials and from society in general. The overall objective is to avoid the damage associated with disclosure. As such, the subject of money laundering is an application of financial secrecy, and has substantially increased in importance as a result of the rise of global terrorism, which needs to be financed in ways that avoid detection.

Besides evasion of taxes and other governmental policies by otherwise honest individuals, money laundering has traditionally been associated with organized crime involved in protection, prostitution, extortion, gambling, and other illegal activities. Much of the growth in the volume of money laundering and its institutionalization at a high level of sophistication has almost certainly been associated with drug trafficking. According to a study by the U.S. Customs Service, "We see narcotics organizations now being set up like major corporations, with an operational arm to move the drugs and a financial arm to handle the money" (Permanent Subcommittee on Investigations 1983, p. 334).

Broadly speaking, money laundering is all about permanently concealing the illicit origins of various forms of criminal money in order for it to re-enter the mainstream of funds flows and subsequently be made available in untainted form to the ultimate owners, their families, and associates. Conversely, it can involve the proceeds of legitimate activities that are channeled through foundations and other fronts into socially-damaging activities. The next section surveys the various money laundering channels that exist and their characteristics (Tanzi 1982).

The Laundering Process

Conversion of financial assets from a form whose discovery would lead to confiscation or create other types of damage into a form in which they are safe from discovery, clearly adds value and must therefore be profitable as an economic process. During the course of 1985 U.S. Congressional hearings, one government witness in testimony explained that laundering was

> ... an extremely lucrative criminal enterprise in its own right. The U.S. Treasury's investigations uncovered members of an emerging criminal class—professional money launderers who aid and abet other criminals through financial activities. These individuals hardly fit the stereotype of an underworld criminal. They are accountants, attorneys, money brokers, and members of other legitimate professions. They need not become involved with the underlying criminal activity themselves except to conceal and transfer the proceeds that result from it. They are drawn to their illicit activity for the same reason that drug trafficking attracts new criminals to replace those who are convicted and imprisoned—greed. Money laundering, for them, is an easy route to almost limitless wealth
>
> (Subcommittee on Crime 1985, p. 331).

Certainly, the bulk of the illicit funds that form the raw material for the money laundering process originate in the form of banknotes. Payment for all manner of illegal transactions, including most forms of tax evasion such as "skimming" taxable revenues, is least likely to leave a paper trail if it is in currency notes. This raises the immediate problem of converting enormous amounts of cash into bankable funds that can be reconfigured though various channels into untainted assets.

To understand the problem that this causes drug dealers, one must consider that drugs are almost invariably sold at the retail level for payment in the form of street money, which generates millions of small-denomination bills resulting from a multitude of street-level sales in the various consuming countries. Currency in small bills is, of course, far bulkier and heavier than money in large bills, and some seizures have involved literally tons of currency notes. In U.S. currency, for instance, $1 million in $20 bills weighs 110 pounds, in $100 bills just 22 pounds. So the drug runner is faced with an initial, very practical problem—how to reduce the volume and weight of narcotics profits for easier manipulation or transportation. A clear trade-off exists between bulk and traceability because of the far fewer large-denomination currency notes in circulation. Bulk and susceptibility to loss or theft also places a premium on converting currency to bankable funds as quickly as possible, which can be accomplished either domestically or in foreign financial jurisdictions.

Currency conversions undertaken domestically require large cash deposits with banks that ask no questions, or through front companies that are involved in cash businesses, such as supermarkets, restaurants, and casinos. Not surprisingly, the law enforcement authorities views domestic cash conversions as a major pressure point in their battle against money laundering and the underlying criminal transactions. The United States, for example, maintains a currency transaction report (CTR) requirement imposed on banks for cash deposits in excess of $10,000. This has given rise to so-called smurfs, couriers who spends their time visiting banks throughout the country, engaging in transactions small enough to avoid the CTR requirement and reduce the currency into manageable and negotiable form. This often involves the purchase of cashier's checks that do not name the payee.

These cashier's checks may then be exchanged a number of times domestically or in Latin America or Europe, in payment of various drug-related or weapons-related transactions. The smurfed checks may also be transported abroad for cashing or for deposit in a secrecy haven. The funds tied up in the cashier's checks, of course, earn no interest for the holder and represent float to the issuing bank.

Unfortunately for the money launderers, domestic currency conversions do not lend themselves to the kinds of economies of scale necessary to handle the enormous cash volumes involved, especially in the drug business. They also leave the assets exposed to loss or disclosure unless the domestic banks themselves are crooked or bankers can be bribed to evade reporting requirements and other banking regulations.

An alternative to domestic conversions is the physical transportation of banknotes to a foreign jurisdiction where they can be converted to bankable funds, either because no reporting requirements exist or because the foreign bank is willing to overlook them. In the absence of exchange controls (so that confidentiality is the only motive for cash as opposed to bank transfers), the rate of exchange legally obtained in this way may not be highly unfavorable, and the transactions and information costs may be quite acceptable. The currency usually finds its way back to the home country and its central bank through interbank transfers.

The more manageable partially laundered cash will follow routes that differ substantially from one case to the next. In some cases, the criminal will want the money to remain in domestic currency. In other cases, she may want it stashed away in an offshore haven and may also want a proportion in the local currency of the country in which she operates.

According to one of the statements submitted in U.S. Congressional hearings in 1985:

> These launderers carry on a number of activities at one time. They arrange for the deposit of illicit cash into domestic financial institutions; arrange for the transportation or delivery of currency into or out of the U.S.; they may buy U.S. dollars in exchange for Colombian pesos; buy pesos in exchange for dollars; buy and sell both Colombian banking instruments as well as U.S. cashier's checks, personal checks or corporate checks; manipulate U.S. domestic narcotics profits from one U.S. bank account to another; arrange for disguised wire transfers of funds from the U.S. to relatively secure havens such as Panama, the Cayman Islands or other havens; set up sham foreign corporations ... sometimes all these things are happening at the same time
>
> (Subcommittee on Crime 1985, p. 333).

Currency movements at times seem to take on very significant proportions. The U.S. dollar appears to be the predominant vehicle currency. Federal Reserve data and the size of reported interbank international currency transactions indicate that a large portion of U.S. currency in circulation is held outside the United States. The media are replete with anecdotes of plane-loads of cash crossing the Caribbean and suitcase-loads crossing European borders.

Currency, traveler's checks, cashier's checks, and other monetary instruments can be supplemented as money laundering vehicles by purchasing bearer bonds and even registered securities that can be endorsed over to the buyer. Another substitute for currency movements is conversion to gold, silver, or other precious metals, precious stones, jewelry, objects of art, and similar assets that are potentially moveable internationally and tend to hold their value. They often lend themselves well to transport and resale for foreign currency. Both alternatives, however, generally involve greater information and transaction costs and therefore tend to be less useful in this context.

Laundering Vehicles

Once the currency conversion process has been completed, or as part of that process, a number of types of financial and nonfinancial organizations come into play. Domestic and foreign financial institutions, lawyers, accountants, airline employees, investment advisers, even government officials will variously provide information and occasionally act as couriers. They make money laundering easier by bending the rules, looking the other way, or violating the law on behalf of a client in return for a payment.

Banks' services in this context may include (1) allowing unidentified clients to make deposits; (2) allowing clients whose funds are not of foreign origin to make investments limited to foreigners; (3) acting without power of attorney to allow clients to manage investments, or to transmit funds, on behalf of foreign-registered companies or local companies acting as conduits; (4) participating in sequential transactions that fall just under national financial reporting thresholds; (5) allowing telephone transfers, without written authorization, or failing to keep to a record of such transfers; and (6) entering false foreign account-number destinations in wire transfers. Failure to exercise due diligence could result in serious costs to the financial institutions themselves. But given the traditional diversity of bank policies and practices, and the relatively small volume of truly questionable transactions as compared to total banking volume, banks have often had difficulty devoting the required substantial resources to filtering procedures.

Beyond payment services of banks and using anonymous accounts, a trust agreement (e.g., in the form of a normal, discretionary, alternative, or disguised trust), may be used to hide the true ownership of banking, securities, or other assets registered in the name of one or more parties with whom the deed of trust has been created. Additionally, an investment company may be set up in a secrecy/tax haven that is nonresident and tax-exempt, free of exchange controls and financial reporting requirements, and possibly subject to only an annual flat tax regardless of the amount of assets or profit. This may involve beneficial ownership that appears in a fiduciary agreement, but nowhere in the records of an official body. The principal's death is an obvious problem with respect to such agreements. Heirs or executors may first have to prove their own standing, as well as the death of the principal, before establishing any right to information about the assets involved.

Owners of laundered assets may also employ shell companies or captive banks. Shares in such entities are normally issued in bearer form where no guarantees are required from the administrators. The name of the ultimate asset holder does not appear anywhere in writing, and even local attorneys who form the company (possibly under instructions from foreign lawyers) may not know the owner's identity. Administrators in some secrecy havens, for example, might give executive powers over a shell company to an unnamed individual without having any idea of what use is being made of the authority conferred.

A *captive bank* is an institution that exists purely for the benefit of one physical or legal person or group of people and may take the form of a shell entity. Captive banks allow the owners to take advantage of substantial leverage in financing their activities. They are normally formed in tax and banking havens with tight disclosure laws, low reserve ratios and withholding tax on interest, and an absence of exchange controls. The true owner of the captive bank can remain anonymous, if necessary. Such banks are often set up as offshore entities, sometimes located in countries with no meaningful banking regulations whatsoever and where all kinds of financial activity are permitted. The use of shell companies with money deposited in overseas banks and recycled into the system through speculative currency or commodity option transactions is one of many supplementary methods employed.

A technique that can be used in conjunction with various kinds of business fronts and shell companies involves the issuance of invoices covering international trade transactions that deviate from agreed prices. On the import side, the foreign supplier issues an invoice in excess of the agreed price of a product. On the export side, the domestic seller issues an invoice for an amount in foreign currency less than the agreed price. The foreign counterparty deposits the difference (less any commission) in an account belonging to the seller and remits the invoice amount. In both cases, false invoicing can succeed in moving laundered funds from one country to another.

Combating Negative Externalities Associated With Financial Secrecy

If financial secrecy facilitates, and in some cases is indispensable for, contact that imposes potentially high costs on society, then a policy toward confidentiality ought to be incorporated into a broad range of financial, economic, and other policies. On the one hand, if such policies succeed in constraining socially damaging conduct, they will necessarily have a negative effect on the demand for financial secrecy. On the other hand, policies that make engaging in financial secrecy practices and supplying financial secrecy services more expensive or risky may well have a constraining effect on the socially damaging activities involved.

Early in the 2000s, national authorities seemed more determined than before in using their economic and political influence to combat both criminal uses of secrecy and tax evasion, and to share information. Consequently, guaranteeing customary levels of offshore secrecy became increasingly difficult. A driving force was governments' appreciation that financial secrecy facilitates both criminal activities and tax evasion, and that one of the best ways to attack these is to increase the cost and reduce the opportunities to launder and hide money.

Governments have undertaken various measures to combat money laundering as a way of damaging the profitability of the underlying criminal transactions. These include currency reporting requirements and various forms of pressure on domestic and foreign bankers to provide insight and disclosure. Good and bad money soon mingle through wire transfers and other interbank transactions, and an unregulated offshore currency market available to all comers. As one Scotland Yard official put it, "Electronic funds transfer has done for money laundering what the washing machine did for clothes washing" (Smith and Walter 1997, p. 151). However, lawyers often appear confident of using their privileged relationships with clients to shield themselves from prosecution in money laundering cases. Bankers may be able to hide behind dense layers of bureaucracy and blame misconduct on lower-level employees. But once the activity becomes large and greed gets the better of caution, defenses may fail.

The 2001 terrorist attacks on New York turbocharged the battle against money laundering and the illicit use of the financial system in furtherance of crime. The Financial Action Task Force (FATF) was created in 1998 primarily to combat money laundering internationally, and ramped up its work after the New York attacks. It has 35 participating countries and an 8-year mandate, with a mission review every 5 years. It does not have a tightly defined constitution, although members are agreed on an overriding commitment to combat terrorism and international crime.

The purpose of FATF, an intergovernmental body, is to develop and foster policies, both at national and international levels, to combat money laundering and terrorist financing. As a "policy-making body," it aims to generate the necessary political will to bring about national legislative and regulatory reforms in these areas.

> The FATF monitors members' progress in implementing necessary measures, reviews money laundering and terrorist financing techniques and counter-measures, and promotes the adoption and implementation of appropriate measures globally. In performing these activities, the FATF collaborates with other international bodies involved in combating money laundering and the financing of terrorism
> (Financial Action Task Force 2011).

Interestingly, application of FATF activities in various ways have surfaced and impeded questionable financial flows in various other areas as well, including drug trafficking, organized crime and tax evasion—sometimes called *bycatch*. Hiding the flows and the assets has become more difficult and more costly, illicit portfolios have become more risky, and those seeking secrecy have become more vulnerable to agency problems in the absence of recourse to adjudication mechanisms or the courts.

Tax Pressures on Financial Secrecy

Indicators suggest that the value of financial confidentiality has been on a gradual decline as a competitive driver in global private banking. This is based on changing attitudes toward financial secrecy and the kinds of pressure that national tax and criminal authorities can bring to bear on foreign jurisdictions. This decline became much more serious in recent years as governments' need for tax revenues to support social programs rose significantly, as well as funding the financial crisis of 2007 to 2009 along with the accompanying bailouts of banks and other firms. Combined with the aforementioned crackdown on money laundering, governments clearly were getting serious about putting heavy pressure on sellers of financial confidentiality, whether countries or institutions.

According to one Organization for Economic Co-operation and Development (OECD) report, secrecy laws and other factors made the use of Swiss bank accounts in particular "attractive to nonresidents" seeking to evade taxes and avoid detection in their home country (Destiny Worldwide Net 1999). Switzerland is the world's biggest offshore banking sector for wealthy individuals, with about a third of the global market. Switzerland's dominant market share in private banking has always been suspected to be partly dependent on its long tradition of banking secrecy, which protected customers who wanted to evade tax in their own country. But until now the OECD's annual country reports on Switzerland have not dealt with the subject. Switzerland and the OECD have, however, clashed once before on the question of tax evasion and bank secrecy. In April 1998, Switzerland, along with Luxembourg, refused to endorse the OECD's guidelines on harmful tax competition. The move was part of an attempt by the OECD to combat unfair fiscal practices. Swiss banks argued that their big market share is primarily due to Switzerland's long tradition of neutrality, political stability, a strong currency, and professional banking services. Switzerland has long provided a home for extremely wealthy foreign individuals who want to minimize their tax bills. Most Swiss bank customers rarely step inside the country and rely on banks there to handle their affairs. The OECD said access to information was essential for effective tax enforcement and that, as globalization and technology continue to advance, it would become increasingly important.

Those concerned with the future of offshore private banking usually focus on (1) tax coordination, cooperation, and alignment among countries of residence of offshore clients; (2) tighter notification and reporting requirements imposed on banks dealing with suspect or under regulated banks and countries; (3) international agreements to expand account investigation related to money laundering, including a more intense focus on accountants and lawyers; and (4) the use of economic and political pressure in the case of noncooperating institutions and countries, including banning them from major financial markets. In 2005, for example, Switzerland signed an agreement with the European Union (EU) for a 30 percent withholding tax on interest income on EU residents' offshore accounts, with the proceeds remitted anonymously to account holders' home countries each year.

These issues came to a head with the disclosure that client data had been stolen in 2002 on a DVD by an employee of a unit of a Liechtenstein bank, LGT Treuhand (partly controlled by the principality of Liechtenstein's royal family and containing a list of some 1,400 customer names). The data were shopped around to various national tax authorities. Germany acquired the stolen data in 2006 for an estimated €5 million and began an aggressive pursuit of tax evaders using a favored technique of establishing Liechtenstein foundations that became the owners of record for assets managed out of Switzerland, and thereby escaped payment of tax on capital income. Other European countries, including France and the United Kingdom showed a keen interest in sharing the German data, causing sleepless nights among European tax evaders.

In 2008, the OECD issued a set of guidelines that defined tax havens, set the outlines of cooperation with countries trying to enforce their tax statutes, and imposed sanctions on tax havens identified as "uncooperative." Criteria for tax haven status include (1) zero or only nominal taxes (generally or in special circumstances) and offer themselves, or are perceived to offer themselves, as a place to be used by nonresidents to escape high taxes in their country of residence; (2) protection of personal financial information, under which businesses and individuals can benefit from strict rules and other protections against scrutiny by foreign tax authorities to prevent disclosure of information about taxpayers who are benefiting from the low tax jurisdiction; and (3) lack of transparency in the operation of the legislative, legal, or administrative provisions.

The OECD was concerned that laws should be applied openly and consistently, and that information needed by foreign tax authorities to determine a taxpayer's situation be available. Lack of transparency in one country can make applying its laws effectively for other tax authorities difficult, if not impossible. Criteria include "secret rulings," negotiated tax rates, limited regulatory supervision, and government's lack of legal access to financial records. A key feature of the OECD Guidelines in identifying tax havens is the lack of information exchange.

To screen countries for tax haven characteristics, the critical factors are therefore zero or nominal taxes, and whether or not an exchange of information and transparency occurs. OECD standards require the exchange of information on all tax matters for the administration and enforcement of domestic tax law. They also provide safeguards for the privacy of any information exchanged.

In order to put pressure on tax haven countries, the OECD issues a blacklist of nations that were not in compliance with the Guidelines. Included were countries such as Malaysia, the Philippines, and Uruguay, which had not committed to the guidelines. It also included the names of eight countries that have committed to the OECD tax haven standards, but had yet to implement them (Austria, Belgium, Brunei, Chile, Guatemala, Luxembourg, Singapore, and Switzerland), and 70 countries were listed as either having "substantially" implemented the proposals or having committed to them without substantial implementation, including Liechtenstein and Andorra. Several countries revised their policies in an effort to get their names removed from the blacklist, although some took time to put the new policies into practice.

By early 2009, only three countries remained on the list. Pressure mounted ahead of the April 2009 meeting of the Group of 20 nations, which had threatened to produce a blacklist of alleged tax havens for targeting with sanctions. Promises made by Lichtenstein and other offshore banking centers just ahead of the meeting caused G-20 leaders to back off, but the threat of sanctions remained if bilateral cooperation deals were not reached. Under the OECD model, for example, Liechtenstein banks subsequently agreed to offer data on clients (but only in response to specific tax fraud investigations by foreign governments) under agreements with Germany, the United Kingdom, and the United States. Comparable agreements were under discussion with the European Union as a whole, allowing Liechtenstein to cooperate with tax investigations in some 27 countries.

The noose confronting tax evaders using financial secrecy was clearly tightening under the fiscal pressures confronting virtually all countries to collect taxes owed. Switzerland has incorporated the new standards into 30 bilateral double-taxation treaties, which are more sophisticated than the ones they replace (including the 2005 withholding agreement with the European Union on interest income), which continued to allow the use of various evasive tactics.

More Pressure on Switzerland

Perhaps the most dramatic breach of offshore financial secrecy involved the U.S. Internal Revenue Service (IRS), UBS, and the government of Switzerland in 2008 and 2009. As noted, Swiss banking secrecy was authorized under the Swiss Banking Act of 1934, making it illegal to reveal information about Swiss bank accounts and their owners with the exception of legal due process involving evidence of a crime recognized under Swiss law. Insight had been permitted as early as 1986 in the case of financial crimes in which the Swiss government forced Bank Leu to reveal data after the U.S. government became aware of insider trading charges. This led to the arrest of Dennis Levine, Ivan Boesky, and others in one of the largest insider trading prosecutions in history, most of which involved Swiss accounts. There followed a period of reluctance by Swiss banks to take on new U.S. accounts, including accounts of ordinary U.S. citizens trying to evade U.S. taxes (not a crime in Switzerland), but not engaged in tax fraud (which is a crime in Switzerland).

In 2000, UBS acquired a major U.S. retail broker, Paine Webber, in its efforts to create a major footprint in the U.S. capital market to match the big domestic securities firms, the domestic commercial banks that had been allowed into investment banking in 1999, and European rivals such as Credit Suisse and Deutsche Bank. In dealing with domestic private clients using its new U.S. platform, UBS had to use extreme caution not to engage in activities on behalf of clients that could be interpreted as aiding and abetting tax evasion. Indeed, within UBS, the widely disseminated rule was that "tax-sensitive" U.S. clients were off-limits given that in the United States, tax evasion is automatically a criminal offense and prosecution would immediately entangle UBS in aiding and abetting allegations.

UBS and other foreign banks were welcome to serve U.S. clients abroad, but had to report transactions and capital income to the IRS on the same basis as did domestic banks, asset managers, and broker-dealers. Foreign banks were expected to comply with this requirement and to have in place proper compliance systems and procedures.

To the surprise of most people both inside and outside UBS, UBS was secretly violating its agreement with the U.S. tax authorities and its own internal compliance policies in its offshore private banking group. Much of this came to light in Florida court testimony by a former UBS private banker in a case brought against a California real estate mogul who had engaged in massive tax evasion. UBS Private Banking had devised a so-called Swiss Solution. Beginning in 2004, UBS aggressively helped affluent U.S. individuals evade taxes involving offshore accounts in "nominee names" or "sham entities" in which the U.S. taxpayer would not be identified as a beneficiary. Because UBS did not disclose these accounts to the IRS, the IRS did not receive any tax payments on the investment income.

The ex-UBS whistleblower, Bradley C. Birkenfield, pleaded guilty in June 2008 to a charge of conspiring to defraud the United States. He gave extensive testimony against former UBS colleagues leading to the arrest in Miami of Western Hemisphere private banking head Martin Liechti (later returned to Switzerland). The evidence that surfaced in this and subsequent investigations was highly incriminating, showing falsification of records, and a clear, systematic intent to deceive the tax authorities.

Following the events in Florida, UBS offshore private bankers' travel to the United States was stopped and the bank shut down all offshore coverage of U.S. wealthy clients. During July 2008, UBS agreed to exit the U.S. cross-border business in non–SEC registered entities. The previous month, the U.S. District Court in Miami had authorized the IRS to serve UBS with John Doe summons seeking records to identify all (unknown) U.S. taxpayers with accounts at UBS in a civil action. In November 2008, former UBS Executive Director Raoul Weil, head of offshore private banking, was indicted by a federal grand jury in Florida along with "unindicted co-conspirators" and declared a "fugitive from justice."

In February 2009, UBS entered into a criminal "deferred prosecution" agreement with the U.S. Department of Justice and was fined $780 million ($380 million disgorgement of profits and $400 million for back withholding taxes, interest and penalties). Additionally, the Swiss government agreed to deliver information on 250 UBS client accounts (furnished by UBS) to the Department of Justice. This was the first major breach of Swiss banking secrecy in broad-gauge tax matters. In the wake of that action, some UBS clients came forward voluntarily to secure more favorable treatment and avoid criminal prosecution under an IRS amnesty program.

Besides the Florida action against UBS, the Department of Justice in February of 2009 filed suit in Miami to enforce the John Doe summons to disclose unknown U.S. taxpayer clients of the bank. Based on discovery of a 2004 UBS document by IRS agents, a demand was put forward for 52,000 offshore accounts held by U.S. private banking clients. UBS refused to comply, citing substantial defenses under Swiss Law to combat such a broad-based request. At the same time, several U.S. clients brought suit in Swiss courts to prevent implementation of their account disclosure, citing that disclosure had to occur case by case, that particulars have to be considered, that government rulings can be appealed in a very time-consuming process, and that the Swiss government had never agreed to provide information in response to broad John Doe–type fishing expeditions.

For UBS, the issue was critical. It was already under deferred criminal prosecution in the Birkenfield case and the bank as a whole faced the prospect of a criminal indictment in which it would almost certainly be fined heavily and *in extremis* forced to withdraw from the United States market altogether.

For the Swiss government, the stakes were equally high. The case was a vital test of the veil of secrecy, on a wholesale basis, without evidence of specific crimes under Swiss law. Moreover, offshore banking based on secrecy was one of the country's key export industries. The same high stakes applied to the U.S. government, strapped for funds and determined to enforce its tax law, especially at a time of recession and massive budget deficits. Some $120 billion was thought to reside in offshore accounts of U.S. residents. Ignoring tax evasion on such a scale was politically impossible. Government tax and finance officials in Europe closely watched all the Swiss-U.S. action, some considering Switzerland effectively a rogue nation by enabling the systematic hiding of taxable wealth.

What is the result? In August 2009, the Swiss and U.S. governments signed an agreement that was negotiated at the highest levels and intended to settle the matter. UBS agreed to turn over to the IRS some 4,450 additional American client names covering some $18 billion in assets, without specifying the selection criteria or timing of disclosure. This presumably induced sleepless nights among tax evaders to encourage self-reporting under the IRS compliance option. Once selected, UBS notified clients that their names were about to be turned over to the IRS. The clients could then appeal under Swiss law, but the appeal itself had to be notified to the U.S. Department of Justice. Switzerland agreed that additional names could be disclosed if the United States presented evidence that other Swiss banks aided and abetted tax evasion.

Procedurally, the United States filed a tax treaty request with the Swiss government for the data on American clients, which then ordered UBS to turn over the data. In return, the United States dropped its John Doe summons. Together, with the earlier UBS client disclosures and the IRS voluntary program, the IRS had some 10,000 names by the end of 2009.

Who are the winners and losers? UBS appeared to get the entire matter behind it in the intergovernmental settlement and was able to continue rebuilding from the disaster of the global financial crisis, reputational losses, and the threat of criminal sanctions. Future embarrassing fallout for the bank included criminal indictments filed against a number of its former private bankers. At the same time, the easy money of hefty charges for financial secrecy ended.

On the other hand, after announcement of the Swiss-American agreement, various smaller Swiss banks that were strategically far less exposed to the United States than UBS, quickly promised former UBS clients (who had been advised by the bank to come forward and take advantage of the IRS self-reporting program before it was too late) more sophisticated tax evasion schemes in the hope of attracting both U.S. and European tax evaders as clients.

For its part, the United States was indeed unlikely to rest on its success in breaching offshore financial secrecy, with other Swiss banks and other alleged financial havens clearly on the radar screen. In August 2011, U.S. prosecutors, investigating aiding and abetting allegations involving offshore tax evasion, issued an indictment against a Zurich accountant who was allegedly a leader in setting up sham corporations, foundations, and other structures with no commercial purpose other than tax evasion by U.S. clients. Also indicted on the same charge were former UBS private bankers who left after the bank stopped serving American clients in 2008. Charges included violation of rules against serving as an investment adviser without registering as such with the Securities and Exchange Commission (SEC). Credit Suisse and at least six additional Swiss banks (unnamed, but including at least one cantonal bank in addition to Baseler Kantonalbank, which had already been named in previous indictments) and a Liechtenstein bank attracted the attention of U.S. prosecutors and were asked for pertinent client information. Thus, a new confrontation with Switzerland arose as court documents were released specifying tax evasion and the active involvement of the additional Swiss banks, building pressure for more client names. The Swiss demanded that all bankers involved be exempt from prosecution, an argument refused by the United States.

Much of the momentum for the U.S. investigations came from the IRS's voluntary disclosure program with information that other Swiss banks were actively soliciting former UBS clients in contravention of the bank's own advice. Moreover, evidence emerged suggesting that some of these clients broke Swiss laws against money laundering.

Meantime, Switzerland agreed to tax treaties with both Britain and Germany to ensure tax compliance without violating Swiss confidentiality statutes. Both countries committed themselves not to use criminal prosecutions against Swiss banks or bankers. Clients are committed to pay tax authorities in their home countries a one-time sum on their capital, plus annual payments on capital gains and dividends. These withholding taxes and remittances substitute for account disclosure to the home country tax authorities. The one-time payment to Germany was estimated at $2.7 billion and the future tax on capital gains and dividends at 26 percent remitted by the Swiss banks and recouped from client accounts (Simonian 2011). In the case of the United States, the lump-sum payment was about $650 million with a future flat-rate tax of 48 percent. Some expect this model be replicated in new tax treaties with other European countries.

The use of Swiss banking seems to be over for U.S. offshore tax evaders, as well as much of Europe. The Swiss government had to concede on a major point of principle, and felt the heat of governments in Europe and elsewhere seeking outcomes similar to that with the United States. Private banking in Switzerland would clearly have to be transformed to rely on the demand for secrecy from non–tax related reasons, plus investment performance, service excellence, and the country's advantages as a stable economic and financial environment. In the process, the Swiss private landscape would change substantially as a key export product, financial secrecy, saw its competitive edge eroded among major segments of the offshore private banking market. Efforts by hard-core secrecy seekers to find refuge in Singapore or Hong Kong will trigger an enforcement effort focusing on an eventual settlement with those financial centers. Nevertheless, estimates surfaced that about 18 percent of offshore private client assets at Credit Suisse, 20 percent at UBS, and 30 to 40 percent at Julius Baer, would migrate to other offshore centers (Saltmarsh 2011). Beyond that, they will be forced into some shaky environments and pay for the tactics through increased risk and lower returns.

SUMMARY AND CONCLUSIONS

Discussions of financial secrecy are usually, and not surprisingly, shrouded in mystery. In contrast, this chapter identifies nondisclosure of financial information as a distinctly commercial service—one having many attributes of the market for ordinary commercial services. There is demand, supply, equilibrium, consumer and producer surplus, agency problems, and a host of other characteristics familiar to students of economics. These concepts help frame discussions of criminal cash flows, flight capital, insider trading proceeds, financing terrorism, and tax evasion. All require financial secrecy, and all are components of the market for financial nondisclosure. If the argument that financial secrecy is associated with a host of social costs is accepted, then regulatory and enforcement intervention in secret financial flows may be a key component in remediation. Indeed, intervention may be more effective than efforts to interdict the socially damaging behavior itself.

DISCUSSION QUESTIONS

1. What impact might the antiterrorist initiatives under FATF have had on global patterns of tax evasion? Explain.

2. Government victories in recent years in the battle against tax evasion have relied on bank data stolen by former employees and purchased by national tax authorities. Explain whether the government's using of such data is ethical.

3. UBS has a clearly stated policy for its private bankers not to deal with offshore accounts of clients subject to U.S. tax laws in ways that might constitute aiding and abetting actions in criminal violation of the law. Yet, UBS private bankers evidently pursued such clients with enthusiasm. How can this be explained?

4. Most insider trading scandals uncovered by the U.S. Securities and Exchange Commission have involved offshore bank accounts. Why? Are the countries where such accounts are housed in any way culpable? Why or why not?

5. Assume that the former finance minister in a small developing country in Africa managed to hide more $700 million in overseas accounts before being ousted from the government and becoming an ordinary private citizen. What could this individual do to keep these funds?

REFERENCES

Blum, Richard H. 1984. *Offshore Haven Banks, Trusts and Companies*. New York: Praeger Publishers.

Chambost, Eduard. 1983. *Bank Accounts: A World Guide to Confidentiality*. London: John Wiley & Sons, Inc.

Cornwell, Rupert. 1983. *God's Banker*. London: Victor Gollancz.

Destiny Worldwide Net. 1999. "Swiss under Pressure in Tax Evasion Battle." Privacy Class Alumni Group. August 6. Available at http://tech.groups.yahoo.com/group/privacy1/message/105.

Diamond, Walter H., and Dorothy B. Diamond. 1984. *Tax Havens of the World*. New York: Matthew Bender.

Financial Action Task Force. 2011. "What Is the FATF?" Available at www.fatf-gafi.org/document/57/0,3746,en_32250379_32235720_34432121_1_1_1_1,00.html.

Kwitney, Jonathan. 1987. *The Crimes of Patriots*. New York: W.W. Norton & Co.

Legarda, Benito. 1984. "Small Island Economies." *Finance and Development* 21:2, 47–49.

O'Neil, David M. 1983. *Growth of the Underground Economy, 1950–1981*. Joint Economic Committee, U.S. Congress. Washington, D.C.: U.S. Government Printing Office.

Permanent Subcommittee on Investigations. 1983. *Crime and Confidentiality: The Use of Off-shore Banks and Companies*. Committee on Governmental Affairs, United States Senate. Washington, D.C.: U.S. Government Printing Office.

Richpuran, Somchai. 1984. "Measuring Tax Evasion." *Finance and Development* 21:4, 12–14.

Saltmarsh, Matthew. 2011. "Swiss Near Tax Treaties with Germany and Britain." *New York Times*, August 9. Available at www.nytimes.com/2011/08/10/business/global/switzerland-moves-to-squeeze-tax-evaders.html.

Simonian, Haig. 2011. "U.S. Presses Switzerland over Secret Accounts." *Financial Times*, August 9. Available at www.ft.com/intl/cms/s/0/fa44976a-c288-11e0-9ede-00144fea bdc0.html#axzz1UpVR5gzm.

Skousen, Mark. 1983. *The Complete Guide to Financial Privacy*. New York: Simon & Schuster.

Smith, Roy C., and Ingo Walter. 1997. *Street Smarts: Linking Professional Conduct with Shareholder Value in the Securities Industry*. Boston: Harvard Business School Press.

Smith, Roy C., Ingo Walter, and Gayle De Long. 2012. *Global Banking*, 3rd ed. New York: Oxford University Press.

Subcommittee on Crime. 1985. *Current Problems of Money Laundering*. Committee of the Judiciary, U.S. House of Representatives, 99th Congress. Washington, D.C.: U.S. Government Printing Office.

Tanzi, Vito. 1982. *The Underground Economy*. Lexington, MA: D.C. Heath.

Walter, Ingo. 1990. *The Secret Money Market*. New York: Harper-Collins.

ABOUT THE AUTHOR

Ingo Walter is the Seymour Milstein Chair in Finance, Corporate Governance and Ethics at the Stern School of Business, New York University. Since joining the faculty, he has served as Chair of International Business, Chair of Finance, Director of the New York University Salomon Center for the Study of Financial Institutions, Director of the Stern Global Business Institute, and Dean of the Faculty. He has had visiting professorial appointments at the Free University of Berlin, University of Mannheim, University of Zurich, University of Basel, the Institute for Southeast Asian Studies in Singapore, IESE in Spain, INSEAD in Fontainebleau, and various other academic and research institutions. His principal areas of academic and consulting activity include international finance and banking. He has published papers in most of the professional journals in the field and is the author, co-author, or editor of 26 books, most recently *Global Banking*, Third Edition, published by Oxford University Press in 2012. Professor Walter received his AB and MS degrees from Lehigh University and his Ph.D. degree in 1966 from New York University.

PART III

Corporate Engagement

CHAPTER 16

Corporate Social Responsibility and Corporate Governance

LORENZO SACCONI
Professor of Economics and Unicredit Chair in Economic Ethics and Corporate
Social Responsibility, University of Trento

INTRODUCTION

In the last decades, the agency model has gained acceptance among corporate governance (CG) scholars and practitioners. The agency model does not acknowledge any basic responsibility of managers or directors' toward any stakeholder beyond shareholders. It is based on shareholders primacy. Corporate social responsibility (CSR), however, involves at least some corporate responsibility toward stakeholders other than shareholders. Not surprisingly, the agency model of CG does not reserve any major role to CSR within CG, but it does not exclude an instrumental use of CSR as far as it may function as a tool that is practical to shareholder value maximization.

The agency model is by no means the only view of CG. A second prominent view sees the board of directors as a largely autonomous body aimed at providing an impartial balance among the different corporate stakeholders and playing the role of a mediating hierarchy. While some suggest that this model is a faithful interpretation of American corporate law, there are also CG institutions that cannot be interpreted according to the shareholder primacy doctrine in Japan, Germany, and most continental European countries.

The purpose of this chapter is to provide a theory of CSR as an extended model of corporate governance whereby entrepreneurs, directors, managers, and owners (as far as they have direct influence on corporate decisions) have fiduciary duties owed to both noncontrolling stakeholders and shareholders. This model understands CSR as a social norm making sense of both existing legal orderings and social reform movements aimed at designing CG so that employees and managers' specific investment in human capital is safeguarded no less than financial capital investments. Moreover, the chapter provides a social contract foundation of the multifiduciary and multistakeholder model of CG along two distinct but convergent lines of argumentation. First, the role that social norms play in the emergence of different CG institutions—a point accepted by both the competing views of CG considered—is taken into account. The social contract is the best potential explanation of how a group of agents can share a social norm and then it may evolve until the equilibrium state of an institution is established. The model of reasoning consisting in an impartial acceptance under a veil of ignorance therefore explains the starting point in the equilibrium selection process of social norms. Accordingly, CSR would endogenously emerge as a social norm from the corporate stakeholders' social contract understood as an equilibrium selection mechanism. The social contract would not explain or predict other CG models as an endogenously emergent institution.

Second, the main criticisms raised from a normative view point against the stakeholder approach to CG are addressed. In fact, the social contract answers all of them. In particular, it furnishes the impartial mode of reasoning that the mediating hierarch should implement in seeking a fair balancing among different legitimate stakeholders' claims. Moreover, it gives a mathematical uniquely defined objective function that the mediating hierarch should strive to maximize.

Finally, multiple fiduciary duties owed to both controlling and noncontrolling stakeholders emerge naturally from a two-step social contract on the firm's constitution. Thus, the CSR model permits specifying the fiduciary duties owed to each category of stakeholders, granting each of them a proper area of fiduciary privilege.

The remainder of this chapter has the following organization. The first section provides an account of the place reserved to CSR in the debate between alternative CG views. The second section presents the definition of CSR as extended multifiduciary CG model. The third section introduces the idea that an economic institution is a summary representation (through a shared mental model) of the equilibrium regularity played in a given domain of interaction and the idea of a social contract based norm as staring point of an equilibrium selection process. The fourth section applies the Binmore-Rawls social contract theory to the prediction that a CSR social norm would emerge from strong and weak stakeholders' interactions, and derives its basic egalitarian principle of fair stakeholder treatment. The fifth section shows that the same social contract model justifies the CSR model of corporate governance and helps deriving multiple fiduciary duties and the objective-function of the corporation governed according to CSR. The last section summarizes and concludes.

THE PLACE OF CSR IN THE CORPORATE GOVERNANCE DEBATE

This section provides a discussion of the place reserved to CSR in the debate between alternative CG views.

The Agency Model of Corporate Governance

One prominent view of corporate governance sees it as a system of contracts, rules, norms, and institutions (legal and social) aimed at assuring the accomplishment of promises that corporate managers implicitly undertake with the investors of financial capital in a corporation, i.e., its shareholders. According to this position, Macey (2008, p. 1) notes:

> the purpose of corporate governance is to persuade, induce, compel, and otherwise motivate corporate managers to keep the promise they make to investors. Another way to say this is that corporate governance is about reducing deviance by corporation where deviance is defined as any actions by management or directors that are

at odds with the legitimate, investment-backed expectations of investors. Good corporate governance, then, is simply about keeping promises. Bad governance (corporate deviance) is defined as promise breaking behavior.

This is a typical statement in the agency view of corporate governance. CG is seen as a game played by two main players linked to each other by a special kind of (agency) contract. The agent is the manager who is in charge of running the corporation on behalf of the principals within the limits set by contracts and legal regulations linking the corporation with all the other stakeholders.

The principal is conceived as a representative player who stands for all the shareholders. Principals delegate to managers the task of running the firm according to their interests (e.g., value maximization), but they cannot control managerial behavior in any detail because of the asymmetry of information that characterizes the principal/agent relationship. In agency theory, the principal/agent asymmetry of information is inherent because ownership is dispersed across many shareholders. Further, no single shareholder has the time, resources, knowledge, or the will to be completely informed about corporate management in which he holds a share. Dispersed and uninformed shareholders consequently lack direct influence on corporate management because of the separation of ownership and control. Thus, rules or incentives that constrain agents to act according to their principals' best interests, preventing agents from behaving opportunistically, are the focus of CG.

Asymmetry of information in the agency model results from both individual and collective causes. At the individual level, the principal may simply lack information on actions performed by the agent because these are unobservable, and he may be confined to observing their outcomes, which are only probabilistically linked to actions. Collectively, shareholders face what economists call a *collective choice problem*. Each shareholder holds too small a fraction of the overall amount of corporate shares to be individually motivated to undertake the cost of becoming sufficiently informed about the company's management. In fact, his individual level of influence on the management would not justify the effort required. If a sufficiently large coalition of shareholders was prepared to actively supervise corporate management, an individual shareholder could profit by free-riding their positive surveillance efforts without bearing the cost of doing it on his own.

According to the nexus-of-contract view of the firm, owing to ex ante and ex post imperfections in bilateral long-term contracts, the entrepreneur or manager centralizes all the contracts with the various categories of stakeholders on the company that he runs, the purpose being to design incentives that minimize contract costs (Alchian and Demestez 1972; Hansmann 1999). The agency approach to CG, however, contends that many stakeholders are related to the company by concrete and quite well-specified contracts that are self-contained and do not require a specific governance structure to protect their parties beyond contract law. By contrast, shareholders are residual claimants that may profit from their financial investment only after the firm has complied with other more concrete contracts, which makes their investments an inherently risky matter. But contractual commitments with shareholders are so indefinite, and the possibility that shareholders can verify respect of those commitments and attainment of their goals is so remote, that they warrant special protection (Jensen and Meckling 1976; Easterbrook and Fischel 1991; Tirole 2001).

Thus, CG only concerns a set of rules providing for the following:

- Protection of shareholders against managerial abuse of the discretion that the separation between ownership and control grants to managers
- Allocation of ownership and residual control rights
- Delegation by shareholders to a board of directors of control to be exercised on their behalf
- Fiduciary duties of due care, and no conflicts of interest, so that directors do not abuse the gaps in the fiduciary relation linking them to shareholders
- Remuneration and incentive schemes whereby the board may induce managers to act according to the shareholders' best interests
- Mergers and acquisitions that align the management's preferences with those of the shareholders by means of the threat that a new entrepreneur who succeeds in taking over the company may fire the incumbent management

From an economist's viewpoint, what is peculiar about this line of thought is how it oversimplifies the main point of Coase (1937) and also Williamson's (1975, 1986) economic analysis of the firm. According to this analysis, the firm is a transaction-governance institution substituting a hierarchical organization for atomistic spot market contracts whereby the incompleteness of all contracts with stakeholders is filled by authority relations (Coase 1937; Williamson 1975, 1986; Grossman and Hart 1986; Hart and Moore 1990). But the agency model reduces governance to the rules that only fill the gaps in the shareholder/management relations. CG thus focuses only on providing a mechanism with which to ensure that promises implicitly made by managers to shareholders are kept.

Unsurprisingly, this view has no room for corporate social responsibility (CSR) insofar as it concerns at least a set of responsibilities and obligations that those with authority in the company owe not just to shareholders but also to other stakeholders within the scope of their legitimate discretion. In fact, according to the agency view of CG, there are by definition no further obligations that may complement those owed to shareholders and that could therefore introduce further and perhaps dissimilar constraints on the managers' and directors' exercise of discretion beyond the responsibility of running the firm in the best interest of the shareholders.

The Mediating Hierarchy Model of CG

The foregoing agency and promissory views do not assign any major role to CSR in defining the firm's objective-function and the principles and goals of CG. This is not true, however, for the mediating hierarchy model of CG.

A second prominent view of CG is that corporate law does not guarantee and does not intend to secure shareholders' absolute priority in defining CG aims and corporate strategies. Instead, boards of directors are granted primacy because they are endowed with broad autonomy based on the business judgment doctrine that insulates them against shareholders' self-interested claims to maximize their share value (Blair and Stout 1999; Elhauge 2005; Stout 2011b). The board is relatively free to frame the corporation's strategy according to its views of the corporation's interests, development, and success, and also to exercise freedom in its decisions about dividends distribution and shareholders' compensation policies, assuming that the corporate interest results from the balance among different stakeholders' claims. A good theory of CG should make sense of this management autonomy, which is characteristic of the corporate form as an institution with a legal personality distinct from the natural persons involved in it (Aoki 2010).

What the agency view regards as inefficiency in the current U.S. CG system and a deviation from its main goal—keeping the promise to protect the shareholders' investments against managers' opportunism—is in this second perspective regarded as empirical proof of the enduring non–shareholder-oriented nature of U.S. corporate law. Consider the historical fact that many states enacted stakeholder-oriented bills during the 1980s allowing the managers of targeted corporations to adopt defensive tactics in order to resist adversarial takeovers. This is cited as evidence that U.S. corporate law incorporates interests that extend well beyond those of shareholders when deciding a change in the corporation ownership and control structure that might be prejudicial to noncontrolling stakeholders such as workers, suppliers, and local communities (Branson 2001; Stout 2011b).

Blair and Stout (1999, 2006) defend this view of CG by contending that the board of directors is a *mediating hierarchy* whose goal is to mediate among the different stakeholders' claims in order to pursue the corporation's overall success. This view is distinctive because it is based on an economic analysis of the firm as team production. Thus, the mediating hierarchy view forestalls the accusation that it is too detached from the economic goal of the firm typically raised by theorists in the agency model tradition against progressive views of CG. In a productive team, different stakeholders—not just financial capital investors but also and mainly human capital investors—undertake specific investments. Because of incompleteness of contracts, due not only to asymmetric information but also to bounded rationality and unforeseen events, these investments can be subjected to hold-up by other stakeholders. This happens especially when these stakeholders have control over decisional variables that are essential for accomplishment of the transactions in relation to which the investments were undertaken. Being afraid that the expected value of their investments will be expropriated, they do not invest at an efficient level (Williamson 1975; Grossman and Hart 1986; Hart and Moore 1990; Rajan and Zingales 1998). Since specific investments are multiple, this may happen for any allocation of residual control, and hence abuse of authority is always a latent risk (Sacconi 1999, 2000). Therefore, the main goal of the board of directors as a mediating hierarchy is to prevent opportunistic behavior within the team and abuse of residual control rights, and to allow each stakeholder to profit from its participation in team production.

Not surprisingly, therefore, the mediating hierarchy theory of CG is much more akin and sympathetic to CSR than agency theory. CSR may be seen as the value or fairness principle directing the board members' discretion in exercising their mediating function.

Diversity of CG Legal Frameworks Regarding the Place Reserved for Stakeholders

The debate between the promissory and the mediating hierarchy views of CG and the role of the board of directors in particular is both normative and descriptive.

In this latter respect, the debate concerns the true nature or goal of corporate law in the United States. However, as far as description is concerned, supporters of the two views may disagree about this point while agreeing that, at an international level, CG systems other than the agency model focus on the protection of a set of interests broader than that of shareholders alone. Macey (2008, p. 11) states the following:

> In many places, particularly Germany and Japan, the fundamental premise behind corporation is not the notion of a promise to maximize value for shareholders. Instead the fundamental corporate promise is that the corporation is a creation of the state whose goals are to serve myriad and often conflicting societal interests.
>
> Macey (2008, p. 35)

In Germany, 82.7 percent of senior managers thought their company belonged to all the stakeholders. France was not much different with 77 percent of top manager giving the corporation to the stakeholders. In Japan, an astonishing 97 percent of managers thought that the company belonged to all stakeholders (see Allen and Gale 2000).

These opinions of managers are complementary to the mandatory labor regulations in many European countries that grant broad protection against arbitrary dismissals. Moreover, the German co-determination model provides for the active representation of at least one of the main nonowner stakeholders (i.e., employees) in the CG structure. In the supervisory board, which is superordinate to the managerial board, unions are represented in a proportion that may equal 50 percent of seats, not including the chairman of the company (Osterloch, Frey, and Zeitoun 2010).

Japan is another well-known anomaly with respect to the agency model of CG. Aoki (2010) notes a major change occurred in the Japanese CG landscape during the past two decades. Specifically, this change is the decline of the traditional role of national banks in both providing financial capital for large corporations and exercising a supervisory and control function on the internal CG and organization structures. Although many large corporations such as Toyota and Canon now resort to the financial market for their capitalization, so that ownership has been dispersed among many shareholders, the emerging model still does not resemble a variant of the agency model. As in the past, the primary orientation of managers was to increase profitability by keeping the corporation's commitment to value human capital investments and to keep the promise of continuity of long-life employment relations with the key skilled employees. What seems to emerge is a hybrid CG model based on the coexistence of dispersed shareholder external ownership and indirect control, and internal governance largely concentrated on making the alliance among the essential cognitive human assets held in the company by managers and core employees maximally profitable and mutually advantageous. Japanese managers discharge a mediating hierarchy function devoted to promoting organizational cooperation among managers' and workers' human cognitive assets, while also being accountable to the surveillance role performed by institutional investors' representatives intended to ensure that the cooperation does not degenerate into opportunistic collusion detrimental to financial capital investors (Aoki 1984, 2010).

Returning to the differences between the United States and Europe, it may seem that the U.S. perspective on CG gives priority to shareholders while the continental European perspective assigns more weight to stakeholders' claims. This interpretation may be inaccurate. On the contrary, such differences may stem from different internally consistent answers to the same problem of preventing hold-up of human capital investments in teams (Deakin and Rebeiroux 2008; Gelter 2009). Thus, the crux of the comparison between the United States and Europe is how much direct influence shareholders have in the two contexts according to their dispersion throughout the financial capital market, and hence the level of autonomy enjoyed by managers. In the United States, a wide dispersion of ownership tightly constrains the direct influence of shareholders on corporate decisions. On the contrary, in Europe, a higher concentration of ownership increases the direct influence of owners—sometimes a single family or a small coalition of investors. This enables the board of directors to function as a mediating hierarchy in the United States, while it entails that a stronger legal protection must have emerged to protect noncontrolling stakeholders (especially workers) and their specific investments in continental Europe. Such legal protection may take the form of strong labor laws protecting workers against arbitrary dismissals. This gives unions information rights and the possibility to bargain on lay-offs and the restructuring of companies and, especially in Germany, the formal proviso of participatory decision rights for unions through the co-determination model, i.e., their participation in the supervisory board.

According to Gelter (2009), these are two local optima based on complementary levels of realization of two variables: concentration of ownership and legal protection of long-lasting labor contracts. When ownership is concentrated, so that shareholders exercise direct influence on the board of directors and corporate management, mandatory labor laws are required as complementary devices with which to protect specific investments in human capital from the threat of expropriation. When ownership is widely dispersed and does not exert any major direct influence, the unions' influence tends to decline, and the mediating hierarchy model of the board of directors emerges as a more flexible solution able to provide a fair balance among all the relevant stakeholders' investment and interests.

If these two local optima are equilibria around which players interacting in the domains of institutional systems of CG tend to gravitate, some institutional, political, or technological change may eventually push systems out of the equilibrium path into situations that are not stable, and even less mutually beneficial. In the past decades, the indirect influence of shareholders over corporate management has been hugely increased by the wide diffusion of so-called incentive contracts for managers' compensation, such as stock-option plans, that are intended to align managers' behavior with shareholders' interests by making the managers' compensation largely dependent on shareholder value as assessed by financial markets. This drove directors and managers to consider themselves as main shareholders and thus to conduct the company, not as trustees acting on behalf of some further group of stakeholders, but as self-interested agents acting in their own self-interest and maximizing the share value as far as it reflected their own self-interest. Under these incentives schemes, managers and directors no longer operate as impartial mediating hierarchs, and their wide discretion and informative advantage with respect to all stakeholders give them the opportunity for holding all them up. Many authors maintain that wide discretion plus the perverse self-interested incentives of managers legitimized under the "maximization of short-term share value" doctrine were among the main causes of the 2007–2008 global financial crisis (Cassidy 2009; Posner 2009; Aoki 2010; Stiglitz 2010).

At the same time, as a consequence of the 2010–2011 sovereign debts crisis in the eurozone, growing political pressure has been exerted for labor law protection against arbitrary dismissals to be reduced in order to give more flexibility to the labor market. In the absence of any major restructuring of ownership concentration in continental Europe, this pressure may push these systems of CG very far from their local optima. Yet the persistence of the co-determination model in Germany and the relative success of German companies even in the context of the global crisis may suggest that this is actually a successful model of CG.

This chapter submits that insofar as the CSR movement is relevant to the shaping of CG models worldwide, it can be interpreted as an equilibrating force that concurs in rolling CG systems back to their optimal equilibrium position, or in changing them by moving toward new equilibria where a new fair balance of stakeholders' protection is reached.

Both sides in the CG debate acknowledge the importance of social norms in shaping CG institutions (Macey 2008; Stout 2006, 2011a). Thus, CSR may be seen as an emerging social norm shaping CG even within different legal frameworks. Social norms satisfy the definition of game-theoretical equilibria, and hence the emergence of CSR as a social norm of CG can be seen as essentially an equilibrium selection process. According to the social contract theory illustrated in this chapter, this process is initiated by the shared acceptance of a normative model of fair treatment among stakeholders. It then receives support from the preferences and beliefs affected by the social contract justification of CSR. These preferences and beliefs make it self-sustaining as the result of the iterated best responses of each stakeholder to the choices of others.

This chapter provides a full-fledged social contract foundation for CSR as a model of multifiduciary CG whereby the protection of the controlling stakeholder's (i.e., shareholders) specific investments is complemented by symmetrical responsibilities for the protection of noncontrolling stakeholders' specific investments, and their cognitive human assets' value as well. Taken into account is the challenge that "there is no legitimate theoretical or moral objection to those who assert that goals of the modern corporation should serve the broad interest of all stakeholders . . . provided that these goals are clearly disclosed to investors before they part with their money" (Macey 2008, p 3). That is, the enlarged goal of the corporation should be construed in terms of a fair agreement. The social contract of the firm precisely shows that the extension of fiduciary duties to all the stakeholders is exactly what they would accept voluntarily by a hypothetical fair agreement.

CSR AS A MULTIFIDUCIARY MODEL OF CG

Various lines of research in new institutional economics, unorthodox law and economics, the stakeholder approach to management studies, and business ethics provide an understating of CSR that relates it to CG (Aoki 1984, 2010; Freeman 1984; Sacconi 1991, 2000; Donaldson and Preston 1995; Clarkson 1999; Blair and Stout 1999, 2006; Evan and Freeman 1993; Freeman and Velamury 2006; Sacconi

2006a, 2006b, 2007, 2010a, 2010b, 2011; Freeman, Harrison, Wicks, Parmar, and De Colle 2010; Stout 2011b; Donaldson 2012). According to these views, CSR is not only a form of corporate strategic management but also a model for governing transactions occuring among the firm's stakeholders. Here, governance is no longer the set of rules simply allocating property rights and defining the owners' control over the company's management. Instead, it relates to the new-institutional economics view whereby firms, as well as contracts and other institutions, are governance structures that establish diverse rights and related responsibilities in order to reduce transaction costs (Coase 1937; Williamson 1975, 1986; Grossman and Hart 1986) and the negative externalities related to economic transactions so as to approximate social welfare.

This view is constitutive because it sees CSR as a constitutive trait inherent to how the corporation functions and to its goal. That is, this view sees CSR as the governance model on the basis of which a company pursues its objective-function, namely, the joint interest and mutual advantage of all its relevant corporate stakeholders. Insofar as CSR is defined as a governance model entailing a multistakeholder definition of the corporate goal, it concerns less the sphere of corporate means than the domain of corporate ends (the corporation's goals) and constitutional rules, i.e., it is constitutive.

Sacconi (2006a, 2006b, 2007, 2010a) defined CSR as a model of extended corporate governance whereby those who run firms, such as entrepreneurs, directors, managers, have responsibilities that range from fulfillment of their fiduciary duties toward the owners to fulfillment of analogous fiduciary duties toward all the firm's stakeholders. Two terms must be defined for the foregoing proposition to be clearly understood. The first term is *fiduciary duties*. The assumption here is that a subject has a legitimate interest but is unable to make the relevant decisions, in the sense that he does not know what goals to pursue, what alternative to choose, or how to deploy his resources in order to satisfy his interest. The trustor therefore delegates decisions to a trustee empowered to choose actions and goals being endowed with wide discretion and authority. The trustee may thus use the trustor's resources and select the appropriate course of action. For a fiduciary relationship to arise, however, the trustor must possess a belief that his/her claim (right) toward the trustee will be met. In other words, the trustor is confident that the trustee directs actions and uses the resources made over to him so that results are obtained that satisfy the trustor's interests. These claims (i.e., the trustor's rights) impose fiduciary duties on the agent who is invested with authority (the trustee) that he is obliged to fulfill. The fiduciary relationship applies in a wide variety of instances such as tutor/minor and teacher/pupil relationships. In the corporate domain, the relationship is between the board of a trust and its beneficiaries or between the board of directors of a joint-stock company and its shareholders, and then more generally between management and owners. The term *fiduciary duty* means the duty or responsibility to exercise authority for the good of those who have granted that authority and are therefore subject to it (Flannigan 1989).

The second term is *stakeholders*. This term denotes individuals or groups with a major stake in the running of the firm and who are able to materially influence it (Freeman and McVea 2001). However, from an economist's point of view, most relevant to defining stakeholders is the following distinction between two categories: stakeholders in the strict sense and stakeholders in the board sense.

Stakeholders in the strict sense are those who have an interest at stake because they have made specific investments in the firm, such as in the form of human capital, financial capital, social capital or trust, physical or environmental capital, or for the development of dedicated technologies. Such investments may substantially increase the total value generated by the firm and are made specifically in relation to that firm so that their value is idiosyncratically related to the completion of the transactions carried out by or in relation to that firm. These stakeholders are reciprocally dependent on the firm because they influence its value but at the same time depend largely upon it for satisfaction of their well-being prospects (lock-in effect). By contrast, *stakeholders in the broad sense* are those individuals or groups whose interest is involved because they undergo the external effects, positive or negative, of the transactions performed by the firm, even if they do not directly participate in the transaction, so that they do not contribute to or directly receive value from the firm.

One can thus appreciate the scope of CSR defined as an extended form of governance: it extends the concept of fiduciary duty from a mono-stakeholder setting where the sole stakeholder relevant to identification of fiduciary duties is the owner of the firm to a multistakeholder one in which the firm owes fiduciary duties to all its stakeholders, including the owners.

CSR SOCIAL NORMS AND SELF-SUSTAINING INSTITUTIONS OF CG

Social norms are nowadays deemed no less important for CG than legal norms. In fact, these two types of norms are complementary (Stout 2011a). Since the adoption of certain contracts or statutes at the corporate level is to some extent voluntary, social norms may be seen as drivers of the voluntary adoption of one or another legal model (e.g., shareholder-oriented vs. stakeholder-oriented). Moreover, even if a legal system makes some legal constraints and principles in CG mandatory, it largely depends on social norms whether the legal constraints will be actually followed and whether adherence will spread at societal level. Certain legal institutions of CG, such as fiduciary duties, may or may not be established in a given context according to how social norms of trust are shaped at societal level. For example, if good social capital and trustworthiness in a given society were very low, assigning the fiduciary duties of autonomous trustees an important role in CG could be pointless (Macey 2008).

Social norms are even more important for the economic rather than legal analysis of institutions because modern economists understand them as *conventions* (Lewis 1969; Schotter 1981; Sudgen 1986). Conventions are coordination game equilibria that may endogenously emerge from repeated strategic decisions among players participating in a given domain of interaction. They are stable and self-enforceable once a system of mutually consistent expectations has formed that sustains the common belief that all participants will maintain behavior consistent with the norm. Because of their self-enforceability and incentive compatibility, conventions are the kind of institutions that economists like more, i.e., *spontaneous orders* (Hayek 1973; Sugden 1986).

Hence, the gist of this section is that, once complementarity with the law has been recognized, and assuming that no mandatory laws are obstructing the emergence of a CSR model of CG, the endogenous beliefs, motivations, and preferences of economic agents such as companies and their stakeholders become the essential forces driving the implementation of the CSR model of multistakeholder governance. In game theoretical terms, the normative model is implementable in equilibrium. This is also the basis for the widely accepted view that CSR implementation is mainly a matter of voluntary self-regulation of self-enforceable principles and norms. Thus, its implementation may rest primarily on soft laws, social standards, codes of ethics, voluntary adoption of contracts, provisos, and statutes, all of which are self-sustaining norms constraining from within the discretion of corporate directors and managers (Wieland 2003; Sacconi 2006a).

The best way to integrate social norms into the emergence and stability of CG models is to resort to Aoki's (2001, 2010) account of institutions. Institutions "are not rules exogenously given by the polity, culture or a meta-game" but "rules created through the strategic interaction of agents, held in the minds of agents and thus self-sustaining" (Aoki 2001, p. 11). An institution is "a self-sustaining system of shared beliefs about a salient way in which the game is repeatedly played" (Aoki 2001, p. 11). The content of shared beliefs is "a summary representation (compressed information) of an equilibrium in a repeated game" (Aoki 2001, p. 11). Thus, the salient feature of the equilibrium played has a symbolic representation inside the agents' minds and coordinates beliefs that in their turn induce behaviors and their replication over time.

Cognitive components (i.e., beliefs deriving from compressed mental representations of salient aspects of ongoing equilibrium play) and behavioral components (i.e., the iterated play of a given set of equilibrium strategies) are interlocked in a recursive scheme (Aoki 2010; also see the inner circle of Exhibit 16.1). The starting point is cognitive, and it consists in pattern recognition whereby given situations of interaction are framed as games of a certain form wherein players are expected

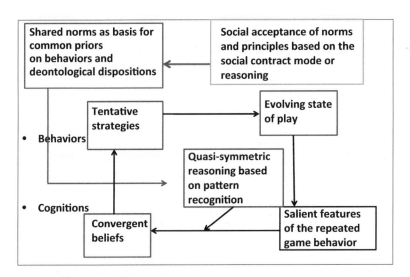

Exhibit 16.1 Modified Aoki Recursive Model

The portion of this exhibit consisting of quasi-symmetric reasoning, convergent beliefs, tentative strategies, evolving state of play, and salient features of the repeated game behavior represents Aoki's recursive model of an equilibrium institution. Overall, the exhibit shows that social acceptance of norms based of social contract reasoning affects initial common beliefs on behaviors and dispositions and hence is the starting point for the emergence process leading to an equilibrium institution.

to reason in a given quasi-symmetrical way. At step two, this framing of the situation induces players to entertain quasi-converging beliefs about a certain mode of playing the game. Thus, at step three, on passing from beliefs to the players' actual behavior, each player adopts a tentative strategy based on the belief that others will also adopt strategies consistent with the aforementioned mode of behavior. Hence, in step four, strategies clash, and some of them prove to be more successful and based on a better prediction. By trial and error, therefore, strategies converge toward an equilibrium of the game. This may be construed as an evolutionary result because the mode of playing attracts more and more players through iterated adaptation to the other players' aggregate behaviors in the long run. At each repetition, however, this evolving equilibrium is summarily represented in its salient features by a compressed mental model resident in the players mind, so the fifth step concluding the circle is again cognitive.

This circle can be recursively iterated so that the ongoing equilibrium mode of playing is repeatedly confirmed by beliefs that translate into equilibrium behaviors, which are represented summarily by mental models, and so on. At some point, this belief system reaches a nearly complete state of common knowledge (Lewis 1969; Binmore and Brandenburger 1990) about how players interact. The resulting equilibrium is an institution: a regularity of behavior played in a domain of interaction and stably represented by the shared mental model resident in all the participants' minds. It is essentially equivalent to the notion of social norm as a convention.

However, a limitation is apparent in this understanding of institutions, and it concerns the normative meaning of an institution. Institutions in the above game-theoretical definition only ex post tell each player what the best action is. Once the players share the knowledge that they have reached an equilibrium state, then playing their best replies is actually a prescription of prudence that confirms the already-established equilibrium. Thus, institutions tell players only how to maintain the existing, already settled, pattern of behavior. They say nothing ex ante about how agents should behave before the mental representation of an equilibrium has settled and a self-replicating equilibrium behavior has crystallized. Institutions only describe regularity of behavior and are devoid of genuine normative meaning and force.

However, institutions including CG (Donaldson 2012) contain norms, such as constitutional principles, laws, statutes, ethical codes, standard rules, and shared social values, which are expressed by explicit utterances in the players' language concerning values, rights, and obligations. These statements have a primarily prescriptive meaning, and if individuals attribute them moral meaning, such prescriptions are also universalizable (i.e., extensible to all similar states of affairs) and overriding with respect to alternative prescriptions expressed in the same context (Hare 1981). Norms thus defined literally have normative meaning independently of the fact that they induce replication of an already-settled collective equilibrium behavior. Thus, a second component of a proper definition of an institution should be the mental representation of the normative meaning of norms.

This makes a great difference. The normative meaning of norms does not depend on knowledge about the ongoing behavior of other players. Instead, norms are able to justify and give first-place reasons for shared acceptance of a mode of behavior addressing all the participants in a given interaction domain before it has been established as an equilibrium point. A norm gives intentional reasons to act independently on the evolutionary benefits of adaptation in the long run because when an individual or a group of agents in a given action domain initiate an institutional change, it cannot stem from the pressure of evolutionary forces, which unfold their attraction only in the long run. Instead, a norm enters the players' shared mental model (Denzau and North 1994) of how the game should be played, shapes the players' reciprocal disposition to act and their default beliefs about common behaviors, and hence becomes the basis for their first coordination on a specific equilibrium. In other words, it works as the first move in a process of equilibrium selection that activates the recursive process outlined by Aoki (2010). According to a line of theorizing in behavioral game theory, because a norm has been (cognitively) commonly accepted it may affect both dispositions to act (preferences) and expectations (default beliefs about how other players behave), so that the norm becomes a game equilibrium (Grimalda and Sacconi 2005; Sacconi 2007, 2011; Sacconi and Faillo 2010; Sacconi, Faillo, and Ottone 2011).

This equilibrium selection function of norms is deployed in two contexts: (1) within a well-defined game, where an old equilibrium path (old institution) has been abandoned for whatever reason and a new equilibrium path (new institution) has to be reached; and (2) when the underlying action domain changes because environmental or technological changes have occurred, or some further action opportunity is simply discovered by players, so that achieving a new equilibrium is necessary.

In these contexts, "the point is that some symbolic system of predictive/ *normative* beliefs [emphasis added] precedes the evolution of a new equilibrium and then becomes accepted by all the agents in the relevant domain through their experiences" (Aoki 2001, p. 19). The key point is, therefore, to explain how a norm (basis for a system of normative beliefs) becomes acceptable by agents before the relevant equilibrium behavior is settled through rational best response, evolution, or other behavioral mechanisms such as reciprocity and conformism. What is required is a collective mode of reasoning (cognition) able to explain how a normative mental model arises before any evolutionary pressure has operated in that direction, and on the basis of which a norm may become commonly accepted in what is not yet an equilibrium state. Therefore, what is needed is a cognitive mechanism of justification for norms that can operate in a similar way in many different contexts, so as to be able to produce a social norm that adapts to diverse situations.

The best justificatory account for the ex ante shared acceptance of norms is the social contract model. Contractarian norms result from a voluntary agreement in a hypothetical choice situation that logically comes before any exogenous institution is superimposed on a given action domain, or before any institution has yet emerged. Thus, a norm arises only because of the voluntary agreement and adhesion of agents, even before it is established as an evolutionary equilibrium. To define the agreement, any social contract model sets aside threats, fraud, and manipulation—resources that would render the parties substantially unequal in terms of bargaining power—and considers all the agents as equal in respect to their rational autonomy, so that many of their arbitrary differences are placed under a *veil of ignorance*. Although a long tradition of contractarian models could be cited, the main reference here is to the Rawlsian model (Rawls 1971).

By introducing the social contract as the cognitive mechanism by which a norm may be accepted and become a shared mental model, Aoki's recursive model can be reformulated. The inner circle of Exhibit 16.1 is retained. What is new (as shown in the upper part of Exhibit 16.1) is that the pattern derives from a shared social norm that categorizes the game as the domain of application of some more general principle. From this categorization it follows that some shared idea of the players' disposition to act (preferences) and common beliefs can be applied in the case under examination. In turn, the social norm derives from social contract reasoning (see Exhibit 16.1) employed by players in order to agree on basic principles and norms when equilibrium institutions are not already established.

SOCIAL CONTRACT AS AN EQUILIBRIUM SELECTION DEVICE

This subsection applies Binmore's (2005) game theoretical vindication of the Rawlsian social contract to the corporate stakeholders' interactions (Sacconi 2010b). Assume that two stakeholders, a poor but skilled worker (Eve) and a rich proprietor of means of production and capital (Adam) meet in a *state of nature* structured as a noncooperative game. Assume that they repeatedly play the same game resulting in a wide set of feasible outcomes. The state of nature precedes the institution of any legal artifice such as the *corporation* under which they could form a regulated team. In Exhibit 16.2 the convex and compact payoff space X_{EA} corresponds to

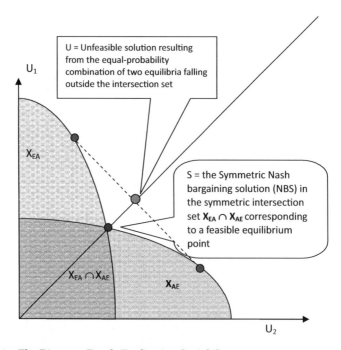

Exhibit 16.2   The Binmore-Rawls Egalitarian Social Contract
The egalitarian solution S equal to the Nash bargaining solution within the symmetric intersection set $X_{EA} \cap X_{AE}$ is also the Rawlsian maximin with respect to the initial outcome space X_{EA}. It is derived by taking jointly the requirements of impartiality and impersonality as well as the stability condition that the solution must be incentive compatible.

the outcome set of the state of nature repeated game. Let these outcomes be all equilibria of the repeated game (i.e., when one player chooses his component of one of these strategy combinations the other has no incentive to deviate from it by changing his strategy component).

Then assume that before agents engage in the relevant interaction (e.g., a largely incomplete contract), they want to agree ex ante on the selection of one of these possible equilibrium points/outcomes. This may be seen as agreeing on a social norm singling out to what they should be entitled by playing their roles under a "corporation." This distributive norm is a skeletal constitution for the corporation that the agents would be prepared to enter. Since the constitution must be fair, impartiality and impersonality of the agreement are required. Taken together, these assumptions are the veil of ignorance hypothesis. In other words, each agent makes his decision "as if" he were ignorant about his true identity, so that in order to reach a deliberation he takes in turn the positions of each possible participant in the game.

In this context, *impersonality* means that acceptance of the solution must not depend on personal and social positions. Thus, players should select a solution that cannot be affected by the symmetrical replacement of social roles and personal positions with respect to individual players. Technically, Exhibit 16.2 depicts this replacement by the symmetric translation of the initial payoff space X_{EA} with respect to the Cartesian axes representing the utility of player 1 and player 2, respectively. Thus, under the initial payoff space X_{EA}, player 1 will have all the possible payoffs of Eve and player 2 all the possible payoffs of Adam. But under the translated payoff space X_{AE}, roles are reserved, and player 1 will then get Adam's possible payoffs and player 2 will get Eve's possible payoffs. Moreover, Exhibit 16.2 illustrates that each player, when taking the other's perspective, exercises perfect empathetic identification. That is, when player 1, who under X_{EA} was Eve, thinks to be Adam under X_{AE}, this player is able to reproduce exactly the same payoffs that player 2 experienced when the player was Adam.

Impartiality means that the players must agree on an outcome under the hypothesis that the reciprocal replacement of positions works in such a way that each stakeholder has an equal probability of finding himself in the position of each of the possible two roles. Equal-probability explains how the solution may not change under the symmetrical translation of the payoff space with respect to the players' utility axes. Take an outcome x_{EA} that by replacing personal positions may realize in two noncoinciding ways (x_{EA} itself and x_{AE}). To make this outcome acceptable requires taking the expected value of an equal probability distribution over the two realization ways: $1/2 x_{EA} + 1/2 x_{AE}$. This would identify a point in the space that is invariant under the players' positions replacement (i.e., an egalitarian solution residing on the bisector).

However, this construction is not meant to be an excessive idealization. Agents retain awareness that the solution must be an equilibrium of the original game. That is, the solution must be a collective behavior that the parties know is self-enforceable and incentive-compatible once they think that they all are playing it. This is a requirement of realism of the agreed solution: agents cannot afford to agree ex ante on a solution if it is not incentive-compatible ex post (beyond the veil of ignorance). The reason is simple. Admit that the impartial solution proves ex post not to be an equilibrium of the original game (does not belong to the original payoff space of the state of nature game). Hence, the player who ex post would be most favored by returning to a solution belonging to the initial equilibrium set would simply deviate to an equilibrium strategy.

Consequently, the stability condition requires that the ex ante solution (agreed behind the veil of ignorance) must correspond to an outcome that under the players' place-permutation would nevertheless belong to the ex post equilibrium set. In other words, the selected outcome must be an equilibrium (say) either if player 1 takes the position of Adam (and player 2 respectively the position of Eve) or in the opposite case when their identification is reversed (player 2 occupies Adam's position, whereas player B takes Eve's position), and all the more so when an equally probable combination of the two identifications is taken.

What has been just set is a new feasibility condition. Owing to the state of nature game's assumptions, only equilibria of the original payoff space X_{EA} are feasible. Any further outcome—potentially subject to agreement—would be wishful thinking because no ex post equilibrium would exist that could implement it (see point U in Exhibit 16.2). Adding the conditions of impersonality and impartiality further restricts feasible outcomes to the symmetric intersection $X_{EA} \cap X_{AE}$ of the two payoff spaces generated by symmetrical translation of the original space, which is a proper subset of the initial outcome (equilibrium) set X_{EA}, as Exhibit 16.2 shows. This is a symmetrical payoff space wherein any bargaining solution necessarily falls on the bisector, which is the geometrical locus of egalitarian solutions (where parties share the bargaining surplus equally). Note that this result takes for granted an egalitarian status quo preceding the agreement, but this assumption too is a consequence of the veil of ignorance.

In particular, players resort to the Nash bargaining solution (NBS), which is the most widely employed solution for bargaining games (Nash 1950). It prescribes picking the point of the efficient (north-east) frontier of the payoff space (representing the outcomes set of possible agreements) where the product $\Pi(u_i - d_i)$ of the utilities u_i of players ($i = 1, 2$), net of utility d_i associated with their status quo, is maximal. Assuming that the players bargain according to the typical rationality assumptions of game theory (Harsanyi 1977), and given that the feasible outcome set is the symmetric intersection sub-space $X_{EA} \cap X_{AE}$, the NBS is by assumption egalitarian and selects the point S of Exhibit 16.2.

The striking result of this construction is that the minimal requirement of social justice (impersonality and impartiality) becomes compatible with realism and ex post stability in an interaction where players are free to choose according to their preferences. In spite of Hayek (1973), freedom of choice and incentive compatibility does not require relinquishing the moral demands of social justice. On the contrary, it entails that the solution must be egalitarian and must coincide with the Rawlsian maximin distribution, even within an originally asymmetrical set of possible outcomes. Thus, given a real-life set of possible outcomes reflecting possible inequality between the participants, the solution falls on the equilibrium that most favors the worst-off player, which in most cases is the egalitarian distribution.

CORRESPONDENCE TO THE MULTISTAKEHOLDER MODEL OF CG

This section employs the social contract theory in a different way. The previous section used social contract theory as an equilibrium selection device able to identify (theoretically predicting) which social norm tends to emerge as the basis for an institution. Here the social contract is used normatively to specify and justify the CSR extended model of CG. This section answers the main normative objections raised against the multistakeholder approach to CG. First, this approach is incapable of providing a bottom line against which managers' conduct can be assessed because the objective function representing the stakeholders' different goals must be multidimensional. Second, no simple exercise of maximization can represent a decision consistently aimed at achieving such incoherent goals (Jensen 2001). Third, since multiple fiduciary duties are too indefinite, they cannot give priority and reserve justified privilege to any one stakeholder's legitimate claim among others, which would be constitutive of fiduciary duties (Marcoux 2003).

The Mediating Hierarch's Mode of Reasoning

In the mediating hierarchy view of CG, the board of directors is an arbiter of the cooperative interaction among the various stakeholders participating in team production. But how should directors mediate among different stakeholders? The suggestion is that they should devise the principle for impartial mediation by working out the social contract that all stakeholders would accept as a fair term of agreement for the implementation of a corporate joint cooperative strategy and the consequent allocation of rights, duties, and payoffs (Sacconi 2006a, 2006b).

The board of directors may construe the stakeholders' social contract by the following procedure of impartial reasoning inspired by the Rawlsian veil of ignorance. This is a decision procedure by which the decision maker accounts for any personal perspective as if he were unable to identify it with his own personal perspective on the problem. This requires establishing the preconditions for a fair agreement. Hence, force, fraud, and manipulation must be set aside, and the only features of each stakeholder accounted for are his capability to contribute to team production under different joint plans, and the utilities that he can derive from each of them. Since any reasonable agreement must grant some advantage to some stakeholder, a fair reference point for advantage must be set. Thus, the agreement status quo must keep each stakeholder immune from hold-up. That is, before discussing the agreement, each stakeholder is granted at least full reimbursement of his specific investment's costs.

In order to calculate the legitimate shares that stakeholders can claim, the impartial director will put himself in the position of each stakeholder in turn (impersonality) and will assign equal probability to each position (impartiality). Thus, by an effort of sympathy, he will accept or reject any available agreement according to each stakeholder's preference. Hence, the terms of agreement deemed acceptable are those that each stakeholder is willing to accept from his own personal point of view. Solutions acceptable to some stakeholder but not to others are then discarded. Thus, the process ends with the nonempty intersection of the allocations acceptable from whichever point of view. An agreement acceptable from whichever point of view must necessarily exist because team production is mutually advantageous with respect to an alternative organization of production where members would split into separate units. If an agreement were impossible, stakeholders would simply organize themselves into separate production units.

Note that the impartial director is applying exactly the same model of the social contract pointed out in the previous section. Thus, assume for simplicity the following: (1) only two stakeholders, (2) their possible agreements define a convex set of possible outcomes, and (3) the director applies the veil of ignorance using his utility function as a tool to simulate in turn possible payoffs of both stakeholders at each possible agreement. Impartiality and impersonality conditions therefore impose invariance of the impartial director's payoff under both perspectives that he may take. For any acceptable agreement, this entails that the impartial director's payoff is the expectation of an equal probability mixture of two stakeholders' payoffs. The solution must be sought in the symmetrical intersection of the two outcome sets that the impartial director reconstructs when taking the two stakeholders' perspectives in turn. Thus, the director must choose the agreement that maximizes the Nash bargaining product within this symmetric set.

Summing up, there is a behavioral and cognitive model of the mediating director. Such a fair mediation also corresponds to a unique and calculable objective function: maximizing the NBS within the symmetrical intersection subset of outcomes. Though abstract, this is by no means more distant from reality than the traditional profit maximization rule. Moreover, it is realistic insofar as the impartial director focuses only on agreements implementable by stakeholders who ex post act according to their individual incentives.

Two-Step Social Contract Derivation of the Multiple Fiduciary Structure

The social contract is now employed to tell a hypothetical story of how the multistakeholder corporation may have justifiably emerged and how it resulted in multiple fiduciary governance. At the beginning, all stakeholders face a state of nature plagued by incomplete contracts and opportunistic behavior. To put an end to this mutually destructive interaction, they agree to form a multistakeholder productive association wherein all stakeholders have the same rights and duties. This avoids the situation where, by exclusive control, some may expropriate the fruits of other stakeholders' investments. In the productive association, therefore, all the stakeholders are confident that if any one of them makes a specific investment, nobody can hold him up with the threat of exclusion from the relevant transaction. This minimizes the contract costs that would derive from incomplete contracts.

Assuming that the multistakeholder association is a possible form of team production, each stakeholder will rationally negotiate his adhesion to the association's plan of action, which requires adhesion by all of them. The association's joint plan is then selected by the first social contract whereby stakeholders decide to coalesce.

This agreement stipulates the following: (1) rejection of (or redress for) joint plans generating negative externalities for broad-sense stakeholders who in fact join the association in order to ensure that they will not be victimized; (2) production of the maximum surplus possible (i.e., the maximal difference between the value of goods and services for consumers, who also belong to the association, and the costs incurred by all other stakeholders to produce them); and (3) fair distribution of the surplus according to a rationally acceptable agreement reached among all the stakeholders in a bargaining process free from force or fraud and based on an equitable status quo insuring each stakeholder against hold-up.

Stakeholders conduct the bargaining process under a veil of ignorance about their possible advantaged or disadvantaged positions in the productive association. The solution is calculated according to maximization of the NBS within the symmetrical payoff space deriving from the association's possible outcomes, when all feasible personal payoffs are equally affordable to all stakeholders given the possibility of reciprocal replacement of their relative positions and roles.

However, once the first social contract has been accomplished, stakeholders immediately realize that the equally inclusive association is plagued by governance costs. Collective choice costs, coordination costs, and also free-riding costs in peer-group-managed teams may greatly reduce its actual output. Thus, they agree to devise an optimal authority structure in order to minimize governance costs.

By a further step in the process, they settle a second social contract on the association's governance structure. This agreement stipulates that authority is delegated to the single stakeholder who is most efficient in governance. This problem has different solutions: either the typical public company with dispersed shareholders, or family-controlled companies, or partnerships or consumer cooperatives may be the most efficient governance solution according to contingencies (Hansmann 1996).

The stakeholders' class invested with authority is remunerated with the residual and is authorized to appoint those who run the firm operationally (managing directors). But an understanding among the association's members is that the authority of the corporate governance structure will be legitimated only in so far as it is instrumental to the first social contract. In other words, the prospective noncontrolling members of the association will accept authority if and only if the association's new ownership and control structure proves to be the best way to implement the first social contact of the firm, which pre-exists the authority relation and gives reasons for accepting it (Raz 1985; McMahon 1989). No constitution of the governance structure may be accepted if minimizing governance costs is not a means to improve the fair remuneration of the association's members. Of course, the remuneration of those appointed to the association's governing roles will impinge on the surplus recovered from reducing governance costs. But no governance structure could be accepted by the second social contract if it were not beneficial in an impartial way to all the stakeholders. Hence, a principle of accountability to noncontrolling stakeholders asking that they participate in some internal committee having supervisory powers must be added, so that they may verify that corporate management does not substantially deviate from the principles settled by the first social contract.

Accordingly, there is a two-step agreement, and the directors' fiduciary duties ensue from each step. They owe special fiduciary duties to residual claimants via a narrow fiduciary proviso replicating the typical duty of due care and non–conflict of interest. But this narrow proviso is obligating only under the constraint of respecting a broader fiduciary proviso owed to noncontrolling stakeholders, which is more fundamental and overriding. In other words, once the three provisos of the first social contract have been met, if two or more courses of action indifferent in terms of broader proviso compliance are still feasible, the directors are obliged to choose the course of action more favorable to the residual claimant (owner or shareholders).

A clear priority order of stakeholders' claims is thus established, and all stakeholders are privileged in some proper respect. Broad-sense stakeholders are assigned priority, but only in the weak sense of restricting the company's range of action to those joint plans that do not engender strong externalities detrimental to them. Second in priority are strict-sense stakeholders, who are granted a wide range of privileges in the discretion area of directors who must protect their specific investments and then arbitrate cooperation according to the symmetric NBS. Last, in the subset of possible corporate decisions indifferent to the NBS, residual claimants are assigned privilege consisting in the decision of pursuing (constrained) shareholder value maximization. Indeed, since the NBS is a uniquely determined solution, substantial discretion in choosing shareholder value maximization strategies that do not also entail improvement of the other stakeholders' positions is quite unrealistic.

SUMMARY AND CONCLUSIONS

Social norms affect CG and have an important role in equilibrium selection because they help define which of many equilibrium behaviors is initially accepted. The social contract is the basic mode of reasoning by which agents initially work out an accepted social norm that then contributes to the affirmation of an equilibrium institution. It applies under conditions in which an endogenous and free agreement among reasonably equally rational agents is admitted. The social contract device entails some form of veil of ignorance reasoning, i.e., some form of impartiality and impersonality with sympathy mechanism is a natural frame of mind available for this social norms acceptance endeavor.

In the domain of CG institutions, CSR is the social norm selected by the social contract, which can then be understood as a social norm affecting the emergence of a CG model. In games that noncontrolling stakeholders play with entrepreneurs or owners of physical assets, the social contract identifies a social norm for the fair (egalitarian) distribution of the corporate surplus among all stakeholders. This is an equilibrium of the game that may then crystallize into an institution for governing these relationships. In particular, the corresponding institution is a CG regime that seems to abide by a social norm of stakeholders' fair treatment. Since the same social contract model also works as a justification for the normative model of extended fiduciary duties, these duties are also owed by directors to all the stakeholders. What is morally justified tends also to emerge as an equilibrium institution (unless an endogenous agreement among free and reasonably equally rational agents is obstructed), and vice versa.

Summing up, the CSR model of CG is supported by the argument that it is an emerging social norm that may crystallize into CG economic institutions when an original position choice over CG institutions is allowed. That is, the CSR model would be an impartial spontaneous order in the domain of CG. No other CG model, especially the agency model giving absolute priority to shareholders, is supported by similar analysis of equilibrium selection in games. Under the agency model, the player interpretable as the entrepreneur or owner would be allowed to try to converge on equilibria such that he would appropriate the entire surplus (for example reaching the bargaining solution in X_{AE} that grants Adam's advantage). The social contract deletes these equilibria from what can be ex ante picked up by a fair equilibrium selection process. Other explanations can be given for the relative success of the agency model as an institution of CG, but not the social contract used to explain the initial acceptance of a social norm that then develops into a CG institution. Ex ante acceptability under fair conditions of agreement cannot be satisfied by the agency model.

Thus, the challenge put forward by Macey (2008) has been accepted and defeated. The CSR model of CG is justified as an acceptable agreement among all the company's stakeholders that can be reached before adopting any particular corporate form. Can the same be said for the promissory model giving absolute priority to shareholder value maximization? Insofar as the argument put forward in this chapter is sound, the answer is no.

DISCUSSION QUESTIONS

1. Is there any definition of CSR that relates it to CG? If so, what is that definition? What do stakeholders and fiduciary duties mean according to this definition?

2. Explain whether the dominant agency model is CG friendly or inimical to CSR. What about the competing model of the board of directors as a mediating hierarchy?

3. Explain whether CSR is a view that needs to be superimposed from outside on what stakeholders may agree by themselves in the field of CG rules, or is it a social norm that may emerge endogenously as an equilibrium from their interaction?

4. Are freedom of choice, stability, and the egalitarian distribution of payoffs incompatible? Explain why or why not. Consider the answer provided by the social contract model of equilibrium selection under a veil of ignorance.

5. What does the social contract model say about the way in which a board of directors should strive for an impartial mediation among all the corporate stakeholders? Can it be mutually advantageous?

6. Explain whether the CSR model of CG puts forth a clearly defined objective function that a socially responsible company should aim to maximize.

7. What fiduciary duties are owed to different stakeholders? Can they be differentiated according to each stakeholder's position?

REFERENCES

Alchian, Armen A., and Harold Demsetz. 1972. "Production, Information Costs and Economic Organization." *American Economic Review* 62:5, 777–795.

Allen, Franklin, and Douglas Gale. 2000. *Comparing Financial Systems.* Cambridge: MIT Press.

Aoki, Masahiko. 1984. *The Cooperative Game Theory of the Firm.* Cambridge: Cambridge University Press.

Aoki, Masahiko. 2001. *Toward a Comparative Institutional Analysis.* Cambridge MA: MIT Press.

Aoki, Masahiko. 2010. *Corporations in Evolving Diversity.* Oxford: Oxford University Press.

Binmore, Ken. 2005. *Natural Justice.* Oxford: Oxford University Press.

Binmore, Ken, and Adam Brandenburger. 1990. "Common knowledge and game theory." In Ken Binmore, ed., *Essays in the Foundation of Game Theory,* 105–150. Oxford: Basil Blackwell.

Blair, Margaret M., and Lynn A. Stout. 1999. "A Team Production Theory of Corporate Law." *Virginia Law Review* 85:2, 247–331.

Blair, Margaret M., and Lynn A. Stout. 2006. "Specific Investment: Explaining Anomalies in Corporate Law." *Journal of Corporation Law* 31, 719–744.

Branson, Douglas M. 2001. "Corporate Governance Reform and the New Corporate Social Responsibility." *University of Pittsburgh Law Review* 62, 605–645.

Cassidy, John. 2009. *How Markets Fail.* New York: Farrar, Strauss and Giroux.

Clarkson Center for Business Ethics. 1999. *Principles of Stakeholder Management.* Toronto: Clarkson Center for Business Ethics, Rothman School of Management, University of Toronto.

Coase, Ronald H. 1937. "The Nature of the Firm." *Economica* 4:1, 386–405.

Deakin, Simon, and Antoine Rebeiroux. 2008. "Corporate governance, labor relations and human resource management in Britain and France: convergence or divergence?" In Jean-Philippe Touffut, ed., *Does Company Ownership Matter?* 126–150. Cheltenham: Edward Elgar Publisher.

Denzau Arthur, and Douglass C. North. 1994. "Shared Mental Models: Ideologies and Institutions." *KIKLOS* 47:1, 3–31.

Donaldson, Thomas. 2012. "The Epistemic Fault Line in Corporate Governance." *Academy of Management Review* 37:2. Forthcoming.

Donaldson Thomas and Lee E. Preston. 1995. "The Stakeholder Theory of the Corporation: Concepts, Evidence, and Implications" The Academy of Management Review, Vol. 20, No. 1. 65–91.

Easterbrook, Frank, and Daniel R. Fischel. 1991. *The Economic Structures of Corporate Law.* Cambridge: Harvard University Press.

Elhauge, Einer. 2005. "Sacrificing Corporate Profit in the Public Interest." *New York University Law Review* 80:3, 733–869.

Evan, William M., and R. Edward Freeman. 1993. "A Stakeholder theory of the corporation: Kantian capitalism." In Tom L. Beauchamp and Norman E. Bowie, eds., *Ethical Theory and Business,* 97–106. Englewood Cliffs, NJ: Prentice Hall.

Flannigan, Robert. 1989. "The Fiduciary Obligation." *Oxford Journal of Legal Studies* 9:3, 285–294.

Freeman, R. Edward. 1984. *Strategic Management: A Stakeholder Approach.* Boston: Pitman.

Freeman, R. Edward, Jeffrey R. Harrison, Andrew C. Wicks, Bidhan L. Parmar, and Simone De Colle. 2010. *Stakeholder Theory: The State of the Art.* Cambridge: Cambridge University Press.

Freeman, R. Edward, and John McVea. 2001. "A Stakeholder approach to strategic management." In Michael A. Hitt, R. Edward Freeman, and Jeffrey S. Harrison, eds., *The Blackwell Handbook of Strategic Management,* 189–207. Oxford: Blackwell.

Freeman, R. Edward. and S. Ramakrishna Velamuri. 2006. "A New Approach to CSR: Company Stakeholder Responsibility," in A. Kakabadse and M. Morsing (eds.), *Corporate Social Responsibility (CSR): Reconciling Aspiration with Application,* New York: Palgrave Macmillan, 9–23.

Gelter, Martin. 2009, "The Dark Side of Shareholder Influence: Managerial Autonomy and Stakeholder Orientation in Comparative Corporate Governance." *Harvard International Law Journal* 50:1, 129–134.

Grimalda, Gianluca, and Lorenzo Sacconi. 2005. "The Constitution of the Not-for-Profit Organization: Reciprocal Conformity to Morality." *Constitutional Political Economy* 16:3, 249–276.

Grossman, Sanford J., and Oliver Hart. 1986. "The Costs and Benefit of Ownership: A Theory of Vertical and Lateral Integration." *Journal of Political Economy* 94:4, 691–719.

Hansmann, Henry. 1996. *The Ownership of the Enterprise.* Cambridge: Harvard University Press.

Hare, Richard M. 1981. *Moral Thinking.* Oxford: Clarendon Press.

Hart, Oliver, and John Moore. 1990. "Property Rights and the Nature of the Firm." *Journal of Political Economy* 98:6, 1119–1158.

Harsanyi, John C. 1977. *Rational Behavior and Bargaining Equilibrium in Games and Social Situations*. Cambridge: Cambridge University Press.

Hayek, Fredrick A. 1973. *Law, Legislation and Liberty*. Chicago: University of Chicago Press.

Jensen, Michael C. 2001. "Value Maximization, Stakeholder Theory, and the Corporate Objective Function." *Journal of Applied Corporate Finance* 14:3, 8–21.

Jensen, Michael C., and William H. Meckling. 1976. "Theory of the Firm: Managerial Behavior, Agency Costs and Ownership Structure." *Journal of Financial Economics* 3:4, 305–360.

Lewis, David. 1969. *Convention: A Philosophical Study*. Cambridge: Harvard University Press.

Macey, Jonathan R. 2008. *Corporate Governance*. Princeton NJ: Princeton University Press.

Marcoux, Alexei M. 2003. "A Fiduciary Argument against Stakeholder Theory." *Business Ethics Quarterly* 13:1, 1–24.

McMahon, Christopher. 1989. "Managerial Authority." *Ethics* 100:1, 33–53.

Nash, John F. 1950. "The Bargaining Problem." *Econometrica* 18:2, 155–162.

Osterloch, Margit, Bruno S. Frey, and Hossam Zeitoun. 2010. "Voluntary co-determination produces sustainable productive advantage." In Lorenzo Sacconi, Margaret Blair, R. Edward Freeman, and Alessandro Vercelli, eds., *Corporate Social Responsibility and Corporate Governance: The Contribution of Economic Theory and Related Disciplines*. 332–352. Basingstoke: Palgrave Macmillan.

Posner, Erik A. 2000. *Law and Social Norm*. Cambridge, MA: Harvard University Press.

Posner, Richard A. 2009. *A Failure of Capitalism*. Cambridge, MA: Harvard University Press.

Rawls, John. 1971. *A Theory of Justice*. Oxford: Oxford University Press.

Rajan, Raghuram G., and Luigi Zingales. 1998. "Power in a Theory of the Firm." *Quarterly Journal of Economics* 113:2, 387–432.

Raz, Joseph. 1985. "Authority and Justification." *Philosophy and Public Affairs* 14:1, 3–29.

Sacconi, Lorenzo. 1991. *Etica degli affari*, Milano: Il Saggiatore.

Sacconi, Lorenzo. 1999. "Codes of Ethics as Contractarian Constraints on the Abuse of Authority within Hierarchies: A Perspective from the Theory of Firm." *Journal of Business Ethics* 21: 2–3, 189–202.

Sacconi, Lorenzo. 2000. *The Social Contract of the Firm: Economics, Ethics and Organization*. Berlin: Springer Verlag.

Sacconi, Lorenzo. 2006a. "CSR as a model of extended corporate governance, an explanation based on the economic theory of social contract, reputation and reciprocal conformism." In Fabrizio Cafaggi, ed., *Reframing Self-Regulation in European Private* Law, 289–346. The Netherlands: Kluwer Law International.

Sacconi, Lorenzo. 2006b. "A Social Contract Account for CSR as Extended Model of Corporate Governance (Part I): Rational Bargaining and Justification." *Journal of Business Ethics* 68:3, 259–281.

Sacconi, Lorenzo. 2007. "A Social Contract Account for CSR as Extended Model of Corporate Governance (Part II): Compliance, Reputation and Reciprocity." *Journal of Business Ethics* 75:1, 77–96.

Sacconi, Lorenzo. 2010a. "A Rawlsian view of CSR and the game theory of its implementation (part I): the multistakeholder model of corporate governance." In Lorenzo Sacconi, Margaret Blair, R. Edward Freeman, and Alessandro Vercelli, eds., *Corporate Social Responsibility and Corporate Governance: The Contribution of Economic Theory and Related Disciplines*, 157–193. Basingstoke: Palgrave Macmillan.

Sacconi, Lorenzo. 2010b. "A Rawlsian view of CSR and the game theory of its implementation (part II): fairness and equilibrium." In Lorenzo Sacconi, Margaret Blair, R. Edward Freeman, and Alessandro Vercelli, eds., *Corporate Social Responsibility and Corporate Governance: The Contribution of Economic Theory and Related Disciplines*, 194–125. Basingstoke: Palgrave Macmillan.

Sacconi, Lorenzo. 2011. "A Rawlsian View of CRS and the game of its implementation (part III): conformism and equilibrium selection." In Lorenzo Sacconi and Giacomo

Degli Antoni, eds., *Social Capital, Corporate Social Responsibility, Economic Behavior and Performance*, 42–79. Basingstoke: Palgrave Macmillan.

Sacconi, Lorenzo, and Marco Faillo. 2010. "Conformity, Reciprocity and the Sense of Justice. How Social Contract-Based Preferences and Beliefs Explain Norm Compliance: The Experimental Evidence." *Constitutional Political Economy* 21:2, 171–201.

Sacconi, Lorenzo, Marco Faillo, and Stefania Ottone. 2011. "Contractarian Compliance and the 'Sense of Justice': A Behavioral Conformity Model and Its Experimental Support." *Analyse & Kritik* 33:1, 273–310.

Schotter, Andrew. 1981. *The Economic Theory of Social Institutions*. Cambridge: Cambridge University Press.

Stiglitz, Joseph E. 2010. *Firewall, America, Free Market and the Sinking of the World Economy*. New York: W. W. Norton & Company.

Stout, Lynn A. 2006. "Social Norms and Other-Regarding Preferences." In John N. Drobak, ed., *Norms and the Law*, 13–35, Cambridge: Cambridge University Press.

Stout, Lynn A. 2011a. *Cultivating Conscience*. Princeton, NJ: Princeton University Press.

Stout, Lynn A. 2011b, "New Thinking On Shareholder Primacy." Law-Econ Research Paper No. 11-04, School of Law, UCLA.

Sugden, Robert. 1986. *The Economics of Rights, Co-operation and Welfare*. Oxford: Basil Blackwell.

Tirole, Jean. 2001. "Corporate Governance." *Econometrica* 69:1, 1–35.

Wieland, Joseph, ed. 2003. *Standards and Audits for Ethics Management Systems: The European Perspective*. Berlin: Springer Verlag.

Williamson, Oliver. 1975. *Market and Hierarchies*. New York: The Free Press.

Willamson, Oliver. 1986. *The Economic Institutions of Capitalism*. New York: The Free Press.

ABOUT THE AUTHOR

Lorenzo Sacconi is professor of Economics and Unicredit Chair in Economic Ethics and Corporate Social Responsibility at the University of Trento. He is also the scientific director of EconomEtica, the inter-university center of research for economic ethics and CSR. In the past, he was a visiting scholar at the LSE (London), and taught game theory, methodology of economics, public choice economics, and business ethics at the University of Pavia, Bocconi University (Milano), and LIUC–Cattaneo University (Castellanza). He has also served as chairman of the Italian Business Ethics Network, EC member of the EBEN (European Business Ethics Network), and scientific director of the Q-RES project. His research areas focus on ethics and economics, institutional economics, theory of the firm, corporate governance, business ethics and CSR. He has recently authored and edited several books including *The Social Contract of the Firm, Corporate Social Responsibility and Corporate Governance: The Contribution of Economic Theory and Related Disciplines*, and *Social Capital, Corporate Social Responsibility, Economic Behavior and Performance*. He holds a laureate cum laude in philosophy from the University of Pisa.

CHAPTER 17

Measuring Responsibility to the Different Stakeholders

AMIR RUBIN
Associate Professor, Simon Fraser University and Interdisciplinary Center (IDC)

ERAN RUBIN
Lecturer, Holon Institute of Technology (HIT)

INTRODUCTION

Corporations are motivated to become more socially responsible because their stakeholders expect them to understand and address the social and community issues that are relevant to them. Unlike traditional financial performance measures, the definition of social performance is hard to conceptualize. This is due to its aspiring, all-encompassing approach to corporate activity. Social performance typically covers an organization's relationship with the natural environment, its employees, and ethical issues concentrating on consumers and products, as well as the relationship with suppliers. Other issues include corporate actions on questions of ethnicity and gender. This leads to much debate over the possibility of developing a reliable and unbiased measure that effectively represents the overall social performance of the firm. This chapter asserts that while an all-encompassing measure for corporate social performance (CSP) is infeasible, measuring the different aspects of corporate social responsibility (CSR) separately can be effective for increasing transparency and aligning the goals of corporations with those of society.

To illustrate the skeptical view that economists typically associate with the ability to measure CSR, referring to an exchange of ideas between John Mackey, the CEO of Whole Foods Market, and the late Nobel Laureate Milton Friedman, may be instructive. Mackey (*Reason Magazine* 2005, p. 1) writes, "It is the function of company leadership to develop solutions that continually work for the common good." Friedman (*Reason Magazine* 2000, p. 2) responds:

> The differences between John Mackey and me regarding the social responsibility of business are for the most part rhetorical. Stripped of the camouflage, and it turns out we are in essential agreement. Whole Foods Market has done well in a highly competitive industry. Had it devoted any significant fraction of its resources to exercising a social responsibility unrelated to the bottom line, it would be out of business by now or would have been taken over. . . .

Mackey (*Reason Magazine* 2000, p. 5) responds:

> But are we essentially in agreement? I don't think so.... In contrast to Friedman, I do not believe maximizing profits for the investors is the only acceptable justification for all corporate actions.

In this exchange, the views of both Friedman and Mackey can be rationalized. Friedman is skeptical on whether a firm can survive if it pays too much attention to its overall footprint on society and suggests that a firm attempting to do so will lose focus on being profitable and fail. Importantly, according to Friedman's view, a firm that concentrates on shareholders' objective (maximizes share price) benefits all stakeholders, not only shareholders, because it makes products or provides services that society values. If the firm engages in harmful activity to society while producing the good, consumers, investors, workers, and suppliers are likely to respond, which in turn should negatively affect the firm's share price. Mackey contends that the firm does not need to concentrate on only share price but should engage in doing good to society. In a frictionless economy, arguing against Friedman's approach is difficult because any good or bad behavior should be reflected in share price (to as much as society cares about these behaviors). However, Mackey has the upper hand if stakeholders are unaware of the firm's CSR practices. Under such circumstances, society may desire the firm to do the right thing socially even if it is not reflected in share price. Hence, measuring CSR is essential for providing transparency and aligning the shareholders' objective (Friedman's view) with the moral compass of society (Mackey's view).

Thinking about how different stakeholders share the firm's cash flow is useful in order to illustrate some of the conceptual problems associated with measuring CSR. This illustration assumes that all firm-effects on stakeholders can be measured in monetary terms. For example, the idea of having diversity in the workforce by employing new immigrants may be perceived by some firm's management as a bad idea if it believes that these workers may be less effective, perhaps because of language difficulties. However, if the firm were to be compensated fairly in monetary terms for the disadvantage, then it should be willing to hire these workers. Hence, the assumption is made here, although arguable, that all CSR issues are measurable in monetary terms.

Exhibit 17.1 illustrates this idea. The different pieces of the pie represent the share of cash flow that a certain group of stakeholders receives. In some cases, if the firm improves the cash flow going to one group of stakeholders (say, the employees), it can also improve the cash flow going to another group (say, the shareholders). While such cases are certainly possible, they do not represent any dilemma for a corporation. Any firm should engage in activities that can increase the cash flow going to one group of stakeholder if it does not come at the expense of another group. Things become economically interesting, however, when improved cash flows to one group come at the expense of another group. Under such circumstances, one could examine approaches for sharing the cash flow among the different stakeholders in such a way that the distribution between the different groups is fair according to the moral view of society.

In essence, each of the stakeholders receives a slice of the corporate pie. The cash flow represented by the shareholders' slice is net income, or earnings of the firm, which manifests itself in either dividends or share price. In the finance

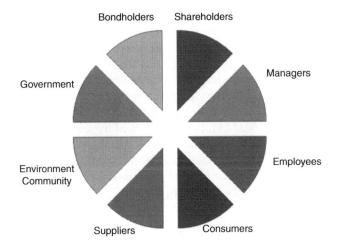

Exhibit 17.1   The Firm and the Different Stakeholders

The figure shows how the cash flow generated by the firm is split between the different stakeholders. An increase in the cash flow going to one group typically requires a decrease in the cash flow going to another group of stakeholders.

governance literature, if the manager does not maximize the shareholder stake, this would be considered an agency problem, and good corporate governance practices are supposed to make sure that shareholders are treated fairly. The interest payments and face value of debt belong to the bondholders. Consumers receive the products or services of the firm, while employees and managers receive wages for their part in helping provide the firm's services or making its products. The government stake in the pie comes in the form of corporate taxes. Typically, a firm is considered socially responsible when it treats society as a whole better than what it is required to do by law. The government's role is to make sure that the firm and its officers obey the law. A reasonable assumption is that any type of law violation affects society as a whole. Hence, any law violation can be seen as an expropriation from the government. However, the CSR literature typically assumes that the environment/community is a different stakeholder from the government. This may be because the government is not sufficiently active in or capable of regulating environmental issues. Another possibility is that a company's operations mostly affect the community residing near the firm's factory. Finally, the suppliers provide raw materials or services to the company. Suppliers derive cash flow from the firm's viability and sometimes by its willingness to pay above market prices in order to provide a reasonable lifestyle to low-income families who provide the raw materials for its products.

Let's see how one can get information on the stake of a particular group. Financial statements offer a summary that is mostly valuable for shareholders, while bond ratings combined with financial statements reflect the stake of the bondholders. The claim of the other stakeholders is typically considered corporate social performance. CSP measures are supposed to measure the cash flow regarding various stakeholders, but most often focus on employees, consumers, and the community. The other groups are rarely mentioned, such as suppliers and the government, even though they are also stakeholders and are affected by the firm's actions in important ways.

A concern with a CSP measure encompassing numerous stakeholders is that while a company may promote its performance in one dimension, it may at the same time engage in another dimension with harmful business practices, which can be perceived as reducing the stake of a different group. For example, a judgment of the *McDonald's Restaurants v. Morris & Steel* case reflects this possibility. Lord Justices Pill, May, and Keane ruled that saying that McDonald's employees worldwide "do badly in terms of pay and conditions" (Appeal Judgment 1999, p. 180) is a fair comment. Since McDonald's is widely known for having environmentally friendly practices, a CSR measure would have to quantify the benefits that McDonald's provides to the environment and at the same time weigh the costs that are associated with the conditions it provides its employees.

Given the above, what is the role of social performance measures? Just as credit ratings enhance transparency in debt capital markets by reducing the information asymmetry between borrowers and lenders, social ratings attempt to provide social investors with accurate information of the extent to which firms' behaviors are socially responsible. Thus, analyzing a firm's CSP for each stakeholder group separately seems appropriate.

The remaining four sections of the chapter are organized as follows. The next section provides a review of the available CSP measures and discusses the shortcomings of an all-encompassing measure. A discussion of the proposed alternative to an all-encompassing measure follows in the next section. The next-to-last section provides a review of the different CSR stakeholders as well as possible measures of a company's social performance with respect to each stakeholder group. The final section offers a summary and conclusions.

MEASURING SOCIAL PERFORMANCE

Measuring social performance has evolved from an area in which few found interest, to an industry of nongovernmental organizations (NGOs), social rating agencies, and different stakeholders—all seeking to get the true measure of CSR. This section provides a review of the available measures and presents some of their pitfalls.

Available CSP Measures

The Association of Certified Chartered Accountants (ACCA) reports that nearly 2,000 firms globally are producing CSR reports (Cheney, Roper, and May 2007). Another study reports that more than 2,300 firms from more than 80 nations participate in the UN Global Compact (Cetindamar and Husoy 2007). Well-known social indices include KLD, FOOTSE4good, and the DOW Jones Social Index. Many, but not all, of these ratings and their underlying criteria are proprietary. Innovest, for example, offers a publicly available global 100 list produced annually since 2005. Some rankings focus on specific sectors, while others rank corporations across all sectors. Some offer numerical orderings, while others provide best-in-class or other benchmarks to signal socially responsible certification. Some are specific to a region of the world, while others are global. Some ratings are based solely on nonfinancial data to assess social responsibility independent from financial performance. Others combine financial and nonfinancial data to measure long-term value and sustainability.

Although many measures and ranking methods are available, the correlation between these rankings is unclear. Conceivably, some rankings are not even at par with the average moral value of an individual in the society. For example, some ranking agencies may consider firms that produce alcohol or weapons, or use nuclear energy as socially irresponsible, while others may not. Generally, inconsistent relationships between the ratings are expected as the definition of socially responsible depends on the belief structure of the rating agency and its customers.

In 1988, the investment firm of Kinder, Lydenberg, Domini, and Company, Inc. (now commonly known as KLD), began offering a mutual fund of U.S. companies that mirrored the Standard & Poor 500 except for being screened for social responsibility factors. The Domini Social Index Fund consisted of about 400 large U.S. companies chosen for lack of participation in such "irresponsible" fields as military contracting, South Africa, tobacco products, gambling, and nuclear power. Over time, KLD added positive screens to their ratings database, including assessments of companies' environmental records, hiring and promotion of minorities and women, charitable giving, community relations and voluntarism, product quality, consumer relations, employee relations, and support for sustainable or organic agriculture. By 1996, KLD included more than 800 firms in its assessments and was releasing the database for scholarly research. RiskMetrics bought KLD Research in November 2009 at a time when the data collection and assessments had become increasingly extensive and sophisticated (Lydenberg and Sinclair 2009). Many researchers now use its SOCRATES database as a way of calculating CSP in empirical studies.

KLD, CSID (Canada), and ARESE (France) ratings studies are all multidimensional and difficult to locate specifically as processes or outcomes. These multidimensional rating schemes incorporate assessments of phenomena that can be used to illustrate company commitment or lack thereof to CSR principles, use of responsive processes, and outcomes for various stakeholders and the company itself. These ratings are achieving great popularity as CSP measures, largely because they are third-party assessments of CSP and do not heavily rely on company self-reports, which is often a problem with the social and environmental reporting studies. Although KLD, the earliest comprehensive rating scheme, began by assessing only U.S.-based firms, the global nature of CSP concerns is now being addressed much better, both by KLD and the other schemes in use.

Despite the many measures and their problems, all rating agencies have a goal of providing some objective and verifiable grounds for assessing social performance. As Dillenburg, Green, and Erekson (2003, p. 3) emphasize, "what gets measured, gets managed." Without effective measurement, seeing how demands for corporate responsibility could translate into a systematic mechanism for affecting corporate behavior and decision making throughout the economic system is difficult (Scalet and Kelly 2010).

Measuring CSP

According to Jon Entine, a leader and author in sustainability practice, social responsible investing (SRI) funds are very sloppy and often wrong in identifying "doing good" (Chatterji, Levine, and Toffel 2009). Debate continues unresolved about what exactly *doing good* means. A central problem of discerning CSP is that good CSP and bad CSP do not appear to be on a single continuum.

Mallott (1993) finds that managers talk about social responsibility and irresponsibility as distinctly different phenomena. Irresponsible acts cause unjustifiable harm or unacceptable increases in risk to certain stakeholders. Responsible acts range from ordinary ethical behavior to extraordinary acts of beneficence. Obviously, the same act can be responsible toward some stakeholders and irresponsible towards others. Also, a single company can have a wildly divergent record on responsible and irresponsible acts. The possibility arises of a highly ranked company that performs abysmally on some key dimension or a low ranking for a company that causes little or no harm but is unremarkable in doing good.

One can attribute harmful outcomes to irresponsible corporate behavior, but this is not necessarily true. Harm can result from lone actors who sabotage safety controls or are careless or reckless, or from acts of nature that cannot be avoided or planned, or from the actions of others unrelated to the organization, who nevertheless manage to cause harm traceable to them. Thus, harm is typically observable but not necessarily attributable to irresponsibility. Qualitative interviews elicited many examples of bad behavior, which researchers categorized in terms of harm to the natural environment, harm to local businesses, violation of societal rules and expectations, employee practices (such as wage, working conditions, discrimination, and benefits), questionable sales practices, dishonesty, selling offensive material, and questionable or unfair pricing policies. Ordinary responsible or ethical behavior is typically not rewarded or even noticed. Ethically responsible conduct often results in nothing more than a lack of visible harmful outcomes, but such a lack might be attributable instead to luck, clever manipulation, or even suppression of the voices of the injured. Another problem is that acts of responsibility or beneficence, no matter how positive in intention, may be incomplete, disingenuous, or outright false.

Ultimately, the appropriateness and power of measures rest on the ability to observe relevant phenomena and on the accuracy and reliability of the observers. In the past, most social screening included the traditional method of negatively screening specific corporations. Thus, the initial CSR movement seemed to be more about screening bad firms than about rewarding good ones. The SRI community first screened out companies that produced "sin and violence" products such as tobacco, firearms, and military weaponry. Then it conducted positive screens such as percentage of pretax earnings given to charities. Additional screens came to be identified with specific types of stakeholders, including measures such as workplace safety records, percentage of women and minorities in higher management, and pollution performance.

Promoting Segregation Instead of an Encompassing Measure

More than 100 studies have examined whether CSR metrics predict financial performance. These studies investigate whether shareholders experience any financial gain when firms extend the cash flow given to other stakeholders. Even if no correlation exists between CSP and CSR, a higher CSP is good because it does not take away from the shareholders. Other relationships among the shares of different stakeholders can also be considered. For example, if the firm is rated highly in environmental performance, does this help the firm's performance with respect to employees? Better CSP on one dimension is always good as long as it does not hurt a different group of stakeholders.

The current practice of CSR rating agencies is ill suited for providing an all-encompassing measure of CSR. Instead, the data supplied by the rating agencies can help provide information about a firm's performance with respect to the different CSR stakeholders.

Breaking down the CSP measure to its components, depending on the different group, can be helpful for different reasons, but mostly because an all-encompassing measure is not sufficiently informative. Studies that find little correlation between an overall CSR metric measure and financial performance may understate the relationship between CSR and financial performance because an overall, encompassing measure of CSR is probably a noisy indicator of true CSR activities. At the same time, other studies, including Orlitzky, Schmidt, and Rynes (2003), that find a positive correlation between an overall encompassing measure of CSR and financial performance may overstate the relationship between actual CSR and financial performance. Stakeholders may be misled by overall encompassing CSR metrics to buy products or invest in shares of companies that can successfully market themselves as socially responsible, when in fact, they are not, or are socially responsible only on some dimensions. In fact, little value may result from conducting any study on the CSR-financial performance relationship before understanding the link between a firm's social rating and actual social performance (Margolis and Walsh 2003). Chatterji et al. (2009) are the first to conduct such a study. These authors, who study the relationship between environmental rating and environmental performance, find that the ratings do a fairly good job on some dimensions but are weak on other dimensions.

CSR COMPONENTS: THE DIFFERENT STAKEHOLDERS AND MEASURES

This section elaborates on the different stakeholders. It reviews major stakeholders discussed in the literature and proposes several measures of performance for each stakeholder.

Measuring Environmental Performance

Environmental measures focus on the cost structure and environmental performance of a company. Different sources can substantiate such an assessment. Some are grounded in legislation while others are voluntary. The Bhopal tragedy of 1984, in which a leak of chemicals in a plant in India resulted in the death of thousands, triggered environmental disclosure legislation, which is associated with the Emergency Planning and Community Right-to-Know Act (EPCRA) of 1986.

Unlike financial controls and legislation, EPCRA does not limit company environmental behavior, but rather requires companies to disclose inventories of dangerous chemicals and provide related emergency plans: namely, the Toxics Release

Inventory (TRI) of the U.S. Environmental Protection Agency, begun in 1987 after the passage of the EPCRA. Over the years, the TRI has undergone many changes including updates on the list of chemicals, required reporting times, and other key variables. TRI data are self-reported by companies and may be based on estimates rather than actual measurements. No penalties exist for false reporting or failure to report (Scorse 2005). Further accounting for environmental impacts may occur within a company's financial statements, relating to liabilities, commitments, and contingencies for the remediation of contaminated lands or other financial concerns arising from pollution. In the United States, securities laws have been interpreted to require environmentally-related disclosures when such information is relevant to financial performance, material regulatory compliance, and material legal proceedings. Despite different standards of disclosure, the predominant standard for disclosures has been developed by the Global Reporting Initiative (GRI), and more than 75 percent of the Global Fortune 250 use GRI guidelines.

In their environmental reports, large companies commonly place primary emphasis on eco-efficiency, referring to the reduction of resource and energy use and waste production per unit of product or service. These reports provide an aggregate figure. Hence, a comprehensive understanding about all inputs, outputs, and wastes of the organization may not necessarily emerge. While companies can often demonstrate high eco-efficiency, their ecological footprint, which is an estimate of total environmental impact, may change independently as output changes.

In short, while the above sources may be imperfect, they reduce ambiguity about a corporation's impact on the environment when compared to a general encompassing CSP measure. By examining behavior on environmental issues, a more grounded conclusion about a firm's performance can be established. Indeed, CSR rating agencies generally adopt this approach and provide much input for research. For example, referring to such ratings, Chatterji et al. (2009) find that the KLD negative environmental performance ratings are fairly good summaries of past environmental performance. Additionally, firms with more KLD concerns have slightly and statistically significantly more pollution and regulatory compliance violations in later years. In contrast, KLD positive environmental factors do not have predictability.

Customer-Related CSR

Customer-related CSR is a somewhat ambiguous term. The term *customer* defines the relationship between this group of stakeholders and the company as a relationship in which the stakeholders value the company's products. Thus, "good" performance with respect to customers is held by definition; otherwise the customer would not buy the product.

The Meaning of Customer-Related CSR

The Council of Economic Priorities (CEP), a nonprofit public interest organization founded in 1969, pioneered the idea of recruiting customers to the cause of CSR with several books. These books—*Guide to Corporations: A Social Perspective* (Zalkind 1974) and *Rating America's Corporate Conscience* (Lydenberg, Marlin, and Strub 1986)—offer discussions of companies and their social responsibility efforts, or lack thereof. The aim of these works was to arm customers with information that could guide their shopping decisions, whether or not that information was directly beneficial to them as product users. Along these lines, increasing evidence shows that consumers value products of socially responsible firms, and that CSR is not merely the right thing to do but also the smart thing to do (Smith 2003). Acting in a socially responsible manner is smart because CSR companies can induce customers to identify with them (Bhattacharya and Sen 2003), and enhance customers' product attitudes (Berens, van Riel, and van Bruggen 2005). However, consumers are typically more concerned with the product they purchase than with CSR. Hence, from the consumer's point of view, having a good product may be the most important social responsibility action that is expected from the company. Therefore, CSR initiatives may reduce purchase intent and induce negative perceptions if consumers believe that CSR investments are at the expense of developing corporate abilities, such as product quality (Sen and Bhattacharya 2001).

The above discussion implies that by effective marketing of CSR activities to consumers, a company can differentiate between a positive CSP–financial performance relationship and a negative one (Luo and Bhattacharya 2006). Of course, this issue gives rise to research associated with the way companies communicate their CSR initiatives to consumers. For example, Nan and Heo (2007) suggest that the fit between the company line of business and social activity may play a role in user perception of the company. Yoon, Zeynep, and Schwarz (2006) provide evidence that both the medium through which consumers learn about CSR and the ratio of CSR contributions to CSR-related advertising affect consumers' perception of a company.

Measuring Customer-Related CSR Performance

Measurement efforts of customer-related social performance have taken two distinct paths—one employing various kinds of perceptual or attitudinal data, and the other using objective indicators such as safety, recalls, false advertising, or product-related regulatory violations. The first group of measures can account for the possibility that consumers may value not only the product but also social responsibility to other stakeholders. The second set of measures is based on the view that the product is the core concern element through which consumer-related social responsibility should be measured.

The marketing field has long been involved in measuring consumer satisfaction. Paul, Downes, Perry, and Friday (1997) developed and validated an 11-item scale measuring consumer sensitivity to CSP. Their eventual aim was to relate consumers' CSP attitudes to actual buying behavior while eliminating the possibility of social desirability bias in attitude measures.

Other scholars have approached the question of consumer effects on the CSP–financial performance relation from various angles. Because of U.S. regulatory requirements, some objective data are available on, for example, Food and Drug Administration recalls and violations, false or misleading advertising charges, discriminatory bank lending practices, automobile safety recalls, and much more.

Surprisingly, few of these data make their way into CSP studies, but this is a gap that could be readily filled. Similar data are also available for European companies.

Measuring Employee-Related Performance

Treatment of employees is an inseparable aspect of CSP. While evaluation of environment performance takes a major stance in CSP today, in its early days the field of CSR focused on assessing corporations with respect to the way firms handle their employees. That is, human resources issues such as communications with employees, training and development, retirement and termination counseling, and health and safety were the factors defining a firms' CSP (Clarkson 1988). An implication was that corporations and their managers should be concerned about these issues if they were to be evaluated as socially responsible. However, even within this narrower scope, measuring positive and negative CSR was always a problem. Early work aiming to guide assessment in this area extended the scope of CSR and suggested that the dimensions of social responsibility are defined as economic, legal, ethical, and discretionary (Carroll 1979). These components of CSR provide some measuring tools, since financial statements help with economic areas, and databases supply information about litigation and allegations of illegal corporate behavior. However, ethical responsibilities are more difficult to define and measure, given that no generally accepted ethical principles can be cited or enforced. As Carroll notes, evaluating discretionary responsibilities is also difficult because they are volitional or philanthropic in nature. Hence, the social elements were better defined, and extended beyond employee-based social performance. However, measuring CSP in general and corporate social performance with respect to employees in particular was still difficult. The problem was acknowledged, and voices called for CSP measures, which should consist of ultimate outcomes or results, rather than with policies or intentions (Preston 1988).

Under this perspective, different units of analysis and respective measurement schemes have been suggested. Regarding units of analysis, Clarkson (1995), for example, suggests including units such as benefits, career planning, health promotion, and employment equity and discrimination. Others suggest different units of measure. For example, both Schwepker (2001) and Edmans (2011) look at job satisfaction. Notably, such units of analysis imply measures that vary in their coherence. Some aspects, such as wages, can be evaluated using exact figures, while others, such as job satisfaction, are more abstract and may encompass several employee-related elements.

Different measurement schemes have been promoted. Using such measures, studies have examined the relationship of employee-related social performance with CSR in general. For example, Schwepker (2001) provides evidence that perceived CSR is positively related to employee job satisfaction. Valentine and Fleischman (2008) bring additional supportive results for this phenomenon. Edmans (2011) analyzes companies of the 100 Best Companies to Work For in America, according to *Fortune Magazine*. He finds that the best companies also exhibit significantly more positive earnings surprises and announcement returns. Thus, Edmans concludes that employee satisfaction is positively correlated with shareholder return, the stock market does not fully value intangibles, and certain socially responsible investing screens (in this case CSP with respect to employees) may improve investment returns.

Others show that effective CSR reporting increases employees' satisfaction (Lee, Ho, Wu, and Kao 2008). Longo, Mura, and Bonoli (2005) examine various employee-related issues as indicators of CSP, including employees' health and safety at work, development of workers' skills, well being and satisfaction of workers, quality of work, and social equity. Using these indicators, they develop a "grid of values" created by small-to-medium enterprises concerned with CSP.

Researchers have also examined the relationships between employee-related social performances and other corporate issues. Corporate reputation and employee recruiting seem to be positively related to employee-related social performance indicators (Greening and Turban 2000). Riordan, Gatewood, and Bill (1997) find that corporate image has both a direct and an indirect relationship with employee turnover. Albinger and Freeman (2000) report that high CSP helps to attract employees who have a high degree of job choice, but for the less skilled, educated, or experience applicants, CSP apparently plays no role. The psychological consequences of layoffs and plant closings, for example, receive attention in other literatures but not so much in CSP research. Government-mandated disclosures of work safety records, discrimination lawsuits, regulatory complaints, ratio of women and minorities in various workforce slices, and much more are typically part of composite ratings such as KLDs. Some CSP studies, including Orlitzky et al. (2003), use such objective measures.

Measuring Supplier-Related Performance

Suppliers are probably the group of stakeholders that are least discussed when evaluating CSR activities. Typically, being socially responsible to suppliers would mean that the firm behaves in an ethical manner with them. Recently, with the increased attention to CSR, suppliers are related to firms through codes of conduct developed by businesses.

Codes of conduct provide guidelines between supply chain entities that are intended to improve the company's social and environmental performance. Because companies are increasingly held responsible for the conditions under which their products are being produced, codes of conduct are increasingly prevalent and therefore provide a tool to examine the relationships companies hold with their suppliers. While the core purpose of the code of conduct is to document the manner by which social responsibility should be improved throughout the supply chain, this section explains how it can also serve as a tool for examining social responsibility to suppliers.

An example that illustrates this approach is IKEA, the Swedish home-furnishing company that has established a code of conduct with its suppliers. A question that rises is whether the code of conduct came to improve company image alone, or whether social responsibility towards suppliers is also a concern for the company. These things can be learned by examining how the burden of improving social image is distributed between IKEA and its suppliers, and how the benefits of improved social image are distributed; that is, by examining how the agreement treats suppliers.

IKEA introduced its code of conduct in the early 2000s and refers to it as The IKEA Way on Purchasing Home Furnishing Products (IWAY). IWAY defines what the suppliers can expect from IKEA and what IKEA requires from its suppliers regarding working conditions, child labor, and environmental management. IWAY includes 19 different areas divided into more than 90 specific issues (Peders and Anderson 2006). According to the severity of sanctions suggested in the code of conduct on the supplier, in case the supplier does not meet code expectations, one can learn how motivation for social responsibility is distributed between improved company image/environment and responsibility towards the suppliers. For instance, if the code of conduct suggests immediate breaking of supply relationships in case of noncompliance, this would suggest that the motivation for social responsibility towards the suppliers is very limited. Often, the future of the supplying company depends on continuous co-operation with the buyer (Buvik and Reve 2002). In contrast to immediate termination, less severe procedures may be suggested in the code of conduct. For example, in IWAY, IKEA does not break supply relations due to noncompliance, as long as the supplier shows a willingness to improve conditions. In fact, IKEA demonstrates what seems to be a well balanced distribution of responsibility towards company image/environment and suppliers.

If a supplier fails to abide by the code of conduct, IKEA requires the supplier to prepare an action plan detailing how it will rectify the noncompliance issues. Even if requirements are unfulfilled within a specified time frame, the time for implementation is extended as long as the supplier shows a positive attitude towards implementation of IWAY (Pedersen and Andersen 2006). Thus, examining the code of conduct shows that IKEA has a well balanced distribution of interests towards stakeholders and takes a serious stand on CSR.

Besides sanctions, methods for encouragement can also suggest the extent to which the buyer is socially responsible towards its suppliers. For example, the code of conduct may suggest that the buyer compensate the supplier for costs associated with code compliance. Alternatively, the buyer can reward the supplier for complying with the code of conduct. According to such a line of action, additional encouragement methods can be suggested.

Finally, a written code of conduct document can not only provide a measure of social responsibility to suppliers but also indicate the measures that actually took place. For example, with respect to sanctions, Pedersen and Anderson (2006) note that firms terminated 354 supplier contracts in 2005 of which 6 percent were mainly due to noncompliance of IWAY issues, and 11 percent partially due to noncompliance. Such metrics along with those of corrective acts and the average longevity of relationships with suppliers can help devise a measure on social responsibility towards suppliers.

Measuring Community-Related Performance

The community is typically regarded as the group of people that is related to the company mostly through location proximity. Communities can often put pressure on companies, through elected officials, to observe norms of behavior, act according to concerns of the community, and contribute to the community's institutions. Of course, respecting the surrounding environment is part of the contribution related to the community, as well as social responsibility to employees, because both employees and the surrounding environment can be considered part of some proximate community. Related to this, the literature often discusses the responsibility to community when discussing employees and vice versa, as disentangling the two is probably impossible. However, responsibility to the community has a broader meaning and can be defined as including contributions to the arts, efforts directed to the solution of social problems, and assistance with community improvement (Besser 1999). Just as companies need to be a supplier of choice, an employer of choice, and an investor of choice, they should also be a neighbor of choice (Burke 1999). Hence, in order to be socially responsible towards the community, companies have to build sustainable and ongoing relationships with key individuals, groups, and organizations. They should also be responsive to community expectations and concerns, and develop ways that strengthen the community's quality of life.

The crucial role of community-based CSR has intensified over the years as governments and public organizations have increasingly withdrawn from actively providing to the community due to privatization. With this change, community services and projects have to find alternative sources for resources. Corporations' contributions to the community can take many different forms (Boehm 2002), including initiating community projects, supporting educational programs, and establishing sports facilities. Support in this area may be monetary or through direct involvement of managers and employees. Contribution to the community may also take place through economic development in the form of grants and low-interest loans for individuals or community programs.

One approach to measure social responsibility to the community would be to look at the monetary value of the contributions. Unlike other CSR contributions, community-related contributions can arguably be well measured. Another way to measure social responsibility to the community is through interviews and questionnaires. The idea here is that rather than using absolute values, an important aspect of contribution is the mere involvement in some activity, or the amount of time and effort a business puts in advancing the community relative to its resources. For example, Besser (1999) develops a measurement tool in which the variables indicating community responsibility are commitment to the community, support for the community, or participation in community leadership activity.

Measuring Government-Related Performance

Government related CSP is derived from a company's illegal activity. For example, criminal conduct, such as accounting fraud and the backdating scandal, which produced greater executive incomes without the need to report higher expenses to their shareholders, could be considered as violation of federal laws, and hence can be classified as poor government-related CSP. Although such activity could be classified as wrongful action towards the shareholders, criminal activity can have grave consequences to other stakeholders. For example, the Enron case shows major consequences to employees, the community, and the U.S. economy.

Measuring illegal conduct is very different from other measures discussed in this review. Other measures, such as shareholder value, employ benefits, and environmental conduct, cannot be entirely hidden from the public, or may be self-reported by the firm to different degrees. In contrast, problems in measuring illegal conduct originate from the fact that such conduct may be completely un-known, unless exposed by some governing entity. Hence, rather than measuring illegal actions, measures of a firm's illegality may reflect the extent to which the firm is effectively monitored or is less capable of concealing illegal actions.

Under law, a firm is a legal entity that can own property, make contracts, sue, and be sued. Furthermore, the U.S. Supreme Court has held that corporations have constitutional rights (Beale 2009). Under such circumstances, firms have the same possible incentives and disincentives for engaging in illegal conduct as any human entity may have. *Corporate illegality* is defined as an illegal act primarily meant to benefit a firm by potentially increasing revenues or decreasing costs (McKendall and Wagner 1997).

Traditionally, the moral calculator hypothesis has helped to explain decisions to act illegally. According to this hypothesis, which is derived from rational choice theory, confronted with limited access to legitimate means to achieve organization goals, decision makers will calculate the costs and benefits of using illegitimate means. If benefits outweigh the costs, actors will violate the law (Kagan and Scholtz 1984). The negative consequences that a firm may suffer as an outcome of engaging in illegal activities include damaged firm performance (Davidson and Worrell 1988), loss of access to important resources, and severe damage to the reputation of the firm or its managers (Karpoff, Lee, and Martin 2009).

As illegal conduct may take many forms, various measurements can be sug-gested, all based on past illegal behavior exposed. For example, Harris and Bromiley (2007) look at accounting irregularities identified by the U.S. Government Accountability Office that prompted financial restatements. Using this measure, they find empirical support for the notion that top management incentive compen-sation and poor organizational performance relative to aspirations, each increase the likelihood of illegal activity. Another way to measure this type of illegality would be in line with Johnson, Ryan, and Tian (2009), who look at cases of misre-porting that the Securities and Exchange Commission (SEC) chose to prosecute, or to look at securities class action lawsuits (Peng and Roell 2008).

Baucus and Near (1991) investigate only cases in which a firm's managers or employees knowingly engaged in illegal acts. To do so, they analyze cases from legal databases to extract violations in which the law assumed that a firm acted with knowledge or intent, and the courts ruled that the firm was guilty of illegal behavior. Hill, Kelley, Agle, Hitt, and Hoskisson (1992) analyze violations of legal regulations cited by the Environmental Protection Agency (EPA) and Occupation Safety and Health Administration (OSHA). Mishina, Dykes, Block, and Pollock (2010) use various database and news sources, such as "the corporate crime re-porter," to devise a dichotomous variable indicating whether a firm should be considered as acting illegally or not. Although many measures are available that can serve as a proxy for a corporate illegal activity, they have not found their way to databases of SRI rating firms.

SUMMARY AND CONCLUSIONS

A fundamental problem that arises when dealing with CSR is the incoherence of the term. Many constructs are used interchangeably without a clear definition of their meaning or how they differ from one another. For example, corporate so-cial responsibility (CSR), corporate social performance (CSP), and corporate social responsiveness (CSR) are only a few examples of acronyms used interchangeably in numerous studies.

An immediate outcome of this state of affairs is the lack of agreement on what is supposed to be measured when quantifying a firm's social performance. While there may be a general agreement that CSR should be associated with "doing good," many problems are associated with suggesting a measure that follows this notion. First, what constitutes "good" is a matter of perspective. Second, no single continuum or scale exits between "good" and "bad" corporate actions. Third, a single company can have a wildly divergent record on responsible and irresponsible acts. As discussed in this chapter, these are only a few of the challenges faced when attempting to measure CSR.

This chapter advocates viewing CSR as a construct encompassing benefits to different stakeholders of a company. Namely, the different shareholders who may benefit or suffer from the extent of socially responsible actions performed by the company include bondholders, shareholders, employees, managers, the environment, suppliers, and customers. The chapter discusses the different concerns of these stakeholders, how they relate to one another, and how they differ. Most importantly, different measures are often used when considering each stakeholder group. Thus, measuring CSR with respect to a specific stakeholder group appears much more informative than an all-encompassing measure. Extracting true CSR activities performed from an all-encompassing measure is difficult because of various interactions between the different dimensions of CSR activities. Hence, studies employing an overall CSR measure may be limited in their explanatory power regarding the corporate social phenomena.

The appropriateness and power of measures rests on the ability to observe relevant phenomena and on the accuracy and reliability of the observers. When CSR activities are measured separately for each stakeholder group, the meaning of the measure becomes more coherent and knowledge of CSR actions and outcomes can advance.

DISCUSSION QUESTIONS

1. Explain why measuring corporate social performance (CSP) is consistent with both Milton Friedman's view in which firms should maximize shareholder value (share price), and the alternative view that the firm should do what is good for society.

2. Explain some of the problems associated with measuring CSP, and provide an example of where measurement controversy may arise.

3. Explain the focus of the following CSP components: environmental performance, customer performance, employee-related performance, supplier-related performance, and community-related performance.

4. What elements do government-related performance measures aim to capture, and what is the challenge? Provide specific examples of measures used in the literature.

REFERENCES

Albinger, Heather Schmidt, and Sarah J. Freeman. 2000. "Corporate Social Performance and Attractiveness as an Employer to Different Job Seeking Populations." *Journal of Business Ethics* 28:3, 243–253.

Appeal Judgment. 1999. The Supreme Court of Judicature QBENF 97/1281/1. In The Court of Appeal (Civil Division) on Appeal from the Queen's Bench Division (The Hon Mr. Justice Bell) Royal Courts of Justice, Strand, London WC2.

Baucus, Melissa S., and Janet P. Near. 1991. "Can Illegal Corporate Behavior Be Predicted? An Event History Analysis." *Academy of Management Journal* 34:1, 9–36.

Beale, Sara Sun. 2009. "A Response to the Critics of Corporate Criminal Liability." *American Criminal Law Review* 46:1, 1481–1505.

Berens, Guido, Cees B. M. van Riel, and Gerrit H. van Bruggen. 2005. "Corporate Associations and Consumer Product Responses: The Moderating Role of Corporate Brand Dominance." *Journal of Marketing* 69:1, 35–48.

Besser, Terry L. 1999. "The Significance of Community to Business Social Responsibility." *Rural Sociology* 63:3, 412–431.

Bhattacharya, C. B., and Sankar Sen. 2003. "Doing Better at Doing Good." *California Management Review* 47:1, 9–24.

Boehm, Amnon. 2002. "Corporate Social Responsibility: A Complementary Perspective of Community and Corporate Leaders." *Business and Society Review* 107:2, 171–194.

Burke, Edmund M. 1999. *Corporate Community Relations: The Principles of Neighbor of Choice.* Westport, CT: Praeger.

Buvik, Arnt, and Toger Reve. 2002. "Inter-Firm Governance and Structural Power in Industrial Relationships: The Moderating Effect of Bargaining Power on the Contractual Safeguarding of Specific Assets." *Scandinavian Journal of Management* 18:3, 261–284.

Carroll, Archie B. 1979. "A Three-Dimensional Conceptual Model of Corporate Performance." *Academy of Management Review* 4:4, 497–505.

Cetindamar, Dilek, and Kristoffer Husoy. 2007. "Corporate Social Responsibility Practices and Environmentally Responsible Behavior: The Case of the United National Global Compact." *Journal of Business Ethics* 76:2, 163–176.

Chatterji, Aaron K., David I. Levine, and Michael W. Toffel. 2009. "How Well Do Social Ratings Actually Measure Corporate Social Responsibility?" *Journal of Economics and Management Strategy* 18:1, 125–169.

Cheney, George, Juliet Roper, and Steven K. May. 2007. "Overview." In Steven K. May, George Cheney, and Juliet Roper, eds. *The Debate Over Corporate Social Responsibility*, 3–12. Oxford: Oxford University Press.

Clarkson, Max B. E. 1988. "Corporate social performance in Canada, 1976–86." In Lee E. Preston, ed., *Research in Corporate Social Performance and Policy* 10, 241–265. Greenwich, CT: JAI Press.

Clarkson, Max. B. E. 1995. "A Stakeholder Framework for Analyzing and Evaluating Corporate Social Performance." *Academy of Management Review* 20:1, 92–117.

Davidson, Wallace N., and Dan L. Worrell. 1988. "The Impact of Announcements of Corporate Illegalities on Shareholder Returns." *Academy of Management Journal* 31:1, 195–200.

Dillenburg, Stephen, Timothy Greene, and O. Homer Erekson. 2003. "Approaching Socially Responsible Investment with a Comprehensive Ratings Scheme: Total Social Impact." *Journal of Business Ethics* 43:3, 167–177.

Edmans, Alex. 2011. "Does the Stock Market Fully Value Intangibles? Employee Satisfaction and Equity Prices." *Journal of Financial Economics* 101:3, 621–640.

Greening, Daniel W., and Daniel B. Turban. 2000. "Corporate Social Performance as a Competitive Advantage in Attracting a Quality Workforce." *Business and Society* 39:3, 254–280.

Harris, Jared D., and Philip Bromiley. 2007. "Incentives to Cheat: The Influence of Executive Compensation and Firm Performance on Financial Misrepresentation." *Organization Science* 18:3, 350–367.

Hill, Charles W. L., Patricia C. Kelley, Bradley R. Agle, Michael A. Hitt, and Robert E. Hoskisson. 1992. "An Empirical Examination of the Causes of Corporate Wrongdoing in the United States." *Human Relations* 45:10, 1055–1076.

Johnson, Shane A., Harley E. Ryan, and Yisong S. Tian. 2009. "Managerial Incentives and Corporate Fraud: The Sources of Incentives Matter." *Review of Finance* 13:1, 115–145.

Kagan, Robert A., and John T. Scholz. 1984. "The Criminology of the corporation and regulatory enforcement strategies." In Keith Hawkins and John Thomas, eds., *Enforcing Regulation*, 67–95. Boston: Kluwer-Nijhoff.

Karpoff, Jonathan M., D. Scott Lee, and Gerald S. Martin. 2009. "The Cost to Firms of Cooking the Books." *Journal of Financial and Quantitative Analysis* 43:3, 581–611.

Lee, Tzai Zang, Ming-Hong Ho, Chien-Hsing Wu, and Shu-Chen Kao. 2008. "Relationships between Employees' Perception of Corporate Social Responsibility, Personality, Job Satisfaction, and Organizational Commitment Marketing." Proceedings of the International Conference on Business and Information (BAI), Kuala Lumpur, Malaysia, July 6–8, 1–17.

Longo, Mariolina, Matteo Mura, and Alessandra Bonoli. 2005. "Corporate Social Responsibility and Corporate Performance: The Case of Italian SMEs." *Corporate Governance* 5:4, 28–42.

Luo, Xueming, and C. B. Bhattacharya. 2006. "Corporate Social Responsibility, Customer Satisfaction, and Market Value." *Journal of Marketing* 70:4, 1–18.

Lydenberg, Steve D., Alice Tepper Marlin, and Sean O'Brien Strub. 1986. *Rating America's Corporate Conscience: A Provocative Guide to the Companies behind the Products You Buy Every Day*. Reading, MA: Addison-Wesley.

Lydenberg, Steve D., and Graham Sinclair. 2009. "Mainstream or Daydream? The Future for Responsible Investing." *Journal of Corporate Citizenship* 33:April, 47–67.

Mallott, Mary J. 1993. "Operationalizing Corporate Social Performance." Unpublished Doctoral Dissertation, University of Pittsburgh.

Margolis, Joshua D., and James P. Walsh. 2003. "Misery Loves Companies: Rethinking Social Initiatives by Business." *Administrative Science Quarterly* 48:2, 268–305.

McKendall, Marie A., and John A. Wagner. 1997. "Motive, Opportunity, Choice, and Corporate Illegality." *Organization Science* 8:6, 624–647.

Mishina, Yuri, Bernadine J. Dykes, Emily S. Block, and Timothy G. Pollock. 2010. "Why Good Firms Do Bad Things: The Effects of High Aspirations, High Expectations and Prominence on the Incidence of Corporate Illegality." *Academy of Management Journal* 53:4, 701–722.

Nan, Xiaoli, and Kwangjun Heo. 2007. "Consumer Responses to Corporate Social Responsibility (CSR) Initiatives: Examining the Role of Brand-Cause Fit in Cause-Related Marketing." *Journal of Advertising* 36:2, 63–74.

Orlitzky Marc, Frank L. Schmidt, and Sara L. Rynes. 2003. "Corporate Social and Financial Performance: A Meta-Analysis." *Organization Studies* 24:3, 403–441.

Paul, Karen, Lori M. Zalka, Meredith Downes, Susan Perry, and Shawnta Friday. 1997. "U.S. Consumer Sensitivity to Corporate Social Performance." *Business and Society* 36:4, 408–418.

Pedersen, Esben Rahbek, and Mette Andersen. 2006. "Safeguarding Corporate Social Responsibility (CSR) in Global Supply Chains: How Codes of Conduct Are Managed in Buyer-Supplier Relationships." *Journal of Public Affairs* 6:3–4, 228–240.

Peng, Ling, and Ailsa Roell. 2008. "Executive Pay and Shareholder Litigation." *Review of Finance* 12:1, 141–184.

Preston III, Lee. E. 1988. *Research in Corporate Social Performance and Policy 10*. Greenwich, CT: JAI Press.

Reason Magazine. 2005. "Rethinking the Social Responsibility of Business." Available at http://reason.com/archives/2005/10/01/rethinking-the-social-responsi.

Riordan, Christine M., Robert. D. Gatewood, and Jodi Barnes Bill. 1997. "Corporate Image: Employee Reactions and Implications for Managing Corporate Social Performance." *Journal of Business Ethics* 16:4, 401–412.

Scalet, Steven, and Thomas F. Kelly. 2010. "CSR Rating Agencies: What Is Their Global Impact?" *Journal of Business Ethics* 94:1, 69–88.

Schwepker, Charles H. 2001 "Ethical Climate's Relationship to Job Satisfaction, Organizational Commitment, and Turnover Intention in the Salesforce." *Journal of Business Research* 54:1, 39–52.

Scorse, Jason David. 2005. "The Effects of Social and Environmental Information on Firm Behavior." Unpublished Doctoral Dissertation, University of California, Berkeley.

Sen, Sankar, and C. B. Bhattacharya. 2001. "Does Doing Good Always Lead to Doing Better? Consumer Reactions to Corporate Social Responsibility." *Journal of Marketing Research* 38:2, 225–244.

Smith, Craig N. 2003. "Corporate Social Responsibility: Whether or How?" *California Management Review* 45:4, 52–76.

Valentine, Sean, and Gary Fleischman. 2008. "Ethics Programs, Perceived Corporate Social Responsibility and Job Satisfaction." *Journal of Business Ethics* 77:2, 159–172.

Yoon, Yeosun, Gürhan-Canli Zeynep, and Norbert Schwarz. 2006. "The Effect of Corporate Social Responsibility (CSR) Activities on Companies with Bad Reputations." *Journal of Consumer Psychology* 16:4, 377–390.

Zalkind, Joe. 1974. *Guide to Corporations: A Social Perspective.* Chicago: Swallow Press/Council on Economic Priorities.

ABOUT THE AUTHORS

Amir Rubin is an associate professor at the Beedie School of Business, Simon Fraser University (Canada) and the Arison School of Business, Interdisciplinary Center (IDC) Herzliya (Israel). After five years as an economist with the Israeli Security Authority regulating mutual funds and designing risk analysis tools, Professor Rubin switched to academic research and teaching. His research interests include corporate finance, corporate governance, and corporate social responsibility. He has published in various finance and sustainability journals such as the *Journal of Banking and Finance, Journal of Business Ethics, Journal of Financial Intermediation,* and *Journal of Financial Markets.* Professor Rubin received his Ph.D. in Finance from the University of British Columbia.

Eran Rubin is currently a lecturer at the Faculty of Technology Management at the Holon Institute of Technology (HIT). His research interests include financial impacts of information systems, environmental information systems, decision support systems, and corporate social responsibility. Professor Rubin has published in various journals concerning information systems and sustainability including the *Journal of Business Finance and Accounting, International Journal of Social Environmental and Economic Sustainability,* and *Requirements Engineering Journal.* He received his Ph.D. in Management Information Systems from the University of British Columbia.

CHAPTER 18

Corporate Philanthropy

JANET KIHOLM SMITH
Von Tobel Professor of Economics, Robert Day School of Economics and Finance,
Claremont McKenna College

INTRODUCTION

Most large corporations throughout the world engage in some type of philanthropy. This includes gifts to social and charitable causes such as support for education, the arts, environmental causes, social services, and relief funds. Many firms also support programs where employees engage in volunteer activities. Some companies direct their charitable giving to the communities in which they are located or do business; others have a broader reach, even extending to international aid efforts. In the United States, corporate giving is about evenly split between *in kind* (e.g., product donations, and *pro bono* work by corporate employees) and monetary (cash) gifts.

Not surprisingly, the recent economic downturn has negatively affected corporate giving. Nonetheless, by one estimate, after substantial declines in 2008 and 2009, U.S. total corporate giving grew by an annual (inflation-adjusted) 8.8 percent in 2010 to $15.29 billion (Giving USA Foundation 2011). To provide perspective, corporate giving, including giving through corporate foundations and direct giving by corporations, accounts for only a small fraction of total philanthropy in the United States. In 2010, it represented 5 percent of total giving ($290.89 billion), a percentage that has remained approximately constant over time. According to the Giving USA Foundation, this 5 percent figure compares to charitable giving by individuals (73 percent), foundations (14 percent), and bequests (8 percent). To provide additional perspective on potential economic impact, total corporate philanthropy (both cash and noncash) currently represents about 1.0 percent of total pre-tax corporate income and a much smaller fraction of total revenue (computation for income based on data from the *Economic Report of the President* 2011).

This chapter explores a myriad of issues involving corporate giving. The first section describes the evolution of views about corporate giving. This section also lays the groundwork for the two primary hypotheses (rationales) for giving programs—the *value enhancement* theory and the *agency cost* theory. Corporate donations to charitable causes are a visible and measurable component of what some consider the firm's social responsibility to add value in ways that go beyond the traditional objective of making profits for shareholders. The alternative, but not mutually exclusive, view of charitable giving is that corporations can enhance shareholder value through strategic spending on philanthropy. The second section describes common attributes of corporate giving programs and corporate foundations, identifies giving priorities of large corporations, and documents the governance features of the programs. The third section contains a survey of empirical evidence about corporate giving, with a particular emphasis on two questions: What are the determinants of corporate giving? Does giving have a positive impact on firm performance? Various methodological and data-related challenges for research on corporate philanthropy are briefly mentioned. The final section concludes.

EVOLVING VIEWS OF CORPORATE PHILANTHROPY

While early industrialists, notably John Rockefeller and Andrew Carnegie, became well-known philanthropists, their giving was private, funded with personal profits derived as owners of their businesses, and not direct expenditures of their corporations. Still, these industrialists set the stage for corporate giving through their views about responsibilities of the wealthy to give back a substantial fraction of their wealth to society. Carnegie (1889, p.1), for example, in his essay, "The Gospel of Wealth," acknowledges that opportunities for accumulating wealth depended in part on society and that the "man of wealth thus becoming the mere trustee and agent for his poorer brethren."

In the early nineteenth century, numerous company towns emerged throughout the United States, such as textile mill towns in the northeast and isolated mining towns, and the owners of these businesses began to invest business resources in the health, education, and welfare of workers. The rationale was that such expenditures are legitimate costs of doing business because they helped to attract and retain workers and to possibly enhance productivity. As Soskis (2010) documents, many of these firms assumed a paternalistic regard for their employees, often providing them with housing, schools, and even churches. Workers' lives, however, were highly proscribed and workers were often paid in company script that could only be used in the town for goods and services that were sold at controlled prices. Ultimately, these efforts did not lead to better employer-employee relationships. Soskis cites the Pullman Town social experiment outside of Chicago as an example.

Marshand (1998) notes that the nature of giving changed as professional managers began replacing the founders of large business. Some of the managers shared similar interests in improving the welfare of employees and the community but lacked extensive fortunes or renown within a specific local community, and could not develop reputations for professional service apart from their roles in the corporations. Instead, they built internal structures within the company to provide "welfare" benefits to employees, such as calisthenics classes, free lunches, and pension funds. Managers viewed these company-provided benefits as worker "welfare" because they were benefits that most firms did not offer and were unnecessary to be competitive. Moreover, the benefits sometimes produced spillover effects for the community generally. Soskis (2010) documents that in the 1890s, the president of National Cash Register Company, which invested heavily in "welfare work," attempted to validate the investments by hanging signs around the factory, declaring IT PAYS. Soskis also points out that these efforts to be charitable were partly preemptive—responding to concerns of government intervention in the workplace and with unionization.

During the first half of the twentieth century, companies throughout the United States continued to provide modest amounts of philanthropy, generally in the form of improvement of local communities. Prominent examples included the railroad companies' contributions to local Young Men's Christian Associations (YMCAs), which supported the potential pool of employees, and business gifts to the Community Chest and social welfare organizations (Soskis 2010).

While the U.S. government granted a charitable gift deduction to individuals in 1917, many more years passed before the government applied this deduction to business. The Internal Revenue Bureau (IRB), which later became the Internal Revenue Service (IRS), impeded business giving under a revenue ruling that cast substantial doubt on the legality (tax deductibility) of corporate gifts to community chests and similar organizations. In 1932, the IRB ruled that contributions are legitimate businesses expenses so long as the taxpayer corporation can show it reasonably contemplated a financial return commensurate with the payments, and was motivated by such expectation of a financial return in making the payment. This ruling, requiring that corporate philanthropy be treated as an investment decision with the view toward creating value for investors, clearly stipulated a higher bar than firms face today.

To illustrate the tension and controversy surrounding corporate philanthropy during the Great Depression period, Franklin D. Roosevelt, as governor of New York, vetoed a bill that would have authorized public utility companies to con-tribute to charities. The *New York Times* reported that Roosevelt defended his position by stating that authorization of such contributions would sanction two unsound practices—purchasing goodwill by corporations and substituting the au-thority of corporate officials to bestow gifts that belong properly to the individual stockholders. In spite of this setback, the lobbying effort for a corporate charita-ble gift deduction intensified, and, ironically, Roosevelt, as president, signed the deduction into law in 1935. Still, even though the law allowed deductions for con-tributions that could be directly tied to a business purpose, most corporations in this era did not participate in philanthropy.

Court Cases, the Indirect Benefit Rationale, and the Growth of Corporate Giving

A major boost to philanthropy resulted from what appeared to be a minor dis-pute over a small corporate gift to Princeton University. Before the mid-1950s, the prevailing legal view was that philanthropy was beyond the power of the corpora-tion, and contributions not *directly* related to the purposes of the corporation were illegal (Kahn 1997). This view changed following a key decision of the New Jersey Supreme Court in 1953 (*A. P. Smith Mfg. Co. v. Barlow* 1953). In 1950, New Jersey had amended its laws to allow corporations to make contributions to educational institutions. The following year, Barlow, among other shareholders of A. P. Smith Company, challenged the legality of a $1,500 gift that the company had made to Princeton University. Upon appeal, the Supreme Court ruled that the gift was le-gal and articulated an indirect benefit justification, noting that such contributions benefited the corporation indirectly by improving public relations and creating favorable publicity.

The *A. P. Smith Mfg.* decision also articulated views about philanthropy that provide useful insights as to why, in the 1950s and 1960s, a push occurred for additional business philanthropy. The period followed a substantial build up in government spending and health and welfare regulation, and also encompassed the Cold War. The narrative that accompanied the court's decision points to the potential for corporate philanthropy as a means of reducing the scope of government's involvement in the economy. An influential book by Richard Eells (1956), a former GE executive, as quoted in Soskis (2010, p. 19), supports this view when Eells wrote that the aim of corporate philanthropy is "... to protect and preserve the donor's autonomy by protecting and preserving those conditions within the greater society which ensure the continuity of a system of free, competitive enterprise." This sentiment is reflected *A. P. Smith Mfg. Co. v. Barlow*, 98 A.2d 581, 590 N.J. (1953) with respect to education:

> There is now widespread belief throughout the nation that free and vigorous non-governmental institutions of learning are vital to our democracy and the system of free enterprise and that withdrawal of corporate authority to make such contributions... would seriously threaten their continuance. Corporations have come to recognize this and with their enlightenment have sought... to insure and strengthen the society which gives them existence.

Also, the growth and prominence of large corporations had altered the nature of the pool of potential donors. The court noted in *A. P. Smith Mfg. Co. v. Barlow* 98 A.2d 581, 590 (1953), that the wealth of the nation had changed hands and

> ... with the transfer of most of the wealth to corporate hands and the imposition of heavy burdens on individual taxation, [individuals] have been unable to keep pace with increased philanthropic needs. They have therefore, with justification, turned to corporations to assume the modern obligations of good citizenship....

Miller (2009) analyzes the motivation and political underpinnings of several important corporate philanthropy cases during this early era. He points out that a surprising number of luminaries were witnesses for A. P. Smith in the $1,500 gift case, including the chairman of the board of the Standard Oil Company of New Jersey, a former chairman of the board of the United States Steel Corporation, and the president of Princeton University. In his analysis of corporate philanthropy cases, Miller comments on the political nature of the case and is prompted to ask, "What was really going on?" He concludes that this was a "collusive lawsuit" brought and funded for the twin purposes of establishing a precedent that would enable companies to make charitable gifts and encourage them to make such gifts in the future.

Following the *A. P. Smith* decision and other cases with similar outcomes, individual states reinforced the court rulings by enacting philanthropy statues that validated corporate authority to make contributions (Kahn 1997). Moreover, various corporations created foundations to facilitate giving. Corporations set up these foundations as tax-exempt institutions that receive funds (to build an endowment) from their affiliated corporation and often share employees and officers. The foundations set criteria for funding, screen proposals, administer the funding, and evaluate the results. One perceived advantage of establishing a foundation is that the endowment can shelter the giving from business cycle fluctuations, allowing a corporation to maintain a constant level of giving over time. The federal tax laws that require private foundations to annually distribute 5 percent of the value of their net investment assets foster this practice.

Modern Concerns with Corporate Involvement in Philanthropy

Still, in spite of the growth in corporate philanthropy, Lankford (1964) reflects a basic uneasiness towards it. A famous critique of corporate giving came from economist, Milton Friedman. In a *New York Times* magazine article, Friedman (1970) challenged the corporate sector's embrace of philanthropy by asking whether corporations should engage in philanthropy at all. In the article, Friedman reiterates his earlier argument (Friedman 1963, p. 133) that "corporate officials are in no position to determine the relative urgency of social problems or the amount of organizational resources that should be committed to a given problem." His contention is that businesses should produce goods and services efficiently and leave the solving of social problems to concerned individuals and government agencies. Friedman's main argument is that corporate executives, when acting in their official capacity, and not as private persons, are agents of the corporation's stockholders and as such have an obligation to make decisions in the interest of the stockholders. According to Friedman (1963, 1970), the corporation is an instrument of the stockholders who own it. If the corporation makes a contribution in lieu of a distribution, it prevents the individual stockholder from deciding how to dispose of the funds. The implication is that individuals, such as stockholders and employees, should make charitable contributions and not the corporation.

Others express similar views including management scholar, Peter Drucker, who, though often misinterpreted, regards economic performance as the overriding social responsibility of an enterprise. Drucker (1962, p. 63) notes, "In any society... the first and overriding social function and responsibility of the enterprise is economic performance. Drucker (2001, pp. 59–60) also comments:

> Whenever a business has disregarded the limitation of economic performance and has assumed social responsibilities that it could not support economically, it has soon gotten into trouble.... This, to be sure, is a very unpopular position to take. It is much more popular to be "progressive." But managers, and especially managers of key institutions of society, are not being paid to be heroes in the popular press. They are being paid for performance and responsibility.... To take on tasks for which one lacks competence is irresponsible behavior. An institution, and especially a business enterprise, has to acquire whatever competence is needed to take responsibility for its impacts. But in areas of social responsibility other than impacts, right and duty to act are limited by competence.

Like Friedman, Drucker (2001, pp. 61–62) questions whether corporations are suited for making decisions about social causes:

> But where business... is asked to assume social responsibility for... the problems or ills of society..., management needs to think through whether the authority implied by the responsibility is legitimate. Otherwise it is usurpation and

irresponsible.... Every time the demand is made that business take responsibility for this or that, one should ask, Does business have the authority and should it have it? If business does not ... then responsibility on the part of business should be treated with grave suspicion. It is not responsibility; it is lust for power.... Management must resist responsibility for a social problem that would compromise or impair the performance capacity of its business.... It must resist when the demand goes beyond its own competence. It must resist when responsibility would ... be illegitimate authority....

Does Philanthropy Reflect Agency Costs?

The corollary of the Friedman and Drucker views about corporate involvement in social causes is that such involvement reflects agency costs. While managers can usually make an argument that charitable giving enhances a firm's goodwill, agency cost theory recognizes that managers do not fully internalize the opportunity cost of such expenditures in their decision making. Managers can derive substantial personal benefits from the activities such as networking opportunities. Directors, who are presumably monitoring managers on behalf of shareholders, may not be in a good position to do so, as directors generally are also involved in these philanthropic activities. For example, directors may be invited to such events as charity art galas, museum openings, and golf and tennis tournaments. As described below, empirical studies examine the agency cost hypothesis for giving and its alternative—the value-enhancement hypothesis.

Can Giving Be "Strategic"?

The concept of *strategic giving* became popular with businesses in the 1980s and 1990s (Wulfson 2001). The concept is that giving can simultaneously enhance firm performance and benefit society. Related to this, many companies began to link their corporations to specific and visible social causes and to charitable organizations, such as the early association of the Marriott Corporation with the March of Dimes. The perception was that some consumers would see value in corporate philanthropy and hence the objective was to find a means to differentiate the firm's products and create a strategic advantage (Varadarajan and Menon 1988; Wulfson 2001). Cause-related marketing (CRM) typically involves marketing and advertising campaigns that promote both the corporation and the cause or social issue. By contrast, *pure* philanthropy is concerned with assistance to education, arts and culture, health and social services, civic and community projects, without regard to creating firm value. CRM is aimed at enhancing the firm's competitive advantage and creating a higher "willingness to pay" for consumers.

Consistent with Friedman's (1963, 1970) reasoning, Porter and Kramer (2002) assert that most corporate philanthropy, including most types of CRM and strategic giving, does not reap benefits for stakeholders. Despite claims to the contrary, Porter and Kramer (p. 5) point out that in today's environment, "most companies feel compelled to give to charity" and contend that most charity is "diffuse and unfocused." Yet, they argue that justification exists for corporate philanthropy if the firm's social and economic goals are aligned and if charitable giving improves the firm's long-term business prospects. This alignment is more likely to occur if the giving can be leveraged so that social benefits exceed those provided by individual donors or even governments. While the latter point is more of a social comment than an economic comment, competitive advantage is more likely to be obtained if others cannot replicate the benefits of corporate giving at a lower cost.

Porter and Kramer (2002) believe that accepting the corporate claims that their giving is "strategic" lets corporations off too easily. They argue for a higher bar. Strategic giving that only enhances a firm's goodwill is not truly strategic and is wasteful in the Friedman sense. To be value enhancing, it must improve a company's ability to compete. Giving that is truly strategic implies that shareholders should not expect to sacrifice financial returns for philanthropic reasons.

CORPORATE PHILANTHROPIC PRACTICES

As noted above, corporations make two types of gifts to charity—cash gifts and in-kind gifts. For example, through programs they sponsor, some airlines provide complimentary airfares for cancer sufferers, and hotel chains provide free rooms. Some companies also donate their employees' time, advice, and service instead of cash. Other companies provide computer equipment, software, drugs, and other products and services. Oracle, for instance, gives the bulk of its donations (more than $2 billion annually) as computer software.

Giving Priorities

The Conference Board tracks annual U.S. corporate giving trends. It documents that a small number of large companies are responsible for most corporate giving. Of the 166 companies surveyed, 32 gave 80 percent of total contributions (Conference Board 2009). In terms of geographic allocation, they report a shift, with increases in corporate contributions to both Africa and China. The study also indicates that contributions to environmental concerns by corporations have been increasing over time.

The Conference Board (2009) study confirms other findings. For example, in recent years, the pharmaceutical industry had the most in total giving, which occurs largely in noncash contributions. Recently, noncash gifts from large pharmaceutical companies totaled around $2 billion (83.4 percent of all industry contributions). Internationally, the impact of pharmaceuticals is also dramatic. Noncash gifts totaled nearly 80 percent of all international giving. IRS tax deduction rules for in-kind gifts, which are generous with regard to gifts of drugs made by pharmaceutical companies, can explain some of this giving. Webb (1996) documents tax advantages associated with corporate giving.

Brown, Helland, and Smith (2006) study giving priorities by industry. Exhibit 18.1 shows a summary of their results of cash-only giving by corporations. It indicates the percentage of charitable contributions that firms in a given industry allocate to various categories. This exhibit lists only those categories where firms report more than 1 percent of their total monetary donations. Religion, international, and science each account for less than 1 percent, on average, and are thereby excluded from the table. Some interesting patterns emerge of which most indicate that firms find giving opportunities that complement their business. For example, pharmaceutical companies give the bulk of their contributions to health-related

Exhibit 18.1 Giving Priorities by Industry

Industry (SIC codes)	Arts	Civic	Education	Environment	Health	Matching	Social Services	Other	General
Mining, construction	7.9	4.4	32.3	0.0***	21.9*	0.0***	11.2	0.9***	17.7
Manufacturing	8.0**	6.5	31.5***	1.0	14.8	1.6	14.2	4.0***	17.7***
Transportation	12.7	2.4***	7.4***	0.6	17.3	0.0***	5.4***	0.6***	52.0***
Pharmaceuticals	6.2***	5.6	19.8***	0.6**	42.6***	1.4	6.1***	4.1	11.1*
Petroleum	9.5	5.2	33.2**	3.8***	10.9	0.0***	13.7	1.7	16.1
Communications	7.2	6.9	47.0***	0.0***	7.2***	0.9	8.7**	2.7	13.0
Utilities	8.6	8.6	22.6	1.8	7.6***	0.0***	12.9	0.3***	36.4*
Wholesale trade	8.5	7.7	30.1	0.9	14.8	0.0***	12.5	4.4	20.0
Retail trade	5.0***	3.7***	10.2***	0.3***	12.2	0.0	21.7*	1.7*	44.7***
Depository institutions	10.7	8.9	21.0	0.4***	13.3	2.5	19.8*	1.8*	20.4
Insurance carriers	11.1	7.7	2.7	2.7	14.3	0.8	10.7	1.9	24.0
Financial, insurance, real estate	21.8***	0.9***	25.4	0.8	20.1	5.8***	22.5*	0.0***	0.0***
Services	8.8	0.9***	23.5	0.8	14.4	2.5	3.2***	2.2	43.8
Mean	8.85	6.33	27.28	1.10	15.21	1.35	13.88	2.88	21.83

Based on a sample of Fortune 500 firms, the exhibit shows the percentage of contributions that firms allocate to various causes, categorized by industry. The t-tests show the significance of the difference between the value of the industry's mean percentage given to a category relative to the mean reported for all other industries, adjusted for multiple-year observations for a firm. ***, **, *, indicate significance at 0.01, 0.05, 0.10 levels, respectively, using two-tailed tests.

Source: Adapted from Brown et al. (2006).

causes and education. Petroleum firms account for the largest percentage contributions (3.82 percent, on average) to the environment, which is significantly higher than other industries. While giving to the arts is the third most popular category of giving opportunities, it is especially popular with financial firms. They give 21.8 percent of their total contributions to the arts. The authors point out that giving to the arts is a likely candidate for agency cost interpretations because finding a link for such spending to bottom-line profitability is difficult. Nonetheless, firms in every industry report giving something to the arts. Also striking is the finding that the second-most-popular category for giving is "general." This category is one that firms may select if they do not want to report details on their giving. As shown, transportation firms and utilities are significantly more likely to select this category rather than to provide details.

Governance of Corporate Giving Programs

Many large corporations have chosen to establish foundations through which they make charitable contributions. While the foundation funding comes from their associated for-profit corporation, foundations are legally separate entities. This suggests that the foundation may have more autonomy to pursue interests that are not aligned with the corporation. The presence of corporate officers on the foundation's board may mitigate concerns with agency problems, but officers may also receive nonpecuniary benefits from these foundation positions.

Exhibit 18.2 shows some comparative statistics on the use of foundations by the Fortune 500 sample used by Brown et al. (2006). Some striking differences are evident between those firms that choose to have a foundation versus those that do not. Older firms and firms with more employees and more assets are more likely to have a foundation. The data suggest that agency costs are related to the presence of a foundation, as traditional monitoring variables are negatively associated with foundations (i.e., the percentage of equity held by institutions and by blockholders, and the debt-to-value ratio for the firm). The data also indicate that foundations may result in more focused giving for the corporation as a whole because corporations with foundations are more likely to give to specific categories rather than to the "general" category.

Most firms in the Brown et al. (2006) sample have a charitable foundation (83.9 percent). Of those, 62.4 percent identify a corporate officer as running the foundation. For instance, the chief executive officer (CEO) runs the foundation in 42.0 percent of the cases. In contrast, for those firms that choose not to have a foundation, only 6.2 percent identify a corporate officer as running the giving program. Here, the CEO oversees the program in only 2.7 percent of the firms.

EVIDENCE ON THE MOTIVATION AND IMPACT OF CORPORATE PHILANTHROPY

Managers and directors can usually make a plausible and legally defensible case for how charitable spending can bolster the firm's image and goodwill with employees, the local community, and customers. This type of argument, however, begs the question of whether identifying meaningful economic benefits for

Exhibit 18.2　Corporate Foundations, Firm Governance, and Giving Statistics

	Foundation	No Foundation	t-statistic
Selected variables			
Firm attributes:			
Assets (millions)	29,059.00	18,280.00	2.002**
Employees (thousands)	59.24	43.74	1.725*
Firm age (since IPO)	96.31	86.24	2.149**
Ratio of advertising to sales	0.02	0.01	1.412
Ratio of R&D to sales	0.02	0.01	1.922*
Governance (monitoring) variables:			
Total directors	12.58	12.11	1.672*
Ratio of (inside + gray directors) to total directors	0.24	0.26	−1.647*
Percent equity held by institutions	59.00	63.20	−2.741***
Percent equity held by blockholders	13.40	20.67	−4.261***
Ratio of debt to total firm value (book)	0.17	0.22	−3.524***
Giving rates:			
Annual dollar giving	11,100.00	8,368.53	1.454
Annual giving per 1000 employees	278.91	279.59	−0.014
Annual giving per $ assets	747.84	526.79	2.169**
Annual giving per director	876.85	685.62	1.252

Based on a sample of Fortune 500 firms, the exhibit shows differences in variables for firms that have established a foundation and those that have not. The last column shows the t-tests of the significance of the difference in the means. ***, **, * indicate significance at 0.01, 0.05, 0.10 levels, respectively, using two-tailed tests.
Source: Adapted from Brown et al. (2006).

stockholders is possible. For example, do workers accept lower wages or become more productive when working for a firm they perceive to be socially responsible, so that shareholders benefit on net? Do customers respond to corporate philanthropy by their willingness to pay higher prices for the company's products, other things constant? Do investors, particularly institutions, accept lower returns from firms that are known for pursuing corporate philanthropy? Are local communities or regulators more likely to respond with a more favorable regulatory environment for such firms?

Empirical studies spanning multiple disciplines, including economics, finance, marketing, accounting, law, management, and ethics, have addressed aspects of these questions. Many studies address two overarching empirical questions: (1) Do corporations give to charity because the motivation is value-enhancement or agency costs? (2) Does corporate philanthropy affect firm performance? The findings of the empirical studies that address these questions appear below.

The Determinants of Corporate Giving

Researchers use various methods, datasets, and time frames to ascertain the determinants of corporate giving. Many of these studies are framed in terms of testing a value-enhancement theory for giving and an agency cost theory (manager/

director utility maximization). In a natural experiment approach, Boatsman and Gupta (1996) study changes in firm contributions in response to a change in marginal corporate tax rate. Their results are consistent with managerial utility maximization being an important driver for corporate contributions, in that contributions go beyond what would be profit maximizing. They also find that business cycles, resulting in a low income elasticity of corporate contributions, do not greatly affect corporate charity. Overall, the findings are inconsistent with the hypothesis that corporations optimally consider the tax consequences of their giving programs; instead, they lend support to the agency cost theory.

Brown et al. (2006) test the value-enhancement theory and agency cost theory for why firms give to charity. Their results provide some evidence that giving enhances shareholder value, as firms in the same industry tend to respond to competitive pressure by adopting similar giving practices, and firms that advertise more intensively also give more to charity. Galaskiewicz and Burt (1991) also discuss the possibility of competitive "contagion" in philanthropy, which would account for similar practices.

Much of the evidence from Brown et al. (2006) is consistent with agency costs and managerial discretion in corporate giving. They find that firms with larger boards give significantly more cash than those with smaller boards. Larger boards are also associated with the establishment of a foundation. In terms of other possible agency cost variables, they examine the impact on giving of firm governance attributes that can provide evidence of effective monitoring. The evidence suggests that firms with higher debt-to-value ratios give less in cash contributions and are less likely to have foundations. The authors also find support for the idea that the presence of economic rents contributes positively to corporate giving, as suggested by Tobin's Q being positively related to giving.

Seifert, Morris, and Bartkus (2004), who find that firms with more slack resources (cash flow/sales) contribute more to charity as a fraction of sales, provide related evidence supporting the agency cost theory. They also find a negative effect on ownership concentration (number of blockholders) on donations, and report that higher levels of giving are associated with the percentage of insider stock ownership, ratio of inside to outside board members, and proportion of female and minority board members. Wang and Coffey (1992) also show that more diverse boards are associated with more giving, perhaps because more diversity leads to supporting more and varied causes.

Rubin and Barnea (2010) do not measure corporate giving directly, but classify firms as having a large or small corporate social responsibility (CSR) index, for which giving is a component. They find that average insiders' ownership and leverage are negatively related to the firm's social ratings, while institutional ownership is uncorrelated with it. They interpret their results as supportive of the agency cost hypothesis, as insider ownership (managers and large blockholders) are associated with higher CSR measures.

Bartkus, Morris, and Seifert (2002) provide evidence that large investors may perceive corporate giving as excessive and act to curtail it. Using a small sample that is matched on industry and firm size, they find weak evidence that corporations giving more are associated with fewer blockholders and less institutional ownership than are those giving smaller amounts. However, using a U.K. data set, Adams and Hardwick (1998) find no connection between giving and shareholder concentration. They do find that firm size, profits, and low leverage are associated with more charitable giving.

Most studies find a positive relationship between giving and firm size using alternative measures of number of employees, net income, and assets. For example, Amato and Amato (2007), who explore possible nonlinearities in the relationship between firm size and giving, find evidence of a cubic relationship, suggesting large firms and small firms giving relatively more, as a fraction of their revenue than medium-size firms. The authors suggest that smaller firms may give more because they tend to be local, with high visibility in their communities, and perhaps this increases net benefits from philanthropy. Brammer and Millington (2006) document a positive relationship between giving and firm size that also holds for a sample of more than 300 U.K. firms.

Finally, many studies document a positive relationship between advertising and giving. Using firm-level data, Navarro (1988) concludes that corporate contributions represent a form of advertising because firms that spend more on advertising also tend to give more to charity. Other studies find a positive relationship between research and development (R&D)/sales and charitable giving. The R&D intensity variable takes on a higher value for firms that depend more on intangible assets such as intellectual property. These findings regarding advertising intensity and R&D intensity are both consistent with value enhancement because spending on advertising and R&D appears to complement charitable giving. Having significant intangible assets may make these firms more vulnerable to appropriation from lawsuits and governmental regulation. This may create incentives for these firms to "buy" protection by creating goodwill with potential jurors, judges, and regulators.

THE IMPACT OF CORPORATE GIVING ON FIRM PERFORMANCE

Studies examine several mechanisms by which corporate giving could increase shareholder wealth. One mechanism may be to establish a reputation for product quality, which presumably would increase customer willingness to pay. Fisman, Hall, and Nair (2006) suggest a signaling model whereby a firm with a high-quality product uses philanthropy to signal its aversion to depreciating quality, thereby generating trust with the consumer. They set out testable implications that predict a positive relationship between profits and corporate giving only in competitive industries and in cases where firms can use philanthropy to signal their type. This reasoning is similar to the Klein and Leffler (1981) bonding argument in that the expenditure is akin to brand name advertising. The challenge is to explain why building a brand name with giving is a more efficient a way to signal than alternative ways to assure quality.

Related to building a reputation for selling high-quality products or services, studies establish that firms lose market value when information is revealed about possible firm misdeeds such as fraud allegations, information about product recalls, oil spills, and other types of environmental law infractions. For example, Karpoff, Lott, and Wehrly (2005) study the reputational costs of environmental standard infractions. The findings of large losses in value imply that firms may want to find ways to repair their reputations, including, as Williams and Barrett (2000) argue, by making visible philanthropic gifts. Some studies investigate this possibility. For example, Williams and Barrett find that the positive relationship between philanthropy and a survey-based reputation measure is stronger for companies that have a track record of violating Environmental Protection Agency (EPA) and Occupational Safety and Health Administration (OSHA) regulations. Consistent with this, Chen, Patten, and Roberts (2008) find that levels of corporate giving are higher among those companies with the lowest rankings on the KLD index for environment issues and product safety. Gan (2005) finds a significant relationship between governmental scrutiny, proxied by court cases, and corporate giving rates. However, whether giving more to charity to restore firm reputation is necessarily value-enhancing behavior is unclear. It may reflect agency costs if managers view philanthropy as guilt payments for their misdeeds rather than investments in reputation that translate into increased shareholder value.

Another mechanism by which philanthropy could increase firm value is to reduce labor costs, other things constant, by catering to employee tastes for working for a philanthropic firm, implying that employees of such firms would work for lower salaries. Alternatively, a culture of philanthropy may engender employee *esprit de corps* and increase productivity per dollar of wages. A few studies examine the relationship between firms' social performance, which includes charitable giving, and prospective employees' perception of the attractiveness of the employer. Vaidyanathan (2008) provides a discussion of these studies. The evidence is mixed, however, and does not directly address the question of how charitable giving may affect the perception of the firm as an employer, or whether employees of philanthropic for-profit firms accept lower wages, indicating their preference for working for firms with greater social awareness.

The ultimate concern of studies of giving and firm performance is whether corporate giving enhances shareholder wealth. Many studies address aspects of this issue, but the results are not dispositive. For example, Margolis, Elfenbein, and Walsh (2007) conduct a meta-analysis of studies examining the relationship between measures of CSR and corporate financial performance (CFP). They note that researchers typically use two measures of CFP: (1) accounting-based measures such as return on assets (ROA) or return on equity (ROE), and (2) market-based measures such as stock returns. Researchers also use hybrid measures such as Tobin's Q. The authors point out that studies vary by whether they adopt contemporaneous measures of CSR and CFP, employ lagged measures, and hypothesize a particular direction of causality. That is, good financial performance could lead to more philanthropy as it is more affordable for a firm that is doing well. But, philanthropy could also lead to improved financial performance. Margolis et al. report on 13 studies that examine the relationship between CFP and CSR. Despite mixed results, the studies generally find a positive effect, which is stronger when measuring CFP before the philanthropic giving than when concurrently measuring it. Studies using accounting measures show larger effects than those using market-based measures. The authors conclude, as do Seifert et al. (2004), that slack resources promote generosity towards charitable endeavors, which is consistent with agency cost explanations.

Some of the ambiguity in the findings about the relationship between CFP and CSR may be explained by the possibility that the relationship is nonlinear.

For example, Barnett and Solomon (2006) and Wang, Choi, and Li (2008) contend that the relationship between philanthropy and financial performance may be curvilinear. Wang et al. hypothesize that this relationship will vary with the level of industry dynamism (a sales volatility measure). Using monetary and nonmonetary giving as well as a matched-sample technique (by sales and industry), they find evidence that when interacted with a measure of dynamism, giving has a positive effect on lagged measures of ROA and Tobin's Q. Consistent with a U-shaped relationship, they find diminishing returns to giving.

Using a large sample of U.S. public companies from 1989 through 2000, Lev, Petrovits, and Radhakrishan (2010) examine the causality issue by regressing growth in corporate philanthropy on sales growth. Applying Granger causality tests, they conclude that charitable contributions are significantly associated with future revenue, whereas the association between revenue and future contributions is only marginally significant. The results are particularly pronounced for goods where individual consumers are the predominant customers. The authors also find a positive relationship between contributions and customer satisfaction. The evidence suggests that philanthropy, under certain circumstances, furthers firms' economic objectives of increasing sales. However, even if sales respond positively to corporate philanthropy, the result is not necessarily higher profit. They do not address the question of whether a link exists between giving and enhanced firm value.

Chai (2010) uses a panel data set of 1,017 publically-listed Korean firms. In Korea, unlike the United States, firms are required to identify their contributions in their accounting disclosures. He shows that larger firms with higher advertising intensity and lower export intensity give more, suggesting that charitable donations are both strategic and discretionary. Chai also finds a positive relationship between charitable donations and foreign ownership. However, he does not find a significant effect of philanthropy on firm financial performance.

Not surprisingly, the results regarding the relationship between firm philanthropy and performance have been inconclusive. Corporations spend only a small percentage of their income on giving programs. Thus, the effects of philanthropy are unlikely to be large enough to be detected in stock returns or changes in firm value. Even if some studies show correlations between giving and performance, overcoming the causality issue is difficult. Hence, the challenge that results may be due to omitting a variable that is positively correlated with performance. McWilliams and Siegel (2000) explain that the relationship between corporate philanthropy and financial performance is possibly spurious if R&D is not included as a control. Similar arguments apply to advertising. Other important issues that are difficult to overcome involve measurement, sample selection, missing accounting data, endogeneity of key variables, and reverse causality.

Recap of Findings

Some common themes emerge from studying the determinants of giving and the impact of giving. Charitable giving is positively associated with larger firms, larger and more diverse boards of directors, and those with higher R&D-to-sales ratios, higher advertising-to-sales ratios, and higher Tobin's Q measures. Giving is inversely related to leverage and to the percentage of shares held by blockholders.

The evidence suggests that giving may be causally related to sales for some firms but no study has established a definitive causal link to financial performance. Some findings suggest that better-performing firms give more to charity. Overall, the results suggest that enhanced financial performance is not the overriding concern of managers when making contributions. Instead, most evidence points to the prevalence of agency costs in corporate giving. Managers and directors and perhaps even some large shareholders are in positions to pursue their own interests with these programs. Still, although perhaps not shown on the bottom line, the evidence cannot refute the notion that some firms align their philanthropy with an underlying strategy and may be successful at leveraging their giving to differentiate their product or work environment.

Data and Methodological Issues

Data on corporate philanthropy are hard to obtain. Most studies use hand-collected databases that merge several sources of information. Even estimates of aggregate giving vary by reporting organization because several organizations attempt to track giving, but each uses a different method and sampling technique. Generally, researchers survey individual firms but report findings in a company-blind aggregated format. Because most survey only large firms, a dearth of data exists on privately-held firms and smaller organizations such as law firms. Philanthropy is correlated with advertising and R&D, but a firm's financial statements do not include advertising and R&D unless they are material. Hence, most panel or cross-sectional studies either assume that if a firm reports nothing for advertising or R&D, the actual expenditure is zero. Studies may also exclude those firms that do not report advertising or R&D, which creates another form of bias and reduces the sample size. Finally, studies adopt varying approaches for including or excluding in-kind gifts when measuring corporate giving. As Seifert et al. (2004) and Brown et al. (2006) point out, there are self-reporting valuation issues. Further, these types of gifts can serve instrumental purposes such as tax avoidance, marketing, or the disposal of obsolete inventory and are not necessarily reflective of philanthropy per se.

SUMMARY AND CONCLUSIONS

Corporate philanthropy is controversial in several respects. First, on a philosophical level, some economists and social thinkers argue that corporations are not well-suited for addressing social problems. Some view addressing such problems as a breach of a fiduciary responsibility to shareholders. Why not allow shareholders to use their own discretion and direct their own charitable contributions? Related to this argument is the concern that business leaders are neither positioned nor particularly well-suited for solving social problems. Second, no compelling body of evidence points to charitable giving as having a positive impact on firm performance. This is not surprising as firm managers may have other motives for giving. Further, the effect may be undetectable, given that philanthropy is a tiny fraction of firm profits, and an even smaller fraction of revenue. Third, if corporate giving does reflect agency costs (the evidence is more compelling in this regard), how could shareholders guard against inappropriate use of funds? Fourth, some evidence indicates that firms can create a competitive advantage with their charitable giving programs. Yet, not all customers or all employees are likely to be willing to "pay" for corporate philanthropy. Without a specific mechanism for how the philanthropy translates into value for shareholders, determining whether corporate giving is generally warranted is unclear. Perhaps a sensible approach for ensuring alignment of business goals and philanthropy is to call for managers and directors to be specific about what they expect from their philanthropic spending. In this way, the philanthropy can be evaluated by whether the firm is achieving its expected results and milestones.

DISCUSSION QUESTIONS

1. Identify the early historical reasons for business firm participation in philanthropy. How have those motivations changed over time?

2. Should a firm make contributions to a charity when shareholders may prefer to receive dividends and make their own philanthropic decisions? Explain why or why not.

3. Based on empirical studies reviewed in this chapter, identify evidence that is consistent with the value enhancement hypothesis and the agency cost hypothesis.

4. What variables are related to the choice of firms to give to charity and what are the signs of those relationships?

5. Identify the data and methodological challenges for researchers analyzing the impact of corporate philanthropy on firm performance. What is the status of the research?

REFERENCES

A. P. Smith Mfg. Co. v. Barlow, 98 A. 2d 581—NJ: Supreme Court. 1953.

Adams, Mike, and Philip Hardwick. 1998. "An Analysis of Corporate Donations: United Kingdom Evidence." *Journal of Management Studies* 35:5, 641–654.

Amato, Louis H., and Christie H. Amato. 2007. "The Effects of Firm Size and Industry on Corporate Giving." *Journal Business Ethics* 72:3, 229–241.

Barnett, Michael, and Robert Solomon. 2006. "Beyond Dichotomy: The Curvilinear Relationship between Social Responsibility and Financial Performance." *Strategic Management Journal* 27:11, 1101–1122.

Bartkus, Barbara R., Sara A. Morris, and Bruce Seifert. 2002. "Governance and Corporate Philanthropy: Restraining Robin Hood?" *Business and Society* 41:3, 319–349.

Boatsman, John, and Sanjay Gupta. 1996. "Taxes and Corporate Charity: Empirical Evidence from Micro-level Panel Data." *National Tax Journal* 49:2, 193–213.

Brammer, Stephen, and Andrew Millington. 2006. "Firm Size, Organizational Visibility and Corporate Philanthropy: An Empirical Analysis." *Journal of Business Ethics* 15:1, 6–18.

Brown, William O., Eric Helland, and Janet Kiholm Smith. 2006. "Corporate Philanthropic Practices." *Journal of Corporate Finance* 12:5, 855–877.

Carnegie, Andrew. 1889. "The Gospel of Wealth." University of Wisconsin Archives. Available at http://us.history.wisc.edu/hist102/pdocs/carnegie_wealth.pdf.

Chai, Dominic H. 2010. "Firm Ownership and Philanthropy." Working Paper No. 400, Center for Business Research, University of Cambridge.

Chen, Jennifer, Dennis Patten, and Robin Roberts. 2008. "Corporate Charitable Contributions: A Corporate Social Performance or Legitimate Strategy?" *Journal of Business Ethics* 82:1, 131–144.

Conference Board. 2009. *The 2009 Corporate Contributions Report.* New York: The Conference Board, Inc.

Drucker, Peter F. 1962. *The New Society.* New York: Harper & Row.

Drucker, Peter F. 2001. *The Essential Drucker.* New York: Harper Collins.

Economic Report of the President. 2011. Washington, D.C.: Government Printing Office.

Eells, Richard. 1956. *Corporate Giving in a Free Society.* New York: Harper & Bros.

Fisman, Ray, Geoffrey Hall, and Vinay Nair. 2006. "A Model of Corporate Philanthropy." Working Paper, Columbia University, Graduate School of Business, and University of Pennsylvania, Wharton School.

Friedman, Milton. 1963. *Capitalism and Freedom.* Chicago: University of Chicago Press.

Friedman, Milton. 1970. "The Social Responsibility of Business Is to Increase Its Profits." *New York Times Magazine* (September 13), 32–33.

Galaskiewicz, Joseph, and Ronald Burt. 1991. "Interorganziation Contagion in Corporate Philanthropy." *Administrative Science Quarterly* 36:1, 88–105.

Gan, Ailan. 2005. "The Impact of Public Scrutiny on Corporate Philanthropy." *Journal of Business Ethics* 69:3, 217–236.

Giving USA Foundation. 2011. *Giving USA 2011: The Annual Report on Philanthropy for the Year 2010.* Available at www.givingusareports.org.

Kahn, Faith Stevelman. 1997. "Pandora's Box: Managerial Discretion and the Problem of Corporate Philanthropy." *UCLA Law Review* 44:579, 479–676.

Karpoff, Jonathan M., John R. Lott, and Eric W. Wehrly. 2005. "The Reputational Penalties for Environmental Violations: Empirical Evidence." *Journal of Law and Economics* 68:2, 653–675.

Klein, Benjamin, and Keith B. Leffler. 1981. "The Role of Market Forces in Assuring Contractual Performance." *Journal of Political Economy* 89:4, 615–641.

Lankford, John. 1964. *Congress and the Foundations in the Twentieth Century.* River Falls, WI: Wisconsin State University.

Lev, Baruch, Christine Petrovits, and Suresh Radhakrishnan. 2010. "Is Doing Good Good for You? How Corporate Charitable Contributions Enhance Revenue Growth."*Strategic Management Journal* 31:2, 181–200.

Margolis, Joshua, Hillary Elfenbein, and James P. Walsh. 2007. "Does It Pay to Be Good? A Meta-Analysis and Redirection of Research on the Relationship between Corporate Social and Financial Performance." Working Paper, Harvard University, University of Michigan, and University of California.

Marshand, Roland. 1998. *Creating the Corporate Soul: The Rise of Public Relations and Corporate Imagery in American Big Business.* Berkeley: The University of California Press.

McWilliams, Abigail, and Donald Siegel. 2000. "Corporate Social Responsibility and Financial Performance: Correlation or Misspecification." *Strategic Management Journal* 21:5, 603–609.

Miller, Geoffrey. 2009. "Narrative and Truth in Judicial Opinions: Corporate Charitable Giving Cases." Working Paper 09-56, New York University, School of Law.

Navarro, Peter. 1988. "Why Do Corporations Give to Charity?" *Journal of Business* 61:1, 66–93.

Porter, Michael, and Mark R. Kramer. 2002. "The Competitive Advantage of Corporate Philanthropy." *Harvard Business Review* 12:80, 5–16.

Rubin, Amir, and Amir Barnea. 2010. "Corporate Social Responsibility as a Conflict between Shareholders." *Journal of Business Ethics* 97:1, 71–86.

Seifert, Bruce, Sara A. Morris, and Barbara R. Bartkus. 2004. "Having, Giving and Getting: Slack Resources, Corporate Philanthropy, and Firm Financial Performance." *Business and Society* 43:2, 135–161.

Soskis, Benjamin J. 2010. "The Pre- and Early History of American Corporate Philanthropy." Working Paper No. 3, History of Corporate Responsibility Project, Minneapolis, MN: Center for Ethical Business Cultures, University of St. Thomas.

Vaidyanathan, Brandon. 2008. "Science of Generosity, Corporate Giving: A Literature Review." Working Paper, Center for the Study of Religion and Society, University of Notre Dame.

Varadarajan, P. Rajan, and Anil Menon. 1988. "Cause-Related Marketing: A Coalignment of Marketing Strategy and Corporate Philanthropy." *Journal of Marketing* 52:3, 58–74.

Wang, Heli, Jaepil Choi, and Jiatao Li. 2008. "Too Little or Too Much? Untangling the Relationship between Corporate Philanthropy and Firm Financial Performance." *Organization Science* 19:1, 143–159.

Wang, Jia, and Betty Coffey. 1992. "Board Composition and Corporate Philanthropy." *Journal of Business Ethics* 11:10, 771–778.

Webb, Natalie J. 1996. "Corporate Profits and Social Responsibility: Subsidization of Corporate Income under Charitable Giving Tax Laws." *Journal of Economics and Business* 48:4, 401–421.

Williams, Robert J., and Douglas J. Barrett. 2000. "Corporate Philanthropy, Criminal Activity, and Firm Reputation: Is There a Link?" *Journal of Business Ethics* 26:4, 341–350.

Wulfson, Myrna. 2001. "The Ethics of Corporate Social Responsibility and Philanthropic Ventures." *Journal of Business Ethics* 29:1, 135–145.

ABOUT THE AUTHOR

Janet Kiholm Smith is the Von Tobel Professor of Economics at Claremont McKenna College (CMC). She has been on the faculties of Arizona State University, University of Southern California, and Oberlin College. At CMC, she has served as the founding dean of the Robert Day School of Economics and Finance, chair of the Department of Economics, and director of the Financial Economics Institute. Current research interests are in the areas of financial economics and new venture economics. She is coauthor of *Entrepreneurial Finance: Strategy, Valuation and Deal Structure* (2011), Stanford University Press. Her publications have appeared in journals such as the *Journal of Finance*, *Journal of Financial & Quantitative Analysis*, *Journal of Corporate Finance*, *Journal of Law and Economics*, *Journal of Law, Economics & Organization*, and *Journal of Industrial Economics*. Professor Smith received a Ph.D. in economics from UCLA.

CHAPTER 19

Institutional Investor Activism

DIANE DEL GUERCIO
Associate Professor of Finance, University of Oregon

HAI TRAN
Finance Ph.D. Student, University of Oregon

INTRODUCTION

While much has been written about institutional investor activism in the corporate governance arena, much less is known about their advocacy activities in the realm of environmental and social issues. In fact, at least six survey articles summarize the voluminous research on corporate governance shareholder activism in the United States (Black 1997; Gillan and Starks 1998, 2007; Karpoff 2001; Romano 2001; Ferri 2011). Notably, most of the research surveyed in these articles appears in mainstream finance journals. In contrast, only Sjostrom (2008) surveys the social responsibility shareholder activism literature; she reports that of 34 studies, only one appears in a finance journal.

Yet many parallel and common issues arise when examining the role of institutional investors in both shareholder activism arenas. Two defining features of institutional investors have important implications for their potential to be effective shareholder activists. First, the fact that institutional investors often manage pools of assets on the order of billions of dollars implies that they tend to have sizable equity ownership stakes in individual companies and in the capital markets in general. As a result, they are potentially influential shareholders who are able to effect change at the companies in which they invest, and they are influential enough to command the attention of regulators or legislators to lobby for market-wide reforms. Second, institutional investors are financial fiduciaries who invest on the behalf of others and as a result, have a legal duty to invest in the best interests of their clients or beneficiaries. This traditionally means that activism can only be justified if clients specifically authorize it, or if the enhanced investment return is greater than any additional cost. While the early studies on corporate governance shareholder activism generally failed to find measurable valuation effects on target firms or on activist portfolios, the later evidence summarized in Ferri (2011) suggests that institutional activists have recently enjoyed much greater success. Evidence on how this success translates to institutional activism in the social responsibility arena, however, is sparse.

This chapter describes how institutional investors incorporate environmental, social, and governance (ESG) criteria into their investment and activism programs. A unifying theme is that socially responsible institutional investment and activist activity is best understood through the lens of their roles as fiduciaries and large investors. The chapter begins by first defining socially responsible investing as discussed in the literature and among practitioners, followed by an overview of the empirical evidence on institutional social activism activities. First, in the context of prodding individual companies to make operating changes or new disclosures, common tactics are discussed, such as engaging in dialogue with corporate management, submitting shareholder proposals to the corporate proxy statement, and participating in active and informed voting. Second, in promoting market-wide reforms, institutional activists have leveraged resources through joining investor networks to lobby the Securities and Exchange Commission (SEC) and Congress for regulatory change.

Using a comprehensive database, this chapter describes the nature of the shareholder proposals submitted by institutional investor sponsors over the period 1992 to 2010, highlighting the key sponsors, the most common actions requested and proposal topics, and measures of success in achieving activist goals. The patterns for institutional sponsors are compared to those of noninstitutional sponsors. Based on this analysis of historical trends and current developments, the chapter ends with a discussion of possible future directions for institutional investor social activism and for future research on their role and effectiveness.

HOW INSTITUTIONAL INVESTORS DEFINE SRI

A careful reading of the literature suggests that socially responsible investment (SRI) means different things to different people. In the United States, the SRI movement has its roots among religious investors who believed their capital should not fund companies that produce products considered immoral, such as tobacco or weapons, or that operate in unethical environments, such as South Africa in the apartheid era or Sudan today. Today, this is often labeled *ethical investing* or *negative screening* because "unethical companies" are excluded or screened from consideration for the portfolio. Constraining the investment universe can have negative implications for portfolio diversification and risk-adjusted performance (Geczy, Stambaugh, Levin 2005; Renneboog, Ter Horst, and Zhang 2008). Still, some investors are willing to sacrifice financial performance to achieve their ethical objectives. According to the Social Investment Forum Foundation Report (2010), negative screening is still a popular strategy among socially responsible asset managers. Consistent with this, Hong and Kacperczyk (2009) find that enough socially conscious investors screen out *sin stocks* to negatively affect their equilibrium pricing.

An emerging variety of SRI labeled *sustainable* or *responsible* investing is likely more appealing to fiduciary institutions. Kerste, Rosenbloom, Sikken, and Weda (2011, p. 157) define sustainable investing as "an investment approach that integrates long-term ESG criteria into investment and ownership decision-making with the objective of generating superior risk-adjusted financial returns." The purely financial motive behind the investment strategy distinguishes it from negative screening. The logic is that climate change, natural resource scarcity, public awareness and consumer sentiment, and potentially looming regulations have material economic and financial consequences for firms. Heal (2005) argues that firms taking actions to anticipate and minimize conflicts with society or stake-holders are consistent with a pure profit motive. For example, firms conflict with society when their social costs exceed their private costs, such as when their pro-duction processes pollute the air and water, or their products have long-term health consequences. Firms that can proactively address these issues and mini-mize societal conflicts can successfully deter costly regulation, mitigate litigation risk, and enhance their reputation with consumers who might consequently favor their products rather than boycott them.

In other words, responsible corporate management focused on long-term shareholder value should carefully consider these business risks. In turn, savvy investors should incorporate information on how well companies are managing these business risks much as they would any other value-relevant information. Some label this approach *positive screening* since investors evaluate companies on ESG criteria as part of their risk management and stock selection decisions. Edmans (2011) shows that applying a positive portfolio screen incorporating em-ployee satisfaction among a firm's workforce is associated with positive abnormal performance. His analysis shows that the market only incorporates the value of this intangible over time, suggesting a profit opportunity for investors who are first aware of its relation to firm profitability.

Social activism can be viewed using this framework as well. Whereas activism on corporate governance issues prods firms to minimize agency conflicts, activism on social issues encourages firms to minimize societal conflicts, with both varieties potentially fully consistent with a profit motive on the part of the activist.

SHAREHOLDER PROXY PROPOSALS AS ACTIVISM TOOLS

Submitting shareholder proposals for inclusion in the corporate proxy statement is one of the most common tools used by institutional investors to push firms to make changes in policies and strategies. Rule 14a-8 of the Securities and Exchange Act of 1934 allows any shareholder owning at least $2,000 in market value or 1 percent of the company's securities for at least one year to include a specific request and 500-word supporting statement in the corporate proxy. Thus, shareholder proposals are included in proxy materials and sent to all shareholders at company expense, a feature that makes them particularly low-cost and appealing to activists. However, ownership requirements for submitting proposals necessarily imply that this tool is incompatible with negative screening.

Upon receiving a shareholder proposal, corporate managers have three op-tions: (1) petition the SEC to allow the proposal to be omitted from the proxy, (2) implement the requested action to the satisfaction of the activists so that they voluntarily withdraw the submitted proposal, or (3) include the proposal to be voted on by shareholders at the annual meeting. By law, even proposals that re-ceive a majority of shareholder vote support are only advisory and need not be implemented by the board of directors. Critics point to the nonbinding nature of shareholder proposals as a reason to be skeptical about their effectiveness in eliciting companies to change. Still, even the early corporate governance activism literature that failed to find valuation effects recognizes the potential for this tool to begin productive dialogues between targeted firms and investors, raise awareness of issues of broad importance, and possibly lead to spillover effects on nontargeted firms that proactively adopt policies to avoid future scrutiny from activists. These ancillary effects are, of course, much harder to measure.

In about 10 to 20 percent of submitted proposals, companies are successful in convincing the SEC to issue a *no-action letter*, which allows them to omit a proposal from the proxy statement. By far the most common reason for omission is that the subject of the proposal involves an *ordinary business decision* relating to the company's day-to-day operations, which are allowed to remain under managers' discretion. An important exception is if the proposal topic is of broad public policy importance or, in the language of the SEC, the issue "transcends day-to-day business matters" (SEC Exchange Act Release No. 40018 5/28/98, 1998).

Brown (2011) argues that the particular topics that constitute public policy importance are subject to SEC staff interpretation and, as a result, evolve over time as the political climate changes. For example, shareholder proposals calling for shareholder approval of equity executive compensation plans were considered ordinary business and thereby excludable before 2002, but allowed thereafter on the grounds that the issue was the subject of widespread public debate (SEC Staff Legal Bulletin No. 14A 7/12/02, 2002). Similarly, the SEC changed its stance on proposals requesting that companies assess the risk they face from major environmental and public health issues, no longer considering this topic ordinary business after October 2009 (SEC Staff Legal Bulletin No. 14E 10/27/09, 2009). Not surprisingly, SEC no-action letter trends affect the observed trends in proposal topics that come to a vote. For example, Ertimur, Ferri, and Muslu (2011) show a jump in compensation-related shareholder proposals after 2002.

The focus of this chapter is confined to activity in the United States. However, Cziraki, Renneboog, and Szilagyi (2010) report that shareholder proposals are not a major tool in other countries. They find that corporate governance shareholder proposals in the United Kingdom and in Continental Europe are rare, and even rarer on social issues. The authors identify only 21 social responsibility proposals across 43 country-years.

SOCIAL RESPONSIBILITY PROPOSALS SUBMITTED BY INSTITUTIONAL INVESTORS

The sections below provide an overview and analysis of how activist institutions have used shareholder proposals on social responsibility topics as a tool to promote corporate reforms. Besides providing an historical context and review of the literature, the chapter contains analysis of a comprehensive sample of social responsibility proposals from 1992 to 2010.

Historical Background on Social Responsibility Shareholder Proposals

While Gillan and Starks (2007) trace the earliest shareholder proposals in the United States to the 1940s, social responsibility proposals did not become an important tool for activists until the 1970s. From the 1940s through the 1980s, sponsoring shareholder proposals was the nearly exclusive realm of "gadflies," namely, individual investors such as the Gilbert brothers and Evelyn Davis, who each sponsored hundreds of proposals at target firms. Not until the 1980s did institutional investors, such as the California Public Employees' Retirement System (CalPERS) and other public pension funds, begin to increasingly use the shareholder proposal tool.

Glac (2010) provides an historical account of the important early victories for social activists in both the court room and the boardroom against two of the largest corporations of the day. First, a landmark 1970 federal appeals court decision ruled in favor of activists that Dow Chemical must include on their proxy a proposal calling for them to cease manufacturing napalm (*Medical Committee for Human Rights v. SEC* 1970). This decision, along with a flurry of social proposal submissions, prompted the SEC to broaden the scope of allowed proposal topics. Second, a group of lawyers organized the Project for Corporate Responsibility and sponsored nine social issue proposals, two of which shareholders voted on at General Motor's 1970 annual meeting. While both proposals received less than 3 percent vote support, the campaign received enormous publicity, including more than 100 reporters covering GM's annual meeting. Despite the low vote support, General Motors ultimately complied with the requests in the two proposals.

Proffitt and Spicer (2006) provide a detailed analysis of the early use of social shareholder proposals on issues of labor and human rights such as apartheid in South Africa. Using a comprehensive sample from 1969 to 2003, they report that religious groups, such as the Interfaith Council on Corporate Responsibility (ICCR), were early adopters and innovators in using proposals as a tool for social change, as well as the most dominant sponsor type, accounting for nearly all proposals on human and labor rights before 1984. Public pension funds enter the scene in 1984 and, as shown in the following sections, remain one of the dominant champions of social issues to this day.

Data Source

The social responsibility shareholder proposal sample used in this chapter is originally from the Investor Responsibility Research Center (IRRC), now available through RiskMetrics. The database contains details on shareholder proposals that are omitted, withdrawn, or voted on at corporate annual meetings from 1992 through 2010, including target firm name, proposal topic, and sponsor name(s). The database also contains the reason for omission for omitted proposals (e.g., ordinary business and the sponsor did not meet ownership requirements) and the vote outcome for proposals that came to a vote. The 1992 through 1996 sample is from Tkac (2006), as the RiskMetrics sample begins in 1997.

A total of 5,818 social responsibility proposals are identified over this 19-year period of which institutional investors sponsor 2,149, or 37 percent. Excluded in these totals are 86 proposals that are classified as *anti-socially responsible*. For example, proposals sponsored by the Free Enterprise Action fund, which states that its mission is to challenge companies that support social causes, are excluded. In generating proposal counts, co-sponsored proposals are adjusted to avoid double-counting. Exhibit 19.1 shows the time trend of proposal submissions by institutional versus noninstitutional sponsors. While the individuals and religious

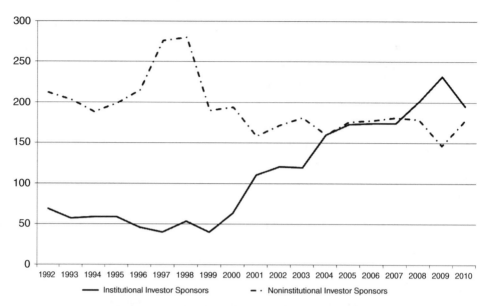

Exhibit 19.1   Socially Responsible Shareholder Proposal Submissions

This exhibit provides an annual count of all socially responsible SEC Rule 14a-8 shareholder proposals from the 1992 to 2010 proxy seasons. The totals include all proposals submitted to target firms for placement on the proxy, including proposals that were subsequently omitted due to an SEC rule violation or withdrawn by the proposal sponsor. In generating proposal counts, co-sponsored proposals are adjusted to avoid double-counting. Institutional investor sponsors include public pension funds, union pension funds, socially responsible mutual funds, and investment advisers. Noninstitutional investors include individuals, religious organizations, and nongovernmental organizations (e.g., Sierra Club). The data from 1997 to 2010 are from RiskMetrics (originally from the Investor Responsibility Research Center), while the sample from 1992 to 1996 is from Tkac (2006).

organizations that comprise the majority of noninstitutional sponsors have been prolific throughout, institutional investor activity began in earnest in 2001 and even exceeds that of noninstitutional sponsors in recent years. The next section provides more details about these sponsors.

Key Institutional Investor Players and Their Motivations for Activism

The sponsors of social policy shareholder proposals can be categorized into four distinct institutional investor categories: public pension funds, union pension funds, socially responsible mutual funds, and investment advisers; and three noninstitutional investor categories: individuals, religious organizations, and nongovernmental organizations (NGOs) (e.g., Sierra Club). While some religious organizations might be categorized as institutional because they are investing pension or endowment assets, they are included in the noninstitutional category for two reasons. First, the corporate governance activism literature has categorized them either separately or pooled with individuals (Gillan and Starks 2000). Second, the current interest is in understanding the activism of institutional investors whose

Exhibit 19.2 Number of Socially Responsible Shareholder Proposals by Sponsor (1992 to 2010)

Sponsor Name	1992 to 2000	2001 to 2010	Total	% of Category
New York City Pension Funds	196	584	780	86.0
Minnesota State Board of Investment	25	31	56	6.2
Connecticut Retirement Plans and Trust Funds	0	32	32	3.5
All other public pension funds (N = 7)	2	37	39	4.3
Total public pension funds	223	684	907	100.0
AFL-CIO	3	82	85	21.4
LongView Collective Investment Fund	30	32	62	15.6
International Brotherhood of Teamsters	5	48	53	13.4
All other union pension funds (N = 25)	97	100	197	49.6
Total union pension funds	135	262	397	100.0
Calvert Group	12	192	204	48.0
Domini Social Investments	9	93	102	24.0
Green Century	4	57	61	14.4
All other SRI mutual funds (N = 7)	19	39	58	13.6
Total SRI mutual funds	44	381	425	100.0
Walden Asset Management	11	153	164	26.5
Trillium Asset Management	53	116	169	27.3
Harrington Investments	22	105	127	20.5
All other SRI investment advisers (N = 10)	38	121	159	25.7
Total SRI investment advisers	124	495	619	100.0

This exhibit summarizes submitted proposals by sponsor and time period for four institutional investor sponsor types. In each sponsor type category, summary information is provided in addition to a listing of the top three individual sponsors. The final column provides the percentage of all proposals in that sponsor-type category represented by the sponsor in that row. For this exhibit, no adjustment is made for co-sponsored proposals. In the case of a co-sponsored proposal, the proposal for each co-sponsor is counted.

primary focus is presumably on financial performance, rather than on investors with an a priori focus on nonfinancial goals. Readers interested in social activism by religious groups can refer to Proffitt and Spicer (2006), Tkac (2006), and Logsdon and Van Buren (2008, 2009). The remainder of this chapter focuses on the institutional sponsors.

Exhibit 19.2 lists the number of proposals over the periods 1992 to 2000 and 2001 to 2010 for each of the four institutional investor types, as well as the names and number of proposals for the top three sponsors within each type. Two patterns quickly emerge. Proposal activity has increased dramatically over time for each of the four sponsor types, and only a few sponsors are responsible for the bulk of this activity. A comparison of columns two and three shows that the most dramatic increase in proposal activity is for the socially responsible mutual funds, where an eight-fold increase occurs in the more recent period.

Proposal activity is highly concentrated. In three of the four types, the top three sponsors account for between 74 percent and 96 percent of all proposals. Notably, the New York City Pension funds account for 86 percent of all activity among public pension funds and the Calvert Family of Funds account for 48 percent of all

SRI mutual fund activity. By comparison, the labor union pension fund category is less concentrated. The top sponsor, the AFL-CIO, accounts for only 21 percent of all labor union proposals, and the top three accounts for only 50 percent. Consistent with this, there are only 10 unique public pension fund sponsors over the 19-year period and 28 unique labor union pension funds.

Public and Labor Union Pension Funds

Given their sheer size, pension funds are important players in the capital markets. According to the U.S. Census Bureau, the 100 largest public pension funds have $2.7 trillion in assets as of March 2011, including $896 billion in domestic equities. Private pension funds control another $4.7 trillion, including $2 trillion in defined-benefit plans (U.S. Department of Labor 2010). Pension funds are also important from the standpoint that they represent the retirement assets of millions of beneficiaries who rely on the prudent investment of those assets for their future security and well-being. A traditional defined-benefit pension plan places the decision-making power with the pension trustees, who are charged with a fiduciary duty to invest the pension assets prudently and in the best interests of the beneficiaries. The Employee Retirement Income Security Act (ERISA) governs private pension plans, while state or local law governs public pension plans. Fiduciary standards for trustees of both types tend to be similar.

A long-standing legal issue is which investment practices are consistent with prudent investments in the best interests of plan beneficiaries. The issue of whether SRI and activism are consistent with properly fulfilling fiduciary duties is currently an open question. No clear consensus exists on whether trustees can incorporate ESG factors into their investment decisions if doing so is detrimental to financial performance. The Department of Labor in the 1998 "Calvert Letter" has taken the view that trustees can consider collateral benefits such as in a SRI, but the investment return must still be commensurate to alternative investments having similar risks (U.S. Department of Labor Advisory Opinion 1998-04A 1998). Given both the legal uncertainty surrounding whether SRI is compatible with fiduciary duties and the size of the asset pool affected by these legal issues, advocates have not surprisingly formed at least two working groups in 2005 and 2009 to study and report on these matters (United Nations Environment Program Finance Initiative 2005, 2009).

If SRI could reliably be justified on a risk-adjusted return basis, ESG considerations would not conflict with beneficiaries' best interests. However, the empirical link between financial performance and SRI by either firms or portfolio managers is weak, and therefore remains an open question, as the surveys by Margolis, Elfenbein, and Walsh (2009), Renneboog et al. (2008), and Capelle-Blancard and Monjon (2011) attest. Absent a purely financial justification, Barber (2007) and Richardson (2010) suggest that SRI may still be appropriate for pension plans if it reflects the preferences of the beneficiaries. Richardson provides a discussion of practical obstacles to implementation, such as how to assess beneficiary preferences and what to do if not all beneficiaries agree on a policy.

In the sample of social proposal sponsors included in this chapter, private pension plans are notably absent. Instead, public pension funds and union pension funds dominate the list of social proposal sponsors, much as they dominate the list of corporate governance proposal sponsors. The literature has hypothesized reasons for this that can apply to the SRI context as well. Hess (2007) provides a summary of these arguments. Some contend that activism is most suited to these two types because they tend to passively index more than other institutional investors and therefore cannot simply sell stocks that they believe are poorly managed or have governance problems. A related point is that these types tend to be *universal owners* that naturally internalize society-wide (market-wide) issues because they are long-term investors who own highly diversified portfolios. Others point to the fact that public and union pension funds are unconcerned with antagonizing corporate management through activism because they do not provide financial services to corporations, unlike banks, investment banks, insurance companies, and investment advisers. Similarly, corporate pension fund trustees may be reluctant to antagonize their fellow corporate managers.

An alternative view is that public and union pension funds pursue activism because their trustees have personal or political motives, and the nature of defined-benefit plans with dispersed uninformed beneficiaries allows trustees to place their own preferences ahead of beneficiaries (Romano 1993, 2001; Woidtke 2002). For example, populist bashing of chief executive officers (CEOs) or advocating a hot-button social issue such as diversity may not lead to performance improvements for the fund, but it may lead to media attention for an activist who has an eye toward a future run at political office. A similar argument holds for union pension funds. They may place current union member collective bargaining goals ahead of beneficiary interests.

The sample included in this chapter finds that New York City (NYC) pension funds are by far the most prolific sponsor of social proposals throughout the period 1992 to 2010. The NYC pension funds are headed by the NYC Comptroller, an elected city official, and governed by a board of trustees that has a majority of political appointees rather than beneficiary-elected representatives. Interestingly, all of the former NYC Comptrollers since the 1970s have run for either NYC mayor or for the U.S. Senate. Romano (1993) argues that a board dominated by political appointees infuses politics into pension fund management, and empirically shows that public pension plan performance is inversely related to the percentage of political appointees on pension boards. Barber (2007) makes a similar argument and points to CalPERS' divestment of tobacco stocks in 2000 as politically motivated and inconsistent with maximizing beneficiary wealth. In sum, while the literature has discussed many possible motives behind labor and union pension fund activism, definitively assessing their true motives in an empirical manner is difficult.

Investment Advisers and Mutual Funds (Asset Managers)

Investment advisers and mutual funds share the characteristic that they provide portfolio management services to clients who have the ability to hire and fire them at will, as well as to mandate any special investment considerations. For example, the client can specify that the manager can only invest in small-capitalization growth stocks. Or the client can mandate that the manager not invest in companies that manufacture tobacco products or weapons. Clients with millions of dollars to invest, such as a wealthy individual or pension plan, can hire an investment adviser and contractually stipulate specific investment guidelines. Small investors

can identify a mutual fund or exchange traded fund (ETF) that states in its prospectus the investment principles that match their own preferences or values. The
SEC monitors whether funds comply with the investment policies stated in their
prospectuses. In 2008, Pax World paid a $500,000 penalty for purchasing stocks of
companies that manufacture alcohol, tobacco, and gambling products, in violation
of its prospectus (SEC Administrative Proceeding No. IA-2761 7/30/08, 2008).

Unlike the case for pension plan trustees, no legal ambiguity exists for investment managers to incorporate ESG principles into their investment decisions, as
long as their clients approve of the strategy. This effectively means that expected
superior investment returns are not a necessary condition for pursuing ESG principles or activism strategies. Some investors are perfectly willing to accept lower
financial returns for advancing positive social changes or better aligning their
personal values with their investment choices. Thus, from the perspective of asset
managers, SRI investing is inherently client driven. Survey and anecdotal evidence
certainly support this view. For example, in a 2010 survey of 107 managers conducted by the Social Investment Forum Foundation (2010), 85 percent listed client
demand as the reason for incorporating ESG factors into their investment strategy, while 60 percent stated a desire to bring about societal benefits. Wen (2009)
reports a similar finding in a survey of European asset managers and analysts
(CSR Europe 2003).

Sponsoring shareholder proposals could serve as a credible signal to investors
that the manager is firmly committed to ESG principles, and therefore could help
market the manager's services to its target clientele. Using a comprehensive sample
of social proposals, the authors of this chapter identify 23 unique investment manager sponsors. Using the managers' web sites to gather background information
on their investment strategies, the authors find that all 23 of the proposal sponsors
market themselves as specializing in SRI. The results show that conventional asset
managers sponsor no social proposals and rarely sponsor corporate governance
shareholder proposals.

The absence of mainstream investment managers among proposal sponsors
is consistent with a motivation among SRI managers that this activity will attract
assets from a clientele with social concerns, rather than by a belief that activism will
enhance portfolio returns. Some contend, however, that the real reason investment
managers avoid activism is that they do not want to alienate target companies that
might potentially hire them to invest their defined-benefit pension assets or 401(k)
plans (Black and Coffee 1994; Taub 2009). Along these same lines, mainstream
investment advisers may avoid activism because their target clientele do not reward this activity. Overall, the same types of institutional investors are important
advocates for both corporate governance and social issues, suggesting that similar
forces spur their activism in both arenas.

Contents of the Proposals

Heal (2005) provides a useful framework for understanding economic motivations
behind social responsibility activism. He views corporate social responsibility as
important whenever inherent conflicts occur between the firm and society, which
he contends arise under two conditions: when the firm's social costs exceed private
costs such as pollution, or when disagreements exist over what is fair, such as

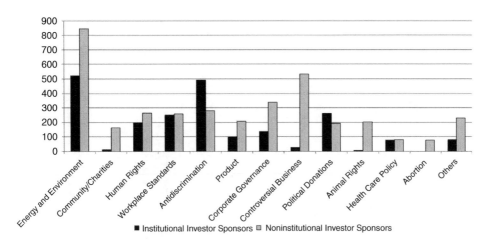

Exhibit 19.3 Socially Responsible Shareholder Proposal Topics (1992 to 2010)

This exhibit shows the range of topics sponsored by institutional and noninstitutional investors during the sample period. Typical proposals for each category are given in parentheses following the category name: energy and environment (issue sustainability report and endorse Ceres principles); community/charities (issue community reinvestment report and disclose charitable contributions); human rights (adopt human rights policy; no purchase of forced labor products); workplace standards (implement International Labor Organization standards and third-party monitoring); antidiscrimination (adopt sexual orientation antibias policy and implement MacBride principles); product (report on genetically-engineered food); corporate governance (report board diversity and link executive pay to social criteria); controversial business (divest tobacco holdings and report on foreign military sales); political donations (disclose political donations); animal rights (stop animal testing), health care policy (adopt principles of health care reform); and abortion (do not contribute to abortion providers). For this exhibit, co-sponsored proposals are adjusted to avoid double-counting.

sweatshop labor conditions. As mentioned earlier, firms that successfully minimize these conflicts with society can reap benefits that enhance performance. Thus, profit-minded investors can prod firms to pay more attention to addressing these conflicts and thus avoid future problems. The chapter now examines the issues and specific requests of activists using shareholder proposals, and analyzes whether they focus on minimizing conflicts between firms and society.

Issues Addressed and Actions Requested in the Proposals

Exhibit 19.3 places each shareholder proposal topic into one of 13 issue categories and provides a summary of the number of proposals in each category that institutional investors and noninstitutions sponsor. The top two issues of institutional sponsors are energy and environment and antidiscrimination, both consistent with institutions prodding firms to pay greater attention to potential business risks. Climate change can lead to major disruptions to company operations, and discriminatory practices have the potential for costly lawsuits. While institutional investors and noninstitutional investors share an interest in sponsoring proposals on energy and environmental matters, the second-most-popular issue for noninstitutional sponsors is controversial business, such as tobacco and firearms. This issue, which is related to the production of unethical products that some socially responsible

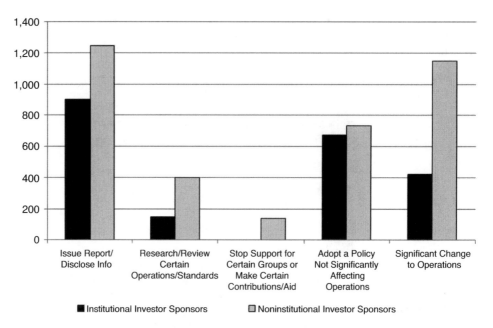

Exhibit 19.4   Actions Requested by Sponsors (1992 to 2010)
This exhibit reports the types of action requested by institutional and noninstitutional investors during the sample period of 1992 to 2010. Institutional investor sponsors did not submit any proposals in the category of "stop support for certain groups or make certain contributions/aid." Co-sponsored proposals are adjusted to avoid double-counting.

investors use as negative screens, ranks only tenth in the list of issues advocated by institutional investors.

Exhibit 19.4 places the actions requested in social policy proposals into five categories and summarizes them. Across both institutional and noninstitutional sponsors, the most common action requested is to issue a report or disclose information to investors. Also similar across both investor types is a request for firms to adopt a policy not substantially affecting their operations, which is primarily antidiscrimination proposals asking companies to adopt sexual orientation antibias policies or to implement the MacBride principles, which encourage fair treatment for minority employees. Institutions differ substantially from noninstitutional sponsors regarding proposals requesting firms to make major changes to operations. A common example for this request is under the topic of workplace standards, where sponsors typically ask firms to implement the International Labor Organization standards and use third-party monitoring. Finally, a category where institutions differ from noninstitutions is under proposals requesting that the firm stop supporting certain named groups including abortion providers and political campaigns. There are 140 such requests from noninstitutional sponsors, but not a single request from an institution.

Success Rate of the Proposals

An old question in the shareholder activism literature is how to measure success. Both researchers and activists alike have applied various definitions but no broad consensus has emerged. At the opposite extreme, most agree that a clear failure is when a company successfully petitions the SEC to omit the shareholder proposal from its proxy statement.

This section provides a discussion of the definitions of success from the literature and applies them to the sample of proposals. One measure of success occurs when proposals come to a vote at the annual meeting and is measured by the percentage of votes cast in favor. Beyond the obvious show of support that a high percentage of votes conveys, vote support is important because SEC rules stipulate thresholds for a proposal to be resubmitted in subsequent years. In the first year, a proposal must receive at least 3 percent of votes in favor in order to be resubmitted the next year. The minimum threshold increases with subsequent submissions, eventually to the level of 10 percent in the third year and beyond. Gaining enough support for resubmission is considered a success for many shareholder activists, as it allows them to keep the issues alive and raise shareholder awareness. The current study finds that only 10 percent of submitted proposals are omitted because vote thresholds are not met. However, this does not capture the proposals not submitted because the sponsor is aware that it did not meet the SEC thresholds.

Over the sample period, the evidence finds increasing vote support in favor of social proposals, especially for those sponsored by institutional investors. Exhibit 19.5 shows the time trend in average vote support for proposals sponsored by institutions versus noninstitutions. For institution-sponsored proposals, the average support is 9.9 percent in 1992 and 25.8 percent in 2010. Not surprisingly, a comparison to corporate governance proposals reveals that social proposals garner much lower shareholder support. While the current study finds average vote support for social proposals of 10.5 percent in 2001, Renneboog and Szilagyi (2010) report an average level of vote support three-times higher (32.2 percent) for

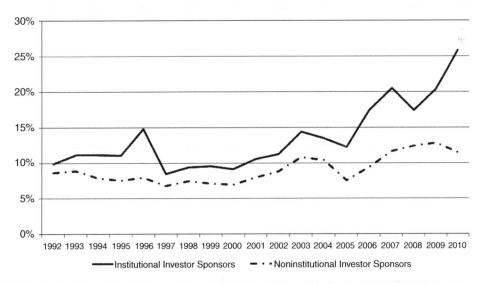

Exhibit 19.5 Average Vote Support for Socially Responsible Shareholder Proposals
This exhibit displays the trend in the average percentage of votes cast in favor of the shareholder proposal for proposals by institutional and by noninstitutional investor sponsors. In computing the average percentage vote support, a co-sponsored proposal is included once for a group if it is sponsored by at least one member of the group.

corporate governance shareholder proposals that same year. Similarly, while Renneboog and Szilagyi report that 27 percent of corporate governance shareholder proposals between 1996 and 2005 received majority vote support, the current study finds that less than 1 percent of social proposals do so, no matter which sample or sub-sample period is examined.

Another common definition of success is if the target firm makes the desired changes or at least some changes that move toward the activists' goals. Because proposals are nonbinding on the board of directors, proposals that pass with high vote support need not be implemented. However, several studies of corporate governance proposals find that majority vote support is associated with a significantly higher implementation rate (Thomas and Cotter 2007; Ertimur, Ferri, and Stubben 2010; Renneboog and Szilalgyi 2010). All three studies find that implementation rates have risen over time, suggesting that target firms are increasingly responsive to shareholder concerns. The current study finds that of the 20 social proposals that receive a majority of voter support, the board of directors implemented 14 (70 percent) within one year of the annual meeting. This compares with a 32.5 percent implementation rate between 1996 and 2005 reported by Renneboog and Szilagyi.

Although precisely determining the outcome is much more difficult for researchers, proposals that are not voted on but are instead withdrawn by the proposal sponsor are potentially highly successful. An activist may withdraw its proposal when the target firm demonstrates to the activist's satisfaction that it will take the necessary actions to address the issues raised in the proposal. Thus, issues may get resolved well before the annual meeting through private dialogue, prompting observers to label proposals that are included in the proxy statement as "failed negotiations." However, activists may also voluntarily withdraw their proposals because they anticipate an SEC omission or very low vote support. Thus, withdrawn proposals are not necessarily unqualified successes. Tkac (2006) investigates the outcomes of withdrawn proposals over the period 1992 to 2002, and is only able to obtain information on the outcomes of 35 percent of these proposals. Out of this smaller sample, 79 percent resulted in a concrete action by the target firm, and 19 percent led to a dialogue between the firm and the shareholder activist but no commitment to action. Given the high degree of target firm actions associated with these withdrawn proposals, Tkac maintains that the percentage of withdrawn proposals across all proposals is a good measure of activist success, and reports a 30 percent success rate.

Rojas, M'zali, Turcotte, and Merrigan (2009) question the relatively high success rate reported by Tkac (2006). They classify a withdrawn social proposal as a "success" only if they find an announcement by any party claiming that the proposal will be implemented. Of 657 withdrawn proposals from 1997 to 2004, they report that only 36 percent fall in this category, and most withdrawn proposals are due to activists conceding that their proposal is unlikely to survive SEC scrutiny or gain support from shareholders. Overall, the authors report that a success rate of 10 percent of all submitted social policy proposals better reflects proposals that are both withdrawn and implemented.

Although information on whether the target firms implemented the activists' requests for the withdrawn proposals is unavailable, the percentage of withdrawn and omitted proposals is used in the sample as rough estimates of activist success and failure. Not surprisingly, the results show substantial differences in these rates

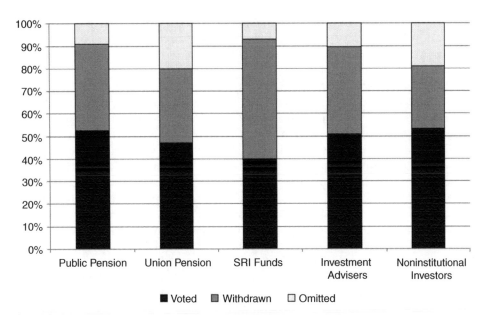

Exhibit 19.6 Distribution of Proposal Outcomes by Sponsor (1992 to 2010)
This exhibit illustrates the differences in proposal outcomes across sponsor types. For each sponsor type, the percentage of submitted proposals is reported that: (1) come to a vote at the annual meeting; (2) are voluntarily withdrawn by the sponsor before the annual meeting and therefore do not appear on the proxy; and (3) are allowed to be omitted from the proxy by the SEC. This exhibit excludes 196 proposals or 3 percent of the sample with other outcomes (e.g., not in proxy, not presented, and meeting cancelled). Co-sponsored proposals are not adjusted for double-counting.

across sponsor types, suggesting that institutional sponsors enjoy greater success as activists. For institutional sponsors, 40.2 percent of all proposals are withdrawn and 11.0 percent are omitted. In contrast, for noninstitutional sponsors, 27.7 percent of all proposals are withdrawn and 19.1 percent are omitted. Exhibit 19.6 summarizes the breakdown of omitted, withdrawn, and voted-on proposals by sponsor type. By this measure, SRI mutual funds are the most successful type, with the highest rate of withdrawal and the lowest rate of omission, while investment managers and public pension funds are not far behind. Union pension funds and noninstitutional investors are least successful by this measure. Rojas et al. (2009) report a similar pattern showing that socially responsible mutual funds and public pension funds have a success rate of about 25 percent versus 10 percent for the full sample.

Using withdrawn proposals as a metric for success suggests that shareholders with sizeable ownership stakes are much more likely to gain the attention of management and reach a compromise. Alternatively, the success of socially responsible mutual funds and public pension funds may be due to their policy of publicizing the outcome of their advocacy and dialogue with target firms. For example, the New York City pension funds, which sponsor 86 percent of public pension fund proposals in the current sample, post a report on their web site every proxy season summarizing the topic and outcome of their proposals. Calvert Funds, which sponsors almost half of all socially responsible mutual fund proposals, also regularly provides similar details on their web site. Companies may be more responsive to these sponsors to avoid negative publicity, as they both regularly publish the names of the leaders and the laggards among their target firms. As Del Guercio, Seery, and Woidtke (2008) and Ertimur et al. (2011) find for corporate governance activism, public shame can be a powerful tool.

David, Bloom, and Hillman (2007) contend that a withdrawn proposal, whether or not implemented by the firm, is only a symbolic victory for activists who care about true social change. The authors find that a composite summary score on the firm's corporate social performance (CSP) is negatively associated with social responsibility shareholder proposals that were either omitted or withdrawn the previous year. One interpretation is that target firms may expend resources to resist external pressure from activists, lowering resources available for performance improvement on other dimensions.

Neubaum and Zahra (2006) address a similar question and use a similar composite score to measure a firm's CSP. Instead of proposal submission, however, they create a measure of institutional activist activity by compiling news stories on incidents of activism by 421 institutional investors. The authors find that institutional ownership by long-term institutional investors (public pension funds) is positively correlated with CSP three years later, while ownership by short-term institutional investors (mutual funds and investment advisers) is not. Further, while their measure of activism is unrelated to CSP, an interaction term of activism with long-term institutional ownership is significantly positively related to CSP.

Finally, the measure of success of greatest interest to researchers and investors alike is whether this activity leads to improvements in financial performance. Gillan and Starks (2007) and Ferri (2011) provide a thorough review of the corporate governance literature's findings and limitations in answering this question. While little evidence is available of a relationship between shareholder activism and positive share price effects or improved operating performance, standard assessment methods are fraught with measurement problems. For example, short-term stock price reactions to shareholder proposals are difficult to interpret because they could either reveal the valuation consequences of activist intervention or a failed negotiation between the activist and the firm. Also, researchers have great difficulty accurately timing when the market learned about the activists' efforts. In short, while evidence consistent with positive valuation effects of corporate governance activism is more common in the recent literature, this remains an open question. Thus, a ripe area for future research is determining the valuation effects of social responsibility activism.

VOTING AS AN ACTIVISM TOOL

Besides filing shareholder proposals, institutional investors can also exercise their influence by actively voting their shares. Because properly researching the issues and deciding how to vote requires substantial time and effort, many institutions hire proxy consultants, such as Institutional Shareholder Services (ISS) or Glass Lewis, to advise them or facilitate voting. According to the Council of Institutional Investors' (2011) primer on proxy voting, most institutions historically delegated their voting authority to external managers, who tended to vote with company management. In 1988, in its famous letter to Avon Products' retirement plan, the Department of Labor ruled that under ERISA, proxy voting rights are considered pension plan assets and therefore trustees have a fiduciary duty to vote in the best interests of beneficiaries (U.S. Department of Labor Advisory Opinion 2/23/88 1988). The Department continued to issue interpretative bulletins, encouraging pension funds to develop written proxy voting guidelines and to exert their influence on corporate management when the benefits of doing so exceed the costs.

In 2002, mutual funds came under SEC scrutiny due to a perceived conflict of interest in voting their proxies in the interests of fund shareholders. Critics argued that funds routinely vote with corporate management out of a desire to gain investment management business from corporate 401(k) plans. In 2003, the SEC adopted new rules requiring mutual funds to disclose their voting policies as well as a full listing of their votes at individual companies. Despite the common view that disclosure would prompt funds to vote against management more often, Cremers and Romano (2011) find no evidence of a decline in support for management proposals due to the rule change but instead find an increase in support.

Morgan, Poulsen, Wolf, and Yang (2011) analyze mutual fund voting patterns on shareholder proposals from 2003 to 2005, including separate statistics on social proposals and on voting by socially responsible funds. They find that funds vote in favor of corporate governance shareholder proposals 49 percent of the time, but only 5 percent of the time for environmental and social proposals. ISS recommended a vote in favor 75 percent of the time for corporate governance proposals, but only 11 percent of the time for social proposals. Morgan et al. find socially responsible funds to be 31 percent more likely to vote in favor of a shareholder proposal than conventional funds. Finally, they find that mutual fund vote support is strongly positively related to the likelihood of a proposal's passage and subsequent implementation of the activist's request, suggesting that mutual funds are influential shareholders.

Morgan et al.'s (2011) evidence that social funds vote differently is unsurprising in light of the current finding that only social funds sponsor social proposals, which are attributed to their incentive to market their social advocacy to their target clientele. Presumably, socially-minded investors would like to verify that their funds are investing and voting according to their stated principles. Two free web sites use official votes disclosed on SEC N-PX filings to aggregate mutual fund voting on management and shareholder proposals (fundvotes.com and proxydemocracy.org), providing investors with summary information to compare across funds. For example, using the Overall Activism Score that proxydemocracy.org assigns to funds based on how often they vote against management, the socially responsible fund sponsors in the current sample range from the 85th percentile (Pax World) to the 98th percentile (Calvert Group) of all mutual funds. In contrast, the two largest fund families, Fidelity and Vanguard, are at the 48th and 13th percentiles, respectively. Thus, socially responsible funds appear to have internally consistent voting and advocacy programs.

COLLECTIVE EFFORTS TO PROMOTE MARKET-WIDE CORPORATE REFORMS

Similar to the group of institutions that co-founded the Council of Institutional Investors in 1985 in order to pool resources and more cost-effectively influence corporate governance practices, several investor networks on social issues have recently formed. For example, 100 institutional investors with $10 trillion in assets are part of the Investor Network on Climate Risk, a project initiated by Ceres, a nongovernmental organization. In 2007, this network petitioned the SEC to require companies to disclose details about their exposure to climate change risk. In February 2010, the SEC issued an interpretative release outlining new disclosure requirements for all public companies.

In 2006, groups within the United Nations set a goal of having institutional investors sign on as signatories to the Principles for Responsible Investment (UN PRI), which means that they agree to incorporate six principles of integrating ESG and of active ownership into their investment processes, ultimately aligning the objectives of investors with society at large. The number of institutional investor signatories worldwide has gone from 73 in May 2006 to 1050 in May 2012. Notably, U.S. signatories include mainstream asset managers such as BlackRock, Capital Group, and T. Rowe Price in addition to the traditional SRI asset managers such as Calvert and Domini.

THE FUTURE OF ESG-FOCUSED INVESTMENT AND ACTIVISM STRATEGIES

Client demand inherently drives institutional investment managerial behavior. By several measures, client demand for SRI and incorporation of ESG factors are rapidly growing. For example, according to the Social Investment Forum Foundation Report (2010), both the number and assets of ETFs incorporating ESG criteria grew from only eight with $2.3 billion in assets in 2007 to 26 ETFs with $4.0 billion in assets in 2009, a 74 percent increase over just two years. Similarly, companies are beginning to provide a socially responsible fund option in their 401(k) plans, presumably due to plan participant interest. According to the *Global Defined Contribution Survey* (Mercer 2009), 12 percent of surveyed plans currently offer a SRI option. States have been adding SRI options to 529 College Savings Plans as well. Currently, California, Illinois, Oregon, Pennsylvania, Virginia, and the District of Columbia offer SRI options in their 529 plans. These trends suggest that small investors are gaining interest in ESG issues, which could presage sufficient interest from beneficiaries to ultimately induce their defined-benefit pension plan trustees to consider SRI as well. In a 2009 survey of investment consultants to pension plans conducted jointly by the Social Investment Forum and *Pensions & Investments*, 88 percent of surveyed respondents stated that client interest in ESG strategies is likely to grow over the next three years. None of the respondents believed client interest would decrease (Social Investment Forum Foundation 2009).

A major obstacle for SRI to emerge from its current status as a market niche to the mainstream of institutional investments is the fiduciary duty of pension plans to invest in the best interests of beneficiaries. The massive scale of global pension plan assets has drawn the attention of ESG advocates as a resource to harness toward achieving their goals. If incorporating ESG gains widespread acceptance among pension funds, this will have profound consequences for the external asset managers they hire as well. The effort by the UN PRI toward studying the legal and practical issues fiduciaries face in justifying a sustainable investment focus is an important move in this direction. One leading indicator of increased acceptance by pension funds is CalPERS' recent web site announcement that it considers ESG factors to be "an essential part of our risk management" and will begin implementing a plan to integrate ESG factors across all asset classes (CalPERS Press Release 2011). After commissioning Mercer Consulting to study the issue, the investment committee of CalPERS' board held a workshop to outline the launch of the Total Fund Strategy for Environmental, Social, & Governance (CalPERS Circular Letter, 2011). Given CalPERS' track record as a pioneer of corporate governance activism, this appears to be an important development.

SUMMARY AND CONCLUSIONS

The predominant perception in the academic finance literature is that SRI and activism are activities in the realm of the gadflies and financial fringe. For example, Starks (2009, p. 467) concludes that "... a minority of investors believe that social responsibility issues have important implications for a firm's actions and value." In a similar vein, Thomas and Cotter (2007, p. 389) conclude that "shareholders view corporate governance proposals as connected to firm value and therefore worthy of support, whereas their beliefs about social responsibility proposals are precisely the opposite."

After 25 years of institutional investor advocacy regarding corporate governance issues, once radical notions, such as having a majority of the board and key committees independent of management, are mainstream today. A review of the current institutional social activist activity and trends suggests a similar sea change in investor attitudes toward social issues. If practitioner interest is a leading indicator, much more research on the understudied economic and financial impact of social issues is likely to occur in the future.

DISCUSSION QUESTIONS

1. Contrast a pension plan trustee's decision to invest according to ESG principles compared to a mutual fund manager's decision. Explain whether different factors should drive each decision.

2. From the perspective of an activist, what are the advantages and disadvantages of submitting shareholder proposals to the corporate proxy as a tool for activism?

3. Compare and contrast socially responsible shareholder proposals with corporate governance proposals in terms of success rates, proposal sponsors, and sponsor motivations.

4. Discuss whether socially responsible activism among institutional investors is likely to increase, decrease, or stay the same in the next 10 years and provide a rationale for this view.

REFERENCES

Barber, Brad M. 2007. "Monitoring the Monitor: Evaluating CalPERS' Activism." *Journal of Investing* 16:4, 66–80.

Black, Bernard. 1997. "Shareholder Activism and Corporate Governance in the United States." In Peter Newman, ed., *The New Palgrave Dictionary of Economics and the Law*, Vol. 3, 459–521. New York: Palgrave Macmillan.

Black, Bernard, and John C. Coffee Jr. 1994. "Hail Britannia?: Institutional Investor Behavior under Limited Regulation." *Michigan Law Review* 92:7, 1997–2087.

Brown Jr., J. Robert. 2011. "The Politicization of Corporate Governance: Bureaucratic Discretion, the SEC, and Shareholder Ratification of Auditors." Working Paper, Sturm School of Law, University of Denver.

CalPERS Circular Letter. 2011. "Meeting Notice of the CalPERS Board of Administration, Its Committees and Advisory Panels," August 4, 2011. Available at www.calpers.ca.gov/eip-docs/about/board-cal-agenda/archives/notices/201108.pdf.

CalPERS Press Release. 2011. "Workshop to Explore Integrating Environmental, Social, Governance Issues into Investment Process." August 9. Available at www.calpers.ca.gov/index.jsp?bc=/about/press/pr-2011/aug/envrnmtl-wkshp.xml.

Capelle-Blancard, Gunther, and Stephanie Monjon. 2011. "The Performance of Socially Responsible Funds: Does the Screening Process Matter?" Working Paper, Université Paris.

Council of Institutional Investors. 2011. "Everything You Ever Wanted to Know about Proxy Voting But Were Afraid to Ask." Available at www.cii.org/UserFiles/file/resource%20center/publications/Proxy%20Voting%20Primer%2003-01-2011%20FINAL.pdf.

Cremers, K. J. Martijn, and Roberta Romano. 2011. "Institutional Investors and Proxy Voting on Compensation Plans: The Impact of the 2003 Mutual Fund Voting Disclosure Regulation." *American Law and Economics Review* 13:1, 220–268.

CSR Europe. 2003. "Investing in Responsible Business: The 2003 Survey of European Fund Managers, Financial Analysts and Investor Relations Officers." Available at www.deloitte.com/assets/DcomBelgium/Local%20Assets/Documents/CSREInvestinginresponsiblebusiness1%281%29.pdf.

Cziraki, Peter, Luc Renneboog, and Peter G. Szilagyi. 2010. "Shareholder Activism through Proxy Proposals: The European Perspective." Working Paper, Tilburg University.

David, Parthiban, Matt Bloom, and Amy J. Hillman. 2007. "Investor Activism, Managerial Responsiveness, and Corporate Social Performance." *Strategic Management Journal* 28:1, 91–100.

Del Guercio, Diane, Laura Seery, and Tracie Woidkte. 2008. "Do Boards Pay Attention When Institutional Investor Activists 'Just Vote No'?" *Journal of Financial Economics* 90:1, 84–103.

Edmans, Alex. 2011. "Does the Stock Market Fully Value Intangibles? Employee Satisfaction and Equity Prices." *Journal of Financial Economics* 101:3, 621–640.

Ertimur, Yonca, Fabrizio Ferri, and Volkan Muslu. 2011. "Shareholder Activism and CEO Pay." *Review of Financial Studies* 24:2, 535–592.

Ertimur, Yonca, Fabrizio Ferri, and Stephen R. Stubben. 2010. "Board of Directors' Responsiveness to Shareholders: Evidence from Shareholder Proposals." *Journal of Corporate Finance* 16:1, 53–72.

Ferri, Fabrizio. 2011. "'Low Cost' Shareholder Activism: A Review of the Evidence." In Claire Hill and Brett McDonnell, eds., *Research Handbook on the Economics of Corporate Law*, forthcoming. Northampton: Elgar Publishers.

Geczy, Christopher C., Robert F. Stambaugh, and David Levin. 2005. "Investing in Socially Responsible Mutual Funds." Working Paper, Wharton Business School, University of Pennsylvania.

Gillan, Stuart, and Laura Starks. 1998. "A Survey of Shareholder Activism: Motivation and Empirical Evidence." *Contemporary Finance Digest* 2:3, 10–34.

Gillan, Stuart, and Laura Starks. 2000. "Corporate Governance Proposals and Shareholder Activism: The Role of Institutional Investors." *Journal of Financial Economics* 57:2, 275–305.

Gillan, Stuart, and Laura Starks. 2007. "The Evolution of Shareholder Activism in the United States." *Journal of Applied Corporate Finance* 19:1, 55–73.

Glac, Katherina. 2010. "The Influence of Shareholders on Corporate Social Responsibility." Working Paper, University of St. Thomas.

Heal, Geoffrey. 2005. "Corporate Social Responsibility: An Economic and Financial Framework." *The Geneva Papers on Risk and Insurance* 30:3, 387–409.

Hess, David. 2007. "Public Pensions and the Promise of Shareholder Activism for the Next Frontier of Corporate Governance: Sustainable Economic Development." *Virginia Law & Business Review* 2:2, 221–264.

Hong, Harrison, and Marcin Kacperczyk. 2009. "The Price of Sin: The Effects of Social Norms on Markets." *Journal of Financial Economics* 93:1, 15–36.

Karpoff, Jonathan. 2001. "The Impact of Shareholder Activism on Target Companies: A Survey of Empirical Findings." Working Paper, Foster School of Business, University of Washington.

Kerste, Marco, Nicole Rosenbloom, Bernd Jan Sikken, and Jarst Weda. 2011. *Financing Sustainability: Insights for Investors, Corporate Executives, and Policymakers.* Amsterdam: VU University Press.

Logsdon, Jeanne M., and Harry J. Van Buren III. 2008. "Beyond the Proxy Vote: Dialogues between Shareholder Activists and Corporations." *Journal of Business Ethics* 87:Supplement 1, 353–365.

Logsdon, Jeanne M., and Harry J. Van Buren III. 2009. "Justice and Large Corporations: What Do Activists Want?" *Business & Society* 47:4, 523–548.

Margolis, Joshua D., Hillary Anger Elfenbein, and James P. Walsh. 2009. "Does It Pay to Be Good . . . and Does It Matter? A Meta-Analysis of the Relationship between Corporate Social and Financial Performance." Working Paper, Harvard University.

Medical Committee for Human Rights v. SEC. 1970. 432 F 2d, 659 (DC Cir 1970).

Mercer. *Global Defined Contribution Survey.* 2009. Available at www.mercer.com/globalDCsurvey.

Morgan, Angela, Annette Poulsen, Jack Wolf, and Tina Yang. 2011. "Mutual Funds as Monitors: Evidence from Mutual Fund Voting." *Journal of Corporate Finance* 17:4, 914–928.

Neubaum, Donald O., and Shaker A. Zahra. 2006. "Institutional Ownership and Corporate Social Performance: The Moderating Effects of Investment Horizon, Activism, and Coordination." *Journal of Management* 32:1, 108–131.

Proffitt, W. Trexler, and Andrew Spicer. 2006. "Shaping the Shareholder Activism Agenda: Institutional Investors and Global Social Issues." *Strategic Organization* 4:2, 165–190.

Renneboog, Luc, Jenke Ter Horst, and Chendi Zhang. 2008. "Socially Responsible Investments: Institutional Aspects, Performance, and Investor Behavior." *Journal of Banking & Finance* 32:9, 1723–1742.

Renneboog, Luc, and Peter G. Szilagyi. 2010. "The Role of Shareholder Proposals in Corporate Governance." *Journal of Corporate Finance* 17:1, 167–188.

Richardson, Benjamin J. 2010. "From Fiduciary Duties to Fiduciary Relationships for Socially Responsible Investment." Working Paper, York University.

Rojas, Miguel, Bouchra M'zali, Marie-France Turcotte, and Philip Merrigan. 2009. "Bringing about Changes to Corporate Social Policy through Shareholder Activism: Filers, Issues, Targets, and Success." *Business and Society Review* 114:2, 217–252.

Romano, Roberta. 1993. "Public Pension Fund Activism in Corporate Governance Reconsidered." *Columbia Law Review* 93:4, 795–853.

Romano, Roberta. 2001. "Less Is More: Making Institutional Investor Activism a Valuable Mechanism of Corporate Governance." *Yale Journal on Regulation* 18:2, 174–252.

SEC Administrative Proceeding No. IA-2761 7/30/08. 2008.

SEC Exchange Act Release No. 40018 5/28/98. 1998.

SEC Staff Legal Bulletin No. 14A 7/12/02. 2002.

SEC Staff Legal Bulletin No. 14E 10/27/09. 2009.

Sjostrom, Emma. 2008. "Shareholder Activism for Corporate Social Responsibility: What Do We Know?" *Sustainable Development* 16:3, 141–154.

Social Investment Forum Foundation. 2009. *Investment Consultants and Responsible Investing Current Practice and Outlook in the United States.* December. Available at http://ussif.org/resources/pubs/.

Social Investment Forum Foundation. 2010. *2010 Report on Socially Responsible Investing Trends in the United States*. Available at http://ussif.org/resources/pubs/.

Starks, Laura. 2009. "EFA Keynote Speech: Corporate Governance and Corporate Social Responsibility: What Do Investors Care About? What Should Investors Care About?" *Financial Review* 44:4, 461–468.

Taub, Jennifer S. 2009. "Able but Not Willing: The Failure of Mutual Fund Advisers to Advocate for Shareholders' Rights." *Journal of Corporation Law* 34:3, 843–893.

Thomas, Randall S., and James F. Cotter. 2007. "Shareholder Proposals in the New Millennium: Shareholder Support, Board Response, and Market Reaction." *Journal of Corporate Finance* 13:2, 368–391.

Tkac, Paula. 2006. "One Proxy at a Time: Pursuing Social Change through Shareholder Proposals." *Economic Review Federal Reserve Bank of Atlanta* 91:3, 1–20.

United Nations Environment Program Finance Initiative. 2005. "A Legal Framework for the Integration of Environmental, Social, and Governance Issues into Institutional Investment." Available at www.unepfi.org/fileadmin/documents/freshfields_legal_resp_20051123.pdf.

United Nations Environment Program Finance Initiative. 2009. "Fiduciary Responsibility: Legal and Practical Aspects of Integrating Environmental, Social, and Governance Issues into Institutional Investment." Available at www.unepfi.org/fileadmin/documents/fiduciaryII.pdf.

U.S. Department of Labor Advisory Opinion 2/23/88. 1988. Available at http://governanceanalytics.com/content/menutop/content/subscription/AppA.PDF.

U.S. Department of Labor Advisory Opinion 98-04A 5/28/98. 1998. Available at www.dol.gov/ebsa/programs/ori/advisory98/98-04a.htm.

U.S. Department of Labor. 2010. *2008 Private Pension Plan Bulletin*, December. Available at www.dol.gov/ebsa/PDF/2008pensionplanbulletin.PDF.

Wen, Shuangge. 2009. "Institutional Investor Activism on Socially Responsible Investment: Effects and Expectations." *Business Ethics: A European Review* 18:3, 308–333.

Woidkte, Tracie. 2002. "Agents Watching Agents? Evidence from Pension Fund Ownership and Firm Value." *Journal of Financial Economics* 63:1, 99–131.

ABOUT THE AUTHORS

Diane Del Guercio is an associate professor of Finance and the Peter W. and Maryanne L. Powell Distinguished Research Scholar at the Lundquist College of Business at the University of Oregon. She has published several articles on the investment practices and activism activities of institutional investors in the *Journal of Financial Economics* and continues to conduct research in this area. Her research comparing the investment flows of pension fund and mutual fund managers with Paula A. Tkac won the William F. Sharpe Award for Best Paper published in the *Journal of Financial and Quantitative Analysis* in 2002. She received her Masters and Ph.D. degrees in Economics from the University of Chicago and her Bachelor's degree in Economics from the University of California, Santa Barbara.

Hai Tran is a finance Ph.D. student at the University of Oregon. His research interests include institutional investors, corporate governance, and corporate social responsibility. He has worked as an auditor for Ernst & Young in the United States and a planning analyst for PepsiCo in Vietnam, where he conducted financial analyses on strategic initiatives for top management. He holds a BA in Business Administration and an MBA from Washington State University.

CHAPTER 20

Social Activism and Nongovernmental Organizations

JONATHAN P. DOH
Herbert G. Rammrath Endowed Chair in International Business,
Villanova University

DEBORAH ZACHAR
MBA Student, Villanova University

INTRODUCTION

Social activism is the process by which individuals, acting alone or as part of a collective, express opposing views on social issues such as labor, environmental, human rights, and poverty. Typically, activists seek to change the behavior of companies or individuals, or encourage the approval or implementation of legislation or regulation. Activism can take a wide range of forms from writing letters to newspapers or politicians, political campaigning, economic activism such as boycotts or preferentially patronizing businesses, rallies, street marches, strikes, sit-ins, and hunger strikes. This chapter focuses primarily on more formal examples of social activism that occur when individuals combine in movements or organizations to advance specific causes.

In the realm of social investment and finance, activism is often targeted at individual companies through various forms of campaigns, financial institutions, or investors and shareowners. Through the process of socially responsible investing (SRI), especially shareholder advocacy, social activists have leveraged the instruments of corporate governance and power to exploit the tools of investment in order to change corporate behavior.

This chapter provides an overview of the role of social activism in the realm of socially responsible finance and investing. It begins with a brief review of various perspectives on corporate social responsibility (CSR), focusing especially on the role of stakeholder theory and stakeholder management. The chapter then documents the emergence of civil society actors such as nongovernmental organizations (NGOs) as critical players in the process by which stakeholders influence financial decisions through their activism. Next, it describes the various mechanisms through which activists influence finance and investments. The chapter concludes with suggestions for further research.

CSR IN FINANCE AND INVESTMENT: STAKEHOLDERS AND STRATEGIES

CSR has both its supporters and detractors. This section focuses not on the legitimacy of the concept, but rather on two theoretical perspectives that provide the basis for understanding why and how social activists influence finance and investments.

Stakeholder Management

In addition to the core ethical foundations of CSR, a broader concept of *stakeholder management* emerged in the 1960s and 1970s. Stakeholder theory is discussed at length in Chapter 2. It focuses on an even broader and more holistic view of CSR and the obligations of corporations to society. A number of variants have emerged that attempt to isolate *normative* and *instrumental* underpinnings of the stakeholder approach and a *convergent* perspective that attempts to show how the two could be integrated (Jones and Wicks 1999). Further, scholars have attempted to develop highly actionable frameworks of stakeholder theory that would allow managers to classify or stratify stakeholders according to their relative salience (Mitchell, Agle, and Wood 1997).

At its core, Jones and Wicks (1999) describe several key elements of stakeholder theory:

1. The corporation has relationships with many constituent groups (*stakeholders*) that affect and are affected by its decisions (Freeman 1984).
2. The theory is concerned with the nature of these relationships in terms of both processes and outcomes for the firm and its stakeholders.
3. The interests of all (legitimate) stakeholders have intrinsic value, and no set of interests is assumed to dominate the others (Clarkson 1995; Donaldson and Preston 1995).
4. The theory focuses on managerial decision making (Donaldson and Preston 1995)

Of relevance for the discussion here, the instrumental view of stakeholder management fully includes shareholders as key stakeholders, going so far as to identify them as one of the firm's most critical, primary stakeholders. Yet, stakeholder theory also suggests that stakeholder groups such as NGOs and community groups also have legitimacy.

Strategic CSR

Most recently, CSR has evolved even further to be viewed as a strategic or instrumental tool of the firm. This view has become more dominant in the CSR literature with important implications for collective understanding about the role of business in society. Strategic theories of CSR (McWilliams, Siegel, and Wright 2006) assert that a company's social practices are integrated into its business and corporate-level strategies. Baron (2001), who coined the term *strategic CSR*, argues that companies compete for socially responsible customers by explicitly linking their social contribution to product sales.

The strategic or instrumental view of CSR has generated more than 100 studies that have sought to link various aspects of the social performance of firms to their financial performance. Waddock and Graves (1997) find that corporate social performance (CSP) and corporate financial performance (CFP) are positively related, reasoning that good performance in the social arena is indicative of good management practice, which, in turn, yields better financial performance. Orlitzky, Schmidt, and Rynes (2003), who conducted a comprehensive meta-analysis of the relationship of CSR and CFP, conclude that CSR generates positive financial returns, although alternate operationalizations of CSP and CFP moderate the positive association. Specifically, CSR appears to be more highly correlated with accounting-based measures of CFP than with market-based indicators. This meta-study finds that the path through which CSR leads to CFP is via reputational effects rather than other operational influences.

A recent meta-analysis by Margolis, Elfenbein, and Walsh (2007) finds that the overall effect of CSP on CFP is positive but small. Further, the study finds as much evidence for reverse causality (e.g., CFP leading to CSP) as the opposite. The authors conclude that the exhaustive and never-ending efforts to establish a CSP-CFP link would be better directed at understanding why companies pursue CSP, the mechanisms connecting prior CFP to subsequent CSP, and how companies manage the process of pursuing both CSP and CFP simultaneously.

Nonetheless, strategic CSR provides the foundation for understanding why corporations are motivated to respond to stakeholder pressure, either to benefit from positive reputation that may accrue from "doing the right thing" or, more likely, to forestall negative reputational events that can have costs to the bottom line in the form of consumer boycotts, share price declines, or other negative impacts. For example, Doh, Howton, Howton, and Siegel (2010, p. 1466) contend that "consideration as a socially responsible firm constitutes a form of organizational legitimacy that is operationalized in a comparative sense (reputation) through inclusion in (or exclusion from) a social index." They also maintain that under conditions of evaluative uncertainty, the capabilities of social actors are assessed by certification contests or endorsements from reputable third parties. The authors further report on the growing number and impact of third-party CSR and corporate citizenship rankings and ratings undertaken by journals, financial institutions, and other organizations.

Stakeholder, Stockholders, and Activism

The emergence of stakeholder management as a unifying concept of corporate strategy and behavior, combined with the increasing "strategic" view of CSR thus provide the basis for understanding how social activism and social activists have come to influence finance and investment. The next section outlines the emergence of NGOs as critical organizations that have become a primary mechanism for channeling social activism and discusses some of the tools and techniques used to advance specific causes.

SOCIAL ACTIVISM AND THE RISE OF CIVIL SOCIETY ORGANIZATIONS AND NGOS

Social activism requires social actors, and in the case of activism related to finance and investment, these actors are primarily nongovernmental organizations. NGOs are also known as civil society organizations. NGOs constitute an important and influential set of actors within the broad context of business and society and corporate citizenship, and have emerged as critical players in shaping governmental policy and practice, influencing legal and governance structures globally, and directly shaping corporate and business activities. Although NGOs or their equivalents have been part of human societies for centuries, in recent decades NGOs have grown in number, power, and influence. NGOs have been influential in a range of key public policy debates, and NGO activism has been responsible for major changes in public policy, law and regulation, and reform of corporate behavior and governance (van Tuijl 1999; Doh and Teegen 2003).

The Rise of NGOs as Social Actors

Although estimates of the number of NGOs vary widely, almost all analysts agree that the number is dramatically increasing. In 1993, the United Nations Development Program identified 50,000 NGOs worldwide (Kellow 2000). In 2002, the total size of the 'independent sector' (nonfirm, nongovernment) in the United States was estimated at 1.4 million organizations, with revenues of nearly $680 billion and an estimated 11.7 million employees (Independent Sector 2004). Despite differences in estimates, most observers agree that NGOs are important organizations within society. Hart and Milstein (2003, p. 58) note, "as the power of national governments has eroded in the wake of global trade regimes, nongovernmental organizations (NGOs) and other civil society groups have stepped into the breach."

   Civil society, also referred to as the *third sector* or the *nonprofit sector*, is used to broadly describe all aspects of society that extend beyond the realm of the public sector and the traditional private sector. When individuals or groups within civil society work together to advance a broad common set of interests and these interests become an important force in shaping the direction of society, social movements emerge as the outcomes of this process. *Social movements* are broad societal initiatives organized around a particular issue, trend or priority. Modern examples include the environmental and feminist movements. When civil society groups band together to form organized relationships, the emergent entities are often referred to as NGOs.

NGOs and Social Activism

Yaziji and Doh (2009) distinguish between two types of advocacy campaigns. The first, which they term *watchdog campaigns*, attempts to hold firms accountable to some set of social, economic, or political expectations. The second type of advocacy campaign, which Yaziji and Doh term *proxy war* campaigns, seeks to achieve some broader social change. According to these authors, the two types of campaigns have dissimilar goals, often select their targets in opposing manners and use different kinds of rhetoric and tactics with diverse audiences.

A watchdog campaign is one in which the goal is to pressure the targeted firm to comply with dominant institution standards. These standards may or may not be formalized in regulation. Watchdog campaigns are often run by local organizations that are responding to a perceived threat or harm to their narrow interests. An example of such campaigns would be local NGOs campaigning against a firm for its local impact such as polluting a river in violation of existing normative and/or regulative standards.

A proxy war, also called a *social movement* campaign, is designed to challenge and change the institutional framework, whether in terms of formal regulatory and legal systems or accepted social norms and values. As carriers of a challenging ideology, the social movement organizations (SMOs, a subcategory of NGOs) behind a campaign often engage in institutional proxy campaigns in which opposing institutions generate a proxy conflict between organizations that strategically interact to promote, sustain or represent the opposing institutions. In proxy war campaigns, the goals of the targeting organization are (1) to extend the application of the campaigning organization's own "home" institutions (whether values or regulations) to a new context; (2) to delegitimize the competing institution; and/or (3) to establish a meta-institutional rule holding that the home institution dominates or takes precedence over the competing institution in cases where the two institutions are in apparent conflict. All proxy wars concern the truth, appropriateness, applicability, and importance of the beliefs, norms, and values in conflict.

Although advocacy campaigns come in several forms, one notable means by which social activism creates policy change, especially in corporations, is through protests. King and Soule (2007) consider this form of action as an *extra-institutional tactic*, bringing light to the fact that those involved in this type of activism are typically not organizational insiders. Due to the fact that corporations especially have no requirements toward stakeholders, protests have proven to be a successful means by which stakeholder groups create necessary change in rigid corporate structure.

According to Hirschman (1970), disgruntled stakeholders attempt to pressure corporations via either *exit* strategies, such as boycotts, or *voice* strategies, such as protests (King and Soule 2007). However, the voice typically creates the most impact because of its controversial nature. Protesting creates a situation in which grievances are aired publicly, oftentimes resulting in detrimental consequences for the targeted firm.

Some protests appear to cause more harm (influence) than others. Research shows that certain characteristics must be present in order for this form of activism to be successful in creating change and garnering the necessary attention. For instance, media coverage is considered one of the biggest influencers of success, not only because of its immense reach, but also because of its public connation of importance (King 2008). Also, the size of the protest can be linked to its importance: the larger the protest, the more important the issue is perceived to be by the public and various stakeholders.

Another influencing factor corresponds to the party holding the protest. If many organizations collaborate to protest against a firm or issue, the perceived value of the issue is heightened. The topic also makes a difference, given that petty issues can be ignored, especially when brought against large, powerful, and financially sound companies. Thus, protesters are most likely attempting not to create an immediate financial burden on the firm, but to decrease reputational legitimacy that will end up affecting revenue in the longer term (King and Soule 2007).

Legitimacy and reputation are seen as indirect qualities of a firm that enable it to stand apart from competitors on a level other than stock price (King 2008). Therefore, protesters often aim to destroy those reputational benefits by bringing to light grievances on important stakeholder issues in a public manner, which according to King and Soule (2007, p. 399), could ultimately "threaten to denigrate their [the target firm's] public image and constrain access to institutional resources." As a result, especially when protests are applied in conjunction with boycotts, King and Soule (p. 420) note that social activism "may constrain future revenue and directly threaten profitability."

According to Bostrom and Hallstrom (2010, p. 5), NGOs have the potential to impose four different types of power on multistakeholders, where the term *power* is referred to on a relational basis as opposed to a *thing* that can be possessed. Bostrom and Hallstrom (p. 5) define power as a form of "socioeconomic resource or the ability" of the firm used "to shape an agenda, debates, and discourses through issue framing." There are four types of NGO power described: symbolic, cognitive, social, and monitoring power.

As Bostrom and Hallstrom (2010, p. 5) note, *symbolic power* refers to the status that comes with an organization that has reached a particular state, usually that of "sustainability, responsibility, and quality." This type of power is important for those firms that are seeking a stronger trust with customers due to the sizable confidence that comes along with NGOs in most cases. Further, some claim that a high level of trust can lead to a higher customer base and in turn higher economic performance. Hence, this symbolic power can create the legitimacy firms desire, as described earlier, which can lead to enhanced CSR practices.

Another type of power that NGOs often exert is *cognitive power*, which Bostrom and Hallstrom (2010, p. 7) refer to as the "ability . . . to provide unique knowledge and information." As Bostrom and Hallstrom (p. 7) note, this includes "language skill, on-the-ground experience, sensitivity to cultural traditions, and the ability to provide theoretical or technical expertise in matters that are subject to standard-setting." In other words, a cognitive power strategy gives the firm the ability to act as a knowledge or technical expert on whatever subject it is working to improve or change.

The third type of power described by Bostrom and Hallstrom (2010) is *social power*, which includes all of the networks, alliances, and collaboration partners involved with the action taking place. This is an extremely beneficial tactic because it is often a situation that involves many players. This type of strategy aims to include everyone across a wide array of industries. As Bostrom and Hallstrom (2010, p. 47) note, "The trick is to find collaborating partners both *within* and *across* categories," and in doing so, the alliance will tap into necessary skills and coalitions.

The final type of power described is *monitoring power*, which Bostrom and Hallstrom (2010) describe as the ability to measure performance against what was promised by the organization. This form of influence not only monitors current action but also develops the necessary processes for evaluating future performance against targets.

NGOs, Civil Society, and Social Movements

NGO is a broad term that loosely refers to all organizations that are neither official parts of government (at any level) nor private, for-profit enterprises. Within the NGO category, however, are many different types, characteristics, and purposes. According to Teegen, Doh, and Vachani (2004), *social purpose* and *club* NGOs are those that arise from social movements. Social purpose NGOs are accountable primarily to the clients that they serve such as environmental, human rights, poverty relief and health NGOs. Club NGOs are membership associations designed primarily to provide a benefit to their members, generally because of pooling interests. Examples of club NGOs are unions, business associations, sports clubs, and other voluntary associations. Most of the contemporary literature on NGOs focuses on those who operate within the social purpose realm.

The United Nations (2003, Paragraph 1) describes an NGO as:

> Any non-profit, voluntary citizens' group which is organized on a local, national, or international level. Task-oriented and driven by people with a common interest, NGOs perform a variety of services and humanitarian functions, bring citizens' concerns to governments, monitor policies and encourage political participation at the community level. They provide analysis and expertise, serve as early warning mechanisms, and help monitor and implement international agreements.

Teegen et al. (2004, p. 466) offer a more succinct definition by describing social purpose NGOs as "private, not-for-profit organizations that aim to serve particular societal interests by focusing advocacy and/or operational efforts on social, political and economic goals, including equity, education, health, environmental protection and human rights." Broadly speaking, NGOs contribute to codes of conduct, provide training, offer resource access and knowledge concerning the delivery of goods and services, share best practices, and create and support institutional settings that promote social welfare.

Teegen et al. (2004) further differentiate among various functions of NGOs. *Advocacy NGOs* work on behalf of others who lack the voice or access to promote their interests. They engage in lobbying, serve as representatives and advisory experts to decisionmakers, conduct research, hold conferences, and stage citizen tribunals. Advocacy NGOs also monitor and expose actions and inactions of others, disseminate information to key constituencies, set and define agendas, develop and promote codes of conduct and organize boycotts or investor actions. In these ways, NGOs give voice and provide access to institutions to promote social gain or mitigate negative spillovers from other economic activity.

Operational (or programmatic or service-oriented) *NGOs* provide goods and services to clients with unmet needs. NGOs have long stepped in to serve as critical safety nets, where politically challenged, indebted or corrupt states are unable or unwilling to provide for unmet needs and where global problems defy neat nation-state responsibilities. Examples of such operational activities include relief efforts provided by the Red Cross or Red Crescent, environmental monitoring and programming by the World Wide Fund (WWF) for Nature, and the distribution of medicinal drugs by Doctors without Borders.

Although some NGOs focus primarily on advocacy or operational service delivery, many pursue both sets of activities simultaneously, or evolve from one to the other. For example, Oxfam, the global development and poverty relief organization, advocates for changes in public policy that would provide greater support to its efforts while also contributing directly to health, education and food security in the developing countries in which it operates. Similarly, Doctors without Borders and WWF are active on the ground, delivering services in their respective domains, but they also simultaneously lobby in the political and regulatory arenas.

A brief example illustrates the relationship among civil society, social movements, and the emergence (and convergence) of different types of NGOs. Environmental conservation has long been of concern to civil society in North America. A strong and ongoing conservation movement gave rise to two service-oriented environmental organizations, the Nature Conservancy (founded in 1951) and the World Wildlife Fund (founded in 1961). This longstanding movement, in conjunction with a growing social movement and related activism over civil rights and the Vietnam War in the early and mid-1960s, gave rise to the environmental movement of the 1960s.

This movement gained momentum after the publication of Carson's (1962) *Silent Spring*, which exposed the hazards of the pesticide DDT, eloquently questioned humanity's faith in technological progress, and helped set the stage for the environmental movement. This movement, in turn, paved the way for the creation of various environmental advocacy organizations such as the Environmental Defense Fund (founded in 1967) and the National Resource Defense Council (founded in 1970). Over time, many environmental advocacy organizations developed more of a service focus, and many service NGOs began to take positions on environmental policy issues, creating some convergence in these organizations and their missions.

An important milestone in the role of NGOs in social activism as it relates to finance and investments occurred in 1984 when a range of NGOs, including church and community groups, human rights organizations and other anti-apartheid activists, built strong networks and pressed U.S. cities and states to divest their public pension funds of companies doing business in South Africa. The Comprehensive Anti-Apartheid Act banned new U.S. investment in South Africa, export sales to the police and military, and new bank loans, except to support trade. The combination of domestic unrest, international governmental pressures and capital flight posed a direct, sustained, and ultimately successful challenge to the white minority rule, resulting in the collapse of apartheid (Doh and Guay 2006).

NGO Collaboration

Besides activism, NGOs may seek to collaborate with companies. Oftentimes this collaboration follows a period of more aggressive advocacy toward the focal company. Spar and La Mure (2003, p. 81) explain this pattern as "an NGO identifies a problem that it and its supporters feel passionately about redressing. In an effort to gain maximum impact from their finite resources, they select a target with the greatest potential to affect the problem at hand and the greatest susceptibility to external pressure." Their external pressure can take various forms and usually involve one of the following: utilizing the Internet, employing grassroots methods, playing up the media, or collaborating with the organization (Li 2001).

The Internet has become a powerful tool in the past decade that has given NGOs the power to reach an ever-expanding audience. Messages are communicated in realtime, and the vast nature of the medium has increased the influence these organizations can hold over corporations. Further, grassroots methods have also been intensified through Internet exposure by widening the reach of a message. For instance, Li (2001, p. 12) notes that "the international environmental group has an e-mail list of over 5,000 activists who are prepared to protest against any number of issues" at any given time. This has been a huge motivator for corporate change, especially because of the media who are interested in exploiting issues at the expense of the corporation.

Some corporations avoid such negative publicity by collaborating with NGOs from the start. For instance, Novartis, though not the target of activism in 2000, actively took the necessary steps to comply with NGO beliefs. According to Spar and La Mure (2003, p. 93), the company asserted that it plans to "act the same way that a mature, responsible and conscientious citizen would act in the community." Novartis continued to make active efforts to comply with NGO complaints even though these complaints were not specifically aimed at the company. As Spar and La Mure (p. 94) note, Novartis concluded that "reputation is one of the most valuable assets of a company. It is not only closely linked to economic performance, but even more to employee behavior." This type of collaboration between corporations and NGOs creates long-lasting and sustainable ethical practices.

Peloza and Falkenberg (2009), who also support long-term collaboration efforts between multinational enterprises (MNEs) and NGOs posit that the most beneficial and lasting NGO-firm relationships occur for those partnerships that go beyond a simple monetary donation. Their research separates the different types of relationships into four categories. The first, called *focused contribution*, is the partnership between a single firm and a single NGO, which is often categorized as a type of surface-level partnership aimed at the ownership of a particular issue at hand. It also has potential to result in a deep collaboration between the partners, given that their work becomes meaningful and highly focused. An example is the partnership between Unilever, "the world's largest tea company," and Rainforest Alliance. As Peloza and Falkenberg note, the collaboration ensures that Unilever's tea is purchased from sustainable sources, thus protecting the environmental and the financial health of participating partners and locations.

The second form of partnership, called *shared contribution*, exists between a single NGO and multiple firms. An example of this type of partnership occurs when many industries operating within the same community join together with a single NGO in hopes of correcting a common issue. According to Peloza and Falkenberg (2009), this has the potential to create a system of best practices across an industry, which can be highly beneficial to a community, as demonstrated by the collaboration between those in the chemical industry in Ecuador with a single

NGO, FundacionNatura. The partnership provides benefits for self-regulation and has established best practices over a variety of categories.

The third form of collaboration between NGOs and firms is referred to as *diffused contribution*, given that a single company works with various NGOs at the same time in order to fulfill specific CSR initiatives. According to Peloza and Falkenberg (2009, p. 104), this form of partnership is the most advantageous when "firms have significant, focused operations in a local area with voids in the business infrastructure." In such instances, "basic infrastructure can be improved through partnerships with a range of NGOs with local knowledge." An example of diffused contribution is Shell's Camisea project, in which the company tries to limit its footprint in Peru by identifying over "350 relevant stakeholders including indigenous populations, environmental NGOs and local governments, which resulted in formal collaborations with over 40 organizations" (Peloza and Falkenberg 2009, p. 104).

The fourth type of collaboration is *communal contribution*, which encompasses the extensive relationship between multiple firms with multiple NGOs. This type of alliance is most appropriate for what Selsky and Parker (2005) call *meta-problems*, which they define as beyond the capacity of what a single organization or NGO can accomplish. The authors also note that such collaborations can be highly complex, require a long-term focus for both the firm and NGO, and the result has an impact on various areas across a range of industries. An example of this type of collaboration is the Fair Labor Association, made up of more than 20 apparel manufacturers and a wide range of NGOs, with "each member playing a vital role in areas such as consultation, monitoring, and verification" (Peloza and Falkenberg 2009, p. 107).

These four types of partnerships between firms and NGOs represent an important factor when researching the overall impact on CSR. Yet, how firms choose the NGO with which they want to collaborate, as well as the means by which they influence each other, also raises important questions. According to Margolis and Walsh (2003), the initial step in determining with which NGO an organization should partner is to assess which *social ills* the firm should focus on. According to their research, both internal and external agents of a firm give MNEs reason to act in a particular manner. Focusing on who these agents are, where they originate, how they communicate, and the standards they employ enables a company to select the NGO with which it wants to form a partnership. Margolis and Walsh (p. 285) use the term *extant theory* to explain how an "appellant's power, legitimacy, and urgency might determine the extent to which managers attend to a claim."

This type of reasoning is essential to understand the relationship between a firm and an NGO when the firm is making a rational decision to partner with an NGO. However, this is not always the case. Oftentimes the NGO exerts power over the firm, leaving the firm with little choice.

In sum, NGOs have emerged to become important players in the broader process of social activism. They launch formal campaigns against companies, or they may partner with them or both. The next section explores the more specific ways in which NGOs have sought to influence social finance and investment.

SRI AND SOCIAL ACTIVISM

The rise of NGOs has not only had a substantial impact on corporate responsibility generally, but it has also had specific affects on SRI. Although NGO activism in the financial realm has taken on various forms and exploited a range of strategies, the results are similar: many firms turn their attention toward investment practices highlighting nonfinancial metrics and practices. This new focus has created challenges for boards and managers that were previously focused solely on shareholder returns. The rise of socially responsible funds has proven to be a force destined to have a long-term presence.

Growth of SRI

Socially responsible investing (SRI) is an investment approach that uses both financial and nonfinancial criteria to determine which assets to purchase, but whose distinguishing characteristic is the latter. In SRI, investors typically look at a company's internal operating behavior (such as employment policies and benefits) and external practices and policies (such as effects on the environment and indigenous people), as well as its product line (such as tobacco or defense equipment) to determine whether they should become owners of the firm. Schueth (2003) traces the origins of SRI to early biblical times. However, the contemporary notion of using the power of financial markets to signal displeasure with certain corporate practices or to encourage others dates to the 1920s when various religious groups stipulated that their investments would not be used to support "sin" shares including liquor, tobacco, and gambling. SRI gained more widespread appeal in the 1960s, when the Vietnam War, civil rights and women's movements, environmental concerns, and other controversial political and social issues became factors in investment decisions. More broadly, some argue that all investments inherently possess ethical dimensions, whether explicitly or implicitly (Domini and Kinder 1986). Hence, SRI may be viewed as a subset of broader investment theory, with the ethical component made explicit and expressly specified.

In its *Report on Socially Responsible Investing Trends*, the Social Investment Forum (SIF) (2010) identified $3.07 trillion in total assets under management using one or more of the three core SRI strategies: screening, shareholder advocacy, and community investing. From 2007 to 2010, social investing enjoyed a growth rate of more than 13 percent, increasing from $2.71 trillion in 2007. According to the SIF, nearly one out of every eight dollars under professional management in the United States today—12.2 percent of the $25.2 trillion in total assets under management tracked by Thomson Reuters Nelson—is involved in SRI. Most of the assets are managed in separate accounts for institutional and individual clients.

As of 2010, the 250 socially screened mutual fund products in the United States had assets of $316.1 billion. By contrast, there were just 55 SRI funds in 1995 with $12 billion in assets. SRI mutual funds span a range of investments, including domestic and international investments, and a growing range of products are available, including hedge funds and exchange-traded funds (ETFs).

Of the various methods used to invest responsibly, investors primarily turn to screening and shareholder advocacy (Harrington 2003). *Screening* is the process by which investors seek out or avoid certain investments based on their social criteria (Glac 2009). For instance, SRI originally meant avoiding companies that partook in questionable activities such as tobacco and gambling. This practice started to change as more corporations advanced their SRI habits. Now, investors have taken on a different approach of actually pursuing those companies that invest responsibly. Given that many corporations no longer publicly advertise their SRI practices, extra effort is required to seek out those in the CSR arena.

Shareholder advocacy, which combines SRI with corporate stakeholder capitalism, is a means by which shareholders actively voice their opinions when they believe the corporation is not acting in a way that is consistent with stakeholder beliefs (Guay, Doh, and Sinclair 2004). For example, whereas the primary result of nonstakeholder action used to be the sales of those shares, investors now feel passionately about having themselves heard and creating change. MacLeod (2009. p. 79) explains that "In the aftermath of the well-publicized corporate scandals in the 1990s and early 2000s, we are increasingly focused on improving transparency and accountability of corporations." The underlying logic here is that investors, especially the largest institutional ones, have a more viable option in exercising voice (i.e., active governance in corporate activities and operations) rather than exit (selling shares in the company) (Hirschman 1970; MacLeod 2009). As a result, shareholders, often in conjunction with NGOs and other advocacy groups, have been an extremely powerful force in shaping corporate governance.

NGOs serve as advisors, information analysts, and consultants to funds focused on SRI. Socially-active clearinghouses such as the Investor Responsibility Resources Center (IRRC), Interfaith Center for Corporate Responsibility (ICCR), and Shareholder Action Network, often working with socially-responsible mutual funds and pensions funds, serve as coordinating mechanisms.

NGO Advocacy toward Institutional Investors and Pension Funds

NGO influencing strategies may simply take the form of advocacy efforts designed to press other shareholders, particularly institutional investors, to urge changes in managerial behavior or management officers. Two examples are the pressure exerted by NGOs during the South Africa divestment campaign and the efforts of student groups to persuade institutional investment funds (particularly university endowments) to remove certain stocks from their portfolios. NGOs concerned about human rights abuses and the antidemocratic orientation of Burma's military junta played an important role in persuading Massachusetts and 23 municipalities including New York City to pass selective purchasing legislation in the mid-1990s (Guay 2000). When the U.S. Supreme Court ruled the Massachusetts law unconstitutional in 2000, NGOs turned to these local governments with divestment plans, many of which were adopted. Breast Cancer Action, a San Francisco–based advocacy organization, has lobbied investment managers to co-author a resolution requiring the cosmetics company, Avon Products, to study the feasibility of removing possible carcinogens from its products. Domini Social Investments, Trillium Asset Management, and Walden Asset Management are sponsoring the resolution.

Social Investors, NGOs, and Shareholder Activism

NGO shareholder activism constitutes a direct challenge to boards and managers and draws attention to shareholder demands and by extension, the inadequacy of managerial actions (Parthiban, Hitt, and Gimeno 2001). Although managers can neutralize boards through control of director nominations (Walsh and Seward 1990), activism may upset the relationship between managers and a cooperative board. The human capital of directors depends on their performance as custodians of shareholder rights (Fama and Jensen 1983), but is increasingly tied to broader stakeholder interests, whether such stakeholders are themselves shareholders or not (Parthiban et al. 2001).

NGOs can influence corporate management and policy, and this influence can take several forms: public announcements, shareholder proposals, direct negotiations with managers, and proxy contests. NGO influence as shareholders may be limited where the dominance of large block shareholders such as institutional investors provides them with voting majorities and constrains the voice of minority shareholders. On the other hand, because of their public profile and stakeholder status, NGOs may influence corporate governance to a degree disproportionate to the shares owned, although some minimal number of ownership shares is required to engage in any of these activities.

The U.S. Securities and Exchange Commission (SEC) recognizes that generally any shareowner holding at least $2,000 in stock, for a minimum of one year before the company's annual submission deadline, may introduce a shareholder resolution. In recent years, shareholders, including NGOs working with or as part of public pension funds and socially responsible investment firms, have been able to withdraw dozens of resolutions asking companies to make pledges on a broad range of social, environmental, governance, and executive compensation (The Forum for Sustainable and Responsible Investment 2010).

For example, in 2006, activist shareholders achieved a major victory when Wal-Mart agreed to substantially expand its diversity reporting, including posting to its website its entire EEO-1 form, the statistical report large employers are required to file annually with the U.S. government. ICCR members successfully won management backing in 2004 for a resolution asking Coca-Cola Co. to report on the impact that HIV/AIDS was having on its African operations. In 2007, advocates of corporate sustainability reporting were able to withdraw proposals at 19 firms, reports SIF member RiskMetrics Group, when those firms agreed to report on their sustainability initiatives. Since the start of a shareholder campaign in 2004, an organization focusing on corporate political activity and its allies have persuaded 52 large companies, including 35 in the S&P 100, to disclose and require board oversight of political spending with corporate funds. Regarding executive pay, in 2006, a coalition of activist investors filed resolutions requesting Say on Pay at more than 60 companies (Social Investment Forum 2010).

Exhibits 20.1 through 20.5 present data on recent shareholder resolutions. Exhibit 20.1 shows the top corporate recipients of shareholder resolutions. While Exxon Mobil is the leading recipient of shareholder proposals, several large banks and financial institutions follow. Oil and gas companies are major targets of shareholder resolutions due to their potential impact on the natural environment. Also, Exxon Mobil was the target of extensive campaigning around rights and benefits for same-sex couples. Banks and financial institutions are popular targets for resolutions due to the impact they have on other companies and organizations. Given the rising nature of socially responsible investment practices, activists have focused on the environmental impact of financial investments by banks.

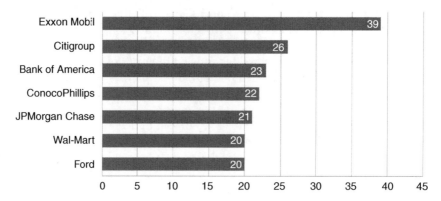

Exhibit 20.1   Top Recipients of Outside Shareholder Proposals during the Period 2008 to 2010

This exhibit shows the most frequent targets (recipients) of shareholder proposals during the period 2008 to 2010.

Source: Adapted from Social Investment Forum (2010). *Shareholder Resolutions Advance Social, Environmental and Corporate Governance Issues.* Available at www.socialinvest.org.

Exhibit 20.2 shows the leading sources of shareholder resolutions sponsors of shareholder proposals. Evelyn Davis is the largest source of such proposals. For almost 50 years, she has been fighting on behalf of shareholders and has been especially active on issues related to executive pay and corporate performance (Strauss 2003). The AFL-CIO, the largest union in the United States, ranks second, followed by John Cheveden, an author and activist fighting for management accountability and shareholder value.

Exhibit 20.3 shows the distribution of proposals by type, while Exhibit 20.4 shows the success rate of boards and shareholders adopting the resolutions. Together, Exhibits 20.3 and 20.4 show that, while social issues are the largest category of proposals, they are also the most difficult with which to achieve success.

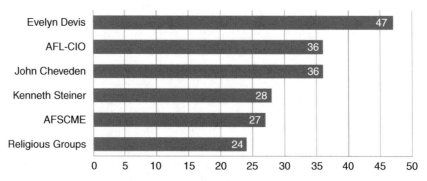

Exhibit 20.2   Most Active Sponsors of Shareholder Proposals and the Number of Shareholder Proposals Sponsored during the Period 2008 to 2010

This exhibit shows the most active sponsors (organizations and individuals) of shareholder proposals and the number of proposals each sponsored during the period 2008 to 2010.

Source: Adapted from Social Investment Forum (2010). *Shareholder Resolutions Advance Social, Environmental and Corporate Governance Issues.* Available at www.socialinvest.org.

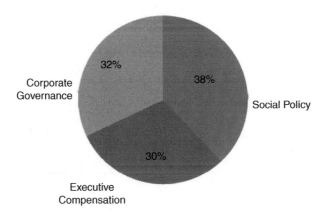

Exhibit 20.3 Types of Shareholder Proposals and Their Distribution
This exhibit shows the three main types of socially-oriented shareholder proposals and the percentage each constitutes of the total.
Source: Adapted from Social Investment Forum (2010). *Shareholder Resolutions Advance Social, Environmental and Corporate Governance Issues.* Available at www.socialinvest.org.

Exhibit 20.5 shows the small percentage, when compared to the whole amount of shareholder proposals, of adoption rates. In 2010 alone, target companies actually enacted only 8.4 percent of the more than 275 proposals. However, as the number of activists and proposals increase, this number could also rise.

NGO Sponsorship of SRI Funds

NGOs themselves are beginning to initiate SRI funds. In the mid-1990s, when the Sierra Club, the oldest, largest, and one of the most influential environmental advocacy groups in the United States, began looking to invest in socially responsible mutual funds, it was unable to find a fund that met its very strict definition of

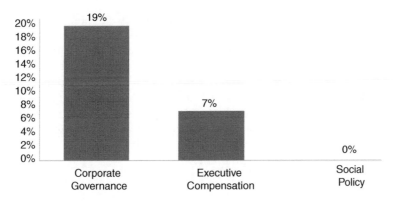

Exhibit 20.4 Adoption Rate of Shareholder Proposals by Type
This exhibit shows the adoption rates of the three most frequent types of social action shareholder proposals.
Source: Adapted from Social Investment Forum (2010). *Shareholder Resolutions Advance Social, Environmental and Corporate Governance Issues.* Available at www.socialinvest.org.

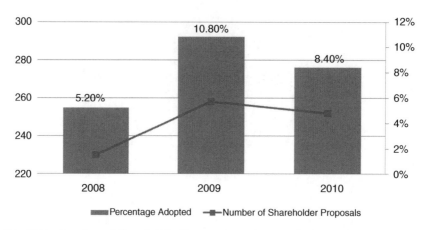

Exhibit 20.5   Number of Shareholder Proposals per Year and Their Adoption Rate during the Period 2008 to 2010

This exhibit presents the overall number of shareholder proposals (bar; left scale) and the percentage adopted by target companies (line, right scale) during the period 2008 to 2010.

Source: Adapted from Social Investment Forum (2010). *Shareholder Resolutions Advance Social, Environmental and Corporate Governance Issues.* Available at www.socialinvest.org.

social and environmental responsibility (Belsie 2001). All the funds invested in one or more companies the group could not support. Hence, the Sierra Club's investment advisory committee decided to hire outside financial advisors and screen the organization's recommendations according to its internal criteria. The Sierra Club had previously established a separate investment fund to use for buying small holdings in companies it views as particularly harmful to the environment. This enabled representatives from the Sierra Club to attend meetings of those corporations as shareholders and sponsor shareholder resolutions urging the companies to change their practices. In 2001, the group started its own mutual fund so that environmentally-minded investors could invest using the same screen (Cushman 2001).

In January of 2003, the Sierra Club officially launched The Sierra Club Stock Fund and the Sierra Club Balanced Fund. Forward Management, a San Francisco–based firm, manages the funds. Both funds use screens that were originally developed for use with the Sierra Club endowment's equity investments to exclude companies with poor environmental performance. Forward Management pays a portion of its management fees to the Sierra Club for identifying securities that meet the established environmental screening guidelines (SocialFund.com 2003). The Sierra Club uses this monetary infusion to support its ongoing environmental activism. This arrangement between the two organizations provides another way for these funds to promote a healthier environment.

Evolution, Progression, and Multiple Use of NGO Influencing Strategies

The influencing strategies described above can be viewed along a continuum reflecting an evolution of NGO involvement in efforts to affect corporate behavior through various investment vehicles. In the early stages of NGO activity, NGOs simply lobby or pressure other investors to take into account the NGOs' views in their investment behavior. As SRI funds became part of the financial landscape, NGOs worked with those funds to develop more credible screening approaches and investment strategies. These first two strategies are largely indirect; they reflect NGOs working through intermediaries—moderators or mediators of their agenda. Once NGOs themselves become shareholders, they may have a direct impact on corporate behavior through their shareholder status. As NGOs themselves have established mutual funds, they have the opportunity to leverage the investment funds of others to influence changes in corporate behavior. These strategies are more direct, and in the case of the latter, allow NGOs to amplify their influence.

NGOs often use several of these influencing strategies to accomplish their goals. In the case of Friends of the Earth (FOE), multiple advocacy and activism strategies occur simultaneously. One common outcome of shareholder resolutions appears to be their withdrawal once boards agree to consider or act on the issues that are the focus of the resolutions. For example, shareholders withdrew resolutions from Duke Energy, Cinergy, Goodyear, and Texaco when they agreed to enter into discussion on global warming. Resolutions at Alcoa and Hasbro were withdrawn pending discussion on the Coalition for Environmentally Responsible Economies (CERES) principles, the global environmental reporting standard and an important element of which is the Global Reporting Initiative. The resolution regarding criteria for underwriting the Three Gorges Dam, a controversial project in China, was withdrawn from Citigroup, as was a resolution concerning fuel consumption at Ford and General Motors. Hence, even when resolutions fail to garner a majority of shareholder votes, the combination of activism and the public messages associated with it can accomplish NGO goals. In the case of the Sierra Club, the mutual fund initiative complements and reinforces its other activism and advocacy efforts, providing a comprehensive multiple-front influencing strategy that takes advantage of the range of tools and techniques available to it. By founding a mutual fund, NGOs such as the Sierra Club may be better able to recruit and retain members.

SUMMARY AND CONCLUSIONS

Social activism, particularly through the use of NGOs or other advocacy groups, has had an immense impact on socially responsible finance and investing. Their powerful influence and growing numbers have begun to shape CSR practices within corporations, which in turn can have an influence on further CFP performance, as research has shown. Also, NGO power, reach, and advocacy tactics create a strong voice and presence in the corporate arena. This can be seen in the rise of SRI and shareholder advocacy, oftentimes in which boards are directly challenged on topics related to SRI. Although NGOs were once known for their indirect strategic influence in the financial realm, their current power and often controversial approaches have created a new way of doing business in today's complex environment. The reach and power and these groups will continue to evolve, and with that the financial and investment organizations will continuously change as well.

This chapter suggests several possible avenues for future research. First, social actors clearly use and employ alternate tactics for influencing finance and investment. Further research should examine the substitution and complementary effects of such tactics including interactions among them. Second, social media provide a new platform for social actors to mobilize and influence. How have social networks affected the growth, influence and strategies of social activists? Finally, the coordination and collaboration among social activists should be more deeply examined, as well as the evolution of engagements between social actors and their corporate counterparts.

DISCUSSION QUESTIONS

1. What is the relationship among social activism, social actors, civil society, and NGOs?
2. What are the two types of NGOs, and how do they differ?
3. Compare and contrast the two different types of advocacy campaigns.
4. Bostrom and Hallstrom (2010) present a theory of NGO power in their research and differentiate among the four types. Explain what is meant by *power* and detail the different categories.
5. Explain the different mechanisms by which NGOs influence SRI.

REFERENCES

Barnett, Michael L., and Andrew J. Hoffman. 2008."Beyond Corporate Reputation: Managing Reputational Interdependence."*Corporate Reputation Review* 11:1, 1–9.

Baron, David P. 2001. "Private Politics, Corporate Social Responsibility, and Integrated Strategy." *Journal of Economics and Management Strategy* 10:1, 7–45.

Belsie, Laurent. 2001. "Rise of the Name-Brand Fund: A Few Affinity Groups Help Investors Put Their Money Where Their Hearts Are." *Christian Science Monitor* 13:August, 16.

Bostrom, Magnus, and Kristina T. Hallstrom. 2010. "NGO Power in Global Social and Environmental Standard-Setting." *Global Environmental Politics* 10:4, 36–59.

Carson, Rachel.1962. *Silent Spring*. New York: First Mariner Books.

Clarkson, Max B. E. 1995. "A Stakeholder Framework for Analyzing and Evaluating Corporate Social Performance." *Academy of Management Review* 20:1, 92–117.

Cushman, John H. 2001."Sierra Club Considers a Mutual Fund." *New York Times*, July 20, A19.

Doh, Jonathan P., and Terrence Guay. 2006. "Corporate Social Responsibility, Public Policy, and NGO Activism in Europe and the U.S.: An Institutional-Stakeholder Perspective." *Journal of Management Studies* 43:1, 47–73.

Doh, Jonathan P., Shawn D. Howton, Shelly W. Howton, and Donald S. Siegel. 2010. "Does the Market Respond to an Endorsement of Social Responsibility? The Role of Information, Institutions, and Legitimacy." *Journal of Management* 36:6, 1461–1485.

Doh, Jonathan P., and Hildy Teegen. 2003. *Globalization and NGOs: Transforming Business, Governments, and Society*. Westport, CT: Praeger.

Domini, Amy L., and Peter D. Kinder. 1986. *Ethical Investing*. Reading, MA: Addison Wesley.

Donaldson, Thomas, and Lee E. Preston. 1995. "The Stakeholder Theory of the Corporation: Concepts, Evidence, and Implications."*Academy of Management Review* 20:1, 65–91.

Fama, Eugene F., and Michael C. Jensen. 1983. "Separation of Ownership and Control." *Journal of Law and Economics* 26:2, 301–325.

Freeman, R. Edward. 1984. *Strategic Management: A Stakeholder Approach*. Boston: Pittman.

Glac, Katherina. 2009. "Understanding Socially Responsible Investing: The Effect of Decision Frames and Trade-off Options." Journal of Business Ethics 87:1, 41–55.

Guay, Terrence. 2000. "Local Government and Global Politics: The Implications of Massachusetts 'Burma Law.'" *Political Science Quarterly* 115:3, 353–376.

Guay, Terrence, Jonathan Doh, and Graham Sinclair. 2004. "Nongovernmental Organizations, Shareholder Activism, and Socially Responsible Investments: Ethical, Strategic, and Governance Implications." *Journal of Business Ethics* 52:1, 125–139.

Harrington, Cynthia. 2003. "Socially Responsible Investing: Balancing Financial Needs with a Concern for Others." *Journal of Accountancy* 195:January, 52–57.

Hart, Stuart, and Mark Milstein. 2003. "Creating Sustainable Value." *Academy of Management Executive* 17:2, 56–69.

Hirschman, Albert. 1970. *Exit, Voice, and Loyalty*. Cambridge: Harvard University Press.

Independent Sector. 2004. *The New Nonprofit Almanac*. Washington, D.C.: The Independent Sector.

Jones, Thomas M., and Andrew C. Wicks. 1999. "Convergent Stakeholder Theory." *Academy of Management Review* 24:2, 206–221.

Kellow, Ansley. 2000. "Norms, Interests and Environmental NGOs: The Limits of Cosmopolitanism." *Environmental Politics* 9:3, 1–22.

King, Brayden G. 2008. "A Political Mediation Model of Corporate Response to Social Movement Activism." *Administrative Science Quarterly* 53:3, 395–421.

King, Brayden G., and Sarah A. Soule. 2007. "Social Movements as Extra-Institutional Entrepreneurs: The Effect of Protests on Stock Price Returns." *Administrative Science Quarterly* 52:3, 413–442.

Li, Gina. 2001. "An Analysis: The Impact of Non-Governmental Organizations on the Practice of Public Relations." *Public Relations Quarterly* 46:4, 11–14.

MacLeod, Michael R. 2009. "Emerging Investor Networks and the Construction of Corporate Social Responsibility." *Journal of Corporate Citizenship* 34: Summer, 69–96.

Margolis, Joshua, and James Walsh. 2003. "Misery Loves Companies: Rethinking Social Initiatives by Business." *Administrative Science Quarterly* 48:2, 268–305.

Margolis, Joshua D., Hillary A. Elfenbein, and James P. Walsh. 2007. "Does It Pay to Be Good? A Meta-Analysis and Redirection of Research on the Relationship between Corporate Social and Financial Performance." Paper Presentation, Academy of Management. Philadelphia, PA.

McWilliams, Abagail, Donald S. Siegel, and Patrick M. Wright. 2006. "Corporate Social Responsibility: Strategic Implications." *Journal of Business Strategies* 23:1, 1–12.

Mitchell, Ronald, Bradley R. Agle, and Donna J. Wood. 1997. "Toward a Theory of Stakeholder Identification and Salience: Defining the Principle of Who and What Really Counts." *Academy of Management Review* 22:4, 853–866.

Orlitzky, Marc, Frank L. Schmidt, and Sara L. Rynes. 2003. "Corporate Social and Financial Performance: A Meta-analysis." *Organization Studies* 24:3, 403–441.

Parthiban, David, Michael A. Hitt, and Javier Gimeno. 2001. "The Influence of Activism by Institutional Investors on R&D." *Academy of Management Journal* 44:1, 144–157.

Peloza, John, and Loren Falkenberg. 2009. "The Role of Collaboration in Achieving Corporate Social Responsibility Objectives." *California Management Review* 51:3, 95–113.

Schueth, Steve. 2003. "Socially Responsible Investing in the United States." *Journal of Business Ethics* 43:3, 189–194.

Selsky, John, and Barbara Parker. 2005. "Cross-Sector Partnerships to Address Social Issues: Challenges to Theory and Practice." *Journal of Management* 31:6, 849–873.

Socialfund.com. 2003. "Sierra Club Launches SRI Mutual Funds."Available at http://www.socialfunds.com/news/article.cgi/article1006.html).

Social Investment Forum. 2010. "Shareholder Resolutions Advance Social, Environmental and Corporate Governance Issues." Available at www.socialinvest.org.

Spar, Debora L., and Lane T. La Mure. 2003. "The Power of Activism: Assessing the impact of NGOs on Global Business." *California Management Review* 45:3, 78–101.

Strauss, Gary. 2003. "Queen of the Corporate Jungle Stalks Annual Meetings." *USAToday.com.* Available at www.usatoday.com/money/companies/management/2003-04-27-shareholders-davis_x.htm.

Teegen, Hildy, Jonathan P. Doh, and Sushil Vachani. 2004. "The Importance of Nongovernmental Organizations (NGOs) in Global Governance and Value Creation: An International Business Research Agenda." *Journal of International Business Studies* 35:6, 463–483.

The Forum for Sustainable and Responsible Investment. 2010. "Advocacy & Public Policy: Shareholder Resolutions." Available at http://ussif.org/projects/advocacy/resolutions.cfm.

United Nations. 2003. "NGO Committee Concludes 2002 Resumed Session, with Final Recommendations on Economic and Social Council Consultative Status." UN Press Release NGO/494.

vanTuijl, Peter. 1999. "NGOs and Human Rights: Sources of Justice and Democracy." *Journal of International Affairs* 52:2, 493–512.

Waddock, Sandra A., and Samuel B. Graves. 1997. "The Corporate Social Performance–Financial Performance Link." *Strategic Management Journal* 18:4, 303–319.

Walsh, James P., and James K. Seward. 1990. "On the Efficiency of Internal and External Corporate Control Mechanisms." *Academy of Management Review* 15:3, 421–458.

Yaziji, Michael, and Jonathan P. Doh. 2009. *NGOs and Corporations: Conflict and Collaboration.* Cambridge: Cambridge University Press.

ABOUT THE AUTHORS

Jonathan P. Doh is the Herbert G. Rammrath Endowed Chair in International Business, founding director of the Center for Global Leadership, and professor of Management and Operations at the School of Business, Villanova University. Previously, he was on the faculty of American University and Georgetown University and a senior trade official with the U.S. government. Professor Doh is author or co-author of more than 50 refereed articles published in the top international business and management journals, 30 chapters in scholarly edited volumes, and more than 50 conference papers. Recent articles have appeared in journals such as *Academy of Management Review, California Management Review, Journal of International Business Studies, Management Information Systems Quarterly, Organization Science, Sloan Management Review,* and *Strategic Management Journal.* He is co-editor and/or co-author of seven books, including *Globalization and NGOs* with Hildy Teegen (Praeger, 2003), *Handbook on Responsible Leadership and Governance in Global Business* with Steve Stumpf (Elgar, 2005), *Multinationals and Development* with Alan Rugman (Yale University Press, 2008), *NGOs and Corporations: Conflict and Collaboration* with Michael Yaziji (Cambridge University Press, 2009), and *International Management: Culture, Strategy, and Behavior,* 8th edition (McGraw-Hill/Irwin, 2012). Professor Doh received his Ph.D. from George Washington University in strategic and international management.

Deborah Zachar is an MBA candidate at the School of Business, Villanova University. She has worked in the hospitality and pharmaceutical industries, traveled extensively, and has made presentations and/or written on diverse topics including social media, American history, childhood development, and food and wine. She received her undergraduate degree in business administration with a concentration in marketing from the Lerner College of Business at the University of Delaware.

PART IV

Socially Responsible Investing

CHAPTER 21

Corporate Socially Responsible Investments

JOHN R. BECKER-BLEASE
Assistant Professor of Finance, Oregon State University

INTRODUCTION

Few topics in business garner as much widespread interest as the debate over the social responsibility of corporations. Discussion of corporate social responsibility (CSR) permeates both the popular press and academia. Research articles related to the antecedents that affect the legality and definition of CSR populate academic journals across all of the business disciplines, economics, law, engineering, and the sciences. The breadth and depth of coverage suggests not only the importance placed on the corporate form of business, but also the unsettled status of the wisdom and impact of CSR on business and society.

This chapter explores how CSR affects and is affected by a firm's investment decisions. The discussion focuses primarily on a firm's real and financial asset investment decisions, frequently called socially responsible investing (SRI). The chapter begins with a discussion of CSR and the definition of a corporate socially responsible investment (CSRI). The chapter then briefly discusses some of the empirical challenges faced in exploring the link between CSRI and corporate financial performance (CFP). Next, five commonly hypothesized sources of CSRI's impact on the firm are discussed, and an overview of the empirical evidence associated with each source is presented. The final section provides a summary and conclusions.

DEFINING CSRI

This section reviews various definitions of what constitutes CSR and CSRI. It also describes some of the challenges empiricists face when attempting to measure CSRI.

CSR

Although CSR has no single generally accepted definition, most conceptualizations center on the relationships that exist between the corporation and those parties whose interests are tied to the corporation. Freeman (1984, p. 25) describes the stakeholders of the corporation as "any group of individual who can affect or is affected by the achievement of the organization's objectives." The question of why stakeholders, particularly nonshareholder stakeholders, might warrant exceptional attention from management harkens back to the role of for-profit corporations in society. Beginning with Adam Smith (1776) and the concept of the "invisible hand," economic theory has generally evolved to demonstrate that under certain assumptions, optimization of overall social welfare occurs when the value of the firm is optimized, which, in turn, results when shareholders' wealth is optimized. In the context of these perfect market assumptions, nonshareholders deserve, or perhaps more accurately, need no special attention. This situation underlies Friedman's (1970, p. SM17) assertion that "there is one and only one social responsibility of business—to use it its resources to engage in activities designed to increase its profits so long as is stays within the rules of the game, which is to say, engages in open and free competition without deception or fraud."

Yet, most economists would agree that the assumptions necessary for Friedman's guidance to be taken literally are too strong under current conditions. Most notably, present contracting technology is insufficient to uniformly link stakeholders' interests to the firm's interests. Markets are frequently incomplete and result in externalities that government oversight cannot adequately resolve, and monopolistic and monopsonistic power persist. The presence of these factors leads to a tension between maximizing shareholder wealth and maximizing social welfare.

Some view CSR as strictly focused on nonshareholder stakeholder interests, irrespective of the impact on shareholder wealth or firm value. Hopkins (2004, p. 1), for instance, suggests that CSR relates specifically to the treatment of stakeholders in an ethical or responsible manner "acceptable in civilized societies." Similarly, the Commission of the European Communities (2001, p. 4) defines CSR as a concept by which "companies decide voluntarily to contribute to a better society and a cleaner environment." McWilliams and Siegel (2001, p. 117) extend this definition to include "actions that appear to further some social good, beyond the interests of the firm and that which is required by law." Each of these is consistent with Friedman's (1970) notion of corporate social responsibility.

According to Baron (2001), social performance alone is insufficient to identify CSR because intent is also a necessary component. That is, if the firm engages in actions with the intent to maximize firm value, but in the process creates spillovers that benefit stakeholders, then the firm has created a "social good," but has not taken a "socially responsible action." Conversely, if the firm elects to expend resources beyond the level required to optimize firm value with the intent of creating a spillover, then this altruism is deemed CSR. Beltratti (2005) notes that CSR as altruism necessarily implies a negative relationship between CSR and firm value.

Others view the apparent dichotomy between shareholders' interests and society's interests as false; CSR in this view can be a necessary consideration in shareholder wealth maximization. Termed *strategic CSR* by Baron (2001), this view suggests that pursuing activities associated with CSR can improve a firm's financial prospects. For example, Heal (2005, p. 393) defines CSR as "taking actions which reduce the extent of externalized costs or avoid distributional conflicts." He notes that society views corporations as having entered implicit contracts with various stakeholders, as well as the explicit contracts already protected by law. Hence, society will maintain the status quo as long as the corporation does not violate these implied contracts. Similarly, Martin, Petty, and Wallace (2009) suggest that CSR is linked to honoring the implicit contracts with stakeholders, which leads to an enhanced reputation for the firm that can result in better access to employees and capital markets as well as the ability to charge premium prices. Thus, strategic CSR suggests that the relationships between the firm and stakeholders can be important elements of a firm's overall competitiveness.

CSR as a strategy is largely consistent with Jensen's (2010) formulation of enlightened value maximization. Jensen contends that firms should consider all stakeholders in order to optimize long-term value. Exploiting stakeholders, while potentially benefitting short-term value, is likely to result in ex post settling up by these or other stakeholders in a manner that ultimately harms long-term value.

CSRI

Defining CSRI is challenging for two reasons. First, CSR is broadly defined by executives. For example, according to a survey by Grant Thorton (2007) of U.S. firms' officers and directors, greater than 50 percent of respondents believe that firms should be, or that their firm is, "extremely" or "very" responsible in the sale of safe products/services to the public, transparency of business and financial operations, safe and clean environment, employee/worker rights, and human rights. Further, of those that employed a corporate responsibility officer, greater than 45 percent indicate their firm was very/extremely responsible in providing affordable health care, economic stability to communities, philanthropy, improved educational standards, and an adequate standard of living for society. Thus, many activities such as personnel policies, design and production choices, community investments, and accounting choices contribute to managers' perception of CSR, and could be considered investments in that they require the commitment of firm resources.

The second challenge relates to identifying CSR activities. If, as Baron (2001) contends, CSR is to be understood as the product of action and intent, then observing CSR is essentially impossible. Instead, researchers are typically forced to focus on what is commonly termed corporate social performance (CSP) or corporate responsibility performance (CRP). *CSP* is defined as the strategies and practices firms implement that affect their relationships with various stakeholders, and is functionally the same as CSRI.

In this chapter, CSRI is broadly defined in a manner that is consistent with the Grant Thorton (2007) survey data. That is, CSRI represents are policies or actions that require the commitment of firm resources that target at some level the relationship between a firm and its nonshareholder stakeholders.

One common criticism of early research efforts into the relationship between CSRI and firm performance is the limited nature of the data on CSRI. Surroca, Tribo, and Waddock (2010) and Wood and Jones (1995) describe the limitations of a single-item approach. CSRI is generally understood to be a complex nexus of relationships among stakeholders and the firm. Examining the impact of a single measure of CSRI can lead to *stakeholder mismatching*. This is particularly true when the measures are applied across industries without controls since the relative importance of relationships with stakeholders likely varies. The criticisms are somewhat allayed by the introduction of the broad-based index measures such as Kinder Lyndenburg Domini (KLD), Ethical Investment Research Service (EIRIS), and Sustainanalytics. These databases provide an independent source of externally collected data that encompasses multiple dimensions of CSRI and has consistency across time.

CSRI AND FIRM PERFORMANCE

A substantial empirical literature has evolved over the past three decades investigating the impact of CSRI on firm performance. As has been widely discussed, this literature has been plagued with many issues, including evolving empirical methodologies, data sources, theoretical underpinnings, and regulatory regimes. Further, as Tirole (2001) discusses, an evolution has occurred over the period towards a *stakeholder society* that involves an expanding public perception of the role of business in society. This evolving awareness likely affects all of the markets in which a firm and its stakeholders interact. For instance, the growing awareness and agreement regarding humans' deleterious impact on the environment has caused customers, suppliers, communities, and governments to alter their contracting with businesses over the past several decades. This section describes five manners in which increased CSRI can positively affect long-term firm value.

Potential Benefits of CSRI to the Firm

Overall, a broad consensus exists within the literature of a positive link between CSR and firm value. For instance, the meta-analyses and literature reviews reported in Margolis and Walsh (2001); Orlitzky and Benjamin (2001); Orlitzky, Schmidt, and Rynes (2003); Wu (2006), Dam (2008); and Blanco, Rey-Maquieira, and Lozano (2009) report varied but generally confirmatory evidence that CSRI is positively associated with CFP.

If managers are able to create long-term value through stakeholder relationships, then what are the potential sources of this value? In other words, what kind of CSRI can lead to improvements in overall value? Based loosely on Heal (2005), this chapter identifies five commonly hypothesized sources of a relationship between CSRI and CFP, including the relationships with employees, customers, and regulators, careful consideration of resource use, and a firm's cost of capital.

Employees

Barney (1997) suggests that competitive advantage, which is the cornerstone of superior financial performance, is derived from a firm's ability to create unique and difficult-to-duplicate resources that improve its ability to identify and exploit market opportunities and diminish threats. Lado and Wilson (1994) and Wright, Ferris, Hiller, and Kroll (1995), among others, suggest that human capital is one of the most important sources of competitive advantage.

Moskowitz (1972) is among the first to suggest a relationship between CSR and human resources. He contends that firms with favorable CSR reputations are likely to benefit from high employee morale and productivity without bearing the full direct cost. Similarly, Davis (1973) and Kreps and Spence (1983) suggest that firms developing a good reputation with employees are better able to attract and retain them, and are able to do so at lower costs than less reputable competitors. The proposed relationship among stakeholder engagement, human capital, and firm value has also begun to appear in the finance academic literature. Zingales (2000) and Jensen (2010), for instance, both suggest that investments in stakeholder welfare can provide important improvements in a firm's reputational and human capital.

Jiao (2010) suggests that such investments in intangibles can have a material and positive impact on firm value. In a sample of 4,027 firm-years across 822 firms, he documents a positive relationship between firm value, as measured by Tobin's Q, and stakeholder engagement, as captured by KLD data. Jiao also finds that the relationship between value and CSRI is strongest for employee relations and the environment. Galema, Plantinga, and Scholtens (2008), who report excess returns associated with employee relations within the KLD data universe, find similar evidence.

One manner in which a positive CSR program can benefit a firm is through improved recruiting outcomes. Specifically, if CSRI reduces recruiting costs or increases the pool of qualified applicants, firms can benefit. Some empirical evidence supports this link. Gatewood, Gowan, and Lautenschlager (1993), for instance, find that corporate image is an important determinant of recruiting attractiveness. Turban and Greening (1997) report that a firm's attractiveness as an employer is positively linked to its KLD ranking in "employee relations" and "product quality."

CSR can also positively affect current employees' perception and treatment of the firm. Riordan, Gatewood, and Bill (1997) find that employees' perception of their employer's external reputation affects their own assessment of the firm. In a sample of 174 employee interviews, the authors discover that negative external images of the firm are associated with a significantly higher likelihood of employee departure and higher job satisfaction. Similarly, Hansen, Dunford, Boss, Boss, and Angermeier (2011) find that employees respond to their perceptions of CSR activities. In two separate experiments with a total of 3,538 observations, they report a positive perception of the firm's CSR standing by employees significantly increases retention likelihood. The authors conclude that the driver of employees' desire to stay is the establishment and enhancement of trust felt by the employee towards the firm. Further evidence, including Valentine and Fleischman (2008), Jose and Thibodeaux (1999), and Koh and Boo (2001), finds a positive association between perceived organizational ethics and employees' attitudes towards work and the organization.

Evidence also suggests that firms can benefit from direct investments that target employees' interests. For instance, a literature has evolved around employer efforts to attract and retain underrepresented groups of employees such as women and minorities. To the extent that discrimination has resulted in underutilizing the talent found in these populations, CSRI efforts can benefit the firm.

The empirical evidence of the performance impact of such employee-focused policies is generally consistent with a positive CSRI-CFP link. For instance, related to gender, Weber and Zulehner (2010) examine the effect of start-ups adopting a proactive policy of having women among the first hires. In a sample of 29,879 start-up firms, their results show that hiring a woman within the first year of operations is positively related to the proportion of the future workforce that consists of women, is consistent with a positive financial impact, and has a significantly greater survival rate of the venture.

Specific investment in infrastructure, such as on-site childcare facilities, or policies, such as flex-time, that ease the work-family balance can also help to attract and retain valuable talent (Goodstein 1994). Although not widely investigated in the literature, empirical evidence is generally supportive of this notion. For instance, Perry-Smith and Blum (2000) investigate a sample of 727 firms with varying levels of investment in work-family systems. Their evidence indicates that firms with strong work-family systems are associated with accounting performance improvements and market performance. Similarly, Arthur and Cook (2004) find that 231 family-friendly announcements are associated with generally positive announcement returns. Interestingly, the effect is most pronounced for early-adopters rather than late-adopters.

The evidence is not uniform, however. Filbeck and Preece (2003a), for instance, investigate the impact of a firm's inclusion on the *Working Mother Annual Survey of Family-Friendly Firms* on the firm value. In their sample of 329 nonconfounded events, they report a negative two-day response by the market to a firm's inclusion in the list. The general pattern of negativity persists over longer event-windows up to 10 days, which leads them to conclude that the market does not value family-friendly initiatives.

In a related study, Filbeck and Preece (2003b) investigate the impact of inclusion in the *Fortune 100 Best Companies to Work For* list in 1998. Based on a sample of 57 firms for which sufficient financial data are available, the authors document an overall positive return in the two weeks leading up to and including the announcement date of the composition of the list. However, the positive returns are largely, but not entirely, reversed during the subsequent two weeks of trading. Their overall conclusion is that the market interprets inclusion in the list as good news about the satisfaction of the firms' workforces, and that workforce contentment is associated with firm value.

In a follow-up study, Ahmed, Nanda, and Schnusenberg (2010) expand the sample to include *Fortune 100 Best Companies to Work For* firms listed between 1998 and 2003. Similar to Filbeck and Preece (2003b), they find a positive announcement returns associated with inclusion in the sample during the six-year period. They also document limited evidence that ex post operating performance improves, and suggest that higher social responsibility towards employees results in superior financial performance.

Additional evidence suggests that firms are responsive to the employment concerns of their workers. Verwijmeren and Derwall (2010), for instance, examine the relationship between firms' reputation for addressing employee well-being and the capital structure decisions that firms make. In a sample of 7,494 firm-years, the authors find that leverage is negatively related to a given firm's KLD rankings in employee well-being. Bae, Kang, and Wang (2011) report similar results for both additional KLD data and when employee treatment is based on *Fortune* magazine's 100 Best Companies to Work For. These results are consistent with the insights offered by Berk, Stanton, and Zechner (2010) that bankruptcy costs and the resulting loss in human capital are a critical indirect cost of bankruptcy. Firms appear to be rewarded for this loyalty to employees, as Verwijmeren and Derwall also document a positive relationship between leverage-adjusted credit ratings and employee relations.

Customers

A considerable literature has evolved around the impact that CSRI efforts have on customer relations and firm performance. While much of the early evidence is anecdotal, Esrock and Leichty (1998) report compelling evidence that firms consider information about their CSRI efforts to be important to current and potential customers based on their findings that more than 80 percent of Fortune 500 companies specifically address CSR issues on their web sites. Generally, CSRI is hypothesized to influence firm performance through its impact on customer behavior including broadening the customer base, permitting suppliers to charge premium prices, and increasing perceived switching costs (Barnett 2007).

Early survey evidence is largely consistent with customers stating a preference for firms and products with positive CSR reputations (Smith 2003). However, despite reporting a preference for CSR-inspired products and suppliers, very little empirical evidence supports a direct relationship between CRSI and customer purchasing decisions (Bhattacharya and Sen 2004; Castaldo, Perrini, Misani, and Tencati 2009). Further, customer beliefs about the importance of CSRI seem primarily self-centered or at least lacking in altruism. For instance, Page and Fearn (2005, p. 307) find wide-spread agreement among customers that "it's up to companies to find ways to produce goods in a responsible way without increasing prices."

Researchers have hypothesized that the relationship between CSRI and purchase decisions is likely more nuanced than a direct effect. For instance, Brown and Dacin (1997) find that consumer beliefs about the company, rather than specific beliefs about a product, seem most important in consumption decisions. That is, only if a consumer had formed a positive impression of the company would that person be influenced by specific beliefs regarding the product. Similarly, Sen and Bhattacharya (2001) find that CSRI can affect both consumers' evaluation of the company and the relative attractiveness of its products, but only along specific pathways. For instance, congruence must exist between customer's beliefs and company CSR positioning in order for CSRI to affect behavior.

Porter and Kramer (2006), who suggest a *license to operate* component to CSRI activities, highlight an interesting dimension between CSRI and consumption choices, That is, CSRI efforts are intended to allow a firm to cluster with other firms in the industry and not become the target of social penalties. Although strong CSRI may not differentiate a firm, failure to do so could. Brown and Dacin (1997) and Castaldo et al. (2009) report confirmatory evidence of this relationship. Sen and Bhattacharya (2001, p. 238) state that "all consumers react negatively to negative CSR information, whereas only those most supportive of the CSR issues react positively to positive CSR information."

Researchers have also considered whether CSRI affects how firms view and transact with one another. For instance, Murray and Vogel (1997) find that managers are more willing to transact with another firm after they have been informed about that firm's CSR efforts. Similarly, Lai, Chiu, Yang, and Pai (2010) examine whether CSRI can affect firm reputation and brand value in business-to-business markets. Based on a survey sample of 179 Taiwanese manufacturing and service companies, they find that CSRI is positively associated with industrial brand equity and performance.

Evidence also suggests that firms consider the nature of the buyer-supplier relationship when making important corporate decisions. For instance, Titman (1984) suggests that a firm's optimal capital structure is influenced by the nature of its relationships with stakeholders when switching costs are high. Banerjee, Dasgupta, and Kim (2008) provide a test of this hypothesis using a sample of manufacturing firms between 1979 and 1997. Specifically, they hypothesize that when the customer-supplier relationship is bilateral, as would occur when a customer constitutes a sizeable portion of a given supplier's sales, both the customer and supplier are interested in minimizing financial risk and thus reducing the potential switching costs associated with liquidation. Their results confirm that when a supplier and customer are in a bilateral relationship, both tend to maintain relatively low levels of leverage. They find this relationship is most pronounced within durable goods industries, where bilateral relationships are most likely to lead to relationship-specific investments or physical asset specificity.

CSRI efforts can also have a deleterious effect on customer relations in certain contexts. Speed and Thompson (2000), for instance, find that sponsorships can harm value when perceived tension exists between the sponsored cause and the firm's reputation. Brady (2003) cites the case of McDonald's efforts to team with UNICEF in fundraising efforts. The proposed partnership led to an outcry from some community members due to the perceived tension between UNICEF's promotion of good nutrition and McDonald's reputation in this regard.

Luo and Bhattacharya (2006) provide additional evidence on the intricacies of the customer relation with CSRI. In their sample of 339 firm-years, they find that customer satisfaction mediates the relationship between CSRI and Tobin's Q. However, if the firm is a low-innovator, CSRI can actually lower satisfaction and harm value. The authors interpret this result as customers interpreting CSRI efforts by constrained firms as squandering scarce resources.

One particularly interesting area in which CSRI and customer relations appear particularly strong is in the area of green real estate. Eichholtz, Kok, and Quigley (2010) suggest that green construction can influence customer behavior of commercial properties and result in higher rents. Potential tenants may view a green facility as providing a better work environment for their employees, enhancing the firm's reputation with potential clients, and providing a longer-lasting, more stable location.

Green construction, however, likely comes at a cost. The direct costs associated with acquiring materials, services, and consultants can be more expensive than for a traditionally built structure and frequently indirect costs are associated with having a building officially certified as green. The two most widely known indicators of green construction are the Energy Star label and a Leadership in Energy and Environmental Design (LEED) rating. Fuerst and McAllister (2011a) report a relative scarcity of examinations into the added cost of green-building, especially within academic outlets. However, several industry-based analyses suggest green buildings can be constructed at a 0 to 2 percent premium compared to traditional construction costs.

Researchers have explored three potential sources of value from green construction: higher rental rates, higher sale price, and higher occupancy rates. The evidence is generally consistent with green-building providing economic value. For instance, Eichholtz et al. (2010) find that in a sample of 10,000 LEED or Energy Star buildings rental rates are, on average 3 percent higher for green buildings, and sale prices are up to 16 percent higher. In additional analyses, the authors report that the increased energy efficiency of the sites explains much of the premiums, but a residual impact appears from intangible benefits of the listing. Fuerst and McAllister (2011b) find in a similar sample that the LEED (Energy Star) certification adds approximately 5 percent (4 percent) to rental values and 25 percent (26 percent) to sale price.

Fuerst and McAllister (2011a) examine occupancy rates as well as dual-certificates. Similar to previous results, they find a 3 to 5 percent rental premium for LEED or Energy Star–rated buildings, which increases to approximately 9 percent when buildings are dual-certified. Sale premiums are similarly affected by dual-certification with a single-rated premium of 18 to 25 percent and a dual-rated premium of 28 to 29 percent. They do not document any measurable difference in occupancy rates for LEED buildings and a 1 percent for Energy Star.

Resource Efficiency

Pollution is a common example of how corporate profitability and society's interests can conflict. Pollution is a classic example of a negative externality in that the social costs exceed the private costs and is the product of ill-defined or unenforceable property rights. Although a Pigouvian tax, or a tax levy tied directly to the magnitude of a negative externality, set at the private-social cost difference will theoretically rectify this problem by essentially forcing the polluter to internalize the externality, correctly assessing the tax is difficult.

How firms use and dispose of resources and byproducts is an important component of most business decisions. Some suggest that careful consideration of resource use and disposal efforts that are consistent with CSRI can help to improve financial performance. As discussed below, some researchers previously discussed various pathways for improved performance as they relate to reputational effects and improved relations with employees and customers, as well as potentially reducing the likelihood or impact of shareholder activism or government regulation. In this section, the chapter focuses on how CSRI can lead to improved resource efficiency and its effect on firm performance.

Multiple anecdotes help to illustrate how CRSI targeted at resource efficiency can benefit a firm's bottom line. Heal (2005) describes the case of British Petroleum (BP), which in 1997 took a proactive stance on the environmental impact of fossil-fuel on global greenhouse gas emissions. The firm adopted an emissions trading system and imposed a system-wide cap on emissions. Rather than being harmed by these necessary outlays, BP reports a net positive impact of $600 million. The savings derive from quantifying the opportunity costs of previously undocumented losses due to pollution. For instance, some initially considered the flaring natural gas from wells a "costless" venting, resulting in pollution. When BP attempted to capture the natural gas to lower emissions, the firm gained a valuable commodity. As Heal points out, the social cost of releasing the natural gas was also an unrecognized opportunity cost for the firm (that is, a private cost).

Sharfman, Meo, and Ellington (2000) provide a more detailed but similar example based on Conoco's early 1990s response to the 1990 Clean Air Act and the looming 1994 pollution permit program (Title V). When faced with the new air quality standards found in the regulation, Conoco conducted an audit and found that 16 facilities would require Title V permits. Rather than face the costs and monitoring associated with this path, Conoco sought to improve its distribution system through rethinking existing technologies. At a total cost of $560,000, the firm was able to avoid the permit costs plus several other operational costs plus reap additional revenue. The overall economic impact was a gain of several millions of dollars.

Porter and Kramer (2011) discuss another example from Wal-Mart. In 2009, Wal-Mart, through careful supply chain analysis, was able to redesign its distribution network, resulting in a reduction of 100 million trucking miles and saving $200 million in costs. Wal-Mart achieved the savings despite an actual increase in the quantity delivered. Combined with Wal-Mart's 2005 Zero Waste Program, which has resulted in a redirection of 120 million pounds of plastic from landfills in 2009, the results suggest that through innovation and re-evaluation, firms' financial performance can improve through enhanced resource efficiency.

A common theme among these examples is waste reduction. A substantial literature suggests managers tend to systematically underestimate the economic benefits of waste prevention. For instance, Klassen and Whybark (1999) examine facility-level data for 83 furniture manufacturing plants and determine the mix of pollution prevention efforts versus pollution control efforts (or "end-of-pipe" technologies). They find significantly better manufacturing performance for facilities that adopt pollution prevention rather than controls.

King and Lenox (2002) examine 614 firms over 2,837 firm-years based on Toxic Release Inventory (TRI) levels. Their results confirm that prevention technologies are associated with higher levels of return on assets (ROA) and Tobin's Q. Their interpretation of this result is that managers are systematically underutilizing opportunities for profitable waste prevention.

Dangelico and Pujari (2010) explore additional dimensions of eco-efficiency. Based on in-depth interviews with executives from 12 small to mid-size companies in Canada and Italy, they identify eco-efficiency efforts related to reduce energy consumption, reduced packaging, making use of and more effectively conducting of recycling programs as important sources of efficiency improvements. Interestingly, they report that the motivation for some of these efforts could not be linked to the business-case justification of improving firm performance. Rather, several of the managers report personal or company-culture-based explanations for the policies. Regardless of the motivation, emerging evidence suggests that eco-efficiency benefits firm performance beyond simply waste reduction. Similarly, Hellstrom (2007) suggests a much broader interpretation of eco-efficiency (specifically eco-innovation) than simple waste reduction.

Dowell, Hart, and Yeung (2000), for example, examine the broad-based Investor Responsibility Research Center's Corporate Environmental Profile for multinational enterprises between 1994 and 1997. They partition the sample based on whether each firm adopts multiple (local), a single U.S.-based, or a single more stringent internal environmental standard policy across its operations and examine value as measured by Tobin's Q. According to their evidence, firms adopting a single "most stringent" policy across jurisdictions are associated with the highest Tobin's Q. The authors further claim a causal link based on two-stage analysis.

Derwall, Guenster, Bauer, and Koedijk (2005) analyze the returns of two portfolios constructed based on firms' Innovest scores. Based on market returns between 1995 and 2003, they report that the portfolio comprised of firms with the highest eco-efficiency scores significantly outperform the lowest portfolio. They also find that in the presence of transactions costs, a long-short zero-investment portfolio will yield a positive return of 3 to 6 percent. Guenster, Bauer, Derwall, and Koedijk (2011) further examine this issue and find that the sensitivity between eco-efficiency and Tobin's Q has strengthened over time. They interpret their results as consistent with eco-efficiency being a potentially important underutilized source of value for managers.

Regulatory

The creation of value through heightened regulation can be a difficult case. To the extent that regulation seeks to reduce negative externalities, the cost should be strictly negative to the firm. In some instances, however, firms can benefit from regulatory pressures. The previously described case of Conoco provides one explanation for regulations leading to value enhancement. As Sharfman et al. (2000) describe, regulatory pressure induced the firm to conduct an environmental audit that resulted in identifying several instances of heretofore unrecognized opportunity costs to lost product and operating cost reductions through greater efficiency. In this case, management is guilty of underestimating the private costs of pollution.

Arora and Gangopadhyay (1995) suggest a second possibility, which Denicolo (2008) develops more completely. In this instance, firms can view regulatory pressures as a strategic opportunity to differentiate themselves from competitors. Particularly, if a firm appears to voluntarily overcomply with existing regulations, it may signal to regulators the ability to tighten existing standards. To the extent that the firm's proactive adoption of the necessary technologies or procedures reduces its costs relative to competitors, then the overcomplying firm will benefit.

Sharfman, Shaft, and Tihanyi (2004) develop a model that helps to explain why many firms appear to adopt an overly cautious environmental compliance policy based on extant regulations. They contend that the changing and unpredictable nature of environmental policies across regions can lead to a very heterogeneous program within a single firm. If improvement costs are high and changes are deemed likely, then their model shows that firms are incented to adopt rigorous environmental policies across the entire firm rather than attempt to race to the bottom in each of the markets in which the firm operates. Viewed from this lens, apparent overinvestment in environmental compliance and standards is simply a proactive measure to reduce expected future costs.

These results are consistent with the theoretical model and empirical evidence reported by Maxwell, Lyon, and Hackett (2000), who suggest that firms self-regulate in the presence of regulatory threats. Similarly, Khanna, Deltas, and Harrington (2009) find that S&P 500 firms respond to the threat of anticipated environmental regulation in motivating their current environmental innovation efforts.

Lutz, Lyon, and Maxwell (2000), however, suggest that overcompliance can be detrimental under certain circumstances. In particular, they find that in an environment where regulatory standards are anticipated, the proactive commitment to higher standards before regulation can induce weaker standards, resulting in a decline in welfare.

Cost of Capital

CSRI may also affect a firm's cost of capital by either reducing perceived information asymmetry or minimizing risks. Merton (1987) suggests that information asymmetry can lead to price discrepancies. In Merton's original formulation, discrepancies arise from a "shadow cost" associated with certain firms not being in some investors' opportunity set. Specifically, the lesser-known firms, depending on size and idiosyncratic factors, will have higher risk-adjusted returns related to their shadow cost. In the context of CSRI, this can manifest as either additional awareness due to CSR efforts or intentional neglect. Odean (1999), for instance, finds that awareness, or more accurately attention, is an important determinant of investors' buying decisions. Thus, CSRI, whether positive or negative, is more likely to attract investors' attention than lack of activity. Related to discretionary neglect, Hong and Kacperczyk (2009) suggest that poor CSRI can detract from investors' interest in holding a security.

An additional consequence of shareholder neglect (or lack of awareness) derived from Merton (1987) is the economic consequences from idiosyncratic factors. That is, because firms are no longer held as a part of a well-diversified portfolio, investors demand compensation for both systematic and certain firm-specific risks. Starks (2009) suggests risks could include regulatory, supply chain, product and technology, reputation, litigation, and physical, several of which have been previously discussed. However, in the context of this section, each of these risks could potentially affect a firm's cost of capital.

Heinkel, Kraus, and Zechner (2001) model the impact of exclusionary ethical investment on corporate behavior. Consistent with Merton (1987), they show that investor aversion to the securities of nongreen firms will result in lower prices for these firms and higher required returns. They also estimate the proportion of the potential investor-base that must shun polluting firms, on average, in order for the valuation consequence to be sufficiently large to induce the firm to reform. Their evidence shows too few green investors during the 1990s to lead to widespread reforms.

Jo (2003) examines one dimension of the information asymmetry hypothesis as it relates to coverage by analysts. Analysts are an important source of information for both institutional and individual investors. Jo suggests that analysts have incentives to follow securities from socially responsible firms in order to meet the (growing) demand from investors. He employs a sample of 1,320 firm-year observations of firms rated by *Fortune* between 1990 and 1998. Jo finds a positive relationship between the Community and Environmental Responsibility scores in *Fortune* and the number of analysts who follow a firm's stock.

Hong and Kacperczyk (2009), who examine the "price of sin," report complementary evidence. In a sample of 193 firms between 1976 and 2006 that are involved in the three "sin" industries (alcohol, tobacco, and gaming), they find a significantly lower number of analysts than for comparable firms in other industries. These results suggest that CSRI can either attract additional analyst interest or avoid a reduction in interest.

Dhaliwal, Li, Tsang, and Yang (2011) report a similar effect of CSRI on analyst coverage. However, in their analysis, they examine firms initiating a CSR disclosure. Using a sample of 1,190 CSR disclosure initiations, they find that firms with superior CSRI attract greater analyst coverage following the initiation of CSR disclosures. Further, the authors also report significantly low error and dispersion of forecast errors following disclosures for high-quality firms. Overall, the evidence appears consistent that CSRI is associated with greater analyst coverage.

CSRI efforts also appear to affect the number of investors who are willing to hold particular securities. Hong and Kacperczyk (2009), for instance, analyze 193 firms that operate in one or more "sin" industries (alcohol, tobacco, and gaming). They hypothesize that institutional investors who are most constrained by social norms, including banks, insurance companies, and pension funds, will disproportionately neglect these "sin" stocks relative to other institutions, such as hedge funds and mutual funds, who are not so constrained. Their analysis confirms this pattern. Dhaliwal et al. (2011) report complementary results. Specifically, for firms initiating CSR disclosures, those with relatively high CSRI ratings experience a significant increase in institutional holdings compared to other firms.

Sharfman and Fernando (2008) examine the impact of perceived risk, specifically environmental risk, on the cost of equity capital. They hypothesize that, consistent with Starks' (2009) suggestion, greater environmental risk management efforts will result in lower risk, and a resulting lower cost of capital. The authors examine this question in a sample of 267 U.S. firms employing KLD data to measure environmental strength or weakness. Consistent with their expectations, Sharfman and Fernando report that great efforts are associated with lower risk and cost of equity capital. In a less formal experiment, Feldman, Soyka, and Ameer (1997) provide additional confirming evidence using a sample of 330 firms between 1980 and 1994. El Ghoul, Guedhami, Kwok, and Mishra (2011) expand on these analyses to include a wider range of possible risks, including employee relations, environmental policies, and product strategies. In their large sample analysis of 12,915 firm-years for U.S. firms between 1992 and 2007, they find that greater CSRI is negatively related to an ex ante estimate of cost of equity.

The impact of CSRI on risk is consistent with the risk management hypothesis of Godfrey (2005); Gardberg and Fombrun (2006); and Godfrey, Merrill, and Hansen (2009). This hypothesis suggests that CSRI efforts send a credible signal to the market that management considers its relationships with stakeholders to be important. As a result, the firm (or managers) accrues moral capital with stakeholders. These stakeholders, in turn, are more likely to give the firm the benefit of the doubt in future interactions if stakeholders feel harmed. As a result, stakeholders are less likely to seek redress or to be satisfied with reduced sanctions if they do. Thus, CSRI acts as an insurance policy. Much of the extant literature of the relationship between CSRI and cost of equity can be interpreted in this light.

The evidence of CRSI efforts on debt financing is more mixed. Verwijmeren and Derwall (2010), who explore the relationship between the strength of employee relations and credit ratings, present some suggestive evidence. They find that firms with strong relations have significantly higher credit ratings and suggest, but do not test, that this will affect a firm's cost of capital.

Goss and Roberts (2011) examine the link between cost of debt capital and CSRI within the context of bank debt. Employing bank debt provides a favorable environment because of banks' quasi-insider status, which should better enable the lender to disentangle sincere CSRI efforts from agency-related policies. Using a sample of 3,996 loans, they find a premium charged to poor CSRI borrowers of 7 to 18 basis points. They find that banks also punish firms for agency-related CRSI. Specifically, for low-quality borrowers, spreads are higher when these firms undertake CSRI.

Sharfman and Fenando (2008) report similarly mixed results. Specifically, in their sample of 267 firms, they find that exposure to environmental risk, as defined by Bloomberg, is not directly related to the cost of debt, but is linked to the firm's choice of capital structure and the relative benefits of tax-shields. Thus, overall, the results suggest little evidence that firms are rewarded for CSRI efforts by reducing their cost of debt. However, firms do appear to be punished for poor CSRI efforts through an increased cost of debt.

SUMMARY AND CONCLUSIONS

The evidence discussed in this chapter is generally consistent with the notion that firm value and shareholders' interest are frequently aligned with the interests of stakeholders. Along many dimensions, managers appear to be able to create value through increased or conscientious consideration of the firm's relationship with its stakeholders. This is consistent with the guidance of Jensen (2010) that enlightened shareholder maximization offers an improvement over strict shareholder-primacy as guidance to best management practices. A recent study provides some interesting evidence on this question. Benson and Davidson (2010) find that a link exists between stakeholder management, measured in terms of KLD data, and firm value, measured as market-to-book. However, managerial compensation is not directly linked to stakeholders' interests, but compensation is linked to firm value, and the link disappears in the presence of controls for endogeneity. The authors interpret this pattern as consistent with firms rewarding managers for enlightened value-maximizing behavior, not strictly shareholder- or stakeholder-centric behavior. Although considerable research remains to be done, especially in more carefully examining the pathways through which CSRI may affect value, the general evidence, literature review, and meta-analyses suggest a generally positive and strengthening relationship between the CSRI and CFP.

DISCUSSION QUESTIONS

1. Why is innovation such a critical component of gains from eco-efficiency?
2. Provide two explanations for why CSRI may lead to a reduction in the cost of capital.
3. What is the distinction between shareholder wealth maximization and enlightened value maximization?
4. Identify five ways in which CSRI can affect CFP.
5. How might management's CSR goals influence capital structure choice?

REFERENCES

Ahmed, Parvez, Sudhir Nanda, and Oliver Schnusenberg. 2010. "Can Firms Do Well While Doing Good?" *Applied Financial Economics* 20:11, 845–860.

Arora, Seema, and Shubhashis Gangopadhyay. 1995. "Toward a Theoretical Model of Voluntary Overcompliance." *Journal of Economic Behavior and Organization* 28:3, 289–309.

Arthur, Michelle M., and Alison Cook. 2004. "Taking Stock of Work-Family Initiatives: How Announcements of 'Family-Friendly' Human Resource Decisions Affect Shareholder Value." *Industrial and Labor Relations Review* 57:4, 599–613.

Bae, Kee-Hong, Jun-Koo Kang, and Jin Wang. 2011. "Employee Treatment and Firm Leverage: A Test of the Stakeholder Theory of Capital Structure." *Journal of Financial Economics* 100:1, 130–153.

Banerjee, Shantanu, Sudipto Dasgupta, and Yungsan Kim. 2008. "Buyer-Supplier Relationships and the Stakeholder Theory of Capital Structure." *Journal of Finance* 63:5, 2507–2552.

Barnett, Michael L. 2007. "Stakeholder Influenced Capacity and the Variability of Financial Returns to Corporate Social Responsibility." *Academy of Management Review* 32:3, 794–816.

Barney, Jay. 1997. *Gaining and Sustaining Competitive Advantage.* Reading, MA: Addison Wesley.

Baron, David. 2001. "Private Politics, Corporate Social Responsibility and Integrated Strategy." *Journal of Economics and Management Strategy* 10:1, 7–45.

Beltratti, Andrea. 2005. "The Complementarity between Corporate Governance and Corporate Social Responsibility." *The Geneva Papers* 30:3, 373–386.

Benson, Bradley W., and Wallace N. Davidson. 2010. "The Relation between Stakeholder Management, Firm Value, and CEO Compensation: A Test of Enlightened Value Maximization." *Financial Management* 39:3, 929–964.

Berk, Jonathan B., Richard Stanton, and Josef Zechner. 2010. "Human Capital, Bankruptcy, and Capital Structure." *Journal of Finance* 65:3, 891–926.

Bhattacharya, C. B., and Sankar Sen. 2004. "Doing Better at Doing Good: When, Why, and How Consumers Respond to Corporate Social Initiatives." *California Management Review* 47:1, 9–24.

Blanco, Esther, Javier Rey-Maquieira, and Javier Lozano. 2009. "The Economic Impacts of Voluntary Environmental Performance of Firms: A Critical Review." *Journal of Economic Surveys* 23:3, 462–502.

Brady, Arlo Kristjan O. 2003. "How to Generate Sustainable Brand Value from Responsibility." *Brand Management* 10:4-5, 279–289.

Brown, Tom J., and Peter A. Dacin. 1997. "The Company and the Product: Corporate Associations and Consumer Product Responses." *Journal of Marketing* 61:1, 68–84.

Castaldo, Sandro, Francesco Perrini, Nicola Misani, and Antonio Tencati. 2009. "The Missing Link between Corporate Social Responsibility and Consumer Trust: The Case of Fair Trade Products." *Journal of Business Ethics* 84:1, 1–15.

Commission of the European Communities. 2001. *Green Paper: Promoting a European Framework for Corporate Social Responsibility.* COM (2001) 366. Brussels: European Commission.

Dam, Lammertjan. 2008. "Corporate Social Responsibility and Financial Markets." Ph.D. Thesis, University of Groningen, Groningen.

Dangelico, Rosa Maria, and Devashish Pujari. 2010. "Mainstreaming Green Production Innovation: Why and How Companies Integrate Environmental Sustainability." *Journal of Business Ethics* 95:3, 471–486.

Davis, Keith. 1973. "The Case For and Against Business Assumption of Social Responsibilities." *Academy of Management Journal* 16:2, 312–322.

Denicolo, Vincenzo. 2008. "A Signaling Model of Environmental Overcompliance." *Journal of Economic Behavior and Organization* 68:1, 293–303.

Derwall, Jeroen, Nadja Guenster, Rob Bauer, and Kees Koedijk. 2005. "The Eco-Efficiency Premium Puzzle." *Financial Analysts Journal* 61:2, 51–63.

Dhaliwal, Dan S., Oliver Zhen Li, Albert Tsang, and Yong George Yang. 2011. "Voluntary Nonfinancial Disclosure and the Cost of Equity Capital: The Initiation of Corporate Social Responsibility Reporting." *Accounting Review* 86:1, 59–100.

Dowell, Glen, Stuart Hart, and Bernard Yeung. 2000. "Do Corporate Global Environmental Standards Create or Destroy Market Value?" *Management Science* 46:8, 1059–1074.

Eichholtz, Piet, Nils Kok, and John M. Quigley. 2010. "Doing Well by Doing Good? Green Office Buildings." *American Economic Review* 100:5, 2494–2511.

Eichholtz, Piet, Nils Kok, and John M. Quigley. 2011. "The Diffusion of Energy Efficient Building." *American Economic Review* 101:2, 77–82.

El Ghoul, Sadok, Omrane Guedhami, Chuck C. Y. Kwok, and Dev R. Mishra. 2011. "Does Corporate Social Responsibility Affect the Cost of Capital?" *Journal of Banking and Finance* 35:9, 2388–2406.

Esrock, Stuart L., and Greg B. Leichty. 1998. "Social Responsibility and Corporate Web Pages: Self-Presentation or Agenda-Setting?" *Public Relations Review* 24:3, 305–319.

Feldman, Stanley J., Peter A. Soyka, and Paul G. Ameer. 1997. "Does Improving a Firm's Environmental Management System and Environmental Performance Result in a Higher Stock Price?" *Journal of Investing* 6:4, 87–97.

Filbeck, Greg, and Dianna C. Preece. 2003a. "Announcement Effects of the Working Mother Annual Survey of Family-Friendly Firms." *Journal of Investing* 12:3, 87–95.

Filbeck, Greg, and Dianna C. Preece. 2003b. "*Fortune's* Best 100 Companies to Work for in America: Do They Work for Shareholders?" *Journal of Business Finance and Accounting* 30:5-6, 771–797.

Freeman, R. Edward. 1984. *Strategic Management: A Stakeholder Approach*. Boston: Pitman.

Friedman, Milton. 1970. "The Social Responsibility of Business Is to Increase Its Profits." *The New York Times Magazine*, September 13, SM17.

Fuerst, Franz, and Patrick McAllister. 2011a. "Eco-Labeling in Commercial Office Markets: Do LEED and Energy Star Offices Obtain Multiple Premiums?" *Ecological Economics* 70:6, 1220–1230.

Fuerst, Franz, and Patrick McAllister. 2011b. "Green Noise or Green Value? Measuring the Effects of Environmental Certification on Office Values." *Real Estate Economics* 39:1, 45–69.

Galema, Rients, Auke Plantinga, and Bert Scholtens. 2008. "The Stocks at Stake: Return and Risk in Socially Responsible Investment." *Journal of Banking and Finance* 32:12, 2646–2654.

Gardberg, Naomi A., and Charles J. Fombrun. 2006. "Corporate Citizenship: Creating Intangible Assets across Institutional Environments." *Academy of Management Review* 31:2, 329–346.

Gatewood, Robert D., Mary A. Gowan, and Gary J. Lautenschlager. 1993. "Corporate Image, Recruitment Image, and Initial Job Choice Decisions." *Academy of Management Journal* 36:2, 414–427.

Godfrey, Paul C. 2005. "The Relationship between Corporate Philanthropy and Shareholder Wealth: A Risk Management Perspective." *Academy of Management Review* 30:4, 777–798.

Godfrey, Paul C., Craig B. Merrill, and Jared M. Hansen. 2009. "The Relationship between Corporate Social Responsibility and Shareholder Value: An Empirical Test of the Risk Management Hypothesis." *Strategic Management Journal* 30:4, 425–445.

Goodstein, Jerry D. 1994. "Institutional Pressures and Strategic Responsiveness: Employer Involvement in Work-Family Issues." *Academy of Management Journal* 37:2, 350–382.

Goss, Allen, and Gordon S. Roberts. 2011. "The Impact of Corporate Social Responsibility on the Cost of Bank Loans." *Journal of Banking and Finance* 35:7, 1794–1810.

Grant Thorton. *Survey of U.S. Business Leaders, 2007. Corporate Responsibility: Burden or Opportunity?* Chicago: Grant Thorton LLP.

Guenster, Nadja, Rob Bauer, Jeroen Derwall, and Kees Koedijk. 2011. "The Economic Value of Corporate Eco-Efficiency." *European Financial Management* 17:4, 679–704.

Hansen, S. Duane, Benjamin B. Dunford, Alan D. Boss, R. Wayne Boss, and Ingo Angermeier. 2011. "Corporate Social Responsibility and the Benefits of Employee Trust: A Cross-Disciplinary Perspective." *Journal of Business Ethics* 102:1, 29–45.

Heal, Geoffrey. 2005. "Corporate Social Responsibility: An Economic and Financial Framework." *The Geneva Papers* 30:3, 387–409.

Heinkel, Robert, Alan Kraus, and Josef Zechner. 2001. "The Effect of Green Investment on Corporate Behavior." *Journal of Financial and Quantitative Analysis* 36:4, 431–449.

Hellstrom, Tomas. 2007. "Dimensions of Environmentally Sustainable Innovation: The Structure of Eco-Innovation Concepts." *Sustainable Development* 15:3, 148–159.

Hong, Harrison, and Marcin Kacperczyk. 2009. "The Price of Sin: The Effects of Social Norms on Markets." *Journal of Financial Economics* 93:1, 15–36.

Hopkins, Michael. 2004. "Corporate Social Responsibility: An Issues Paper." Working Paper. International Labor Organization, Geneva.

Jensen, Michael C. 2010. "Value Maximization, Stakeholder Theory, and the Corporate Objective Function." *Journal of Applied Corporate Finance* 22:1, 32–42.

Jiao, Yawen. 2010. "Stakeholder Welfare and Firm Value." *Journal of Banking and Finance* 34:10, 2549–2561.

Jo, Hoje. 2003. "Financial Analysts, Firm Quality, and Social Responsibility." *Journal of Behavioral Finance* 4:3, 172–183.

Jose, Anita, and Mary S. Thibodeaux. 1999. "Institutionalization of Ethics: The Perspective of Managers." *Journal of Business Ethics* 22:2, 133–143.

Khanna, Madhu, George Deltas, and Donna Ramirez Harrington. 2009. "Adoption of Pollution Prevention Techniques: The Role of Management Systems and Regulatory Pressures." *Environmental Resource Economics* 44:1, 85–106.

King, Andrew, and Michael Lenox. 2002. "Exploring the Locus of Profitable Pollution Reduction." *Management Science* 48:2, 289–299.

Klassen, Robert D., and D. Clay Whybark. 1999. "Environmental Management in Operations: The Selection of Environmental Technologies." *Decision Sciences* 30:6, 601–631.

Koh, Hian Chye, and El'fred H.Y. Boo. 2001. "The Link between Organizational Ethics and Job Satisfaction: A Study of Managers in Singapore." *Journal of Business Ethics* 29:4, 309–324.

Kreps, David M., and A. Michael Spence. 1983. "Modeling the Role of History in Industrial Organization and Competition." Discussion Paper, Volume 992 of Harvard Institute of Economic Research, Harvard University.

Lado, Augustine A., and Mary C. Wilson. 1994. "Human Resource Systems and Sustained Competitive Advantage: A Competency-Based Perspective." *Academy of Management Review* 19:4, 699–727.

Lai, Chi-Shiun, Chih-Jen Chiu, Chin-Fang Yang, and Da-Chang Pai. 2010. "The Effects of Corporate Social Responsibility on Brand Performance: The Mediating Effect of Industrial Brand Equity and Corporate Reputation." *Journal of Business Ethics* 95:3, 457–469.

Luo, Xueming, and C. B. Bhattacharya. 2006. "Corporate Social Responsibility, Customer Satisfaction, and Market Value." *Journal of Marketing* 70:4, 1–18.

Lutz, Stefan, Thomas P. Lyon, and John W. Maxwell. 2000. "Quality Leadership When Regulatory Standards Are Forthcoming." *Journal of Industrial Economics* 48:3, 331–348.

Margolis, Joshua Daniels, and James Patrick Walsh. 2001. *People and Profits? The Search for a Link Between a Company's Social and Financial Performance.* Mahwah, NJ: Erlbaum.

Martin, John, William Petty, and James Wallace. 2009. "Shareholder Value Maximization: Is There a Role for Corporate Social Responsibility?" *Journal of Applied Corporate Finance* 21:2, 110–118.

Maxwell, John W., Thomas P. Lyon, and Steven C. Hackett. 2000. "Self-Regulation and Social Welfare: The Political Economy of Corporate Environmentalism." *Journal of Law and Economics* 43:2, 583–617.

McWilliams, Abagail, and Donald S. Siegel. 2001. "Corporate Social Responsibility: A Theory of the Firm Perspective." *Academy of Management Review* 26:1, 117–127.

Merton, Robert C. 1987. "A Simple Model of Capital Market Equilibrium with Incomplete Information." *Journal of Finance* 42:3, 483–510.

Moskowitz, Milton R. 1972. "Choosing Socially Responsible Stocks." *Business and Society* 1:1, 71–75.

Murray, Keith B., and Christine M. Vogel. 1997. "Using a Hierarchy of Effects Approach to Gauge the Effectiveness of CSR to Generate Goodwill Towards the Firm: Financial Versus Non-Financial Impacts." *Journal of Business Research* 38:2, 141–159.

Odean, Terrance. 1999. "Do Investors Trade Too Much?" *American Economic Review* 89:5, 1279–1298.

Orlitzky, Marc, and John D. Benjamin. 2001. "Corporate Social Performance and Firm Risk: A Meta-Analytic Review." *Business and Society* 40:4, 369–396.

Orlitzky, Marc, Frank L. Schmidt, and Sara L. Rynes. 2003. "Corporate Social and Financial Performance: A Meta-Analysis." *Organization Studies* 24:3, 403–441.

Page, Graham, and Helen Fearn. 2005. "Corporate Reputation: What Do Consumers Really Care About?" *Journal of Advertising Research* 45:3, 305–313.

Perry-Smith, Jill E., and Terry C. Blum. 2000. "Work-Family Human Resource Bundles and Perceived Organizational Performance." *Academy of Management Journal* 43:6, 1107–1117.

Porter, Michael E., and Mark R. Kramer. 2006. "Strategy and Society: The Link between Competitive Advantage and Corporate Social Responsibility." *Harvard Business Review* 84:12, 78–92.

Porter, Michael E., and Mark R. Kramer. 2011. "Creating Shared Value." *Harvard Business Review* 89:1–2, 62–77.

Riordan, Christine M., Robert D. Gatewood, and Jodi Barnes Bill. 1997. "Corporate Image: Employee Reactions and Implications for Managing Corporate Social Performance." *Journal of Business Ethics* 16:4, 401–412.

Sen, Sankar, and C. B. Bhattacharya. 2001. "Does Doing Good Always Lead to Doing Better? Consumer Reactions to Corporate Social Responsibility." *Journal of Marketing Research* 38:2, 225–243.

Sharfman, Mark P., and Chitru S. Fernando. 2008. "Environmental Risk Management and the Cost of Capital." *Strategic Management Journal* 29:6, 569–592.

Sharfman, Mark P., Mark Meo, and Rex T. Ellington. 2000. "Regulation, Business, and Sustainable Development." *American Behavioral Scientist* 44:2, 277–302.

Sharfman, Mark P., Teresa M. Shaft, and Laszlo Tihanyi. 2004. "A Model of the Global and Institutional Antecedents of High-Level Corporate Environmental Performance." *Business and Society* 43:1, 6–36.

Smith, Adam. 1776. *An Inquiry into the Nature and Cause of the Wealth of Nations*. Chicago, IL: University of Chicago Press.

Smith, N. Craig. 2003. "Corporate Social Responsibility: Whether or How?" *California Management Review* 45:4, 52–76.

Speed, Richard, and Peter Thompson. 2000. "Determinants of Sports Sponsorship Response." *Journal of the Academy of Marketing Science* 28:2, 226–238.

Starks, Laura T. 2009. "EFA Keynote Speech: 'Corporate Governance and Corporate Social Responsibility: What Do Investors Care About? What Should Investors Care About?'" *Financial Review* 44:4, 461–468.

Surroca, Jordi, Josep A. Tribo, and Sandra Waddock. 2010. "Corporate Responsibility and Financial Performance: The Role of Intangible Resources." *Strategic Management Journal* 31:5, 463–490.

Tirole, Jean M. 2001. "Corporate Governance." *Econometrica* 69:1, 1–35.

Titman, Sheridan. 1984. "The Effect of Capital Structure on a Firm's Liquidation Decision." *Journal of Financial Economics* 13:1, 137–151.

Turban, Daniel B., and Daniel W. Greening. 1997. "Corporate Social Performance and Organizational Attractiveness to Prospective Employees." *Academy of Management Journal* 40:3, 658–672.

Valentine, Sean, and Gary Fleischman. 2008. "Ethics Programs, Perceived Corporate Social Responsibility, and Job Satisfaction." *Journal of Business Ethics* 77:2, 159–172.

Verwijmeren, Patrick, and Jeroen Derwall. 2010. "Employee Well-Being, Firm Leverage, and Bankruptcy Risk." *Journal of Banking and Finance* 34:5, 956–964.

Weber, Andrea, and Christine Zulehner. 2010. "Female Hires and the Success of Start-up Firms." *American Economic Review: Papers & Proceedings* 100:2, 358–361.

Wood, Donna J., and Raymond E. Jones. 1995. "Stakeholder Mismatching: A Theoretical Problem in Empirical Research on Corporate Social Performance." *International Journal of Organizational Analysis* 3:3, 229–267.

Wright, Peter, Stephen P. Ferris, Janine S. Hiller, and Mark Kroll. 1995. "Competitiveness Through Management of Diversity: Effects on Stock Price Valuation." *Academy of Management Journal* 38:1, 272–287.

Wu, Meng-Ling. 2006. "Corporate Social Performance, Corporate Financial Performance, and Firm Size: A Meta-Analysis." *Journal of American Academy of Business* 8:1, 163–171.

Zingales, Luigi. 2000. "In Search of New Foundations." *Journal of Finance* 55:4, 1623–1653.

ABOUT THE AUTHOR

John R. Becker-Blease is an assistant professor of Finance at Oregon State University. Previously he held positions at Washington State University and the University of New Hampshire, where he held the Reginald Atkins Chair. Professor Becker-Blease has published numerous articles in journals from multiple disciplines such as *Journal of Corporate Finance, Journal of Business Venturing, Economic Inquiry, Financial Management, Entrepreneurship Theory & Practice,* and *Journal of Regulatory Economics.* His research interests include corporate governance, angel capital, and gender-equality. He is recipient of the 2011 Aspen Institute Faculty Pioneer Award as well as other teaching and research awards. He is active in efforts to better incorporate a stakeholder-perspective into finance courses at the graduate and undergraduate levels, and holds a Ph.D. from the University of Oregon.

CHAPTER 22

SRI Mutual Fund and Index Performance

HALIL KIYMAZ
Bank of America Chair and Professor of Finance, Rollins College

INTRODUCTION

The rise of social and ethical investments has received the attention of both practitioners and academicians and has become an important development in the financial community over the last few decades. Individuals have increased levels of awareness for the social issues that affect the quality of their lives. For example, people have a better understanding of health hazards associated with nicotine and tobacco smoke and hence have distanced themselves from these products, including divesting from firms that produce them. Although the origin of social investing goes back several centuries, modern social investing can be traced to the 1960s. The foundation of social investing stems from the concerns of investors on human rights abuses, environmental degradation, and exploitation of workers. These investors harbor the notion that companies should be accountable for their actions in these areas. Managers who take into account social responsibility criteria in selecting securities for their portfolios have received attention from investors. For example, the Social Investment Forum (2010) reports that the total net assets of funds incorporating socially responsible criteria to their investment decisions increased from $12 billion in 1995 to $569 billion in 2010, while the number of socially responsible funds increased from 55 funds in 1995 to 493 funds in 2010.

According to finance theory, the fundamental goal of a business firm is to maximize shareholder wealth as reflected in the market price of the firm's stock. Most firms are so focused on the bottom line that they do not consider the issues raised above unless forced to by government regulations or activists. The question is whether shareholder wealth maximization is consistent with the best interest of society in the long run. Some people believe that firms cannot use their resources to develop the environment without adversely affecting shareholder value. The rationale behind this logic is that any expense used to improve the environment will increase costs, and thus increase product prices and reduce profits. Others believe that investment in social and environmental issues can increase a firm's efficiency and potentially generate new markets (Schueth 2003).

Socially responsible investing (SRI) includes ethical investing and green investing. The growth of investments in socially responsible funds has been getting attention from both practitioners and academics. As a result of the increased interest, investment companies have created funds to meet the needs of those investors. The question of whether active portfolio management investing in socially responsible firms can generate better performance results is an unresolved issue.

This chapter starts with a review of the background of SRI including historical roots, definition, and recent industry trends. This is followed with the screens used by SRI funds and hypotheses associated with returns from SRI. Then, the chapter reviews the literature and synthesizes the performances of SRI in mutual funds as well as the performances of index funds. This section also includes international evidence on SRI return performance. The chapter concludes with a summary.

SRI

SRI has evolved over a long period of time. A brief background on SRI helps to put it into perspective. During this review, various SRI definitions and screening processes are defined.

Background

The foundation of SRI lies in the desires of investors to match their belief schemes with their investment policies. Ethical investing has ancient origins in religion including Jewish, Christian, and Islamic traditions. For example, based on the teachings of the Koran and *Shariah* (Islamic principles of living), Islamic investors avoid investing in companies involved in pork production, pornography, gambling, and in interest-based (*riba*) banking. Islam focuses instead on partnerships and risk-sharing. Islam does not allow investments in bonds or preferred stocks because they both promise a fixed rate of return. Under Islamic principles, all shareholders should be on an equal footing (Ghoul and Karam 2007).

Other historical examples of ethical investing include the Quakers refusing to profit from the weapons and slaves trade when they settled in North America (Kinder and Domini 1997). The Methodist Church in the United Kingdom avoided investing in sinful companies involved in the production of alcohol, tobacco, and weapons and in gambling during 1920s. Apart from religious traditions, modern SRI is based on personal ethical and social convictions of individual investors. For example, the opposition to the Vietnam War inspired creating in 1971 the PAX Fund, which avoids investments in weapon producers and contractors. In the 1980s, South Africa, with its racist apartheid system, received the attention of social investors who pressured investment firms not to include South African firms in their portfolios and companies doing business with such firms.

The SRI industry has experienced a rapid growth in the United States and the rest of the world during the last two decades. During this period, issues such as environmental protection, human rights, and labor relations have become common themes in the SRI investment screens. As a result of various corporate scandals, corporate governance, transparency, and responsibility have recently become the center of attention. Exhibit 22.1 reports the number of SRI funds available to investors, total assets under management, and net assets under management in the United States. The number of funds increased almost tenfold from 44 in 1995 to 493 in 2010. The net assets under management rose even more sharply from

Exhibit 22.1   SRI in the United States, 1995 to 2010

Year	Total Assets under Management (U.S. $ billion)	Net Assets under Management (U.S. $ billion)	Number of Funds
1995	639	12	55
1997	1185	96	144
1999	2159	154	168
2001	2323	136	181
2003	2164	151	200
2005	2290	179	201
2007	2711	202	260
2010	3069	569	493

This exhibit outlines the development of SRI funds in terms of the number of funds and both total and net assets under management.
Source: Social Investment Forum Foundation (2010).

$12 billion in 1995 to $569 billion in 2010, for an astonishing 4,641.67 percent increase. These figures are likely to increase as investors become more aware of issues including corporate governance, emission control, global warming, and community investing that funds use to screen firms.

Over the past decade, the following factors have contributed to SRI growth in U.S. financial markets. First, as a result of increased demand by their clients, money managers are increasingly incorporating environment, social, and governance (ESG) factors into their investment analysis, decision making, and portfolio construction. Second, public funds incorporate ESG factors into their investment decisions as a result of legislative mandates. Third, innovation in new products and fund styles are also reasons for the growth in SRI, including exchange-traded funds (ETFs) and alternative investment funds, such as social venture capital and responsible property funds. Other reasons accounting for the rapid growth in SRI funds and assets include environmentally themed investment products and services, exploration opportunities in clean and green technology, alternative and renewable energy, green building and responsible property development, and other environmentally driven businesses. Finally, U.S. investors are generally well educated and informed, which helps them make better and more responsible investment decisions. Also, women are highly involved in the growth of SRI. The social investment industry estimates that roughly 60 percent of socially conscious investors are women (Schueth 2003). Recently, investors have been attracted to SRI funds because more studies show that investors do not have to sacrifice returns in their SRI.

Definition of SRI and Screening

The definition of SRI varies greatly. A screen is applied to a universe of investment alternatives to identify candidates. But this is a nonfinancial social screen, not a financial screen. According to Kinder and Domini (1997), a social screen is the expression of an investor's social, ethical, or religious concern in a form that permits an investment manager to apply it in the investment decision-making process along with other screens. Schueth (2003) defines SRI as the process of integrating personal values and societal concerns into investment decision making. The World Economic Forum (2011, p. 12) suggests the following definition: "Sustainable investing is as an investment approach that integrates long-term environmental, social, and governance (ESG) criteria into investment and ownership decision-making with the objective of generating superior risk-adjusted financial returns." Responsible investing is most commonly understood to mean investing in a manner that takes into account the impact of investments on wider society and the natural environment, both today and in the future. Another common definition describes SRI as an investment process in which sustainability criteria relating to a company's social and/or environmental behavior play a decisive role in the admittance of that company's stocks to the investment portfolio.

SRI decisions involve various investment screens. Many funds use multiple screens to select securities. Exhibit 22.2 reports both negative and positive screens used by SRI funds. Most funds use negative screening, which is the oldest screening strategy. *Negative screening* refers to excluding certain groups of stocks or industries from SRI portfolios based on social, environmental, and ethical criteria. This group constitutes the largest portion of assets employed by SRI funds. Alcohol, tobacco, and gambling typically represent the most common restrictions that SRI investors use. These restrictions include exclusion from investing in manufacturers, distributors, and retailers of such products. The second-most-common restrictions involve military contracting and weapons producers, including suppliers of all parts. Similar arguments apply to nuclear power plants and firms that design, supply parts, and provide services. Panel A of Exhibit 22.2 defines these restrictions and provides an example of each. Additional negative screens may include adult entertainment, genetically modified organisms, violation of human rights, and animal testing.

Positive screening, which is the second major screening process, involves selecting certain types of investments based on positive characteristics. Panel B of Exhibit 22.2 reports selected positive screens. These qualitative positive screens include community involvement, environment, diversity, product, employee relations, among others. For example, firms with strong commitments to their community are known for generous giving and support for education and housing. Environmental issues include involvement with pollution prevention, recycling, use of alternative fuels, and beneficial products and services. Socially responsible investors use both positive and negative investment criteria in their decision-making process.

Hypotheses Associated with SRI Performance

Modern portfolio theory suggests that diversification reduces the total risk in a portfolio. A policy to exclude certain types of investments (negative screening) limits a manager's ability to diversify; hence a lower risk-adjusted return should be expected. In reality, this reasoning may not hold because negative screening may also eliminate lower-return stocks due to their business or industry characteristics.

The literature contains three major hypotheses about the performances of socially responsible funds compared to conventional funds. The first hypothesis is that the risk-adjusted expected returns of socially responsible funds are equal to the

Exhibit 22.2   SRI Screening Criteria

Panel A. Selective Negative Screens

Screen	Definition	Example
Alcohol	Avoid firms that are involved in the production, distribution, or promotion of alcoholic beverages	"Producer" companies earning 5 percent or more of revenues from alcohol-related activities
Gambling	Avoid casinos and suppliers of gambling equipment	"Operations" and "support" companies earning 5 percent or more of revenues from gambling-related activities
Tobacco	Avoid manufacturers of tobacco product	All companies classified as "producer" "distributor," "retailer," and "supplier" earning 15 percent or more from tobacco products
Military Weapons	Avoid manufacturers of weapons or firearms	All companies classified as "nuclear weapons systems" and "nuclear weapons components" "Chemical and biological weapons systems" and "chemical" and "biological weapons components" All companies classified as "cluster bomb" and "landmine" manufacturer All companies earning 5 percent or more from military weapons
Nuclear Power	Avoid manufacturers of nuclear reactors or related products and firms operate power plants	All companies classified as nuclear "utility" and "essential supplier" earning 5 percent or more revenues from nuclear-related activities" All companies involved in uranium mining and in designing nuclear reactors
Civilian Firearm	Avoid manufacturer of firearms	All companies classified as "producer" and "retailer" earning 15 percent or more from civilian firearms
Adult Entertainment	Avocid publishers of adult magazines, videos, tapes	All companies classified as "producer" earning more than 5 percent of revenues from these activities
Genetically Modified Organisms	Avoid firms operating in genetically modified organism	Companies that genetically modify plants, such as seed and crops, and other organisms intended for agricultural use or human consumption.

(continued)

Exhibit 22.2 *(Continued)*

Panel B. Selected Positive Screens

Screen	Definition	Example
Community	Involve proactive activities with the community	Generous giving Support for education
Diversity	Have active policy towards employment of minorities	Women and minority contracting Family benefits Employment of disabled Gay and lesbian policies
Labor Relations	Seek empowering employee and employee profit sharing Avoid exploiting workforce	Strong union relations Cash profit sharing Strong retirement and health benefits
Environment	Seek to involve in recycling, environmental clean-up, and waste reduction Avoid producing toxic products	Pollution prevention Recycling Alternative fuel and renewable energy
Product	Seek higher-quality products	Quality Research and development and innovation

This exhibit outlines selected negative and positive screens used in the SRI screening process.
Source: MSCI Research (2001).

risk-adjusted expected returns of conventional portfolios (no significant difference in returns). This would be the case where the value added with social responsibility is not priced in the performance. Socially responsible investors do not differentiate the cost of capital of socially responsible firms by requiring lower returns.

The second hypothesis contends that the expected returns of socially responsible portfolios are lower than the expected returns of conventional portfolios. This would indicate that the market clearly prices the social responsibility of a firm. The impact of a social screen is nonrandom, and social screens can create uncompensated risk. Applying screens may limit the full diversification potential and could shift the mean-variance frontier towards less favorable risk-return tradeoffs than those of conventional portfolios. For instance, excluding part of the stock market, such as firms producing alcohol, tobacco, and pornography, may negatively influence the risk-return tradeoffs of SRI funds.

For example, Grossman and Sharpe (1986) find that a South Africa–free portfolio had a residual standard deviation of 2.52 percent relative to the New York Stock Exchange (NYSE) index during the period 1960 to 1983. Furthermore, eliminating a portion of the total universe of stocks would result in suboptimal portfolios. Some maintain that imposing ethical constraints on the equity investment process will come at the cost of inferior portfolio performance. Other concerns include a potential increase in volatility, reduced diversification, and other costs associated with the screening process. Bauer, Derwall, and Otten (2007) explain the rational for this hypothesis. They contend that an ethical investment opportunity set is a subset of the entire investment universe. Developing any kind of ethical screen may be an expensive practice and, hence, can be a drain on net return.

The third hypothesis is that the expected returns of stocks of socially responsible funds provide higher returns than conventional counterparts. Negative news associated with firms that are not socially responsible would cause underestimation of expected returns of these firms. Advocates of SRI argue that evaluating potential investments with financial and social screens makes good social and economic sense. This provides investors with two advantages. First, investment decisions are in line with their personal values, and socially responsible investors will notice and place pressure on firms that are nonresponsive to social concerns.

A set of literature investigates the impact of environmental performance on stock price performance. For instance, Konar and Cohen (2001) study the impact of environmental performance on the market value of firms in the S&P 500. After controlling for variables traditionally thought to explain firm-level financial performance, they find that bad environmental performance is negatively correlated with the intangible asset value of firms. A 10 percent reduction in emissions of toxic chemicals results in a $34 million increase in market value. Yamashita, Sen, and Cohen (1999) also report that the release of information on a company's environmental conscientiousness has an insignificant but a positive impact on stock prices. Rewards for upgrading the environmental conscientiousness score by one rank could result in a 2.66 percent increase in the 10-year average of risk-adjusted returns. Their environmentally highest-ranked stocks performed significantly better than the lowest-ranked stocks.

The second advantage of socially responsible firms may be that they are financially stronger and more profitable because they will be less likely to be subject to product liability suits and settlements, along with environmental fines and lawsuits (Sauer 1997). Additionally, Reyes and Grieb (1998) and Hickman, Teets, and Kohls (1999) demonstrate that socially responsible screens may be valuable contributors to portfolio risk reduction and hence could potentially provide economic benefits to investors.

SRI PERFORMANCE EVALUATION

The performance of SRI can be evaluated through the analysis of either an index or mutual funds. Index analysis includes forming portfolios from screens or using an existing SRI index, while SRI mutual funds allow for existing portfolio evaluation.

SRI Index and Portfolio-Level Analysis of Performance

Various studies investigate the performances of SRI funds and indexes. Studies analyzing either funds or indexes report conflicting results with respect to the superiority of SRI. Several early studies focus on the performances of indices, and some report the dominant performance of SRI indices over conventional indices. For example, Grossman and Sharpe (1986) compare the performance of the NYSE Composite Index with the performance of a value-weighted NYSE portfolio that excludes companies with operations in South Africa. The findings indicate that the risk-adjusted South Africa–free portfolio outperformed the NYSE portfolio by about 0.19 percent per year during 1960 to 1983.

Diltz (1995) also provides partial support for the effectiveness of environmental and military business screens during 1989 to 1991. Studying return characteristics of portfolios formed using various ethical performance indicators, Diltz finds that many screens did not improve portfolio performance, with the exception of environmental and military screens. Hutton, D'Antonio, and Johnsen (1998) investigate the performance of bonds issued by socially responsible firms and compare risk and return characteristics with those of a bond index. The findings indicate that the SRI portfolio provided slightly higher returns than the broader bond index. Furthermore, the duration of the SRI portfolio was also slightly higher.

Luck and Pilotte (1993) find that the Domini Social Index (DSI) outperformed the S&P 500 Index during the period 1990 to 1992. Using the BARRA Performance Analysis package, the authors find that the 400 securities in the DSI produced an annualized return of 233 basis points relative to the S&P 500, and that specific asset selection accounts for 199 basis points of the return. They further note that this period is characterized by a positive growth factor and size returns (smaller stocks outperformed larger capitalized stocks in general during this period). Statman (2000) also reports that the DSI did better than the S&P 500 Index during 1990 to 1998.

Derwall, Guenster, Bauer, and Koedijk (2005) construct two mutually exclusive portfolios by using eco-efficiency characteristics of firms and rank them based on their most recent economic efficiency ratings. They find that a portfolio consisting of stocks with high ranked eco-efficiency performs better than its low-ranked counterpart by about 3 percentage points during 1995 to 2003. This difference is not explained by the differences in market risk sensitivity, investment style, or industry bias.

Other studies do not find any significant differences in returns of SRI portfolios and conventional portfolios. For example, Guerard (1997) examines the average returns of a socially screened equity universe of 950 stocks and compares it to 1,300 unscreened equity stocks during 1987 to 1994. Guerard uses the following social investing screens: military, nuclear power, product (alcohol, tobacco, and gambling), and environment. The findings show that a socially screened universe return is not significantly different from an unscreened universe return. Kurtz (1997) also does not find any statistically significant performance difference between returns of socially screened and unscreened portfolios.

DiBartolomeo and Kurtz (1999) use two separate multifactor models and document that the DSI outperforms the S&P 500 Index, with a total return of 470 percent versus 389 percent over the period of May 1990 through January 1999. The authors do not attribute the higher performance to the social screening process. Instead, they report that sector exposures of the selected companies lead to DSI outperformance.

Sauer (1997) compares the performance of the DSI to the performance of the S&P 500 Index and the Chicago Center for Research in Security Prices (CRSP) Value Weighted Market Indexes. Sauer argues that by using the DSI, the study avoids the confounding effects of transaction costs and management fees that are critical factors when comparing individual mutual fund returns. A comparison of the raw and risk-adjusted performance of the DSI with two benchmark portfolios suggests that applying social responsibility screens does not necessarily yield lower investment performance. A further comparison of the performance of the Domini Social Equity Mutual Fund to the performance of the Vanguard S&P 500 Index and Vanguard Extended Market Index Mutual Funds appears to be favorable, reinforcing the previous findings. Sauer's empirical evidence indicates that investors can choose socially responsible investments that are consistent with their value system and beliefs without being forced to sacrifice performance.

Schröder (2005) analyzes the performances of 29 SRI stock indexes using single-factor models and reports how the SRI screening process affects the performance of underlying equities compared to relevant conventional benchmark indexes. Schröder maintains that focusing on SRI indexes, as opposed to investment funds, has the advantage of measuring the direct performance of indexed firms without taking into account the transaction costs of funds, timing activities, and the skill of the fund managers. The findings are similar to those of previous studies. SRI screens for equities do not lead to a significant performance difference compared to conventional investments. While some would argue that the screening process should lead to a reduction in the risk-adjusted return, the results from these studies show that the SRI stock indexes do not exhibit a different risk-adjusted return from their conventional benchmarks. This implies that an investment in SRI equity indexes does not seem to impose additional costs in terms of a performance reduction to investors.

A few studies report relatively lower performance for an SRI index compared to a conventional index. Among them, Rudd (1979) reports lower returns for a screened portfolio. Comparing the characteristics of the S&P 500 Index with the characteristics of an optimized S&P 500 portfolio that excludes companies with operations in South Africa, Rudd finds that the extra market covariance induced by excluding firms with operations in South Africa results in lower annual returns compared to returns on the S&P 500 Index.

Ghoul and Karam (2007) investigate the extent of overlap between the objectives and components of Christian funds, Islamic funds (faith-based), and ethical funds. Their study shows that Christian, Islamic, and SRI funds have much in common. The screening criteria are generally similar. However, the authors point out that Islamic funds have grown sharply during the last 10 years and differ in one important feature of finance and investment, namely, the prohibition of *riba* (charging of interest). Islam focuses instead on partnerships and risk-sharing. Another distinct feature is the fact that Islamic principles do not allow investments in bonds or preferred stocks because both promise a fixed rate of return. Ghoul and Karam further report a comparison of the performance measures for the Dow Jones Islamic (U.S.) Index, the Domini Social 400 Index, and the S&P 500 Index. The Dow Jones Islamic Index outperformed both the Domini Social 400 Index and the S&P 500 Index in a one-year window. The returns for all three indices seem to be more comparable over longer periods, although both the Dow Jones Islamic Index and the Domini Social 400 Index slightly underperformed the S&P 500 Index during the three-year period ending September 2005.

Adler and Kritzman (2008) quantify the cost that socially responsible investors incur as a result of limiting their investment universe to those companies they deem socially responsible. Some proponents of SRI claim that responsible companies perform as well, or better, than others and, thus, SRI is without cost. However, Adler and Kritzman contend that some cost must be associated with SRI, as socially responsible investors exclude some attractive firms from their portfolios for acting in socially irresponsible manner. By using Monte Carlo simulation, the authors estimate the cost of SRI. Their results show that investors could be giving up somewhere between 0.17 percent and 2.4 percent return per year as a result of the imposed restriction on investable securities. They do not make a case against SRI itself, but rather simply assert that investors should be informed of its associated cost.

Galema, Plantinga, and Scholtens (2008) investigate the relationship between SRI and stock returns. First, they form 12 equally weighted portfolios based on SRI dimensions. The examination of risk-adjusted returns indicates that SRI stocks do not generate risk-adjusted excess returns. The cross-sectional regression results show that only one of the SRI dimensions (employee relations) has a significant positive effect on monthly excess returns. Finally, the authors conclude that SRI affects stock returns by lowering book-to-market ratios and not by generating positive alphas.

SRI Mutual Fund Analysis of Performance

Several studies investigate the performance of SRI mutual funds. The empirical findings are unable to reach a definitive conclusion on the performance of SRI. One group of empirical studies does not find any statistically significant difference between SRI and non-SRI funds. These studies mostly conclude that SRI, at minimum, does not perform any worse than non-SRI or conventional funds. Among them, Hamilton, Jo, and Statman (1993) provide empirical evidence on the performance of 32 socially responsible mutual funds relative to a conventional benchmark. The results indicate that the market does not price social responsibility characteristics of firms. Social responsibility factors have no effect on expected returns or the cost of capital. For example, the average alphas for SRI funds are slightly higher than for non-SRI funds, but the difference is not statistically significant.

Statman (2000) also supports these findings. The average alpha is computed as −0.42 percent for SRI funds compared to −0.62 percent for conventional funds. Although SRI funds performed better than conventional funds of equal assets size, the difference was not statistically significant during the study period of 1990 to 1998.

Goldreyer, Ahmed, and Diltz (1999) examine a sample of 49 mutual funds and compare them with a random sample of conventional funds. Their findings support previously reported results of no significant difference. Among SRI funds, funds that employ positive screens outperform the sample that does not employ such a screening.

Shank, Manullang, and Hill (2005) analyze both short- and long-run performances of SRI mutual funds from 1993 to 2003. The study further makes comparisons among SRI mutual funds, the NYSE Composite Index, and a portfolio made up of firms most valued by SRI mutual fund managers. The findings indicate that most valued socially responsible funds did no better or no worse in terms of performance compared to the overall market during three to five year periods. However, in the longer (10-year) performance comparison, the most valued socially responsible funds outperform the other two indices. The lack of any significant short-term performance reinforces the belief that investors can obtain little financial benefit by selecting the socially responsible investments in the short run. The findings of the study also imply that investors dedicated to SRI may not realize great financial returns, but they will not be economically penalized for their investment philosophy. The most valued mutual funds with positive and significant returns experience greater long-run performance.

A second group of studies investigating the performance of SRI reports significant cost associated with selecting suboptimal portfolios due to the screening of certain groups of stocks. Among them, Geczy, Stambaugh, and Levin (2006) use a sample of 106 SRI equity mutual funds to illustrate a cost associated with imposing the SRI constraint on a portfolio. They contend that the importance of SRI costs depends on the investor's view about the asset pricing model, along with the stock selection ability of fund managers. If investors do not believe in asset pricing models and the ability of managers to beat the market, then the cost is low and negligible. For example, the monthly alpha of the SRI portfolio is higher than that of the non-SRI portfolio, but the difference is insignificant. To a well-diversified investor, the financial cost of the SRI constraint is 5 basis points per month. If investors use an individual fund's track record to predict its future performance, then the cost of SRI is large, about 1.5 percent per month. By restricting the SRI universe to keep out alcohol, tobacco, or gambling related stocks, the monthly cost of the SRI constraint increases by an additional 10 basis points.

Girard, Rahman, and Stone (2007) report similar results. They examine whether a cost exists for the social constraint in SRI mutual funds and try to ascertain whether a component of this cost stems specifically from poor portfolio management skills. Using a sample of 116 Lipper-style mutual funds, their study provides evidence about the relationship between financial and social performance and gives information about the social constraint cost. The authors examine mutual fund managers' performance in terms of selectivity, net selectivity, diversification, and market timing and tie these to social constraint costs. Their findings include evidence of poor selectivity, net selectivity, and market timing ability on the part of socially responsible mutual fund managers. Finally, they conclude that SRI funds have significant costs as a result of the lack of diversification and poor selection skills directly related to the ethical screening process, as well as a higher cost for the lack of diversification unwarranted by social screens.

Gil-Bazo, Ruiz-Verdu, and Santos (2010) provide evidence on whether mutual funds constrained by a SRI strategy underperform mutual funds not subject to constraints. The authors analyze before- and after-fees financial performance by using a matching estimator methodology. They also investigate the importance of the fund management companies in determining these variables. The authors show that the SRI mutual funds do not have any reduced performance and earn a premium in terms of superior risk-adjusted performance relative to that of similar conventional funds both before and after fees, with no evidence indicating that SRI funds charge higher fees. This study further reports that SRI funds operated by firms specializing in the management of SRI significantly outperform the conventional funds. The implications of this study for investors are that they should take into account management company characteristics when selecting SRI funds. SRI funds are cheaper than conventional funds run by the same management company.

Blanchett (2010) tests the raw performance of the SRI funds versus their respective category medians. He reports that SRI funds slightly underperform their non-SRI peers during the study period and that SRI funds have historically cost slightly more than non-SRI funds. This is demonstrated by the gross returns being more favorable than the net returns. On the other hand, at the index level, SRI indexes outperform their respective indices.

Chang and Witte (2010) analyze the performance and risk of socially responsible funds in the United States during 1993 to 1998. They determine that SRI funds have had a relative advantage over conventional funds regarding certain performance measurements. However, the study also concludes that SRI funds provide lower returns and have inferior reward-to-risk performance. Domestic stocks did not prove to be highly competitive when generating returns compared to conventional funds in the same categories during the study period. These results are inconsistent with previous SRI studies concluding that SRI has little or no cost. The study provides other insights about SRI funds and determines that their performance can vary depending on its type. As a whole, these funds appear to have lower expense ratios, lower turnover rates, and lower tax cost ratios than the averages of all mutual funds in the same category. Yet, a closer look at each SRI fund category reveals important information about the success of these investments. SRI funds in balanced fund and fixed-income fund categories perform better than the category averages and have lower risk, higher returns, and higher risk-adjusted returns.

International Evidence on SRI Index and Mutual Fund Performance

SRI is also a growing international phenomenon. Various studies investigate the performance of SRI funds in other countries. Within Europe, SRI funds operate in Austria, Belgium, Finland, France, Germany, Italy, Norway, Spain, Sweden, Switzerland, the Netherlands, and the United Kingdom. Early international studies compare SRI funds to various indices and several use UK data. In one of these early studies, Luther, Matatko, and Corner (1992) investigate the return performances of 15 ethical unit trusts. Their results provide some weak evidence that ethical funds tend to outperform the Financial Times All-Share Index. For example, their study reports mean alphas for ethical funds of 0.03 percent per month. Furthermore, the study documents a bias towards smaller companies for ethical funds. Luther and Matatko (1994) confirm this small cap bias by using an appropriate small cap benchmark. Their evidence shows that ethical funds perform even better relative to the small cap benchmark.

In another UK study, Mallin, Saadouni, and Briston (1995) analyze the performance of ethical trusts relative to the performance of nonethical trusts and the market. Contrary to previous UK studies, analysis of excess returns shows that ethical trusts tend to underperform both nonethical trusts and the market. For example, the alphas of ethical funds range from −0.28 percent to 1.21 percent with most of them (22 out of the 29) positive. Alphas of nonethical funds, on the other hand, range from −0.41 percent to 1.56 percent per month. On a risk-adjusted basis, however, both the ethical and nonethical trusts underperform the market index, and the ethical trusts outperform the nonethical trusts.

In a follow-up study, Gregory, Matatko, and Luther (1997) re-evaluate the Mallin et al. (1995) study using a size and risk-adjusted benchmark. The findings show that alphas of ethical funds are not statistically different from zero (ranging from −0.71 percent to 0.24 percent per month). Furthermore, they demonstrate that ethical dummy variables do not influence fund performance after controlling for age, size, and market risk of fund.

More recently, Mill (2006) analyzes the financial performance of a UK unit trust that was initially a conventional fund and later adopted SRI principles. Mill's compares the financial performance of this investment with three similar conventional funds whose investment objectives remained unchanged. The results show that the mean risk-adjusted performance is unchanged by the switch to a SRI orientation, with no evidence of over- or under-performance in comparison to the benchmark market index.

Mill (2006) also shows similar performance of the unit trust with the control funds because both could match, but not exceed, the performance of the market index. This performance is very similar both before and after adoption of SRI. The variability of SRI fund returns provides interesting results. Mill shows that an increase in variability of trust returns occurs over a period of almost four years from the adoption of SRI in March 1996 followed by a decline to pre-SRI levels. The data do not support the alternative explanation that the increased volatility is linked to a change in fund management occurring in September 1997.

Bauer, Koedijk, and Otten (2005) review the performances of a group of ethical mutual funds from Germany, the United Kingdom, and the United States. By applying a multifactor Carhart (1997) model and controlling for investment style, they report the following results. First, German and U.S. ethical funds underperform both their relevant indices and conventional peers, while UK ethical funds outperform. These differences are not statistically significant after controlling for size, book-to-market, and momentum. Second, ethical indices perform worse than standard indices in explaining ethical fund performance. Third, German and UK ethical funds exhibit significantly less market exposure compared to conventional funds and are heavily exposed to small caps, which is contrary to U.S. funds that are relatively more invested in large caps. Furthermore, all ethical funds tend to be more growth-oriented than value-oriented relative to conventional funds. Introducing time-variation in betas into the analysis leads to a significant underperformance of domestic U.S. funds and a significant outperformance of UK ethical funds relative to their conventional peers. Finally, the authors look at the age of funds and provide evidence on the learning effect of these funds. The findings show younger funds underperform both the index and conventional peers.

Kreander, Gray, Power, and Sinclair (2005) also analyze the performance of 60 European funds from 4 countries and report no difference between ethical and nonethical funds. Furthermore, neither the ethical nor nonethical funds could time the market during the study period. Among explanatory variables, Bauer et al. find that the management fee is the only variable influencing the performance measures. Scholtens (2005) similarly reports that SRI funds in the Netherlands outperform conventional funds, but the difference is not significant.

A few studies examine the performance of ethical funds in Australia. Among them, Cummings (2000) examines whether financial advantage exists for ethical unit trusts and three market-based indices. The findings support the view that ethical screening of portfolios neither helps nor hinders the portfolio performance, regardless of the type of market index used.

Tippet (2001) shows that Australia's three major public ethical investment funds achieve mixed financial success during the 1991 to 1998 period, while underperforming relative to the market on average. Furthermore, during the early years, the average holding-period returns for the three funds was less than the risk-free rate. Tippet interprets these results as strong evidence of investors incurring a financial discount for investing ethically.

Bauer, Otten, and Rad (2006) provide evidence on the performance and investment style of retail ethical funds in Australia. After controlling for investment style, time-variation in betas, and home bias, they report no evidence of significant differences in risk-adjusted returns between ethical and conventional funds during 1992 to 2003. Dividing the entire time period into two parts, the findings change drastically. While during the subperiod of 1992 to 1996, domestic ethical funds significantly underperform their conventional counterparts. During 1996 to 2003, ethical funds match the performance of conventional funds more closely. Bauer et al. interpret these results as ethical mutual funds going through a catching up stage, before delivering returns similar to those of conventional mutual funds.

Bauer et al. (2007) provide evidence on the performance of Canadian ethical mutual funds by comparing these funds with their relative conventional peers. Findings indicate that using a single-factor model provides no significant performance difference between ethical and conventional mutual funds. The results remain the same even after controlling size, book-to-market, and stock price momentum. The implication of this study is that imposing an ethical constraint does not lead to weaker investment performance.

Finally, Renneboog, Horst, and Zhang (2008a) provide a comprehensive review of the international literature. They note that despite research on SRI, many issues remain unsolved, including whether capital markets prices corporate social responsibility (CSR), and whether CSR affects firm value and the cost of capital. They conclude that, based on existing literature, no uniform conclusion exists that SRI investors are willing to accept lower returns to pursue social or ethical objectives. In a follow up study, Renneboog, Horst, and Zhang (2008b) investigate the performance of SRI across the world, including the United States, the United Kingdom, Europe, and Asia-Pacific countries. They document that for most countries, SRI funds underperform their domestic benchmark (ranging from −2.2 percent to −6.5 percent), but only a few of them, specifically funds in France, Japan, and Sweden, are statistically different from the performance of conventional funds.

SUMMARY AND CONCLUSIONS

SRI in equities is no longer a negligible segment of international capital markets. In the United States, investors place a sizeable portion of their funds under management in socially screened portfolios in recent years, surpassing $3 trillion in 2010. As the awareness of investors to ESG issues increases, this segment of the market has become more important. For investors, the key issue is to know whether equities selected by an SRI screening process exhibit different performance from conventional investments in stocks.

This chapter provides an overview of the academic literature in the SRI mutual funds and indices areas. Academic research into the performance of socially responsible mutual funds produces mixed results. Several studies report little evidence of a difference in risk-adjusted returns between ethical and conventional funds. However, other studies find that SRI funds can be a valuable source of portfolio risk reduction, even for investors who are not driven by social values. On the other hand, some researchers report a statistically significant cost associated with socially responsible mutual fund investing. In the end, this research reaches different conclusions, largely because of the varying methodology and time periods. Furthermore, the sustainable indices and funds have not been in existence long enough for anything but short-term performance studies.

DISCUSSION QUESTIONS

1. What are the major findings of U.S. studies on the performance of socially responsible funds?

2. The number of funds and net assets managed by SRI funds rose tremendously during the last decade. What are the factors responsible for the growth of funds and net assets?

3. What are some critical issues that SRI studies find challenging in reaching a conclusion about the performance of SRI?

4. How does the empirical evidence on international SRI differ from that of U.S. studies?

REFERENCES

Adler, Timothy, and Mark Kritzman. 2008. "The Cost of Socially Responsible Investing." *Journal of Portfolio Management* 35:1, 52–56.

Bauer, Rob, Jeroen Derwall, and Roger Otten. 2007. "The Ethical Mutual Fund Performance Debate: New Evidence from Canada." *Journal of Business Ethics* 70:1, 111–124.

Bauer, Rob, Kees Koedijk, and Roger Otten. 2005. "International Evidence on Ethical Mutual Fund Performance and Investment Style." *Journal of Banking and Finance* 29:7, 1751–1767.

Bauer, Rob, Roger Otten, and Alireza Taurani Rad. 2006. "Ethical Investing in Australia: Is There a Financial Penalty?" *Pacific-Basin Finance Journal* 14:1, 33–48.

Blanchett, David M. 2010. "Exploring the Cost of Investing in Socially Responsible Mutual Funds: An Empirical Study." *Journal of Investing* 19:3, 93–103.

Carhart, Mark M. 1997. "On Persistence in Mutual Fund Performance." *Journal of Finance* 52:1, 57–82.

Chang, C. Edward, and H. Dough Witte. 2010. "Performance Evaluation of U.S. Socially Responsible Mutual Funds: Revisiting Doing Good and Doing Well." *American Journal of Business* 25:1, 9–21.

Cummings, Lorne S. 2000. "The Financial Performance of Ethical Investment Trusts: An Australian Perspective." *Journal of Business Ethics* 25:1, 79–92.

Derwall, Jeroen, Nadja Guenster, Rob Bauer, and Kees Koedijk. 2005. "The Eco-Efficiency Premium Puzzle." *Financial Analysts Journal* 61:2, 51–63.

DiBartolomeo, Dan, and Lloyd Kurtz. 1999. "Managing Risk Exposures of Socially Screened Portfolios." Working Paper, Northfield Information Services.

Diltz, J. David. 1995. "Does Social Screening Affect Portfolio Performance?" *Journal of Investing* 4:1, 64–69.

Galema, Rients, Auke Plantinga, and Bert Scholtens. 2008. "The Stocks at Stake: Return and Risk in Socially Responsible Investment." *Journal of Banking and Finance* 32:12, 2646–2654.

Geczy, Christopher C., Robert F. Stambaugh, and David Levin. 2006. "Investing in Socially Responsible Mutual Funds." Working Paper, Wharton School.

Ghoul, Wafica, and Paul Karam. 2007. "MRI and SRI Mutual Funds: A Comparison of Christian, Islamic (Morally Responsible Investing), and Socially Responsible Investing (SRI) Mutual Funds." *Journal of Investing* 16:2, 96–102.

Gil-Bazo, Javier, Pablo Ruiz-Verdu, and Andre A. P. Santos. 2010. "The Performance of Socially Responsible Mutual Funds: The Role of Fees and Management Companies." *Journal of Business Ethics* 94:2, 243–263.

Girard, Eric, Hamid Rahman, and Brett Stone. 2007. "Socially Responsible Investments: Goody-Two-Shoes or Bad to the Bone?" *Journal of Investing* 16:1, 96–110.

Goldreyer, Elizabeth F., Parvez Ahmed, and J. David Diltz. 1999. "The Performance of Socially Responsible Mutual Funds: Incorporating Sociopolitical Information in Portfolio Selection." *Managerial Finance* 25:1, 23–36.

Gregory, Alan, John Matatko, and Robert Luther. 1997. "Ethical Unit Trust Financial Performance: Small Company Effects and Fund Size Effects." *Journal of Business Finance and Accounting* 24:5, 705–725.

Grossman, Blake R., and William F. Sharpe. 1986. "Financial Implications of South Africa Divestment." *Financial Analyst Journal* 42:4, 15–29.

Guerard, John B. 1997. "Is There a Cost to Being Socially Responsible in Investing?" *Journal of Investing* 6:2, 11–18.

Hamilton, Sally, Hoje Jo, and Meir Statman. 1993. "Doing Well While Doing Good? The Investment Performance of Socially Responsible Mutual Funds." *Financial Analysts Journal* 49:6, 62–67.

Hickman, Kent A., Walter R. Teets, and John J. Kohls. 1999. "Social Investing and Modern Portfolio Theory." *American Business Review* 17:1, 72–78.

Hutton, R. Bruce, Louis D'Antonio, and Tommi Johnsen. 1998. "Socially Responsible Investing: Growing Issues and New Opportunities." *Business and Society* 37:3, 281–305.

Kinder, Peter D., and Amy L. Domini. 1997. "Social Screening: Paradigms Old and New." *Journal of Investing* 6:4, 12–19.

Konar, Shameek, and Mark A. Cohen. 2001. "Does the Market Value Environmental Performance?" *Review of Economics and Statistics* 83:2, 281–289.

Kreander, Niklas, Rob H. Gray, David M. Power, and C. Donald Sinclair. 2005. "Evaluating the Performance of Ethical and Non-Ethical Funds: A Matched Pair Analysis." *Journal of Business Finance & Accounting* 32:7–8, 1465–1493.

Kurtz, Lloyd. 1997. "No Effect or No Net Effect? Studies on Socially Responsible Investing." *Journal of Investing* 6:4, 37–49.

Luck, Christopher, and Nancy Pilotte. 1993. "Domini Social Index Performance." *Journal of Investing* 2:3, 60–62.

Luther, Robert G., and John Matatko. 1994. "The Performance of Ethical Unit Trusts: Choosing an Appropriate Benchmark." *British Accounting Review* 26:1, 77–89.

Luther, Robert G., John Matatko, and Desmond C. Corner. 1992. "The Investment Performance of UK Ethical Unit Trusts." *Accounting, Auditing and Accountability Journal* 5:4, 57–70.

Mallin, Chris A., Brahim Saadouni, and Richard J. Briston. 1995. "The Financial Performance of Ethical Investment Funds." *Journal of Business Finance & Accounting* 22:4, 483–496.

Mill, Greig A. 2006. "The Financial Performance of a Socially Responsible Investment over Time and a Possible Link with Corporate Social Responsibility." *Journal of Business Ethics* 63:2, 131–148.

MSCI Research. 2011. "MSCI Global Socially Responsible Indices Methodology." May. Available at www.msci.com/eqb/methodology/meth_docs/MSCI_Global_Socially_Responsible_Indices_Methodology_May2011.pdf.

Renneboog, Luc, Jenke Ter Horst, and Chendi Zhang. 2008a. "Socially Responsible Investments: Institutional Aspects, Performance, and Investor Behavior." *Journal of Banking and Finance* 32:9, 1723–1742.

Renneboog, Luc, Jenke Ter Horst, and Chendi Zhang. 2008b. "The Price of Ethics and Stakeholder Governance: The Performance of Socially Responsible Mutual Funds." *Journal of Corporate Finance* 14:3, 302–322.

Reyes, Mario G., and Terrance Grieb. 1998. "The External Performance of Socially-Responsible Mutual Funds." *American Business Review* 16:1, 1–7.

Rudd, Andrew. 1979. "Divestment of South African Equities: How Risky?" *Journal of Portfolio Management* 5:3, 5–10.

Sauer, David A. 1997. "The Impact of Social-Responsibility Screens on Investment Performance: Evidence from the Domini 400 Social Index and Domini Equity Mutual Fund." *Review of Financial Economics* 6:2, 137–149.

Scholtens, Bert. 2005. "Style and Performance of Dutch Socially Responsible Investment Funds." *Journal of Investing* 14:1, 63–72.

Schröder, Michael. 2005. "Is There a Difference? The Performance Characteristics of SRI Equity Indexes." *Centre for European Economic Research*, Discussion Paper No. 05-50.

Schueth, Steve. 2003. "Socially Responsible Investing in the United States." *Journal of Business Ethics* 43:3, 189–194.

Shank, Todd, Daryl Manullang, and Ron Hill. 2005. "Doing Well While Doing Good Revisited: A Study of Socially Responsible Firms' Short-Term versus Long-term Performance." *Managerial Finance* 31:8, 33–46.

Social Investment Forum Foundation. 2010. "2010 Report on Socially Responsible Investing Trends in the United States." Available at http://ussif.org/resources/research/documents/2010TrendsES.pdf

Statman, Meir. 2000. "Socially Responsible Mutual Funds." *Financial Analyst Journal* 56:3, 30–39.

Tippet, John. 2001. "Performance of Australia's Ethical Funds." *Australian Economic Review* 34:2, 170–178.

World Economic Forum. 2011. "Accelerating the Transition towards Sustainable Investing: Strategic Options for Investors, Corporations and Other Key Stakeholders." Available at http://www3.weforum.org/docs/WEF_IV_AcceleratingSustainableInvesting_Report_2011.pdf.

Yamashita, Miwaka, Swapan Sen, and Mark Cohen. 1999. "The Rewards for Environmental Conscientiousness in the U.S. Capital Markets." *Journal of Financial and Strategic Decisions* 12:1, 73–82.

ABOUT THE AUTHOR

Halil Kiymaz is Bank of America Chair and Professor of Finance at the Crummer Graduate School of Business, Rollins College. He also holds visiting professor positions at several international universities. Before joining the Crummer School, Professor Kiymaz taught at the University of Houston–Clear Lake, Bilkent University, and the University of New Orleans. He holds the Chartered Financial Analyst (CFA) designation and has served as a grader for the CFA Institute. Professor Kiymaz maintains an extensive research agenda focusing on international mergers and acquisitions, emerging capital markets, linkages among capital markets of developing economics, IPOs, and financial management of multinationals. He is the co-author of *The Art of Capital Restructuring: Creating Shareholder Value through Mergers and Acquisition* (Wiley, 2011). He has published more than 60 articles in scholarly and practitioner journals. Professor Kiymaz received his BS in Business Administration from the Uludag University and an MBA, MA in Economics, and Ph.D. in Financial Economics from the University of New Orleans.

CHAPTER 23

Performance Implications of SR Investing: Past versus Future

NADJA GUENSTER
Assistant Professor of Finance, Maastricht University
Visiting Faculty Fellow, University of California at Berkeley

INTRODUCTION

Traditional finance theory assumes that investors only care about the expected payoffs on their assets. Well-known asset pricing models such as the capital asset pricing model (CAPM) and its extensions, rest on this assumption. In contrast to this traditional view, many investors also care about other attributes of their asset holdings (Fama and French 2007). Probably the most prominent example of investor taste affecting portfolio choice is *socially responsible* or *ethical investing*. Socially responsible investors not only care about the financial return on their investment, but also are concerned about whether the companies in their portfolio act in line with their religious, ethical, and political values.

Socially responsible investing (SRI) has experienced tremendous growth over the last two decades. In the United States, SRI assets under management are currently $3.07 trillion of $25.2 trillion invested. Major institutional investors worldwide such as pension funds have started incorporating ethical principles in their portfolio selection process. As of April 2011, more than 850 investment institutions with assets under management of about US $25 trillion have signed the United Nations Principles for Responsible Investment (Principles for Responsible Investment 2011a). By signing this document, institutional investors commit to including a firm's environmental, social, and governance (ESG) standards in their investment analysis and decisions. Institutional investors have a fiduciary duty to act in the best interest of their beneficiaries, but they motivate becoming signatories by stating that they believe that environmental, social, and corporate governance (ESG) issues can affect the performance of investment portfolios (Principles for Responsible Investment 2011b). Similarly, large pension funds, prominently, the California Public Employees' Retirement System (CALPERS), explain their decision to divest from tobacco firms since the late 1990s or early 2000 with the poor performance of these firms and not with moral or ethical considerations (Investing Diary 2000).

The arguments put forward by institutional investors stand in stark contrast to the predictions of finance theory. Instead of being superior, the risk-return tradeoff of an SRI strategy should be similar or worse for two reasons. First, the efficient market theory hypothesizes that all publicly available information is fully reflected in stock prices (Fama 1970). If firms with better ESG standards have higher earnings (Gompers, Ishii, and Metrick 2003; Orlitzky, Schmidt, and Rynes 2003; Guenster, Derwall, Bauer, and Koedijk 2011), this effect should be accounted for in stock prices, and these firms should trade at a higher price. The higher earnings should not translate into higher long-run returns. Second, if investors constrain their universe, for example by excluding certain industries such as tobacco, they should incur diversification costs. In combination, these two arguments imply that SRI investors should at best perform similarly to conventional investors and potentially worse. Based on finance theory, why institutional investors, or anyone else, would follow an SRI strategy is hard to understand.

To gain insights on how the performance of an SRI portfolio compares to a conventional portfolio, this chapter summarizes the empirical literature on the risk-return characteristics of different SRI strategies. It not only reviews the past, but also uses currently available empirical evidence to predict potential future developments.

There are as many SRI strategies as people have different religious, political, and ethical views, but two strategies are the most prominent. The first strategy is ESG-investing, which refers to including or overweighting firms that have high environmental, social, or governance standards and excluding or underweighting firms with low standards. The second widely applied strategy is to avoid investing in firms that are involved in sin or controversial industries. Classical examples of sin industries are the alcohol, tobacco, gambling, and weapon industries. This chapter focuses on these two frequently applied strategies.

The empirical literature on the performance of these two investment strategies provides unexpected results. In contrast to the predictions of finance theory, an ESG investment strategy earned positive abnormal returns or alpha in the 1980s and 1990s. The terms *alpha* and *abnormal return* are used interchangeably and refer to the intercept in an asset pricing model, such as the CAPM, Fama and French (1993) model, or Carhart (1997) model. For the environmental firms, the evidence is probably least pronounced with only Derwall, Guenster, Bauer, and Koedijk (2005) providing evidence of positive abnormal returns. In other studies using different measures of environmental performance, returns are positive though not statistically significantly different from zero (Kempf and Osthoff 2007; Statman and Glushkov 2009). The social dimension covers many different policies, but evidence on positive abnormal returns is limited to firms with strong labor policies or high employee satisfaction scores. Edmans (2011) also investigates different explanations for these abnormal returns. His results suggest that investors underestimate the positive relationship between employee satisfaction and earnings. As firms with very high employee satisfaction scores release higher than expected earnings, these firms earn positive abnormal returns. A similar effect has been documented for well-governed versus poorly governed firms during the 1990s. Several studies such as Gompers et al. (2003) provide evidence of positive abnormal returns to a strategy that buys well-governed firms and sells poorly governed firms. These abnormal returns are rather large. Depending on the exact strategy and information set used, returns are up to 18 percent.

Overall, in contrast to the theoretical predictions, the empirical literature on ESG investment strategies provides evidence of positive abnormal returns.

Institutional investors following an ESG strategy should have performed well in the 1980s and 1990s, in line with their motivation put forward in the United Nations-backed Principles for Responsible Investment Initiative (PRI). Excluding sin firms, however, harmed portfolio performance. As Hong and Kacperczyk (2009) show, firms in the alcohol, gambling, and tobacco industries outperform comparable firms by about 3 to 4 percent annually. Because SRI investors lost out on the high returns of sin stocks, but benefitted from tilting their portfolio towards high ESG firms, they perform, on average, similarly to conventional investors.

Whether SRI investors will be able do so in the future is questionable. For the governance dimension, Bebchuk, Cohen, and Wang (2010) document that abnormal returns vanished in recent years because investors learned to appreciate the positive relationship between governance and returns. Evidence provided by expected return studies shows that firms with high corporate social responsibility (CSR) standards have a lower cost of capital (Chava 2011; El Ghoul, Guedhami, Kwok, and Mishra, 2011). These findings suggest that returns on firms with superior ESG standards are likely to be similar or even lower than returns of firms with low ESG standards. If SRI investors continue excluding sin firms, they are likely to perform worse than conventional investors.

This chapter is organized as follows. The next section discusses the empirical evidence on the performance implications of following different ESG strategies. The second section focuses on how excluding sin firms affects SRI portfolio returns. The nest section discusses the combined effect of both strategies on SRI portfolio performance and provides expectations of how SRI portfolios might perform in the future. The last section concludes this chapter.

Return Implications of ESG Investment Strategies

Although recent studies look at the environment and social dimensions together, the empirical literature on governance and stock returns has developed independently. Following the sequence of ESG, this section discusses the empirical evidence on the portfolio performance implications of each dimension with a focus on potential explanations for the abnormal returns.

Environmental Performance and Stock Returns

Many researchers have tried to study the relationship between stock returns and environmental performance. Ultimately, however, only three studies pertaining to the U.S. market have a sufficiently long time-series of information and use commonly accepted asset pricing models to account for differences in portfolio risk. Exhibit 23.1 provides a summary of the main findings of these studies.

Derwall et al. (2005) conducted the first comprehensive analysis of the relationship between long-term returns and environmental performance. This study uses environmental ratings, called eco-efficiency ratings developed by Innovest (nowadays Riskmetrics). These ratings are designed for institutional investors and attempt to capture environmental performance beyond basic pollution statistics. The ratings also incorporate qualitative and forward-looking information on a firm's environmental strategies. Based on these ratings, Derwall et al. form one portfolio consisting of the best environmental performers and one portfolio

Exhibit 23.1   Environmental Performance and Stock Returns

Study	Period	Dataset	α (top)%	α (bottom)%	α (top-bottom)%
Derwall et al. (2005)	1995 to 2003	Innovest	3.98*	−1.08	5.06*
Kempf and Osthoff (2007)	1991 to 2004	KLD	3.60*	0.59	3.02
Statman and Glushkov (2009)	1992 to 2007	KLD	NA	NA	2.47

This table summarizes the findings of studies relating environmental performance to stock returns. Alpha (α) refers to the intercept of a factor model, such as the CAPM, Fama and French (1993), or Carhart (1997) model and can be interpreted as an abnormal return. If a study reports several specifications, the table displays the α of the main specification or most advanced model. The column "α (top)" refers to the alpha of a portfolio containing the best environmental performers; "α (bottom)" refers to the alpha of a portfolio containing the worst environmental performers; and "α (top-bottom)" refers to the alpha of a zero investment portfolio that is long in the best environmental performers and short in the worst ones. A star (*) indicates that the reported alpha is statistically significant at least at the 0.10 level. NA is not available.

including the worst environmental performers. They compare the returns on these two portfolios after accounting for differences in market risk, size, and value versus growth exposure using performance attribution models. The authors also adjust for industry effects. Even after correcting for these different factors, high-ranked firms earn a positive alpha while low-ranked firms slightly underperform. A portfolio that is long in the best environmental performers and shorts the worst performers earns a statistically significant annual abnormal return of 5 to 6 percent.

Following Derwall et al. (2005), two other studies examine the link between environmental performance and stock returns. Both studies, Kempf and Osthoff (2007) and Statman and Glushkov (2009), use data provided by Kinder, Lydenberg, and Domini (KLD). An advantage of the KLD versus Innovest data is that KLD has a longer history and covers a wider cross-section of firms. In contrast to the Innovest data, KLD environmental data focus more on quantitative information on firms' environmental liabilities and emissions as opposed the more qualitative nature of some information incorporated in Innovest ratings. Similar to Derwall et al., the studies build portfolios of the best and worst environmental performers. Both studies find a positive, albeit not statistically significant, difference between the portfolio of top environmental performers and the bottom portfolio. Statman and Glushkov find an annual alpha of 2.47 percent after adjusting for a market factor, size factor, value versus growth exposure, and momentum. Similarly, Kempf and Osthoff report an alpha of about 3 percent annually.

Only one study finds statistically significant abnormal returns. The other two studies find insignificantly positive abnormal returns. Based on this evidence, tilting a portfolio towards the best environmental performers should in the best case scenario have led to higher returns. In the worst case scenario, it should not have done any harm.

Social Performance and Stock Returns

The social performance dimension is probably the most broadly defined dimension comprising a large variety of policies. Kempf and Osthoff (2007) and Statman and Glushkov (2009) investigate the link between social performance and long-term

Exhibit 23.2 Social Performance and Stock Returns

Study	Period	Data Source	Social Criterion	α (top)%	α (bottom)%	α (top-bottom)%
Statman and Glushkov (2009)	1992 to 2007	KLD	Community			3.96*
			Diversity			0.34
			Employee Relations	NA	NA	3.73*
			Human Rights			−2.57
			Product			2.02
Kempf and Osthoff (2007)	1992 to 2004	KLD	Community			3.09*
			Diversity			0.74
			Employee Relations	NA	NA	3.52
			Human Rights			1.96
			Product			0.58
Derwall et al. (2011)	1992 to 2004	KLD	Employee Relations	NA	NA	5.62
	1992 to 2008					2.81
Edmans (2011)	1984 to 2009	*Fortune* Magazine	100 Best Companies to Work for in America	2.1* to 3.7*	NA	NA

This table summarizes the findings of studies relating social performance to stock returns. Alpha (α) refers to the intercept of a factor model, such as the CAPM, Fama and French (1993), or Carhart (1997) model and can be interpreted as an abnormal return. If a study reports several specifications, the table displays the α of the main specification or most advanced model. The column "α (top)" refers to the alpha of a portfolio containing the best performers for each social criterion; "α (bottom)" refers to the alpha of a portfolio containing the worst performers for each social criterion; and "α (top-bottom)" refers to the alpha of a zero investment portfolio that is long in the best performers and short in the worst ones. A star (*) indicates that the reported alpha is statistically significant at least at the 0.10 level. NA is not available.

abnormal returns by looking at five different dimensions of social performance: community, diversity, employee relations, human rights, and product. The studies again use the KLD dataset and construct portfolios of the worst and best performing firms for each dimension. The first two rows of Exhibit 23.2 compare the annual abnormal returns for the different dimensions of social performance as reported by these two studies.

Statman and Glushkov (2009) report only statistically and economically significant outperformance on strategies based on two criteria: community and employee relations. The alpha on a long-short strategy based on the community criteria is close to 4 percent per year. A zero-investment portfolio based on employee relations earns an abnormal return of 3.7 percent annually. Long-short strategies based on other criteria are not associated with significant abnormal returns. Although Kempf and Osthoff (2007) employ a different portfolio construction method and look at a slightly earlier time-period, their results are largely similar to Statman and Glushkov. Consistent with Statman and Glushkov, only the long-short portfolios based on employee relations and community earn sizable abnormal returns. These returns are of similar magnitude as in Statman and Glushkov but the statistical significance is slightly weaker for employee relations. Derwall, Koedijk, and ter Horst (2011) complement the studies of Statman and Glushkov and Kempf and Osthoff by showing that a long-short portfolio based on employee relations indeed earns a sizable alpha of 5.62 percent, which is statistically significant at the 0.10 level from 1992 to 2002. Derwall et al. stress, however, that the alpha strongly decreases over time and diminishes to 2.81 percent for the period 1992 to 2008.

Edmans (2011) probably conducts the most comprehensive analysis on the relationship between employee relations and stock returns. He analyses the returns on a portfolio that contains the "100 Best Companies to Work for in America" (hereafter BCs) from 1984 to 2009. This portfolio earns a significantly positive abnormal return of about 3.5 percent after adjusting for market risk, size, style, and momentum. After additionally accounting for industry exposure, the abnormal return is still 2.1 percent annually. Edmans explicitly tests different explanations for these abnormal returns and provides evidence in favor of mispricing. His results show that analysts significantly underestimate the future earnings of the BCs. He also finds that the positive abnormal returns cluster around the earnings announcements of the BCs, suggesting that investors are consistently surprised by higher than expected earnings.

Institutional investors may have been able to perform financially well, and definitely no worse, when they invested in socially engaged firms. The empirical evidence consistently reports positive abnormal returns for two dimensions, employee relations and community involvement. Investors could likely forecast that these two dimensions would outperform. Most SRI investors probably followed a strategy of tilting their portfolio towards better performing firms along all social dimensions. Despite that, these SRI investors should have performed no worse than conventional investors, and maybe slightly better, because the abnormal returns on the other three dimensions are indistinguishable from zero.

Corporate Governance and Stock Returns

Gompers et al. (2003) conduct the first and probably most prominent study on corporate governance and stock returns. The study uses data on 24 shareholder rights provisions, many of which can be thought of as antitakeover amendments, to build an index (the G-index) and form portfolios. The portfolio consisting of firms with the fewest antitakeover amendments (i.e., strongest rights) is called the "democracy portfolio." Its counterpart, the "dictatorship portfolio" contains the firms with the worst shareholder rights (i.e., the most antitakeover amendments). Comparing the returns on these portfolios from 1990 to 1999 reveals a surprising result. The democracy portfolio earns much higher returns than the dictatorship portfolio, even after accounting for differences in the portfolios' risk, size, value, and momentum exposures. While the dictatorship portfolio earns a significantly negative abnormal return of about −5 percent, the democracy portfolio earns a positive abnormal return of about 3.5 percent, implying a return difference of an amazing 8.5 percent. These strong and surprising results alerted researchers and inspired many studies on governance and returns. Exhibit 23.3 provides an overview.

Bebchuk, Cohen, and Ferrell (2009) show that six of the 24 provisions in Gompers et al. (2003) have attracted substantial shareholder attention and opposition.

Exhibit 23.3 Corporate Governance and Stock Returns

Study	Period	Corporate Governance Data	α (top)%	α (bottom)%	α (top-bottom)%
Gompers et al. (2003)	1990 to 1999	Shareholder rights data (IRRC)	3.48*	−5.04	8.5*
Bebchuk et al. (2009)	1990 to 1999	Shareholder rights data (IRRC)	NA	NA	7.40* to 14.70*
Johnson et al. (2009)	1990 to 1999	Shareholder rights data (IRRC)	NA	NA	−0.12 to 3.12
Lewellen and Metrick (2010)	1990 to 1999	Shareholder rights data (IRRC)	NA	NA	0.60 to 7.56*
Core et al. (2005)	1990 to 1999	Shareholder rights data (IRRC)	NA	NA	8.25*
	2000 to 2003				−1.56
Bebchuk et al. (2011)	1990 to 1999	Shareholder rights data (IRRC)	NA	NA	5.88* to 14.76*
	2000 to 2008				−3.60 to 4.2
Cremers and Nair (2005)	1990 to 2001	Shareholder rights data (IRRC) combined with blockholder and pension fund ownership (Thomson Reuters/CDA)	NA	NA	10.00* to 15.00*
Giroud and Mueller (2011)	1990 to 1999	Shareholder rights data (IRRC) combined with measures of product market competition (Herfindahl Index)	NA	NA	8.64* to 17.65*

This table summarizes the findings of studies relating corporate governance to stock returns. Alpha (α) refers to the intercept of a factor model, such as the CAPM, Fama to French (1993), or Carhart (1997) model and can be interpreted as an abnormal return. If a study reports several specifications, the table displays the α of the main specification or most advanced model. Alternatively, if the paper reports several important specifications, the table indicates the range for alpha. The column "α (top)" refers to the alpha of a portfolio containing the well-governed firms; and "α (bottom)" refers to the alpha of a portfolio poorly governed firms; "α (top-bottom)" refers to the alpha of a zero investment portfolio that is long in the top portfolio and short in the bottom portfolio. A star (*) indicates that the reported alpha is statistically significant at least at the 0.10 level. NA is not available.

Based on these six provisions, the authors build a new index, the E-index, and form portfolios. A strategy of being long in firms with the highest E-index (i.e., most entrenched managers) and being short in firms with the lowest E-index (i.e., the least entrenched managers) is associated with abnormal returns of 7.4 percent to about 14.7 percent depending on exact model specification. These results are even economically stronger than the findings of Gompers et al. The abnormal returns reported by Bebchuk et al. also have a higher statistical significance, suggesting that streamlining the index indeed resulted in a less noisy identification.

The puzzling results of Gompers et al. (2003) and subsequently Bebchuk et al. (2009) call for an explanation. Gompers et al. put two possible explanations forward. First, the results could be time-period–specific or due to imperfections of the asset pricing model. The G- or E-index may be correlated with a latent (risk) factor that affected returns during the 1990s. In line with this argument, Johnson, Moorman, and Sorescu (2009) suggest that industry effects can explain the return difference. Comparing the industry exposures of the democracy and dictatorship portfolio to the market portfolio, Johnson et al. find that both portfolios' industry exposures deviate substantially from the benchmark, as well as each other. They also show that the abnormal returns documented by Gompers et al. vanish if one uses narrower industry classifications. Lewellen and Metrick (2010) provide evidence to the contrary. They re-examine the results of Gompers et al. using a large variety of industry classifications ranging from wide to narrow. Their results show that no clear pattern exists and that the results of Gompers et al. are robust to some very narrow and well-specified classifications.

A second explanation is that investors underestimated the agency costs of weak shareholder rights. As the best (worst) firms realized higher (lower) earnings than expected and investors adapted their expectations, these firms earned positive (negative) abnormal returns. Core, Guay, and Rusticus (2006), who first examined this hypothesis, do not find any support for it.

More recently, Bebchuk et al. (2010) investigate this proposition again, using a longer time-series of information from 1990 to 2008. For the 1990-to-1999 sample period used by Gompers et al. (2003), Bebchuk et al. estimate statistically and economically significant annual abnormal returns of 6 to 15 percent for a strategy that is long in the best governed firms and short in the worst governed firms. After 2000, the results change dramatically. The annual abnormal returns to the same strategy range from −3.6 to 4.2 percent, depending on the exact performance attribution model used, and they are statistically indistinguishable from zero. Bebchuk et al. conduct various tests to support the hypothesis that investors are initially surprised about the positive relationship between governance and performance, but learned to appreciate it over time. The authors start by confirming that governance is indeed positively related to operating performance. If investors systematically underestimated this relationship between 1990 and 1999, they should have been more positively surprised by the earnings announcements of firms with strong shareholder rights. This is indeed the case. Bebchuk et al. document higher positive abnormal returns to the earnings announcements of well-governed firms up to the end of 2001. In line with the learning hypothesis, these abnormal returns cease to exist after 2001. Further, tests show that even analysts who are likely to be better informed market participants underestimate, on average, the positive effect of governance on earnings.

Two important papers complement the Gompers et al. (2003) index with other governance information. Because the G-index contains many provisions that firms use as antitakeover amendments, it can be thought of as a measure of external governance. Cremers and Nair (2005) complement the G-index with information on blockholder and pension fund ownership. They double sort portfolios using both criteria and find that they are complements. A strategy that is long in a portfolio with a low G-index and shorts firms with a high G-index earns positive abnormal returns of 10 to 15 percent if blockholder (public pension fund) ownership is high. However, the same strategy does not yield any abnormal returns if the blockholder (public pension fund) ownership of the firms in both portfolios is low. Giroud and Mueller (2011) show that competition in product markets and the G-index act as substitutes. For competitive industries, a strategy of investing in firms with a low G-index and shorting firms with a high G-index does not earn abnormal returns. However, as the competitiveness of the industry declines, shareholder rights become more important. A strategy of investing in well-governed firms and shorting poorly governed firms in the least competitive industries earns an abnormal return of up to 17.65 percent. Giroud and Mueller show that weakly governed firms in uncompetitive markets have low earnings and analysts underestimate this effect.

The governance literature provides strong evidence that investors in the 1990s and early 2000 could earn high abnormal returns, particularly if they combined information on several dimensions of a firm's governance. However, as governance has been a well-publicized topic in the academic and popular press in the last decade (Bebchuk et al., 2010), abnormal returns ceased to exist. Going forward, investors following a governance strategy are unlikely to be able to outperform.

RETURNS ON SIN STOCKS

Many investors exclude so-called sin stocks from their investment universe. Theoretically, the Merton (1987) model proposes that stocks that are neglected by a sufficiently large fraction of investors trade at a lower price and earn a higher return. Because of limited risk-sharing, idiosyncratic risk becomes priced for these stocks.

Hong and Kacperczyk (2009) empirically analyze the extent to which investors neglect or shun sin stocks and the resulting asset pricing implications. They find that sin stocks have less institutional ownership. In particular, insurance companies, banks, and other investors, such as pension funds and university endowments, seem to shun sin companies, in line with the anecdotal evidence of CALPERS divesting tobacco stocks. However, justifying the divestment with poor performance is difficult. Consistent with the theoretical predictions of Merton (1987), sin stocks earn positive annual abnormal returns of about 3 percent after accounting for other determinants of stock returns. Such stocks trade at a discount relative to their fundamental value of about 15 percent.

Kim and Venkatachalam (2011) add further evidence that sin stocks are a good investment opportunity. They analyze whether sin stocks may be subject to information risk, which may explain the positive abnormal returns. To the contrary, Kim and Venkatachalam find that the accounting policies of sin firms are very conservative and prudent. The earnings of sin firms have a high predictive power for future cash flows and sin firms recognize losses in a timely manner. Apparently, the public scrutiny and attention to which sin firms are exposed induces them to behave well, and sin stocks are a great investment opportunity.

THE PAST VERSUS FUTURE PERFORMANCE OF SRI STRATEGIES

According to the empirical evidence to date, socially responsible investors earn positive returns from tilting their portfolio towards high ESG firms and negative returns from shunning sin stocks. Not surprisingly, little difference exists historically in the performance between conventional mutual funds and SRI funds (Bauer, Koedijk and Otten 2005). Along the same line, Statman and Glushkov (2009) show that the DS 400, an index designed for socially responsible investors, earned similar returns as the S&P 500 from 1992 to 2007.

Contrary to the predictions of classical finance theory, investors have been able to do well while doing good over the last two decades. Yet, this effect is unlikely to persist in the future. As more investors become aware on the positive relationship between ESG and earnings, an ESG strategy will not continue to earn abnormal returns. Bebchuk et al. (2010) already document a learning effect for corporate governance and show that abnormal returns to a strategy of investing in well-governed firms and shorting poorly governed firms ceased to exist. Similarly, for the social dimension, abnormal returns declined in recent years (Derwall et al., 2011).

Studies provide further evidence of lower returns on an ESG strategy once the market reaches equilibrium by focusing on *ex ante* expected returns or cost of equity capital. Using various methods to estimate the expected cost of capital, two studies find that the cost of capital is lower for firms with high ESG standards. For the environmental dimension, Chava (2011) reports that firms that are emitters of toxic chemicals, produce hazardous waste, or have climate change concerns, face a significantly higher cost of capital. El Ghoul et al. (2011) provide evidence that better environmental performance and employee relations are associated with a lower cost of capital.

In contrast to the positive abnormal returns on an ESG investment strategy, the positive returns on sin stocks persist in equilibrium. As derived by Merton (1987), shunned firms earn in equilibrium higher returns to compensate investors for limited risk sharing. Therefore, the positive returns on the sin firms can be expected to persist as long as these firms are shunned. Combining the evidence on the sin stocks and ESG strategies, SRI investments are likely to earn lower returns than conventional strategies in the future. SRI investors will be unable to earn positive abnormal returns on an ESG strategy anymore and will lose out on the high returns on sin stocks.

SUMMARY AND CONCLUSIONS

This chapter provides evidence that SRI investors have been able to earn positive abnormal returns during the last few decades by following an ESG strategy. Strong evidence suggests that well-governed firms earned positive abnormal returns compared to poorly governed firms. For the environmental and social dimensions, the evidence is a little weaker, but it still points to positive abnormal returns. A very conservative interpretation for these dimensions is that investors were not harmed by overweighting top performers and underweighting the worst performers. In line with the fiduciary duty and motivation put forward in the Principles for Responsible Investment, institutional investors following an ESG strategy achieved good performance on behalf of their beneficiaries. That cannot be said about investors excluding sin stocks. Pension funds and other investors shunning sin stocks lost out on high returns. Given these two counter-weighting effects, SRI investors performed, in sum, similar to conventional investors. This is likely to change in the long run. As firms with high ESG standards are correctly priced and have a lower expected cost of capital, SRI investors will be unable to outperform when following an ESG strategy, but they will continue incurring the costs from shunning sin stocks. At that point, SRI investors face a choice between expected payoffs and investing in line with their values.

DISCUSSION QUESTIONS

1. Explain how to construct an optimal SRI portfolio.
2. Should investors follow a SRI investment strategy? Why or why not?
3. Is the growth in socially responsible investments likely to continue over the next decades? Discuss.
4. Do institutional investors act in the best interest of their beneficiaries when following SRI strategies? Why or why not?

REFERENCES

Bauer, Rob, Kees Koedijk, and Roger Otten. 2005. "International Evidence on Mutual Fund Performance and Investment Style." *Journal of Banking and Finance* 29:7, 1751–1767.

Bebchuk, Lucian A., Alma Cohen, and Allan Ferrell. 2009. "What Matters in Corporate Governance?" *Review of Financial Studies* 22:2, 783–827.

Bebchuk, Lucian A., Alma Cohen, and Charles C. Y. Wang. 2010. "Learning and the Disappearing Association between Governance and Returns." Working Paper 15912, National Bureau of Economics.

Carhart, Mark M. 1997. "On Persistence in Mutual Fund Performance." *Journal of Finance* 52:1, 57–82.

Chava, Sudheer. 2011. "Environmental Externalities and Cost of Capital." Working Paper, College of Management, Georgia Institute of Technology.

Core, John E., Wayne R. Guay, and Tjomme O. Rusticus. 2006. "Does Weak Governance Cause Weak Stock Returns? An Examination of Firm Operating Performance and Investors' Expectations." *Journal of Finance* 61:2, 655–687.

Cremers, K. J. Martijn, and Vinay B. Nair. 2005. "Governance Mechanisms and Equity Prices." *Journal of Finance* 60:6, 2859–2894.

Derwall, Jeroen, Nadja Guenster, Rob Bauer, and Kees Koedijk, 2005. "The Eco Efficiency Premium Puzzle." *Financial Analysts Journal* 61:2, 51–63.

Derwall, Jeroen, Kees Koedijk, and Jenke ter Horst. 2011. "A Tale of Value-Seeking versus Profit-Driven Investors." *Journal of Banking and Finance* 35:8, 2137–2147.

Edmans, Alex. 2011. "Does the Stock Market Fully Value Intangibles? Employee Satisfaction and Equity Prices." *Journal of Financial Economics* 101:3, 621–640.

El Ghoul, Sadok, Omrane Guedhami, Chuck C. Y. Kwok, and Dev R. Mishra. 2011. "Does Corporate Social Responsibility Affect the Cost of Capital?" *Journal of Banking and Finance* 35:9, 2388–2406.

Fama, Eugene F. 1970. "Efficient Capital Markets: A Review of Theory and Empirical Work." *Journal of Finance* 25:2, 383–417.

Fama, Eugene F., and Kenneth R. French. 1993. "Common Risk Factors in the Returns on Stocks and Bonds." *Journal of Financial Economics* 33:1, 3–56.

Fama, Eugene F., and Kenneth R. French. 2007. "Disagreement, Tastes and Asset Prices." *Journal of Financial Economics* 83:3, 667–689.

Giroud, Xavier, and Holger M. Mueller. 2011. "Corporate Governance, Product Market Prices and Competition." *Journal of Finance* 66:2, 563–600.

Gompers, Paul, Joy Ishii, and Andrew Metrick. 2003. "Corporate Governance and Equity Prices." *Quarterly Journal of Economics* 118:1, 107–155.

Guenster, Nadja, Jeroen Derwall, Rob Bauer, and Kees Koedijk. 2011. "The Economic Value of Corporate Eco-Efficiency." *European Financial Management* 17:4, 679–704.

Hong, Harrison, and Marcin Kacperczyk. 2009. "The Price of Sin: The Effects of Social Norms on Markets." *Journal of Financial Economics* 93:1, 15–36.

Investing Diary. 2000. "Calpers Puts Tobacco Behind It." *New York Times*, October. 29. Available at www.nytimes.com/2000/10/29/business/investing-diary-calpers-puts-tobacco-behind-it.html.

Johnson, Shane A., Theodore C. Moorman, and Sorin Sorescu. 2009. "A Reexamination of Corporate Governance and Equity Prices." *Review of Financial Studies* 22:11, 4753–4783.

Kempf, Alexander, and Peer Osthoff. 2007. "The Effect of Socially Responsible Investing on Portfolio Performance." *European Financial Management* 13:5, 908–922.

Kim, Irene, and Mohan Venkatachalam. 2011. "Are Sin Stocks Paying the Price for Their Accounting Sins?" *Journal of Accounting, Auditing and Finance* 26:2, 415–442.

Lewellen, Stefan, and Andrew Metrick. 2010. "Corporate Governance and Equity Prices: Are Results Robust to Industry Adjustment?" Working Paper, Yale University.

Merton, Robert C. 1987. "A Simple Model of Capital Market Equilibrium with Incomplete Information." *Journal of Finance* 42:3, 483–510.

Orlitzky, Marc, Frank L. Schmidt, and Sara L. Rynes. 2003. "Corporate Social and Financial Performance: A Meta-Analysis." *Organization Studies* 24:3, 403–441.

Principles for Responsible Investment. 2011a. "About Us." Available at www.unpri.org/about/.

Principles for Responsible Investment. 2011b. "The Principles for Responsible Investment." Available at www.unpri.org/principles/.

Statman, Meir, and Denys Glushkov. 2009. "The Wages of Social Responsibility." *Financial Analysts Journal* 65:4, 33–46.

ABOUT THE AUTHOR

Nadja Guenster is a visiting assistant professor at the Haas School of Business, University of California, Berkeley, and assistant professor of Finance at Maastricht University. Her two main research areas are the intersection of corporate social responsibility and finance, and asset price bubbles. Her papers have been published in such journals the *Financial Analysts Journal*, *Journal of Asset Management*, and *European Financial Management*. She received the 2005 Moskowitz Prize for the best quantitative study in the SRI domain, 2005 European Finance and Sustainability Research Award, and the 2011 Crowell Prize by Panagora Asset Management.

Professor Guenster obtained her Ph.D. from RSM Erasmus University in 2009.

CHAPTER 24

Money-Flows of Socially Responsible Investment Funds around the World

LUC RENNEBOOG
Professor of Corporate Finance, Tilburg University

JENKE TER HORST
Professor of Portfolio Management, Tilburg University

CHENDI ZHANG
Associate Professor of Finance, University of Warwick

INTRODUCTION

Over the past two decades, socially responsible investments (SRI), also frequently called ethical investments or sustainable investments, have grown rapidly around the world. SRI is an investment process that integrates social, environmental, and ethical considerations into investment decision making. Unlike conventional types of investments, SRI apply a set of investment screens to select or exclude assets based on ecological, social, corporate governance, or ethical criteria, and often engage with local communities and in shareholder activism to further corporate strategies towards these aims. This chapter is based on Renneboog, Ter Horst, and Zhang (2008a; 2008b; 2011).

If investors derive nonfinancial utility from investing in SRI funds or in companies meeting high standards of corporate social responsibility (CSR), then they care less about financial performance than conventional (non-SRI) investors. Bollen (2007) contends that investors may have a multiattribute utility function that is not only based on the standard risk-reward optimization, but also incorporates a set of personal and societal values. If such values matter to investors, the expectation is for (1) further SRI growth even if the risk-adjusted SRI returns are lower than those of conventional investments, and (2) less sensitive SRI money flows to past performance. Consistent with the intuition that the socially responsible attribute smoothes allocation decisions, Bollen finds that volatility in SRI funds is lower than conventional funds flow volatility.

Whether or not investors select funds with explicit nonfinancial attributes is a fundamental question. Because SRI screening plays a central role in the SRI fund industry, this chapter describes how nonfinancial attributes influence SRI money flows and the flow-return relation. This is done by using an international data set of SRI funds. Since investors who follow different tenets of social responsibility choose different types of SRI funds, the flow-return relation may depend on the various types of SRI screens. This chapter also investigates whether SRI investors are good at identifying funds that will do well in the future and how future returns depend on various types of SRI screens and screening intensity. On the one hand, investors can derive nonfinancial utility from investing in companies implementing corporate policies that are congruent with the investors' social or ethical concerns. On the other hand, the fact that SRI screens constrain the investment universe can negatively influence fund returns. The prior literature has studied the performance of SRI funds across countries (Bauer, Koedijk, and Otten 2005; Renneboog et al. 2008a). Further, the chapter analyzes the predictive power of money flows for future fund returns, after controlling for various fund characteristics and SRI screens in particular. Hence, the chapter examines whether ethical money is financially smart.

INSTITUTIONAL BACKGROUND

Modern ethical investing is based on investors' social awareness and has grown substantially over the past decades. Because SRI investors have diverse social objectives, SRI funds usually bring into play a combination of negative and positive SRI screens to construct portfolios. An SRI fund typically applies negative (i.e., exclusion) screens to an initial asset pool, such as the Standard and Poor's (S&P) 500 stocks, from which it excludes specific sectors, e.g., alcohol, tobacco, and defense industries. SRI funds use positive (i.e., selection) screens to select companies that meet superior standards on issues such as corporate governance or environmental protection. The funds often use positive screens with a best in class approach ranking firms within each industry based on, for example, social criteria. The funds include in their portfolios only those firms that pass a minimum threshold in each industry. Moreover, some SRI funds engage in *shareholder activism*, defined as when fund managers attempt to influence a company's actions through direct dialogue with the management (Becht, Franks, Mayer, and Rossi, 2010) or by voting at annual general meetings (Renneboog and Szilagyi, 2011).

The introduction of new investment products such as SRI funds can be motivated by fund families' strategic considerations including product differentiation. Massa (2003, p. 250) finds that the degree of product differentiation negatively affects fund returns, but that fund families have incentives to invent new funds because "the more fund families are able to differentiate themselves in terms of non-performance-related characteristics, the less they need to compete in terms of performance." Khorana and Servaes (2004) confirm that product innovation does indeed generate business if the new fund is sufficiently differentiated from the other funds and is in a specific niche.

CONJECTURES

Berk and Green (2004) present a model in which rational investors use past fund returns to update beliefs about management's ability to generate returns. They derive a positive relationship between fund flows and past returns. However, ample empirical evidence suggests that investors deviate from the standard risk-return optimization (where risk is defined as return volatility) when they choose investment products (Statman 1999). An adverse change of fund performance may have a smaller impact on the investment behavior of an SRI investor than on that of a conventional fund investor. Negative returns could indeed be less important for those SRI investors who attach more importance to nonfinancial attributes. Hence, an SRI investor may be less willing to withdraw money from poorly performing funds than would a conventional investor. Also, an SRI investor many be unable to switch easily because of the availability of a restricted number of SRI funds with investment screens sufficiently close to the investor's ethical, social, or environmental profile. This first conjecture implies that the flow-return relation of SRI funds is weaker than that of conventional funds.

The more averse investors are to specific types of (unethical) corporate behavior, the more moral satisfaction they derive from investing in SRI funds that comply with the investor's personal views on societal/ideological issues. Consequently, SRI funds can attract specific types of investors. For example, Beal and Goyen (1998) report that Australian investors in SRI funds are more likely to be female, older, and more highly educated than those investing in the entire universe of stocks listed on the Australian Stock Exchange. Recent studies by Kumar, Page, and Spalt (2009) and Renneboog and Spaenjers (2009) report on the differences in economic behavior related to saving and consumption, bequests, and risky investments by people with different religious backgrounds. Similarly, a clientele effect can arise between SRI funds that focus on sin or ethical issues and those that target social or environmental issues. Derwall, Koedijk, and Ter Horst (2010) provide evidence on the existence of values-driven and profit-seeking SRI investors. Besides the differences in the flow-return relation across the different types of SRI funds, cultural differences between countries or regions affect this relation. For instance, the World Values Survey reports on the heterogeneity of sociocultural and political values around the world. Hence, this second conjecture states that the types of screens activity influence the flow-return relation of SRI funds (relative to conventional funds).

DATA AND METHODS

This section discusses the sample selection, describes the variables, performance benchmarks matching procedure, and develops the methodology.

Sample Selection

A data set is constructed of socially responsible equity mutual funds domiciled in 17 countries and four offshore jurisdictions: (1) the United States; (2) the United Kingdom including Guernsey and the Isle of Man; (3) Europe including Austria, Belgium, France, Germany, Ireland, Italy, Luxembourg, Sweden, Switzerland, and

Exhibit 24.1   Socially Responsible Investment (SRI) Screens

Categories	Type	Screens	Definitions
Sin	Neg	Tobacco	Avoiding manufacturers of tobacco products
	Neg	Alcohol	Avoiding producers of alcoholic beverages
	Neg	Gambling	Avoiding casinos and suppliers of gambling equipment
	Neg	Weapons	Avoiding firms producing weapons or firearms
	Neg	Pornography	Avoiding publishers of pornographic magazines or video tapes, or firms that provide adult-entertainment services
Ethical	Neg	Animal Testing	Avoiding firms that provide animal-testing services or involved in intensive farming of animals
	Neg	Abortion	Avoiding providers of abortion and manufacturers of abortion drugs or insurance companies that pay for elective abortions
	Neg	Genetic Engineering	Avoiding firms that develop genetically modified products
	Pos	Health care	Selecting firms whose products improve human health
	Neg	Nonmarital	Avoiding insurance companies that provide coverage to nonmarried couples
	Neg	Islamic	Avoiding pork producers and commercial banks. (Used by funds managed according to Islamic principles.)
Social	Pos	Business Practices	Selecting firms emphasizing product safety and quality
	Pos	Corporate Governance	Selecting firms demonstrating best practices related to board independence, executive compensation, or other governance issues
	Pos	Community	Selecting firms with an active involvement in local communities
	Pos/Neg	Diversity	Selecting firms pursuing active policies in employing minorities, women, gays/lesbians, and/or disabled persons; or avoiding firms discriminating on gender/race
	Pos/Neg	Labor Relations	Selecting firms that provide good workplace conditions, empowering employee and/or strong union relations; or avoiding firms with poor labor relations
	Pos/Neg	Human Rights	Selecting firms with policies to protect human rights; or avoiding firms with bad records on human rights issues

Exhibit 24.1 (*Continued*)

Categories	Type	Screens	Definitions
	Pos/Neg	Foreign Operations	Selecting firms with human rights policies for foreign operations; or avoiding firms employing child labor overseas or operating in countries with oppressive regimes
Environmental	Pos/Neg	Environment	Selecting firms with high environmental/ecological standards; or avoiding firms with low environmental standards
	Pos	Renewable Energy	Selecting firms producing power from renewable energy
	Neg	Nuclear	Avoiding companies operating nuclear power plants

This table reports the 21 investment screens used by SRI funds around the world, which are classified into four broad categories. SRI funds often use a combination of the screens. "Neg" represents a negative screen (funds avoid specific industries or firms); "Pos" denotes a positive screen (funds select firms based on relative criteria).
Source: Renneboog, Ter Horst, and Zhang (2008a, 2011)

the Netherlands but excluding the United Kingdom; and (4) the rest of the world, comprising Australia, Cayman Islands, Japan, Malaysia, Singapore, South Africa, and the Netherlands Antilles. The data include the monthly net asset value (NAV), monthly assets under management (AUM), monthly total returns, and fund characteristics such as the management fees, load fees, and the inception date. *NAV* is defined as the per share value of a fund's portfolio. The fund return is net of operating expenses but includes any distributions, and is denoted in local currency. A list of SRI screens from various sources is constructed to compile the dataset of fund screens used by SRI funds around the world, as shown in Exhibit 24.1.

To investigate the behavior of SRI investors relative to that of conventional fund investors, a control group of conventional U.S. and UK equity mutual funds is created using 3,113 U.S. and 419 UK funds. The U.S. and UK SRI funds are much larger than those in Europe and the rest of the world. While the average size of U.S. SRI funds is €249 million, European funds are smaller at €39 million. In terms of total assets under management, the United States has the largest SRI mutual equity funds industry, which manages assets of €13.2 billion. In contrast, the combined assets managed by SRI funds in all the other countries amount to €13.0 billion.

Sample Description

Fund flows are defined as the net change in fund assets beyond asset appreciation. As in Sirri and Tufano (1998), the computed money flows of fund i during month t are:

$$Flow_{i,t} = \frac{AUM_{i,t} - AUM_{i,t-1}(1 + r_{i,t})}{AUM_{i,t-1}} \qquad (24.1)$$

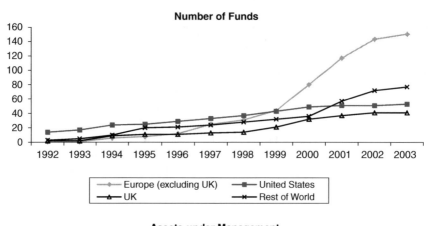

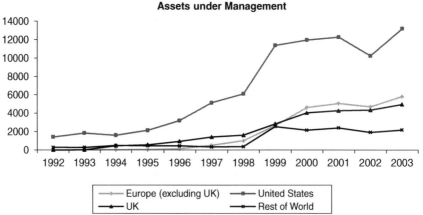

Exhibit 24.2   Growth of the SRI fund Industry

The figure shows the year-end number of funds and assets under management (in € million) of the SRI fund industry in the United States, the United Kingdom, Europe (excluding the United Kingdom), and the Rest of the World (RestW).

Source: Renneboog, Ter Horst, and Zhang (2011).

where $AUM_{i,t}$ and $AUM_{i,t-1}$ are the assets under management (in the local currency) for fund i at the end of months t and $t-1$; and $r_{i,t}$ is the raw return for fund i during month t, which is defined as the discrete returns based on the NAVs of fund i at the end of months t and $t-1$. The returns are net of operating expenses, inclusive of any distributions, and denoted in local currency. This measure of fund flows assumes that all flows occur at the end of the month. To reduce the effect of outliers, the observations of fund flows beyond the 99.5th percentile or below the 0.5th percentile are removed. Other studies on fund flows often apply such criteria (Barber, Odean, and Zheng, 2005; Bollen, 2007).

Exhibit 24.2 shows the number of SRI funds and their total AUM over time. The data show that in just one decade, the number of SRI equity funds around the world has grown rapidly to 321, and that the total AUM has increased from €1.7 billion in December 1992 to €26.2 billion by December 2003. Europe experienced the highest growth in the number of SRI funds, but the fastest growth in SRI assets occurred

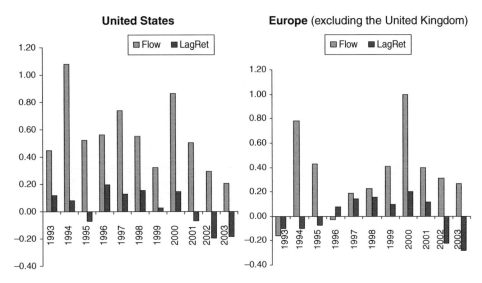

Exhibit 24.3   Flows and Lagged Returns
The figure shows the annual net flows (Flow) and the one-year-lagged annual returns (LagRet) of SRI funds in the United States, the United Kingdom, Europe (excluding the United Kingdom.) and the Rest of the World.
Source: Renneboog, Ter Horst, and Zhang (2011).

in U.S. equity mutual funds. Exhibit 24.3 depicts the average annual flows against the prior-year's average annual returns. The average flows are positive and for all four regions depend on the recent returns of SRI funds. Although the average return of SRI funds around the world was strongly negative in 2001 and 2002 (i.e., –16 percent and –21 percent, respectively), the SRI fund industry still experienced a strong inflow of new money of 41 percent and 38 percent during the next two years.

Exhibit 24.4 presents the summary statistics. Panel A reports the average and standard deviation of the money flows; the returns; the flow volatility, as measured in 12-month rolling windows; the return volatility, which is the standard deviation of returns in 12-month rolling windows; the fund size, as the natural logarithm of fund assets; the total fees, as the annual management fee and the load fees as a percentage of the money invested; and the fraction of funds investing abroad. Load fees consist of front-end fees (share subscription fees) and back-end fees (share redemption fees). SRI funds mainly use load fees to pay for trading costs and marketing expenses such as distribution of payments to brokers or advertising. They use management fees to cover operating expenses comprising managerial compensation, as well as part of the marketing or distribution expenses. SRI funds amortize the load fees over a seven-year holding period, which is the average holding period for equity mutual funds. The variable *Total Fees* is the sum of the management fees and one-seventh of the load fees.

These statistics are computed over time and across funds. Panel A of Exhibit 24.4 shows that the SRI industry experienced strong growth throughout the world; the average monthly growth rate ranges from 2.2 percent in the United

Exhibit 24.4 Summary Statistics

Panel A. SRI Funds by Region

Variable	United States Mean	United States Std. Dev.	United Kingdom Mean	United Kingdom Std. Dev.	Europe (excluding the United Kingdom) Mean	Europe (excluding the United Kingdom) Std. Dev.	Rest of World Mean	Rest of World Std. Dev.
Flow	0.024	0.082	0.022	0.084	0.027	0.110	0.030	0.127
Return	0.005	0.055	0.002	0.048	−0.003	0.059	0.003	0.048
Flow volatility	0.061	0.110	0.089	0.151	0.094	0.129	0.096	0.141
Size	3.669	1.802	3.863	1.644	2.659	1.573	1.730	2.743
Return volatility	0.049	0.022	0.044	0.015	0.054	0.020	0.042	0.021
Total fees	0.019	0.008	0.018	0.006	0.017	0.006	0.021	0.005
Management fees	0.016	0.007	0.013	0.004	0.013	0.005	0.015	0.005
Load fees	0.018	0.024	0.035	0.022	0.028	0.020	0.040	0.027
Direct Invest abroad	0.161	0.370	0.442	0.502	0.934	0.248	0.169	0.377

Panel B. Screening Activity by SRI Funds

	World	United States	United Kingdom	Europe (excluding the United Kingdom)	Rest of World
By fund: Average number of					
Screens	6.79	7.25	9.10	6.62	5.57
Negative screens	3.72	4.21	5.80	3.07	3.59
Positive screens	3.06	3.04	3.29	3.55	1.97
Fraction of funds with					
Negative screens	0.71	0.94	0.85	0.58	0.75
Positive screens	0.77	0.66	0.83	0.91	0.55
Sin screens	0.68	0.91	0.85	0.55	0.70
Ethical screens	0.51	0.53	0.83	0.40	0.53
Social screens	0.68	0.64	0.83	0.77	0.45
Environmental screens	0.77	0.66	0.93	0.86	0.58
Islamic screens	0.12	0.06	0.02	0.03	0.38
Activism policy	0.21	0.45	0.27	0.20	0.04
In-house SRI research	0.24	0.47	0.24	0.22	0.09

Panel A reports the average and standard deviation of monthly money flows measured as the rate of change in the fund assets under management beyond asset appreciation; the monthly returns; the flow volatility, measured over 12-month rolling windows; the return volatility, which is measured by the standard deviation of returns over 12-month rolling windows; the fund size, which is the natural logarithm of fund assets in €; the total fees, which are the sum of the annual management fee and one-seventh of the load fees, expressed as a percentage of the money invested; and the fraction of funds investing abroad. The statistics are computed over time (1992 to 2004) and across funds. Panel B shows the average number of screens used per fund and the average number of negative or positive screens. Panel B also reports the fraction of the funds that use negative, positive, Sin, Ethical, Social, Environmental, or Islamic screens, and the fraction of those funds that engage in activism or base their screening activity on in-house research.

Source: Renneboog, Ter Horst, and Zhang (2011).

Kingdom to 3.0 percent in the rest of the world. The average fund size is largest in the United Kingdom. Moreover, when one-seventh of the load fees is added to the management fees, the average annual total fees range from 1.7 percent in Europe (excluding the United Kingdom) to 2.1 percent in the rest of the world. Important differences occur in the components of fund fees across regions. For example, SRI funds in the United States have the highest average management fee of 1.6 percent per year and the lowest load fees at 1.8 percent. The load fees are the highest in the rest of the world, averaging 4 percent. European SRI funds are the most internationally diversified, as 33 percent of the funds invest across Europe, 61 percent invest outside Europe, and 6 percent invest only in their native country. In contrast, only 16 percent of the SRI funds in the United States invest abroad.

Panel B of Exhibit 24.4 highlights the differences in screening activity across the four regions. SRI funds in the United Kingdom use, on average, about 9.1 investment screens simultaneously, six of which are negative screens that exclude firms or industries with undesirable ethical characteristics. In contrast, SRI funds in the rest of the world apply an average of 5.6 screens. More than 94 percent of SRI funds in the United States use negative screens. In particular, 91 percent of U.S. SRI funds use at least one of the sin screens, banning tobacco, alcohol, gambling, weapons, and pornography. Positive screens are more popular in the United Kingdom and the rest of Europe, and are used by 83 percent and 91 percent of the funds, respectively.

Performance Benchmarks

To measure an individual fund's exposures to a set of benchmarks, monthly returns of benchmark portfolios are constructed for each country in the sample. The benchmark factors for the United States are the three Fama and French (1993) factors and the Carhart (1997) momentum factor. The one-month Treasury-bill rate or the interbank interest rate is used as the risk-free rate.

For each SRI and conventional fund in the sample that has a performance history of at least 24 months, the capital asset pricing model (CAPM) and the Fama-French-Carhart (FFC) models are estimated as:

$$r_t - r_{f,t} = \alpha_1 + \beta_{MKT}(r_t^m - r_{f,t}) + \delta_t \tag{24.2}$$

$$r_t - r_{f,t} = \alpha_4 + \beta_{MKT}(r_t^m - r_{f,t}) + \beta_{SMB}r_t^{smb} + \beta_{HML}r_t^{hml} + \beta_{UMD}r_t^{umd} + \varepsilon_t \tag{24.3}$$

where r_t is the return of a fund in month t; $r_{f,t}$ is the return on a local risk-free deposit; r_t^m is the return of a local equity market index; r_t^{smb}, r_t^{hml}, and r_t^{umd} are the following factors: SMB (the size factor; Small minus Big), HML (the value versus growth factor; High book-to-market minus Low book-to-market) and UMD (the Momentum factor); $\alpha_1 + \delta_\tau$ is the CAPM-adjusted return of ethical/conventional fund portfolios; $\alpha_4 + \varepsilon_\tau$ is the FFC-adjusted return of ethical/conventional fund portfolios; and β_{MKT}, β_{SMB}, β_{HML}, and β_{UMD} are the factor loadings. Fund performance is evaluated on a country basis from a local investor perspective.

Matching Method for the Univariate Analysis

In the univariate analysis on the flow-return relation for SRI funds and conventional funds, a matching procedure is applied between SRI and conventional funds similar to that of Bollen (2007). First, to control for fund age, conventional funds must be no more than two years older or younger than the SRI fund. This exclusion criterion ensures that the funds experience similar life-cycle effects and macroeconomic time-series effects. Second, only those conventional funds without load fees are eligible candidates for no-load SRI funds. This restriction controls for the impact of fund fees and investors' transaction costs on money flows. Third, for each SRI fund, the scores are calculated for all eligible conventional funds that satisfy the above requirements by using two alternative least-squares algorithms with one- or four-factor loadings:

$$Score(a)_{i,j} = (AUM_i - AUM_j)^2/\sigma^2_{AUM} + (\beta_{MKT,i} - \beta_{MKT,j})^2/\sigma^2_{MKT} \qquad (24.4)$$

$$Score(b)_{i,j} = (AUM_i - AUM_j)^2/\sigma^2_{AUM} + (\beta_{MKT,i} - \beta_{MKT,j})^2/\sigma^2_{MKT}$$
$$+ (\beta_{SMB,i} - \beta_{SMB,j})^2/\sigma^2_{SMB} + (\beta_{HMI,i} - \beta_{HMI,j})^2/\sigma^2_{HML} \qquad (24.5)$$
$$+ (\beta_{UMD,i} - \beta_{UMD,j})^2/\sigma^2_{UMD}$$

where i represents an SRI fund and j for a conventional one; AUM is the maximum size of the fund during its life; σ^2_{AUM} is the cross-sectional variance of AUM; β_{MKT}, β_{SMB}, β_{HML}, and β_{UMD} are the risk exposures to the four factors; and σ^2_{MKT}, σ^2_{SMB}, σ^2_{HML}, and σ^2_{UMD} are the cross-sectional variances of the risk exposures. Scaling the squared deviations by the variance normalizes the weights on each matching criterion.

For each SRI fund, two conventional funds with the lowest *Score* are added to the control group. The univariate sample consists of 885 equity mutual funds: 295 SRI funds with a performance history of at least 24 months and two samples of 590 conventional funds, matched by fund age, size, load fees, and risk exposures based on either the CAPM or the Fama-French-Carhart (FFC) four-factor model.

DETERMINANTS OF MONEY FLOWS

This section begins by discussing the results of a univariate analysis of the relationship between past fund performance and the funds' money flows. Next, the flow-return relation is analyzed in a multivariate framework with a particular emphasis on the role of investment screens and screening intensity.

Univariate Flow-Return Analysis

A univariate analysis is first performed on the flow-past return relation of money flows for SRI funds and a sample of matched conventional funds. This test is similar to that conducted by Bollen (2007) for U.S. funds. Sirri and Tufano (1998) show that individual investors use rudimentary performance measures such as raw historical returns to select mutual funds. Therefore, the following flow-return regression is estimated for SRI and matched conventional funds, respectively:

$$Flow_{i,t} = \gamma_0 + (\beta_1 R^+ + \beta_2 R^-)Return_{i,[t-1,t-12]} + \gamma_3 Country_i + u_{i,t} \quad (24.6)$$

where $Flow_{i,t}$ is the money flow of fund i in month t in local currency; $Return_{i,[t-1,t-12]}$ is the average raw return of fund i over the months $t-1$ to $t-12$ in local currency; R^+ and R^- are indicator variables that equal one if $Return_{i,[t-1,t-12]}$ is non-negative or negative, respectively; and $Country_i$ represents the country dummy variables that control for country fixed effects. Fund returns are lagged by one year to focus on the impact of the most recent information available to investors. Indicator variables R^+ and R^- are added in Equation 24.6 to allow for different flow-return sensitivities subsequent to positive or negative returns. This also implies that β_1 and β_2 correspond to money inflows and outflows, respectively.

Regardless of which asset pricing model (be it the CAPM in Equation 24.2 or the FFC four-factor model in Equation 24.3) is used to match SRI funds with conventional ones, the SRI flows are found to be less sensitive to negative returns than are the flows of matched conventional funds (Exhibit 24.5). This pattern applies for both the full sample of SRI funds and for the four regional samples. For the full sample (the world) and for the United States and United Kingdom, the difference between SRI and FFC four-factor matched conventional funds is statistically significant. For the CAPM-matched conventional funds, the difference is significant for the full sample, the United States, and the rest of the world. The sensitivity of SRI flows to positive returns shows more variation over the different regions. SRI flows are less sensitive to positive returns for the full sample and the U.S. subsample. This finding that SRI fund flows are less sensitive to negative past returns supports the first conjecture.

The Flow-Return Relation and SRI Screens

Besides considering past returns, investors in SRI funds may consider other factors, such as a fund's size and age, its return volatility, its fee structure, and the reputation of the fund family. All this information is readily available to investors through newspapers, web sites of issuing financial institutions, and specialized data providers such as Morningstar and Standard & Poor's (S&P). Therefore, the analysis is extended to a multivariate setting using the full sample of SRI and conventional funds. The following equation is estimated to examine in more detail the effect of different types of SRI screens on the flow-return sensitivity:

$$\begin{aligned}
Flow_{i,t} = \gamma_0 &+ (\beta_1 R^+ + \beta_2 R^-)Return_{i,[t-1,t-12]} \\
&+ (\beta_3 R^+ + \beta_4 R^-)Return_{i,[t-1,t-12]} * D(Sin/Ethical_i) \\
&+ (\beta_5 R^+ + \beta_6 R^-)Return_{i,[t-1,t-12]} * D(Social_i) \qquad (24.7) \\
&+ (\beta_7 R^+ + \beta_8 R^-)Return_{i,[t-1,t-12]} * D(Environmental_i) \\
&+ \gamma_1 ScreeningTypes_i + \gamma_2 SRIAttributes_i + \gamma_3 Controls_{i,t-1} + u_{i,t}
\end{aligned}$$

where $Flow_{i,t}$ is the money flow of fund i in month t in local currency; $Return_{i,[t-1,t-12]}$ is the average raw return, average CAPM-adjusted return, or average FFC-adjusted return of fund i over the months $t-1$ to $t-12$ in local

Exhibit 24.5 Flow-Return Relation: Matched-Pair Comparisons

	World	United States	United Kingdom	Europe	Rest of the World
SRI Funds					
Flow Sensitivity to Positive Returns	1.014	0.980	0.825	1.508	1.323
t-statistic	[6.59]***	[2.90]***	[2.86]***	[4.07]***	[4.58]***
Flow Sensitivity to Negative Returns	0.121	0.193	0.124	0.104	0.043
t-statistic	[0.24]	[2.34]**	[0.67]	[0.29]	[0.17]
Matched Conventional funds: FFC					
Flow Sensitivity to Positive Returns	1.104	1.136	0.830	1.248	1.258
t-statistic	[11.92]***	[11.30]***	[3.80]***	[2.77]***	[2.89]***
Flow Sensitivity to Negative Returns	0.285	0.278	0.363	0.280	0.068
t-statistic	[4.08]***	[3.67]***	[2.20]**	[3.60]***	[0.77]
Difference (p-value)					
Flow Sensitivity to Positive Returns	(0.08)*	(0.00)***	(0.21)	(0.53)	(0.11)
Flow Sensitivity to Negative Returns	(0.02)**	(0.07)*	(0.02)**	(0.43)	(0.59)
Matched Conventional funds: CAPM					
Flow Sensitivity to Positive Returns	1.202	1.256	0.820	1.239	1.220
t-statistic	[12.31]***	[11.52]***	[4.44]***	[10.02]***	[10.62]***
Flow Sensitivity to Negative Returns	0.294	0.322	0.264	0.283	0.255
t-statistic	[2.38]**	[2.48]**	[2.10]**	[3.19]***	[2.79]***
Difference (p-value)					
Flow Sensitivity to Positive Returns	(0.03)**	(0.00)***	(0.31)	(0.63)	(0.19)
Flow Sensitivity to Negative Returns	(0.02)**	(0.00)***	(0.43)	(0.40)	(0.03)**

This table presents the flow-return sensitivity (see Equation 24.6) for SRI funds and matched conventional funds around the world. The matching is based on either the four-factor or one-factor models. The dependent variable is the money flow of fund i in month t in local currency as in Equation (1). $Return_{i,[t-1,t-12]}$ is the average return of fund i over the months $t-1$ to $t-12$ in local currency. R^+ and R^- are indicator variables that equal one if $Return_{i,[t-1,t-12]}$ is non-negative or negative, respectively. The estimation includes country fixed effects. The significance levels are calculated by using clustered standard errors over two dimensions (by month and by fund) to account for cross-sectional and time-series dependence. The absolute values of t-statistics and the p-values are reported in brackets and parentheses, respectively. *, **, and *** indicate significance at the 0.10, 0.05, and 0.01 level, respectively.
Source: Renneboog, Ter Horst, and Zhang (2011).

currency; and R^+ and R^- are indicator variables that equal one if the average raw return is non-negative or negative, respectively. *Screening Types* of SRI funds are measured by $D(Sin/Ethical_i)$, $D(Social_i)$, and $D(Environmental_i)$. These three indicator variables equal one if the fund uses at least one of the SRI screens from a broad screening area, i.e., Sin/Ethical, Social, or Environmental screens, respectively. The reason past returns are interacted with measures of screening types is to allow for different flow-return sensitivities by type of SRI fund.

The coefficients in Equation 24.7 are defined as follows: β_1 (β_2) captures the sensitivity of flows to positive (negative) average returns over the previous year for conventional funds. Likewise, ($\beta_1 + \beta_3$) and ($\beta_2 + \beta_4$) represent the sensitivity of flows to past positive and negative average returns, respectively, for those SRI funds with Sin/Ethical screens. The coefficients ($\beta_1 + \beta_5$) and ($\beta_2 + \beta_6$) capture the flow sensitivity to past positive and negative average returns, respectively, for those SRI funds that use Social screens. The coefficients ($\beta_1 + \beta_7$) and ($\beta_2 + \beta_8$) represent the flow sensitivity to past positive and negative average returns for those SRI funds with screens based on environmental criteria.

The *SRI Attributes* comprise the following variables for the SRI funds: (1) $D(Activism\ Policy_i)$ equals one if the fund intends to influence corporate behavior through direct engagement or proxy voting; (2) $D(In\text{-}House\ SRI\ Research_i)$ is an indicator variable that equals one if the screening activities of the fund are based on in-house SRI research; and (3) $D(Islamic\ Fund_i)$ is an indicator variable that shows whether the fund is designed for Islamic investors. All of these variables are equal to zero for conventional funds.

The vector of control variables in Equation 24.7, denoted as $Controls_{i,t-1}$, captures the impact of five groups of variables: *Fund Characteristics, Fund Fees, Fund Family, Investment Styles*, and *Country and Time Effects*. The *Fund Characteristics* are lagged by one month and comprise (1) $Age_{i,t-1}$ is the number of years since the fund's inception; (2) $Size_{i,t-1}$ is the fund size (the natural logarithm of AUM) at month $t-1$; (3) $Return\ Volatility_{i,[t-1,t-12]}$ is the total risk of the fund measured as the standard deviation of monthly fund returns from months $t-1$ to $t-12$; and (4) an indicator variable, $D(Investing\ Abroad_i)$, that equals one if the fund invests in foreign countries. Furthermore, *Fund Fees* comprise *Management Fees$_i$*, (the annual management fee) and the *Load Fees$_i$* (the sum of the front- and back-end load fees). The *Fund Family* consists of *Family Size$_{i,t-1}$*, the size of the fund's family (the natural logarithm of the AUM of all funds belonging to the same family) at month $t-1$, which is the proxy for the visibility and reputation of fund families in the SRI and conventional fund industries. Additionally, the *Investment Styles* variables comprise the exposures to the market, size, book-to-market, and momentum style factors: β_{MKT}, β_{SMB}, β_{HML}, and β_{UMD} as estimated by Equation 24.3. Fixed *Country and Time Effects* are added as 20 country dummies and 150 month dummies, denoted as $D(Country_t)$ and $D(Month_i)$, to control for unobservable differences in money flows across countries, and for the bubble and recession periods. To account for the cross-sectional and time-series dependence between fund observations, the standard errors of the regressions are clustered over two dimensions (Petersen 2009). The procedure imposes 150 clusters by month and 3,853 clusters by fund. In doing so, potential dependence, across funds and months, is allowed in the error terms of the regressions.

Exhibit 24.6 presents the estimation results of Equation 24.7. Columns (1)–(3) show the results for the full sample of conventional and SRI funds (World)

Exhibit 24.6 Flow-Return Relation and Screening Types

		World Raw Return (1)	World CAPM-adjusted (2)	World FFC-adjusted (3)	U.S. Raw Return (4)	U.K. Raw Return (5)	Europe Raw Return (6)	Rest of World Raw Return (7)
	Constant	0.039 [11.04]***	0.067 [16.65]***	0.055 [15.21]***	0.05 [12.90]***	0.032 [1.91]*	0.049 [12.43]***	0.05 [12.70]***
Past Return	Return* R+	1.557 [15.66]***	1.137 [14.52]***	1.747 [18.20]***	1.834 [14.20]***	0.619 [6.19]***	1.832 [14.17]***	1.827 [14.09]***
	Return* R−	0.553 [5.64]***	0.742 [10.64]***	0.856 [9.48]***	0.612 [5.40]***	0.319 [2.76]***	0.618 [5.55]***	0.615 [5.50]***
Return* Screen Types	Return* R+ *D Sin/Ethical	−0.117 [0.66]	0.317 [1.35]	0.019 [0.07]	−0.803 [3.81]***	0.275 [1.38]	0.09 [0.27]	−0.211 [0.62]
	Return* R− *D Sin/Ethical	−0.411 [2.64]***	−0.544 [2.84]***	−0.329 [1.67]*	−0.444 [2.12]**	−0.218 [1.46]	−0.003 [0.02]	−0.434 [3.80]***
	Return* R+ *D Social	−1.059 [4.89]***	−0.882 [2.88]***	−0.96 [2.71]***	−0.984 [3.38]***	−0.564 [1.02]	−0.982 [2.89]***	−0.882 [1.30]
	Return* R− *D Social	0.162 [0.91]	−0.28 [1.02]	0.048 [0.20]	0.882 [1.12]	−0.315 [0.35]	−0.124 [0.55]	0.219 [1.60]
	Return* R+ *D Environmental	0.759 [2.68]***	1.207 [3.38]***	0.819 [2.08]**	0.681 [1.99]**	−0.216 [0.09]	0.839 [2.57]**	−0.139 [1.14]
	Return* R− *D Environmental	−0.007 [0.04]	−0.185 [0.70]	−0.108 [0.42]	−0.523 [1.74]*	0.139 [1.06]	−0.166 [0.65]	−0.092 [0.34]

Screening Types		(1)	(2)	(3)	(4)	(5)	(6)	(7)
	D Sin/Ethical	0.009	0.002	0.005	0.016	0.001	0.004	0.006
		[0.76]	[1.07]	[2.56]**	[4.46]***	[0.61]	[0.81]	[0.84]
	D Social	0.007	−0.004	0.000	0.008	0.007	0.005	0.024
		[1.98]**	[1.48]	[0.16]	[1.11]	[0.43]	[0.81]	[2.44]**
	D Environmental	−0.003	−0.004	0.002	−0.012	0.015	−0.005	0.019
		[0.80]	[1.46]	[0.68]	[1.71]*	[0.84]	[0.78]	[2.93]***
SRI Attributes	D Activism Policy	0.002	0.002	0.002	0.001	0.001	0.000	−0.017
		[1.08]	[1.13]	[0.94]	[0.44]	[0.17]	[0.09]	[0.55]
	D In-House SRI Research	0.005	0.006	0.006	0.003	0.013	0.002	0.009
		[2.62]***	[3.06]***	[2.91]***	[1.43]	[2.39]**	[0.51]	[1.02]
	D Islamic Fund	−0.013	−0.019	−0.013	−0.013	−0.001	−0.015	−0.006
		[3.55]***	[4.99]***	[3.51]***	[3.19]***	[0.08]	[1.98]**	[0.50]
Control variables	Fund Characteristics	Yes	Yes	Yes	Yes	Yes	Yes	Yes
	Fund Fees and Family	Yes	Yes	Yes	Yes	Yes	Yes	Yes
	Investment Styles	Yes	Yes	Yes	Yes	Yes	Yes	Yes
	Country/Time Effects	Yes	Yes	Yes	Yes	Yes	Yes	Yes
	Observations	172558	172355	172399	133382	31469	133589	132078
	R^2	0.06	0.05	0.05	0.07	0.06	0.07	0.07

This table presents the estimates of the impact of screening types on flow-return relation (see Equation 24.7) for SRI funds and non-SRI funds around the world. Columns (1)–(3) show the full sample results (World) with different measures of past performance. Columns (4)–(7) report the subsample results where past performance is measured by raw returns. The dependent variable is the money flow of fund i in month t in local currency as in Equation 24.1. The explanatory variables are lagged by one month. The indicator variables are denoted with a prefix "D." All regressions include fixed country and time (month) effects. The significance levels are calculated by using clustered standard errors over two dimensions (by month and by fund) to account for cross-sectional and time-series dependence. *, **, and *** indicate significance at the 0.10, 0.05, and 0.01 level, respectively.
Source: Renneboog, Ter Horst, and Zhang (2011).

469

with different performance measures, and the columns (4)–(7) show the estimation results for the four regions where past performance is measured by raw returns. The table shows that the flow-return relation of SRI funds around the world depends on the types of screens.

First, at the World level, SRI funds using Sin/Ethical screens are significantly less sensitive to past returns, especially to negative returns, than are conventional funds and other types of SRI funds. The flow sensitivity of conventional funds is 0.55 for past negative returns, but for Sin/Ethical SRI funds the sensitivity is only 0.14 (= 0.55 − 0.41) for past negative returns (see Column (1)). Social screens also reduce the flow sensitivity to past returns, especially when average past returns are positive. Specifically, the flow sensitivity of conventional funds is 1.6 for past positive returns, but SRI funds with Social screens are significantly less sensitive to past positive returns (0.5). Environmental screens seem to have a different impact on flow sensitivity than do Sin/Ethical or Social screens. Environmental screens enhance the flow-return sensitivity when past returns are positive, but U.S. and European SRI funds drive the results. For Environmental SRI funds, this higher sensitivity implies that if the past return is positive, then for a 1 percent increase in the average monthly return over the prior year, the money flows increase by about 2.3 percent per month (= 1.56 + 0.76). This finding of the enhanced flow-return sensitivity for Environmental screens suggests that the environmental attribute is complementary to good fund performance. They are not substitutes to each other as investors derive utility from the environmental attribute only when returns are positive. This finding is also consistent with that of Bollen (2007), who finds that U.S. SRI funds have higher flow-return sensitivity than conventional funds, but only when past performance is good. SRI screens appear to significantly influence the flow-return relation. In general, the differential impact of SRI screens on the flow-return relation provides evidence on the heterogeneity of investor clienteles for SRI funds.

Second, at the regional level, U.S. SRI funds that use Sin/Ethical screens are significantly less sensitive to past returns, be they positive or negative. For the UK SRI funds, no significant impact of screening types on flows is found. For Europe, money flows to Social SRI funds are significantly less sensitive to positive past returns, while money flows to Environmental SRI funds are more sensitive to positive past returns. For the Asian-Pacific region SRI funds, Sin/Ethical screens are the only type of screen that influences the flow-return relation. Clearly, the flow-return relation varies across the different regions. The results show strong indications for the presence of a clientele effect for different types of SRI funds, particularly for the United States and in contrast to the United Kingdom. The different findings by screening type imply the presence of clientele effects that vary across the four regions.

DETERMINANTS OF FUTURE RETURNS

Although SRI investors chase past returns, a question of considerable importance is whether the SRI funds that receive most of the cash inflows perform well in the future. Renneboog et al. (2008b) construct portfolios of SRI funds by tracking investors' fund selection decisions, i.e., the decisions of investing or withdrawing money. They find little evidence that SRI investors can predict future fund performance. However, their study does not take into account the effects of fund characteristics such as fund fees and size. In this section, the predictive power of money flows is analyzed for future fund returns, after controlling for various fund characteristics including SRI screens.

Some studies on conventional mutual funds document a smart-money effect, since money flows can predict short-term fund performance (Gruber 1996; Zheng 1999), but Sapp and Tiwari (2004) show that this effect can be explained by the momentum effect in stock returns. In contrast to the smart money effect, Frazzini and Lamont (2008) document a dumb-money effect, when individual investors invest their money in mutual funds with stocks that prove to be underperforming over the subsequent years. In their model with rational investors and competitive capital markets, Berk and Green (2004) assume that the mutual fund industry has decreasing returns to scale, i.e., that fund returns decrease with fund size, and that new money-inflows chasing past returns can have a negative impact on future performance. Chen, Hong, Huang, and Kubik (2004) confirm that fund size erodes performance due to liquidity and organizational diseconomies, and that this effect becomes more pronounced for funds that invest in small and illiquid stocks.

Because SRI screens constrain the funds' investment universe, this effect is expected to be even stronger for SRI mutual funds. This limitation can force large funds or funds that are receiving substantial money flows to invest part of their inflow in firms with lower risk-adjusted returns. The counterargument is that the SRI funds' screening process generates value-relevant information that is not otherwise available to investors, and that this information can yield superior fund performance. Investors then use the SRI screens as filters to identify managerial competence and superior corporate governance, or to avoid potential costs of corporate social crises and environmental disasters. Therefore, to investigate the impact of SRI screens on future fund returns, the following regression is estimated:

$$Abnormal\ Return_{i,t} = \gamma_0 + \beta_1\ Flow_{i,[t-1,t-12]} + \beta_2\ Flow_{i,[t-1,t-12]} * SRI_i$$
$$+ \gamma_1\ ScreeningTypes_i + \gamma_2\ SRIAttributes_i \qquad (24.8)$$
$$+ \gamma_3\ Controls_{i,t-1} + u_{i,t}$$

where $Abnormal\ Return_{i,t}$ is defined as the risk-adjusted return of fund i in month t in local currency estimated as in Equation 24.3 using the FFC four-factor model as the benchmark, or as in Equation 24.4 using the four factors and an international equity factor. $Flow_{i,[t-1,t-12]}$ is the average money flow of fund i from months $t-1$ to $t-12$ in local currency, and the other explanatory variables are defined as above in Equation 24.7.

Exhibit 24.7 reports the estimation results of Equation 24.8, where Equation 24.4 is used to calculate five-factor-adjusted returns. Similar results are found when the FFC-adjusted returns are calculated based on Equation 24.3. An important finding is that no relationship exists between past average flows and next month's return for either conventional funds or SRI funds. The funds that receive more flows will neither outperform nor underperform in the future.

At the global level, SRI funds with Sin/Ethical or Environmental screens significantly underperform conventional funds. The risk-adjusted return of those SRI funds is, on average, 0.2 percent lower per month (about 2 percent per annum)

Exhibit 24.7 Determinants of Fund Performance

		World	United States	United Kingdom	Europe	Rest of the World
	Constant	0.006 [2.34]**	0.007 [2.16]**	0.001 [0.13]	0.006 [1.99]**	0.007 [2.09]**
Past Flows	Money Flow	0.002 [0.86]	0.003 [1.02]	-0.009 [0.86]	0.003 [0.95]	0.003 [1.08]
	Money Flow*D SRI	0.012 [1.60]	0.001 [0.21]	0.023 [1.55]	0.026 [1.39]	0.023 [1.59]
Screening Types	D Sin/Ethical	-0.002 [4.06]***	-0.004 [2.78]***	0.000 [0.17]	-0.001 [0.62]	0.000 [0.01]
	D Social	-0.001 [1.32]	-0.004 [1.59]	0.002 [1.59]	-0.001 [0.91]	0.000 [0.21]
	D Environmental	-0.002 [2.08]**	-0.002 [1.69]*	-0.005 [2.68]***	0.000 [0.03]	0.000 [0.19]
SRI Attributes	D Activism Policy	0.000 [0.02]	0.004 [2.94]***	-0.002 [1.20]	-0.001 [0.72]	-0.001 [0.34]
	D In-House SRI Research	0.001 [0.82]	0.002 [1.32]	-0.001 [0.39]	0.003 [2.56]**	0.001 [0.21]
	D Islamic Fund	0.001 [0.90]	0.000 [0.15]	-0.013 [1.85]*	0.007 [1.36]	0.002 [0.58]
Fund Characteristics	Age	0.000 [0.45]	0.000 [0.53]	0.000 [0.84]	0.000 [0.91]	0.000 [1.03]
	Size	-0.000 [1.68]*	-0.000 [2.07]**	-0.001 [2.56]**	-0.000 [2.48]**	-0.000 [2.48]**
	Return Volatility	-0.011 [0.32]	0.008 [0.20]	-0.030 [0.33]	0.005 [0.13]	0.007 [0.19]
	D Investing Abroad	-0.001 [0.45]	-0.001 [0.53]	-0.001 [0.55]	-0.001 [0.63]	-0.001 [0.56]

472

Fund Fees					
Management Fees	−0.101	−0.110	0.083	−0.109	−0.109
	[5.27]***	[5.87]***	[1.38]	[5.79]***	[5.87]***
Load Fees	0.002	0.000	0.015	0.000	0.000
	[0.60]	[0.14]	[1.13]	[0.13]	[0.11]
Fund Family					
Family Size	0.000	0.000	0.000	0.000	0.000
	[0.31]	[0.38]	[2.13]**	[0.41]	[0.46]
Investment Styles					
Beta MKT	−0.004	−0.005	−0.002	−0.004	−0.005
	[1.40]	[1.61]	[0.25]	[1.53]	[1.60]
Beta SMB	0.000	0.000	0.001	0.000	0.000
	[0.05]	[0.08]	[0.48]	[0.04]	[0.02]
Beta HML	−0.001	−0.001	−0.005	−0.001	−0.001
	[0.40]	[0.24]	[0.65]	[0.27]	[0.28]
Beta UMD	−0.007	−0.008	0.006	−0.008	−0.008
	[2.12]**	[2.31]**	[0.89]	[2.15]**	[2.13]**
Beta INTERN	−0.006	−0.011	−0.005	−0.010	−0.011
	[1.36]	[1.55]	[1.14]	[1.48]	[1.52]
Fixed Effects					
D Country	Yes	Yes	Yes	Yes	Yes
D Month	Yes	Yes	Yes	Yes	Yes
Observations	144054	124930	12350	124652	123322
R^2	0.06	0.07	0.16	0.07	0.07

This table presents the estimates of the determinants of the abnormal returns (see Equation 24.11) for SRI funds and non-SRI funds around the world. The dependent variable is the five-factor-adjusted return of fund i in month t in local currency. The explanatory variables are lagged by one month. The indicator variables are denoted with a prefix "D." All regressions include fixed country and time (month) effects. The significance levels are calculated by using clustered standard errors over two dimensions (by month and by fund) to account for cross-sectional and time-series dependence. The absolute values of t-statistics are reported in brackets.
*, **, and *** indicate significance at the 0.10, 0.05, and 0.01 level, respectively.
Source: Renneboog, Ter Horst, and Zhang (2011).

than that of conventional funds with otherwise similar fund characteristics and investment styles. This result supports the idea that these SRI screens constrain the risk-return optimization. At the regional level, significant underperformance is found only for U.S. Sin/Ethical funds and for U.S. and UK Environmental SRI funds. Social screens do not have a significant impact on fund performance. Apparently only SRI funds with a strong focus on sin/ethical or environmental issues underperform their conventional counterparts. Only these specific cases support the second conjecture.

Exhibit 24.7 also shows U.S. funds that have a policy of activism can expect 4 percent higher annual returns on a risk-adjusted basis. Although only significant for European SRI funds, some evidence shows that using an in-house SRI research team increases the risk-adjusted return by 30 basis points per month (about 3 percent per annum). This finding supports the argument that the screening process generates some value-relevant information otherwise unavailable to investors.

Similar to Berk and Green (2004) and Chen et al. (2004), the results here show that fund size has a negative impact on future returns of funds. This is consistent with decreasing returns to scale in fund management. The size of fund families is positively associated with fund performance in the United Kingdom, which supports the view that larger fund families have higher organizational efficiency. Finally, expensive funds (with high management fees) are no guarantee of superior abnormal results; on the contrary, these funds perform significantly worse.

SUMMARY AND CONCLUSIONS

This chapter studies the behavior of the so-called ethical investors, i.e., those individuals or institutions that invest in SRI funds around the world. This group of investors cares about the nonfinancial attributes of investment funds. Whether SRI screens affect the money flows and flow-return sensitivity is analyzed in a multivariate framework across different institutional settings that comprise fund characteristics, such as investment styles, fee structure, and role of the fund family to which they belong. Also studied is whether money flows and nonfinancial fund attributes can predict future fund returns. The comprehensive data set consists of nearly all SRI equity funds in the United States, the United Kingdom, Europe (excluding the United Kingdom), Asia, and the Pacific-Rim countries. Conventional mutual funds from the United States and the United Kingdom serve as benchmarks.

The chapter investigates three main areas. First, the chapter examines whether the sensitivity of money flows differs between investors in SRI funds and conventional funds based on past returns. Evidence shows that SRI investors are less concerned about negative returns than are investors in conventional funds. The fact that SRI flows are significantly less sensitive to past negative returns suggests that SRI investors consider nonfinancial fund attributes in their investment decisions. The flow-return relation depends on the types of screens used and on screening intensity. In particular, SRI funds that use negative screens or screens based on specific Sin/Ethical issues to constrain their investment universe (e.g., limiting investments in firms using animal testing or in firms that produce genetically modified food) have a weaker flow sensitivity to negative returns. Social screens (e.g., used to select firms with an active involvement in local communities or with policies to protect human rights) induce a weaker flow-return relation if past returns are positive. In contrast, flows of SRI funds with Environmental screens (e.g., used to select investments in firms that produce or use renewable energy) are more sensitive to past returns. The conclusion is that SRI screening activities induce clientele effects that vary across the four regions used in this study.

Second, this chapter investigates the relationship between the money flows and specific SRI attributes that comprise in-house SRI research, fund age and size, fee level, fund family membership, and the degree of internationalization in a fund's investments. In-house SRI research builds trust, as funds with in-house SRI expertise attract 0.5 percent higher money flows per month, and for UK funds by as much as 1.3 percent a month. Younger and smaller funds as well as funds with lower fees or lower return volatility attract more inflows than do the bigger, older, more expensive, or riskier funds. Funds belonging to a large fund family take on significantly more money flows. This finding can be partly explained by the low switching costs between funds of one family and the more visible brand name of large fund families. The investment profile of funds also matters since funds that invest abroad attract less money flows than do those that invest in their local markets.

Finally, this chapter examines whether ethical money is financially smart, i.e., are SRI investors able to select those SRI funds that will generate high future performance? The evidence suggests that this is not the case, because no relationship exists between past average flows and future returns for either conventional funds or SRI funds. High inflow funds neither outperform nor underperform in the future. This finding is in line with the efficient market hypothesis, which states that investors cannot predict future fund returns, and with the fact that funds are confronted with decreasing returns to scale. While SRI funds with Sin/Ethical screens or Environmental screens (at the world level) significantly underperform matched conventional funds, some SRI attributes have a positive impact on future returns. In particular, U.S. funds with a policy of activism can expect 4 percent higher returns per annum on a risk-adjusted basis. Although only significant for European SRI funds, some evidence indicates that using an in-house SRI research team increases the risk-adjusted return by about 3 percent per annum. This finding supports the argument that the screening process generates some value-relevant information otherwise unavailable to investors.

DISCUSSION QUESTIONS

1. Should SRI funds have higher or lower returns than conventional funds? Explain.
2. What is the difference between positive and negative SRI screening. Give some examples of different types of screens.
3. Give an example of an empirical test that can be conducted to determine whether the money flows of SRI funds are different for past positive and past negative fund performance.
4. What is the smart-money effect?

REFERENCES

Barber, Brad M., Terrance Odean, and Lu Zheng. 2005. "Out of Sight, Out of Mind: The Effect of Expenses on Mutual Fund Flows." *Journal of Business* 78:6, 2095–2120.

Bauer, Rob, Kees Koedijk, and Roger Otten. 2005. "International Evidence on Ethical Mutual Fund Performance and Investment Style." *Journal of Banking and Finance* 29:6, 1751–1767.

Beal, Diana, and Michelle Goyen. 1998. "Putting Your Money Where Your Mouth Is: A Profile of Ethical Investors." *Financial Services Review* 7:2, 129–143.

Becht, Marco, Julian Franks, Colin Mayer, and Stefano Rossi. 2010. "Returns to Shareholder Activism: Evidence from a Clinical Study of the Hermes UK Focus Fund." *Review of Financial Studies* 23:8, 3093–3129.

Berk, Jonathan, and Richard Green. 2004. "Mutual Fund Flows and Performance in Rational Markets." *Journal of Political Economy* 112:6, 1269–1295.

Bollen, Nicolas. 2007. "Mutual Fund Attributes and Investor Behavior." *Journal of Financial and Quantitative Analysis* 42:3, 683–708.

Carhart, Mark. 1997. "On the Persistence of Mutual Fund Performance." *Journal of Finance* 52:1, 57–82.

Chen, Joseph, Harrison Hong, Ming Huang, and Jeffrey Kubik. 2004. "Does Fund Size Erode Performance? The Role of Liquidity and Organization." *American Economic Review* 94:5, 1276–1302.

Derwall, Jeroen, Kees Koedijk, and Jenke Ter Horst. 2010. "A Tale of Values-Driven and Profit-Seeking Social Investors." *Journal of Banking and Finance*, forthcoming.

Fama, Eugene, and Kenneth French. 1993. "Common Risk Factors in the Returns on Stocks and Bonds." *Journal of Financial Economics* 33:1, 3–53.

Frazzini, Andrea, and Owen Lamont. 2008. "Dumb Money: Mutual Fund Flows and the Cross-section of Stock Returns." *Journal of Financial Economics* 88:2, 299–322.

Gruber, Martin. 1996. "Another Puzzle: The Growth in Actively Managed Mutual Funds." *Journal of Finance* 51:3, 783–810.

Khorana, Ajay, and Henri Servaes. 2004. "Conflicts of Interest and Competition in the Mutual Fund Industry." Working Paper, London Business School.

Kumar, Alok, Jeremy Page, and Oliver Spalt. 2009. "Religious Beliefs, Gambling Attitudes and Financial Market Outcomes." *Journal of Financial Economics*, forthcoming.

Massa, Massimo. 2003. "How Do Family Strategies Affect Fund Performance? When Performance-maximization Is Not the Only Game in Town." *Journal of Financial Economics* 67:1, 249–304.

Petersen, Mitchell. 2009. "Estimating Standard Errors in Finance Panel Data Sets: Comparing Approaches." *Review of Financial Studies* 22:2, 435–480.

Renneboog, Luc, and Christophe Spaenjers. 2009. "Religion, Economic Attitudes, and Household Finance." *Oxford Economic Papers*, forthcoming.

Renneboog, Luc, and Peter Szilagyi. 2011. "The Role of Shareholder Proposals in Corporate Governance." *Journal of Corporate Finance* 17:1, 167–188.

Renneboog, Luc, Jenke Ter Horst, and Chendi Zhang. 2008a. "The Price of Ethics and Stakeholder Governance: The Performance of Socially Responsible Mutual Funds." *Journal of Corporate Finance* 14:3, 302–328.

Renneboog, Luc, Jenke Ter Horst, and Chendi Zhang. 2008b. "Socially Responsible Investments: Institutional Aspects, Performance, and Investor Behavior." *Journal of Banking and Finance* 32:12, 1723–1742.

Renneboog, Luc, Jenke Ter Horst, and Chendi Zhang. 2011. "Is Ethical Money Financially Smart? Nonfinancial Attributes and Money Flows of Socially Responsible Investment Funds." *Journal of Financial Intermediation* 20:4, 562–588.

Sapp, Travis, and Ashish Tiwari. 2004. "Does Stock Return Momentum Explain the Smart Money Effect?" *Journal of Finance* 59:6, 2605–2622.

Sirri, Erik, and Peter Tufano. 1998. "Costly Search and Mutual Fund Flows." *Journal of Finance* 53:5, 1589–1622.

Statman, Meir. 1999. "Behavioral Finance: Past Battles and Future Engagements." *Financial Analysts Journal* 55:1, 18–27.

Zheng, Lu. 1999. "Is Money Smart? A Study of Mutual Fund Investors' Fund Selection Ability." *Journal of Finance* 54:6, 901–933.

ABOUT THE AUTHORS

Luc Renneboog is professor of Corporate Finance at Tilburg University. His research areas include corporate finance, corporate governance, initial public offerings, mergers and acquisitions, rights issues, law and economics, the economics of sports, ethical investing, financial distress, and the economics of art. He has published in journals such as the *Journal of Finance, American Economic Review, Journal of Financial Intermediation, Journal of Law and Economics, Journal of Corporate Finance, Strategic Management Journal, Management Science, Oxford Economic Papers*, and *Journal of Banking and Finance*. He holds a B.A. in Philosophy and a BSc/MSc in Management Engineering from the Catholic University of Leuven, an MBA from the University of Chicago, and a Ph.D. in from the London Business School.

Jenke Ter Horst is professor of Portfolio Management and vice-dean of Education at Tilburg University. His research areas include behavioral finance, performance analysis of mutual funds and hedge funds, and socially responsible investments. He has published in journals such as the *Journal of Financial Intermediation, Journal of Financial and Quantitative Analysis, Journal of Corporate Finance, Journal of Banking and Finance, Journal of International Money and Finance*, and *Financial Analysts Journal*. He holds a Ph.D. in Financial Econometrics from Tilburg University.

Chendi Zhang is associate professor of Finance at the University of Warwick. His research areas include corporate finance, behavioral finance, and socially responsible investments. He has published in journals such as the *Journal of Financial Intermediation, Journal of Corporate Finance, Journal of Banking and Finance*, and *Economics Letters*. He has served as consultant and researcher at the World Bank and the International Finance Corporation in Washington, D.C. He holds a Ph.D. in Financial Economics from Tilburg University.

Answers to Chapter Discussion Questions

CHAPTER 2   STAKEHOLDER ANALYSIS

1. Several issues are worth considering regarding objections to a stakeholder worldview. First, investments in stakeholder relationships may take resources away from other potentially worthwhile opportunities and/or reduce the pool of funds available for compensation of owners and managers. Second, the input/output model is a serviceable approximation for the functioning of the firm, and in some cases may be all that is needed to solve the problem at hand. Some firms, particularly in the earlier stages of their development, may not need to have an intense focus on stakeholders not described by the input/output model.

2. Many empirical studies suggest that attention to stakeholder relationships can be financially beneficial to the firm. For example, Orlitzky, Schmidt, and Rynes (2003) find a general positive relationship and address the issue of causality. Edmans (2011) shows that companies with superior employee relations have a higher propensity to deliver earnings above Wall Street forecasts. Guenster, Derwall, Bauer, and Koedijk (2010) report that companies with superior sustainability policies have higher returns on capital. All of these studies suggest that investments in stakeholder relationships can yield tangible financial benefits.

3. Stakeholder theorists generally agree on two primary points. First, virtually all stakeholder theorists agree that the company is in some way accountable to stakeholders beyond those described in the input/output model. Second, most agree that stakeholder relationships go beyond simple supply-and-demand logic and incorporate, to varying degrees, sociopolitical factors.

4. Instrumental stakeholder theory would be most likely to be useful to performance oriented investors. Instrumental stakeholder theory uses a stakeholder framework in the service of some particular objective, in this case the maximization of the firm's value. By contrast normative stakeholder theory idealizes firm behavior in light of a particular values system or ethical standpoint. Descriptive stakeholder theory offers a vocabulary for describing the firm independent of any ethical norm or particular financial objective.

5. Stakeholder analysis might be useful in assessing management quality in several ways. From a stakeholder perspective, management quality may be defined in two general dimensions. First, firms that manage their network of stakeholder relationships efficiently are likely to have more capital left over for compensation of managers and owners. Second, noncontrolling owners must assess the integrity and intentions of those controling the firm to ascertain whether the rewards offered are worth the risk they are being asked to bear. Therefore, the assessment of management quality is not only a question of skillful management but also of integrity.

CHAPTER 3   CORPORATE SOCIAL RESPONSIBILITY

1. Instrumental approaches treat stakeholders as ends to firm performance while intrinsic approaches treat them as ends in themselves. Friedman's (1962, 1970) claims are essentially instrumental—treating stakeholders as ends to firm performance. Freeman (2002) adds in intrinsic concerns suggesting the need to treat stakeholders as ends in themselves, given their status both as humans and stakeholders. Phillips (2003, p. 95) emphasizes the additional obligations owed stakeholders given the firm's acceptance of the stakeholders' voluntary contributions to the firm, vs. duties "owed by all to all simply by virtue of being human."

2. The separation thesis suggests that business can be separated from ethics. Many business ethicists such as Freeman (1994) explicitly reject this thesis while some ethicists such as Carroll (1979, 1991) delineate economic and ethical responsibilities, though Schwartz and Carroll (2003) allow for some overlap. Finance scholars appear to at least implicitly accept the separation thesis.

3. If social and financial performance are not independent, conceptual and methodological issues plague these investigations. Attempting to measure the total value created by firms may be a more interesting and useful endeavor than attempting to measure social and financial performance separately and attempting to establish causality between them. Attempting to measure social and financial performance separately buys into the separation thesis (see above), and many scholars such as Margolis and Walsh (2003) suggest moving beyond rehashing the CSP/CFP debate and onto new research into the relationship between business and society.

4. Phillips (2003) emphasizes the reciprocal nature of moral obligations. Thus, corporate responsibility requires stakeholder responsibility and vice versa. Without stakeholder responsibility, as evidenced, for example, by demands for responsible behavior from corporations through such actions as purchasing, employment, and investment decisions, corporations are unlikely to behave responsibly. Corporate responsibility requires that stakeholders value responsibility, and corporate responsibility becomes endogenous in markets in which they do.

5. The dominance of agency theory in finance approaches to CSR means the finance literature tends to describe CSR, unless directly associated with shareholder value maximization, as either a misappropriation of resources by management, or a misallocation of resources to stakeholders or both. However, recent contributions to the finance literature such as Zingales (2000) recognize that shareholder value is not the only value that firms create. Hennessy and Livdan (2009), Jiao (2010), and Edmans (2011) all find that investments in stakeholders including employees and suppliers, increase the intangible value of the firm, but short-term market valuations do not necessarily reflect this value.

6. If CSR is understood broadly as value creation for stakeholders, as it is by some business ethicists, then value creation necessarily depends on the expertise found in the various functional areas of the firm. The business ethics research on CSR would similarly benefit from the functional expertise of the finance, accounting, and marketing literatures. For example, these literatures' measurement sophistication might assist in quantifying value creation and distribution to stakeholders. In order to address more of the key issues associated with CSR, those literatures in turn might take the discussions occurring in the business ethics literature into greater account, thus better addressing stakeholder value creation, avoiding treating stakeholders as instruments, rejecting the separation thesis, moving past the CSP/CFP debate, recognizing the relationship between corporate and stakeholder responsibility, and detailing the content of those responsibilities.

CHAPTER 4   BUSINESS MODELS AND SOCIAL ENTREPRENEURSHIP

1. *Social entrepreneurship* is a broad term for organizations that aim to solve social problems by entrepreneurial means. According to Alter (2006), the hallmark of social entrepreneurship lies in its ability to combine social interests with business practices to effect social change. Hence, the crux of the individual social enterprise lies in the specifics of its dual objectives—the depth and breadth of social impact to be realized and the amount of money to be earned (the business model). Simms and Robinson (2009) propose that social entrepreneurs may be involved in both for-profit and not-for-profit activities and specifically mention that social enterprises are those that pursue dual or triple bottom line objectives. Elkington and Hartigan (2008) further expand the notion of social entrepreneurship, suggesting that Google is a social enterprise because it has a social mission of making the world's information accessible. The inclusivity of the previously mentioned definitions of social entrepreneurship highlights the question of the boundaries of social and traditional entrepreneurship. While some definitions specifically include the notion of shared value creation, most scholars maintain that a maximization of social value creation represents the definitional difference of social and traditional entrepreneurship (Dacin, Dacin, and Matearm 2010).

2. As a result of the 2007–2008 financial crisis, many started to question the basic premises of the current business system. In the current crisis of legitimacy, Porter and Kramer (2011) suggest that corporations can increase their legitimacy by creating shared value instead of only maximizing shareholder value. They also suggest that corporate leaders look at social entrepreneurs to learn how to create such shared value. Arguably, social entrepreneurs are often ahead of established corporations in discovering shared value opportunities because they are not locked into narrow traditional business thinking. Social entrepreneurship provides alternative organizational logics that enable innovation around products and services that serve formerly underserved and unserved communities.

3. Although a wide range of social enterprises has emerged, Alter (2006) suggests that three main categories be defined by the emphasis and priority given to financial and social objectives: (1) external, (2) integrated, and (3) embedded social enterprises.
   - *External.* In external social enterprises, social value–creating programs are distinct from profit-oriented business activities. The business enterprise activities are external from the organization's social operations and programs such as Alcoa Foundation.
   - *Integrated.* In integrated social enterprises, social programs overlap with business activities, but are not synonymous. Social and financial programs often share costs, assets, and program attributes. The social enterprise activities are thus integrated even as they are separate from the organization's profit-oriented operations. This type of social enterprise such as the Aravind Eye Clinics often leverages organizational assets such as expertise, content, relationships, brand, or infrastructure as the foundation for its business.
   - *Embedded.* In the embedded social enterprise, business activities and social programs are synonymous. Social programs are self-financed through enterprise revenues and thus the embedded social enterprise can also be a stand-alone sustainable program. Because the relationship between business activities and social programs is comprehensive, financial and social benefits are achieved simultaneously. As Prahalad (2005) notes, businesses that serve the base of the pyramid could be regarded as such embedded social enterprises, and the group of enterprises structured by the Grameen and BRAC groups present other approaches.

4. Microfinance is one area that many traditional actors of the financial service industry have examined. Starting out as an attempt to provide small credits to break the vicious cycle of predatory lending, microfinance has become a widely accepted way banking can create financial and social value. Another area where traditional financial service providers could learn from social entrepreneurs is the area of impact investing. Organizations such as Acumen Fund and Calvert Social Investors have presented innovative approaches to creating both social and financial returns.

CHAPTER 5   FIDUCIARY AND OTHER LEGAL DUTIES

1. The duty of loyalty that trustees owe beneficiaries can facilitate SRI when beneficiaries consent to SRI or when the governing trust deed mandates SRI. The former situation might arise in a fund with few members who share similar ethical values. The latter would occur in a charitable foundation that is obliged by its constitution to follow an ethical investment mandate. The duty of care can stimulate SRI when it is a prudent financial investment strategy or it is at least financially comparable to a conventional investment portfolio. However, these legal duties can also hinder SRI. In most investment funds with thousands of beneficiaries, having beneficiaries be unanimous in their views about SRI is unlikely and many might not want to sacrifice financial returns. The duty of loyalty can prevent trustees from considering wider societal interests even if their investments create social and environmental problems. The duty to invest prudently can hinder SRI if its financial benefits are not apparent, such as when they are too long-term or uncertain.

2. Trustees may lawfully practice SRI if beneficiaries consent, regardless of financial returns, unless the trust is established with explicit financial objectives or if governmental regulation creates overriding statutory duties. Trustees are obliged to treat beneficiaries even-handedly (the duty of impartiality), and therefore would be restricted from practicing SRI if there were major differences of opinion among the beneficiaries. In most jurisdictions, beneficiaries tend to lack firm legal rights to be consulted or to instruct trustees, although investment fund regulations, especially in the case of pension funds, sometimes give beneficiaries rights to voice their opinions or to elect representatives to boards of trustees.

3. Trustees are legally obliged to act in the best interests of beneficiaries, and therefore cannot take into account wider societal interests except in limited circumstances. Those circumstances include if an investment policy that is in the beneficiaries' best interests provides incidental social benefits, or if beneficiaries' best interests are defined primarily in ethical terms. Furthermore, because trustees must obey the purpose of the trust and any overriding statutory duties, they may be legally obliged to take into account specific charitable or ethical goals.

4. Financial investing is already subject to an array of regulations and some governments have legislated measures to promote SRI. There is presently a lack of extensive empirical research on the most effective policy instruments to reform for override fiduciary law in order to promote SRI. Taxation incentives may provide a powerful financial subsidy for SRI. Informational policy instruments, such as mandatory corporate environmental reporting, can help social investors to discriminate between companies on their environmental performance. Existing obligations on some public sector funds to practice SRI may be appropriate in a society where broad agreement exists on social and environmental values, and as a way to enable public funds to set an example for private investors. However, regulatory intervention can create additional compliance costs for investors and reduce the efficiency of the market.

CHAPTER 6   INTERNATIONAL AND CULTURAL VIEWS

1. Four major institutional theories that have been used to explain differences in financial developments around the world are legal origin, endowments, religion, and cultural values. Until recently, national characteristics have been largely ignored in the finance literature. Lately, however, numerous papers document that national characteristics are important factors for variations in financial development around the world. The theory of law and finance seems to be the most influential among the four theories. The economic consequences of legal origin have been extended to virtually all fields of financial theory, and to date, the legal origin is prominently important when explaining cross-country differences in finance.

2. Existing research primarily focuses on religion and culture as factors for socially and environmental sustainable developments. The usefulness of these theories seems intuitively plausible. Both theories rely on intrinsic values – internalized either by religion or national culture – that are highly likely to guide attitudes toward ethical issues. Many regard religion as a source of moral standards. As a key personal trait, religiosity is generally expected to influence ethical attitudes in a positive way. Culture is defined as "the collective programming of the mind," and is composed of basic values that shape people's beliefs and attitudes. Consequentially, people from different cultural backgrounds have different beliefs about what is right or wrong, which potentially results in differences in ethical decision making.

3. The theory of law and finance is based on differences between the two prevailing legal traditions: the British common law and the French civil law. Both systems differ substantially in the degree of investor protection originating from their basic underlying ideas. The common law promotes private property rights and is thus particularly supportive for financial development in general. The two major legal traditions spread around the world through conquest and colonization, and the fundamentals of each legal tradition have survived until today. Countries with a common law tradition usually exhibit better developed financial markets than countries with a civil law tradition.

   Although the endowments theory also originates from the legal institutions set up by colonizers, it emphasizes a completely different causal mechanism. The endowment theory focuses on the conditions and environment faced in the colonies. If colonialists encountered hospitable environments where settling was convenient, they set up sound institutions that secured property rights and fostered financial developments. In hostile disease environments where settlers died in large numbers, they created worse institutions facilitating government control and tried to extract as much from the colony as possible. The colonial institutions continue to influence financial development today.

4. Hofstede (1983) advanced one of the most influential frameworks to characterize cultures. In his original research, he identified four cultural dimensions: power distance, uncertainty avoidance, individualism and collectivism, and masculinity and femininity. Later he added a fifth dimension – long-term versus short-term orientation. Several researchers attempt to establish improved models to measure national culture. Schwartz (1994) recognizes seven culture-level dimensions: conservatism, intellectual autonomy, affective autonomy, hierarchy, egalitarianism, mastery, and harmony. Other frameworks that describe national cultures are the GLOBE study and the World Values Survey.

   To date, several studies use the Hofstede or GLOBE cultural dimensions to explain variations in social and environmental sustainability. All studies could reveal an important effect of culture. Using the Schwartz cultural dimension of harmony as an explanatory variable for sustainability might seem particularly fruitful. This cultural dimension refers to a harmonious relationship with the surrounding environment that seems to be notably related to business ethics.

CHAPTER 7   SOCIAL, ENVIRONMENTAL, AND TRUST ISSUES IN BUSINESS AND FINANCE

1. Three distinctive changes have occurred within SET issues over time. First, as Exhibits 7.1 and 7.3 show, a change took place from social issues with a near focus to general social issues and social issues with a far focus. Second, as Exhibits 7.1 and 7.2 indicate, a change from social issues to environmental issues also happened. Lastly, as Exhibits 7.1 and 7.2 reveal, trust issues appeared more recently.

2. Generally, two main reasons explain the changes within the SET agenda: issues being addressed and solved, and a shift in the general socio-economic environment. Consider the shift from near social to general and far social issues. Several of the near social issues, such as safety at the workplace, were targeted and improved. The perceived importance of far social issues, such as massacres of the Apartheid regime, also increased. Both reasons led to the shift of attention from near social issues towards far and general social issues. The shift from social issues (near, far, and general) towards environmental issues is based on the awareness and consequences of reckless business activities mainly through accidents. One milestone is the publication of the Club of Rome report, which highlights the consequences of unsustainable growth.

    Trust appears increasingly on the agenda as globalization and deregulation lead to an increase in company power and a decrease of governmental control. In the late 2000s and early 2010s, the financial crisis and then the Eurozone crisis increased skepticism of the population and the mistrust in companies and whole sectors, especially the financial sector.

3. The most important message for the future is that neither the specific SET issues nor the categories into which they fall are static. They are adaptable and change as the world and society change. The history outlined in the first part of the chapter shows that SET issues in the past involved various players with many different motivations. The same can be expected in the future. New players will enter and with them new SET issues. Furthermore, the rapid development of worldwide communication will support this process and enable movements to reach a global scale within days.

4. This chapter contends that SET considerations appear to be less a flavor of the moment, but rather performance relevant aspects in business and finance. The basis of this view is two gradual changes in contextual factors. First, corporations, especially financial institutions, have become increasingly complex, which creates societal concerns. Second, the instant exchange of opinions on social networking websites is leading societies to become increasingly critical and collaborative. Both developments increase the likelihood of making societal critiques of perceived misbehavior of businesses in general and financial institutions in particular. Such critiques can lead to losses in client trust, which appear highly performance relevant, because trust is a key product differentiation factor of many financial service providers. In contrast, utilizing social media correctly can build trust and enhance business opportunities.

CHAPTER 8   RELIGION AND FINANCE

1. In the early 20th century, Max Weber claimed that the Protestant work-and-save ethic led to a 'spirit of capitalism' in Protestant regions. Weber's thesis has been the subject of fierce debates in the literature for many years. Iannaccone (1998, p. 1474) writes that "the most noteworthy feature of the Protestant ethic thesis is its absence of empirical support."

2. Hilary and Hui (2009) investigate how the religiosity of a firm's environment affects its investment decisions. Firms located in highly religious areas exhibit lower risk exposures, investment rates, and growth rates, but higher undiscounted profits. Shu, Sulaeman, and Yeung (2011) link local religiosity to organizational risk-taking. They find that mutual funds located in regions with low Protestant (or high Catholic) population have higher return volatilities, mainly because of less diversification and more aggressive trading. Kumar, Page, and Spalt (2011) find more ownership of lottery-type stocks by institutional investors and more widespread use of employee stock option plans in regions with a high Catholic-Protestant ratio. Golombick, Kumar, and Parwada (2011) find that fund managers in Catholic counties tilt their portfolio towards Catholic stocks.

3. Various studies examine the role of religion in household finance. For example, Salaber (2009) relates the religious environment to the ownership and returns of sin stocks in a European cross-country study. Protestants appear to be more 'sin averse' than Catholics. Hood, Nofsinger, and Varma (2010) confirm the higher ownership of sin stocks by Catholics for the United States. Kumar, Page, and Spalt (2011) show that Catholic regions invest more in lottery-type securities. Peifer (2011) shows that investors in religious SRI funds are less responsive to past return performance than those in secular SRI funds. Georgarakos and Furth (2011) find a positive correlation between the fraction of religious people and timely repayment of loans in Europe. Crowe (2009) documents a negative relationship between the population share of Evangelical Protestants and regional house price volatility in the United States. However, a lack of research exists on whether individual differences in religious background are also translated into differences in general savings and investment decisions on the level of the household.

4. Religious household heads are more likely to put aside money than non-religious individuals, and especially Catholic households are less likely to invest in stocks. Whether these results can be generalized worldwide is unclear. The possibility exists that the impact of religiosity differs not only across denominations but also across regions. For example, the finding that Catholics are more risk averse than Protestants in the Netherlands goes against recent evidence for the United States that Catholics or firms in Catholic regions exhibit less risk aversion.

CHAPTER 9   SOCIAL FINANCE AND BANKING

1. Generally, social finance and banking try to achieve a positive social impact by means of finance and banking. A positive social impact affects society, the environment, or sustainable development. The finance and banking products and services are loans, investments, venture capital, or microfinance. In contrast to social finance, socially responsible investment integrates social or environmental criteria into the set of conventional investment indicators in an attempt to create a financial return outperformance compared to conventional investment that does not integrate social, environmental, or sustainability performance criteria into the investment process.

2. Usually, these types of banks offer products and services related to social banking, such as loans for social enterprises, renewable energy projects or social housing. In contrast to conventional banks, social banks provide loans that create a social or environmental benefit. Besides loans, social banks offer investment funds, fixed deposits, and other investment products and services that support projects and enterprises that have a positive impact on society. Additionally, many social banks offer usual banking products and services such as credit and debit cards and different types of accounts.

3. Impact investors typically invest in the equity of social enterprises or charitable organizations. They strive to maximize both social and financial return. This objective is based on

the concepts of blended return or the shared value proposition. Both state that social and financial returns are not a trade-off but may be concurrently maximized. Most impact investors are "for profit" and thus create both social and financial return. Some focus on poverty reduction, development, or microfinance in developing countries. Others provide access to financial services for non- or underserved people at the bottom of the socio-economic pyramid.

4. To avoid donor reliance, yet scale up the lending business, some microfinance institutions cooperate with traditional banks and become "commercialized" or even go public to increase their capital base. Because of this, many experts worry that microfinance will depart from its social mission and only focus on financial returns. This change is called *mission drift* and often happens because of the challenge to scale-up the business and to control the costs of lending. On the one hand, the consequences of higher profits could lead to lower outreach. In order to gain higher financial returns, microfinance may prefer doing business with wealthier customers. On the other hand, commercialized microfinance could provide more opportunities to explore new markets.

5. To measure the success of social finance, a social return on investment (SROI) analysis could be done. SROI is a set of practices and indicators that are used to measure the social impact of a business or activity. It can be used to measure both positive and negative impacts on society. The development of SROI indicators consists of collecting social performance data, prioritizing the data with respect to their importance, incorporating these data in decision-making processes and reporting, and valuing the amount of social values that are created or destroyed. Thus, SROI can show the efficiency of social finance and can help investors make the right investment decision.

CHAPTER 10   MANAGERIAL COMPENSATION

1. The surge of stock options beginning in the early 1980s is the main reason for the exponential increase in CEO pay in the United States. From the mid-1990s to the end of 2005, stock options were the major portion of executive compensation. After the 2000 bubble burst, the use of stock options started to lose its appeal and was gradually replaced by restricted stocks, which in 2008 became the most important element in CEO compensation package. The substantial increase in CEO pay is mainly limited to large public firms such as S&P firms.

2. Recent studies show that executives in the United States are paid higher than their foreign counterparts. Yet, the difference becomes statistically insignificant after considering the structures and characteristics of compensation packages in the United States, and in particular the higher risk associated with equity-based compensation.

3. The literature is inconclusive as to whether the high observed level of CEO compensation is fair and ethical. The most supported view, however, is that CEOs are excessively paid. The substantial increase in CEO pay is mainly limited to large public firms such as S&P firms. Moreover, recent studies show that similar increases in average market capitalization over the same period can fully explain the sizeable increases in average CEO pay between 1980 and 2003.

4. Weak internal governance is the main factor that seems to induce executive compensation manipulation. The common view is that enough, if not too many, regulations exist on executive compensation. Recent evidence suggests that the lack of enforcement by the Internal Revenue Service and the Securities and Exchange Commission seems to have encouraged entrenched CEOs to engage in such unethical behavior.

CHAPTER 11   EXTERNALITIES IN FINANCIAL DECISION MAKING

1. Externalities occur in financial decision making when the decision to invest supports an activity or product that causes an external benefit or cost to third-party stakeholders that were not directly involved in the transaction. An externality is a cost generated by the activities of one or more market players, where the cost is borne by individuals or groups that did not agree to the activities. Externalities are the social effects of economic activity derived from productive or other activity that affect parties other than the originator of such activity, which do not work through the price system. There can be individual or systemic externalities.

2. Securitization through collateralized debt obligations (CDOs) was developed to manage risk. Securitization allows financial market players to take debt they have acquired, break it into tranches of varying degrees of risk, and sell it to purchasers at prices commensurate with the potential risk and return. The originating lender under this *originate and distribute* model of financing arguably had hedged its own risk and was able to free up that capital to relend into the market. Securitization of debt through CDOs and other products creates incentives for the originating lender not to be duly diligent in its lending decisions, as it can off load the risk to the purchasers of various tranches of the debt. Securitization generates few incentives for the originating lender to exact protective covenants, or to undertake monitoring on an ongoing basis, given that other parties bear the risk of default. Over multiple similar transactions, these disincentives caused a market crisis. The subprime mortgage lending in the United States and consequent foreclosure and housing crisis is an example.

3. Share lending uncouples legal and economic interest in equity investment. The market for share lending includes 20 percent or more of all the outstanding shares of most large U.S. corporations. Hu and Black (2008) suggest this *soft parking* of shares means that shares are held in friendly hands that have voting rights but no economic ownership, but provide access to shareholder rights when desired under an informal arrangement either to vote as directed or unwind the shares back to the hidden owner. Shareholders with substantial shareholdings are in a position to potentially influence the decisions of directors and officers because of their voting power even though they may have no economic risk in the outcome of those decisions. For fundamental transactions, this disconnection may mean that votes on such transactions do not truly represent the wishes of those whose interest is allied with the corporation's long-term sustainability. Equally important, when large shareholders have little or no economic interest, their influence on corporate officers may not be in the best interests of investors or the corporation and is likely to detract from investing that is aimed at socially responsible behavior by the company. In turn, negative externalities exist for the employees, smaller investors, and the community in which the company is located. Investors with little stake in the company are unlikely to care about its long-term financial health or decisions that reflect SRI goals.

4. SRI investors could avoid buying derivatives products that are part of the speculative market and that lead to negative externalities. They could require companies to disclose the degree to which the firm is invested in derivatives and the degree to which it has the capital to back any calls on its liquidity. Socially responsible investors could also ensure that investments in firms engaging in securitization require those firms to retain sufficient economic interest in the distributed loans that incentives are present to conduct the due diligence, monitoring, and oversight of the debtor company's governance and finance. Socially responsible investors could advocate for corporate compensation structures that

reduce incentives to take excessive risk and create negative externalities; instead, rewarding effective oversight of regulatory compliance, independent monitoring of audit and operational functions, and long-term sustainability. They could insist that officers be incentivized to better identify risks of particular structured financial products; understand inappropriate risk concentration; shift risk stress tests from focus on past events to identifying new risks and potential outcomes; and ensure a continuous understanding the firm's risk position. Socially responsible investors could also advocate remuneration systems that focus on staff whose activities can have a material impact on both the risk exposure of the company and on its externalizing activities.

CHAPTER 12   REAL ESTATE AND SOCIETY

1. Building-level research shows substantial financial benefits of sustainability investments in real estate. Green buildings have higher rents, better occupancy, and higher values than conventional, but otherwise comparable buildings. Research by a McKinsey team also suggests that carbon abatement initiatives in real estate mostly have positive financial value. These results show that investments in green buildings generally do not conflict with the fiduciary responsibility of institutional investors. However, investments into the further improvement of a building's sustainability have diminishing marginal benefits beyond a certain point. When costs start exceeding benefits, a conflict with the fiduciary responsibility of the investor emerges.

2. An investor in commercial office buildings has exposure to the business cycle in two ways. First, the rental cash flow is related to it. Rent flows are the product of contract rent and occupancy, and especially the latter is known to fluctuate with the business cycle. Research discussed in the chapter shows that the occupancy is higher and more stable in green buildings than in conventional buildings, which implies less exposure to the business cycle through that route. Second, after rents, the next biggest expense in commercial buildings is the energy bill. Energy prices are known to fluctuate with the business cycle. Because green buildings have lower energy bills, they are less exposed to cyclical movements in energy prices. Both of these effects lead to a lower exposure to the business cycle and therefore to lower systematic risk.

3. The research examined in the chapter shows that green buildings are generally newer and taller, and have a higher quality rating than conventional buildings. Because such buildings are also newer, taller, and of higher quality, they generally have higher rents and prices than other buildings. Failing to control for these building characteristics could lead to falsely attributing rent and price effects to the greenness of the buildings, while in reality, their age, size, and quality would be partly driving these effects.

4. Many sustainability investments into real estate already have a positive net present value at current energy prices; the current state of technological developments; and current technology prices for heating, cooling, lighting, insulation, and onsite energy generation. Thus, rational investors should make these investments without waiting for any sort of government intervention after having made the appropriate cost-benefit analyses. A government policy of subsidies and tax breaks may actually harm these investments, as it incentivizes decision makers to wait for bigger hand-outs in the future. However, investors might not act fully rationally. In that case, a government policy of nudges, for example by providing green labels in countries and markets where they do not yet exist, would help investors see the benefits of green real estate investments where they do not currently do so. As for regulation, requiring people by law to make investments they

should make in their own best financial interests does not make sense. Given enough time, they will invest without that regulation.

5. The research examined in this chapter suggests that consumer decisions regarding green properties are quite rational. For example, buyers of homes in the Netherlands seem to value energy efficiency because they pay higher prices for very energy-efficient homes. The lower energy costs of these houses partly drive this behavior. Although Japanese home buyers do not pay a premium for green homes, this also seems rational because Japanese homes are generally quite green. Thus, additional green measures taken in Japan create a financial burden rather than a benefit, which would make a premium for these buildings irrational. Commercial property investors have taken the initiative for a global information tool on green property portfolios—GRESB. This tool allows them to make rational and informed decisions about the sustainability of their real estate investments. The strong growth in the number of GRESB users suggests that investors are increasingly taking rational green decisions in real estate.

CHAPTER 13 FEDERAL HOUSING POLICIES AND THE RECENT FINANCIAL CRISIS

1. Two important reasons explain why the federal government first became involved in reviving homeownership in the Great Depression. The first was to stimulate the economy by preventing further collapse and loss of wealth in the housing sector and by putting people back to work in building houses. At a time of nearly 25 percent unemployment, this was an important goal of housing policies. The second goal was both social and political—the desire to give more people a stake in the American way of life at a time when political extremism and Communist agitation were quite strong in many countries.

2. Whether the Community Reinvestment Act (CRA) played an important role in the financial crisis of 2008 is unclear. Under the CRA, community needs are to be met in a manner consistent with the safe and sound operation of the institution, and the resulting loans must meet various bank supervisory standards, including supervisory guidance on appropriate loan-to-value limits for real estate loans. Consequently, depository institutions may have faced more risk constraints than other entities lending to new and low-income homebuyers. Moreover, data on higher-priced loans to lower-income borrowers suggest that depository institutions covered by the CRA may have played only a modest role in this segment of the market.

3. Studies indicate that low-income homeowners are unlikely to receive the same level of housing tax incentives as other income groups. As a result, the housing tax incentives may do little to increase homeownership rates because the vast majority of the tax benefits flow to households that should be able to purchase homes without such assistance. A good case could be made for reducing or eliminating homeowner tax deductions and lowering tax rates in a revenue-neutral manner. However, a politically strong real estate lobby and misperceptions about how much the average taxpayer benefits from such deductions have stood in the way of such reform.

4. Alternatives to current policies include homeowner tax credits, first-time homeowner grants and down payment assistance, and alternative mortgage instruments. These policies could be more carefully focused than recent policies were and involve far less public intervention into mortgage markets. These alternatives also would entail less financial risk on the part of first-time and lower-income homebuyers, thus helping to provide a

better path for building household wealth and financial security. Other ways are available to make homeownership more affordable, but the key tests for any new proposals should be whether they are consistent with sustainable housing markets, avoid putting homeowners and lenders at undue risk, and provide a supportive and appropriate blend of public and private interests.

CHAPTER 14 PREDATORY LENDING AND SOCIALLY RESPONSIBLE INVESTORS

1. The causes of the home mortgage crisis are complex and have been subject to much debate. Most commentators point to the financial industry's creation of problematic credit products and poor underwriting. Mortgage brokers and origination companies marketed mortgage loans that were unsuitable for borrowers, and then resold these loans to investors through the process of securitization. Credit rating agencies, including Standard and Poor's, Moody's, and Fitch Investment Services encouraged the purchase of the securities funded with problematic mortgage loans by granting high quality bond ratings to mortgage-backed securities. Some commentators have also pointed to the Federal Reserve Board's fiscal policy of maintaining low interest rates, which made the spread between cost of funds and the potential yield from subprime mortgage securities too tempting to resist. Still some other commentators have criticized Congress and federal banking regulators for failing to adopt regulations that inhibit the origination and sale of unaffordable mortgage loans.

2. Psychologists and behavioral economists have identified at least seven borrower characteristics that tend to cause inefficiency in consumer finance markets: (1) borrowers' unrealistic optimism about their ability to pay; (2) borrowers' discounting the value of future consumption because of a present-focused bias; (3) borrowers often make borrowing decisions under distress-induced abbreviated reasoning patterns; (4) borrowers, who often lack basic qualitative and quantitative literacy, have difficulty processing finance-related information and often suffer from *information overload*; (5) lenders frame credit prices and marketing information in ways that distort borrowers' perception of value and over-rely on inaccurate first impressions; (6) some lenders may extract inefficiently high prices out of borrowers that are irrationally averse to losses; and, (7) consumer credit can be negatively interrelated with addictive and compulsive consumer behaviors such as alcoholism, pathological gambling, and compulsive spending.

3. Just because a loan is legal does not necessarily mean that purchasing it is socially responsible. The financial industry is constantly evolving and the law is very often one step behind. Moreover, the financial industry often plays a key role in shaping the law through lobbying and government relations. Some critics of existing law believe that industry manipulates the law to facilitate socially irresponsible, yet profitable, financial products.

4. Because many different types of financial products are available to consumers, finding criteria that reliably distinguish socially harmful loans in every case is difficult. However, some warning signs that may lead to socially harmful outcomes include:
   - Exorbitant interest rates. Many scholars and advocates believe that interest rates in excess of 36 percent per annum tend to do borrowers more harm than good.
   - Loan products that generate substantial revenue from hidden pricing features.
   - Loans that exceed traditional debt-to-income ratios. Historically lenders and consumer finance counselors were skeptical of debt payments that exceeded 36 percent of a household's gross income. Virtually all consumer finance counselors agree that

debt payments in excess of 45 percent of borrowers' gross income are dangerously unsustainable.

- Loans that result in negative equity in borrowers' collateral.
- Negatively amortizing loans.

CHAPTER 15   USE AND MISUSE OF FINANCIAL SECRECY IN GLOBAL BANKING

1. The terrorist attacks on New York City in 2001 triggered renewed interest in cross-border financial transfers that are necessary to carry out acts of terrorism. The amounts involved are very small, but nevertheless crucial in enabling terrorism—the classic needle in a haystack problem. Terrorist funding must be kept secret, usually disguised as commercial transactions, foundations, and personal remittances. The FATF represents a systematic attempt by the OECD countries of rooting out terrorism-related financial flows and promoting cooperation among governments engaged in this task. In the process, investigators inevitably come across substantial financial assets that are unrelated to terrorism, but are nevertheless the proceeds of criminal activity such as organized crime, extortion, and the drug trade. Discovering these kinds of financial flows and assets represents a valuable byproduct of the FATF initiative.

2. Governments use all kinds of sources of information to go after criminal activity. This includes undercover police, stool pigeons, eavesdropping, and other clandestine information sources. In some cases, they are sanctioned by law; in other cases, by court order before the fact, and in still other cases by a judge's determination at trial regarding the admissibility of evidence. Evidence regarding financial secrecy enabling tax evasion would be covered by the same standards anchored in the law and the administration of justice, so there are no ethical questions once the rules are set. This applies to cases where tax evasion is a criminal offense and prosecuted under criminal law. Where tax evasion is a civil offense, the ethics issue becomes debatable since standards of prosecution tend to be much lower.

3. As in other large organizations, business units dealing with private clients in banks and financial conglomerates are under heavy pressure to make the numbers. So despite general policies that play well in public, and may be genuinely supported by senior management and boards of directors, line staff members looking to make the numbers and generate performance bonuses have the incentive to increase the volume of business that offers attractive margins. Sometimes these opportunities push very close to the edge of acceptability and/or legality. Imperfect markets, after all, are where the money is. So UBS private bankers clearly overstepped the limits imbedded in the bank's own policies. The question is how far up the management hierarchy this behavior went. Testimony in a Florida court led to an indictment of the global head of the private banking business and an extradition request to the Swiss government, which has not been honored. Whether the Bank's Global Executive Board or its Supervisory Board knew of the issue is open to question.

4. Insider trading needs secrecy to work. Financial operations require substantial exposures and sometimes leverage, which have to remain confidential. The proceeds likewise need the protection of secrecy at the time of the transactions and thereafter. Consequently, using offshore accounts routed through channels with no commercial purpose other than secrecy is virtually ubiquitous. Suspicious trades are usually flagged by brokers to the authorities (the Securities and Exchange Commission in the United States) who will decide whether an investigation is warranted. If the insider trading ring is large, prosecution may be facilitated by cutting deals with peripheral members in return for

leniency. This is a tactic that can blow up an insider trading ring remarkably efficiently, and is followed by requests to foreign financial authorities for information relevant to a criminal investigation.

5. The task of keeping these ill-gotten funds is difficult. Increasingly, even the most hard-nosed secrecy havens want to stay well clear of clients who are corrupt politicians. Their behavior will ultimately come out, often involving heinous crime committed on their watch, and this is very bad for the private banking business. Legitimate wealthy clients, and even otherwise respectable tax evaders, want nothing to do with a bank that has aided and abetted political suppression of crimes against humanity. So finding secrecy havens becomes increasingly tough, involving stacks of intermediaries, shell companies, foundations, and using financial centers that are not as particular about dealing with crooks. But these actions are also more risky from an investment perspective. So the ex-government official would do best to leave the country and establish residence, and possibly buy citizenship, to impede later extradition. Another step would be to employ a "secret agent" (who in turn is likely to have loose values of integrity and morality) to construct a secrecy edifice with as many defenses as possible. Spending a third of the investable assets (after adjusting for increased risk) spent in this endeavor would not be surprising.

CHAPTER 16   CORPORATE SOCIAL RESPONSIBILITY AND CORPORATE GOVERNANCE

1. As defined in the chapter, corporate social responsibility (CSR) is a model of extended corporate governance (CG) whereby those who run firms, such as entrepreneurs, directors, and managers, have responsibilities that range from fulfillment of their fiduciary duties towards the owners to fulfillment of analogous fiduciary duties towards all the firm's stakeholders. Two economic concepts help to explain stakeholders: (1) those stakeholders who are responsible for specific investments and consequently may be subjected to hold-up, and (2) those who undergo externalities. Fiduciary duties are correlated to rights and legitimate claims held by trustors entering into a trust relationship with a trustee. By this relationship, trustors delegate authority and discretion concerning the decision that must be ultimately functional to the pursuance of their goals. Thus, fiduciary duties fill gaps in the fiduciary relationship whereby stakeholders delegate authority to the company management, directors, and entrepreneurs as a precondition to its legitimization.

2. Agency theory, as applied to CG, excludes having managers discharge any further fiduciary duty towards stakeholders other than owners or shareholders. CG is about keeping management's promises to further the best interests of owners or shareholders. As far as CSR enters the inner dimension of management strategic choices, it can only play an instrumental role functional to the main goal of shareholder value maximization. On the contrary, the mediating hierarchy model of CG is by definition a view within which corporate managers and the board of directors play the role of an impartial and fair mediator among different stakeholder interests. CSR specifies a value or criterion for this mediating role, which is necessary to a firm's success as a form of team production, and is inspired by the idea of having a social contract among the corporate stakeholders. Without the hypothesis that corporate directors and managers have to play a balancing role amongst different stakeholders in order to prevent reciprocal opportunistic behavior, CG would have no place in CSR.

3. The chapter presents economic institutions as game equilibria based on mutually consistent belief systems describing the ongoing equilibrium behavior of agents in a given domain of interaction—a behavior that confirms these same beliefs. Therefore, an

institution is self-supporting and self-enforceable. An institution emerges from a multiplicity of possible equilibria through a cognitive process. It starts from the acceptance of a social norm by means of a social contract reasoning, which is in turn represented by the shared mental (normative) model of agents participating in the given interaction domain and ends with establishing an equilibrium institution.

CSR is the only social norm of CG that emerges from a fair social contract among the firm's stakeholders. Hence, it may endogenously emerge and be voluntarily accepted as a social norm that then develops in an equilibrium institution. No need exists to superimpose it because it is the CG norm that would emerge endogenously when agents undertake an ex ante perspective whereby they select by agreement one equilibrium among the many possible in the free interaction domain of CG. On the contrary, other CG institutions would not emerge endogenously in the sense that could not be chosen by stakeholders equally and freely capable to enter a voluntary agreement on the CG form. In particular, agency models, based on the primacy of shareholders could not emerge endogenously through the voluntary agreement of all the stakeholders because such models allow substantial abuse of authority towards noncontrolling stakeholders.

4. The Binmore-Rawls social contract model shows the following. Assume that two agents, facing an interaction situation, want ex ante to agree on an equilibrium that could emerge from their free strategic interaction (i.e., a repeated noncooperative game). Moreover, assume that they want to keep to a basic and elementary form of morality consisting of making choices under a veil of ignorance so that any chosen solution must be robust against an impartiality and impersonality test. Hence, the chosen solution must be necessarily egalitarian. A mathematical proof is available for this result. This solution is based on the idea that a choice under a veil of ignorance can be represented as follows: (1) by considering as a choice set the outcome space of a basic game and its symmetric translation with respect to the player positions, and (2) by requiring, in order to satisfy the request of stability and free players' incentive compatibility, that the solution must belong to the symmetric intersection of these two outcome spaces. This is equivalent to adopting the symmetric Nash bargaining solution in this symmetric outcome space. Freely choosing interacting players committed to a very basic form of morality and to any solution that is ex post stable and incentive compatible results in an egalitarian solution.

5. The social contract approach provides a model of reasoning that a mediating hierarch may implement in order to work out the impartial balance among the corporate stakeholders' claims. It consists in taking in turn each stakeholder's viewpoint and calculating agreements that are invariant under all these permutations of personal viewpoints. This is essentially the same idea of making choices about the corporate strategy under a veil of ignorance with respect to the identity of the stakeholder whose interest is to be maximized.

Because a firm is a form of team production that engenders a surplus deriving from the cooperation among stakeholders undertaking specific investments, such a procedure reaches a mutually beneficial agreement. That is, at least one (but normally many) agreement exists such that any stakeholder gains a positive share of the corporate surplus by adhering to the agreement rather than rejecting it. The veil of ignorance ensures that at least one of these mutually advantageous agreements may be acceptable by whichever point of view.

6. The CSR model of CG provides a clearly defined objective function that a socially responsible company should aim to maximize. According to the social contract approach, the objective function of the socially responsible corporation is the Nash bargaining product of stakeholders' payoffs derivable from the stakeholders' agreements over cooperative joint strategies. These are the strategies according to which the company can be led by implementing a feasible form of stakeholders' cooperation. In particular, under the

hypothesis of impartiality and impersonality, the relevant payoff space to be considered is the symmetric intersection set resulting from the symmetrical translation of a basic outcome space (representing all possible equilibria) that are reachable by joint strategies. A rational conduit of the firm will then strive to maximize the symmetric Nash bargaining product of all the stakeholders' payoffs. The outcome space can be defined by taking for each cooperative strategy the difference (surplus) between the costs borne by all stakeholders in order to produce the good and the good's value for consumers. The solution grants each stakeholder that the costs borne in order to participate in cooperation will be refunded, so that nobody can be held up. Moreover, the solution consists of choosing the joint strategy that maximizes the product of all stakeholders' shares of the corporate surplus.

7. The socially responsible corporation results from a two-step social contract among all the corporate stakeholders. The first social contract establishes a multistakeholder cooperative association including *broad-sense stakeholders*, who are interested in the association only in so far as it may prevent negative externality against them, and *strict-sense stakeholders*, who are interested in the association because it may prevent opportunistic expropriation of their specific investments undertaken in the cooperative activities they carry out with other members of the association. The second social contract provides a structure of ownership and control, i.e., a CG structure, to the same association. A fiduciary proviso follows from each of these steps. From the latter a narrow fiduciary proviso derives about the obligation that managers and directors have towards the stakeholder category that is selected as the governing one at the second step. But a broad fiduciary proviso derives from the first step about extended fiduciary duties that the CG structure owes to all the stakeholders participating in the cooperative association.

A clear priority order of stakeholders' claims is thus established in which all stakeholders are privileged in some proper respect. Broad-sense stakeholders are assigned priority but only in the weak sense of restricting the company's range of action to those joint plans that do not engender strong externalities detrimental to them. Second in priority are *strict-sense stakeholders*, who are granted a wide range of privileges in the discretion area of directors who must protect their specific investments and then arbitrate cooperation according to the symmetric Nash bargaining solution. Last, in the subset of possible corporate decisions indifferent to the criterion, residual claimants are assigned privilege consisting in the decision of pursuing (constrained) shareholder value maximization.

CHAPTER 17   MEASURING RESPONSIBILITY TO DIFFERENT SHAREHOLDERS

1. According to Milton Friedman, firms providing services and products that society values are profitable in a free market-economy. If the firm engages in harmful activity and the different stakeholders know about such activity, share price should decline. Hence, maximizing share price is equivalent to doing good within society. However, essential to this equivalence result is that stakeholders are aware of the firms' effects on society, or corporate social performance (CSP). If these effects are unknown, stakeholders will not react and affect the firm's profitability, which ultimately affects share price accordingly. Thus, measuring corporate social responsibility (CSR) is essential for providing transparency and aligning the share price objective with the moral view of society. One can claim that measuring CSP is important no matter whether the firm attempts to maximize share price or has a broader objective and considers its affects on society. As Dillenburg, Green, and Erekson (2003, p. 170) emphasize, "What gets measured, gets managed." Without effective measurement, claiming that "maximizing share price" is equivalent to "doing good with society" is difficult.

2. A concern with a CSP measure encompassing many stakeholders is that while a company may promote its performance in one dimension, it may at the same time engage in another dimension in harmful business practices. Another major concern is that social responsibility and irresponsibility are distinctly different phenomena and tend to change over time depending on beliefs in society. For example, a liberal society may not approve of companies producing weapons, while a conservative society may disapprove of companies producing alcohol.

3. Environmental performance measures focus on the cost structure and environmental performance of a company. Customer-related performance measurement relates to the customers' perceptual attitude towards the company and customers' valuation of the company's products. Employee performance measurement looks into the way companies treat their employees. These measures focus on issues such as job satisfaction or human resources issues such as communications with employees, and training and development. Supplier-related performance measures focus on the way a company treats its suppliers such as whether the company fairly shares with its suppliers the costs and benefits of supply chain initiatives. Community-related performance focuses on measuring the way a company treats the group of people that is related to the company mostly through their location proximity. This measure aims to capture issues such as contributions to the arts, efforts directed to the solution of social problems, and assistance with community improvement.

4. Government-related CSP is derived from a company's illegal activity. For example, criminal conduct, such as accounting frauds and the backdating scandal, could be considered as violation of federal laws, and hence can be classified as poor government-related CSP. The challenge in measuring illegal conduct is rooted in the fact that extended efforts may be involved in concealing such conduct from governing entities. Examples of measurements used in the literature include accounting irregularities, looking at cases of misreporting that the Securities and Exchange Commission (SEC) chooses to prosecute, and looking at securities class action lawsuits.

CHAPTER 18   CORPORATE PHILANTHROPY

1. Early historical reasons for business firm participation in philanthropy include a desire to provide benefits to potential and existing employees and to create spillover benefits for communities in which the firm is located. The philanthropy included gifts, such as to community chests and the Young Men's Christian Association. There was a historical reluctance to allow firms to make contributions that did not have a direct tie to the firm's profits. This changed in the 1950s with the case decision in *A. P. Smith Mfg. Co. v. Barlow,* and with federal and state laws that facilitated giving and provided tax deductibility. The writings of Milton Friedman, Peter Drucker, and Michael Porter, among others, reflect concerns about corporate involvement in philanthropy. Today, corporate giving is often justified as a means for the firm to create a competitive advantage; to generate publicity and visibility; to take advantage of tax benefits associated with deductibility; and to build its reputation with consumers, employees, regulators, and government entities that can impact the competitive conditions in which the firm operates.

2. Several perspectives exist on whether a firm should make contributions to a charity when shareholders may prefer to receive dividends and make their own philanthropic decisions. On the one hand, corporations may potentially benefit if they can create a competitive advantage through their giving programs by either lowering cost or increasing value relative to their competitors, and whether firm managers have special expertise in evaluating social needs. Contributions may enhance the utility of managers and directors and what that implies for shareholders. On the other hand, managers may be

well-positioned to find ways to create a competitive advantage with their giving programs and whether the giving will lead to benefits for stakeholders and ultimately for shareholders.

3. Evidence is available to support either the value enhancement hypothesis or the agency cost hypothesis. Concerning value enhancement, firms from the same industry have similar priorities that appear to complement their business, such as petroleum firms contributing to environmental causes or pharmaceutical companies giving drugs to consumers in poor countries. This giving appears to be aimed at enhancing value and/or reducing costs, perhaps by improving employee relations and protecting firm reputation, and by taking advantage of tax code deductions. Evidence of relationships between giving and sales is consistent with a positive value impact, but it is not dispositive because no persuasive evidence is available that giving has an impact on profits. Corporate philanthropy may be too small to detect impact on shareholder value, however. Regarding evidence consistent with agency costs, findings of empirical studies across disciplines suggest that more giving to philanthropic causes (measured as giving per dollar sales or assets) is associated with larger board size, more diverse boards, and low leverage (lower creditor monitoring).

4. Different variables are related to the choice of firms to give to charity. Charitable giving is positively associated with larger firms, larger and more diverse boards of directors, and firms with higher R&D-to-sales ratios, advertising-to-sales ratios, and Tobin's Q measures. Giving is inversely related to leverage and to the percentage of shares held by blockholders. Overall, the results suggest that enhanced financial performance is not the overriding concern of managers when making contributions. Instead, most evidence points to the prevalence of agency costs in corporate giving.

5. Various data and methodological challenges face researchers who are attempting to analyze the impact of corporate philanthropy on firm performance. Reliable data on firm-specific philanthropy are hard to obtain, and most data sets are necessarily hand collected and restricted to short time periods. Aggregated data are generated based on different survey methods that are not directly comparable, making trends in philanthropy difficult to track. Empirical issues facing researchers include the following: the endogeneity of independent variables in cross-sectional and panel models of philanthropic giving and in models designed to evaluate the impact of philanthropy; consistency of treatment of in-kind gifts; and self-reporting of giving amounts.

CHAPTER 19   INSTITUTIONAL INVESTOR ACTIVISM

1. A pension plan trustee has a fiduciary duty to invest the plan assets in the best interests of the beneficiaries. This typically means that trustees should pursue prudent investment strategies such as holding diversified portfolios and maximizing expected returns given the level of risk appropriate for the pension plan. Therefore, a pension plan trustee should pursue environmental, social, and governance (ESG) principles only if doing so is consistent with the fund's investment strategies. Thus, whether applying ESG principles is associated with performance improvements relative to a traditional portfolio approach is a question trustees must consider. The academic evidence on this question, however, is mixed and therefore still unanswered. In contrast, a fund prospectus governs mutual fund managers. In this document, the fund states its investment policies, and investors who desire a portfolio selected according to these policies could choose to invest in this fund. Thus, mutual fund managers are free to invest according to ESG principles as long

as they disclose this to investors in their prospectus. The SEC monitors whether funds actually follow the policies outlined in their prospectus.

2. According to SEC Rule 14a-8, shareholders who meet a minimal ownership requirement can submit a proposal to be placed on the corporate proxy and voted on at the company's annual meeting. The firm prepares and distributes the proxy materials at no explicit cost to the activist. Thus, a big advantage here is the low cost of this activity. Activists can easily share their concerns with other shareholders, who can register their support for the issue by voting in favor of the proposal. If the proposal sponsor is large and influential enough to gain the attention of management, activists can use the proposal as a starting point to set up a face-to-face meeting with corporate management and discuss shareholder concerns. The disadvantage of this approach is that the proposal is only advisory to the board of directors. Even if the proposal receives a majority of vote support, the board need not comply with the activist's request. Another disadvantage is that the topic of the proposal needs to be relatively narrow in scope. The activists also need to make sure that they comply with all the SEC rule requirements or their proposals will be allowed to be omitted from the proxy.

3. Many similarities exist between socially responsible and corporate governance proposals in terms of sponsors and sponsor motivations. For example, public pension funds and union pension funds commonly sponsor both types of proposals. Similarly, private pension funds sponsor very few shareholder proposals of either type. Some contend that incentives of both groups drive this pattern. For example, public and union pension funds tend to passively index and hold highly diversified portfolios. Thus, such funds cannot sell the stock when they are unhappy with the way the company is being run and therefore will find activism more appealing than other types of investors. However, others maintain that other things motivate these investor types. For example, some public pension fund officials have political aspirations and might become activist just to raise their public profile, not because they believe the activism will result in higher returns for the fund. Similarly, some believe that union pension funds are activist because it helps them gain concessions from firms in union negotiations. Corporate governance proposals tend to have much higher vote support than socially responsible proposals. However, a recent increase in vote support has occurred for social proposals, especially for the ones sponsored by institutional investors.

4. A few recent developments suggest that socially responsible activism among institutional investors is likely to increase. First, institutional investors are now placing more emphasis on positive screening. Thus, such investors choose firms for a portfolio based on ESG factors that identify which firms are best equipped to thrive when faced with such issues as climate change, natural resource scarcity, and demographic concerns. Previously, social investing meant applying negative screens that tended to negatively affect return performance and the portfolio's diversification. For these reasons, social investing and activism are now more appealing to fiduciary institutions that can point to an economic and financial reason to incorporate ESG principles into their risk management and security selection decisions. Firms that pro-actively address "social" issues can successfully deter costly regulation, mitigate litigation risk, and enhance their reputations with consumers who might consequently favor their products rather than boycott them.

Three recent developments suggest that institutional investors' increased interest in ESG principles and social activism might gain momentum and legitimacy. First, individual investors are gaining interest in social issues. In turn, these investors will demand more financial products such as mutual funds, 529 plans, 401(k) plans, and ETFs. Second, the United Nations Principles for Responsible Investments is gaining the support of hundreds of institutional investors worldwide, including mainstream investors, not just socially responsible asset managers. Finally, pioneers such as CalPERS are starting to show interest and leadership in incorporating ESG principles across the billions of dollars of pension assets they control. Given the news coverage that actions by CalPERS receive, other pension funds may follow its lead.

CHAPTER 20   SOCIAL ACTIVISM AND NONGOVERNMENTAL ORGANIZATIONS

1. *Social activism* is the process by which individuals, acting alone or as part of a collective, express their views in opposition or support of social issues such as labor, environmental, human rights or poverty. Social activism requires social actors. In the case of activism related to finance and investment, these actors are primarily nongovernmental organizations (NGOs), also known as civil society organizations. Civil society, also referred to as the *third sector* or the *nonprofit sector*, broadly describes all aspects of society that extend beyond the realm of the public sector and the traditional private sector. When individuals or groups within civil society work together to advance a broad common set of interests and these interests become an important force in shaping the direction of society, social movements emerge as the outcomes of this process. Social movements are broad societal initiatives organized around a particular issue, trend, or priority. Modern examples include the environmental movement and the feminist movement. When civil society groups band together to form organized relationships, the emergent entities are often called NGOs.

2. The two types of NGOs are advocacy and operational NGOs. The first type of NGO, works on behalf of others who lack the voice or access to promote their interests. The actions of advocacy NGOs take various forms from lobbying to protests or research. These groups work to promote social gains or mitigate negative spillovers from economic activity. Operational NGOs provide goods and services to clients with unmet needs. An example of an operational NGO is the Red Cross.

3. According to Yaziji and Doh (2009), the two different types of advocacy campaigns are watchdog campaigns and proxy wars. A watchdog campaign is one in which the social organization attempts to hold the target firm accountable for some set of social, economic, or political expectations. Such campaigns are typically run by local organizations in response to a perceived threat or harm to their local interests. In contrast, proxy wars are designed to challenge and change the institutional framework, whether in terms of the formal regulatory and legal systems or accepted social norms and values.

4. Power, in terms of NGOs, is referred to on a relational basis and not an object that is possessed. The first type, *symbolic power*, is the status that comes with an organization that has reached a high level of sustainability, responsibility, and quality. The second type is referred to as *cognitive power*, meaning that the organization has considerable knowledge, allowing it to act as an expert. The third type, *social power*, includes all networks, alliances, and collaboration partners involved with the action, creating an influential group around the action at hand. Fourth, *monitoring power* is the ability to measure performance against what was promised by the organization.

5. Socially responsible investing (SRI) refers to an investment approach that uses both financial and nonfinancial criteria to determine which assets to purchase. Once, the purpose of SRI was to avoid those organizations promoting "sinful" behaviors such as tobacco or alcohol. More recently, researchers seek out those firms that promote socially responsible causes in order to show support. NGOs oftentimes aid in this process by acting as advisors, information analysts, and consultants to funds concerned with SRI.

CHAPTER 21 CORPORATE SOCIALLY RESPONSIBLE INVESTMENTS

1. Gains from eco-efficiency can derive from better or creative use of existing technologies or from innovation. The chapter describes an example of the former, where Conoco was able to increase bottom-line performance. However, there are typically few barriers to entry for competitors to respond when the technology is widely available. Thus, firms may be unable to achieve a long-term competitive advantage. With innovation, however, a firm may be able to protect the efficiency gain or sell the technology to competitors.

2. Cost of capital can be reduced through CSRI activities by reducing the extent or impact of asymmetric information or idiosyncratic risk factors. As described by Merton (1987), investor awareness can affect required returns. To the extent that CSRI can make investors aware of a firm's securities or make the firm a palatable investment opportunity, the firm's cost of capital should decline. Further, due to investors' unwillingness or inability to fully diversify their portfolios, they likely demand compensation for some degree of idiosyncratic risk. CSRI efforts can reduce the firm's exposure to various sources of risk, thus reducing the cost of capital.

3. The distinction between shareholder wealth maximization and enlightened value maximization primarily is involved with the assumptions and the managerial implications. The traditional shareholder-primacy argument relies on well-functioning markets and governments to lead to optimal levels of social welfare. However, in the presence of market failures, firms have the ability to expropriate wealth from nonshareholder stakeholders and to the benefit of shareholders, in particular, short-term shareholders. The enlightened wealth maximization paradigm seeks to optimize aggregate social welfare through long-term value maximization. It encourages managers to consider stakeholders' response to short-term firm decisions and the impact this settling-up will have on long-term value.

4. Five ways in which CSRI can affect CFP are through (1) improved relations with customers who will show greater loyalty and potentially a willingness to pay a premium price; (2) improved relations with employees who will potentially be easier to recruit and retain; (3) improved or reduced use of resources and control of pollution, which can often provide insights into unrecognized opportunity costs; (4) improved relations with regulators that can reduce the likelihood and severity of future regulatory changes; and (5) a reduced cost of capital for the firm.

5. Management's CSR goals could influence a firm's capital structure choice. Greater leverage is associated with both fewer resources available to management and an increase in the likelihood of financial distress. If contracts are not efficient between stakeholders and the firm, the greater risk associated with leverage can effectively transfer wealth from stakeholders to shareholders. Firms wanting to honor the implicit nature of their contracts with stakeholders may do so by using less debt financing. Although mixed, empirical evidence suggests that firms with particularly valuable contracts with nonshareholders make more limited use of debt to protect those relationships.

CHAPTER 22 SRI MUTUAL FUND AND INDEX PERFORMANCE

1. Socially responsible investing (SRI) continues to get the attention of both practitioners and academicians. At the center of the discussion is the performance of SRI relative to conventional funds. The academic literature is unable to reach a consensus on this issue

and empirical results are mixed. Several studies report little evidence of a difference in risk-adjusted returns between ethical and conventional funds. This is interpreted as SRI performing no worse than conventional funds. Some studies even suggest that SRI funds can be a valuable source of portfolio risk reduction, even for investors who are not driven by social values. On the other hand, some researchers report a statistically significant cost associated with socially responsible mutual fund investing as investors settle for suboptimal portfolios from the screening process.

2. SRI has experienced an incredible growth over the last 10 years. Several factors contribute to this growth. First, as a result of increased awareness of investors on environmental, social, and governance (ESG) issues has increased the products offered by financial institutions. Money managers follow the desires of their clients. U.S. investors seem to be better educated and informed about social responsibility, which helps them make better and more responsible investment decisions. Moreover, women are becoming highly involved in investment, including SRI criteria. For example, the social investment industry estimates that roughly 60 percent of socially conscious investors are women.

   Second, institutions, especially public funds, are incorporating ESG criteria in their investment decisions as a result of legislative mandates. Third, fund managers and institutional investors' responses to certain countries also represent an important reason for the growth of SRI. For example, crises in Sudan are influencing many institutional investors and money managers' decision to divest firms that are doing business in such a volatile, repressive regime. The Social Investment Forum reports that Sudan-related investment policies have displaced tobacco as the most prevalent criteria incorporated into investment management, affecting more than $1.3 trillion in institutional assets.

   Third, new products and innovation fund styles are also contributing to the growth of SRI. For example, environmentally themed investment products and services explore opportunities in clean and green technology.

   Finally, shareholder advocacy is becoming very popular. Growing numbers of institutional investors and money managers are joining investor networks not only to coordinate their work on shareholder resolutions but also to advance their shareholder advocacy through public statements and other policy initiatives.

3. Several issues prevent researchers from reaching a conclusion about the performance of SRI. First, some relate to the measurement and choice of appropriate benchmarks, which is critical to measuring the performance of SRI. Second, the composition of ethical funds may differ drastically in terms of their holdings and degree of international diversification. This would impose currency risk and other nonethical influences on realized returns of ethical funds. Third, the capitalization of the stocks in SRI funds may be an issue. Ethically sound companies may tend to be smaller in market capitalization than others. This may confound possible ethical effects. Fourth, the number of screens used may be quite different in similar funds. Using multiple screens would reduce the available stock universe and hence be subject to more severe suboptimal portfolios. Fifth, using single versus multiple indices in models could change the significance level of the findings. Finally, the fee structure of funds, age of funds, and study period may influence research findings.

4. Earlier international studies mostly provide evidence on ethical funds in the United Kingdom. The findings show that ethical funds outperform conventional funds. This is similar to the results reported by earlier U.S. studies. The follow-up studies in the United Kingdom find no significant differences between ethical and nonethical funds. Similar results are reported for Australian, Canada, and Germany. On the other hand, ethical funds in a few countries such as France, Japan, and Sweden significantly overperform relative to conventional funds. The empirical studies of international SRI also report mixed results in most countries.

CHAPTER 23 PERFORMANCE IMPLICATIONS OF SOCIALLY RESPONSIBLE INVESTING: PAST VERSUS FUTURE

1. An optimal SRI portfolio depends on the utility function of the investor. For example, if an investor feels strongly about excluding tobacco stocks, he may increase his utility to do so even if it hurts his portfolio's performance. In that sense, the "optimal" SRI portfolio is different for every investor. Some investors may only care about expected payoffs. A SRI portfolio that tilted towards firms with high ESG standards over the past decades, but excluded sin stocks would have harmed performance.

   Going forward, there may be no "optimal" SRI portfolio if investors consider only expected payoffs. Investors who only care about expected payoffs are likely better off not following an SRI strategy. However, investors who feel strongly about certain issues may still be better off incorporating ethical values in their portfolio decisions. The loss in utility from earning potentially lower returns may be outweighed by the gain in utility from investing consistently with their ethical values.

2. Whether investors should follow a SRI investment strategy has many possible answers to this question. The main disadvantage of following an SRI strategy is a potentially lower expected return in the future. The main advantage is that SRI investors can invest in line with their values.

3. Arguments are available on both sides about whether the growth in socially responsible investments is likely to continue over the next decades. Due to the high return on ESG strategies over the last decades, the SRI market may have attracted many investors who actually care more about expected payoffs than about investing using ethical or social values. If an SRI strategy earns lower returns in the future, these investors are likely to leave the SRI segment.

   Firms' ESG standards have increasingly attracted attention not only by investors but also by the general public. More people are becoming interested and care about ESG issues. They may be willing to incorporate ESG standards at the expense of performance and, thus, would contribute to a growth of the SRI market, even if expected returns are lower.

4. Whether institutional investors act in the best interest of their beneficiaries when following SRI strategies depends on several factors. Institutional investors with a clear mandate to invest in a socially responsible manner, for example, SRI mutual funds, are clearly acting in their clients' interest. Answering this question for pension funds and other investors who have no explicit mandate is more difficult. Excluding sin stocks has harmed portfolio performance. That would only be in the beneficiaries' best interest if the beneficiaries had strong ethical concerns about sin industries. Otherwise, not investing in sin stock would only have lowered the beneficiaries' pension, which is clearly not in their best interest. Because ESG strategies have earned positive abnormal returns in the past, following an ESG strategy did not interfere with the beneficiaries' financial interests.

CHAPTER 24 MONEY-FLOWS OF SOCIALLY RESPONSIBLE INVESTMENT FUNDS AROUND THE WORLD

1. An adverse change of fund performance may have a smaller impact on the investment behavior of an SRI investor than on that of a conventional fund investor. Negative returns may be less important for those SRI investors who attach more importance to nonfinancial

attributes. Hence, an SRI investor may be less willing to withdraw money from poorly performing funds than would a conventional investor. The more averse investors are to specific types of (unethical) corporate behavior, the more moral satisfaction they derive from investing in SRI funds that comply with the investor's personal views on societal/ideological issues. Therefore, SRI investors are expected to be satisfied with lower returns than conventional investors as the former are expected to get a moral dividend. The counterargument is that SRI screening discloses firm-specific information that is not yet priced. Hence, SRI funds could yield higher returns than conventional funds.

2. Because SRI investors have diverse social objectives, SRI funds usually bring into play a combination of negative and positive SRI screens to construct portfolios. An SRI fund typically applies negative (i.e., exclusion) screens to an initial asset pool, such as the Standard and Poor's (S&P) 500 stocks, from which it excludes specific sectors (e.g., alcohol, tobacco, and defense industries). SRI funds use positive (i.e., selection) screens to select companies that meet superior standards on issues such as corporate governance or environmental protection. The funds often use positive screens with a best in class approach ranking firms within each industry based on social criteria. The funds include in their portfolios only those firms that pass a minimum threshold in each industry.

Environmental	Positive/ Negative	Environment	Selecting firms with high environmental/ ecological standards; or avoiding firms with low environmental standards
	Positive	Renewable Energy	Selecting firms producing power from renewable energy
	Negative	Nuclear	Avoiding companies operating nuclear power plants

3. The following is an example of an empirical test to determine whether the money flows of SRI funds differ for past positive and past negative fund performance: $Flow_{i,t} = \gamma_0 + (\beta_1 R^+ + \beta_2 R^-) Return_{i,[t-1,t-12]} + u_{i,t}$, where $Flow_{i,t}$ is the money flow of fund i in month t in local currency; $Return_{i,[t-1,t-12]}$ is the average raw return of fund i over the months $t-1$ to $t-12$ in local currency; and R^+ and R^- are indicator variables that equal one if $Return_{i,[t-1,t-12]}$ is nonnegative or negative, respectively. Fund returns lagged by one year are used to focus on the impact of the most recent information available to investors. The indicator variables R^+ and R^- allow for different flow-return sensitivities to subsequent positive or negative returns.

4. The smart-money effect signifies that money flows can predict short-term future fund performance. Empirically, the returns are correlated on lagged money flows. If a positive correlation exists, the investors in these funds are classified as smart. Frazzini and Lamont (2008) document a dumb-money effect, when individual investors invest their money in mutual funds with stocks that prove to be underperforming over the subsequent years.

Index

Stay in touch!

Subscribe to our free Finance and Accounting eNewsletters at
www.wiley.com/enewsletters

Visit our blog: **www.capitalexchangeblog.com**

Follow us on Twitter
@wiley_finance

"Like" us on Facebook
www.facebook.com/wileyglobalfinance

Find us on LinkedIn
Wiley Global Finance Group

WILEY Global Finance
WHERE DATA FINDS DIRECTION

Printed and bound by CPI Group (UK) Ltd, Croydon, CR0 4YY

24/04/2025

14661395-0001